Tafsīr al-Qurṭubī

Vol. 8

Sūrat al-Anfāl – Booty

Sūrat at-Tawbah – Repentance

& *Sūrah Yūnus* – Jonah

Tafsīr al-Qurṭubī

The General Judgments of the Qur'ān and Clarification of what it contains of the *Sunnah* and *Āyah*s of Discrimination

Abū 'Abdullāh Muḥammad ibn Aḥmad ibn Abī Bakr ibn Farḥ al-Anṣārī al-Khazrajī al-Andalusī al-Qurṭubī

Vol. 8

Sūrat al-Anfāl – Booty
Sūrat at-Tawbah – Repentance
& *Sūrah Yūnus* – Jonah

translated by
Aisha Bewley

Diwan Press
Classical and Contemporary Books on Islam and Sufism

Published by: Diwan Press Ltd. 2024

Website: www.diwanpress.com
E-mail: info@diwanpress.com

By: Abu 'Abdullah Muhammad ibn Ahmad al-Qurtubi
Translated by: Aisha Abdarrahman Bewley
Edited by: Abdalhaqq Bewley

A catalogue record of this book is available from the British Library.

ISBN 13: 978-1-914397-32-5 (PB)
978-1-914397-33-2 (CB)
978-1-914397-34-9 (eBook)

Contents

Table of Transliterations

ء	’	ض	ḍ
ا	a	ط	ṭ
ب	b	ظ	ẓ
ت	t	ع	‘
ث	th	غ	gh
ج	j	ف	f
ح	ḥ	ق	q
خ	kh	ك	k
د	d	ل	l
ذ	dh	م	m
ر	r	ن	n
ز	z	ه	h
س	s	و	w
ش	sh	ي	y
ص	ṣ		

Long vowel		Short vowel	
ا	ā	ـَ	a [*fatḥah*]
و	ū	ـُ	u [*ḍammah*]
ي	ī	ـِ	i [*kasrah*]
أَوْ	aw		
أَيْ	ay		

Translator’s note

The Arabic for the *āyats* is from the Algerian State edition of the *riwāyah* of Imam Warsh from the *qirā’ah* of Imam Nāfi‘ of Madīnah, whose recitation is one of the ten *mutawātir* recitations that are mass-transmitted from the time of the Prophet ﷺ.

There are minor omissions in the text. Some poems have been omitted which the author quotes to illustrate a point of grammatical usage or as an example of orthography or the usage of a word, often a derivative of the root of the word used in the *āyah*, but not the actual word used. Often it is difficult to convey the sense in English. Occasionally the author explores a grammatical matter or a tangential issue, and some of these may have been shortened. English grammatical terms used to translate Arabic grammatical terms do not have exactly the same meaning, sometimes rendering a precise translation of them problematic and often obscure.

The end of a *juz’* may vary by an *āyah* or two in order to preserve relevant passages.

8. Sūrat al-Anfāl – Booty

It is Madinan and about Badr according to al-Ḥasan, 'Ikrimah, Jābir and 'Aṭā'. Ibn 'Abbās said that it is Madinan except for seven *āyah*s from *āyah* 30 to *āyah* 37.

يَسْـَٔلُونَكَ عَنِ ٱلْأَنفَالِ ۖ قُلِ ٱلْأَنفَالُ لِلَّهِ وَٱلرَّسُولِ ۖ فَٱتَّقُوا۟ ٱللَّهَ وَأَصْلِحُوا۟ ذَاتَ بَيْنِكُمْ ۖ وَأَطِيعُوا۟
ٱللَّهَ وَرَسُولَهُۥٓ إِن كُنتُم مُّؤْمِنِينَ ۝١

1 They will ask you about booty. Say: 'Booty belongs to Allah and the Messenger. So have *taqwā* of Allah and put things right between you. Obey Allah and His Messenger if you are believers.'

'Ubādah ibn aṣ-Ṣamit related: 'The Messenger of Allah ﷺ went out to Badr and confronted the enemy. When Allah routed them, a group of the Muslims pursued them to kill them, another group surrounded the Messenger of Allah ﷺ, and yet another group reached the enemy camp and looted it. When Allah dispersed the enemy, and those who went after them returned, they said, "We should have the booty. We are the ones who went after the enemy and Allah has negated them and defeated them." Those who surrounded the Messenger of Allah ﷺ said, "You have no more entitlement to it than us. We should have it. We surrounded the Messenger of Allah ﷺ so that the enemy could not attack him." Those who actually got to the army and booty said, "You are no more entitled to it than us. It should be ours. We came upon it and impounded it."' So Allah revealed this *āyah* and the Messenger of Allah ﷺ divided it immediately between them.

Abū 'Umar said that the people who have knowledge of the Arabic language say that *istalwaw* means to surround. The verb is used for death overcoming people. 'He divided it immediately' means quickly. They said that *fuwāq* is the period between two milkings of a she-camel. It is pronounced as *fuwāq* or *fawāq*. This was before the revelation of: *'Know that when you take any booty, a fifth of it belongs to Allah…'* (8:41) Scholars say that it means that Allah and the Messenger have judgment regarding it and do with it what will bring one close to Allah.

Muḥammad ibn Isḥāq related from 'Abd ar-Raḥmān ibn al-Ḥārith and others of our companions from Sulaymān ibn Mūsā al-Ashdaq from Makḥūl that Abū

Umāmah al-Bāhilī said, 'I asked 'Ubādah ibn aṣ-Ṣāmit about this *āyah* and he said, "It was revealed about us, the people of Badr, when we disagreed about the booty and our behaviour was poor. So Allah took it from our hands and gave it to the Messenger and the Messenger of Allah ﷺ divided it equally."' That was *taqwā* of Allah, obeying the Messenger and preventing division.

It is related in the *Ṣaḥīḥ* that Sa'd ibn Abī Waqqās said, 'The Companions of the Messenger of Allah ﷺ took an immense amount of booty. There was a sword in it. I took it to the Prophet ﷺ and said, "Give me this sword as booty. You know my state." He said, "Take it back to where you took it from." I went until I was about to throw it in the common booty. My soul got at me and I returned to him and said, "Give it to me." He said to me in a fierce voice, "Take it back to where you took it from." I went until I was about to throw it in the common booty. My soul got at me again and I returned to him and said, "Give it to me." He said to me in a fierce voice, "Take it back to where you took it from." Then Allah revealed: "*They will ask you about booty.*"' This is the wording of Muslim, and there are many variants about it. We have said enough. Allah gives success in guidance.

The singular of booty (*anfāl*) is *nafl*. It is said:

Tawqā of our Lord is the best booty.
My slowness and haste is by the permission of Allah.
It is the best of spoils.

Nafl means an oath and an example of it is found in the *ḥadīth*: 'The Jews are free of you by fifty oaths (*nafl*).' *Nafl* also means denial as in the *ḥadīth*: "He denied [paternity of] her child.' *Nafl* also means a particular plant (trefoil). *Nafl* is also doing more than the obligatory: the supererogatory. A grandchild is called *nāfilah* because it he is an addition to the child. Spoils are *nāfilah* because they are an addition to what Allah has made lawful for this Community which was unlawful for others. The Prophet ﷺ said, 'I was preferred over the Prophets by six.' One of them was: 'Spoils were made lawful for me.' *Anfāl* are the actual spoils. 'Antarah said:

When the fight is hot, we are quenched by the canal
And we are abstinent in the division of the spoils (*anfāl*).

Scholars have four different views about what constitutes booty. The first is that it is what is wrested from the unbelievers for the Muslims or taken without fighting. The second is that it is the fifth (*khums*). The third is that it is a fifth of the fifth. The fourth is that it is initial spoils about which the ruler acts as he sees fit.

The position of Mālik is that booty is in the gift of the ruler from the fifth according to how he sees fit. There is no booty in the other four-fifths. He did not think that booty came from the initial spoils themselves because the people who receive it are specified. They are those who obtain it on mounts. The fifth is returned and divided according to the discretion of the ruler. The people who receive it are not specified. The Messenger of Allah ﷺ said, 'I only have a fifth of the spoils Allah gives you and that fifth is returned to you.' After this, no one has a right to the booty. It is part of the right of the Messenger of Allah ﷺ. It is a fifth. This is known in his school. It is related that he said, 'That is from the fifth of the fifth.' That is the position of Ibn al-Musayyab, ash-Shāfi'ī and Abū Ḥanīfah.

The reason for the disagreement is the *ḥadīth* of Ibn 'Umar which Mālik related: 'The Messenger of Allah ﷺ sent an expedition towards Najd and they plundered many camels, their shares being eleven or twelve camels each. They were given them camel by camel.' That is how Mālik related it with some uncertainty in the transmission from Yaḥyā. A group of the transmitters of the *Muwaṭṭā'* corroborate that except for al-Walīd ibn Muslim. He related it from Mālik from Nāfi' from Ibn 'Umar. He said in it: 'Their shares were twelve camels and they were given them camel by camel.' He had no uncertainty.

Al-Walīd ibn Muslim and al-Ḥakam ibn Nāfi' mentioned from Shu'ayb ibn Abī Ḥamzah from Nāfi' that Ibn 'Umar said, 'The Messenger of Allah ﷺ sent us in an expedition towards Najd…' Al-Walīd's version has 'consisting of four thousand' and 'an expedition was sent out from the army.' Al-Walīd's version has: 'I was one of those who went out in it, and the shares of the army were twelve camels each, and the people on the expedition got a camel each [in addition] and so their shares were thirteen camels.' Abū Dāwūd mentioned it.

This is used as evidence by those who say that booty is part of the fifth. They explain that if this expedition had been ten people, for instance, and they had taken 150 as booty, the fifth, which is 30, would have been taken from it and they would have had 120. That divided between ten would be twelve camels each. Then the people would be given from the fifth a camel each because a fifth of thirty does not have eleven camels. When you know what ten have, you know what a hundred or a thousand or more have.

Those who say that it is a fifth of the fifth use as evidence that it is permitted for there to be clothes and goods which were sold besides the camels and so those who did not get a camel were given the value of a camel from those goods. This is supported by what Muslim related of this *ḥadīth* by various paths, 'We got camels and booty.'

Muḥammad ibn Isḥāq said about this *ḥadīth* that the leader gave them booty before the distribution. This demands that booty is from the initial spoils which differs from Mālik's position. The position of those with a different position is more appropriate because they are *ḥuffāẓ*, as Abū 'Umar said. Makḥūl and al-Awzā'ī said, 'More than a third is not given as booty.' That is the position of the majority of scholars. Al-Awzā'ī said, 'If they are given more, it is given to them and made part of the fifth.' Ash-Shāfi'ī said, 'There is no limit in the fifth which the leader can exceed.'

The *ḥadīth* of Ibn 'Umar indicates what al-Walīd and al-Ḥakam mentioned from Shu'ayb from Nāfi' that when an expedition goes out from the army and gets the booty, the army share in it. This is an issue whose ruling is not mentioned in other than the *ḥadīth* of Shu'ayb from Nāfi'. Scholars do not disagree about it. Praise belongs to Allah.

Scholars disagree about when the leader says before the fight, 'Whoever destroys that fortress will receive such-and-such. Whoever reaches that spot will receive such-and-such. Whoever brings a head will receive such-and-such. Whoever brings a captive will receive such-and-such.' It is related that Mālik disliked it and said, 'This is fighting for this world.' He did not permit it. Ath-Thawrī said that it is permitted and there is nothing wrong with it. This possibility is taken from the *ḥadīth* of Ibn 'Abbās who said, 'In the Battle of Badr, the Prophet ﷺ said, "Whoever has killed someone has such-and-such and whoever takes a prisoner will have such-and-such."'

'Ikrimah reported from the Prophet ﷺ: 'Whoever does such-and-such and comes to such-and-such place, will have such-and-such.' The young men went quickly and the old men stood firm. When there was victory, the young men came asking for what he had allotted them and the old men said, 'Do not take it leaving us out. We were your support.' Allah revealed, *'Put things right between you'"* Ismā'īl ibn Isḥāq mentioned it. it. Ath-Thawrī said, 'That is permitted and there is nothing wrong with it.'

It is related that 'Umar ibn al-Khaṭṭāb said to Jarīr ibn 'Abdullāh al-Bajalī when he came to him with his people wanting to go to Syria, 'Will you go to Kufa if you have a third of every land grant and captives after the fifth has been taken?' A group of the *fuqahā'* said that: al-Awzā'ī, Makḥūl, Ibn Ḥaywah and others. They thought that the fifth was from the entire spoils (*ghanīmah*) and that booty (*nafl*) was after the fifth. Then the spoils were shared between the people of the army. Isḥāq, Aḥmad and Abū 'Ubayd said that. Abū 'Ubayd said, 'People today believe that there is no booty from the spoils until the fifth has been taken.' Mālik said,

'It is not permitted for the leader to say to an expedition, "You can have a third of what you take."' Saḥnūn said, 'When a leader says to an expedition, "You can have what you take. You do not have to pay the fifth on it," that is not permitted. If it occurs, what was taken has to be returned because this ruling is aberrant and not permitted or carried out.'

Mālik recommended that the leader only take the fifth from what is openly visible, such as turbans, horses and swords. Some scholars forbade the ruler to give booty in the form of gold, silver, pearls and the like. Some said that it is permitted in any form and that is sound based on the statement of 'Umar and what is demanded by the *āyah*. Allah knows best.

Have *taqwā* of Allah and put things right between you. Obey Allah and His Messenger if you are believers.'

Allah commands *taqwā* and putting things right. It means: 'Collaborate on the command of Allah in making the supplication, "O Allah, heal division!"' It means the state by which there is gatheredness. This indicates that there is disagreement between people or that they incline to quarrelling with one another as is stated in the *ḥadīth*. *Taqwā* has already been discussed (2:2). It means: 'Have *taqwā* of Allah in respect of your words and deeds and put things right between you.' '*Obey Allah and His Messenger*' regarding the matter of spoils and the like and the phrase '*if you are believers*' indicates that the path of the believers is to obey what has been commanded. It is said that the conjunction '*in – if*' here means 'when'.

إِنَّمَا ٱلْمُؤْمِنُونَ ٱلَّذِينَ إِذَا ذُكِرَ ٱللَّهُ وَجِلَتْ قُلُوبُهُمْ وَإِذَا تُلِيَتْ عَلَيْهِمْ ءَايَٰتُهُۥ
زَادَتْهُمْ إِيمَٰنًا وَعَلَىٰ رَبِّهِمْ يَتَوَكَّلُونَ ﴿٢﴾ ٱلَّذِينَ يُقِيمُونَ ٱلصَّلَوٰةَ وَمِمَّا رَزَقْنَٰهُمْ يُنفِقُونَ ﴿٣﴾
أُوْلَٰٓئِكَ هُمُ ٱلْمُؤْمِنُونَ حَقًّا لَّهُمْ دَرَجَٰتٌ عِندَ رَبِّهِمْ وَمَغْفِرَةٌ وَرِزْقٌ كَرِيمٌ ﴿٤﴾

2-4 The believers are those whose hearts tremble when Allah is mentioned, whose faith is increased when His Signs are recited to them, and who put their trust in their Lord; those who establish the prayer and give of what We have provided for them. They are in truth the believers. They have high ranks with their Lord and forgiveness and generous provision.

Scholars say that this *āyah* is encouragement to cling to obedience to the Messenger ﷺ in respect of what he commands regarding dividing up the booty. *Wajal* is fear. In the present tense of the verb there are four dialectical forms:

yawjalu, *yājalu*, *yayjalu*, and *yiyjilu*. Sībawayh related that. The verbal noun is *wajil*, *wajal* and *mawjal*. *Mawjil* is a place and a noun. If someone says *yājilu*, he makes the *wāw* an *alif* because there is a *fatḥah* before it. The usage of the Qur'an gives it a *wāw*, as in 15:53. *Yiyjilu* is the dialect of Asad. They used to say '*anā ījil, naḥnu nījil, anta tījil*.' All have a *kasrah*. Someone who says '*yayjal*' bases it on this dialect although there is a *fatḥah* on the *yā'* and not a *kasrah* since it is heavy to have a *kasrah* on a *yā'*.

Sufyān related from as-Suddī about this *āyah*, 'When someone desires to commit an injustice, he is told, "Have *taqwā* of Allah," and he will then refrain and his heart tremble.' In this *āyah* Allah Almighty described the believers as people who have fear and tremble when He is mentioned. That comes from the strength of their faith and their awareness of their Lord. It is as if they were in front of Him. Similar to this *āyah* is: *'Give good news to the humble-hearted, whose hearts quake at the mention of Allah'* (22:34-35) and *'Only in the remembrance of Allah can the heart find peace.'* (13:28) This refers to full recognition and the trust of the heart.

Wajal is fear of Allah's punishment and there is no contradiction. Allah combines both ideas when He says: *'The skins of those who fear their Lord tremble at it and then their skins and hearts yield softly to the remembrance of Allah.'* (39:23) It means that their souls are at peace with Allah out of certainty, even though they fear Allah. This is the state of the gnostics of Allah who fear His might and punishment. It has no connection with what the ignorant common people and silly innovators do, when they shriek and roar and bray like donkeys. Those who do that and claim that it is ecstasy and humbleness need to be told, 'You have not reached the state of the Messenger nor that of the Companions in respect of gnosis of Allah, fear of Him and esteem for His majesty.' Allah described the state of the people of true knowledge when they hear His remembrance and recitation of His Book in His words: *'When they listen to what has been sent down to the Messenger, you see their eyes overflowing with tears because of what they recognise of the truth. They say, 'Our Lord, we believe! So write us down among the witnesses.'* (5:83) This is a description of their state and what they say.

If someone is not like that, they are not following the guidance of such people nor are they on their path. Whoever follows a *sunnah* is on the *sunnah*. Anyone who practises the states of the mad and insane is someone with the basest kind of state. There are various types of madness. Muslim related from Anas ibn Mālik that some people went to the Prophet ﷺ and enquired about this matter. He came out one day and went up the *minbar* and said, 'Ask me. While I am standing here, I will make clear to you anything you ask me about.' When the people heard that, they were silent and feared that they were facing something that was about to happen. Anas said, 'I began to look right and left and everyone had their heads in their garments weeping.' He mentioned the *ḥadīth*. At-Tirmidhī related it and had it as sound from al-'Irbāḍ ibn Sāriyah: 'The Messenger of Allah ﷺ admonished us eloquently and our hearts trembled at it.' He said not say, 'We shouted or danced or cried out or stood.'

whose faith is increased when His Signs are recited to them

They increase in affirmation. So their faith today is greater than their faith was yesterday. Someone who affirms twice or three times continues to increase in their affirmation. It is said that the breasts are expanded by the great number of Signs and proofs. This is found in *Āl 'Imrān* (3:172). The meaning of *tawakkul* was already discussed in *Āl 'Imrān* (3:123-124).

those who establish the prayer and give of what We have provided for them. They are in truth the believers

This was already discussed in *al-Baqarah* (2:3). *'They are in truth the believers'* means: they are those who are the same inwardly and outwardly with respect to Islam. This indicates that every truth has a tangible reality. The Prophet ﷺ said to Ḥārithah, 'Every truth has a reality, so what is the reality of your faith?' A man asked al-Ḥasan, 'Abū Sa'īd, are you a believer?' He said to him, 'There are two types of faith. If you ask me about faith in Allah, His angels, His Books, Messengers, the Garden and the Fire, the Resurrection and Reckoning, I believe in those things. If you ask me about the words of Allah: *"The believers are those whose hearts tremble when Allah is mentioned…,"* by Allah, I do not know if I am one of them or not.'

Abū Bakr al-Wāsiṭī said, 'If someone says, "I am truly a believer in Allah," he is told, "The reality of belief is having a thorough grasp, complete knowledge and comprehension. If someone lacks this, his claim is invalid."' He means by that what the people of the Sunnah say: 'The true believer is the one destined for the Garden. If someone does not know that [he corresponds to that which he finds] in the secret of Allah's wisdom, then his claim to truly be an believer is not sound.'

كَمَآ أَخْرَجَكَ رَبُّكَ مِنۢ بَيْتِكَ بِٱلْحَقِّ وَإِنَّ فَرِيقًا مِّنَ ٱلْمُؤْمِنِينَ لَكَٰرِهُونَ ﴿٥﴾

5 Just as your Lord brought you out from your house with truth, even though a group of the believers disliked it,

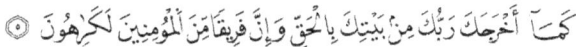

Az-Zajjāj said that the *kāf* (*just as*) at the beginning of the sentence is as if it were in the accusative, meaning, 'Booty is confirmed for you as your Lord brought you out of your house with truth.' It means: 'It is like your Lord brings you out of your house with truth.' Therefore it means: 'Carry out what you have been commanded to do regarding the spoils and booty as you wish, even if they dislike it,' because some of the Companions spoke to the Messenger of Allah ﷺ when he allotted something to all of those who brought a captive while most of the people remained without anything. So the position of the *kāf* in *kamā* is accusative as we mentioned. Al-Farrā' also said that.

Abū 'Ubaydah said that it is an oath, meaning, 'Yes, by the One Who brought you out,' and the *kāf* means 'and' and *mā* means 'Who'. Sa'īd ibn Mas'adah said, 'It means: those are truly believers, as your Lord brought you out from your house with the truth.' Some scholars said, 'As your Lord brought you out from your house with the truth, have *taqwā* of Allah and put things right between you.'

'Ikrimah said that it means: 'Obey Allah and His Messenger as He brought you out.' It is said that *'as your Lord brought you out'* is connected with Allah's words: *'They have high ranks,'* and it means: they have high ranks with their Lord, forgiveness and generous provision. This promise to the believers is true in the Next World just as your Lord brought you out of your house with the obligatory truth. He fulfilled His promise and gave you success over your enemy as in His words: *'When Allah promised you that one of the two parties would be yours.'* (8:7) As He carried out this promise in this world, so He will carry out what He promised in the Next World. This is a good view which an-Naḥḥās mentioned and preferred.

It is said that the *kāf* in *kamā* is comparative and it is by way of requital as one says to his slave, 'As I made you face my enemies and they found you weak and you asked for help, so I have reinforced and strengthened you and removed your defect. Seize them now and punish them like that. As I clothed you and gave you provision, do such-and-such. As I was good to you, be grateful to me for it.' He said, 'Your Lord brought you out of your house with the truth and made you succumb to sleep – giving you and those with you a feeling of security – and He sent you down water from heaven to purify you and angels from heaven to aid you, so strike their necks and strike all their finger-joints!' It is as if he were saying, 'I have removed your defects and reinforced you with angels, so strike these places on them, which will be fatal for them, so that Allah's desire to realise the truth and make the false invalid will be achieved.' Allah knows best.

The words: *'even though a group of the believers disliked it'* means that they disliked leaving Makkah and leaving their property and houses.

يُجَٰدِلُونَكَ فِي ٱلۡحَقِّ بَعۡدَ مَا تَبَيَّنَ كَأَنَّمَا يُسَاقُونَ إِلَى ٱلۡمَوۡتِ وَهُمۡ يَنظُرُونَ ٦

6 arguing with you about the Truth after it had been made clear as though they were being driven to their death with open eyes.

Their *arguing* was what they said when he ﷺ commanded them to fight after encouraging them to go after the caravan which they failed to catch. They did not have many provisions with them and that was hard on them and they said, 'If only you had told us about fighting, we would have made provision for it.' *'The Truth'* refers to the fighting. *'After it had been made clear'* to them that you do not command anything except with the permission of Allah. It is said that it means after it was clear to them that Allah promised them either victory over the caravan or the people of Makkah. If it was not the caravan, then it must have been referring to the people of Makkah and victory over them. The words are an objection to their arguing.

'As though they were being driven to their death' out of their dislike of encountering the people. *'With open eyes'* means that they know that that will happen to them. Allah says, *"On the Day when a man will see what he has done."* (78:40)

وَإِذۡ يَعِدُكُمُ ٱللَّهُ إِحۡدَى ٱلطَّآئِفَتَيۡنِ أَنَّهَا لَكُمۡ وَتَوَدُّونَ أَنَّ غَيۡرَ ذَاتِ
ٱلشَّوۡكَةِ تَكُونُ لَكُمۡ وَيُرِيدُ ٱللَّهُ أَن يُحِقَّ ٱلۡحَقَّ بِكَلِمَٰتِهِۦ وَيَقۡطَعَ دَابِرَ
ٱلۡكَٰفِرِينَ ٧ لِيُحِقَّ ٱلۡحَقَّ وَيُبۡطِلَ ٱلۡبَٰطِلَ وَلَوۡ كَرِهَ ٱلۡمُجۡرِمُونَ ٨

7-8 When Allah promised you that one of the two parties would be yours and you would have liked it to have been the unarmed one, whereas Allah desired to verify the Truth by His words and to cut off the last remnant of the unbelievers. This was so that He might verify the Truth and nullify the false, even though the evildoers hate that.

'One of' is in the accusative as a second object, and *'would be yours'* is also in the accusative as an appositive for *'one of'*. *'Tawaddūna'* means 'love'. Abū 'Ubaydah said that *'unarmed'* means without edged weapons. *Shawkah* means weapons. *Shawk* is also a plant with thorns and so you say that a man is bristling (*shā'ik*) with sharp weapons. It is also reversed and *shākī* is used in the same way. So it means: 'You want to defeat the group without weapons so that it means not having to fight.' Az-Zajjāj said that.

Allah desired to verify the Truth by His words.

This means: make Islam victorious. The *Truth* is always true, but its victory is its verification since if it was not made clear, it would be like the false. *'By His words'* means His promise. Allah promised that to His Prophet ﷺ in *Sūrat ad-Dukhān* where He says: *'On the day We launch the Great Assault, We will certainly take Our revenge'* (44:16), meaning on Abū Jahl and his fellows. And He also says: *'to exalt it over every other* dīn.*"* (9:33) It is said that *'by His words'* is by His command to you to strive against them. The phrase *'cut off the last remnant of the unbelievers'* means eradicating them by their destruction. The verification of the Truth is giving victory to the *dīn* of Islam and making it strong. *'The false'* refers to disbelief and its nullification is by eliminating it just as verifying the truth is by making it manifest. Allah says: *'Rather We hurl the truth against falsehood and it cuts right through it and it vanishes clean away.'* (21:18)

إِذْ تَسْتَغِيثُونَ رَبَّكُمْ فَاسْتَجَابَ لَكُمْ أَنِّي مُمِدُّكُم بِأَلْفٍ مِّنَ الْمَلَائِكَةِ
مُرْدِفِينَ ﴿٩﴾ وَمَا جَعَلَهُ اللَّهُ إِلَّا بُشْرَىٰ وَلِتَطْمَئِنَّ بِهِ قُلُوبُكُمْ
وَمَا النَّصْرُ إِلَّا مِنْ عِندِ اللَّهِ إِنَّ اللَّهَ عَزِيزٌ حَكِيمٌ ﴿١٠﴾

9-10 Remember when you called on your Lord for help and He responded to you: 'I will reinforce you with a thousand angels riding rank after rank.' Allah only did this to give you good news and that so your hearts would be at rest. Victory comes from no one but Allah. Allah is Almighty, All-Wise.

Remember when you called on your Lord for help

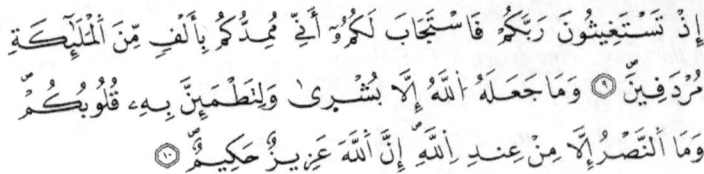

Calling for help is seeking succour and aid. It is when a man calls out for help. The noun is *ghawth*, *ghuwāth* and *ghawāth*. Form X is asking for help and Form IV is giving help. The noun is *ghiwāth*. Al-Jawharī said that. Muslim related that 'Umar ibn al-Khaṭṭāb said, 'At the Battle of Badr, the Messenger of Allah ﷺ looked at the idolaters. They numbered a thousand and his Companions numbered three hundred and seventeen. The Prophet of Allah ﷺ turned towards the *qiblah* and raised his hands and began to call on his Lord: "O Lord, fulfil for me what you promised! O Allah, if You destroy this group of the people of Islam, You will not be worshipped on the earth!" He continued to call on his Lord, facing the *qiblah*, until his cloak fell from his shoulders. Abū Bakr went to him and took his cloak, putting it back over his shoulders. He then clasped him from behind him and said, "O Prophet of Allah, you have entreated your Lord enough. He will give you what He promised you!" Then Allah revealed this. Allah helped him with the angels.'

'Riding rank after rank' is recited by Nāfi' as *'murdafīn'* and as *'murdifīn'* by the others, which is an active participle meaning to follow one after the other. One group came after another. That is more frightening to the eyes. If it is *'murdafīn'*, the doer is not named because the people who fought in the Battle of Badr were followed by a thousand angels who descended to help them against the unbelievers. *'Murdafīn'* is an adjective of 'a thousand angels'. It is also said that it is a *ḥāl* modifying the accusative pronoun in *'mumiddukum,'* i.e. reinforcing you with a thousand angels. This is the position of Mujāhid.

Abū 'Ubaydah related that the verbs *radafa* and *ardafa* mean the same. Abū 'Ubayd did not recognise that they had the same meaning because Allah says: *'the second blast follows (*rādifa*) it'* (79:7) and did not say *'murdifa'*. An-Naḥḥās, Makkī and others said that the reading with the *kasrah* is more appropriate because the people of interpretation according to this reading explain it as 'they followed one another' and because it contains the meaning of the *fatḥah* according to what Abū 'Ubaydah related and because most reciters have that.

Sībawayh said that it is recited with *rā'* and double *dāl* with a *kasrah* (*muraddifīn*). Some of them have a *kasrah* on the *rā'* (*murriddifīn*) and some have it with a *ḍammah* on the *rā'* (*muruddifīn*). All three readings have a doubled *dāl* with a *kasrah*. According to Sībawayh it implies *murtadifīn* and then the *tā'* is incorporated into *dāl* and its vowel moved to the *rā'* so that two silent letters are not together. The second position is that the *rā'* has a *kasrah* because of the meeting of two silent letters. The *rā'* has a *ḍammah* in the third to follow the *ḍammah* of the *mīm*.

Ja'far ibn Muḥammad and 'Āṣim al-Jaḥdarī said that *ālf* is the plural of *'alf'* (a thousand), like *fils* and *aflas*. The descent of the angels, their marks and fighting were already mentioned in *Āl 'Imrān* (3:126). What is meant is support. It is possible that it is reinforcement. Allah points out that victory comes from Allah, not from the angels. If it had not been for His help, the number of angels would have been of no use. Victory from Allah can be by the sword or by the definitive proof.

إِذْ يُغَشِّيكُمُ ٱلنُّعَاسَ أَمَنَةً مِّنْهُ وَيُنَزِّلُ عَلَيْكُم مِّنَ ٱلسَّمَآءِ مَآءً لِّيُطَهِّرَكُم
بِهِۦ وَيُذْهِبَ عَنكُمْ رِجْزَ ٱلشَّيْطَٰنِ وَلِيَرْبِطَ عَلَىٰ قُلُوبِكُمْ وَيُثَبِّتَ
بِهِ ٱلْأَقْدَامَ ﴿١١﴾

11 And when He overcame you with sleep, making you feel secure, and sent you down water from heaven to purify you and remove the taint of Shayṭān from you, and to fortify your hearts and make your feet firm.

And when He overcame you with sleep, making you feel secure,

'Yughshīkumu'n-nu'āsa' has two objects and is the reading of the people of Madīnah. It is good because of the attribution of the verb to Allah since He was already mentioned in *'Victory comes from no one but Allah'* and because after it is *'He sent down on you'* and the action is ascribed to Allah. 'Overcoming with sleep' is ascribed to Allah because of the structure of the words. Ibn Kathīr and Abū 'Amr recite *'yaghshākumu'n-nu'āsu'* which makes sleep the subject of the verb. His evidence is found in *'security, restful sleep overtaking'* (3:154) in the recitation of those who recite it with *yā'* or *tā'* and the action is ascribed to sleep or security. Security (*amanah*) is sleep. Allah says that sleep is what overpowered the people.

The rest recite *'yughashshīkum*" with a *fatḥah* on the *ghayn* and double *shīn*. 'Sleep' is in the accusative in the reading of Nāfi'. There are two dialectical forms with the same meaning: *ghashshā* and *aghshā*. Allah says: *'blindfolding them (aghshaynāhum)'* (36:9) and He says: *'what enveloped it (ghashshā) enveloped it'* (53:54). Makkī said, 'What is preferred is a *ḍammah* on the *yā'*, doubled and in the accusative because Allah says after it: *'amanatan minhu'* and the *hā'* refers to Allah and so He was the One Who overcame them with sleep, and because that is the position of most people. It is said that it means security from the enemy.

'Security' is a direct object or a verbal noun. The forms are *amanah*, *amn* and *amān*. All mean the same. Sleep is a state of security in which one is not afraid. This is sleeping at night before the fighting. Their managing to sleep is extraordinary in view of the important business that lay ahead of them. But Allah made them tranquil. 'Alī said, 'There was no horseman among us in the Battle of Badr other than al-Miqdād on a piebald horse. I remember that there was none of them who did not sleep except for the Messenger of Allah ﷺ who was praying under the tree and weeping until morning.' Al-Bayhaqī mentioned it.

Al-Māwardī said: 'There are two reasons for bestowing sleep on them on this night. One of them is that Allah strengthened them through rest for the following day. The second is that He made them feel secure by removing terror from their hearts.' It is as it is said, 'Security makes one sleep and fear keeps one awake.' It is said that Allah made them sleep at the moment when the two battle lines met. This was discussed about Uḥud in *Āl 'Imrān* (3:154).

and sent you down water from heaven to purify you and remove the taint of Shayṭān from you, and to fortify your hearts and make your feet firm.

The literal meaning of the Qur'an indicates that they slept before it rained. But Ibn Abī Nujayh said, 'The rain was before they slept.' Az-Zajjāj related that in the Battle of Badr, the unbelievers reached Badr before the believers and camped there. The believers remained without water, so they were frightened, thirsty, in a state of *janābah* and prayed like that. Some of them said to themselves because of what Shayṭān suggested to them, 'We claim that we are the friends of Allah and His Messenger is among us and yet this is our state. It is the idolaters who have the water!' Allah sent down rain on the night of Badr, the 17th of Ramaḍān until the wadis flowed with it. They drank, purified themselves and watered the camels. It made the sand firm between them and the idolaters so that the feet of the Muslims were firm at the time of the fighting. It is said that these states took place before they reached Badr. This is sounder. It is what Ibn Isḥāq mentioned in his *Sīrah* as did others. This is a summary.

Ibn 'Abbās said, 'When the Messenger of Allah ﷺ was informed that Abū Sufyan was coming from Syria, he encouraged the Muslims to go out to them. He said, "This is the caravan of Quraysh which contains wealth. Go out to them and perhaps Allah will grant you victory over them." Those who were eager went with him and some people were slow and disliked going out. The Messenger of Allah ﷺ went quickly, not paying any attention to those who made excuses or waiting for those who were absent. He went with three hundred and thirteen of the Companions, Muhājrūn and *Anṣār*.'

We find in al-Bukhārī that al-Barā' ibn 'Āzib said, 'At the Battle of Badr there were about eighty *Muhājirūn* and about two hundred and forty *Anṣār*.' It is also transmitted from him: 'We used to say that the Companions of Muḥammad ﷺ were about three hundred and ten, the same as the number of the companions of Ṭālūt who crossed the river with him, and only believers crossed the river.' Al-Bayhaqī mentioned that Abū Ayyūb al-Anṣārī said, 'We went out to Badr. When we had travelled a day or two, the Messenger of Allah ﷺ commanded us to take a count. We did so and we were three hundred and thirteen. We told the Prophet ﷺ what our number was and he was happy about that, praised Allah and said, "The number of the companions of Ṭālūt."'

Ibn Isḥāq said, 'Everyone thought that the Messenger of Allah ﷺ would not go to war without having made prior preparation for it. When Abū Sufyān was near Hijaz, he sent out spies to get information and he questioned any riders he met out of fear for people's property. Then he got news from one of the riders that Muḥammad, the Messenger of Allah ﷺ, had called the people against him. He took precautions then and hired Ḍamḍam ibn 'Amr al-Ghifārī and sent him to Makkah and commanded him to bring Quraysh to defend their property and to inform them that Muḥammad ﷺ was waiting for it with his Companions. Ḍamḍam did that.

'So the people of Makkah came out with about a thousand men and the Prophet ﷺ set out with his Companions. Word reached Quraysh that they should come out to protect their caravan. The Prophet ﷺ consulted the people. Abū Bakr rose and spoke well. 'Umar rose and spoke well. Then al-Miqdād ibn 'Amr rose and said, "Messenger of Allah, do what Allah has commanded you and we are with you. By Allah, we will not say as the tribe of Israel said, *'You and your Lord go and fight. We will be sitting here.'* (5:24) Rather we say, 'You and your Lord go and fight and we will fight with you.' By the One Who sent you with the Truth, if you were to travel to Bark al-Ghimād (a city in Abyssinia), we would fight resolutely with you against it." The Messenger of Allah ﷺ was happy at that and prayed for good for him. Then he said, "Give me advice, people!" by which he meant the *Anṣār*. That was because they were the majority of people and when they pledged allegiance at 'Aqabah, they had said, "Messenger of Allah, we are not responsible for your safety until you reach our houses. When you reach us, then you are our responsibility. We will defend you from what we defend ourselves, our wives and children."

'The Messenger of Allah ﷺ was afraid that the *Anṣār* might think that they only had to support him in Madīnah and that they did not have to travel with them against an enemy who was not in their territory. When the Messenger of Allah ﷺ said that, Sa'd ibn Mu'ādh (or Sa'd ibn 'Ubādah, or perhaps both of them on that day) spoke and said, "Messenger of Allah, it is as if you mean us, the company of the *Anṣār*." The Messenger of Allah ﷺ said, "Yes." He said, "We have believed in you and followed you. Carry out what Allah has commanded you. By the One Who sent you with the truth, if you were to ask us to cross this sea and you plunged into it, we would plunge into it with you." The Messenger of Allah ﷺ said, "Go forward with Allah's blessing. It is as if I can see the enemy lying prostrate."

'The Messenger of Allah ﷺ proceeded and got to the water of Badr before Quraysh. Quraysh were prevented for getting there first by a heavy rain which Allah sent down on them while the Muslims only got from it that which made the surface of the wadi compact and helped them to travel. The Messenger of Allah ﷺ stopped at the water that was nearest to Madīnah. Al-Ḥubāb ibn al-Mundhir ibn 'Amr indicated something else to him. He asked, "Messenger of Allah, is this a place which Allah has revealed that you should stop so that we can neither go forward or back, or is it a matter of opinion and military tactics?" The Messenger of Allah ﷺ answered, "It is a matter of opinion and military tactics." He said, "Messenger of Allah, this is not the place to stop. Take us to the closest water to the enemy and camp there. Close up the wells beyond it and then build a cistern and fill it and we will have water and they will not." The Messenger of Allah ﷺ thought the idea was good and did it. Then they met and Allah helped His Prophet and the Muslims. Seventy of the idolaters were killed and seventy captured. The believers took revenge on them. Allah healed the heart of His Messenger and his Companions of their ire. Ḥassān said about that:

I recognise the houses of Zaynab on the sand hill,
    like the lines of the Revelation on clean paper.
The winds pass over them and every dark cloud
    pours out spring rain.
Its houses are mere tatters
    which were once the home of the beloved.
Stop remembering them every day.
    Quench the heat of the grieving heart.
Recount that concerning which there is no shame,
    telling the truth, not the reports of a liar,
About what Allah did on the day of Badr
    in giving us victory over the idolaters.
A day when their company was like Ḥirā'
    whose foundations appear at sunset.
We met them with a company
    like the lions of the wood, young and old
Before Muḥammad, helping him
    against the enemy in the heat of battle.
Sharp swords were in their hands
    and well-tried spears with knots,
The Banū Aws, the nobles, helped by
    the Banū an-Najjār in the strong *dīn*.
We left Abū Jahl fallen flat
    and we left 'Utbah on the ground.

We left Shaybah among men
of noble lineage.
The Messenger of Allah called to them
when we threw them headfirst into the pit,
"Have you not found my words to me true?
Allah's command takes hold of the heart."
They did not speak. If they had spoken, they would say,
"You were right. You had the correct opinion."'

There are three points in this. The first is that Mālik said, 'I heard that Jibrīl asked the Prophet ﷺ, "How are the men of Badr thought of among you?" He answered, "The best of us." He said, "They are the same with us."' This indicates that the honour of creatures is not achieved by essences but by actions. The angels have noble actions through persevering in constant glorification while we have actions through sincere obedience and thinking that the best obedience is what the *Sharī'ah* commands. The best of actions is *jihād*, and the best *jihād* was in the Battle of Badr because it was the foundation of Islam.

The second point is the fact that the Prophet ﷺ went out to meet the caravan which indicates that it is permitted to go out for booty and that it is lawful earning. It refutes what Mālik disliked regarding that when he said, 'That is fighting for this world,' and what has come about the fact that someone fighting to make the Word of Allah uppermost is in the Way of Allah whereas someone who fights for booty is not. That is only true when booty is his sole aim and the *dīn* has no portion in it. 'Ikrimah related that Ibn 'Abbās said, 'The people said to the Prophet ﷺ when Badr was over, "You must take the caravan. There is nothing protecting it." Al-'Abbās, who was one of the captives, called out, "That is not good." The Prophet ﷺ asked, "Why?" He answered, "Because Allah promised you one of the two parties and Allah has given you what He promised." The Prophet ﷺ said, "You have spoken the truth."' Al-'Abbās had been informed about what the Companions of the Prophet ﷺ said and the business of Badr.

The third point is that Muslim related from Anas ibn Mālik that the Messenger of Allah ﷺ left those killed for three days and then he stood over them and said, 'Abū Jahl ibn Hishām! Umayyah ibn Khalaf! 'Utbah ibn Rabī'ah! Shaybah ibn Rabī'ah! Have you found what your Lord promised you to be true? I have found what my Lord promised me to be true.' 'Umar heard what the Prophet ﷺ said and asked, 'Messenger of Allah, how can they hear and answer when they are corpses?' He answered, 'By the One Who has my soul in His hand, you do not hear what I say better than they hear, but they cannot answer.' Then he commanded that they be dragged and thrown into the pit of Badr.

'*Jayyafū*' means to become stinking corpses. 'Umar's question, 'How can they hear?' is thinking it unlikely based on the what normally happens, and the Prophet ﷺ told 'Umar that the dead hear just like the living. This indicates that death is not simply non-existence and pure effacement. It is the cutting off and departure of the spirit from the body and the placing of a barrier between them. It is a change of state and moving from one abode to another. The Messenger of Allah ﷺ said, 'When a dead person is placed in his grave and his companions leave him, he hears the sound of their [departing] sandals.' It has a sound transmission.

make your feet firm by it.

The pronoun in '*by it*' refers to the water which made the ground of the wadi firm. It is also said that it refers to fortifying hearts and so making feet firm designates help and support in war.

إِذْ يُوحِي رَبُّكَ إِلَى الْمَلَائِكَةِ أَنِّي مَعَكُمْ فَثَبِّتُوا الَّذِينَ آمَنُوا سَأُلْقِي فِي
قُلُوبِ الَّذِينَ كَفَرُوا الرُّعْبَ فَاضْرِبُوا فَوْقَ الْأَعْنَاقِ وَاضْرِبُوا مِنْهُمْ
كُلَّ بَنَانٍ ١٢

12 And when your Lord revealed to the angels, 'I am with you so make those who believe firm. I will cast terror into the hearts of those who disbelieve, so strike their necks and strike all their finger joints!'

The regent in '*when*' is in making the feet firm at that time. It is said that the regent is in '*to fortify their hearts*'. It can imply: 'Remember when your Lord revealed to the angels, "I am with you,"' which is in the accusative. It means: 'I am with you (or present with you) with help and support.' '*With you*' has a *fatḥah* on the '*ayn* as an adverb. If it has a *sukūn*, then it is a particle.

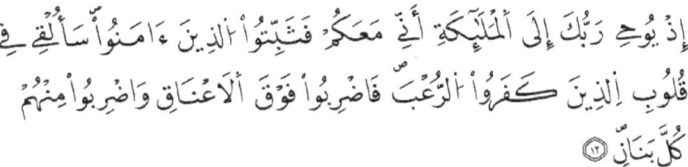

The words '*make those who believe firm*' mean: give them the good news of victory, or fighting with them, or being present with them without fighting. An angel would go to the front of the row in the form of a man and say, 'Go! Allah is your helper!' The Muslims thought that it was one of them. It was already mentioned in *Āl 'Imrān* (3:125-126) that the angels fought on that day and the Muslims saw heads separated from necks without seeing who struck the blow. Some of them heard someone saying, 'Advance, Ḥayzūm!' but did not see the person saying it. It is said that this making firm was the Messenger of Allah ﷺ reminding them that the angels had descended as reinforcements.

I will cast terror into the hearts of those who disbelieve, so strike their necks and strike all their finger joints!'

This was explained in *Āl 'Imrān* (3:151). *'Strike their necks'* is a command to the angels. It is also said that it is a command to the believers. The word 'above' (*fawq*) (lit. 'above their necks') is redundant, as al-Afkhash, aḍ-Ḍaḥḥāk and 'Aṭiyyah said. Al-Mas'ūdī related that the Messenger of Allah ﷺ said, 'I was not sent to punish with Allah's punishment. I was sent to strike the necks and tighten the bonds.' Muḥammad ibn Yazīd said, 'This is an error because the preposition "above" gives the meaning and it is not permitted to go beyond it. The meaning is that they are permitted to strike the faces and what is close to them.' Ibn 'Abbās said, 'Every head and skull.' It is said that it is what is above the neck: the heads. 'Ikrimah said that. Striking the head is more effective because it is most likely to affect the brain. Something like this is found in *an-Nisā'* (4:11) where 'above' is not redundant when Allah says: *'more than two.'*

In the phrase *'strike all their finger joints,'* az-Zajjāj said that the word *banān* is the plural of *banānah*. Here it means the fingers and other limbs. *Banān* is derived from the verb *abanna*, to remain in a place. *Banān* is used for residence and life. It is also said that what is meant are the ends of the fingers and toes. It is an expression which indicates being firm in the fighting and war. When the fingers are struck, then the person so struck cannot fight, which is not the case with other limbs. 'Antarah said:

The lad of Hayjā' defends its honour
and strikes off every finger (*banān*) in the fight.

There are also the words of 'Antarah about *banān* meaning fingers:

Death obeys the authority of my hand
when it reaches its fingertips (*banān*) with the Indian blade.

'Banān' is often used for fingers in Arabic poems. Ibn Fāris said that *banān* are fingers or the extremities. One of them mentioned that they are called *banān* because they are that by which a person puts circumstances in order, making a person settled and stable. Aḍ-Ḍaḥḥāk said that *banān* refers to every joint.

ذَٰلِكَ بِأَنَّهُمْ شَآقُّوا۟ ٱللَّهَ وَرَسُولَهُۥ ۚ وَمَن يُشَاقِقِ ٱللَّهَ وَرَسُولَهُۥ فَإِنَّ
ٱللَّهَ شَدِيدُ ٱلْعِقَابِ ﴿١٣﴾ ذَٰلِكُمْ فَذُوقُوهُ وَأَنَّ لِلْكَٰفِرِينَ عَذَابَ
ٱلنَّارِ ﴿١٤﴾

13-14 This was because they were hostile to Allah and His Messenger. If anyone is hostile to Allah and His Messenger, Allah is Severe in Retribution. That is your reward, so taste it. The unbelievers will also have the punishment of the Fire.

The pronoun '*This*' is in the nominative for the inceptive. It implies: 'this matter' or 'the matter is like that'. '*Hostile to Allah*' means hostile to His friends. *Shiqāq* is a split so that each is on one side. It was already mentioned (2:137). *'That is your reward…'* Az-Zajjāj said that the pronoun '*that*' is in the nominative by the implication of the command or the story, i.e. 'The business is like that, so taste it.' It can also be in the accusative by the effect of '*taste*' as you say: 'Zayd: I hit him.' The meaning of the words is to rebuke the unbelievers. '*Anna*' is in the nominative as added to '*that*'. Al-Farrā' said that it can be in the accusative, meaning, 'the unbelievers will have.' He said that it is permitted for it to imply: 'know that.' Az-Zajjāj said, 'If the implication of "know" had been permitted, then it would be permitted to say, "Zayd going [nominative] and 'Amr sitting [accusative]." It is rather permitted to have "Zayd going [accusative]" in the inceptive, because the one reporting is informing. This is not allowed by any grammarian.'

يَٰٓأَيُّهَا ٱلَّذِينَ ءَامَنُوٓا۟ إِذَا لَقِيتُمُ ٱلَّذِينَ كَفَرُوا۟ زَحْفًا فَلَا تُوَلُّوهُمُ ٱلْأَدْبَارَ ﴿١٥﴾
وَمَن يُوَلِّهِمْ يَوْمَئِذٍ دُبُرَهُۥٓ إِلَّا مُتَحَرِّفًا لِّقِتَالٍ أَوْ مُتَحَيِّزًا إِلَىٰ فِئَةٍ فَقَدْ
بَآءَ بِغَضَبٍ مِّنَ ٱللَّهِ وَمَأْوَىٰهُ جَهَنَّمُ ۖ وَبِئْسَ ٱلْمَصِيرُ ﴿١٦﴾

15-16 You who believe! when you encounter those who disbelieve advancing in massed ranks into battle, do not turn your backs on them. Anyone who turns his back on them that day, unless he is withdrawing to rejoin the fight or withdrawing to support another group, brings Allah's anger down upon himself. His refuge is Hell. What an evil destination!

You who believe! when you encounter those who disbelieve advancing in massed ranks into battle, do not turn your backs on them.

Zaḥf (*advancing*) is to approach slowly. Its root is to creep forward on the buttocks. Then it is used for anyone who walks while advancing in battle. *Tazāḥif* is to approach one another. *Zaḥf* is used for approaching the enemy and *iztiḥafa* is for some to walk towards others. *Ziḥāf* in poetry is to shorten a syllable between two syllables in order to bring them closer together. It is said that it is when you approach and help one another and do not flee or turn your backs. Allah forbade that for the believers and made *jihād* and fighting the unbelievers obligatory for them. Ibn 'Aṭiyyah said that the word *adbār* (*backs*) is the plural of *dubur*. The use of the word '*backs*' in this *āyah* may be a turn of phrase because it is ugly for someone to flee and he is censured for it.

In this *āyah* Allah commands the believers not to turn their backs in the face of the unbelievers. This command is subject to the condition, for which there is a text, about them being no more than twice the number of the believers. If the believers meet a group of idolaters who are twice their number, there is an obligation not to retreat before them. If someone flees from two, he is fleeing from the press of battle. If someone flees from three, he is not fleeing from the press of battle and so the threat is not directed at him. Flight is a major and serious wrong action based on the literal text of the Qur'an and the consensus of most of the *imāms*.

One group, including Ibn al-Mājishūn in *al-Wāḍiḥah* said that weakness, strength and numbers should be taken into account. According to them, it is permitted for a hundred cavalry to flee a hundred cavalry if they know that the idolaters have twice the vigour and courage of the Muslims. The position of the majority, however, is that it is not permitted for a hundred to flee from less than two hundred. When a Muslim is faced with more than two of the enemy, he is permitted to retreat, but steadfastness is better. The army of Mu'tah stood firm and they were 3000 against 200,000, including 100,000 Greeks and 100,000 of the Arabs of Lakhm and Judhām. In the history of al-Andalus it is recorded that Ṭāriq, the client of Mūsā ibn Nuṣayr, went there in Rajab 93 AH with 1700 men when the king of Andalusia, Roderic, had 70,000 men. Ṭāriq advanced against him and was steadfast and Allah defeated the tyrant Roderic and victory was achieved.

Ibn Wahb said, 'I heard Mālik being asked about people who meet the enemy or are keeping guard when the enemy comes to them and they are few: should they fight or go and inform their companions?' He said, 'If they are strong enough to fight them, then they fight them. Otherwise they go to their companions and inform them.'

People disagree about whether fleeing in battle is specific to the Battle of Badr or is general to all fighting until the Day of Rising. It is related from Abū Sa'īd al-Khudrī that it is specific to the Battle of Badr, and Nāfi', al-Ḥasan, Qatādah, Yazīd ibn Abī Ḥabīb and aḍ-Ḍaḥḥāk also said that. That is the position of Abū Ḥanīfah as well. According to them it was particularly directed to the people of Badr and they were not permitted to run away. If they had, they would have run away to the idolaters and on that day there were no Muslims except them and the Muslims had no group except that of the Prophet ﷺ. Aṭ-Ṭabarī said, 'This is debatable because in Madīnah there were many of the *Anṣār* whom the Prophet ﷺ had not ordered to go out and who did not think that there would be fighting. They thought that it was just a matter of the caravan. The Messenger of Allah ﷺ went out with those who responded quickly.' And it is related from Ibn 'Abbās and other scholars that the *āyah* remains binding until the Day of Rising.

The first group cite what we mentioned as evidence as well as Allah's words '*on that day*', saying that it indicates the Battle of Badr and that the ruling of the *āyah* was abrogated by the *āyah* of twice the number. The ruling about fleeing from battle is that it is not a major wrong action. People fled in the Battle of Uḥud and Allah pardoned them. Allah says about them in the Battle of Ḥunayn: '*you turned your backs*'. (9:25) and there was no blame connected to that. Most scholars say that any day of battle is intended, as indicated by Allah's words: '*when you encounter those who disbelieve…*', so the ruling of the *āyah* will remain until the Day of Rising provided there is no more than twice their number as Allah made clear in another *āyah*. This is what Mālik, ash-Shāfi'ī and most scholars believe.

We find in *Sahih Muslim* from Abū Hurayrah that the Messenger of Allah ﷺ said, 'Avoid the seven major sins.' They include fleeing from battle. If someone flees, he should ask for Allah's forgiveness. This is a text regarding this matter. As for Uḥud, the enemy was more than double. In spite of that, they were blamed. The same is true of Ḥunayn. Those who fled, fled from superior numbers.

Ibn al-Qāsim said, 'The testimony of someone who has fled from battle is not allowed. It is not permitted for them to flee, even if their leader flees, since Allah says: "*Anyone who turns his back on them that day.*"' He said, 'It is permitted to flee if they are more than twice their number.' This is when the number of Muslims does not reach 12,000. When their number reaches 12,000, it is not lawful to flee even if the idolaters are more than double that number since the Messenger of Allah ﷺ said, '12,000 will not be defeated due to lack of numbers.' Most of the people of knowledge say that this number shows the *āyah* to be of a general nature. Abū Bishr and Abū Salamah al-'Āmilī related it. He is al-Ḥakam ibn

'Abdullāh ibn Khaṭṭāf and is not considered reliable. They related from Anas ibn Mālik that the Messenger of Allah ﷺ said, 'Aktham ibn al-Jawn! Go on expedition with other than your people and your character will become good and you will become generous to your companions. Aktham ibn al-Jawn! The best number of companions is four and the best number of scouts is forty. The best size of expedition is four hundred. The best size of army is four thousand. Twelve thousand will not be defeated for lack of numbers.' What is related from Mālik indicates that that is the position of his school. He said that to al-'Umarī al-Ābid when he asked if there was scope to abandon fighting against someone who altered and changed rulings. He said, 'If you have twelve thousand with you, there is no option to do that.'

If someone does flee, he should ask Allah for forgiveness. At-Tirmidhī related from Bilāl ibn Yasār from his father that his grandfather heard the Prophet ﷺ say, 'If anyone says, "There is no god but Him, the Living, the Self-Sustaining, and I turn in repentance to Him," Allah will forgive him, even if he fled from battle.' He said that this *ḥadīth* is *gharīb* and only known by this path.

unless he is withdrawing to rejoin the fight or withdrawing to support another group.

'Withdrawing' (*taḥarruf*) is moving away from the battlefront, and it involves moving from one side to another which is part of the tactics of war and is not being routed. The same is true of withdrawing to another group of Muslims to help them. So he resumes the fight and is not overcome. Abū Dāwūd related that 'Abdullāh ibn 'Umar was in one of the expeditions of the Messenger of Allah ﷺ. He said, 'The people turned away and I was one of those who turned away. When we did that, we said, "What are we doing? We have fled from the battle and brought wrath on ourselves!" Then we said, "We will enter Madīnah and go cautiously in it, so that no one will see us." We entered and then said, "We should present ourselves to the Messenger of Allah ﷺ. If we can repent, we will do so. If that is not possible, we will leave." We sat before *Fajr* to wait for the Messenger of Allah ﷺ. When he came out, we rose and went to him and stated, "We fled." He turned to us and said, "No, you are those withdrawing to attack [with another group]." We approached him and kissed his hand and he said, "I am the group of Muslims."'

Tha'lab said, 'The word [in the *ḥadīth*] *'akkārūn* is referring to those who turn in order to rejoin.' Others said that when someone retreats in war and then comes back again, the verb used is *'akara, i'takara*. Jarīr related from Manṣūr that Ibrāhīm said, 'A man retreated in the Battle of al-Qādisiyyah and went to 'Umar in Madīnah and said, "Amīr al-Mu'minīn, I am destroyed! I fled from the battle" 'Umar stated, "I am your group."' Muḥammad ibn Sīrīn said, 'When Abū 'Ubaydah was killed, the news reached 'Umar and he said, "If he had retreated to me, I would have been his group! I am the group for every Muslim!"'

According to these *ḥadīths*, flight is not a serious sin because the group here consists of Madīnah, the leader and the Muslim community wherever they are. According to the other view, it is a serious sin because the group with them is the group present in the battle. This is the position of the majority: that flight from battle is a serious wrong action. They said, 'The statements of the Prophet ﷺ and 'Umar are showing judicious concern for the believers since at that time they stood firm many times against double their number.' Allah knows best.

brings Allah's anger down upon himself.

This means he merits Allah's anger. The root meaning of *bā'a* is to return. He will abide in Hell. This indicates eternity as he says elsewhere. The Prophet ﷺ said, 'If someone says, "I ask forgiveness of Allah. There is no god but Him, the Living, the Self-Sustaining," he will be forgiven, even if he fled from the press of battle.'

فَلَمْ تَقْتُلُوهُمْ وَلَٰكِنَّ ٱللَّهَ قَتَلَهُمْ ۚ وَمَا رَمَيْتَ إِذْ رَمَيْتَ وَلَٰكِنَّ ٱللَّهَ رَمَىٰ ۚ
وَلِيُبْلِيَ ٱلْمُؤْمِنِينَ مِنْهُ بَلَآءً حَسَنًا ۚ إِنَّ ٱللَّهَ سَمِيعٌ عَلِيمٌ ﴿١٧﴾ ذَٰلِكُمْ وَأَنَّ ٱللَّهَ
مُوهِنُ كَيْدِ ٱلْكَٰفِرِينَ ﴿١٨﴾

17-18 You did not kill them; it was Allah who killed them; and you did not throw when you threw; it was Allah who threw: so He might test the believers with this excellent trial from Him. Allah is All-Hearing, All-Knowing. That is your reward. Allah always confounds the schemes of the unbelievers.

You did not kill them; it was Allah who killed them;

This is about the Battle of Badr. It is related that when the Companions of the Messenger of Allah ﷺ left Badr, each of them mentioned what he had done, saying, 'I did this' and another, 'I did that.' There was mutual boasting about that and so the *āyah* was revealed to inform them that it is Allah Almighty Who causes death and decrees all things and that His slave participates by his acquiring it and by his intention. The *āyah* refutes those who say that the actions of people are created by themselves. It means: 'You did not kill them, but Allah killed them by driving them to you so that you had power over them.' It is said that Allah killed them by the angels with whom He reinforced you.

and you did not throw when you threw; it was Allah who threw:

Scholars have four different positions about this throwing.

The first is that this throwing refers to the pebbles thrown by the Messenger of Allah ﷺ at Ḥunayn. Ibn Wahb related that from Mālik. Mālik said, 'There was no one who was not hit by that on that day.' That is also related from Ibn al-Qāsim.

The second is that it was in the Battle of Uḥud when he threw the spear at the neck of Ubayy ibn Khalaf who turned in retreat. The idolaters said, 'By Allah, there is nothing wrong with you!' He said, 'By Allah, if he had spat on me, he would have killed me! Did he not say, "I will kill him"?' Ubayy had threatened to kill the Messenger of Allah ﷺ in Makkah and the Messenger of Allah ﷺ said to him, 'Rather I will kill you.' The enemy of Allah died at a placed called Sarif on his return to Makkah from the blow struck by the Messenger of Allah ﷺ. Mūsā ibn 'Uqbah said that Ibn Shihāb said, 'In the Battle of Uḥud, Ubayy advanced in his armour and helmet, saying, "I will not be saved if Muḥammad is saved!" He attacked the Messenger of Allah ﷺ intending to kill him'. Mūsā ibn 'Uqbah said that Sa'īd ibn al-Musayyab said, 'Two of the believers went to confront him and the Messenger of Allah ﷺ commanded them to let him go. Muṣ'ab ibn 'Umayr met him in defence of the Messenger of Allah ﷺ and was slain. The Messenger of Allah ﷺ saw the collar-bone of Ubayy ibn Khalaf through a gap between his helmet and chain-mail and stabbed him with his spear, Ubayy fell from his horse but the wound did not bleed. Sa'īd said that he broke a rib and that the *āyah* was revealed about that.' This is weak because the *āyah* was revealed after Badr.

The third is that what is meant is the arrow that the Messenger of Allah ﷺ shot at the fortress of Khaybar which flew and hit Ibn Abī al-Ḥuqayq while he was on his bed. This is also false. The conquest of Khaybar occurred much later than the Battle of Uḥud. What is sound is that the manner in which Ibn Abī al-Ḥuqayq was killed was other than this.

The fourth is that this throwing took place in the Battle of Badr. Ibn Isḥāq said that. This is sounder because the *sūrah* is about the Battle of Badr. That was when Jibrīl said to the Prophet ﷺ, 'Take a handful of dust.' He took a handful of dust and threw it in their faces. There was no idolater whose eyes were not affected by it in his eyes, nose and mouth. Ibn 'Abbās said that. Tha'lab said that it means: 'You threw alarm and terror into their hearts when you threw the pebbles' and they were defeated. The words '*it was Allah Who threw,*' mean He helped and supported you. The Arabs say, 'Allah threw for you,' meaning that He helped you and gave you success and worked for you. Abū 'Ubaydah related this. Muḥammad ibn Yazīd said, 'You did not throw by your own power when you threw, but you threw by the power of Allah.'

so that He might test the believers with this excellent trial from Him.

'Trial' here means blessing. The *lām* is connected to something elided, i.e. 'so that He might test the believers in that way.'

Allah always confounds the schemes of the unbelievers.

The people of Makkah and Madīnah and Abū 'Amr read '*muwahhinu kayda*' while the people of Kufa read '*mūhinu kaydi*'. The form with the *shaddah* conveys added emphasis. It means that Allah casts terror into their hearts and splits them up so that they become weak. *Kayd* is plotting. It was already mentioned (4:76).

إِن تَسْتَفْتِحُوا فَقَدْ جَآءَكُمُ الْفَتْحُ وَإِن تَنتَهُوا فَهُوَ خَيْرٌ لَّكُمْ وَإِن
تَعُودُوا نَعُدْ وَلَن تُغْنِيَ عَنكُمْ فِئَتُكُمْ شَيْئًا وَلَوْ كَثُرَتْ وَأَنَّ اللَّهَ
مَعَ الْمُؤْمِنِينَ ١٩

19 If it was a decisive victory you were seeking, that victory has clearly been won. If you desist, it will be better for you; but if you return, We also will return. Your troops will not help you at all, however many they are. Allah is with the believers.

If it was a decisive victory you were seeking, that victory has clearly been won.

This sentence is a precondition and its apodosis. Three things are said about it. The first is that this is addressed to the unbelievers because they asked for victory and said, 'O Allah, give victory to whichever of us has cut off kin and wronged his companion.' Al-Ḥasan, Mujāhid and others said that. They said that at the time they left to support the caravan. It is said that Abū Jahl said it at the moment of fighting. An-Naḍr ibn al-Ḥārith said, 'O Allah, if this is the truth with You, then send down stones from heaven on us or bring us a painful punishment.' He was one of those killed at Badr. 'Seeking victory' (*istiftāḥ*) is to seek for help. It means:

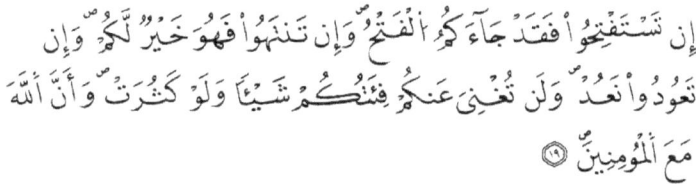

'The victory you requested has come, but it is for the Muslims against you. So that which makes the matter clear has come to you and the truth has been revealed to you.' *'If you desist'* from disbelief, 'it will be better for you.' *'If you return'* to these words and to fighting Muhammad ﷺ, '*We also will return*' to helping the believers. Your gathering will not help you, even if they are numerous. Allah helps those who believe and a group will not overcome them, however many.

The second view is that this is addressed to the believers and so it means: 'If you sought victory, victory has come to you. *'If you desist'* from what you did in terms of taking booty and captives without permission, '*it will be better for you*'. *'If you return'* to doing the same thing, '*We will return*' to rebuking you, in the way Allah makes clear in a later *āyah*: *'Were it not for a prior decree…'* (8:68)

The third view is that the first part is addressed to the believers while what is after it is addressed to the unbelievers, in other words 'if you return to fighting, We will return to the like of Badr.'

Al-Qushayrī said that what is sound is that it is addressed to the unbelievers. When they went out to help the caravan, they held on to the curtains of the Ka'bah and said, 'O Allah, give victory to the most guided of the two parties and the best of the two religions!' Al-Mahdawī said that it is related that the idolaters went out carrying the curtains of the Ka'bah, seeking victory by them. There is no contradiction because of the possible that they did both things.

Allah is with the believers.

It can be read as '*inna*' at the beginning, indicating a new sentence, or as '*anna*' as added to *'Allah always confounds the schemes of the unbelievers'* or to *'I am with You'*, in which case it means 'because Allah.' What is implied is that, in spite of their great number, Allah will help him ﷺ and he will not be defeated, even though they are numerous.

يَٰٓأَيُّهَا ٱلَّذِينَ ءَامَنُوٓاْ أَطِيعُواْ ٱللَّهَ وَرَسُولَهُۥ وَلَا تَوَلَّوْاْ عَنْهُ وَأَنتُمْ تَسْمَعُونَ ﴿٢٠﴾

20 You who believe! obey Allah and His Messenger. And do not turn away from him when you are able to hear.

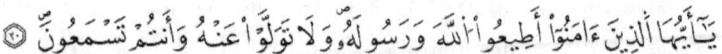

This is addressed to the true believers. Allah singled them out rather than the hypocrites in order to exalt them. Allah reiterated for them the command to obey Allah and His Messenger and forbade them to turn away. This is the view of most people. One group said that this is addressed to the hypocrites and it means: 'O you who believe only on your tongues.' Ibn 'Aṭiyyah said, 'Even if this is vaguely possible, it is very weak indeed because Allah described the one addressed in this *āyah* as having faith, and faith is affirmation. Hypocrites are not described as affirming anything. Even more unlikely is the view of those who say that it is addressed to the tribe of Israel. It is further away from the *āyah*.'

Turning away is to turn back. He said, 'from him' and not 'from the two of them' because obeying the Messenger is obeying Allah. It is like His words: *'it would be more fitting for them to please Allah and His Messenger.'* (9:62) The meaning of *'when you are able to hear'* is: 'when you are able to hear the proofs recited to you in the Qur'an.' It acts as an adverbial *ḥāl*.

وَلَا تَكُونُوا۟ كَٱلَّذِينَ قَالُوا۟ سَمِعْنَا وَهُمْ لَا يَسْمَعُونَ ﴿٢١﴾ إِنَّ شَرَّ
ٱلدَّوَآبِّ عِندَ ٱللَّهِ ٱلصُّمُّ ٱلْبُكْمُ ٱلَّذِينَ لَا يَعْقِلُونَ ﴿٢٢﴾

21-22 Do not be like those who say, 'We hear,' when they do not hear. The worst of beasts in Allah's sight are those who are deaf and dumb and have no intellect.

Do not be like the Jews, hypocrites or idolaters. 'Hearing' here refers to the hearing of the ears. The meaning of the words *'when they do not hear'* is that they do not reflect on or contemplate what they hear. They are in the position of the one who does not listen and turns from the truth. Allah forbids the believers to be like that. The *āyah* indicates that the words of a believer, 'I hear and obey' are useless unless the effect of that appears on him through his obedience in actions. When he falls short where commands are concerned and fails to carry them out and turns to committing prohibited matters, what hearing does he have and what obedience does he have? He is then in the position of a hypocrite who makes a show of faith while concealing his disbelief. That is what is meant here. Those who say, 'We hear' and do not hear are the hypocrites, either from the Jews or idolaters. Then Allah tells us that the unbelievers are the worst beasts on the earth. It refers to some people of the Banū-d-Dār. The root of 'worst *(sharr)*' is *asharr* and the *alif* is elided. It is similar with 'best *(khayr)*' whose root is *akhyar*.

وَلَوْ عَلِمَ ٱللَّهُ فِيهِمْ خَيْرًا لَّأَسْمَعَهُمْ ۖ وَلَوْ أَسْمَعَهُمْ لَتَوَلَّوا۟ وَّهُم مُّعْرِضُونَ ﴿٢٣﴾

23 If Allah knew of any good in them, He would have made them able to hear. But even if He had made them able to hear, they would still have turned away.

'He would have made them able to hear' the proofs and arguments and understand them, but He already knew that they would be among the wretched. If they had been *'able to hear'* meaning 'understand', they still would not have believed after He knew before-time that they would be unbelievers. It is said that it means that He would have enabled them to hear the words of the dead when they asked that Quṣayy ibn Kilāb and others be brought back to life to testify to the Prophethood of Muḥammad ﷺ. Az-Zajjāj said, 'so that they could hear the answer to all they asked for.' *'They would still have turned away'* since Allah already knew that they would not believe.

يَٰٓأَيُّهَا ٱلَّذِينَ ءَامَنُوا۟ ٱسْتَجِيبُوا۟ لِلَّهِ وَلِلرَّسُولِ إِذَا دَعَاكُمْ لِمَا
يُحْيِيكُمْ ۖ وَٱعْلَمُوٓا۟ أَنَّ ٱللَّهَ يَحُولُ بَيْنَ ٱلْمَرْءِ وَقَلْبِهِۦ
وَأَنَّهُۥٓ إِلَيْهِ تُحْشَرُونَ ﴿٢٤﴾

24 You who believe! respond to Allah and to the Messenger when He calls you to what will bring you to life! Know that Allah intervenes between a man and his heart and that you will be gathered to Him.

There is no disagreement that this is addressed to the true believers. *Istijābah* is to respond. The root form of the verb in *'what will give you life'* is *yuḥyīyukum*" and the *ḍammah* is elided from the *yā'* since it is heavy and *idghām* is not permitted. Abū 'Ubaydah said that the meaning of *'respond'* is answer, but linguistically it is known that *istijāba* is transitive with a *lām* and *ajāba* is transitive without a *lām* as we see in 46:31. [POEM] The verbal noun of Form IV is *ijābah* and the noun is *jābah*. *Mujāwabah* and *tawājub* mean conversation. One says, 'a good answer (*jībah*)'.

'To what will bring you to life' is connected to *'respond'*. It means: 'respond to what will bring you to life when He calls you.' It is said that the *lām* has the meaning of 'to', in other words *'to what will bring you to life'*, implying that Allah gives life to your *dīn* and teaches you. It is said that He calls you to what will give life to your

hearts so that you proclaim His Unity. This giving of life is metaphorical because it is from the death of disbelief and ignorance.

Mujāhid and the majority said that it means: 'Respond with obedience to the commands and prohibitions which the Qur'an contains. There is eternal life and timeless blessing in it.' It is also said that what is meant is *jihād*. It is the cause of life outwardly because when the enemy is not attacked he attacks and there is death in his attack. Death in *jihād* is eternal life. Allah says: *'Do not suppose that those killed in he Way of Allah are dead. No indeed! They are alive.'* (3:169) What is sound is that it is general and undefined as the majority say.

Al-Bukhārī related that Abū Sa'īd al-Mu'allā said, 'I was praying in the mosque and the Messenger of Allah ﷺ called me and I did not respond. Then I went to him and said, "Messenger of Allah, I was praying." He said, "Does not Allah Almighty say, 'Respond to Allah and to the Messenger when He calls you to what will bring you to life'?"' This was already mentioned in the *Fātiḥah*. Ash-Shāfi'ī said, 'This is evidence that an obligatory action or word in the prayer does not invalidate it because the Messenger of Allah ﷺ commanded him to respond while he was praying.' This also contains the proof of the position of al-Awzā'ī that if a man is praying and sees a child about to fall into a well, and shouts at him and goes and rebukes him, there is no harm in that. Allah knows best.

Know that Allah intervenes between a man and his heart

This is textual evidence from Allah that He creates disbelief and faith and can come between the unbeliever and the faith which He has commanded him to have, so that he does not acquire it because it has not been decreed for him. Instead Allah has decreed the opposite for him: which is disbelief. The same is true of the believer: Allah comes between him and disbelief. Therefore it is clear by this text that the Almighty creates all that His slaves procure, both good and evil. This is the meaning of the words of the Prophet ﷺ, 'No, by the Overturner of hearts.' That action of Allah is justice for whomever He misguides and disappoints because He did not deny them anything which was obliged on Him so as to remove the quality of justice. He denied His grace to them, not what was obliged for them.

As-Suddī said, 'Allah comes between a man and his heart so that he can only believe with His permission or disbelieve with His permission, in other words by His will.' The heart is the place of reflection and it is in the Hand of Allah. When He wishes, He comes between someone and their heart by means of illness or misfortune, preventing them from understanding. So it means: 'Hasten to respond before you are unable to do so through lack of mental capacity.' Mujāhid said that it means that Allah comes between a man and his mind so that he does not know what he does. We find in revelation: *'There is a reminder in that for anyone who has a heart,'* (50:37) meaning someone with intelligence. It is said that Allah comes between a person and their heart through death so they cannot acquire anything they had earlier failed to obtain.

It is said that on the day of the Battle of Badr the Muslims feared the great number of the enemy and Allah informed them that He comes between a man and his heart by replacing fear with security and changing what their enemies feel from security to fear. It is said that the meaning is that He changes things from one state to another. This is comprehensive. Aṭ-Ṭabarī preferred it to be a report from Allah that He controls the hearts of His slaves and He comes between them and their hearts when He wishes so that a man only perceives anything by the will of Allah.

and that you will be gathered to Him.

This is added to what is before it. Al-Farrā' said, 'If it had been a new sentence, it would be correct to have "*innahu*" rather than "*annahu*".

وَاتَّقُوا فِتْنَةً لَّا تُصِيبَنَّ الَّذِينَ ظَلَمُوا مِنكُمْ خَاصَّةً وَاعْلَمُوا
أَنَّ اللَّهَ شَدِيدُ الْعِقَابِ ٢٥

25 Be fearful of trials which will not afflict solely those among you who do wrong. Know that Allah is Severe in Retribution.

Ibn 'Abbās said, 'Allah commanded the believers not to affirm the wrong among them lest the punishment envelop them.' That is how az-Zubayr ibn al-'Awwām interpreted this. He said in the Battle of the Camel in 26 AH, 'I did not know until today that I was one of those intended by this *āyah*. I thought that it was only about those who were being addressed at that time.' That is how al-Ḥasan al-Baṣrī, as-Suddī and others interpreted it as well. As-Suddī said, 'The *āyah* was revealed about the people of Badr in particular. They underwent a trial and fought one another in the Battle of the Camel.' Ibn 'Abbās said, 'This *āyah* was revealed about the Companions of the Messenger of Allah ﷺ.' He said, 'Allah commanded the believers not to affirm the wrong among them lest Allah envelop all of them with the punishment.' Ḥudhayfah ibn al-Yamān said that the Messenger of Allah ﷺ said, 'There will be trial (*fitnah*) between some of my Companions. May Allah forgive them because they are my Companions. Some people after them will establish a custom in respect of it on account of which Allah will admit them to the Fire.'

These are interpretations which are supported by some *ḥadīth*s. We find in *Ṣaḥīḥ Muslim* that Zaynab bint Jaḥsh asked the Messenger of Allah ﷺ, 'Messenger of Allah! Will we be destroyed while there are righteous people among us?' 'Yes,' he replied, 'if there is a lot of corruption.' We find in the *Ṣaḥīḥ* of at-Tirmidhī: 'If people see someone committing an injustice and do not seize his hands to stop him, Allah will very soon envelop them with a punishment from Him.' These *ḥadīth*s were already discussed. We find in *Ṣaḥīḥ Bukhārī* and at-Tirmidhī from an-Nu'mān ibn Bashīr that the Prophet ﷺ said, 'The metaphor of someone who stops at the limits of what Allah has ordained and someone who transgresses them is that of some people who are together on a ship. Some of them are at the top and some at the bottom. When those at the bottom want to drink, they have to pass by the people above them, so they say, "If we make a hole in our part, we will not annoy those above us." If they are allowed to do what they want, they will all be destroyed. If they are prevented from doing it, they will be saved and all will be saved.' This *ḥadīth* shows that the masses are punished for the sins of the few. Punishment is warranted when commanding the right and forbidding the wrong are abandoned.

Our scholars say that when *fitnah* is acted upon, then all are destroyed. That is when acts of disobedience appear and the wrong spreads and is not changed. When it is not changed, it is mandatory for the believers who object to it in their hearts to emigrate from that land and flee from it. This is the ruling for the nations before us. An example of that is the story of the Sabbath when some of them shunned the disobedient and said, 'We will not live with you.' This is what the Salaf said. Ibn Wahb related that Mālik said, 'Emigrate from a land in which wrong is done openly and do not reside in it.' His argument was that that was what Abū ad-Dardā' did in leaving the land of Mu'āwiyah when usury became public practice. He had allowed the sale of gold goblets for more than their weight. This was transmitted in the *Ṣaḥīḥ*.

Al-Bukhārī related from Ibn 'Umar that the Messenger of Allah ﷺ said, 'When Allah sends down a punishment on a people, the punishment strikes everyone among them and then they will be resurrected according to their actions.' This indicates that general destruction from Him is purification for the believers and retribution against the impious. Muslim related from 'Abdullāh ibn az-Zubayr that 'Ā'ishah said, 'The Messenger of Allah ﷺ started in his sleep and I said, "Messenger of Allah, you did something in your sleep which you have not done before." He replied, "Something extraordinary! Some people of my community attacked this house seeking a man of Quraysh who had taken refuge in it. When they are at al-Baydā', the earth will swallow them up." We said, "Messenger of Allah, there are many people on the road." He replied, "Yes, they include those who are striving for something, those who are forced and travellers. They will all be destroyed and have different ends and Allah Almighty will resurrect them according to their intentions."'

If it is said that Allah says: *'No burden-bearer will bear another's burden'* (6:164), *'Every soul is held in pledge against what it earned'* (74: 37) and *'For it is what it has earned; against it was it has merited'* (2:286), and that this means that no one can be punished for the sin of someone else and that the punishment is connected to the one who commits it, the answer is that, when people support one another in wrongdoing, part of the obligation of all who see it is to change it. If they are silent about it, they are all considered disobedient. One actually does it and the other is happy with it. Therefore, in His judgment and wisdom, Allah puts the one who consented to it in the same position as the one who committed it and he is included in the punishment. Ibn al-'Arabī said that. It is contained in *ḥadīths* as we said. The aim of the *āyah* is: 'Be fearful of a trial which goes beyond the wrongdoers and afflicts all, good and bad.'

Grammarians disagree about the addition of the *nūn* to '*tuṣībanna*'. Al-Farrā' said that it is the same as when someone says, 'Descend from your mount and do not let it throw you off [with the *nūn*].' It is the apodosis of the command in the negative, meaning, 'Descend from it and it will not throw you off.' It is like Allah's words: *'enter your dwellings so that Sulaymān and his troops do not crush you,'* (27:18) meaning: 'Enter so that they do not crush you.' The *nūn* is added because it contains the meaning of the result (*jazā'*). It is said that it is like an oath, and the *nūn* is only added to a negative action or the apodosis of an oath.

Abū al-'Abbās al-Mubarrad said that it is prohibition after a command. It has the meaning of a prohibition to the wrongdoers. It means: 'Do not approach wrongdoing.' Sībawayh related, 'I should not see you here,' i.e. 'Do not be here. I will not see anyone here.' Al-Jurjānī said, 'It means: "Fear trials which will afflict those who do wrong in particular" and "*lā tuṣībanna*" is a prohibition in the position of an adjective of something indefinite. It is interpreted as talking about the punishment afflicting those who did wrong.'

'Alī, Zayd ibn Thābit, Ubayy and Ibn Mas'ūd recited *'la-tuṣībanna'* without an *alif.* Al-Mahdawī said, 'If someone recites "*la-tuṣībanna*", it is possible that it is a shortening of "*lā tuṣībanna*" and the *alif* is elided as it is elided from "*mā*" which is the sister of "*lā*" in the like of "*ama wa-llāhi la-af'alanna*" and expressions like it. It is possible that it differs from the majority reading and so it means that it will afflict the wrongdoer in particular.'

وَٱذْكُرُوٓا۟ إِذْ أَنتُمْ قَلِيلٌ مُّسْتَضْعَفُونَ فِى ٱلْأَرْضِ تَخَافُونَ أَن يَتَخَطَّفَكُمُ
ٱلنَّاسُ فَـَٔاوَىٰكُمْ وَأَيَّدَكُم بِنَصْرِهِۦ وَرَزَقَكُم مِّنَ ٱلطَّيِّبَٰتِ لَعَلَّكُمْ
تَشْكُرُونَ ﴿٢٦﴾

26 When you were few and oppressed in the land, afraid that the people would snatch you away, He gave you refuge and supported you with His help and provided you with good things so that hopefully you would be thankful.

Al-Kalbī said that this was revealed about the *Muhājirūn*, describing their situation before *Hijrah* and at the beginning of Islam. '*In the land*' means the land of Makkah. The verb '*snatch*' (*khiṭf*) is to grab someone suddenly. Qatādah and 'Ikrimah said that '*people*' here means the idolaters of Quraysh. Wahb ibn Munabbih said that it is the Persians and Greeks. Ibn 'Abbās said that the refuge in the verb '*gave you refuge*' was with the *Anṣār*. As-Suddī said that it refers to Madīnah, and the meaning is the same. The verb '*support*' here means strengthen and '*with His help*' means 'with His direct aid' or it is said that it is by means of the angels in the Battle of Badr. The '*good things*' is a reference to the booty which was already mentioned.

يَٰٓأَيُّهَا ٱلَّذِينَ ءَامَنُوا۟ لَا تَخُونُوا۟ ٱللَّهَ وَٱلرَّسُولَ وَتَخُونُوٓا۟ أَمَٰنَٰتِكُمْ وَأَنتُمْ
تَعْلَمُونَ ﴿٢٧﴾

27 You who believe! do not betray Allah and His Messenger, and do not knowingly betray your trusts.

It is related that this was revealed about Abū Lubābah ibn 'Abd al-Mundhir when he indicated to the Banū Qurayẓah that they would be killed. Abu Lubābah said, 'By Allah, my feet did not move before I knew that I had betrayed Allah and His Messenger.' So this *āyah* was revealed. When it was revealed, he tied himself to one of the pillars of the mosque and said, 'By Allah, I will not taste food or drink until I die or Allah turns to me.' The report is well-known.

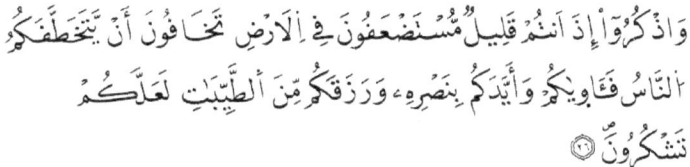

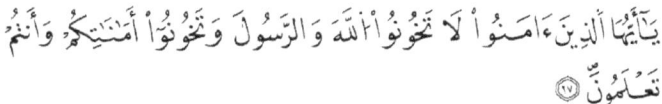

'Ikrimah said, 'When the business of Qurayẓah arose, the Prophet ﷺ sent 'Alī [to them] with the people who accompanied him. When they reached Qurayẓah, they slandered the Messenger of Allah ﷺ. Jibrīl came on a piebald horse.' 'Ā'ishah said, 'I can still see the Messenger of Allah ﷺ wiping the dust from the face of Jibril. I said, "This is Diḥyah, Messenger of Allah." He said, "This is Jibrīl." He asked, "Messenger of Allah, what keeps you from going to the Banū Qurayẓah?" The Messenger of Allah ﷺ said, 'How will I deal with their fortresses?' Jibrīl said, "I will enter against them with this horse of mine." The Messenger of Allah ﷺ rode a horse without a saddle. When 'Alī saw him, he said, "Messenger of Allah! You should not go to them. They are insulting you." He said, "No, it will be a greeting." The Prophet ﷺ went to them and said, "Brothers of monkeys and pigs." They said, "Abū al-Qāsim, we are not used to hearing abusive language from you!" They said, "We will not come down for the judgment of Muḥammad, but we will come down for the judgment of Sa'd ibn Mu'ādh." He came and judged that their fighters should be killed and their dependents taken as captives. The Messenger of Allah ﷺ said, "That is what the angel told me at dawn."' Then this was revealed and it was revealed about Abū Lubābah. He indicated to the Banū Qurayẓah when they said, 'We will submit to the judgment of Sa'd ibn Mu'ādh.' It meant: 'Do not do it. It means slaughter,' and he pointed to his throat.

It is said that the *āyah* was revealed about the fact that they heard something from the Prophet ﷺ and then disclosed it to the idolaters. And it is also said that it refers to stealing from the booty and it was ascribed to Allah because He is the One Who commanded its division and to the Messenger of Allah ﷺ because he conveyed from Allah and carried it out.

'Betrayal' (*khayānah*) is treachery and concealing something. Exemplification of that is found in the words of Allah: *'He knows the eyes' deceit (khā'inah).'* (40:19) The Prophet ﷺ used to say, 'O Allah, I seek refuge with You from hunger which is a terrible bedmate and from betrayal (*khayānah*) which is a terrible close companion.' An-Nasa'ī transmitted it from Abū Hurayrah. The verb in '*betray your trusts*' is in the jussive tense to correspond to the first. '*Trusts*' are the actions which Allah has entrusted to His servants. They are called '*trusts*' because the one who has them is secure from denying rights. It is derived from the word *amn* (security). The adverb '*knowingly*' means: knowing the ugliness and shame in betrayal. It is said that it means knowing that it is a trust.

وَٱعْلَمُوٓا۟ أَنَّمَآ أَمْوَٰلُكُمْ وَأَوْلَٰدُكُمْ فِتْنَةٌ وَأَنَّ ٱللَّهَ عِندَهُۥٓ أَجْرٌ
عَظِيمٌ ﴿٢٨﴾

28 Know that your wealth and children are a trial and that there is an immense reward with Allah.

Abu Lubābah had wealth and children among the Banū Qurayẓah. That is what moved him to be lenient to them. This indicates being tested by that. '*There is an immense reward with Allah,*' so prefer His right to their right.

يَٰٓأَيُّهَا ٱلَّذِينَ ءَامَنُوٓا۟ إِن تَتَّقُوا۟ ٱللَّهَ يَجْعَل لَّكُمْ فُرْقَانًا وَيُكَفِّرْ عَنكُمْ
سَيِّـَٔاتِكُمْ وَيَغْفِرْ لَكُمْ ۗ وَٱللَّهُ ذُو ٱلْفَضْلِ ٱلْعَظِيمِ ﴿٢٩﴾

29 You who believe! if you have *taqwā* of Allah, He will give you discrimination and erase your bad actions from you and forgive you. Allah's favour is indeed immense.

Taqwā has already been mentioned (2:2). Allah knows whether or not they will have *taqwā*. He mentions that condition because He addresses His slaves in the same way that they might address themselves. When someone fears his Lord, which is by following His commands and avoiding His prohibitions, leaving doubtful things out of the fear of falling into forbidden things, filling the heart with sincere intention and engaging his limbs in righteous actions, preserving himself from being sullied by hidden and outward *shirk* by considering other than Allah where actions are concerned, and dealing with this world with abstinence in respect of wealth, Allah will give him discrimination between truth and falsehood and provide him with the ability to obtain the good he desires. Ibn Wahb said that he asked Mālik about this *āyah* and he recited: '*Whoever has taqwā of Allah, He will give him a way out.*' (65:2) Ibn al-Qāsim and Ashhab related the like of that from Mālik and Mujāhid also said that. A poet said:

You have no parting (*furqān*) from long-lasting sorrow
after the residents have travelled on and left.

Another said:

How can I hope for immortality when death seeks me
and I cannot part (*furqān*) from the cup of fate.

Ibn Isḥāq said that *furqān* is to distinguish between the truth and falsehood. Ibn Zayd said that. As-Suddī said that it is salvation. Al-Farrā' said that it is victory and conquest. It is said that it is in the Next World when Allah will admit you to the Garden and others to the Fire.

وَإِذْ يَمْكُرُ بِكَ ٱلَّذِينَ كَفَرُوا۟ لِيُثْبِتُوكَ أَوْ يَقْتُلُوكَ أَوْ يُخْرِجُوكَ ۚ
وَيَمْكُرُونَ وَيَمْكُرُ ٱللَّهُ ۖ وَٱللَّهُ خَيْرُ ٱلْمَـٰكِرِينَ ٣٠

30 When those who disbelieve were plotting against you to imprison you or kill you or expel you: they were plotting and Allah was plotting, but Allah is the Best of Plotters.

This reports about what the idolaters agreed to in their plotting against the Prophet ﷺ in the Dār an-Nadwah. They agreed to kill him, so they waited for him in the night and lay in ambush at the door of his house throughout the night so that they could kill him when he emerged. The Prophet ﷺ instructed 'Alī ibn Abī Ṭālib to sleep in his bed and prayed to Allah to conceal his tracks from them. Allah covered up their eyes and he went out when they had fallen asleep and put dust on their heads and went on his way. In the morning 'Alī came out to them and they knew that the Messenger of Allah ﷺ had eluded them. The report is well-known in the *Sīrah* and elsewhere.

The verb *athbata* means to imprison. Qatādah said that it means to tie up. He and 'Abdullah ibn Kathīr said that it means to put in prison. Abān ibn Taghlib and Abū Ḥātim said that it means to cover with wounds and beat severely. The verb '*they were plotting*' begins a new sentence. *Makr* is secret plotting about something. The plotting on the part of Allah referred to in the words: *'Allah is the Best of Plotters,'* is repaying them with the punishment for their plotting from a direction they did not expect.

وَإِذَا تُتْلَىٰ عَلَيْهِمْ ءَايَـٰتُنَا قَالُوا۟ قَدْ سَمِعْنَا لَوْ نَشَآءُ لَقُلْنَا مِثْلَ هَـٰذَآ ۙ
إِنْ هَـٰذَآ إِلَّآ أَسَـٰطِيرُ ٱلْأَوَّلِينَ ٣١

31 When Our Signs are recited to them, they say, 'We have already heard all this. If we wanted, we could say the same thing. This is nothing but the myths of previous peoples.'

This was revealed about an-Naḍr ibn al-Ḥārith. He went to trade in Ḥīra and brought back stories like that of *Kalīlah and Dimnah* and tales about Khusrau and Caesar. When the Messenger of Allah ﷺ relayed information about those in the past, an-Naḍr said, 'If I had wanted to, I could have done the same as this.' This was insolence and a lie. It is said that they imagined that they had the like of it as the magicians imagined in the case of Mūsā. Then they attempted to do it and were unable to and so they said stubbornly, '*This is nothing but the myths of previous peoples.*'

وَإِذْ قَالُوا۟ ٱللَّهُمَّ إِن كَانَ هَٰذَا هُوَ ٱلْحَقَّ مِنْ عِندِكَ فَأَمْطِرْ عَلَيْنَا
حِجَارَةً مِّنَ ٱلسَّمَآءِ أَوِ ٱئْتِنَا بِعَذَابٍ أَلِيمٍ ٣٢

32 And they say, 'Allah, if this is really the truth from You, rain down stones on us out of heaven or send a painful punishment down on us.'

The noun '*the truth*' is recited as *al-ḥaqqa* in the accusative by the effect of the verb *kāna* and the *huwa* is added for separation. It is also permissible for it to be in the nominative (*al-ḥaqqu*). Az-Zajjāj said, 'I do not know of anyone who recited that. Grammarians do not disagree that it is permitted, but the reading is *sunnah* and it is only recited with a pleasing recitation.'

There is disagreement about this statement. Mujāhid and Ibn Jubayr said that the one who said it was an-Naḍr ibn al-Ḥārith. Anas ibn Mālik said that the one who said it was Abū Jahl. Al-Bukhārī and Muslim related that. Then it is possible that they said that out of the uncertainty in their hearts, or it was by way of obduracy and making things obscure for people who thought that they had insight. Then what they asked for actually happened to them in the Battle of Badr. It is related that one of the Jews met Ibn 'Abbās and asked, 'Who are you from?' 'Quraysh,' he answered. He said, 'You are from the people who said, *"Allah, if this is really the truth from You…"* Why did they not say, "If this is really the truth from You, then guide us to it!"? Those are an ignorant people.' Ibn 'Abbās said, 'And you, Israelite, are from a people whose feet were not dry from the sea in which Pharaoh and his people were drowned and Mūsa and his people were saved before they said, *"Give us a god as these people have gods."* (7:138) Mūsā told them, "You are indeed an ignorant people."' The Jew was speechless. In the phrase '*rain down stones*' the verb *amṭara* is used because it is punishment; when it is a matter of mercy the verb *maṭara* is used according to Abū 'Ubaydah. This was already mentioned (6:25) .

وَمَا كَانَ ٱللَّهُ لِيُعَذِّبَهُمْ وَأَنتَ فِيهِمْ وَمَا كَانَ ٱللَّهُ مُعَذِّبَهُمْ وَهُمْ يَسْتَغْفِرُونَ ﴿٣٣﴾

33 Allah would not punish them while you were among them. Allah would not punish them as long as they sought forgiveness.

This was revealed when Abū Jahl said, *'O Allah, if this is the truth from You…'* (8:32) We find that in *Ṣaḥīḥ Muslim*. Ibn 'Abbās said, 'The people of a town will not be punished until the Prophet ﷺ and believers leave it and go where they are commanded.'

Allah would not punish them as long as they sought forgiveness.

Ibn 'Abbās said that they used to say in *ṭawāf*, 'Your forgiveness!' If the impious ask for forgiveness, that removes some evil and harm from them. It is said that asking forgiveness refers to the Muslims who were among them, implying, 'He would not punish them while there are Muslims among them asking for forgiveness.' When they left, then Allah punished them at Badr and elsewhere. Aḍ-Ḍaḥḥāk and others said that. It is said that asking for forgiveness here means Islam, and so it means that they become Muslims. Mujāhid and 'Ikrimah said that. It is said that 'seeking forgiveness' is because there were those future generations in their loins who will ask for forgiveness. That is also related from Mujāhid. It is said that it means, 'If they were to ask for forgiveness, they would not be punished.' So they are called on to ask for forgiveness. Qatādah and Ibn Zayd said that.

Al-Madā'inī mentioned that some scholars said, 'One of the Arabs in the time of the Prophet ﷺ was extravagant to himself and did not restrict himself. When the Prophet ﷺ died, he wore wool and stopped doing what he had been doing and made a display of the *dīn* and practices. He was told, 'You should have done this while the Prophet ﷺ was alive and he would have been happy with you.' He said, 'I had two securities. One is gone and the other still remains. Allah Almighty says: *"Allah would not punish them while you are among them."* That is one security. The other is: *"Allah would not punish them as long as they sought forgiveness."'*'

وَمَا لَهُمْ أَلَّا يُعَذِّبَهُمُ ٱللَّهُ وَهُمْ يَصُدُّونَ عَنِ ٱلْمَسْجِدِ ٱلْحَرَامِ وَمَا كَانُوٓا۟
أَوْلِيَآءَهُۥٓ ۚ إِنْ أَوْلِيَآؤُهُۥٓ إِلَّا ٱلْمُتَّقُونَ وَلَٰكِنَّ أَكْثَرَهُمْ لَا يَعْلَمُونَ ﴿٣٤﴾

34 But why should Allah not punish them now when they bar access to the *Masjid al-Ḥarām*? They are not its guardians. Only people who are godfearing can be its guardians. But most of them do not know that.

It means: What will prevent Him punishing them? They deserved punishment because of the ugly deed they perpetrated and the causes of that. But each of them has a term which is already written for him. So Allah punished them with the sword after the Prophet ﷺ left. The following was revealed about that: *'An inquirer asked about an impending punishment.'* (70:1) Al-Akhfash said that *an* is redundant. *'Most of them do not know'* that the godfearing are its guardians.

وَمَا كَانَ صَلَاتُهُمْ عِندَ ٱلْبَيْتِ إِلَّا مُكَآءً وَتَصْدِيَةً ۚ فَذُوقُوا۟
ٱلْعَذَابَ بِمَا كُنتُمْ تَكْفُرُونَ ﴿٣٥﴾ إِنَّ ٱلَّذِينَ كَفَرُوا۟ يُنفِقُونَ
أَمْوَٰلَهُمْ لِيَصُدُّوا۟ عَن سَبِيلِ ٱللَّهِ ۚ فَسَيُنفِقُونَهَا ثُمَّ تَكُونُ
عَلَيْهِمْ حَسْرَةً ثُمَّ يُغْلَبُونَ ۗ وَٱلَّذِينَ كَفَرُوٓا۟ إِلَىٰ جَهَنَّمَ
يُحْشَرُونَ ﴿٣٦﴾ لِيَمِيزَ ٱللَّهُ ٱلْخَبِيثَ مِنَ ٱلطَّيِّبِ وَيَجْعَلَ ٱلْخَبِيثَ
بَعْضَهُۥ عَلَىٰ بَعْضٍ فَيَرْكُمَهُۥ جَمِيعًا فَيَجْعَلَهُۥ فِى جَهَنَّمَ ۚ أُو۟لَٰٓئِكَ
هُمُ ٱلْخَٰسِرُونَ ﴿٣٧﴾

35-37 Their prayer at the House is nothing but whistling and clapping. So taste the punishment because you disbelieved! Those who disbelieve spend their wealth barring access to the Way of Allah. They will spend it; then they will regret it; then they will be overthrown. Those who disbelieve will be gathered into Hell, so that Allah may sift the bad out from the good, and pile the bad on top of one another, heaping them all together, and tip them into Hell. They are the lost.

Ibn 'Abbās said, 'Quraysh used to perform *ṭawāf* of the House naked, clapping and whistling. They thought that that was worship.' *Mukā'* is whistling and *taṣdīyah* is clapping. Mujāhid, as-Suddī and Ibn 'Umar said that. 'Antarah said:

I left the absent husband of the woman cast down,
the flesh between side and shoulder clapping like the upper jaw.

It means that it makes a sound. *Makā'a* is used for a camel breaking wind. As-Suddī said that it is the tune of white bird found in the Hijaz called *mukā'*. A poet said:

The *mukā'* warbled beyond the meadow

Qatādah said that *mukā'* is clapping the hands and *taṣdīyah* is shouting. According to commentators, this refutes ignorant Sufis who dance, clap and faint. That is objectionable and intelligent people avoid such things. Someone who does that is doing something similar to what the idolaters used to do at the House. Ibn Jurayj and Ibn Abī Najīḥ related from Mujāhid that *mukā'* is a sound made by putting the fingers in the mouth and *taṣdīyah* is whistling and by that they wanted to distract Muḥammad ﷺ from the prayer. An-Naḥḥās said, 'What is known in language is what is related from Ibn 'Umar.' Abū 'Ubayd and others said that the verb *makā, yamkū* is to whistle and *ṣaddā, yuṣaddā* is to clap. Illustrating that are the words of 'Amr ibn al-Iṭnābah:

They continue to make a tumult,
whistling (*mukā'*) at the House while clapping.

Sa'īd ibn Jubayr said that the meaning of *taṣdīyah* is to bar them from the House. The phrase *'sift the bad out from the good'* means the believer from the unbeliever. It is said that it is general to all actions, expenditure and other things.

قُل لِّلَّذِينَ كَفَرُوٓا۟ إِن يَنتَهُوا۟ يُغْفَرْ لَهُم مَّا قَدْ سَلَفَ وَإِن
يَعُودُوا۟ فَقَدْ مَضَتْ سُنَّتُ ٱلْأَوَّلِينَ ٣٨

38 Say to those who disbelieve that if they stop, they will be forgiven what is past; but if they return to it, they have the pattern of previous peoples in the past.

Say to those who disbelieve that if they stop,

The Prophet ﷺ was commanded to say this to the unbelievers whether or not he used those actual words. Ibn 'Aṭiyyah said, 'If it had been as al-Kisā'ī mentioned in the copy of the Qur'an of Ibn Mas'ūd, the Message would not have been conveyed except by these exact words. This is according to what words demand.'

'If they stop' means stop disbelieving. Ibn 'Aṭiyyah said that it must be that. The forgiveness is the apodosis of the precondition. Forgiveness of what an unbeliever did in the past is only granted to someone who stops disbelieving. Excellent are the words of Abū Sa'īd Aḥmad ibn Muḥammad az-Zubayrī:

Forgiveness is obliged for the lad when he confesses
and then stops doing what he did.
That is because of the words of Allah about the one who confesses.
When he stops, he is forgiven what was in the past.

Muslim related that Abū Shumāsah al-Mahri said, 'We were with 'Amr ibn al-'Āṣ when he was dying and weeping profusely …' Among his words he mentioned that the Prophet ﷺ said, 'Do you not know that Islam wipes out what is before it, *hijrah* wipes out what is before it, and *ḥajj* wipes out what is before it?' Ibn al-'Arabī said, 'This is a kindness from Allah to His creatures. That is because the unbelievers professed unbelief and committed crimes, acts of disobedience and sins. If punishment had been ordained for them, they never would have sought repentance or obtained forgiveness. So Allah made acceptance of repentance easy for them on their demonstration of regret. Forgiveness is a gift of Islam and it wipes all that went before, making it more likely that they would enter the *dīn* and more likely that they would accept the word of the Muslims. If they knew that they were going to be punished, they would not repent nor become Muslim.'

We find in *Ṣaḥīḥ Muslim* that a man in an earlier time killed ninety-nine people and then asked whether or not repentance was possible for him. A man of worship told him, 'No, repentance is impossible for you!' So he killed him and completed the hundred. Look at the words of that man of worship: 'No, repentance is impossible for you!' When the man learned that, it made him despair and he killed him as is likely in the case of someone who despairs of mercy. So making someone despair corrupts them and making things easy for them is beneficial for them. It is related from Ibn 'Abbās that when a man who had not killed anyone came to him and asked, 'Can a killer repent?' he said, 'No' in order to make him fear and be cautious. When someone who had killed someone else asked him that, he said, 'Yes, he can repent' to make things easy for him.

Ibn al-Qāsim and Ibn Wahb said that Mālik said about someone who divorced while still an idolater and then became Muslim, 'He has no divorce.' It is the same with someone who makes an oath and then becomes Muslim: he does not break the oath. It is the same if someone is compelled to do things: he is forgiven. If someone lies about a Muslim and then becomes Muslim, or steals, the *ḥadd* punishment for slander and theft is carried out on him. But if he fornicates and then becomes Muslim or rapes a Muslim woman and then becomes Muslim, the *hadd* is cancelled for him. Ashhab related that Mālik said, 'Allah means what has passed before Islam in respect of wealth, blood or any other thing.' Ibn al-'Arabī said, 'This is correct because of the generality of the words *"Say to those who disbelieve that if they stop, they will be forgiven what is past"* and "Islam wipes out what is before it" and what was made clear about that making things easy and not causing people to despair.'

There is no disagreement that the actions committed by an unbeliever in the Abode of War while he was still an unbeliever are cancelled out, but if he is given security to come to us and then slanders a Muslim, he receives the *ḥadd* punishment. If he steals, his hand is cut off. The same is true of a *dhimmī*. If he slanders, he is given the *ḥadd* punishment of eighty lashes. If he steals, his hand is cut off. If he murders someone, he is killed in retaliation. Islam does not cancel that since he broke a contract he made when he was an unbeliever. This is transmitted by Ibn al-Qāsim and others. Ibn al-Mundhir said, 'There is disagreement about a Christian who fornicates and then becomes Muslim and there is clear evidence against him from the Muslims. It is related that ash-Shāfi'ī said when he was in Iraq, 'There is no *ḥadd* punishment imposed on him and no exile because of this *āyah*.' Abū Thawr said, 'If he is a Muslim and admits that he fornicated while he was an unbeliever, the *ḥadd* is carried out.' Al-Kūfī related that it is not.

In the case of an apostate, when he reverts to Islam and has missed prayers, committed crimes and destroyed property, it is said that his ruling is that of an original unbeliever. He is not punished for something he did during the time he was an apostate. In one of his positions, ash-Shāfi'ī said that every right due to Allah and due to a human being is obliged on him, citing as evidence the fact that rights due to human beings are binding on him and so the rights due to Allah must also be binding on him. Abū Ḥanīfah said, 'What is due to Allah is cancelled, but what is due to human beings is not.' Ibn al-'Arabī said, 'That is the position of our scholars because Allah Almighty has no need of the rights due to Him while human beings do.' That is the position of our scholars. Do you not see that rights due to Allah are not obliged on a child while the rights due to human beings are? They said that the words are general to the rights due to Allah Almighty.

but if they return to it,

In other words if they revert to fighting, because when the verb *'āda* is non-specific, it can include both returning to a prior state and then moving from it.

Ibn 'Aṭiyyah said, 'We do not find for these unbelievers in this *āyah* any state of those we have mentioned except that of fighting and it is not permitted to make it refer to unbelief because they have not left it. We said that about *'āda* when it is undefined because in Arabic it can be added to the inceptive and the predicate and take on the meaning of "become" as when you say, "Zayd became (*'āda*) a king" where *'āda* means "became."' [POEM ILLUS.] This does not necessitate returning to a previous state. It is defined by its predicate which is what makes the meaning 'become'.

they have the pattern of previous peoples in the past.

This contains a threat and makes them resemble the nations in the past who were punished by Allah.

وَقَٰتِلُوهُمْ حَتَّىٰ لَا تَكُونَ فِتْنَةٌ وَيَكُونَ ٱلدِّينُ كُلُّهُۥ لِلَّهِ
فَإِنِ ٱنتَهَوْا۟ فَإِنَّ ٱللَّهَ بِمَا يَعْمَلُونَ بَصِيرٌ ﴿٣٩﴾ وَإِن تَوَلَّوْا۟ فَٱعْلَمُوٓا۟ أَنَّ
ٱللَّهَ مَوْلَىٰكُمْ نِعْمَ ٱلْمَوْلَىٰ وَنِعْمَ ٱلنَّصِيرُ ﴿٤٠﴾

39-40 Fight them until there is no more *fitnah* and the *dīn* is Allah's alone. If they stop, Allah sees what they do, but if they turn away, know that Allah is your Master, the Best of Masters, and the Best of Helpers!

Fitnah here means unbelief. This has already been discussed in *al-Baqarah* (2:193) and elsewhere. Praise be to Allah.

وَٱعْلَمُوٓا۟ أَنَّمَا غَنِمْتُم مِّن شَىْءٍ فَأَنَّ لِلَّهِ خُمُسَهُۥ وَلِلرَّسُولِ وَلِذِى ٱلْقُرْبَىٰ
وَٱلْيَتَٰمَىٰ وَٱلْمَسَٰكِينِ وَٱبْنِ ٱلسَّبِيلِ إِن كُنتُمْ ءَامَنتُم بِٱللَّهِ وَمَآ أَنزَلْنَا
عَلَىٰ عَبْدِنَا يَوْمَ ٱلْفُرْقَانِ يَوْمَ ٱلْتَقَى ٱلْجَمْعَانِ وَٱللَّهُ عَلَىٰ كُلِّ شَىْءٍ قَدِيرٌ ﴿٤١﴾

41 Know that when you take any booty a fifth of it belongs to Allah, and to the Messenger, and to close relatives, orphans, the very poor and travellers, if you believe in Allah and in what We have sent down to Our slave on the Day of Discrimination, the day the two groups met – Allah has power over all things –

Know that when you take any booty a fifth of it belongs to Allah, and to the Messenger,

Ghanīmah (booty) linguistically is what a man takes or gathers by effort. That is illustrated by the words of the poet:

I went around all areas until I was pleased to bring booty (*ghanīmah*).

Another said:

The one to whom I send the booty (*ghunm*) on the day it is taken
Who is fed by it is fed by it. The one deprived is deprived.

Maghnam and *ghanīmah* mean the same. *Ghunm* is the verbal noun. Know that there is agreement that what is meant here is the property of the unbelievers when the Muslim gain it through victory and by force. Here this specification is not demanded linguistically as we made clear, but the *Sharī'ah* has defined this word in this manner.

The *Sharī'ah* has two names for property taken from the unbelievers: *ghanīmah* and *fay'*. What the Muslims gain from their enemy by effort and riding horses and camels is called *ghanīmah*. Common usage has necessarily given the noun this meaning. *Fay'* is derived from the verb *fā'a* which means 'to return'. It applies to all the property which comes to the Muslims without fighting or movement, such as *kharāj* on land, *jizyah* on individuals, the *khums* of the booty and similar things. Sufyān ath-Thawrī and 'Aṭā' ibn as-Sā'ib said that. It is also said that *fay'* designates any wealth that goes to the Muslims without force being applied. The meanings are similar.

According to the majority, this *āyah* abrogates the beginning of the *sūrah*. Ibn 'Abd al-Barr claimed that there is a consensus that this *āyah* was revealed after the first *āyah* of the *sūrah* and that the four-fifths of the booty is divided between those who take it and that Allah's words: *'They will ask you about booty…'* were revealed when the people of Badr argued about the booty of Badr as we mentioned at the beginning of the *sūrah*.

This indicates the validity of what Ismā'īl ibn Isḥāq reported from Muḥammad ibn Kathīr from Sufyān from Muḥammad ibn as-Sā'ib from Abū Ṣāliḥ that Ibn 'Abbās said: 'On the Day of the Battle of Badr, the Prophet ﷺ said, "Whoever has killed someone has such-and-such and whoever takes a captive has such-and-such.' They had killed seventy and captured seventy. Abū al-Yasar ibn 'Amr brought two captives and said, "Messenger of Allah, you promised that whoever killed someone has such-and-such and I have brought two captives." Sa'd rose and said, "Messenger of Allah, neither increase in reward nor cowardice towards the enemy kept us back, but we stood in this place out of fear that the idolaters would turn round. If you give to these, nothing will be left for your Companions (who stayed with you)." They each expressed their views and the revelation came: *"They will ask you about booty..."* (8:1) So they handed over the booty to the Messenger of Allah ﷺ. Then the words: *"Know that when you take any booty..."* were revealed.'

It is said that the ruling remains and is not abrogated and the booty went to the Messenger of Allah ﷺ and was not divided between those who took it. That is what is said by the *imāms* after him. Al-Māzirī related it from many of our fellows: the leader can take it from them. They used as evidence the conquest of Makkah and what happened at Ḥunayn. Abū 'Ubayd said, 'The Prophet ﷺ took Makkah by force and returned it to them and did not divide it or turn it into spoils.' Some people think that this is allowed for leaders after him.

According to this understanding of the *āyah*, four-fifths goes to the leader and he can keep it or divide it between those who captured it. This is not in fact the case because of what we mentioned earlier and because Allah ascribed the booty to those who take it in His words: *'Know that when you take any booty...'*. Then He specified the *khums* for those named in His Book. He was silent about the four-fifths as He was silent about the two-thirds in His words: *'if your heirs are your parents your mother receives a third.'* (4:11) It is agreed that the father has two-thirds. So the four-fifths goes to those who take the booty by consensus as Ibn al-Mundhir, Ibn 'Abd al-Barr, ad-Dāwūdī, al-Māzirī, Qāḍī 'Iyāḍ and Ibn al-'Arabī all said. The reports expressing this support one another. Therefore the *āyah* is about what the leader gives, before the division, to whomever he wishes according to what he thinks will be beneficial. 'Aṭā' and al-Ḥasan said that it is particular to what comes in an exceptional fashion from the idolaters to the Muslims in the form of slaves, slave-girls or animals: the leader decides what he wishes about that.

It is said that what is meant is the booty taken by sorties. The leader can take a fifth or let them have it all as spoils. Ibrāhīm an-Nakha'ī said about a ruler who sends out a sortie which takes booty: the leader can make it all booty or he can take a fifth from it. Abū 'Umar related from Makḥūl and 'Aṭā' that 'Alī ibn Thābit said, 'I asked Makḥūl and 'Aṭā' about a ruler allowing people to keep their booty and they said that he can do that.' Abu 'Umar said, 'Whoever believes this interprets the words *"They will ask you about booty..."* as meaning that the Prophet ﷺ can deploy it wherever he wishes and do not think that it was abrogated by the words: *"Know that when you take any booty..."*' Other things are stated which can be found in the book, *al-Qabas*, a commentary on the *Muwaṭṭā'* of Mālik ibn Anas. As far as I know, no scholar said that the words *'They will ask you about booty...'*

abrogate *'Know that when you take any booty...'* Most say what we have relayed about the second one abrogating the first. They do not permit any alteration or change in the Book of Allah.

As for the story of Makkah, it is not a conclusive proof because the scholars disagree about its conquest. Abū 'Ubayd said, 'We think that Makkah is not comparable to any other place for two reasons. One is that Allah singled out booty and spoils for the Prophet ﷺ which He did not give to anyone else, as is clear when He says: *"They will ask you about booty..."* We think that that is specific to him. The other reason is that there are sunnahs about Makkah which do not apply to anywhere else. As for Ḥunayn, the *Anṣār* were compensated when they said, "He gives the booty to Quraysh while our skins and swords are dripping with their blood!" He told them, "Are you not content for people to return with this world while you return to your houses with the Messenger of Allah ﷺ."'' Muslim and others transmitted it. No one else could say this. Allah knows best.

Scholars do not disagree about the fact that Allah's words: *'Know that when you take any booty...'* are not general, but specific. Part of what is specific by consensus is that they agree that the spoils of a slain enemy go to the one who killed him if the leader calls that out. The same is true of captives. The leader has a choice about them without disagreement as will be explained. Another area which is specific is land. So what is meant is any booty you take in the form of gold and silver, goods and captives. Land is not included in the generality of this *āyah* based on what Abū Dāwūd related that 'Umar ibn al-Khaṭṭāb said: 'If it had not been [that I would leave] the last of people [bereft without anything],[1] no town would have been conquered without me dividing it as the Messenger of Allah ﷺ divided Khaybar.'

Verification of this position is found in what the *Ṣaḥīḥ* related from Abū Hurayrah where the Prophet ﷺ said, 'Iraq will withhold its *qafīz*s and dirhams and Syria will withhold its *mudd*s and dinars.' Aṭ-Ṭaḥāwī said that it means 'will withhold'. That indicates that it is not for those who take booty because what the booty-takers own does not have *qafīz*s or dirhams in it. If the earth had been divided, nothing would have remained for those who came after the booty-takers. Allah says: *'...those who come after them'* (59:10) which is added to *'the poor of the Muhājirūn'* (59:8). He said that one distributes that which can be moved from one place to another. Ash-Shāfi'ī said, 'All the booty obtained from the people of war, large or small, house, land, goods or other things is divided up – except adult men. The leader can choose what to do about them: to be gracious to them, to kill them, or to take them captive.' The method followed in what is taken from them

1 Text in brackets from Ibn Ḥajar's explanation in *Fatḥ al-Bārī*.

and captured is that of booty. He uses as proof the generality of the *āyah*. He said that the land is considered as booty and must be divided like other booty. The Messenger of Allah ﷺ divided up all the property of Khaybar he took by force.

They said, 'If it were permitted to make a special case for land, it would be permitted to apply it to other than land and so the ruling of the *āyah* would be invalidated. The *āyah* in *al-Ḥashr* is not valid evidence because it was about *fay'*, not *ghanīmah*. Allah's words: "*...those who come after them...*" (59:10) is an exception to the words which are part of the supplication for those who preceded them in faith and nothing else.' They said that 'Umar's act in making the land a *waqf* was for one of two reasons. Either it is booty which delighted its people and he made it a *waqf*, as Jarīr related, and as the Messenger of Allah ﷺ did with the captives of Hawāzin, when people were happy to give what was in their possession, or the land which 'Umar made a *waqf* was *fay'* and so he did not need anyone's consent.

The Kufans believe that the ruler has a choice about dividing land up or confirming it and imposing *kharāj* on it and it becomes their property, like land taken by truce. Abū al-'Abbās said, 'This is combining the two proofs and taking a middle position. It is absolutely what 'Umar understood. That is why he said what he said. Only the Kufans have reported the abrogation of what the Prophet ﷺ did and did not make it specific to them. They added to what 'Umar did. 'Umar made it a *waqf* in the best interests of the Muslims and did not give its ownership to the people who made a truce who had asked for that.

Mālik, Abū Ḥanīfah and ath-Thawrī believed that spoils from someone killed do not go to the one who killed them and that its ruling is the same as booty, unless the leader states, 'Whoever has killed someone gets his spoils.' Then he is entitled to it. Al-Layth, al-Awzā'ī, ash-Shāfi'ī, Isḥāq, Abū Thawr, Abu 'Ubayd, aṭ-Ṭabarī and Ibn al-Mundhir said that the spoils go to the one who kills in every case, whether the ruler states that or not. Ash-Shāfi'ī said, 'The spoils go to the killer when he kills someone advancing on him. That is not the case when he kills someone retreating.' Abū al-'Abbās ibn Surayj among the people of ash-Shāfi'ī said that the *ḥadīth*, 'Whoever has killed someone gets his spoils' is not general because of the consensus of scholars that if someone kills a captive, a woman or an old man, he has no spoils from any of them. The same is true of someone who finishes off a wounded person or someone who kills someone who has had his hands or feet cut off. He said that that is also the case with someone retreating who is not stopped from retreating. He said that it is known that the *ḥadīth* stating that the spoils go to the one who killed someone has a further meaning or an additional specification regarding the killing, which is that he killed him while he was advancing because of the difficulty involved in that. That is the not case with someone who kills in other circumstances.

Aṭ-Ṭabarī said that the spoils go to the killer whether the one he killed was advancing or retreating, fleeing or coming forward, when that is in battle. This is refuted by what 'Abd ar-Razzāq and Muḥammad ibn Bakr mentioned from Ibn Jurayj who heard Nāfi', the freedman of Ibn 'Umar, say, 'We have heard that when the Muslims and unbelievers meet and one of the Muslims kills one of the unbelievers, he takes his spoils unless it occurs in the confusion of battle because then it is not known who actually killed the person.' The literal meaning of this refutes what aṭ-Ṭabarī said because of the stipulation that spoils come only from killing in battle. Abū Thawr and Ibn al-Mundhir said that the spoils go to the killer in battle or not in battle, advancing or retreating, fleeing or retreating in any manner, because of the generality of the words of the Prophet ﷺ.

Muslim related that Salamah ibn al-Akwa' said, 'We went on an expedition against Hawāzin with the Messenger of Allah ﷺ. While we were eating at mid-morning, a man came on a red camel and made it kneel. Then he removed a leather thong from its girth and tied the camel with it. Then he ate with the people. He began to look around at us. There was some weakness among us and a lack of camels [to ride]. Some of us were on foot. Then he left quickly and went to his camel, untied it, made it kneel, sat it on it and urged it up, and set off quickly on it. A man on a brown camel pursued him [taking him to be a spy]. I hurried out, reached the withers of the brown camel, then the withers of the red camel and then caught the nose-string of the camel and made it kneel. When it put its knees on the ground, I unsheathed my sword and struck the man's head and he fell. Then I led the camel with his baggage and weapons. The Messenger of Allah ﷺ and the people met me. He asked, "Who killed the man?" They said, "Ibn al-Akwa'." He said, "He has all his spoils."' Salamah killed him while he was running away and not advancing and was given his spoils.

Mālik takes that as evidence that a killer is not entitled to the spoils except with the leader's permission. If it had been mandatory for him simply by the act of killing, he would not have needed to repeat this statement. There is further evidence for this in what Abū Bakr ibn Abī Shaybah said that Bishr ibn 'Alqamah said: 'I advanced against a man in the Battle of al-Qādisiyyah and killed him and took his spoils. I went to Sa'd and he said to those with him, "These are the spoils of Bishr ibn 'Alqamah. It is better than 12,000 dirhams. We have given them to him."' If giving the spoils to the killer had been a judgment from the Prophet ﷺ, it would not have been necessary for them to attribute that to themselves through *ijtihād* and the killer would have taken them without being told to. Allah knows best.

We find in the *Ṣaḥīḥ* that Mu'ādh ibn 'Amr ibn al-Jamūḥ and Mu'ādh ibn 'Afrā' both struck Abū Jahl with their swords and killed him. They went to the Messenger of Allah ﷺ and he asked, 'Which of you killed him?' Each of them stated, 'I killed him.' He looked at their swords and said, 'Each of them killed him.' He judged that the spoils went to Mu'ādh ibn 'Amr ibn al-Jamūḥ. This is a text showing that the spoils do not belong to the killer or the Prophet ﷺ would have divided it between them. We also find in the *Ṣaḥīḥ* that 'Awf ibn Mālik said, 'I went out with those who went out with Zayd ibn Ḥārithah in the Mu'tah expedition and a Madadī from Yemen accompanied me.' In the course of the account 'Awf said, 'Khālid, do you not know that the Messenger of Allah ﷺ judged that the spoils go to the killer?' 'Yes,' he answered, 'but I think it is too much for him.' Abū Bakr al-Barqānī transmitted this with the same *isnād* as Muslim, but he added the clarification that 'Awf ibn Mālik said 'The Messenger of Allah ﷺ did not take a fifth from spoils.'

The Madadī was a comrade of theirs on the Mu'tah expedition in part of Syria. He said, 'A Roman on a palomino, with a gilded saddle, a gold-plated belt and a sword embellished with gold attacked the Muslims. The Madadī slipped up beside him and, when he came alongside him, struck the horse's hamstring. The man fell and he killed him with his sword and took his weapons. He gave them to Khālid ibn al-Walīd who kept them. 'Awf said, "Give it all to him. Did you not hear the Messenger of Allah ﷺ say, 'The spoils go to the killer'?" He answered, "Yes, but I think it is too much for him." There were some words between me and him and I told him, "I will tell the Messenger of Allah ﷺ." When we met with the Messenger of Allah ﷺ, 'Awf mentioned that to the Messenger of Allah ﷺ who said to Khālid, "Why did you not give it to him?" He answered, "I thought it too much for him." He ﷺ said, "Give it to him." 'Awf said [to Khalid], "Have I not done what I told you I'd do?" The Messenger of Allah ﷺ became angry and said, "Khālid, do not give it to him. Why do you not leave my commanders alone?"' This is a clear proof that the killer is not entitled to the booty simply on account of his killing, but that it is up to the discretion of the leader. Aḥmad ibn Ḥanbal said, 'The killer only gets the spoils when going forth to fight by individual challenge.'

Scholars disagree about taking a fifth from such spoils. Ash-Shāfi'ī said that there is no fifth. Isḥāq said, 'If the spoils are small in quantity, the killer takes them. If they are a lot, there is a fifth.' That is what 'Umar ibn al-Khaṭṭāb did with al-Barā' ibn Mālik when he went out to fight al-Marzubān and killed him.

The value of his belt and trousers was thirty thousand and he took a fifth of that. Anas reported that al-Barā' ibn Mālik killed a hundred of the idolaters [in the battle] not counting the man who came forth to fight him by individual challenge. When they attacked az-Zāra, the *dihqān* of az-Zāra came out and said, 'Man to man!' Al-Barā' came forth and they fought with their swords and then grappled. Al-Barā' threw him down on his hip and then sat on him and took his sword and killed him. He took his weapons and belt and brought them to 'Umar. He gave him the weapons as spoils and estimated the value of the belt at thirty thousand and took a fifth. He said, 'It is wealth.'

Al-Awzā'ī and Makḥūl said, 'Spoils are booty and there is a fifth due on them.' The same is related from 'Umar ibn al-Khaṭṭāb. Ash-Shāfi'ī's evidence is what Abū Dāwūd related from 'Awf ibn Mālik al-Ashjā'ī and Khālid ibn al-Walīd that the Messenger of Allah ﷺ judged that the killer receives the spoils without a fifth being taken from it. Most scholars believe that the spoils are not given to the killer unless he has definitive proof that he killed the person concerned. Most say that a single witness is sufficient based on the *ḥadīth* of Abū Qatādah. It is said that it requires two witnesses or one witness and an oath. Al-Awzā'ī said that the claim is enough and evidence is not a condition for entitlement. They all agree that it is better in order to remove dispute. Do you not see that the Prophet ﷺ gave Abū Qatādah the spoils of the man he killed without testimony or oath? A single testimony is not sufficient and judgment should not be based on it alone. Al-Layth ibn Sa'd said that. I heard our Shaykh al-Ḥāfiẓ al-Mundhirī ash-Shāfi'ī say, 'The Prophet ﷺ allotted spoils on the basis of the testimony of al-Aswad ibn Khuzā'ī and 'Abdullāh ibn Unays. This removes dispute and uncertainty.' The Mālikīs say that the leader does not need evidence because it is in the gift of the leader with or without testimony.

They disagree about what personal spoils consist of. There is no disagreement that weapons used for fighting and horses are part of the spoils if the enemy fought on a horse and fell from it. Aḥmad says that horses are not part of the spoils. The same is true of waist-bands or belts containing dinars, gems or the like. There is no disagreement that they are not part of the spoils. They disagree about what is worn as adornment for war. Al-Awzā'ī said that all of that is part of the spoils. One group said that it is not. This is related from Saḥnūn, except for belts which he says are part of the spoils. Ibn Ḥabīb said in *al-Wāḍiḥah* that the armbands are also part of personal spoils.

As for Allah's words: *'a fifth of it belongs to Allah,'* Abū 'Ubayd said, 'This abrogates the words of Allah at the beginning of the *sūrah*: *"Booty belongs to Allah and the*

Messenger." (8:1) The Messenger of Allah ﷺ did not receive a fifth of the booty of Badr and so the ruling of not taking the fifth was abrogated by this.' It is clear from what 'Alī said in *Ṣaḥīḥ Muslim*, 'I had an old she-camel as my share of the booty in the Battle of Badr. The Messenger of Allah ﷺ gave me a camel from the fifth on that day,' that the fifth was applied then, and so what Abū 'Ubayd said is rejected. Ibn 'Aṭiyyah said that it is possible that the fifth which 'Alī mentioned was from one of the expeditions between Badr and Uḥud: there was the expedition to the Banū Sulaym, the expedition to the Banū al-Muṣṭaliq, the expedition of Dhū Amarr and the expedition of Baḥrayn. No fighting is recorded in them, but it is possible that there was booty. Allah knows best. This interpretation is refuted by the words of 'Alī that day. It clearly indicates the day of the division of the booty of Badr, although it is possible that the fifth at Badr was not from Badr itself but from the expedition of 'Abdullāh ibn Jaḥsh which was the first booty taken in Islam and the first fifth taken in Islam. Then *Sūrat al-Anfāl* was revealed. This is more appropriate than the first interpretation. Allah knows best.

'Mā' in the phrase *'when you take'* means 'which' and what it refers to is elided, implying 'the booty which you take'. The *fā'* is added because there is a sense of requital in the words. The second *anna* reinforces the first and it can be *inna*. It is related from Abū 'Amr. Al-Ḥasan said, 'This is the key of the words. This world and the Next belong to Allah.' An-Nasā'ī mentioned it. Allah began the discussion of *fay'* and *khums* by mentioning Himself because they are the noblest form of acquisition. He did not ascribe *ṣadaqah* to Himself because it is the detritus of people.

Scholars have six different views about how the fifth is divided.

One group said that the fifth is distributed to six categories: one sixth is given to the Ka'bah, which is for Allah, the second is for the Messenger of Allah ﷺ, the third is for those with kinship, the fourth is for orphans, the fifth is for the poor and the sixth is for travellers. Some of those who espouse this position say that the share for Allah is given to those in need.

The second view is that of Abū al-'Āliyah and ar-Rabī' who said that it is divided into five parts: one share is reserved for Allah and the other four parts are for people. Then someone strikes his hand on the part reserved and nothing is taken from it and it is appointed for the Ka'bah. Then the rest of the shares are divided between five: one share for the Prophet ﷺ, one for his relatives, one for orphans, one for the poor and one for travellers.

The third view is taken from al-Minhāl ibn 'Amr who said that he asked 'Abdullah ibn Muḥammad ibn 'Alī and 'Alī ibn al-Ḥusayn about the fifth who said, 'It is for us. Allah says: *"orphans, the poor and travellers"* and it is our orphans and poor that are meant.'

The fourth view is that of ash-Shāfi'ī who said that it is divided between five. He thought that the share of Allah and His Messenger was one and that it was spent in the best interests of the Muslims, and the four-fifths are given to the categories mentioned in the *āyah*.

The fifth view is that of Abū Ḥanīfah who said that it is divided between three: orphans, the poor and travellers. He thinks that the category of the relatives of the Messenger of Allah ﷺ was removed at his death just as the ruling of his share was removed. They said that in the fifth one begins with putting bridges right and building mosques, paying *qāḍī*s and the army. The like of this is also related from ash-Shāfi'ī.

The sixth view is that of Mālik who said that it is left to the discretion of the ruler and his *ijtihād*. The ruler takes from it without any amount being defined and gives to relatives of the Prophet ﷺ according to his discretion and spends the rest in the best interests of the Muslims. That is what the four Rightly-Guided Caliphs said and they acted on that. It is indicated by the words of the Messenger ﷺ: 'I only have the fifth from the booty which Allah gives you, and that fifth is returned to you.' He said that it is not divided into three or five parts. What is mentioned in this *āyah* is to call attention to them because they are most important category of recipients.

Az-Zajjāj said that the argument of Mālik is based on the words of the Almighty: *'They will ask you what they should give away. Say, "Any wealth you give away should go to your parents and relatives and to orphan, the very poor and travellers."'* (2:215) There is a consensus that a man is permitted to give to other categories if he sees fit. An-Nasā'ī mentioned that 'Aṭā' said, 'The fifth of Allah and the fifth of His Messenger are the same. The Messenger of Allah ﷺ took from it and gave from it wherever he wished and did what he wished with it.'

to close relatives,

The *lām* is not for clarification of entitlement and ownership. It clarifies the expenditure and the place. The evidence for this is found in what Muslim related: 'Al-Faḍl ibn 'Abbās and Rabī'ah ibn 'Abd al-Muṭṭalib went to the Prophet ﷺ and one of them said, "Messenger of Allah, you are the kindest of people and best in maintaining ties of kin. We want to marry and we came so that you could put us in charge of some of this *ṣadaqah* (*zakāt*). We will pay you as the people pay you and have a portion as they do." He was silent for a long time until we wanted to speak to him. Zaynab began to make a sign from behind the curtain that we should not speak. Then he said, "*Ṣadaqah* is not lawful for the family of Muḥammad. It is the detritus of people. Summon Maḥmiyah for me," and he was in charge of the fifth, "and Nawfal ibn al-Ḥārith ibn 'Abd al-Muṭṭalib." They came and he said to Maḥmiyah, "Marry your daughter to this lad," meaning al-Faḍl ibn 'Abbās, and he did so. He said to Nawfal ibn al-Ḥārith, "Marry your daughter to this lad," meaning Rabī'ah ibn 'Abd al-Muṭṭalib. He said to Maḥmiyah, "Take such-and-such from the fifth for the dower."'

The Prophet ﷺ said, 'I only have a fifth from the booty which Allah gives you and that fifth is returned to you.' He gave all or some of it. He also gave some of it to reconcile hearts, and they are not mentioned by Allah in the division. This indicates what we mentioned. Success is by Allah.

Scholars have three different positions about '*close relatives*'. One is that it applies to all of Quraysh, as some of the early generations said, because when the Prophet ﷺ climbed Ṣafā, he began to shout, 'O Banū 'Abd Manāf! O Banū 'Abd al-Muṭṭalib! O Banū Ka'b! O Banū Murrah! O Banū 'Abd Shams! Save yourselves from the Fire.' This will be mentioned in *ash-Shu'arā'*.

Ash-Shāfi'ī, Aḥmad, Abū Thawr, Mujāhid, Qatādah, Ibn Jurayj and Muslim ibn Khālid said that it is the Banū Hāshim and Banū 'Abd al-Muṭṭalib who are intended because, when the Prophet ﷺ divided the share of relatives, it was distributed between the Banū Hāshim and Banū 'Abd al-Muṭṭalib. He said, 'They did not part from me in the Jāhiliyyah or in Islam. The Banū Hāshim and Banū 'Abd al-Muṭṭalib are one thing,' and he intertwined his fingers. An-Nasa'ī and al-Bukhārī transmitted it. In *Sahih Bukhārī*, al-Layth related that Yūnus added, 'The Prophet ﷺ did not give any of the share to the Banū 'Abd Shams or the Banū Nawfal.' Ibn Isḥāq said, "Abd Shams, Hāshim and al-Muṭṭalib were maternal brothers. Their mother was 'Ātikah bint Murrah.' Nawfal was their paternal brother.' An-Nasā'ī said, 'The Prophet ﷺ gave a share to relatives. They are the Banū Hāshim and Banū 'Abd al-Muṭṭalib, both rich and poor.' It is said that it was for their poor rather than their rich, such as orphans and travellers, and so it is like the view which I think is the most likely to be correct. Allah knows best. Young and old, male and female are the same in respect of it because Allah gave them that. And the Messenger of Allah ﷺ divided it between them.'

The third position is that only the Banū Hāshim are meant as Mujāhid and 'Alī ibn al-Ḥasan said. It is the position of Mālik, ath-Thawrī, al-Awzā'ī and others.

When Allah made the ruling of the fifth clear and was silent about the four-fifths, that indicates that it is the property of those who took it. The Prophet ﷺ

made that clear when he said, 'If any town disobeys Allah and His Messenger, the fifth belongs to Allah and His Messenger and the rest to you.' There is no disagreement about this among the Community or Imāms as Ibn al-'Arabī related in *al-Aḥkām* as well as others. However, the leader can decide to be gracious and set the captives free and then the rights of those who took them is cancelled with respect to them, as the Prophet ﷺ did in the case of Thumāmah ibn Uthāl and others. He said, 'If al-Muṭ'im ibn 'Adī had been alive and spoken to me about these captives, I would have left them to him.' Al-Bukhārī transmitted it. That was in repayment for what he did in terms of ending the boycott. He may also kill all of them. The Messenger of Allah ﷺ killed 'Uqbah ibn Abī Mu'ayṭ among the captives. The same is true of an-Naḍr ibn al-Ḥārith. He killed him at aṣ-Ṣufrā'. There is no disagreement about that.

The Messenger of Allah ﷺ had a share of the booty like the rest of those who took it, whether he was present or absent. He had the first choice in respect of swords, share (of any valuables), servants or animals. Ṣafiyyah bint Ḥuyayy was his first choice from the booty of Khaybar. The sword *Dhū al-Fiqār* was also part of the first share. This first choice ended with his death except in the view of Abū Thawr. He thought that the ruler could have it just as the Prophet ﷺ did. The wisdom in that is that the people of the Jāhiliyyah thought that the leader had a fourth of the booty. A poet of theirs said:

> You have a fourth of it and the choice booty,
> by your judgment, leader's booty, and pre-eminence.

The verb *raba'a* is used for taking a fourth of the booty. Al-Aṣma'ī said, 'The fourth was in the Jāhiliyyah and the fifth in Islam. A fourth of the booty used to be taken without *Sharī'ah* or religion and the leader chose from it. After the first choice, he judged whatever he wanted regarding anything. He could have what is separate of it and any furnishings and utensils that were left. Allah made the *dīn* firm by saying: *"Know that what you took of booty..."* The first and prime choice remained for His Prophet ﷺ and the judgment of the Jāhiliyyah was cancelled.

'Āmir ash-Sha'bī said, 'The Messenger of Allah ﷺ had a share called the prime share (*ṣafiyy*) if he wished: slave or slave-girl or horse, which he could choose before the fifth was allotted.' Abū Dāwūd transmitted that. Abū Hurayrah said, '[Allah] will meet His slave and say, "Did I not honour you, make you a chief, give you a wife and subject camels and horses to you and enable you to lead and be entitled to take the fourth?"' Muslim transmitted it. The verb means taking the *mirbā'*, or a fourth of the booty and acquisitions which your people get.

Some of the companions of ash-Shāfi'ī believe that a fifth of the fifth went to the Prophet ﷺ to spend on his wives and children and store up the food for a year from that. He spent the rest on animals and weapons. This is refuted by what Ibn 'Umar related. He said, 'The property of the Banū an-Naḍīr was part of the *fay'* which Allah gave His Messenger for which the Muslims had not ridden horses or camels. It was especially for the Prophet ﷺ. He used to spend out of it for the food for a year and put the rest into animals and weapons as preparation for the Cause of Allah.' Muslim transmitted it. He said, 'The fifth is returned to you.'

There is no evidence in the Book of Allah about a horseman being preferred to a man on foot. They are equal because Allah allotted the four-fifths to them and did not specify a man on foot from a horseman. If it had not been for reports from the Prophet ﷺ, a horseman would be like a footsoldier, a slave like a free man and a child like an adult.

Scholars disagree about the division of the four-fifths. According to Ibn al-Mundhir, the position of most of the people of knowledge is that a horseman gets two shares and a footsoldier one. Those who said that include Mālik ibn Anas and those of the people of Madīnah who follow him. That is also stated by al-Awzā'ī and the people of Syria who agree with him, ath-Thawrī and the people of Iraq who agree with him, and al-Layth ibn Sa'd and the people of Egypt who follow him. It was also stated by ash-Shāfi'ī and his people, Aḥmad ibn Ḥanbal, Isḥāq, Abū Thawr, Ya'qūb and Muḥammad. Ibn al-Mundhir said, 'We do not know of anyone who disagrees with that except an-Nu'mān who disagrees with the customs, new and old, saying that the horseman only gets one share.'

It may be that the *ḥadīth* of Ibn 'Umar was unclear to him. Ibn 'Umar reported that the Messenger of Allah ﷺ gave two shares to a horseman and one share to a footsoldier. Ad-Dāraquṭnī transmitted it. Ar-Ramādī said that it is like what Ibn Numayr said that he was told by an-Naysabūrī, 'I consider this weak from Ibn Abī Shaybah from ar-Ramādī because Aḥmad ibn Ḥanbal, 'Abd ar-Raḥmān ibn Bishr and others related it from Ibn 'Umar differently to this: that the horseman has three shares: one share for him and two for his horse.' That is how 'Abd ar-Raḥmān ibn Bishr related it from 'Abdullāh ibn Numayr from 'Ubaydullāh ibn 'Umar from Nāfi' from Ibn 'Umar.

We find in *Ṣaḥīḥ Bukhārī* from Ibn 'Umar that the Messenger of Allah ﷺ gave two shares to a horse and one to its rider. This is a text. Ad-Dāraquṭnī related that az-Zubayr said, 'The Messenger of Allah ﷺ gave me four shares on the Day of Badr: two shares for my horse, one share for me, and one share for my mother among relatives.' One version has 'a share for my mother as the share of relatives.'

It is transmitted that Bashīr ibn 'Amr ibn Muḥṣin said, 'The Messenger of Allah ﷺ gave four shares to my horse and one share to me and so I took five shares.' It is said that it is left to the discretion of the leader and his opinion is implemented. Allah knows best.

There is no disparity between a horseman and a foot soldier by more than for one horse. Ash-Shāfi'ī said that. Abū Ḥanīfah said that there is a share for more than one horse because it is a greater burden and a greater benefit. Ibn al-Jahm among our companions said that. Saḥnūn related it from Ibn Wahb. Our proof is that it is not related that the Prophet ﷺ gave a share for more than one horse. The same is true of the *Imāms* after him; and the enemy can only be fought on one horse. What is more than that is just extra and so more than two shares is not given. It is like someone who has more swords and spears. It is the same if there are three or four. It is related that Sulaymān ibn Mūsām said that there is a share for each horse in the case of someone with multiple horses.

There is only a share for pure-bred horses because they can attack and retreat; there is also one for work-horses and good horses which have that ability. If the horse does not possess that, it has no share. It is said that they are allowed a share if the leader gives them one because the benefit varies according to the situation. Good horses and pack-horses are good for rough situations like ravines and mountains. Noble horses are good for situations in which there is attack and retreat. That is based on the assessment of the leader. 'Pure-bred' are Arab horses (*'uttāq*) and 'pack and good' horses are Greek horses.

Our scholars disagree about when a horse is infirm. Ashhab and Ibn Nāfi' said that it has no share because it is not possible to fight on it. It is said that it receives a share if it is hoped that it will recover. An emaciated horse gets no share since it is not useful. If a horse is slightly ill, as with an injury to the hoof and similar things which do not prevent a horse from being of use, it gets a share. A horse which has been borrowed or rented gets a share. The same is true of one which is usurped, but its share goes to its actual owner. The horse is entitled to a share, even on ships when booty is taken on a ship because it is moored.

There is no share of the booty for supplementary people such as servants and workers who accompany the army because they do not intend to fight nor go out in *jihād*. It is also said that they receive a share since the Prophet ﷺ said, 'Booty is for those who are present at the battle.' Al-Bukhārī transmitted it. There is no argument in that because it is explained as those who take part in the fighting and go out to it. Allah adequately explains fighters and people of livelihood among the Muslims when he puts them into two different groups, each of which has a state and ruling. He says: *'He knows that some of you are ill and that others are travelling in the land seeking Allah's bounty and that others are fighting in the Way of Allah.'* (73:20) When those people fight, they are not harmed by being engaged in their livelihood because the reason for their entitlement exists in them. Ashhab stated, 'None of them is entitled, even if he fights.' That is the view of Ibn al-Qaṣṣār. This is refuted by the *ḥadīth* of Salamah ibn al-Akwa' who said, 'I was following Ṭalḥah ibn 'Ubaydullāh, watering his horse and foraging for it, serving him and eating his food.... Then the Messenger of Allah ﷺ gave me two shares: the share of a horse and the share of a foot soldier and I had both.' Muslim transmitted it. Ibn al-Qaṣṣār uses as evidence the *ḥadīth* of 'Abd ar-Raḥmān ibn 'Awf in which the Messenger of Allah ﷺ said to him, 'These are three dinars which are his portion and share of his expedition for this world and the Next.'

As for slaves and women, the position of the Book is that they have no share or gift. It is said that they receive gifts, and that is the position of most scholars. Al-Awzā'ī said, 'If a woman fights, she gets a share.' He stated that the Messenger of Allah ﷺ gave shares to the women at Khaybar. He added, 'We believe that the Muslims take this position.' Among our people Ibn Ḥabīb inclined to this view. Muslim transmitted from Ibn 'Abbās in his letter to Najdah, 'You asked me whether the Messenger of Allah ﷺ went on expeditions with women. He used to go with them and they treated the wounded and were given gifts from the booty, but not an actual share.'

If children are capable of fighting, we have three positions. One is that they have a share. The second is that they have no share until they come of age based on the *ḥadīth* of Ibn 'Umar, and that is the position of Abū Ḥanīfah and ash-Shāfi'ī. The third is that there is a difference is between someone who fights and has a share or fights and does not have a share. The first is sound because the Messenger of Allah ﷺ commanded, regarding the Banū Qurayẓah, that those of them who had pubic hair be killed and those who had not be let go. This is based on considering fighting rather than adulthood. Abū 'Umar related in *al-Istī'āb* that Samurah ibn Jundub said, 'Some lads of the *Anṣār* were presented to him and he let those who had reached maturity go [on the expedition]. I presented myself to him one year and he took another lad and sent me back. I said, "Messenger of Allah, you let him go and turned me back. If I wrestled him, I would beat him!" I wrestled him and beat him, so he let me join.' Slaves have no share but are given gifts.

When an unbeliever is present with the permission of the leader and fights, there are three positions about him having a share. The position of Mālik and Ibn al-Qāsim is that he has no share. Ibn Ḥabīb added that such people have no portion. There is a distinction in the third view, which is that of Saḥnūn, between the Muslims being sufficient on their own, in which case he has no share, and not being so and in need of help, in which case he has a share. If he does not actually fight, he is not entitled to anything. That is also the case with slaves fighting along with free men. Ath-Thawrī and al-Awzā'ī said that when *dhimmī*s are asked for help, they get a share. Abū Ḥanīfah and his people say that they have no share, but are given gifts. Ash-Shāfi'ī said, 'The leader can hire them from property which he does not himself own. If he does not do it, he gives to them from the share of the Prophet ﷺ.' He said elsewhere that idolaters are given a gift when they fight with the Muslims. Abū 'Umar said, 'All agree that if a slave, who is one of those whose surety is allowed, fights, he does not get a share but does get a gift. An unbeliever is more entitled to that.'

If slaves or *dhimmī*s go out as thieves and take the property of the enemy, it is theirs and there is no fifth because neither they or women are part of the general meaning of the *āyah*. There is no disagreement that unbelievers are not included. Saḥnūn said that no fifth is owed from what a slave takes. Ibn al-Qāsim said that a fifth is owed because his master allowed him to fight and he fought for the *dīn* which is not the case with an unbeliever. Ashhab said in *The Book of Muḥammad*, 'If a slave or *dhimmī* go out from the army and take booty, the booty belongs to the army and not to them.'

Entitlement to a share is dependent on being present at the battle to help the Muslims. If someone is present at the end of the battle, he is entitled [to a share], but not if he arrives after it is over. The same is true if he is absent due to retreating, but if that is done with the intention of joining another group, he is still entitled to it. Al-Bukhārī and Abū Dāwūd related that the Messenger of Allah ﷺ sent Abān ibn Sa'd out from Madīnah on an expedition towards Najd. Abān ibn Sa'd and his men came to the Messenger of Allah ﷺ at Khaybar after it had been conquered and the reins of their horses were made of palm fibre. Abān said, 'Give us a share, Messenger of Allah.' Abū Hurayrah said, 'Do not give them a share, Messenger of Allah.' Abān said, 'You say this and you are a weasel slipping down to us from the top of a lotus-tree!' The Messenger of Allah ﷺ said, 'Sit down, Abān,' and did not give them a share.

Scholars disagree about someone who goes out to attend the battle but is prevented from doing so by an excuse like getting lost. There are three views: that he has a share; that he does not; and there is a distinction in the third, which is the well-known view: he receives it if he got lost before the fighting but after entering enemy territory. It is the soundest view and it is what Ibn al-'Arabī said. [Another is that] he does not have it if it happened before the fighting. He is like someone whom the general sends out from the army in the interests of the army and that distracts him from attending the battle. He has a share. Ibn al-Mawwāz said that. Ibn Wahb and Ibn Nāfi' related it from Mālik. It is related that he has no share, but has a gift since he lacks the reason for entitlement to a share. Allah knows best.

Ashhab said, 'The one who is taken captive has a share, even if he is in irons.' What is sound is that he has no share because it is property to which one is entitled by fighting. If someone is absent, or is present but ill, he is like someone who is not present. In general, someone who is absent has no share. The Messenger of Allah ﷺ did not give a share to anyone who was absent except at Khaybar. There were shares for the people of al-Ḥudaybīyah, both those present and those absent, by the words of the Almighty: *'Allah has promised you much booty which you take.'* (48:20) Mūsā ibn 'Uqbah said that and it is related from a group of the Salaf.

After the Battle of Badr, a share was given to 'Uthmān, Sa'īd ibn Zayd and Ṭalḥah who were all absent but they were considered like those who were present, Allah willing. 'Uthmān stayed behind to look after Ruqayyah, the daughter of the Messenger of Allah ﷺ, at his command because she was ill. The Messenger of Allah ﷺ gave him his share and reward and so he was like one of those who were present. Ṭalḥah ibn 'Ubaydullāh was in Syria trading and the Messenger of Allah ﷺ gave him his share and reward and so he is counted as one of those who were at Badr. Sa'īd was also absent in Syria and the Messenger of Allah ﷺ gave him his share and reward and so he is also counted as one of those who were at Badr.

About the people of al-Ḥudaybīyah, Ibn al-'Arabī said, 'As for the people of al-Ḥudaybīyah, there was a promise from Allah specific to those people and so no one else shares in it. It is possible that the shares of 'Uthmān, Sa'īd and Ṭalḥah (after Badr) were from the fifth because the community agree that someone who fails to go because of an excuse does not receive a share.' What is clear is that that was particular to 'Uthmān, Sa'īd and Ṭalḥah and not the basis for an analogy with anyone else. Their shares were from the booty itself like the rest of those who were present, not from the fifth. This is evident from the *ḥadīth*s, and Allah knows best. Al-Bukhārī related that Ibn 'Umar said, 'When 'Uthmān was absent from Badr, he was married to the daughter of the Messenger of Allah ﷺ who was ill. The Prophet ﷺ said to him, "You will have the reward and share of someone who was present at Badr."'

if you believe in Allah

Az-Zajjāj said that a group said that it means: 'Know that Allah is your Master if you believe in Him.' So the *'in'* is connected to this promise. One group said that '*in – if*' is connected to '*Know that when you take booty.*' Ibn 'Aṭiyyah said that this is the sound position because the verb '*know*' contains the command to obey and submit to the command of Allah about booty and so *in* is connected to '*know*' with this meaning. It means: 'If you believe in Allah, then obey and submit to the command of Allah in what He teaches you regarding the division of booty.'

in what We have sent down to Our slave

The *mā* is in the genitive as added to the name of Allah. '*The Day of Discrimination*' is the day of distinguishing between truth and falsehood. It was the Battle of Badr. '*The day the two groups met*' refers to the party of Allah and the party of Shayṭān.

إِذْ أَنتُم بِالْعُدْوَةِ الدُّنْيَا وَهُم بِالْعُدْوَةِ الْقُصْوَىٰ وَالرَّكْبُ أَسْفَلَ مِنكُمْ وَلَوْ تَوَاعَدتُّمْ لَاخْتَلَفْتُمْ فِي الْمِيعَادِ وَلَٰكِن لِّيَقْضِيَ اللَّهُ أَمْرًا كَانَ مَفْعُولًا لِّيَهْلِكَ مَنْ هَلَكَ عَن بَيِّنَةٍ وَيَحْيَىٰ مَنْ حَيَّ عَن بَيِّنَةٍ وَإِنَّ اللَّهَ لَسَمِيعٌ عَلِيمٌ ﴿٤٢﴾

42 when you were on the nearer slope, and they were on the further slope and the caravan was lower down than you. If you had made an appointment with them you would have broken the appointment. However, it happened so that Allah might settle a matter whose result was preordained: so that those who died would die with clear proof, and those who lived would live with clear proof. Allah is All-Hearing, All-Knowing.

when you were on the nearer slope, and they were on the further slope and the caravan was lower down than you.

It means: 'We sent revelation when you were in this situation,' or 'Remember when you were…' '*Udwah* is the side of a wadi. It is recited as '*udwah* and '*idwah*. If it is '*udwah*, the plural is '*udā* and if it is '*idwah*, the plural is '*idā*. *Dunyā* here means '*nearer*' and *quswā* means '*further*'. They are the feminine form. *Quṣwā* is also said to be *quṣyā*, but *quṣwā* is the dialect of the Hijaz. The nearer was the one which was in the direction of Madīnah and the further was in the direction of Makkah. So it means: when you stopped at the edge of the wadi closer to Madīnah and your enemy was on the side further from Madīnah.

'The caravan was lower down than you' is a reference to the caravan of Abū Sufyān and others. They were in a lower place than them, on the coast with the goods. It was said that it was the camels on which the goods were: they were in a place in which they were safe, as success from Allah. So He reminded them of His blessings to them.

'Lower down than you' is adverbial in the position of a predicate. Al-Akhfash, al-Kisā'ī and al-Farrā' permit it to be read as *'asfalu'*, meaning much lower than you. *Rakb* is the plural of *rākib*. The Arabs only use *rakb* for a group of riding camels. Ibn as-Sikkīt and most of the people of language say that *rākib* and *rakb* are only used for camels and not for horses. *Rakb*, *arkab*, *rukbān* and *rākibūn* are only used for camels according to Ibn Fāris.

If you had made an appointment with them

It means that there was no agreement because of their great number and your small number. If you had known how many there were, you would have delayed. So Allah gave you success in order *'that Allah might settle a matter'* by helping the believers and making the *dīn* victorious. The *lām* in *'settle'* is connected to something elided. It means: 'He joined them in order that Allah might settle...' Then Allah repeats it, saying *'so that those who died.'* It means: 'He gathered them there in order to settle a matter so that those who died would die.' *'Man'* (who) is in the nominative and *'live'* is in the accusative, added to *'die'*.

The *'clear proof'* is the establishment of the proof and evidence by that. It means: so that those who died would die by a visible clear proof. So this proof is established by being clearly seen. The same is true of those who lived. Ibn Isḥāq said, 'So that those who disbelieved would disbelieve after the proof had been established against them and any excuse cut off, and it is the same with those who believe.'

The verb in *'those who lived'* is read with two *yā*'s based on the root: *ḥayiyā* and also as *ḥayyā*. The first is the reading of the people of Madīnah, al-Bazzī and Abū Bakr, and the second is the reading of the rest. It is preferred by Abū 'Ubayd because it is written like that in the Qur'an.

إِذْ يُرِيكَهُمُ ٱللَّهُ فِى مَنَامِكَ قَلِيلًا ۖ وَلَوْ أَرَىٰكَهُمْ كَثِيرًا
لَّفَشِلْتُمْ وَلَتَنَٰزَعْتُمْ فِى ٱلْأَمْرِ وَلَٰكِنَّ ٱللَّهَ سَلَّمَ ۗ إِنَّهُۥ عَلِيمٌۢ بِذَاتِ ٱلصُّدُورِ ﴿٤٣﴾

43 Remember when Allah showed them to you in your dream as only a few. If He had shown you them as many, you would have lost heart and quarrelled about the matter; but Allah saved you. He knows what your hearts contain.

Mujāhid said that the Prophet ﷺ saw them in a dream as few and recounted that to his Companions and that made them firm. It is said that *manām* means the place of sleep, which is the eye, and so it means 'in the place where you dream' and there is an elision. Al-Ḥasan said that. Az-Zajjāj said, 'This is a good position, but the first is preferable in Arabic because of the rest of the sentence.' It indicates that the dream was about the meeting and it was during sleep. The meaning of '*lost heart*' is to lose the courage to fight. '*Quarrelled*' here is to disagree. '*But Allah saved you*' from disagreement. Ibn 'Abbās said that it is about losing heart. It is said that '*saved*' means: 'He ensured the complete victory of the Muslims.'

وَإِذْ يُرِيكُمُوهُمْ إِذِ ٱلْتَقَيْتُمْ فِىٓ أَعْيُنِكُمْ قَلِيلًا وَيُقَلِّلُكُمْ فِىٓ
أَعْيُنِهِمْ لِيَقْضِىَ ٱللَّهُ أَمْرًا كَانَ مَفْعُولًا ۗ وَإِلَى ٱللَّهِ تُرْجَعُ
ٱلْأُمُورُ ﴿٤٤﴾

44 Remember when Allah made you see them as few when you met them, and also made you seem few in their eyes. This was so that Allah could settle a matter whose result was preordained. All matters return to Allah.

This is in a state of wakefulness. It is possible that the first is also about wakefulness as when you use *manām*, the place of sleep, to mean the eye. According to this, the first is particular to the Prophet ﷺ, and this is for all. Ibn Mas'ūd said, 'I said to a man who was beside me in the Battle of Badr, "Do you see seventy?" He said, "They are about a hundred." We captured a man and asked, "How many are you?" He answered, "We are a thousand."'

'Made you seem few in their eyes' is about the beginning of the fighting until Abū Jahl said on that day, 'They are only what a camel eats. Take them hard and tie them up!' When the fighting started, the Muslims seemed many in their eyes as in

Allah's words: *'You saw them as twice their number with your own eyes.'* (3:13) The phrase *'so that Allah could settle a matter'* is repeated because the meaning the first time is about the encounter and the second time about killing the idolaters and making the *dīn* mighty. It is the completion of the blessing to the Muslims. *'All matters return to Allah'* refers to where they finally end up.

يَٰٓأَيُّهَا ٱلَّذِينَ ءَامَنُوٓاْ إِذَا لَقِيتُمْ فِئَةً فَٱثْبُتُواْ وَٱذْكُرُواْ ٱللَّهَ كَثِيرًا
لَّعَلَّكُمْ تُفْلِحُونَ ﴿٤٥﴾

45 You who believe! when you meet a troop, stand firm and remember Allah repeatedly so that hopefully you will be successful.

You who believe! when you meet a troop, stand firm

Fi'ah is a group. Allah commands them to stand firm when fighting the unbelievers as the previous *āyah* forbids fleeing from the enemy. So the command and prohibition are the same. This stresses standing firm against the enemy and remaining steadfast.

remember Allah repeatedly

Scholars say three things about this remembrance. The first is: 'remember Allah when your hearts are anxious.' Remembering Him helps them to remain firm in hardship. The second: 'make your hearts firm and remember Him with your tongues.' The heart is not still in the encounter and the tongue is confused. So Allah commanded *dhikr* so that the heart is firm in certainty and the tongue is firm in *dhikr*, and the person concerned will say what the companions of Ṭālūt said: *'Our Lord, pour down steadfastness upon us, and make our feet firm, and help us against this unbelieving people.'* (2:250) This state only comes from strength of gnosis and burning insight. It is the courage which is praised by people. The third is: 'remember the promise of Allah to you about selling your selves and rewarding you for it.'

What is most apparent is that the *dhikr* of the tongue brings about the success of the Garden. Muḥammad ibn Ka'b al-Quraẓī said, 'Had anyone been allowed to leave *dhikr*, it would have been Zakariyyā. Allah says: *"Your Sign is not to speak to people for three days, except by gesture. Remember your Lord much."* (2:41) There is an allowance for people in battle as He says here.' Qatādah said, 'Allah obliged *dhikr* on His slaves to distract them from what they experience in the clash of swords.'

The ruling of this *dhikr* is that it should be silent because raising the voice in battle is disliked and ruinous when the one doing so is alone. It is good when it is done by all in the attack because it weakens the enemy. Abū Dāwūd related that Qays ibn 'Ubbād said, 'The Companions of the Messenger of Allah ﷺ disliked shouting in battle. Abū Burdah reported the like of that from his father from the Prophet ﷺ.' Ibn 'Abbās said that it is disliked to veil the face in battle. Ibn 'Aṭiyyah says, 'Allah knows best, but it was the custom of the Murābiṭūn to remove the veil in battle in spite of the fact that they usually wore it.'

وَأَطِيعُوا۟ ٱللَّهَ وَرَسُولَهُۥ وَلَا تَنَٰزَعُوا۟ فَتَفْشَلُوا۟ وَتَذْهَبَ رِيحُكُمْ ۖ
وَٱصْبِرُوٓا۟ ۚ إِنَّ ٱللَّهَ مَعَ ٱلصَّٰبِرِينَ ﴿٤٦﴾

46 Obey Allah and His Messenger and do not quarrel among yourselves lest you lose heart and your momentum disappear. And be steadfast. Allah is with the steadfast.

This continues the instruction to them to stop them disagreeing and arguing about Badr. *'Lest you lose heart'* is in the accusative by the *fā'* in the apodosis of the prohibition. Sībawayh does not permit the elision of the *fā'* and the jussive while al-Kisā'ī does. *Tafshalū* is also recited as *tafshilū*, but is not common. The phrase *'your momentum disappear'* means your strength and victory, as you say, 'The wind is in favour of so-and-so' when he is victorious. A poet said:

When your winds blow, take advantage of them.
Everyone will have a time when they are still.

Qatādah and Ibn Zayd said, 'There is absolutely no victory without a wind that blows and strikes the faces of the unbelievers. Confirmation of that is found in the words of the Prophet ﷺ: "I was helped by the east wind and 'Ād was destroyed by the west wind."' Al-Ḥakam said that *'your momentum disappear'* is a reference to the east wind when Muḥammad ﷺ and his community were helped by it. Mujāhid said that it is the loss of the momentum of the Companions of the Messenger of Allah ﷺ when they disagreed with him at Uḥud. The verb *'be steadfast'* is a command to be steadfast and it is applied to every place, especially the battlefield as in Allah's words above: *'When you meet a troop, stand firm.'* (8:45)

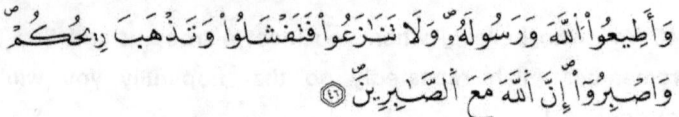

وَلَا تَكُونُوا۟ كَٱلَّذِينَ خَرَجُوا۟ مِن دِيَٰرِهِم بَطَرًا وَرِئَآءَ ٱلنَّاسِ
وَيَصُدُّونَ عَن سَبِيلِ ٱللَّهِ ۚ وَٱللَّهُ بِمَا يَعْمَلُونَ مُحِيطٌ ﴿٤٧﴾

47 Do not be like those who left their homes in arrogance, showing off to people and barring them from the way of Allah – Allah encompasses what they do –

This is a reference to Abū Jahl and his companions who went out on the Day of Badr to assist the caravan. They went out with singing girls and musical instruments. When they reached al-Juḥfah, Khufāf al-Kinānī, a friend of Abū Jahl, sent gifts to him with one of his sons. He said, 'If you wish, I will reinforce you with men, or if you wish, I will reinforce you with myself and those people who are immediately available.' Abū Jahl said, 'If we are fighting Allah, as Muḥammad says, by Allah, we have no power against Allah! If we are fighting people, by Allah, we have strength against people and, by Allah, we will not return from fighting Muḥammad until we reach Badr and drink wine there and the slave-girls play music for us. Badr is one of the festivals of the Arabs and one of their markets, so the Arabs will hear that we came forth, and they will fear us until the end of time.' They came to Badr and their destruction occurred.

Baṭr linguistically means being strengthened by the blessings of Allah and preserved by Him from acts of disobedience. It is a verbal noun used as an adverb: they went out in arrogance, showing off, and barring people, meaning misguiding them.

وَإِذْ زَيَّنَ لَهُمُ ٱلشَّيْطَٰنُ أَعْمَٰلَهُمْ وَقَالَ لَا غَالِبَ لَكُمُ ٱلْيَوْمَ مِنَ
ٱلنَّاسِ وَإِنِّى جَارٌ لَّكُمْ ۖ فَلَمَّا تَرَآءَتِ ٱلْفِئَتَانِ نَكَصَ عَلَىٰ عَقِبَيْهِ
وَقَالَ إِنِّى بَرِىٓءٌ مِّنكُمْ إِنِّىٓ أَرَىٰ مَا لَا تَرَوْنَ إِنِّىٓ أَخَافُ ٱللَّهَ ۚ
وَٱللَّهُ شَدِيدُ ٱلْعِقَابِ ﴿٤٨﴾

48 when Shayṭān made their actions appear good to them, saying, 'No one will overcome you today for I am at your side.' But when the two parties came in sight of one another, he turned right round on his heels saying, 'I wash my hands of you. I see what you do not see. I fear Allah. Allah is Severe in Retribution.'

It is related that Shayṭān appeared to them in the form of Surāqah ibn Mālik ibn Ju'sham on that day. He was from the Banū Bakr ibn Kinānah. Quraysh were afraid that the Banū Bakr would come at them from the rear because they had killed one of their men. When he appeared to them, he said what Allah reports here. Aḍ-Ḍaḥḥāk said, 'Iblīs came on the Day of Badr with his banner and his army and put into their hearts that they would not be defeated as long as they were fighting for the religion of their fathers.'

Ibn 'Abbās said, 'Allah helped His Prophet Muḥammad ﷺ and the believers with a thousand angels. Jibrīl was with five hundred angels on one side and Mīkā'īl with five hundred angels on the other. Iblīs came with an army of *shaytāns* with a banner and they were in the form of men of the Banū Mudlij while Shaytān himself was in the form of Surāqah ibn Mālik ibn Ju'sham. Shayṭān told the idolaters, "You will not be defeated today by the people while I am with you." When the people formed up in ranks, Abū Jahl said, "O Allah, give victory to the side most entitled to the truth!" The Messenger of Allah ﷺ raised his hands and said, "Lord, if this party is destroyed, You will not be worshipped on the earth." Jibrīl said, "Take a handful of earth." He took a handful of dirt and threw it in their faces. There was no idolater who was not hit by it in his eyes, nose and mouth. They turned back in retreat. Jibrīl confronted Iblīs. When he saw him, his hand was in the hand of one of the idolaters, and Iblīs removed his hand and he and his party retreated. A man said to him, "Surāqah! Did you not claim that you would be at our side?" He said, "I am quit of you. I see what you do not see."' Al-Bayhaqī and others mentioned it.

It is reported in the *Muwaṭṭā'* from Ibrāhīm ibn Abī 'Ablah from Ṭalḥah ibn 'Ubaydullāh ibn Kurayz that the Messenger of Allah ﷺ said, 'Shaytan is not more abased, more cast out, more contemptible or angrier on any day than on the Day of 'Arafah. That is only because he sees the descent of Allah's mercy and Allah's disregard of great wrong actions. That is something other than he was shown on the Day of Badr.' Someone said, 'What was he shown on the Day of Badr, Messenger of Allah?' He said, 'Did he not see Jibrīl arranging the ranks of the angels?'

Nakaṣa means to return in the dialect of Sulaym. Mu'arrij and others said that. A poet said:

Turning back on your heels is not a point of honour.
    Honour lies in advancing in the face of arrows.

Someone else said:

Their holding back did not benefit those who turned back.
The people of the forerunners are not harmed by advancing.

Here it is not going backwards, but fleeing as it is said: 'When Shayṭān hears the *adhān*, he flees farting.' It is said that Iblīs lied when he said, '*I fear Allah*,' but he knew that he had no power. The plural of *jār* (at your side) is *ajwār* and *jīran,* and *jīrah* is used for a few.

إِذْ يَقُولُ ٱلْمُنَٰفِقُونَ وَٱلَّذِينَ فِى قُلُوبِهِم مَّرَضٌ غَرَّ هَٰٓؤُلَآءِ دِينُهُمْ وَمَن
يَتَوَكَّلْ عَلَى ٱللَّهِ فَإِنَّ ٱللَّهَ عَزِيزٌ حَكِيمٌ ﴿٤٩﴾

49 And when the hypocrites and those with sickness in their hearts said, 'These people have been deluded by their *dīn*.' But those who put their trust in Allah will find Allah to be Almighty, All-Wise.

The hypocrites were those who made a show of Islam while they concealed disbelief. '*Those with sickness in their hearts*' are the doubters, who are less bad than the hypocrites because they were new to Islam and there was some weakness in their intention. When they set out to fight and when the ranks met, they said, '*These people have been deluded by their dīn.*' It is also said that they are the same, and that is more appropriate. Have you not seen Allah He says: '*those who believe in the Unseen*' (2:3) and then He says: '*those who believe in what was sent down to you.*' (2:4) They are about the same people.

وَلَوْ تَرَىٰٓ إِذْ يَتَوَفَّى ٱلَّذِينَ كَفَرُوا۟ ٱلْمَلَٰٓئِكَةُ يَضْرِبُونَ وُجُوهَهُمْ
وَأَدْبَٰرَهُمْ وَذُوقُوا۟ عَذَابَ ٱلْحَرِيقِ ﴿٥٠﴾ ذَٰلِكَ بِمَا قَدَّمَتْ أَيْدِيكُمْ
وَأَنَّ ٱللَّهَ لَيْسَ بِظَلَّٰمٍ لِّلْعَبِيدِ ﴿٥١﴾

50-51 If only you could see when the angels take back those who disbelieved at their death, beating their faces and their backs: 'Taste the punishment of the Burning! That is for what you did. Allah does not wrong His slaves.'

It means those who remained and were not killed in the Battle of Badr. It is also said that it is about those who were killed in the Battle of Badr. The apodosis of *law* is elided and implies: 'you would see something terrible.' The word '*beating*' is adverbial here. The noun *'backs'* here means their buttocks, alluded to by the fact of turning the backs. Mujāhid and Sa'īd ibn Jubayr said that. Al-Ḥasan said that it is their actual backs. He said that a man said to the Messenger of Allah ﷺ, 'Messenger of Allah, I saw something like the strap of a sandal on the back of Abū Jahl.' He said, 'That was the blow of the angels.' It is said: 'This blow occurs at death, and it may also be on the Day of Rising when they go to the Fire.'

Taste the punishment of the Burning!

Al-Farrā' said that it means: 'They will say, "Taste!" and there is elision.' Al-Ḥasan said, 'This is on the Day of Rising. The guardians of Hell will say to them, "Taste the punishment of burning."' It is related in one of the commentaries that the angels have iron cudgels and whenever they strike, the Fire burns in their wounds and that is the meaning of Allah's words: *'Taste the punishment of the Burning.'* Tasting can be physical and metaphorical. It is testing and trial as you say, 'Ride this horse and test (*dhuq*) it' and 'Look into so-and-so and test (*dhuq*) what he has.' Ash-Shammākh said when describing a bow:

He tested it, so I gave him some leniency.
It is enough when the barrier absorbs the arrow.

The root of *dhawq* is tasting with the mouth.

That is for what you did. Allah does not wrong His slaves.'

The pronoun *'That'* is in the nominative, meaning, 'That is what the matter is' or 'That is your repayment' and the phrase *'for what you did'* means for the sins you committed. *'Allah does not wrong His slaves'* since He made the Path clear and sent the Messengers, so why did you go against it? *'Anna'* is in the genitive added to *mā*, but can also be in the accusative by the elision of *bā'*. It can mean: 'That is the fact that Allah…' It is also be in the nominative by the context.

كَدَأْبِ ءَالِ فِرْعَوْنَ وَالَّذِينَ مِن قَبْلِهِمْ كَفَرُوا بِـَٔايَاتِ اللَّهِ فَأَخَذَهُمُ اللَّهُ
بِذُنُوبِهِمْ إِنَّ اللَّهَ قَوِيٌّ شَدِيدُ الْعِقَابِ ﴿٥٢﴾

52 Such was the case with Pharaoh's people and those before them. They rejected Allah's Signs so Allah seized them for their wrong actions. Allah is Strong, Severe in Retribution.

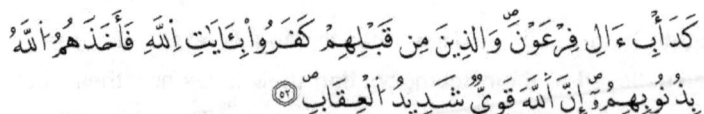

Da'b is the custom which was already mentioned in *Āl 'Imran* (3:11), in other words the pattern of punishing them when their souls are taken and in the graves is like what was done with the people of Pharaoh.

ذَٰلِكَ بِأَنَّ ٱللَّهَ لَمْ يَكُ مُغَيِّرًا نِّعْمَةً أَنْعَمَهَا عَلَىٰ قَوْمٍ حَتَّىٰ يُغَيِّرُوا۟ مَا بِأَنفُسِهِمْ
وَأَنَّ ٱللَّهَ سَمِيعٌ عَلِيمٌ ٥٣

53 That is because Allah would never change a blessing He has conferred on a people until they had changed what was in themselves. Allah is All-Hearing, All-Knowing.

This is the cause, meaning that the reason for this punishment was that they changed and altered things. Quraysh were blessed with fertility, wealth, security and well-being. Allah says of them: *'Do they not see that We have established a safe haven while people all around them are violently dispossessed.'* (29:67) As-Suddī said that the blessing to them was Muḥammad ﷺ and they disbelieved in him and so he was moved to Madīnah and the punishment afflicted the idolaters.

كَدَأْبِ ءَالِ فِرْعَوْنَ وَٱلَّذِينَ مِن قَبْلِهِمْ كَذَّبُوا۟ بِـَٔايَٰتِ رَبِّهِمْ
فَأَهْلَكْنَٰهُم بِذُنُوبِهِمْ وَأَغْرَقْنَآ ءَالَ فِرْعَوْنَ وَكُلٌّ كَانُوا۟ ظَٰلِمِينَ ٥٤

54 Such was the case with Pharaoh's people and those before them. They denied their Lord's Signs so We destroyed them for their wrong actions. We drowned Pharaoh's people. All of them were wrongdoers.

This is not repetition because the first was the case for denial and the second for alteration. The rest of the *āyah* is clear.

إِنَّ شَرَّ ٱلدَّوَآبِّ عِندَ ٱللَّهِ ٱلَّذِينَ كَفَرُوا۟ فَهُمْ لَا يُؤْمِنُونَ ٥٥ ٱلَّذِينَ عَٰهَدتَّ
مِنْهُمْ ثُمَّ يَنقُضُونَ عَهْدَهُمْ فِى كُلِّ مَرَّةٍ وَهُمْ لَا يَتَّقُونَ ٥٦

55-56 The worst of animals in the sight of Allah are those who disbelieve and do not believe, those with whom you make a treaty and who then break it every time. They are not godfearing.

It means: whatever crawls on the face of the earth in the knowledge and wisdom of Allah. This is like the words of Allah: *'those who are dumb and deaf and have no intellect.'* (8:22) Then He describes them saying: *'those with whom you make a treaty...'* The meaning of *'They are not godfearing'* is that they do not fear Allah's vengeance.

The preposition *'min'* in 'with whom' is partitive because the treaty is made with their leaders who then break it. It is a reference to the Banū Qurayẓah and an-Naḍīr according to Mujāhid and others. They broke the treaty and helped the idolaters of Makkah with weapons and then made excuses, saying, 'We forgot.' So the Prophet ﷺ made another treaty with them and again they broke it on the day of the Battle of the Ditch.

فَإِمَّا تَثْقَفَنَّهُمْ فِي الْحَرْبِ فَشَرِّدْ بِهِم مَّنْ خَلْفَهُمْ لَعَلَّهُمْ يَذَّكَّرُونَ ﴿٥٧﴾

57 So if you come upon such people in war, make a harsh example of them to deter those coming after them so that hopefully they will pay heed.

The sentence is a precondition with an apodosis, and the *nūn* at the end of '*come upon*' is included for stress when there is a *mā* according to the Basrans. The Kufans say that the heavy and light *nūn* added in the case of *immā* in the repayment is because of the difference between a protasis and indicating a choice between things. *'Make a harsh example of them'* means 'capture them and make them struggle or put them in a weak state in which you have power over them and conquer them.' This is necessary from Allah's words '*in war*'. Some people said that it means to encounter them. Someone who is described by the verb *thaqifa* is easily found when you seek him. A man is *thaqif* and a woman is described as *thaqāf.* The first view is more fitting since it is connected to the *āyah.* The one who is found may be overcome or not. Linguistically *thiqāf* is one who is firm in the use of a spear and the like. Nābighah said:

You call Quʿayn when steel has bitten them
as the firm wielder (*thiqāf*) grips the knobs.

to deter those coming after them

Saʿīd ibn Jubayr said that the meaning is to warn those behind them. Abū ʿUbayd said that it is in the dialect of Quraysh, and *sharrada* is to make them hear. Aḍ-Ḍaḥḥāk said that it is to make an example of them. Az-Zajjāj said that it is to do an action to them by way of killing which parts them from those behind them.

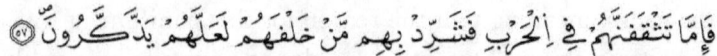

Tashrīd linguistically means scattering and separation. The verb *sharrada* means to wrest people from their place and drag them from it until they separate. A poet of Hudhayl said:

> I go around the valleys every day
> in fear that Ḥakīm will scatter me.

The verb is used for a camel when it leaves its owner. *Sharridh* is related from Ibn Mas'ūd. They are two dialectical forms. Quṭrub said that *tashrīdh* is making an example of and *tashrīd* is separating. Ath-Tha'labī related that. Al-Mahdawī said there is no point to the *dhāl* unless it replaces the *dāl* since they are close and that *sharridh* is not known in language. The pronoun *'man'* means 'which' here according to al-Kisā'ī. *'Man khalfahum'* is also read as *'min khalfihimi'*.

'They will pay heed' means that they will remember your threat to them. It is said that it refers to those after them because someone who is killed does not pay any heed to those after him and so it does not deter him.

وَإِمَّا تَخَافَنَّ مِن قَوْمٍ خِيَانَةً فَانبِذْ إِلَيْهِمْ عَلَىٰ سَوَآءٍ إِنَّ ٱللَّهَ
لَا يُحِبُّ ٱلْخَآئِنِينَ ﴿٥٨﴾

58 If you fear treachery on the part of a people, revoke your treaty with them mutually. Allah does not love treacherous people.

Treachery (*khiyānah*) is deceit and breaking treaties. This *āyah* was revealed about the Banū Qurayẓah and Banū an-Naḍīr. Aṭ-Ṭabarī related this from Mujāhid. Ibn 'Aṭiyyah said, 'What is clear from the words of the Qur'an is that the business about the Banū Qurayẓah ends at Allah's words: *"to deter those coming after them"*. Then in this *āyah* He begins talking about what He will do in the future with those whose treachery is feared and this *āyah* deals with them. The Banū Qurayẓah were not among those whose treachery was feared. Their treachery was clear and well known.'

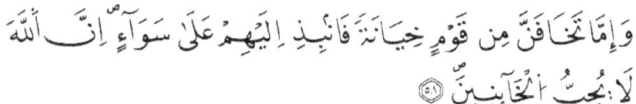

Ibn al-'Arabī said, 'If it is asked how it is possible to break a treaty when there is fear of treachery and treachery is suspected and not certain, so how can a certain treaty be cancelled on account of suspected treachery, there are two points in the answer. One is that fear can mean certainty just as hope can mean knowledge. Allah Almighty says: *"What is the matter with you that you do not hope for honour from Allah?"* (71:13) The second is that when the marks of treachery appear and evidence of them is confirmed, then the treaty must be revoked so that it does not lead to destruction. Lack of certainty is permitted here out of necessity. When there is certainty, it is enough to revoke the treaty. The Messenger of Allah ﷺ went against the people of Makkah in the Year of the Conquest when it was known that they had broken the treaty without revoking it with them.'

The verb *nabdh* means casting away and casting off. Al-Azharī said that it means: 'When you have a treaty with people and know that they have broken the treaty, do not deem them to have broken the treaty until you inform them that they have broken the treaty so that there is equality of knowledge. Then attack them.'

An-Naḥḥās said, 'This is part of the inimitability of the Qur'an whose like does not exist in other language in its brevity and multiple meanings.' It means: 'if you fear treachery from a people with whom you have a treaty, then revoke the treaty with them. Tell them: "You have broken the treaty and I will fight you," so that they know that and have the same knowledge as you. Do not fight them when there is a treaty with them and they trust you. That would be treachery and perfidy.' Allah then makes that clear when He says: *'Allah does not love treacherous people.'*

What al-Azharī and an-Naḥḥās mentioned about revoking the treaty in terms of mutual knowledge is refuted by what the Prophet ﷺ did in the Conquest of Makkah. When they broke the treaty, he did not send anyone to them. He said, 'O Allah, cut off our news from them.' He attacked them. It is the meaning of the *āyah* because when they broke the treaty they knew that they had done that and so there was mutuality with them. When someone does not know that they have broken the treaty, it is not lawful or permitted to attack them.

At-Tirmidhī and Abū Dāwūd related that Sulaym ibn 'Āmir said, 'Mu'āwiyah had a treaty with the Byzantines and he went close to their territory to attack when the treaty ended. A man came on a horse, saying, "Allah is greater! Allah is greater! Fidelity and not treachery." They looked and saw that it was 'Amr ibn 'Anbasah. Mu'āwiyah sent for him and he said, "I heard the Messenger of Allah ﷺ say, 'If someone has a treaty with a people, he should not strengthen it or loosen it until its term ends or it is mutually revoked.'" Mu'āwiyah went back with the people.' At-Tirmidhī said that this is a sound *ḥasan ḥadīth*. *Sawā'* is evenness and balance. A poet said:

Strike the faces of the treacherous enemies
    until they respond to you by being levelled flat (*sawā'*).

Al-Kisā'ī said that it is justice. It may mean being in the middle as Allah says: *'In the middle of Hellfire.'* (37:55) Ḥassān said:

Alas for the Companions and party of the Prophet
after they disappear into the justice (*sawā'*) of the heretic.

It is as He says here: *'revoke your treaty with them mutually,'* meaning both openly and secretly.

Muslim related from Abū Sa'īd al-Khudrī that the Messenger of Allah ﷺ said, 'On the Day of Rising every traitor will have a banner raised [recording] the extent of his treachery. There is no traitor with worse treachery than a ruler betraying his subjects.' Our scholars say that treachery from a ruler is worse than any other form because it entails corruption. When rulers are treacherous and that is known in them – even if they have not broken a treaty – their enemy is not safe from them whether there is a treaty or truce. He gathers his strength and makes his harm great. That makes people averse to entering the *dīn* and obliges the censure of the Muslim leader. If, however, the enemy has no treaty, he should employ every trick against him and every device. That is based on his words ﷺ, 'War is deceit.' Scholars disagree about whether *jihād* should be done under a treacherous leader. There are two views. Most believe that you should not fight with him while some believe that you should. Both views exist in our school.

وَلَا تَحْسَبَنَّ الَّذِينَ كَفَرُوا سَبَقُوا ۚ إِنَّهُمْ لَا يُعْجِزُونَ ﴿٥٩﴾

59 Do not imagine that those who disbelieve have got ahead. They are quite powerless.

This means do not imagine that those who escaped the battle have got ahead by staying alive. Then Allah begins a new sentence: *'They are quite powerless'* in this world so that Allah will bring about their defeat at your hands. It is also said that it is referring to the Next World. That is the position of al-Ḥasan. Ibn 'Āmir, Ḥafṣ and Ḥamzah recited it with *yā'* ('They should not imagine') while the rest recite it with *tā'*. *'Those who disbelieve'* is the first object and *'got ahead'* is the second object. If it is read with *yā'*, a group of grammarians, including Abū Ḥātim, claimed that it is poor Arabic and its recitation is not permitted and it is not countenanced by anyone who knows syntax. Abū Ḥātim said, 'That is because "imagine" does not have an object and it requires two objects.' An-Naḥḥās said, 'This is severe bias. The reading is permitted and the meaning is: "Those behind him should not imagine," and the pronoun refers to what is before. The reading with *tā'* is clearer.'

Al-Mahdawī said, 'If it is read with *yā'*, it is possible that the pronoun in the verb refers to the Prophet ﷺ and *"those who disbelieve have got ahead"* are two objects. It is also possible that *"those who disbelieve"* is one object and the first object is elided. It means: "those who disbelieve should not reckon that they have got ahead."' Makkī said, 'It is permitted that an *"an"* is elided with "got ahead" and so it takes the place of two objects. It implies: "those who disbelieve should not reckon that they have got ahead." So it is like: *"Do people imagine that they will be left"* (29:2) in taking the place of two objects.'

Ibn 'Āmir recited *annahum.* Abū Ḥātim and Abū 'Ubayd think that this reading is unlikely. Abū 'Ubayd said that it is permitted with the meaning: 'Do not imagine that those who disbelieve are not powerless.' An-Naḥḥās said, 'That which Abū 'Ubayd mentioned is not permitted with the Basran grammarians. It is only permitted to say, "I imagine that Zayd left" with *innahu.* It is not permitted because it is in the position of a inchoative as you say, "I reckon that Zayd's father (*Zaydan abūhu*) went out." If it had a *fatḥah*, it would mean, "I reckon that Zayd has gone out (*Zaydan khurūjahu*)." This is impossible. It is also unlikely that it has no sense at all since it necessarily has a meaning because Allah says it, although "*lā*" is redundant. There is no way that a single letter of the Qur'an can be prolix without any evidence which must be accepted. The reading is excellent according to the meaning because they are powerless.'

Makkī said, 'The meaning is that the unbelievers should not imagine that they have got ahead, because they are powerless, meaning they will not succeed. So "*anna*" is in the position of the accusative by the elision of the *lām* or in the position of the genitive by the action of the *lām* since it is frequently elided with *anna*, and that is related from al-Khalīl and al-Kisā'ī. The rest recited it as '*inna'* as a new sentence which is separate from what precedes it. That is preferred because it conveys a sense of emphasis and because that is the position of the majority.

It is related that Ibn Muḥayṣin recited *'yu'ajjazūni'* with a *shaddah* and *kasrah* on the *nūn*. An-Naḥḥās says that this is an error for two reasons. One is that the meaning of Form II is to weaken and the other is that it must have two *nūns*. The meaning of Form IV is to make it impossible to overcome.

وَأَعِدُّوا لَهُم مَّا اسْتَطَعْتُم مِّن قُوَّةٍ وَمِن رِّبَاطِ الْخَيْلِ تُرْهِبُونَ بِهِ عَدُوَّ اللَّهِ
وَعَدُوَّكُمْ وَآخَرِينَ مِن دُونِهِمْ لَا تَعْلَمُونَهُمُ اللَّهُ يَعْلَمُهُمْ وَمَا تُنفِقُوا مِن
شَيْءٍ فِي سَبِيلِ اللَّهِ يُوَفَّ إِلَيْكُمْ وَأَنتُمْ لَا تُظْلَمُونَ ﴿٦٠﴾

60 Arm yourselves against them with all the firepower and cavalry you can muster, to terrify the enemies of Allah and your enemies, and others besides them whom you do not know. Allah knows them. Anything you spend in the Way of Allah will be repaid to you in full. You will not be wronged.

Arm yourselves against them

Allah commanded the believers to gather their strength against their enemies after prioritising piety. If Allah had wished, He could have defeated them with words and spitting in their faces and a handful of dust as the Messenger of Allah ﷺ did, but He wanted to test some of the people by means of others by His prior knowledge and His Decree which was carried out. Preparing good for a friend and evil for an enemy is included in 'arming yourselves'.

with all the firepower

Ibn 'Abbās said that '*firepower*' here means weapons and bows. We find in *Ṣaḥīḥ Muslim* that 'Uqbah ibn 'Āmir said that he heard the Messenger of Allah ﷺ recite while he was on the *minbar*: '*Arm yourselves against them with all the firepower…*' and he said, 'Firepower is shooting! Firepower is shooting! Firepower is shooting!' This is a text which is related from 'Uqbah by Abū 'Alī Thumāmah ibn Shuqayy al-Hamdānī. There is nothing else in the *Ṣaḥīḥ*. There is another *ḥadīth* related about shooting from 'Uqbah who related that he heard the Messenger of Allah ﷺ say, 'Lands will be opened up by conquest for you. Allah is enough for you. None of you lacks the ability to engage in archery.'

The Prophet ﷺ also said, 'Everything with which a man diverts himself is a waste of time except engaging in archery, training his horse and frolicking with his wife. That is the truth.' Allah knows best, but he means by this that all of a man's diversions which do not benefit immediately or in the Hereafter are a waste of time and it is better to turn away from them. If he does these three things by way of diversion and activity, they are true because they are connected to what is beneficial. Shooting and training horses both help in war and frolicking with one's wife can lead to a child who will unify Allah and worship Him, so these three are part of the truth.

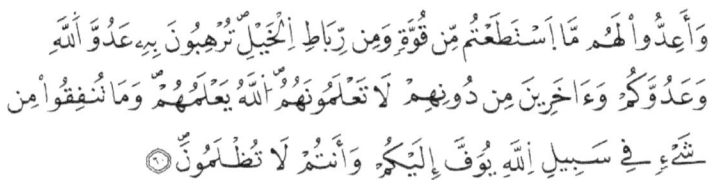

We find in the *Sunan* of Abū Dāwūd, at-Tirmidhī and an-Nasā'ī from 'Uqbah ibn 'Āmir that the Prophet ﷺ said, 'Allah will admit three people to the Garden because of one arrow: its maker who aims for good in making it, its shooter and the one who hands it to the shooter.' The virtue of shooting arrows is immense. It is of great benefit to the Muslims. Its punishment is severe on the unbelievers. Learning horsemanship and the use of arms is a general obligation (*farḍ kifāyah*). It can also be specifically incumbent in certain circumstances.

and cavalry you can muster,

Al-Ḥasan, 'Amr ibn Dīnār and Abū Ḥaywah recited 'cavalry' as '*rubuṭ*', the plural of *ribāṭ*. Abū Ḥātim said that Ibn Zayd said, '*Ribāṭ* is five or more horses. The plural is *rubuṭ*. They are what are tethered.' The verb is *rabaṭa*, *yarbiṭu*, and *irtabaṭa*. *Ribāṭ* is tethering horses and stringing them opposite the enemy. A poet said:

Allah commanded tethering against the enemy in war.
    Allah is the best one to give success.

Makḥūl ibn 'Abdullāh said:

You blame the tethering of horses
    when Allah ordered the Prophet Muḥammad to do it.

Tethering horses is an immense bounty and noble station. 'Urwah al-Bāriqī had seventy horses ready for *jihād*. Mares are recommended. 'Ikrimah and a group said that. It is sound. The womb of a mare is a treasury and its back is might. Jibrīl's horse was a mare. The *imām*s related from Abū Hurayrah that the Messenger of Allah ﷺ said, 'There are three types of horses: one is reward for a man, one is a veil for a man, and one is a burden for a man.' He did not single out male or female. The best of them is the one with the greatest reward and most benefit. The Messenger of Allah ﷺ was asked, 'Which slaves are best?' He answered, 'The dearest in price and most valued by their people'

An-Nasā'ī related from Abū Wahb al-Jushamī, a Companion, that the Messenger of Allah ﷺ, said, 'Name yourselves by the names of the Prophets. The names which Allah loves the most are 'Abdullāh and 'Abd ar-Raḥmān. Tether horses. Stroke their forelocks and haunches. Tether them up but not with string. You should have a bay with a white blaze and white feet or a sorrel with a white blaze and white feet, or a black horse with a blaze and white feet.' At-Tirmidhī related from Abū Qatādah that the Prophet ﷺ said, 'The best horse is a dark horse with a blaze and a white spot on the nose, then one with a blaze and white feet with the right leg free. If it is not dark, then a bay of this description.' Ad-Dārimī also related from Abū Qatādah that a man said, 'Messenger of Allah, I want to buy a horse. What should I buy?' He answered, 'Buy a dark horse with a white spot on the nose and white legs with the right leg free or a bay with this description and you will get booty and be safe.' The Prophet ﷺ disliked horses with white on their right rear leg and left foreleg, or on its right foreleg and left rear leg. Muslim transmitted that from Abū Hurayrah. The horse on which al-Ḥusayn was killed was like that.

If it is asked why shooting and horses are singled out, the answer is that it is because horses are the basis of warfare and bearing its burdens, and good is tied into their forelocks. They are the strongest force and the greatest training and the strongholds of horsemen and on them one moves about in the battlefield. Allah singles them out for honour and swears by their dust: '*By the charging horses panting hard.*' (100:1) Arrows are among the most successful things used in wars and they harass the enemy and take many lives. The Messenger of Allah ﷺ singled them out for mention and called attention to them. That is like '*Jibrīl and Mīkā'īl.*' (2:98) The usage occurs frequently.

Some of our scholars use this *āyah* as a proof of the permissibility of making a *waqf* of horses and weapons and setting up treasuries and store-houses as provision against enemies. Scholars disagree about the permissibility of making a *waqf* of animals like horses and camels, having two positions: one is that it is forbidden, and that is the view of Abū Ḥanīfah; but the sounder view is that of ash-Shāfi'ī, and it is sounder because of this *āyah* and because of the *ḥadīth* of Ibn 'Umar about the horses on which he rode in the Way of Allah and the words of the Prophet ﷺ about Khālid: 'You wrong Khālid. He has made a *waqf* of his armour and devoted it to the Way of Allah.' There is also what was related about a woman assigning a camel to the Way of Allah. Her husband wanted to perform *ḥajj* and she asked the Messenger of Allah ﷺ who said, 'Give it to him to perform *ḥajj*. Ḥajj is one aspect of the Way of Allah.' It is also because it is a useful act of devotion and so it is permitted to make a *waqf* of it, as is the case with land. As-Suhaylī mentioned in *Kitāb al-A'lām*, in connection with this *āyah*, the fact of the Prophet ﷺ giving names to horses and weapons of war.

to terrify the enemies of Allah and your enemies and others besides them

This means: by doing that you frighten the enemies of Allah and your enemies among the Jews, Quraysh and the idolatrous Arabs. The '*others besides them*' are the Persians and the Romans. As-Suddī said that. It is also said that it is the jinn and aṭ-Ṭabarī preferred that. It is said that what is meant by it is anyone whose enmity is not known. As-Suhaylī said that it may refer to the Banū Qurayẓah, and other things are said as well. In fact nothing should really be said about it because Allah says: *'and others besides them whom you do not know.'* So how can anyone claim knowledge of them? There is, however, a sound *ḥadīth* from the Messenger of Allah ﷺ about this *āyah* saying that it is the jinn who are being referred to.

The Messenger of Allah ﷺ said, 'Shayṭān does not confuse anyone who has a noble horse in his house.' A horse is called 'noble' (*'atīq*) because it is free of inferior breeding. This *ḥadīth* has an *isnād* by al-Ḥārith ibn Abī Usāma from Ibn al-Mulaykī from his father from his grandfather from the Prophet ﷺ. It is related that the jinn do not approach a house where there is a horse and they flee from the neighing of a horse.

Anything you spend in the Way of Allah will be repaid to you in full

This means what you give as *ṣadaqah*. It is said that it is what you spend on yourselves or your horses. The words *'repaid to you in full'* refer to the Next World. A good action will be rewarded with ten like it up to seven hundred times or many more.

وَإِن جَنَحُوا۟ لِلسَّلْمِ فَٱجْنَحْ لَهَا وَتَوَكَّلْ عَلَى ٱللَّهِ ۚ إِنَّهُۥ هُوَ ٱلسَّمِيعُ
ٱلْعَلِيمُ ﴿٦١﴾

61 If they incline to peace, you too incline to it, and put your trust in Allah. He is the All-Hearing, the All-Knowing.

If they incline to peace, you too incline to it,

The feminine pronoun *hā* is used here because 'peace' (*salm*) is feminine and it is also possible that it is because the action is considered feminine. *Junūḥ* means 'inclining'. This means towards those whose treaty has been revoked. Mutual peace means a truce. A man inclines to another when he turns to him. This is why ribs are called *jawāniḥ*: they bend towards the abdomen. Camels 'incline' when they stretch out the front of their necks in running. Dhū ar-Rummah said:

When he died on top of the saddle, I revived his spirit
by mentioning you when the swift camels lower their necks (*junnaḥ*).

An-Nābighah said:

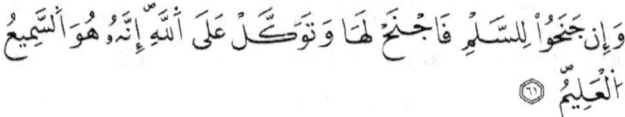

They lower their wings (*jawāniḥ*) certain of their direction
When the first is victorious of two parties who meet.

He means birds. The verb is also used for the night when it advances and extends its covering over the earth. *Salm* and *salām* both mean a truce. Al-A'mash, Abū Bakr, Ibn Muḥayṣin and al-Mufaḍḍil recited *'lis-silm'*. The rest have it *salm*. This was discussed in full in *al-Baqarah* (2:208). *Salām* comes from *taslīm*. The majority recite 'incline' as '*fajnaḥ*', which is the dialect of Tamīm. Al-Ashhab al-'Uqaylī recited '*fajnuḥ*', which is the dialect of Qays.

There is disagreement about whether this *āyah* was abrogated or not. Qatādah and 'Ikrimah said that it was abrogated by Allah's words: '*...kill the idolaters wherever you find them*' (9:5) and '*...fight the idolaters totally.*' (5:36) The two of them said that the freedom entailed by every truce is abrogated until they say, 'There is no god but Allah.' Ibn 'Abbās said that it is abrogated by the words: *'Do not become faint-hearted and call for peace.'* (47:35) It is said that it is not abrogated, but refers to the acceptance of *jizyah* from the people of *jizyah*. The Companions of the Messenger of Allah ﷺ made peace in the time of 'Umar ibn al-Khaṭṭāb, and the leaders after him often did so with non-Arab lands in return for what they took from them, leaving them with what they had in spite of the fact that they were able to destroy them completely. Similarly the Messenger of Allah ﷺ made peace with many people in exchange for what they paid. An example of that is Khaybar, whose people returned to it after its conquest on condition that they paid half of the produce of their work. Ibn Isḥāq said that Mujāhid said that Qurayẓah are meant by this *āyah* because *jizyah* was accepted from them, whereas nothing was accepted from the idolaters. As-Suddī and Ibn Zayd said that the meaning of the *āyah* is: 'If they ask you for peace, accept it,' and there is no abrogation regarding it.

Ibn al-'Arabī said, 'The basis of the different responses to what this means is Allah's words: *'Do not become faint-hearted and call for peace when you are uppermost and Allah is with you.'* (47:35) When the Muslims have might, strength, expansion, vigour, great numbers and great force, there should be no truce. As a poet said:

There is no truce until the horses attack with spears
and strike necks and heads with steel.

When the best interests of the Muslims lie in a truce, on account of the benefit it brings or the harm it averts, there is no harm in the Muslims initiating it if they need to do so. The Messenger of Allah ﷺ made peace with the people of Khaybar on certain conditions which they broke and so the truce was broken. He made a truce with [Makhshī ibn 'Umar] aḍ-Ḍamrī, Ukaydir of Dūmah and the people of Najran. He made a truce with Quraysh for ten years until they broke their treaty. The caliphs and Companions continued in this path which was followed, with the elements we have explained in operation. Al-Qushayrī said, 'When the Muslims possess strength, a truce should only be made for a year. When the unbelievers are strong, it is permitted to make a truce with them for ten years, but more is not permitted. The Messenger of Allah ﷺ made a truce with the people of Makkah for ten years.'

Ibn al-Mundhir said, 'Scholars disagree about the length of the period of the truce made by the Messenger of Allah ﷺ with the people of Makkah after al-Ḥudaybīyah. 'Urwah said that it was four years and Ibn Jurayj said it was three years. Ibn Isḥāq said that it was ten years.' Ash-Shāfi'ī said that it is not permitted to make a truce with the idolaters for more than ten years based on what the Prophet ﷺ did at al-Ḥudaybiyah. If the idolaters make a truce for longer than that, it should be revoked because the basic position is the obligation to fight the idolaters until they believe or pay the *jizyah.*

Ibn Ḥabīb said that Mālik said, 'It is permitted to make peace with the idolaters for one, two or three years.' Al-Muhallab said, 'The Prophet ﷺ gave them the judgment in this case which was outwardly weakness for the Muslims on the basis of the fact that Allah stopped the she-camel of the Messenger of Allah ﷺ from going towards Makkah when he turned it towards Makkah and it knelt. He said, "She has been kept back by the One Who kept the elephant back."' Al-Bukhārī transmitted it from al-Miswar ibn Makhramah. It indicates the permissibility of making peace and a truce with the idolaters without taking any wealth from them when the ruler thinks that proper.

It is permitted, in case of need, for the Muslims to make a peace treaty in exchange for wealth given to the enemy since the Prophet ﷺ made a truce with 'Uyaynah ibn Ḥiṣn al-Fazārī and al-Ḥārith ibn 'Awf al-Murrī on the Day of the Confederates for a third of the fruits of Madīnah and they left with the people of Ghaṭafān, disappointing Quraysh and returning with their people. This was an attempt to bring them round, rather than a truce. When the Messenger of Allah ﷺ saw that they had repented and were content, he consulted Sa'd ibn Mu'ādh and Sa'd ibn 'Ubādah. They said, 'Messenger of Allah, if this is something with which you are pleased, we will do it for you, and if it is something which Allah has commanded you to do, we will hear and obey, or is it something you are doing for us?' He said, 'Rather it is something I do for you. The Arabs have shot at you with a single bow.' Sa'd ibn Mu'ādh said, 'Messenger of Allah, by Allah, we and those people were practising *shirk* and idol worship, not worshipping or knowing Allah. People did not get a single date from us except by purchase or hospitality. So now, after Allah has honoured us with Islam and guided us to it and exalted us by it, why should we give them our wealth? By Allah, we will only give them the sword until Allah judges between us and them.' The Messenger of Allah ﷺ was delighted by that and said, 'So be it.' He said to 'Uyaynah and al-Ḥārith, 'Go. There is nothing but the sword for you from us.' Sa'd took the paper which only had the *shahādah*, 'There is no god but Allah' on it, and erased it.

وَإِن يُرِيدُوٓاْ أَن يَخۡدَعُوكَ فَإِنَّ حَسۡبَكَ ٱللَّهُۚ هُوَ ٱلَّذِيٓ أَيَّدَكَ بِنَصۡرِهِۦ
وَبِٱلۡمُؤۡمِنِينَ ٦٢ وَأَلَّفَ بَيۡنَ قُلُوبِهِمۡۚ لَوۡ أَنفَقۡتَ مَا فِي ٱلۡأَرۡضِ جَمِيعٗا
مَّآ أَلَّفۡتَ بَيۡنَ قُلُوبِهِمۡ وَلَٰكِنَّ ٱللَّهَ أَلَّفَ بَيۡنَهُمۡۚ إِنَّهُۥ عَزِيزٌ
حَكِيمٞ ٦٣

62-63 If they intend to deceive you, Allah is enough for you. It is He Who supported you with His help and with the believers, and unified their hearts. Even if you had spent everything on the earth, you could not have unified their hearts. But Allah has unified them. He is Almighty, All-Wise.

'If they intend to deceive you' by making a show of peace to you, while concealing treachery and perfidy, then incline towards them. You are not responsible for their false intentions. *'Allah is enough for you'* means that Allah will take care of you and protect you. A poet said:

When there is carnage and the staff is broken,
The Indian sword is enough for you and aḍ-Ḍaḥḥāk.

It is He Who supported you with His help and with the believers,

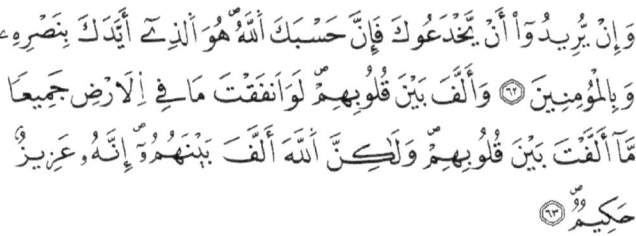

This means He strengthened you with His help, meaning at Badr. An-Nu'mān ibn Bashīr said that *'the believers'* here refer to the *Anṣār*. The phrase *'unified their hearts'* means that He joined together the hearts of Aws and Khazraj. The fact that their hearts became unified, in spite of the intense tribalism of the Arabs, is one of the Signs of the Prophet ﷺ and one of his miracles because previously if one of them had been slapped, he would have fought on that account until he had gained suitable retaliation for it. They were the most fanatic of people in that respect. But Allah unified their hearts so that a man would fight his father and brother for the sake of the *dīn*. It is also said that what is meant is the unification of the *Muhājirūn* and *Anṣār*. The meanings are close.

يَٰٓأَيُّهَا ٱلنَّبِيُّ حَسْبُكَ ٱللَّهُ وَمَنِ ٱتَّبَعَكَ مِنَ ٱلْمُؤْمِنِينَ ٦٤

64 O Prophet! Allah is enough for you, and for the believers who follow you.

This is not repetition. Allah says earlier: *'If they intend to deceive you, Allah is enough for you,'* which is a specific kind of protection. His words here make this protection universal, implying: 'Allah is enough for you in every state.' Ibn 'Abbās said, 'It was revealed about 'Umar becoming Muslim. Thirty-three men and six women had become Muslim with the Prophet ﷺ and when 'Umar became Muslim, they became forty in number.' The *āyah* is Makkan and it was written in a Madinan *sūrah* at the command of the Messenger of Allah ﷺ. Al-Qushayrī mentioned it.

In the *Sīrah* there is something from 'Abdullāh ibn Mas'ūd which differs from what Ibn 'Abbās said about 'Umar becoming Muslim. He said, 'We were not able to pray at the Ka'bah until 'Umar became Muslim. When he became Muslim, he fought with Quraysh until he was able to pray at the Ka'bah and we prayed with him.' 'Umar became Muslim after some of the Companions of the Messenger of Allah ﷺ had gone to Abyssinia. Ibn Isḥāq said, 'The total number of those who went to Abyssinia and emigrated there, not counting their children who went with them or were born there, were eighty-three men if 'Ammār ibn Yāsir was one of them. That is uncertain.' Al-Kalbī said, 'The *āyah* was revealed at al-Baydā' in the expedition to Badr before the fighting.'

'For the believers who follow you' means 'Allah is enough for you and the *Muhājirūn* and *Anṣār* are enough for you.' It is also said that it means: 'Allah is enough for you and those who follow you,' as ash-Sha'bī and Ibn Zayd said. Al-Ḥasan took the first view. An-Naḥḥās and others preferred it. According to the first view, the pronoun *'man'* is nominative as joined to the Name of Allah and means: 'Allah and your followers among the believers are enough for you.' According to the second, it is implied, like the words of the Prophet ﷺ, "Allah and the sons of Qaylah are enough for me against him."[2] It is also said that it is possible that it means, 'Allah is enough for them.' *'Man'* can be in the position of an accusative with the meaning: 'Allah is enough for you and enough for those who follow you' with the predicate elided.

2 The sons of Qaylah means the Aws and Khazraj.

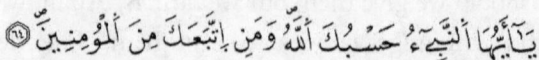

يَٰٓأَيُّهَا ٱلنَّبِيُّ حَرِّضِ ٱلْمُؤْمِنِينَ عَلَى ٱلْقِتَالِ إِن يَكُن مِّنكُمْ عِشْرُونَ
صَٰبِرُونَ يَغْلِبُوا۟ مِا۟ئَتَيْنِ وَإِن تَكُن مِّنكُم مِّا۟ئَةٌ يَغْلِبُوٓا۟ أَلْفًا مِّنَ
ٱلَّذِينَ كَفَرُوا۟ بِأَنَّهُمْ قَوْمٌ لَّا يَفْقَهُونَ ﴿٦٥﴾ ٱلْـَٔـٰنَ خَفَّفَ ٱللَّهُ عَنكُمْ وَعَلِمَ
أَنَّ فِيكُمْ ضَعْفًا فَإِن تَكُن مِّنكُم مِّا۟ئَةٌ صَابِرَةٌ يَغْلِبُوا۟ مِا۟ئَتَيْنِ
وَإِن يَكُن مِّنكُمْ أَلْفٌ يَغْلِبُوٓا۟ أَلْفَيْنِ بِإِذْنِ ٱللَّهِ وَٱللَّهُ مَعَ
ٱلصَّٰبِرِينَ ﴿٦٦﴾

65-66 O Prophet! spur on the believers to fight. If there are twenty of you who are steadfast, they will overcome two hundred; and if there are a hundred of you, they will overcome a thousand of those who disbelieve, because they are people who do not understand. Now Allah has made it lighter on you, knowing there is weakness in you. If there are a hundred of you who are steadfast, they will overcome two hundred; and if there are a thousand of you, they will overcome two thousand with Allah's permission. Allah is with the steadfast.

O Prophet! spur on the believers to fight.

The verb '*spur on*' (*ḥarriḍ*) means to encourage and motivate. There are various similar verbs with this meaning: *ḥāraḍa*, *wāẓaba*, *wāṣaba* and *akabba*. Someone who is described as *ḥāriḍ* is the one who is close to death. An example of that is found in the words of Allah: '*until you waste away* (*ḥaraḍan*)' (12:85), meaning melt away from sorrow until you are close to death.

If there are twenty of you who are steadfast, they will overcome two hundred;

This is a report which contains a promise with a precondition. It means: twenty of you who are steadfast will overcome two hundred. Twenty, thirty and forty are each the name of a something set down in the form of a plural designating this number. This is like the noun *Filisṭīn*.

If it is asked why the beginning of *'ishrīn* (twenty) has a *kasrah* whereas *thalāthīn* and the rest of the numbers up to eighty, with the exception of *sittīn* (sixty) have a *fatḥah,* the answer, according to Sībawayh, is that *'ishrīn* comes from *'ashrah* (ten) as *ithnayn* (two) comes from *wāḥid* and so it has a *kasrah* as does *ithnayn*. The evidence for this is their words, '*sittūn* and *tis'ūn*' and it is said, '*sittah* and *tis'ah*'.

Abū Dāwūd related that Ibn 'Abbās said that when *'If there are twenty of you who are steadfast'* was revealed, it was hard on the Muslims since, by saying that, Allah was making it an obligation on the individual not to flee when faced by ten. Then Allah made that less onerous, saying: *'Now Allah has made it lighter for you.'* When Allah made it lighter for them in respect of number, He decreased the need for steadfastness by that account. Ibn al-'Arabī said, 'Some people said that this was in the Battle of Badr and was then abrogated. This is an error. It is not transmitted at all that the idolaters formed ranks against the Muslims there. However, the Creator originally made it obligatory for the Muslims and connected that to knowing what they are fighting for, which is the reward, while the idolators do not know what they are fighting for.'

The *ḥadīth* of Ibn 'Abbās indicates that it is an obligation. When that was difficult for them, the obligation was reduced to one standing firm against two, and it was lightened for them and ordained for them that one hundred should not flee from two hundred. According to this view, it is easing, not abrogation. This is good. Qāḍī Ibn aṭ-Ṭayyib mentioned that when part of a ruling or some of its elements are abrogated, or the number involved changed, it is permitted to say that it is abrogated because it is not the first ruling. It is different. He was commenting on the disagreement about that.

مَا كَانَ لِنَبِيٍّ أَن يَكُونَ لَهُۥٓ أَسْرَىٰ حَتَّىٰ يُثْخِنَ فِى ٱلْأَرْضِ ۚ
تُرِيدُونَ عَرَضَ ٱلدُّنْيَا وَٱللَّهُ يُرِيدُ ٱلْءَاخِرَةَ ۗ وَٱللَّهُ عَزِيزٌ حَكِيمٌ ﴿٦٧﴾

67 It is not fitting for a Prophet to take captives until he has let much blood in the land. You desire the goods of this world, whereas Allah desires the Next World. Allah is Almighty, All-Wise.

It is not fitting for a Prophet to take captives until he has let much blood in the land.

Asrā (captives) is the plural of *asīr.* It is like *qatīl* (slain) and *qatlā* and *jarīḥ* (wounded) and *jarḥā. Usārā* and *asārā* are also used as the plural of *asīr.* They used to bind captives with straps, one of which is *isār.* So anyone who is captured, even if not bound, is called *asīr.* Al-A'shā said:

Hair bound me in his house,
a strap binds donkeys.

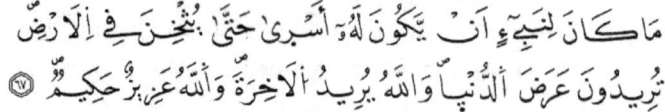

This was already discussed in *al-Baqarah* (2:85). Abū 'Amr ibn al-'Alā said, 'Captives are those bound when they are taken. Captives are those bound with rope.' Abū Ḥātim related that he heard that from the Arabs.

This *āyah* was revealed about Badr to reprimand the Companions of Allah's Prophet ﷺ. The meaning is: 'It was not correct for you to do this action which obliged the Prophet ﷺ to take captives before letting blood.' Allah says of them here: *'You desire the goods of this world.'* The Prophet ﷺ did not order them to leave the men alive at the moment of fighting and he did not desire the goods of this world in any way. The group of those involved in the fighting did that and so the rebuke and reprimand is directed at those who indicated to the Prophet ﷺ that he should accept ransom. This is the position of most commentators and it is the only one which is sound. The Prophet ﷺ is mentioned in the *āyah* since he did not forbid them doing it when he saw from the hut that it was happening, and that Sa'd ibn Mu'ādh, 'Umar ibn al-Khaṭṭāb and 'Abdullāh ibn Rawāḥah disliked it. The Prophet ﷺ was distracted by the suddenness of what happened and the arrival of victory and he did not forbid them to allow the men to stay alive. That is why he and Abū Bakr wept when the *āyahs* were revealed. Allah knows best.

Muslim related the *ḥadīth* of 'Umar ibn al-Khaṭṭāb whose beginning was mentioned in *Āl 'Imrān* (3:122-125). Abū Zumayl said that Ibn 'Abbās said, 'When the captives were taken, the Messenger of Allah ﷺ asked Abū Bakr and 'Umar, "What do you think should be done with these captives?" Abū Bakr said, "Messenger of Allah, they are our cousins and tribe. I think that you should accept ransom for them and that will give us strength against the unbelievers. Perhaps Allah will guide them to Islam." The Messenger of Allah ﷺ asked, "And what do you think, Ibn al-Khaṭṭāb?" He said, "No, by Allah, Messenger of Allah! My opinion is not that of Abū Bakr. I think you should hand over them to us and we will strike off their heads. Hand over 'Aqīl to 'Alī and he can strike off his head. Hand over so-and-so (a relative of 'Umar's) to me and I will strike off his head. These are the leaders and heads of unbelief."' ['Umar said,] 'The Messenger of Allah ﷺ liked what Abū Bakr said and did not like what I said. The following day I went and found the Messenger of Allah ﷺ and Abū Bakr sitting down weeping. I said, "Messenger of Allah, tell me why you and your companion are weeping. If I find reason to weep, I will weep. Otherwise I will imitate your weeping." The Messenger of Allah ﷺ said, "I am weeping about what your companions suggested to me about accepting ransom. Their punishment was shown to me and it was closer than this tree." There was a tree close to the Messenger of Allah ﷺ.'

Allah revealed: *'It is not fitting for a Prophet to take captives until he has let much blood in the land…'* (to *āyah* 69)." So Allah made booty lawful for them.

Yazīd ibn Hārūn related from Yaḥyā from Abū Mu'āwiyah from al-A'mash from 'Amr ibn Murrah from Abū 'Ubaydah that 'Abdullāh said, 'After the Battle of Badr, the captives were brought and they included al-'Abbās. The Messenger of Allah ﷺ asked, "What do you think should be done with these captives?" Abū Bakr said, "Messenger of Allah, your people and your family. You should let them live. Perhaps Allah will turn to them." 'Umar said, "They denied you, expelled you and fought you. Bring them forward and strike off their heads!" 'Abdullāh ibn Rawāḥah said, "Find a valley with many trees and set it alight over them.' Al-'Abbās who was listening exclaimed, "You have cut off ties of kinship!" The Messenger of Allah ﷺ went inside without replying to them at all. Some people said, "He will take the position of Abū Bakr." Others said, "He will take the position of 'Umar." Still others said, "He will take the view of 'Abdullāh ibn Rawāḥah." The Messenger of Allah ﷺ came out and said, "Allah softens the hearts of some men so that they become softer than milk and Allah hardens the hearts of some men so that they become harder than stone. You, Abū Bakr, are like Ibrāhīm who said, *'If anyone follows me, he is with me, but if anyone disobeys me, You are the Ever-Forgiving, Most Merciful.'* (14:36). Abu Bakr, you are like 'Īsā who said, *'If You punish them, they are Your slaves. If You forgive them, You are the Almighty, All-Wise.'* (5:118) You, 'Umar, are like Nūḥ when He said, *'My Lord, do not leave a single one of the unbelievers the earth!'* (71:26) 'Umar, you are like Mūsā when He said, *'O Lord, obliterate their wealth and harden their hearts so that they do not believe until they see the painful punishment.'* (10:88) You are the uppermost. No one should be released except by a ransom or having his head struck off." 'Abdullah said, "Except Suhayl ibn Bayḍā'? I heard him mention Islam." The Messenger of Allah ﷺ was silent. I was never more afraid that a stone from heaven would fall on me than on that day. Then Allah revealed: *"It is not fitting for a Prophet to take captives until he has let much blood in the land…"*' In one variant, the Messenger of Allah ﷺ said, 'We would have been struck by a punishment in opposing Ibn al-Khaṭṭāb which only 'Umar would have evaded.'

Abū Dāwūd related that 'Umar said, 'In the Battle of Badr, when the Messenger of Allah ﷺ took ransom, Allah revealed: *"It is not fitting for a Prophet to take captives until he has let much blood in the land…"* Then booty was made lawful.'

Al-Qushayrī mentioned that Sa'd ibn Mu'ādh said, 'Messenger of Allah, it is our first battle with the idolaters. I prefer shedding much blood.' *Ithkān* is a lot of killing, and Mujāhid and others said that it means killing many idolaters. The

Arabs use the verb *athkhana* for doing something thoroughly. Some said that it means 'until he overpowers and kills.' Al-Mufaḍḍal said:

He prays *Ḍuḥā* and its time is not one of devotion.
　Pharaoh shed much blood in his unbelief.

It is said that '*until he has let much blood*' means to have power. It is said that *ithkān* is strength and force. So Allah Almighty informed that killing the captives taken at Badr was more appropriate than ransoming them.

Ibn 'Abbās said, 'In the Battle of Badr, the Muslims were few. When they became numerous and their power was great, Allah revealed: *"set them free or ransom them"* (47:4)' It will be explained in *Sūrat al-Qitāl* (the *Sūrah of Fighting*, or *Muḥammad*), Allah willing. It is said that they were rebuked because Badr was a pivotal battle and dealt with the leaders, nobles and chiefs and property of Quraysh by killing, enslavement and ownership. All of that was something momentous and they should have waited for Revelation and not been hasty. When they were hasty and did not wait, what was directed at them was directed at them. Allah knows best.

Aṭ-Ṭabarī and others have the *isnād* of a report in which the Messenger of Allah ﷺ said to the people, 'If you wish, you can take the ransom for the captives and seventy of you will be killed in war according to their number, or if you wish, they can be killed and you will be safe.' They said, 'We will accept the ransom and seventy of us will be martyred.' 'Abd ibn Ḥumayd mentioned that Jibrīl descended to the Prophet ﷺ to give people the choice. This was dealt with in *Āl 'Imrān* (3:165). 'Abīdah as-Salmānī said, 'They asked for the best of both and seventy of them were killed at Uḥud.'

Here a problem arises. If it is asked that if there was a choice, how could there have been a rebuke, the answer is that the rebuke occurred first because of their eagerness to accept ransom. Then there was a choice after that. Something that indicates that is that al-Miqdād said, when the Messenger of Allah ﷺ commanded that 'Uqbah ibn Abī Mu'ayṭ be killed, 'My captive, Messenger of Allah!' Muṣ'ab ibn 'Umayr said to the one who had captured his brother, 'Bind his hands well. His mother is wealthy.' There are other accounts that indicate eagerness to take ransom. When those they had captured were taken to Madīnah and the Messenger of Allah ﷺ had finally executed an-Naḍr, 'Uqbah and others, the choice was sent down from Allah. Then the Messenger of Allah ﷺ consulted with his Companions and 'Umar retained his original position about killing them while Abū Bakr thought that the best interest for the strength of the Muslims lay in the wealth obtained by ransom. The Messenger of Allah ﷺ inclined to the view of Abū Bakr. Both views were *ijtihād* after the option of choosing had been given. According to this, no censure was revealed. Allah knows best.

Ibn Wahb said Mālik said that this *āyah* was revealed about the captive idolaters at Badr. They were idolaters on that day and were ransomed and returned. If they had been Muslims, they would have stayed and not returned. Forty-four of them were killed and a like number captured. The martyrs at Badr were few. Abū 'Amr ibn al-'Alā' said, 'Those killed were seventy and the same number captured.' That is what Ibn 'Abbās, Ibn al-Musayyab and others said. It is sound as we find in *Ṣaḥīḥ Muslim*: 'On that day they killed seventy and captured seventy.' Al-Bayhaqī mentioned that they said, 'The captives were brought and Shuqrān, the freedman of the Messenger of Allah ﷺ, was put in charge of them. There were forty-nine men who were counted. There were originally seventy. That is agreed upon and there is no doubt about it.'

Ibn al-'Arabī said, 'Mālik said, "They were idolaters" because commentators related that al-'Abbās said to the Prophet ﷺ, "I am Muslim." In one variant we find that the captives said to the Prophet ﷺ, "We have believed in you." Mālik says that all of this is weak. He cited as evidence for its falsity what was mentioned about their return to Makkah and the fact that they were present at Uḥud.' Abū 'Umar ibn 'Abd al-Barr said, 'They disagree about when al-'Abbās became Muslim. It is said that it was before the Battle of Badr. That is why the Messenger of Allah ﷺ said, "Whoever meets al-'Abbās should not kill him. He was brought out unwillingly." It is reported from Ibn 'Abbās that the Messenger of Allah ﷺ said on the Day of Badr, "Some of the Banū Hāshim and others have been brought out unwillingly without any desire to fight us. Whoever meets one of them from the Banū Hāshim should not kill him. Whoever meets Abū al-Bakhtarī should not kill him. Whoever meets al-'Abbās should not kill him. He was forced to come out."' He mentioned that he became Muslim when he was captured in the Battle of Badr. It is also mentioned that he became Muslim on the day of Khaybar. He used to write to the Messenger of Allah ﷺ with news of the idolaters. He wanted to emigrate, but the Messenger of Allah ﷺ wrote to him: 'Remain in Makkah. Your staying there is more beneficial for us.'

لَّوْلَا كِتَٰبٌ مِّنَ ٱللَّهِ سَبَقَ لَمَسَّكُمْ فِيمَآ أَخَذْتُمْ عَذَابٌ عَظِيمٌ ٦٨

68 Were it not for a prior decree which had already proceeded from Allah, a terrible punishment would have afflicted you on account of what you took.

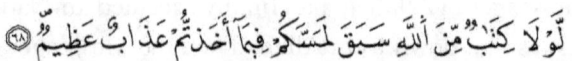

Allah had already decreed that He would not punish a people until it was clear to Him that they would not become godfearing. People disagree about what the *prior decree* from Allah was. The soundest opinion is that it was the making lawful of booty. It was forbidden to those before us. In the Battle of Badr, the people hastened to the booty and Allah revealed this, i.e. making booty lawful.

Abū Dāwūd aṭ-Ṭayālisī related in the *Musnad* from Salām from al-A'mash from Abū Ṣāliḥ that Abū Hurayrah said, 'In the Battle of Badr, people hurried to the booty and got hold of it. The Messenger of Allah ﷺ said, "Before you, booty was not lawful for anyone except the leaders." It used to be that when a Prophet and his companions obtained booty, they would collect it and fire would descend from heaven and consume it. Then Allah revealed, "*Were it not for a prior decree...*"' At-Tirmidhī transmitted it. He said that it is a sound *ḥasan ḥadīth*. Mujāhid and al-Ḥasan said that.

Mujāhid, al-Ḥasan and Sa'īd ibn Jubayr said that the *prior decree* is Allah's forgiveness for the people of Badr as already stated elsewhere, or deferment for their past and future wrong actions. One group said that the *prior decree* is Allah pardoning them for this wrong action in particular. The general meaning is sounder since the Messenger of Allah ﷺ said to 'Umar about the people of Badr, 'What will inform you? Perhaps Allah has looked on the people of Badr and said, "Do what you wish. I have forgiven you."' Muslim transmitted it. It is said that the *prior decree* was that He would not punish them while Muḥammad ﷺ was among them. It is said that the *prior decree* is that Allah does not punish anyone for something he does in ignorance until it has been made clear to him. One group said that the *prior decree* is what Allah has decreed in terms of His effacing someone's minor wrong actions on account of their avoiding major ones. Aṭ-Ṭabarī believed that all these possibilities are included in the expression and did not take one meaning rather than another.

Ibn al-'Arabī said, 'The *āyah* is evidence of the fact that if someone does something he believes to be unlawful when it is in fact something Allah knows to be lawful, he is not punished for it. An example of this is someone who is fasting and says, "I am going to have a fit today and so I will break my fast now," or a woman who says, "This is the day of my period," and breaks her fast. They do that because fits and menstruation do break the fast. The well-known position of the School is that there is *kaffārah* (expiation) for it, and that is the position of ash-Shāfi'ī. Abū Ḥanīfah says that there is no *kaffārah* owed and that is another opinion.

The reasoning behind the first opinion is that the post occurrence arrival of permissibility does not establish an excuse which removes the punishment for doing something that is unlawful when it is actually done, as is the case when someone has sex with a woman and then marries her afterwards. The reasoning behind the second opinion is that the inviolability of that day is cancelled in the sight of Allah, and so the breaking of the fast coincides with what is lawful, not unlawful in the knowledge of Allah. So it is like someone intending to have sex with a woman brought to him, believing that she is not his wife, when she is, in fact, his wife. This is sounder. The first opinion does not hold because where prohibition is concerned, Allah's knowledge and our knowledge are the same, and what we think about this case differs from Allah's prior knowledge of it, and what one relies on is Allah's knowledge as He says here: *'Were it not for a prior decree which had already proceeded from Allah, a terrible punishment would have afflicted you on account of what you took.'*

فَكُلُوا۟ مِمَّا غَنِمْتُمْ حَلَـٰلًا طَيِّبًا ۚ وَٱتَّقُوا۟ ٱللَّهَ ۚ إِنَّ ٱللَّهَ غَفُورٌ رَّحِيمٌ ٦٩

69 So make full use of any booty you have taken which is lawful and good; and have *taqwā* of Allah. Allah is Ever-Forgiving, Most Merciful.

This apparently stipulates that all booty goes to those who take it and that they share equally in it. The words of Allah, however, make it clear that the fifth must be taken from it and spent in the manner mentioned: *'Know that when you take any booty, a fifth of it belongs to Allah…'* (8:41) This has already been discussed in full.

يَـٰٓأَيُّهَا ٱلنَّبِىُّ قُل لِّمَن فِىٓ أَيْدِيكُم مِّنَ ٱلْأَسْرَىٰٓ إِن يَعْلَمِ ٱللَّهُ فِى قُلُوبِكُمْ
خَيْرًا يُؤْتِكُمْ خَيْرًا مِّمَّآ أُخِذَ مِنكُمْ وَيَغْفِرْ لَكُمْ ۗ وَٱللَّهُ غَفُورٌ رَّحِيمٌ ٧٠
وَإِن يُرِيدُوا۟ خِيَانَتَكَ فَقَدْ خَانُوا۟ ٱللَّهَ مِن قَبْلُ فَأَمْكَنَ مِنْهُمْ ۗ
وَٱللَّهُ عَلِيمٌ حَكِيمٌ ٧١

70-71 O Prophet! say to those you are holding prisoner, 'If Allah knows of any good in your hearts, He will give you something better than what has been taken from you and forgive you.' Allah is Ever-Forgiving, Most Merciful. But if they mean to betray you, they have already previously betrayed Allah, so He has given you power over them. Allah is All-Knowing, All-Wise.

O Prophet! say to those you are holding prisoner,

It is said that this is addressed to the Prophet ﷺ and his Companions, and it is said that it is addressed to him alone. Ibn 'Abbās said, 'The prisoners mentioned in this *āyah* were al-'Abbās and his companions. They said to the Prophet ﷺ, 'We believe in what you brought and we testify that you are the Messenger of Allah. We will advise you about your people.' This *āyah* was revealed. The falsity of this has already been made clear in what Mālik said. We find in the *Muṣannaf* of Abū Dāwūd from Ibn 'Abbās that after the Battle of Badr the Prophet ﷺ made the ransom of the people of the Jāhiliyyah four hundred [dirhams].

Ibn Isḥāq said, 'Quraysh sent to the Messenger of Allah ﷺ to ransom their prisoners and each of the people with prisoners ransomed their prisoners for what satisfied them. Al-'Abbās said, "Messenger of Allah, I am a Muslim." The Messenger of Allah ﷺ replied, "Allah knows best whether you are a Muslim. If it is as you say, then Allah will repay you for that. We must go by appearances. Ransom yourself and the sons of yours brothers, Nawfal ibn al-Ḥārith ibn 'Abd al-Muṭṭalib and 'Aqīl ibn Abī Ṭālib, and your ally, 'Utbah ibn 'Amr of the Banū al-Ḥārith ibn Fihr." He said, "I do not have that much, Messenger of Allah." He said, "Where is the money that you and Umm al-Faḍl buried? You told her, 'If I die on this journey, this property is for my sons Faḍl, 'Abdullāh and Qutham.'" He said, "Messenger of Allah, I know that you are the Messenger of Allah. This is something which only Umm al-Faḍl and I know. Messenger of Allah, reckon for me what you took from me of the twenty *ūqiyyah*s I had." The Messenger of Allah ﷺ said, "No, that is something which Allah gave us from you. Ransom yourself, the sons of your brother and your ally." Then Allah revealed, *"O Prophet! Say to those to are holding prisoner..."'* Ibn Isḥaq said, 'The prisoner with the greatest ransom was al-'Abbās ibn 'Abd al-Muṭṭalib because he was a wealthy man. He ransomed himself for a hundred *ūqiyyah*s of gold.' Al-Bukhārī said that Anas ibn Mālik said that some of the *Anṣār* asked permission to speak to the Messenger of Allah ﷺ, and said, 'Allow us to forego the ransom [due to us] for our nephew al-'Abbās.' He said, 'By Allah, you will not forego even a dirham of it.'

An-Naqqāsh and others said that the ransom for each of the prisoners was forty *ūqiyyah*s except for al-'Abbās. The Prophet ﷺ said, 'Double the ransom for al-'Abbās.' He also obliged him to ransom his nephews, 'Aqīl ibn 'Abd al-Muṭṭalib and Nawfal ibn al-Ḥārith and he paid eighty *ūqiyyah*s for them and eighty *ūqiyyah*s for himself, and he took twenty *ūqiyyah*s from him in the fighting. That was because he was one of the ten who was responsible for feeding the people of Badr. Disaster overtook them in the Battle of Badr and they fought before being fed and the twenty *ūqiyyah*s remained with him and was taken from him at the time of the fighting. On that day one hundred and eighty *ūqiyyah*s were taken from him. Al-'Abbās said to the Prophet ﷺ, 'You left me what I am ashamed to ask Quraysh to fulfil.' The Prophet ﷺ said, 'Where is the gold you left with your wife Umm al-Faḍl.' Al-'Abbās asked, 'What gold?' The Messenger of Allah ﷺ said to him, 'You told her: "I do not know what will befall me in this. If something happens to me, it is for you and your son."' He said, 'Nephew, who told you this?' 'Allah informed me,' he answered. Al-'Abbās said, 'I testify to you that you spoke the truth. I have only realised today that you are the Messenger of Allah and I know that only the Knower of secrets informed you. I testify that there is no god but Allah and that you are His slave and Messenger and I disbelieve in what is other than Him.' He commanded his nephews to become Muslim and they did. It is about them that it was revealed: *'O Prophet! say to those you are holding prisoner...'*

The one who captured al-'Abbās was Abū al-Yasar Ka'b ibn 'Amr, one of the Banū Salamah. He was a short man and al-'Abbās was tall and stout. When he brought him to the Prophet ﷺ, he said to him, 'An angel helped you against him.'

He will give you something better than what has been taken from you

The '*something better*' is Islam and '*what has been taken from you*' was the ransom. It is said that this happens in this world and it is said that it is in the Next World. We find in *Ṣaḥīḥ Muslim* that when wealth was brought to the Prophet ﷺ from Baḥrayn, al-'Abbās said to him, 'I ransomed myself and I ransomed 'Aqīl.' The Messenger of Allah ﷺ said to him, 'Take.' So he spread out his garment and took what he could carry. In a source other than the *Ṣaḥīḥ* it is reported that al-'Abbās said to him, 'This is the better than what was taken me and after that I hope that Allah will forgive me.' Al-'Abbās said, 'He gave me Zamzam and I would not like to have all of the wealth of the people of Makkah in exchange for it.' Aṭ-Ṭabarī said that al-'Abbās said, 'It was revealed about me when I informed the Messenger of Allah ﷺ of my Islam and asked him to count the twenty *ūqiyyah*s which were taken from me before the ransom, he refused, saying, "That is booty (*fay'*)." In exchange for that Allah gave me twenty slaves, all of whom carried out trade with my wealth.'

We find in the *Muṣannaf* of Abū Dāwūd that 'Ā'ishah said, 'When the people of Makkah sent what was required to ransom their prisoners, Zaynab sent wealth with which to ransom Abū al-'Āṣ. In it she sent a necklace which had belonged to Khadījah which she had given her when she married Abū al-'Āṣ.' She said, 'When the Messenger of Allah ﷺ saw it, he was greatly moved by it and said, "If you think you should release her captive to her and return her property to her, then do so." They said, "Yes." The Prophet ﷺ made Abū al-'Āṣ promise to let Zaynab come to him [in Madīnah]. The Messenger of Allah ﷺ sent Zayd ibn Ḥārithah and another man of *Anṣār* and told them, "Go to Ya'juj valley and wait until Zaynab comes and then bring her here."'

Ibn Isḥāq said that this happened a month after Badr. 'Abdullāh ibn Abī Bakr related that Zaynab, the daughter of the Messenger of Allah ﷺ, said, 'When Abū al-'Āṣ returned to Makkah, he said to me, "Make preparations to join your father." I went out and made preparations. Hind bint 'Utbah met me and asked, "Daughter of Muḥammad, have I not heard that you are intending to join your father?" I told her, "I do not want to do that." She said, "Niece, do not do it. I am a wealthy woman and I have goods sufficient for your needs. If you need goods, I will sell them to you or I can make you a loan. What comes about between men does not come about between women." By Allah, when she said that, I only thought that she would do it. I was afraid of her, however, and concealed it, saying, "I do not want to do that."'

When Zaynab finished her preparations, she set out, and left and her husband's brother, Kinānah ibn ar-Rabī', led her in the daytime. The people of Makkah talked about that and Habbār ibn al-Aswad and Nāfi' ibn 'Abd al-Qays al-Fihri went out after her. The first to reach her while she was in her howdah was Habbār ibn al-Aswad. Kinānah knelt and took his arrows from his quiver and his bow and said, 'By Allah, if any man comes near me, I will put an arrow in him!' Abū Sufyān came with some nobles of Quraysh and said, 'Put away your arrows so that we can talk to you.' Abū Sufyan stood by him and said, 'You have not done right. You have left with the woman in front of the people. You know the calamity we experienced at Badr. The Arabs will think and say, when you take his daughter to him in front of the people, that this is weakness on our part. Return with the woman and stay a few days. Then take her away secretly at night to join her father. By my life, we have no intention of keeping her from her father and there is no revenge for us in that for what befell us.' He did that and after two or three days, he took her and she continued until she reached the Messenger of Allah ﷺ. They mentioned that she miscarried due to the terror she experienced when Habbār frightened her.

Ibn al-'Arabī said, 'When the idolaters were taken captive, some of them spoke about Islam but did not act with resolve on their words or acknowledge it definitively. It seems that they wanted to be close to the Muslims, but not far from the idolaters either. Our scholars said, "When an unbeliever talks about faith in his heart and on his tongue but does not resolve to carry that out, he is not a believer. If the like of that is found in a believer, he is an unbeliever unless that comes as a result of whispering which he cannot repel. Allah will pardon it and cancel it." Allah made the reality of that clear to His Messenger ﷺ and says: *"If they mean to betray you…"* It means: "if these words of theirs are treachery and plotting, *'they have already previously betrayed Allah'* by their disbelief, plotting against you and fighting you. If what they said is good – and Allah knows it – He will accept that from them and give them better than what they spent and will forgive them for their prior disbelief, treachery and plotting.'"

The plural of *khiyānah* (betrayal) is *khayā'in*. It should be *khawā'in* because its root has *wāw*, but they differentiate between it and the plural of *khā'inah*. It is said: *khā'in*, *khūn*, *khawanah* and *khānah*.

إِنَّ ٱلَّذِينَ ءَامَنُواْ وَهَاجَرُواْ وَجَٰهَدُواْ بِأَمْوَٰلِهِمْ وَأَنفُسِهِمْ فِي سَبِيلِ ٱللَّهِ
وَٱلَّذِينَ ءَاوَواْ وَّنَصَرُوٓاْ أُوْلَٰٓئِكَ بَعْضُهُمْ أَوْلِيَآءُ بَعْضٍۚ وَٱلَّذِينَ ءَامَنُواْ وَلَمْ
يُهَاجِرُواْ مَا لَكُم مِّن وَلَٰيَتِهِم مِّن شَيْءٍ حَتَّىٰ يُهَاجِرُواْۚ وَإِنِ ٱسْتَنصَرُوكُمْ
فِي ٱلدِّينِ فَعَلَيْكُمُ ٱلنَّصْرُ إِلَّا عَلَىٰ قَوْمِۭ بَيْنَكُمْ وَبَيْنَهُم مِّيثَٰقٌۗ وَٱللَّهُ بِمَا
تَعْمَلُونَ بَصِيرٞ ٧٢ وَٱلَّذِينَ كَفَرُواْ بَعْضُهُمْ أَوْلِيَآءُ بَعْضٍۚ إِلَّا تَفْعَلُوهُ تَكُن
فِتْنَةٞ فِي ٱلْأَرْضِ وَفَسَادٞ كَبِيرٞ ٧٣ وَٱلَّذِينَ ءَامَنُواْ وَهَاجَرُواْ وَجَٰهَدُواْ فِي
سَبِيلِ ٱللَّهِ وَٱلَّذِينَ ءَاوَواْ وَّنَصَرُوٓاْ أُوْلَٰٓئِكَ هُمُ ٱلْمُؤْمِنُونَ حَقّٗاۚ لَّهُم مَّغْفِرَةٞ
وَرِزْقٞ كَرِيمٞ ٧٤ وَٱلَّذِينَ ءَامَنُواْ مِنۢ بَعْدُ وَهَاجَرُواْ وَجَٰهَدُواْ مَعَكُمْ فَأُوْلَٰٓئِكَ
مِنكُمْۚ وَأُوْلُواْ ٱلْأَرْحَامِ بَعْضُهُمْ أَوْلَىٰ بِبَعْضٖ فِي كِتَٰبِ ٱللَّهِۚ إِنَّ ٱللَّهَ
بِكُلِّ شَيْءٍ عَلِيمُۢ ٧٥

72-75 Those who believe and have made *hijrah* and done *jihād* with their wealth and themselves in the Way of Allah, and those who have given refuge and help, they are the friends and protectors of one another. But as for those who believe but have not made *hijrah*, you are not in any way responsible for their protection until they make *hijrah*. But if they ask you for help in respect of the *dīn*, it is your duty to help them, except against people you have a treaty with. Allah sees what you do. Those who disbelieve are the friends and protectors of one another. If you do not act in this way there will be turmoil in the land and

great corruption. Those who believe and have made *hijrah* and done *jihād* in the Way of Allah and those who have given refuge and help, they are the true believers. They will have forgiveness and generous provision. Those who believe and make *hijrah* later on and accompany you in doing *jihād* they also are of your number. But blood relations are closer to one another in the Book of Allah. Allah has knowledge of all things.

Those who believe and have made *hijrah*

The *sūrah* ends by mentioning mutual protection (*muwālah*) so that each group knows their protector who will help them. *Hijrah* and *jihād* have already been discussed (2:217-218). *'Those who have given refuge and help'* is added to it, and they are the *Anṣār* who lived in Madinah and *who were already settled in the abode, and in faith*, and the Prophet ﷺ and the *Muhājirūn* joined them. The pronoun '*Those*' is in the nominative by the inceptive, and '*ba'ḍuhum*' is a second inceptive whose predicate is '*awliyā'u ba'ḍ*'. All are the predicate of *inna*.

Ibn 'Abbās said that '*protectors of one another*' refers to inheritance. They used to inherit from one another on the basis of *hijrah*. Those who believed but did not emigrate did not inherit from those who had emigrated. Then Allah abrogated that by mentioning '*blood relations*'. Abū Dāwūd transmitted that. Then inheritance went to blood relations and the people of different religions did not inherit from one another at all. Then the Prophet ﷺ said, 'Give the obligatory shares of inheritance to their people' as was already discussed in the *Āyah* of Inheritance in *an-Nisā'* (4:22). It is also said that there is no abrogation and that it means in respect of help and support. "*Those who believe*" is an inceptive and predicate.

'You are not in any way responsible for their protection': Yaḥyā ibn Waththāb, al-A'mash and Ḥamzah recited '*wilāyatihim*' [instead of *walāyatihim*]. It is said that it is a dialectal usage. It is said that it comes from the verb *waliya*, to be put in charge of a thing. A *walī* has clear governance (*walāyah*). A *wālī* has clear guardianship (*wilāyah*). The reading with the *fatḥah* is clearer and better because the meaning is help and lineage. Both *walāyah* and *wilāyah* are used to mean governance.

But if they ask you for help in respect of the *dīn*

It means: if those believers who have not emigrated from the land of war ask you for help in the form of a party of men or with money to enable their rescue, then help them. That is an obligation on you. Do not disappoint them unless they ask you for help against an unbelieving people with whom you have a treaty. Then do not help them against them and do not break the treaty until its term has been fulfilled. Ibn al-'Arabī added, 'Unless they are oppressed prisoners. Then the duty of guardianship (*walāyah*) over them stands and it is mandatory to assist them so that not one of us should hesitate a moment before going out to rescue them, if our number is sufficient to accomplish that, or we spend all our wealth to bring them out until no one has a single dirham left. That is what Mālik and all the scholars say.' We belong to Allah and to Him we return regarding what happens to people who leave their brothers as prisoners of the enemy while they possess treasuries of wealth, surplus means, power, numbers, strength and resolve. Az-Zajjāj said, 'It is possible that the phrase *"it is your duty to help them"* is in the accusative for encouragement.'

Those who disbelieve are the friends and protectors of one another,

Allah ended the duty of mutual protection between the unbelievers and believers and made the believers protectors of one another, givers of support to one another, and those who work together in their common belief. Our scholars say that if an unbelieving woman has a Muslim brother, he should not give her away in marriage because there is no *walāyah* between the two of them. The people of her religion should give her away in marriage. Similarly, a Muslim woman may only be given in marriage by a Muslim, and an unbelieving woman may only be given in marriage by an unbeliever who is her relative or a bishop, even if she is being married to a Muslim. But it is not valid for a Muslim to act on her behalf in the contract unless she is an emancipated slave. For anyone else, if a Muslim acts in the contract on her behalf, and the one she is marrying is a Muslim, the contract is void. No regard is paid to her marriage to a Christian. Aṣbagh, however, said that it is not annulled since it is better that a Muslim be the contracting party.

If you do not act in this way there will be turmoil in the land and great corruption.

This refers to mutual inheritance and holding to it. It means: 'Do not let them inherit from one another in the manner they used to.' Ibn Zayd said that. It is said that it refers to mutual help, support, and giving assistance. Ibn Jurayj and others said that is the case even if *fitnah* does not arise from it immediately. This view is more likely than the second view.

At-Tirmidhī mentioned from 'Abdullāh ibn Muslim ibn Hurmuz from Muḥammad and Sa'd, the sons of 'Ubayd, from Abū Ḥātim al-Muzanī that the Messenger of Allah ﷺ said, 'If someone comes to you with whose *dīn* and character you are pleased, then give in marriage to him. If you do not do so, there will be turmoil (*fitnah*) in the earth and much corruption.' They said, 'Messenger of Allah, what if there is something in him?' He said three times, 'If someone comes to you with whose *dīn* and character you are pleased, then give in marriage to him.' He said that it is a *gharīb* [*ḥasan*] *ḥadīth.*

It is said that it refers to observing the treaties and agreements included in Allah's words: *'except against people you have a treaty with.'* If this is not done, it is turmoil itself. It is said that it refers to helping the Muslims in the *dīn*. That is the meaning of the second view.

Ibn Isḥāq said, 'Allah made the *Muhājirūn* and *Anṣār* the people protected by Him in the *dīn* as opposed to any others. He made the unbelievers protectors of one another.' Then He says: *'If you do not act in this way,'* meaning by your taking unbelievers as protectors rather than believers, *'there will be turmoil in the land'* caused by war and the attacks, dispossession and capture that accompany it. The *'great corruption'* referred to is the appearance of disbelief. Al-Kisā'ī said that it is possible that the phrase *'there will be turmoil in the land'* means: 'what you do will result in turmoil and great corruption.'

Those who believe and have made *hijrah* and done *jihād* in the Way of Allah and those who have given refuge and help, they are the true believers.

'Ḥaqq' here is a verbal noun, in other words there are those whose faith Allah makes true by emigration and *jihād* and those whose faith is made true by giving refuge and help. They receive the good news in Allah's words: *'They will have forgiveness and generous provision'* which is an immense reward in the Garden.

Those who believe and make *hijrah* later on

This means after al-Ḥudaybīyah and the Pledge of Riḍwān. That is because *hijrah* after that had a lower rank than the first *Hijra*. The second *Hijrah* is the one that was made after the truce took place and war had laid down its burdens for about two years. Then the Conquest of Makkah took place and then the Prophet ﷺ said, 'There is no *hijrah* after the Conquest.' It is clear that anyone who believed and emigrated became joined to them. The words *'they are also of your number'* means that they are the same as you in respect of the duty of assistance and mutual protection.

But blood relations are closer to one another in the Book of Allah.

Ūlū is the plural of *dhū*. *Raḥim* is feminine and the plural is *arḥām*. What is meant here are paternal kin as opposed to maternal kin. Something that makes clear that what is meant by *raḥm* are the paternal relations (*'aṣabāt*) is found in the words of the Arabs: 'Kinship (*raḥim*) is connected you,' by which they did not mean kinship through the mother. According to Ibn Hishām, Qutaylah bint al-Ḥārith, the sister of an-Naḍr ibn al-Ḥārith (and as-Suhaylī said that what is sound is that she was the daughter of an-Naḍr and not his sister) said, when she was lamenting her father whom the Prophet ﷺ executed at aṣ-Ṣafrā':

O rider, I think that you will reach Uthayl
on the morning of the fifth day if you are fortunate.
Once there convey my greeting to a dead man there.
Swift camels continue to carry it
From me to you: tell of flowing tears
welling up, sometimes choked by sobbing.
Can an-Naḍr hear when I call him?
Can the dead who do not speak hear?
O Muḥammad! The best son of a noble mother
among her people, and a sire of noble lineage!
It would not have harmed you if you had been gracious.
Sometimes a warrior will be, even though full of rage and fury.
Had you accepted ransom, I would have ransomed him
with the highest ransom that could possibly be paid.
An-Naḍr was the closest relative of those captured
and the most entitled to be set free.
The swords of his father's sons came against him.
By Allah, kinship here was shattered!
Exhausted he was led to execution,
a shackled prisoner, bound and miserable.

The early generations and those after them disagreed about the inheritance of maternal relatives and those relatives of the deceased who have no share in the Book and who are not paternal kin, such as the children of daughters, the children of sisters, the daughters of brothers, paternal and maternal aunts, an uncle who is the father's maternal half-brother, the maternal grandfather, and the maternal grandmother, and those closer to them.

Some say that those relatives who do not have a share do not inherit. That is related from Abū Bakr aṣ-Ṣiddīq, Zayd ibn Thābit, Ibn 'Umar, and one variant is related from 'Alī. It is the position of the people of Madīnah. It is related from Makḥūl and al-Awzā'ī, and ash-Shāfi'ī took that position. Those who said that they do inherit were: 'Umar ibn al-Khaṭṭāb, Ibn Mas'ūd, Mu'ādh, Abū ad-

Dardā', 'Ā'ishah, and 'Alī in one variant. It is the position of the Kufans, Aḥmad and Isḥāq. They used this *āyah* as evidence and said, 'It includes all relatives for two reasons: kinship and Islam. So they are more entitled to it than those who have only one reason: Islam.'

The first group respond by saying that this is an undefined universal *āyah*. It literally means every relative, near or far. The *āyahs* of inheritance define it. What defines and makes clear rules over what is undefined. They said, 'The Prophet ﷺ made the *walā'* a second reason. The previous master (*mawlā*) is put in the same position as the *'aṣabah* and he said, "The *walā'* belongs to the one who set free." He forbade selling or giving away the *walā'*.'

The others cite as proof what Abū Dāwūd and ad-Dāraquṭnī related from al-Miqdād that the Messenger of Allah ﷺ said, 'Whoever dies without relatives is ascribed to me (and sometimes it is said, 'to Allah and His Messenger'). If someone leaves wealth, it goes to his heirs. I am the heir of those who have no heirs. I pay his blood money and I inherit from him. The maternal uncle is the heir of someone with no heirs. He pays his blood money and inherits from him.'

Ad-Dāraquṭnī related from Ṭāwūs that 'Ā'ishah said, 'Allah is the *mawlā* of the one who has no *mawlā* and the maternal uncle is the heir of the one who has no heirs.' (*mawqūf*)

It is related from Abū Hurayrah that the Messenger of Allah ﷺ said, 'The maternal uncle is an heir.' It is related that Abū Hurayrah said, 'The Messenger of Allah ﷺ was asked about the inheritance of a paternal aunt and maternal aunt and said, "I do not know until Jibrīl comes to me." Later he said, "Where is the one who asked about the inheritance of the paternal aunt and maternal aunt?" A man came and he said ﷺ, "Jibrīl told me that neither of them have anything."' Ad-Dāraquṭnī said, 'Only Mas'adah has an *isnād* for this from Muḥammad ibn 'Amr, and it is weak. What is correct is that it is *mursal*.'

It is related from ash-Sha'bī that Ziyād ibn Abī Sufyān asked someone sitting with him, 'Do you know the judgment of 'Umar regarding paternal and maternal aunts?' 'No,' was the answer. He said, 'I am the creature of Allah with the best knowledge of how 'Umar judged regarding them. He put the maternal aunt in the position of the mother and the paternal aunt in the position of the father.'

9. Sūrat at-Tawbah – Repentance

بَرَآءَةٌ مِّنَ ٱللَّهِ وَرَسُولِهِۦٓ إِلَى ٱلَّذِينَ عَٰهَدتُّم مِّنَ ٱلْمُشْرِكِينَ ١

1 An announcement to those idolaters you have a general treaty with that Allah and His Messenger are free of them:

Sa'īd ibn Jubayr said, 'I asked Ibn 'Abbās about *Sūrat Barā'ah* (*at-Tawbah*) and he said, "It is the Disgracer. Allah continued to reveal '*among them*' until we feared that He would not omit anyone."' Al-Qushayrī Abū Naṣr 'Abd al-Ḥamīd said, 'This *sūrah* was revealed about the Tabūk expedition and it was revealed after it. At the beginning of it Allah revoked the treaties with the unbelievers. The *sūrah* discloses the secrets of the hypocrites. It is called The Disgracer and The Investigation because it investigates the secrets of the hypocrites. It called the Scatterer. It is called the Investigation, and *ba'tharah* is investigation.'

Scholars disagree about the reason why the *basmalah* is omitted at the beginning of this *sūrah*. There are five views about it. The first is because it is said that something the Arabs used to do in the Jāhiliyyah was that when they had a treaty with someone and wanted to break it, they wrote them a letter without the *basmalah*. When *Sūrat Barā'ah* was revealed to break the treaty between the Prophet ﷺ and the idolaters, the Prophet ﷺ sent 'Alī ibn Abī Ṭālib with it and he read it to them in the Festival. He did not use the *basmalah* in it following their custom when breaking treaties.

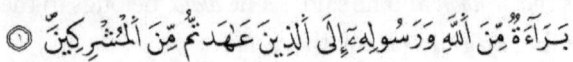

The second view is that an-Nasā'ī related from Aḥmad from Muḥammad ibn al-Muthannā from Yaḥyā ibn Sa'īd from 'Awf from Yazīd ar-Raqqāshī that Ibn 'Abbās said, 'I asked 'Uthmān, "What made you count *al-Anfāl* as one of the *Mathānī* and *Barā'ah* as one of the Hundreds, and then connect them without writing the line 'In the Name of Allah, the all-Merciful, Most Merciful' between them and put them among the Seven Long Ones? What made you do that?" 'Uthmān answered, "When something was revealed to the Messenger of Allah ﷺ, he summoned to him one of those who could write. He would say, 'Put this in the *sūrah* in which is such-and-such.' *Āyahs* were revealed to him and he said, 'Put these *āyahs* in the *sūrah* in which there is mentioned such-and-such.' *Al-Anfāl* was among the first to be revealed and *Barā'ah* was one of the last, and their stories are similar. The Messenger of Allah ﷺ died without making it clear that it is part of it. I think that it is part of it and so I joined the two together and did not write the line '*In the Name of Allah, the all-Merciful, Most Merciful*' between them."' Abū 'Īsā at-Tirmidhī transmitted it and said that it is a *ḥasan ḥadīth*.

The third view is also related from 'Uthmān. Mālik said in what Ibn Wahb, Ibn al-Qāsim and Ibn 'Abd al-Ḥakam related, that when the beginning of it was removed, the *basmalah* was also removed with it. That is related from Ibn 'Ajlān. It reached him that *Sūrat Bara'ah* was equal in length to *al-Baqarah* or close to it. Then some of it was removed and that is why the *basmalah* is not written between them. Sa'īd ibn Jubayr said, 'It was like *Sūrat al-Baqarah*.'

The fourth view was what Khārijah, Abū 'Iṣmah and others said. They said that when they wrote out the copy of the Qur'an during the time that 'Uthmān was caliph, the Companions of the Messenger of Allah ﷺ disagreed. Some of them said that *Bara'ah* and *al-Anfāl* were one *sūrah* and others said that they were two *sūrahs*. Therefore a gap was left between them because of the view of those who said that they were two *sūrahs* and the *basmalah* was omitted because of the view of those who said that they were one *sūrah*. So both groups were satisfied and their arguments upheld in the copy of the text of the Qur'an.

The fifth view is what 'Abdullāh ibn al-'Abbās said, 'I asked 'Alī ibn Abī Ṭālib, "Why is '*In the Name of Allah, the All-Merciful, Most Merciful*' not written in *Barā'ah*?" He answered, "Because '*In the Name of Allah, the All-Merciful, Most Merciful*' is security and *Barā'ah* was sent down with the sword. There is no security in it."' Al-Mubarrad related that explanation and said, 'That is why they are not joined together. "*In the Name of Allah, the All-Merciful, Most Merciful*" is mercy and *Bara'ah* was revealed in anger.' Something similar is reported from Sufyān. Sufyān ibn 'Uyaynah said, '"*In the Name of Allah, the All-Merciful, Most Merciful*" is not written at the beginning of this *sūrah* because the *tasmiyah* is mercy and mercy is security. This *sūrah* was revealed about the hypocrites and with the sword, not with security for the hypocrites.'

What is sound is that the *basmalah* is not written because Jibrīl did not bring it down in this *sūrah*. Al-Qushayrī said that. 'Uthmān said that the Messenger of Allah ﷺ died when he had not made it clear that it was part of it. This indicates that all the *sūrahs* were ordered according to what the Prophet ﷺ said and made clear. *Bara'ah* alone was added to *al-Anfāl* without the instruction of the Prophet ﷺ

since he died before making that clear and they are called 'the two close ones' and so it is obliged to join them because description of how the Messenger of Allah ﷺ joined them together while he was alive demands that that be done.

Ibn al-'Arabī said that this furnishes proof that analogy is a fundamental principle of the *dīn*. Do you not see how 'Uthmān and the notable Companions resorted to analogy in the absence of a text and thought that the narrative content of *Bara'ah* was similar to that of *al-Anfāl* and so they joined them together on that basis? When it is clear that analogy was used in the compilation of the Qur'an, how much more should that be the case with other rulings?

The verb *barā'ah* means to be free of something. You say, 'I am free of it' (*bari'tu*) when you remove it from yourself and sever it from you. *Barā'ah* is in the nominative as the predicate of an implied inceptive. The words imply: 'This is a freeing…' It can also be in the nominative by the inceptive and the predicate is then '*to those*'. It is also permitted for an inceptive to be indefinite because it is descriptive and describes something specific. 'Īsā ibn 'Umar recited '*barā'ah*' in the nominative, implying: 'Hold to freeing,' and so it has the meaning of encouragement. It is a verbal noun on the measure of *fa'ālah*, like *shanā'ah* and *danā'ah*.

to those idolaters you have a general treaty with

Those means those whom the Messenger of Allah ﷺ had made a treaty with because he made treaties and all his Companions were content with that and so it was as if they had also made the treaty and it is ascribed to them. Similarly, treaties which the leaders of unbelief have made for their people are ascribed to them, reckoned against them and they are taken to task for them. Only that is possible. Acceptance by everyone is not possible, so the ruler contracts what he thinks is in their best interest and it is binding on his subjects.

فَسِيحُوا۟ فِى ٱلْأَرْضِ أَرْبَعَةَ أَشْهُرٍ وَٱعْلَمُوٓا۟ أَنَّكُمْ غَيْرُ مُعْجِزِى ٱللَّهِ وَأَنَّ ٱللَّهَ مُخْزِى
ٱلْكَٰفِرِينَ ۝٢

2 'You may travel about in the land for four months and know that you cannot thwart Allah and that Allah will humiliate the unbelievers.'

'You may travel about in the land for four months

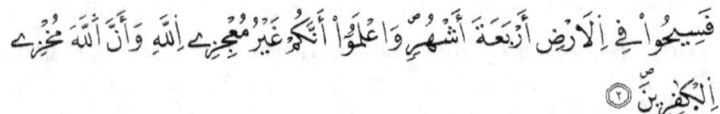

Allah here moves from the third person to the second person: 'Tell them to travel in the land, to and fro, secure and without any fear of any of the Muslims fighting, despoiling, killing or capturing you.' The verb *sāḥa* is used for travelling in the land. The verb is *sāḥa, yasīḥu, siyāḥah, suyūḥ* and *sayḥān*. From it comes the noun *sayḥ*, which is the running of water on the surface of the ground. Corroborating that are the words of Ṭarafah ibn al-'Abd:

> If I were to fear this from you, it would not get me
> before you see horses spreading out (*tasīḥu*) before me.

Scholars disagree about the nature of the four month delay after which Allah and His Messenger are free of those idolaters. Muḥammad ibn Isḥāq and others said that there were two categories of idolaters. One group of them had a treaty which would last for less than four months, and so they were granted a delay of four months. The other group had a treaty without any time stipulation and so it was shortened to four months if they desired that. Then after that there would be war against them from Allah and His Messenger and the believers. Then they would be killed wherever they were caught and captured unless they repented. This term began on the Day of the Greater Hajj and ended on the 10th of Rabī' al-Ākhir. As for those who did not have a treaty, the term was the end of the four sacred months. That was fifty days: twenty of Dhu-l-Ḥijjah and Muḥarram.

Al-Kalbī said, 'It was four months for those who had a treaty with the Messenger of Allah ﷺ of less than four months, and for those who had a treaty of more than four months, those are the ones whose treaty Allah commanded should be given their full time when He says: *"Honour their treaties until their time runs out."* (9:4). This is preferred by aṭ-Ṭabarī and others.

Muḥammad ibn Isḥāq, Mujāhid and others mentioned that this *āyah* was revealed about the people of Makkah. That was because the Messenger of Allah ﷺ made a treaty with Quraysh in the year of al-Ḥudaybīyah that there would be no war for ten years during which the people would be safe and would refrain from fighting one another. Khuzā'ah were part of the treaty with the Messenger of Allah ﷺ and the Banū Bakr were with Quraysh. Then the Banū Bakr attacked Khuzā'ah and broke the treaty. The reason for that was an outstanding blood feud from some time before Islam which the Banū Bakr had against Khuzā'ah. When the truce was made at al-Ḥudaybīyah, people were safe from one another and the Banū ad-Dīl of Banū Bakr, who wanted blood, took advantage of the opportunity and unpreparedness of Khuzā'ah and wanted to take revenge for those of the Banū al-Aswad ibn Razn whom Khuzā'ah had killed. Nawfal ibn Mu'āwiyah ad-Dīlī set out with those who obeyed him from the Banū Bakr ibn 'Abd Manāt and attacked some of Khuzā'ah at night and killed them. Quraysh had helped the Banū Bakr with weapons and some of Quraysh themselves participated. Khuzā'ah retreated to the *Ḥaram* according to the well-known account. That broke the treaty contracted at al-Ḥudaybīyah. 'Amr ibn Sālim al-Khuzā'ī, Budayl ibn Qarqā' and some of Khuzā'ah went to the Messenger of Allah ﷺ to ask for his help because of what the Banū Bakr and Quraysh had done to them. 'Amr ibn Sālim composed:

> O Lord, I entreat Muḥammad
> by the ancient alliance between our fathers!
> You were a father to us and we were the child
> and then we became Muslim and have not withheld our support.
> Help us – may Allah guide you to immediate help
> and summon the servants of Allah to come as reinforcements.
> Among them the Messenger of Allah is prepared
> Bright white, like the sun, rising up.
> The expression on his face becomes clouded
> in an army like a raging sea.
> Quraysh has broken their promise to you
> and violated their firm pledge with you.
> They claim that I cannot call on anyone for help
> when they are lowly and fewer in number.
> They attacked us at night at al-Watīr
> and killed us while we were bowing and in prostration.

The Messenger of Allah ﷺ said, 'I will not help anyone if I do not help the Banū Ka'b!' Then he looked at a cloud and said, 'It will provide an opening for the Banū Ka'b,' meaning Khuzā'ah. The Messenger of Allah ﷺ said to Budayl ibn Warqā' and those with him, 'Abū Sufyān will come to strengthen the treaty and increase its length but will return without achieving it.' Quraysh regretted what they had done and Abū Sufyān went to Madīnah to try and maintain the treaty and increase the time of the truce and returned without achieving it as the Messenger of Allah ﷺ had said. The Messenger of Allah ﷺ made preparations to go to Makkah and Allah conquered it in 8 AH.

When news of the conquest of Makkah reached Hawāzin, Mālik ibn 'Awf an-Naṣrī gathered them to what is known as Ḥunayn. There the Muslims were victorious over the unbelievers. The battle against Hawāzin at Ḥunayn took place at the beginning of Shawwāl 8 AH. The Messenger of Allah ﷺ delayed the division of booty and women and did not distribute them until he went to Ṭā'if.

The Messenger of Allah ﷺ laid siege to them for about twenty days. Other things are said about the length of time. He set up a catapult and used it on them as is famous about that expedition.

The Messenger of Allah ﷺ then went to al-Ji'rānah and divided the booty of Ḥunayn as is well-known. Then he ﷺ left and they separated. 'Attāb ibn Usayd led the people in *ḥajj* that year. He was the first amīr in Islam to be put in charge of the *ḥajj*. The idolaters performed *ḥajj* following their practices. 'Attāb ibn Usayd was good, excellent and scrupulous.

Ka'b ibn Zuhayr ibn Abī Salmā went to the Messenger of Allah ﷺ and eulogised him. He stood in front of him and recited his ode which begins, 'Su'ād is gone and my heart is sick with love...' He recited it to the end and in it he mentioned and praised the *Muhājirūn*. Before that he had written satire about the Prophet ﷺ and the *Anṣār* criticised him because he had not mentioned them. So he came to the Prophet ﷺ with an ode in which he praised the *Anṣār*. He said:

He who loves a noble life, should be
with the horsemen of the righteous *Anṣār*
Who inherit noble traits, from father to son.
They are the best men, sons of the best men,
Throwing with their arms strong spears
like long Indian swords.
Those who look with eyes red as
coals, their eyes not exhausted.
They have pledged themselves to their Prophet to the death
on days of hand-to-hand fighting and cavalry attacks.
They purify themselves with their practices
with blood of the unbelievers.
Their habit is that
of strong-necked lions in hidden valleys.
If you come to seek their protection,
it is as if you were in the haunts of mountain goats.
In the Battle of Badr, they struck 'Alī[3] with a blow
which was close to felling all of Nizār.
If the tribes knew all that I know about them,
those who argue with me would believe me.

3 'Alī ibn Mas'ūd.

They are people who, when the stars have given no rain,
feed well the night-travellers who arrive.

Then after he left Ṭā'if, the Messenger of Allah ﷺ stayed (in Madinah) through Dhu-l-Ḥijjah, Muḥarram, Ṣafar, Rabī' al-Awwal, Rabī' al-Ākhir, Jumāda al-Ūla and Jumāda al-Ākhirah. In Rajab of 9 AH he left with the Muslims to attack the Romans in the Tabūk expedition, which was the last expedition he made.

Ibn Jurayj reported that Mujāhid said, 'When the Messenger of Allah ﷺ left Tabūk, he wanted to perform *ḥajj* and then said, "Naked idolaters are present doing *ṭawāf* of the House. I do not want to perform *ḥajj* until that practice no longer exists." He sent Abū Bakr in command of the *ḥajj* and sent with him forty *āyah*s from the beginning of *Barā'ah* to read to the people of the Festival. He announced that among the people when they gathered and 'Alī came out on the camel of the Prophet ﷺ, al-Aḍbā' and he caught up to Abū Bakr at Dhu-l-Ḥulayfah. When Abu Bakr saw him, he asked, "Commander or commanded?" He replied, "Commanded," and they went on. Abū Bakr oversaw the *ḥajj* for people in their stations which they had in the Jāhiliyyah.'

We find in the book of an-Nasā'ī that Jābir said, 'A day before the day of Tarwīyah, 'Alī recited *Barā'ah* to the end of it to people as well as on the Day of 'Arafah and the Day of Sacrifice after the *khuṭbah* of Abū Bakr: over three days. On the first of *Nafr*, Abū Bakr stood and addressed the people and told them how to hasten and how to stone, instructing them in their practices. When he finished, 'Alī stood and recited *Barā'ah* to the end.' Sulaymān ibn Mūṣā said, 'When Abū Bakr spoke at 'Arafah, he said, "Stand, 'Alī, and convey the Message of the Messenger of Allah ﷺ." 'Alī stood and did it.' He said, 'Then it occurred to me that all the people had not been present for the *khuṭbah* of Abū Bakr. I began to go around to the tents on the Day of Sacrifice.'

At-Tirmidhī related that Zayd ibn Yuthaya' said, 'I asked 'Alī what he was sent with on the *ḥajj*. He answered, "I was sent with four things: no one naked should perform *ṭawāf* of the House; if someone has a treaty with the Prophet ﷺ, it will continue to its end; if someone has no treaty, the term is four months; and only a believer will enter the Garden, and the Muslims and idolaters will not join together after this year."' He said that this is a *ḥasan* sound *ḥadīth*. An-Nasā'ī transmitted it, and he said, 'I called out until my voice was hoarse.'

Abu 'Umar said that 'Alī was sent to revoke every treaty to those with whom it was made and that after that year no idolater should perform *ḥajj* and no one should perform *ṭawāf* of the Ka'bah naked. Abū Bakr led the *ḥajj* in that year, 9 AH. Then the Messenger of Allah ﷺ made *ḥajj* the following year and he did not make any other *ḥajj* from Madīnah. His *ḥajj* took place in Dhu-l-Ḥijjah. He said, 'Time revolves...' according to what comes in the *āyah* about delayed months. The Ḥajj was established in Dhu-l-Ḥijjah and will continue until the Day of Rising. Mujāhid mentioned that Abū Bakr performed *ḥajj* in Dhu-l-Qa'dah 9 AH.

Ibn al-'Arabī said, 'The wisdom in giving *Barā'ah* to 'Alī includes revoking treaties which the Prophet ﷺ had made. The custom of the Arabs was that a contract could only be cancelled by the one who made it and so the Prophet ﷺ, wanting to head off any argument of the Arabs, sent his Hāshimī cousin from his house to revoke the treaty so that no one would be able to say anything.' Az-Zajjāj also said that.

Scholars say that the *āyah* contains the permission to break treaties between us and the idolaters. There are two cases of that. One is when the time specified ends and so we have the choice to declare war. The second is when we fear treachery from them and then their treaty is revoked as has already been said. Ibn 'Abbās said that the *āyah* is abrogated. The Prophet ﷺ made a treaty and then revoked it when he was commanded to fight.

وَأَذَانٌ مِّنَ اللَّهِ وَرَسُولِهِ إِلَى النَّاسِ يَوْمَ الْحَجِّ الْأَكْبَرِ أَنَّ اللَّهَ بَرِيءٌ مِّنَ
الْمُشْرِكِينَ وَرَسُولُهُ فَإِن تُبْتُمْ فَهُوَ خَيْرٌ لَّكُمْ وَإِن تَوَلَّيْتُمْ فَاعْلَمُوا أَنَّكُمْ
غَيْرُ مُعْجِزِي اللَّهِ وَبَشِّرِ الَّذِينَ كَفَرُوا بِعَذَابٍ أَلِيمٍ ﴿٣﴾

3 A proclamation from Allah and His Messenger to mankind on the day of the greater pilgrimage: 'Allah is free of the idolaters, as is His Messenger. If you repent, it will be better for you. But if you turn your backs, know that you cannot thwart Allah.' Give the unbelievers the news of a painful punishment –

There is no disagreement that *adhān* (*proclamation*) linguistically means informing. Here it is added to '*barā'ah*'. '*Mankind*' here is all people. The phrase '*on the day of the greater pilgrimage*' is adverbial and the regent in it is '*adhān*'. It is described by Allah's words, '*from Allah*' and the suggestion of the action remains in it, making it adverbial. It is said that the regent in it is '*humiliate*' (in the previous *āyah*) and it is not valid for '*adhān*' to be the regent because it is descriptive and does not have the action of a verb.

Scholars disagree about what '*the day of the greater pilgrimage*' is. It is said that it is the Day of 'Arafah. That is related from 'Umar, 'Uthmān, Ibn 'Abbās, Ṭāwūs and Mujāhid. It is the position of Abū Ḥanīfah and ash-Shāfi'ī also stated that. 'Alī,

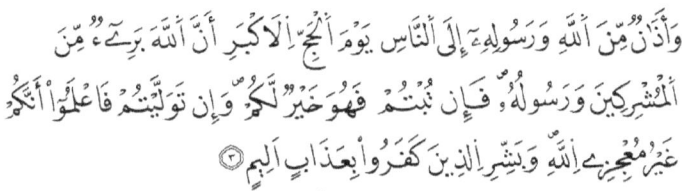

Ibn 'Abbās, Ibn Mas'ūd, Ibn Abī Awfā and al-Mughīrah ibn Shu'bah also said that it is the Day of Sacrifice. Aṭ-Ṭabarī preferred that. Ibn 'Umar related that the Messenger of Allah ﷺ stood on the Day of Sacrifice in the *ḥajj* which he made and said, 'What day is this?' They answered, 'The Day of Sacrifice'. He said, 'This is the day of the greater pilgrimage.' Abū Dāwūd transmitted it. Al-Bukhārī transmitted from Abū Hurayrah: 'Abū Bakr aṣ-Ṣiddīq sent me among those who made the announcement at Minā on the Day of Sacrifice: "After this year no idolater will make *ḥajj* or do *ṭawāf* of the House naked."' The day of the greater pilgrimage is the Day of Sacrifice. It is called '*greater*' because people say 'the lesser pilgrimage'. Abū Bakr revoked it for the people that year. No idolater performed *ḥajj* in the year of the Farewell Ḥajj, in which the Prophet ﷺ performed *ḥajj*. Ibn Abī Awfā said, 'The Day of Sacrifice is '*the day of the greater pilgrimage*' on which blood is shed, the garlands are removed, dishevelment is abandoned and on which the *muḥrim* comes out of *iḥrām*.' This is the position of Mālik because the Ḥajj is all on the Day of Sacrifice because standing occurs in its night and stoning, sacrifice, shaving and *ṭawāf* in its morning.

The first group use as evidence the *ḥadīth* of Makhramah in which the Prophet ﷺ said, 'The Day of the greater pilgrimage is the Day of 'Arafah.' Qāḍī Ismā'īl related it. Ath-Thawrī and Ibn Jurayj said, 'The '*day of the greater pilgrimage*' means all of the days of Minā.' This is as one says about battles, 'The Day of Ṣiffīn', 'The Day of the Camel', and 'The Day of Bu'āth'. It means a time, not a specific day.

It is related from Mujāhid that the greater pilgrimage is *qirān* and the lesser is *ifrād*. There is nothing about this in the *āyah*. He and 'Aṭā' said, 'The greater pilgrimage is that in which one stands at 'Arafah and the lesser is '*umrah*.' Mujāhid also said that it is all of the days of *ḥajj*. Al-Ḥasan and 'Abdullāh ibn al-Ḥārith ibn Nawfal said, 'It is called '*the day of the greater pilgrimage*' because that year both the idolaters and the Muslims performed *ḥajj* and the festivals of the religions coincided on that day: those of the Jews, Christians and Magians.' Ibn 'Aṭiyyah said, 'That would be a weak reason for Allah to describe it as "great" in His Book.' Al-Ḥasan also said that it is called '*greater*' because in it Abū Bakr performed *ḥajj* and revoked treaties. This is similar to the view of al-Ḥasan. Ibn Sīrīn said, 'The *day of the greater pilgrimage* is the year in which the Prophet ﷺ performed the Farewell Ḥajj and tribes performed it with him.'

Allah is free of the idolaters, as is His Messenger

'Anna' is in the accusative, implying '*bi-anna*'. If it is read as *inna*, it implies: 'He said that Allah...' *Barī'* is the predicate of *anna*. '*His Messenger*' is added, if

you wish, to something elided in the nominative in '*free*', or if you wish, it is the inceptive and its predicate is elided. It implies: 'His Messenger is free of them.' If '*Messenger*' is in the accusative, which al-Ḥasan and others have, it is added to the name of 'Allah' in the wording. There is an aberrant reading which has '*Messenger*' in the genitive based on it being an oath. It means 'by the right of His Messenger'. It is also related from al-Ḥasan. The story about 'Umar was mentioned at the beginning of the book (Introduction, p.24).

'*If you repent*' means repent of *shirk*. '*Better for you*' means 'more beneficial.' '*If you turn your backs*' on faith, '*know that you cannot thwart Allah*': be aware that He encompasses you and will send down His punishment on you.

إِلَّا ٱلَّذِينَ عَٰهَدتُّم مِّنَ ٱلْمُشْرِكِينَ ثُمَّ لَمْ يَنقُصُوكُمْ شَيْـًٔا وَلَمْ يُظَٰهِرُوا۟ عَلَيْكُمْ
أَحَدًا فَأَتِمُّوٓا۟ إِلَيْهِمْ عَهْدَهُمْ إِلَىٰ مُدَّتِهِمْ ۚ إِنَّ ٱللَّهَ يُحِبُّ ٱلْمُتَّقِينَ ٤

4 except those among the idolaters you have treaties with, who have not then broken their treaties with you in any way, or granted assistance to anyone against you. Honour their treaties until their time runs out. Allah loves those who are godfearing.

The phrase '*except those among the idolaters...*' is in the accusative by the connected exception. It means: 'Allah is free of the idolaters except for those with whom there is a treaty for the duration of that treaty.' It is said that it is a separate exception, meaning: 'Allah is free of them, but those who have a treaty are confirmed in that treaty and it is allowed to reach its completion.'

The clause '*who have not then broken their treaties with you*' indicates breaking the treaty with those who have broken it and being faithful with those who were faithful to their treaty until it ends. So Allah gave His Prophet ﷺ permission to break the treaty of those who had broken it and to be faithful to those who remained faithful to the end of it.

The phrase '*in any way*' means regarding any of the conditions of the treaty. '*Not granted assistance*' means that they have not aided them. 'Ikrimah and 'Aṭā' ibn Yasār recited '*yanquḍūkum*' based on something elided. It implies: 'they have not broken their treaty.' It is said that this is particular to the Banū Ḍamrah. '*Until their time runs out*', even if it is more than four months.

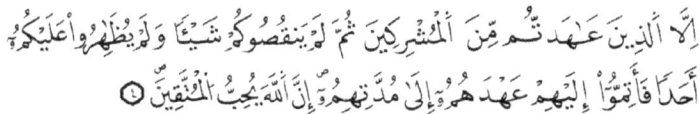

فَإِذَا انسَلَخَ الْأَشْهُرُ الْحُرُمُ فَاقْتُلُوا الْمُشْرِكِينَ حَيْثُ وَجَدتُّمُوهُمْ وَخُذُوهُمْ
وَاحْصُرُوهُمْ وَاقْعُدُوا لَهُمْ كُلَّ مَرْصَدٍ فَإِن تَابُوا وَأَقَامُوا الصَّلَوٰةَ وَءَاتَوُا الزَّكَوٰةَ
فَخَلُّوا سَبِيلَهُمْ إِنَّ اللَّهَ غَفُورٌ رَّحِيمٌ ۝

5 Then, when the sacred months are over, kill the idolaters wherever you find them, and seize them and besiege them and lie in wait for them on every road. If they repent and establish the prayer and pay *zakāt*, let them go on their way. Allah is Ever-Forgiving, Most Merciful.

Then, when the sacred months are over,

The verb *insalakha* means to leave behind. *Salakha* is used of a month when it is in its last days. It means departed. A poet said:

When I leave (*salakhtu*) the month, I destroy what is before it.
My ending and beginning is enough of a killer of months.

The month is over (*insalakha*) and the day is over, divested of the prior night. The verb *salakha* is used for a woman removing her shift. We find in the Revelation: *'A Sign for them is the night – We peel (*naslakhu*) the day away from it.'* (36:37) *Mislākh* is a palm-tree which drops its unripe fruits.

Scholars say two things about the sacred months. It is said that they are the known months: three consecutive ones and one on its own. Al-Aṣamm said that it means the idolaters who have no treaty: it is obliged to refrain from fighting them until the sacred months are finished. That was a period of fifty days according to what Ibn 'Abbās mentioned because that call was made on the Day of Sacrifice. It is said that the months for a treaty are four. Mujāhid, Ibn Isḥāq, Ibn Zayd and 'Amr ibn Shu'ayb said that. It is said that they are called 'sacred' because Allah forbade the believers to shed the blood of the idolaters and confront them except in a good way.

kill the idolaters wherever you find them,

This is general to every idolater, but the *Sunnah* makes exclusions, as was made clear in *al-Baqarah*, women, monks, children and some others. Allah says about the People of the Book: *'until they pay the* jizyah.*'* (9:29) It is, however, possible, that the word '*mushrikūn*' is not applied to the People of the Book. That would mean that *jizyah* may not be taken from idol-worshippers and others as will be explained.

The undefined nature of *'kill the idolaters'* entails permission to kill them in any way, but other reports prohibit mutilation. In addition, the actions of the Ṣiddīq in killing the people of the *Riddah* by burning with fire, stones, being shot at from the tops of mountains, and being thrown into wells, are connected to the undefined nature of the *āyah*. Similarly 'Alī burned some of the people of the *Riddah*. So it is permissible to incline to this position and rely on the undefined nature of the words. Allah knows best.

'*Wherever you find them*' is general to every place, although Abū Ḥanīfah said that it is specific to the Sacred Mosque as was mentioned in *al-Baqarah* (2:191-192). Then they disagree. Al-Ḥusayn ibn al-Faḍl said that this abrogates every *āyah* in the Qur'an which mentions turning away and patience in the face of harm from enemies. Aḍ-Ḍaḥḥāk, as-Suddī and 'Aṭā' said that it is abrogated by Allah's words: '*set them free or ransom them*' (47:4) so prisoners are not executed but either set free or ransomed. Mujāhid and Qatādah said that it abrogates: '*set them free or ransom them*' (47:4) but it is only permitted to kill prisoners who are idolaters. Ibn Zayd said that both *āyah*s are *āyah*s of judgment and that is sound, because setting free, killing and ransom all continued to be practised by the Messenger of Allah ﷺ from the first battle he fought, which was Badr.

The words '*seize them*' refer to capture, and capture can entail killing, ransom or setting free as the ruler wishes. The command '*besiege them*' means prevent them from going to their lands and entering yours unless they have permission and then they enter with security.

lie in wait for them

Ambush (*marṣad*) is a place in which you wait for the enemy, so sit for them in all the places of ambush. You say, '*arṣadtu*' (I laid in wait), *arṣudu*. 'Āmir ibn aṭ-Ṭufayl said:

You know, and do not forget
    that death lies in wait (*marṣad*) for the young man.

'Adī said:

Is it a criticism that ignorance is part of a lad's pleasure?
    Death lies in wait for souls.

This indicates that it is permitted to assassinate them before the call to Islam.

'*Every*' is accusative as an adverb. That is preferred by az-Zajjāj. It implies: 'in every place of ambush and on every place of ambush.' So *marṣad* is a word meaning '*road*'. Abū 'Alī az-Zajjāj erred in making '*road*' an adverb. He said, 'A road is a specific place, like a house and a mosque and so it is not permitted to elide the genitive from it, although there is some elision in what is heard. It is as Sībawayh related, 'I entered Syria' and 'I entered the house.' [POEM]

If they repent

It means that they repent of *shirk*. This *āyah* must be reflected upon, in that in it Allah connects killing to *shirk* and then says, '*If they repent*.' The basic position is that killing on account of *shirk* is cancelled when *shirk* is removed. That means that killing is cancelled on the strength of repentance alone without any consideration of establishing the prayer or paying the *zakāt*. This makes this matter clear. However, Allah mentions repentance but also mentions two other conditions with it and there is no way that they can be abandoned. It is similar to the words of the Prophet ﷺ, 'I was commanded to fight people until they say, "There is no god but Allah," establish the prayer and pay *zakāt*. When they do that, their blood and property is protected from me except for a right and their reckoning is up to Allah.' Abū Bakr aṣ-Ṣiddīq said, 'By Allah, I will fight those who make a distinction between the prayer and *zakāt*. *Zakāt* is what is due on wealth.' Ibn 'Abbās said, 'May Allah have mercy on Abū Bakr! How great his understanding of *fiqh* was!' Ibn al-'Arabī said, 'He joined the Qur'an and the Sunnah without any discontinuity."'

There is no disagreement among the Muslims that anyone who abandons the prayer or any other obligatory practice, considering it to be lawful to do that, has become an unbeliever. Anyone who abandons actions of the *sunnah* out of carelessness is impious (*fāsiq*). Anyone who abandons the *nawāfil* (supererogatory actions) is not to be confined unless he denies their excellence, in which case he is considered an unbeliever because he has rejected what the Messenger ﷺ brought and reported.

There is disagreement about someone who abandons the prayer without denying it or considering that what he does is lawful. Yūnus ibn 'Abd al-A'lā related that Ibn Wahb said that he heard Mālik say, 'If someone believes in Allah and affirms the Messengers but refuses to pray, he should be killed.' That is also what Abū Thawr and all the followers of ash-Shāfi'ī said and it is the position of Ḥammād ibn Zayd, Makḥūl and Wakī'. Abū Ḥanīfah said, 'He should be imprisoned and beaten, but not killed.' That is the position of Ibn Shihāb and Dāwūd ibn 'Alī. He finds evidence for his position in the words of the Prophet ﷺ: 'I was commanded to fight people until they say, "There is no god but Allah." When they do that, their blood and property are protected from me except when there is a legal right.'

They said that there are three legal rights, elucidated when the Prophet ﷺ said: 'The blood of a Muslim man is only lawful in three instances: unbelief after belief, fornication after being *muḥṣan*, or killing someone not in retaliation for another life.'

A group of the Companions and Tābi'ūn believed that if someone abandons a prayer deliberately until its time is gone without excuse and refuses to perform it or make it up, saying, 'I will not pray,' he has become an unbeliever and his life and property can be lawfully taken and his Muslim heirs do not inherit from him. He is asked to repent. If he does not repent, he is killed and his ruling is the same as that of an apostate. That is the position of Isḥāq. Isḥāq said, 'That is what the people of knowledge have thought from the time of the Prophet ﷺ to our time.'

Ibn Khuwayzimandād said, 'Our people disagree about the time when someone who abandons the prayer should be killed. Some people have said that it is at the end of the preferred time and others have said that it is at the end of the *ḍarūrī* time, which is the time needed before *Fajr* to perform two *rak'ahs* for *'Ishā'* and the time needed before sunrise to perform the two *rak'ahs* of *Subḥ*.' Isḥāq said that the departure of the time of *Ẓuhr* is at sunset and the time of *Maghrib* when dawn appears.

This *āyah* indicates that the statement of someone who says, 'I have repented' is not accepted unless he adds to it actions which verify that repentance because Allah here stipulates performing the prayer and paying *zakāt* as preconditions of repentance in order to verify its sincerity. He says in the *āyah* of usury: *'If you repent you may have your capital'* (2:279) and He says: *'except for those who repent and put things right and make things clear.'* (2:160) This matter was already discussed in *Sūrat al-Baqarah* (2:160).

وَإِنْ أَحَدٌ مِّنَ ٱلْمُشْرِكِينَ ٱسْتَجَارَكَ فَأَجِرْهُ حَتَّىٰ يَسْمَعَ كَلَٰمَ ٱللَّهِ ثُمَّ أَبْلِغْهُ
مَأْمَنَهُۥ ذَٰلِكَ بِأَنَّهُمْ قَوْمٌ لَّا يَعْلَمُونَ ٦

6 If any of the idolaters ask you for protection, give them protection until they have heard the words of Allah. Then convey them to a place where they are safe. That is because they are a people who do not know.

If any of the idolaters ask you for protection,

This means: 'If any of those you are commanded to fight ask for protection, security and protection, give it to them so that they can listen to the Qur'an, so as to understand its rulings, commands and prohibitions.' If that person accepts it, it is good. If he refuses, then return him to his place of security. There is no disagreement about this, and Allah knows best. Mālik said, 'When a *ḥarbī* is found on a road in Muslim lands and says, "I have come to seek safe-conduct," these are unclear matters. I think that he must be returned to his place of security.' Ibn al-Qāsim said, 'That is the case with someone who is found having arrived as a merchant on our coast and says, "I thought that you would not attack a person who has come as a merchant so that he can conduct trade."' The literal meaning of the *āyah* indicates that he should be among those who want to hear the Qur'an and look into Islam. Commerce is something else: it is for the benefit of the Muslims and looking into what will bring him benefit.

There is no disagreement among scholars that a ruler is allowed to grant security because his role involves prior investigation and promoting public interest and he represents all his subjects in bringing benefits and deterring harm. They disagree about safe conduct granted by someone other than the caliph. According to most scholars, any free man can give security, although Ibn Ḥabīb said that the ruler must have oversight of it. In the well-known position of the School, a slave may give protection and that is also the position of ash-Shāfi'ī and his people, Aḥmad, Isḥāq, al-Awzā'ī, ath-Thawrī, Abū Thawr, Dāwūd, and Muḥammad ibn al-Ḥasan. Abū Ḥanīfah said that a slave has no right to grant protection. That is the second view of our scholars.

The first position is sounder going by the words of the Prophet ﷺ, 'The blood of the Muslims is equal and the lowest of them can give his protection.' It is said that the word 'lowest' allows the safe conduct granted by a slave. A free woman must be more entitled to do that than a slave and no consideration should be given to the view based on 'they have no share' [the position of Abū Ḥanīfah that anyone who is not entitled to a share of the booty – namely women, slaves and children – should not be able to grant security]. 'Abd al-Malik ibn al-Mājishūn said, 'A woman is not allowed to grant security unless the ruler allows it.' His position is an aberration from that of the majority. If a child is able to fight he can grant safe conduct because he is one of the fighters and part of the fighting party.

Aḍ-Ḍaḥḥāk and as-Suddī believed that this *āyah* abrogated Allah's words: '*fight the idolaters…*' (9:36). Al-Ḥasan said, 'It is an *āyah* of judgment and is a *sunnah* until the Day of Resurrection.' Mujāhid said that. It is said that the ruling of this *āyah* remained for the four months which was the term set, but this position is not valid. Sa'īd ibn Jubayr said, 'One of the idolaters went to 'Alī ibn Abī Ṭālib and said, "If one of our men wants to go to Muḥammad after the four months are up to listen to the Word of Allah or bring him something, he will be killed!" 'Alī replied, "No, because Allah Almighty says: *'If any of the idolaters ask you for protection, give them protection until they have heard the words of Allah.'*"" This is sound and the *āyah* is one of judgment.

In *'if any'*, the word 'any' is in the nominative by an implied verb, like that which is after it. This is good for '*in*' but ugly for its sisters. The position of Sībawayh regarding the difference between '*in*' and its sisters is that since it is the mother of the particles of precondition, it is singled out for this, and because it does not apply to any other. Muḥammad ibn Yazīd said that the statement that it is not true of others is an error because it can mean 'what' which it is in the light form, but undefined. That is not the case with other particles. [POEM ILLUSTRATING]

Scholars have said that Allah's words: *'until they have heard the words of Allah'* indicate that the words of Allah are heard when they are recited. Shaykh Abū al-Ḥasan, Qāḍī Abū Bakr, Abū al-'Abbās al-Qalānisī, Ibn Mujāhid, Abū Isḥāq al-Isfarāyinī and others also said that because of these words of Allah here. Allah states that His words are heard when someone recites them. The consensus of the Muslims indicate that when a reciter recites the *Fātiḥah* or a *sūrah*, the people there say, 'We have heard the words of Allah.' They make a difference between reciting the words of Allah and reciting the poetry of Imru al-Qays. The meaning of *'the words of Allah'* was already discussed in *al-Baqarah* (2:75) and the fact that what is constituted is neither a letter nor a sound. Praise be to Allah.

كَيْفَ يَكُونُ لِلْمُشْرِكِينَ عَهْدٌ عِندَ اللَّهِ وَعِندَ رَسُولِهِۦٓ إِلَّا الَّذِينَ
عَٰهَدتُّمْ عِندَ الْمَسْجِدِ الْحَرَامِ فَمَا اسْتَقَٰمُوا لَكُمْ فَاسْتَقِيمُوا لَهُمْ
إِنَّ اللَّهَ يُحِبُّ الْمُتَّقِينَ ٧

7 How could any of the idolaters possibly have a treaty with Allah and with His Messenger, except for those you made a treaty with at the *Masjid al-Ḥarām*? As long as they are straight with you, be straight with them. Allah loves those who are godfearing.

The word '*how*' is used here to express astonishment, as when you say, 'How could anyone beat me?' which means 'No one will beat me.' '*Ahd*' is the subject noun of *kāna*. There is something elided in the *āyah* which means: 'How can the idolaters have a treaty when they conceal treachery?' It is as it is said:

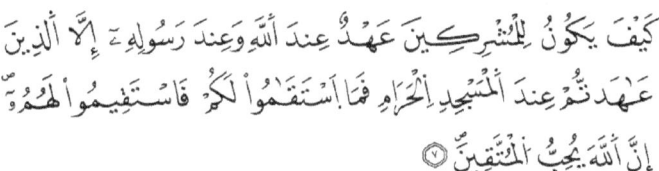

You two told me that death is in the towns.
How can that be when they are strong and sturdy?

Meaning how can there be death there? Az-Zajjāj said that.

It is said that it means: 'How could the idolaters have a treaty with Allah by which they will be secure from His punishment tomorrow and how could they have a treaty with the Messenger by which they are secure from the punishment of this world?' Then Allah makes an exception for those who have a treaty that was made at the Masjid al-*Ḥaram.* Muḥammad ibn Isḥāq said that they are the Banū Bakr. This means: 'The treaty only holds for those who have not broken or violated it.'

As long as they are straight with you, be straight with them.

As long as they remain true to the terms of their treaty, do the same to them. Ibn Zayd said, 'They were not straight, so Allah set a term of four months for them. As for those without a treaty, fight them when you find that they do not repent.'

كَيْفَ وَإِن يَظْهَرُوا عَلَيْكُمْ لَا يَرْقُبُوا فِيكُمْ إِلًّا وَلَا ذِمَّةً
يُرْضُونَكُم بِأَفْوَاهِهِمْ وَتَأْبَىٰ قُلُوبُهُمْ وَأَكْثَرُهُمْ فَاسِقُونَ ﴿٨﴾

8 How indeed! For if they get the upper hand over you, they will respect neither kinship nor treaty. They please you with their mouths but their hearts belie their words. Most of them are deviators.

How indeed! For if they get the upper hand over you,

Allah repeats His expression of astonishment at the fact that they should have a treaty when their actions are dishonourable, meaning 'How could they have a treaty if, when they get the better of you, they respect neither kinship nor treaty?' The verb *ẓahara 'alā* means 'surmount'. An example of its use is found in Allah's words: *'They were, therefore, unable to climb over (yaẓharū) it.'* (18:97)

they will respect neither kinship nor treaty.

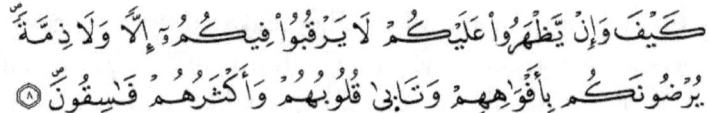

The verb used for '*respect*' here (*yarqubū*) means to preserve. A *raqīb* is a guardian. The noun *ill* denotes a treaty according to Mujāhid and Ibn Zayd. Mujāhid also said that it is one of the Names of Allah. Ibn 'Abbās and aḍ-Ḍaḥḥāk said that it means kinship. Al-Ḥasan said that it means protection and Qatādah said it means an alliance. *Dhimmah* is a treaty. Abū 'Ubaydah said that it is an oath, and he also said that it is a treaty and protection. Al-Azharī said that it is a name of Allah in Hebrew. Its root is *ilīl* which means 'shining'. The verb *alla, ya'ullu* in respect of a colour means to be clear and bright. It is said that its root means sharpness, from which comes *allah* as used for a spear. An ear which is sharp is called *mu'allalah.* In that we find the words of Ṭarafah ibn al-'Abd describing his she-camel with sharpness and being upright:

Sharp (*mu'allalatān*) ears, by which her noble line is recognised,
like those of a solitary wild ox at Ḥawmal.

If *ill* is used to mean treaty, protection and kinship, it implies that ears are directed to that aspect, in other words sharp about it. A treaty is called '*ill*' because of its clarity and clearness. The plural used for few is *ālāl* and the plural for many is *ilāl*. Al-Jawharī and others said that *ill* with *kasrah* means Allah, and *ilāl* is also used for the treaty and kinship. Al-Ḥasan said:

By your life, your kinship (*ill*) with Quraysh
is like the kinship (*ill*) of a young camel to an ostrich.

The noun '*dhimmah*' means a treaty. It is every kind of sanctity, the loss of which necessitates a wrong action. Ibn 'Abbās, aḍ-Ḍaḥḥāk and Ibn Zayd said that *dhimmah* is a treaty. If someone makes *ill* to mean a contract, then it is a repetition of the same thing using different words [which is common in Arabic]. Abū 'Ubaydah Ma'mar said that *dhimmah* is keeping aloof from someone. Abū 'Ubayd said that *dhimmah* is safe conduct going by the words of the Prophet ﷺ, 'The least of them can grant protection (*dhimmah*).' The plural of *dhimmah* is *dhimam*. A well which is described as *dhammah* has little water and the plural is *dhimām*. Dhū ar-Rummah said:

On camels from Ḥimyar, their eyes were like
wells with little water (*dhimām*), exhausted by camels.

The people of *dhimmah* are people with a treaty.

They please you with their mouths

This means that they utter words which please you with their tongues, but they break their treaties. Every unbeliever is a deviator (*fāsiq*), but here Allah means those who do ugly things openly and break treaties.

اشْتَرَوْا بِـَٔايَٰتِ ٱللَّهِ ثَمَنًا قَلِيلًا فَصَدُّوا عَن سَبِيلِهِۦٓ إِنَّهُمْ سَآءَ
مَا كَانُوا يَعْمَلُونَ ٩

9 They have sold Allah's Signs for a paltry price, and they have barred access to His Way. What they have done is truly evil.

This refers to the idolaters when they broke their treaties by consuming what Abū Sufyān fed them. Mujāhid said that. It is said that they exchanged the Qur'an for the goods of this world. The verb '*barred*' means turned away. It is derived from *ṣudūd* or to bar the way of Allah, from *ṣadd*.

لَا يَرْقُبُونَ فِى مُؤْمِنٍ إِلًّا وَلَا ذِمَّةً وَأُولَٰٓئِكَ هُمُ ٱلْمُعْتَدُونَ ١٠

10 They respect neither kinship nor treaty where a believer is concerned. They are the people who overstep the limits.

An-Naḥḥās said, 'This is not repetition. The first time it applies to all idolaters and the second time specifically to the Jews. They sold the proofs of Allah and His clarification by seeking leadership and greed.' *'The people who overstep the limits'* are those who go beyond the lawful to the unlawful by breaking a treaty they have made.

فَإِن تَابُوا وَأَقَامُوا ٱلصَّلَوٰةَ وَءَاتَوُا ٱلزَّكَوٰةَ فَإِخْوَٰنُكُمْ فِى ٱلدِّينِ
وَنُفَصِّلُ ٱلْـَٔايَٰتِ لِقَوْمٍ يَعْلَمُونَ ١١

11 But if they repent and establish the prayer and pay *zakāt*, they are your brothers in the *dīn*. We make the Signs clear for people who have knowledge.

'If they repent' of their *shirk* and hold to the rulings of Islam they are *'your brothers in the dīn'*. Ibn 'Abbās said, 'This makes the blood of the people of the *qiblah* unlawful.' This was discussed earlier.

Ibn Zayd said, 'Allah imposed the prayer and *zakāt* and refused to separate them and refused to accept the prayer without *zakāt*.' Ibn Mas'ūd said, 'You are commanded to pray and pay *zakāt*. Whoever does not pay *zakāt* has no prayer.' The Prophet ﷺ said, 'If anyone separates three things, Allah will separate him from His mercy on the Day of Resurrection: someone who says, "I obey Allah but do not obey the Messenger" when Allah Almighty says: *"Obey Allah and obey the Messenger"* (4:59); someone who says, "I will perform the prayer but not pay *zakāt*" when the Allah Almighty says: *"establish the prayer and pay zakāt"* (2:43); and someone who makes a distinction between gratitude to Allah and gratitude to his parents when the Almighty says: *"Give thanks to Me and to your parents."* (31:14)'

'We make the Signs clear.' Faṣṣala means to make clear. *'People who have knowledge'* are singled out because they are those who benefit from it. Allah knows best.

وَإِن نَّكَثُوٓا۟ أَيْمَـٰنَهُم مِّنۢ بَعْدِ عَهْدِهِمْ وَطَعَنُوا۟ فِى دِينِكُمْ فَقَـٰتِلُوٓا۟
أَئِمَّةَ ٱلْكُفْرِ ۙ إِنَّهُمْ لَآ أَيْمَـٰنَ لَهُمْ لَعَلَّهُمْ يَنتَهُونَ ﴿١٢﴾

12 If they break their oaths after making their treaty and defame your *dīn*, then fight the leaders of unbelief – their oaths mean nothing – so that hopefully they will stop.

If they break their oaths after making their treaty and defame your *dīn*,

The verb *nakatha* means to break. Its root is everything which is entwined together and then unravelled and so it is metaphorical for faith and contracts. He said:

If she makes an oath, the distant one does not break her promise.
A woman with dyed fingers does not have an oath.

after making their treaty and defame your *dīn*,

This is by deprecation, war and other things which idolaters do. The verb *ṭa'ana* is used for both thrusting with a spear and defaming with words. With a *ḍammah* in the imperfect it means to transfix with the eye. It is used metaphorically. An example of its usage is what the Prophet ﷺ said to some when he put Usāmah in command: 'If you attack his command, you attacked the command of his father before him. By Allah, they are both worthy of command.' It is a sound transmission. Some scholars have used this *āyah* as evidence for it being obligatory to kill anyone who defames the *dīn* since doing that reveals him to be an unbeliever. To defame something is to ascribe to it that which is not appropriate for it or to make light of things in the *dīn* when there is definite proof of their basic soundness and the rightness of the secondary rulings connected to them.

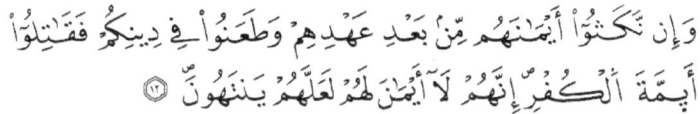

Ibn al-Mundhir said, 'Most of the people of knowledge agree that anyone who insults the Prophet ﷺ should be killed.' Some of those who stated that are Mālik, al-Layth, Aḥmad and Isḥāq. It is the position of ash-Shāfi'ī. It is related that an-Nu'mān said, 'A *dhimmī* who insults the Prophet ﷺ should not be killed.' This will be discussed. It is related that a man said in the assembly of 'Alī: 'It can only be said that Ka'b ibn al-Ashraf was killed treacherously.' 'Alī ordered that his head be cut off. Another man said that in the assembly of Mu'āwiyah and Muhammad ibn Maslamah stood up and said, 'Does this person say this in your gathering while you remain silent? By Allah, I will never live with you under the same roof! If I am alone with him, I will kill him!'

Our scholars say that if someone ascribes treachery to the Prophet ﷺ they should be killed and not asked to repent. That is what 'Alī and Muhammad ibn Maslamah understood from what the man had said because it constitutes *zandaqah*. As for someone who ascribes the treachery to those directly involved in the action, he is killed if he says, 'They gave him safe conduct and then betrayed him,' [implying that the Prophet ﷺ had given them permission to do that] since that ascription is a pure lie. There is nothing in their words which indicate that they gave him security or openly stated that. If they had done that, it would not have been safe-conduct because the Prophet ﷺ sent them to kill him, not to give him safe-conduct. That allowed Muhammad ibn Maslamah to say what he said and the same applies to 'Alī.

There is some investigation and hesitation about killing someone who has ascribed that to them [in particular]. The reason is whether ascribing treachery to them amounts to ascribing it to the Prophet ﷺ because he thought their action correct which would necessarily mean that he was content with treachery. Anyone who explicitly states that is killed. If ascribing treachery to them does not necessarily mean ascribing it to the Prophet ﷺ, the person who does it should not be killed. But even though we say that he should not be killed, nevertheless anyone who says that should be punished by imprisonment, a severe beating and great humiliation.

According to the best known position of the school of Mālik, if a *dhimmī* deprecates the *dīn*, he breaks his treaty, because Allah says: *'If they break their oaths…'* commanding that they then be killed and fought. That is also the position of ash-Shāfi'ī. Abū Ḥanīfah said that he is asked to repent and a simple attack does not break the treaty unless there is oath breaking involved in it, because Allah only commands them to be killed when two conditions are met: breaking the treaty and defaming the *dīn*. We say that when they do anything contrary to the treaty, they break their treaty. Mentioning both matters does not mean hesitating to fight them when either of the two things exist since breaking it on its own allows that both logically and in the *Sharīʻah*. We think that the *āyah* implies: 'If they break their treaty, it is lawful to fight them. If they do not break it, but attack the *dīn* while remaining faithful to the treaty, it is also permitted to fight them.' It is related that a *dhimmī* was brought before 'Umar; he had prodded an animal which a Muslim woman was riding and it galloped and she fell, exposing some of her private parts. He commanded that he be crucified there and then.

When a *dhimmī* makes war, he breaks his treaty and his wealth and children are *fay'* (spoils). Muḥammad ibn Maslamah said, 'His children are not taken because of it since he alone broke the treaty, but his property is taken.' The position of Muḥammad ibn Maslamah does not hold because the *dhimmī*'s treaty entails protection of both his children and his wealth. So when his property is removed from him, his children are as well. Ashhab said, 'When a *dhimmī* breaks his treaty, he remains with his contract, and a free man does not ever revert to slavery.' This is astonishing [that he remains with his contract after breaking it]. It is as if he thought that the treaty constituted an ironclad judgement. The treaty has a ruling which derives from investigation and the Muslims oblige it for him. When he breaks it, it is broken just like other contracts.

Most scholars say that if one of the people of the *Dhimmah* insults the Prophet ﷺ or insinuates that or makes light of his worth or description in any way that is not consistent with the fundamental nature of his unbelief, he should be killed. He was not given the *dhimmah* or treaty on this basis. However, Abū Ḥanīfah, ath-Thawrī and their followers among the people of Kufa say that he should not be killed; the *shirk* he originally commits to is far worse. He should, however, be punished and disciplined. The argument against it is found in the words of Allah: *'If they break…'* Some of them use as evidence the command of the Prophet ﷺ to kill Ka'b ibn Ashraf who had a treaty.

Abū Bakr became exasperated with one of his companions and Abū Barzah asked, 'Should I not strike off his head?' He said, 'That is not permissible for anyone after the Messenger of Allah ﷺ.' Ad-Dāraquṭnī related from Ibn 'Abbās that a blind man had an *umm walad* who had two sons like pearls. She used to abuse and insult the Prophet ﷺ. He forbade her to do that but she did not stop. He rebuked her but to no avail. One night she mentioned the Prophet ﷺ and her master could bear it no longer and he took a pickaxe, put it on her stomach and leaned on it until it pierced her. The Prophet ﷺ said, 'Bear witness that blood was shed which has no legal consequence.' The variant of Ibn 'Abbas has, 'killed her.' In the morning, that was mentioned to the Messenger of Allah ﷺ and the blind man stood and said, 'Messenger of Allah, I was her owner. She insulted you and attacked you. I forbade her but she did not stop. I rebuked her to no avail. I have two sons like pearls by her. She was kind to me. Yesterday she began to insult and attack you and I killed her.' The Prophet ﷺ said, 'Bear witness that blood was shed without legal consequence.'

They disagree about what happens when a *dhimmī* insults him ﷺ and then becomes Muslim: is he safe from execution? It is said that his Islam cancels his killing and this is the well-known position in the School because Islam removes what is before it. This is not the case with a Muslim who insults him and then repents. Allah says: *'Say to those who disbelieve that if they stop, they will be forgiven what is past.'* (8:38) It is also said that Islam does not cancel his killing. That is stated in *al-'Utbiyyah* because it is a right of the Prophet ﷺ demanded by the violation of his sanctity and by the intention of attaching shortcoming and disgrace to him. His reverting to Islam does not cancel it, even though there is no better state than that of a Muslim.

fight the leaders of unbelief

A'immah is the plural of *imām*. It means, according to some scholars, the leaders of Quraysh, such as Abū Jahl, 'Utbah, Shaybah and Umayyah ibn Khalaf. This is unlikely. The *āyah* is in *Sūrat Barā'ah*. When it was revealed and recited to the people, Allah had eradicated the leaders of Quraysh and only Muslims or one with a truce remained. It is possible that *'fight the leaders of unbelief'* means those who advocate breaking treaties and attacking the *dīn*; that is the basis and core of disbelief and so they are among of the leaders of unbelief according to this. It is also possible that it means: 'the chiefs and the leaders among them' and fighting them is fighting their followers and they have no sanctity.

The root of the word is *a'mimah*, like *mithāl* and *amthilah* and the *mīm* is assimilated into the second *mīm* and the vowel accepts the *hamzah* and so two *hamzah*s are joined and the second is changed into a *yā'* [as *ayimmah*]. Al-Akhfash claimed that one says, 'this one is *ayammu*[4] than this' with *yā'* and al-Māzinī said *awammu*[3] with *wāw*. Ḥamzah recited *a'immah* and most grammarians believe this is incorrect because it combines two *hamzah*s in one word.

their oaths mean nothing

This means that no treaty can be made with them because their treaties are false in that they would not fulfil them. Ibn 'Āmir recited it as *'lā īmān'* meaning 'they have no Islam'. It is possible that the verbal noun of *āmana* is *īmān* from

4 Instead of *a'ammu* 'more effective as an *imām*'.

which comes *amn* which is opposite fear, i.e. 'they do not believe'. This is why He says, '*fight the leaders of unbelief*'.

so that hopefully they will stop.

So that they will abandon *shirk*. Al-Kalbī said, 'The Prophet ﷺ made an agreement with the people of Makkah for a year at al-Ḥudaybīyah when they prevented him from reaching the House. Then they made a peace on the basis that he could return and remained true to that as long as Allah wished. Then the allies of the Messenger of Allah ﷺ, Khuzā'ah, fought the allies of the Banū Umayyah of Kinānah. The Banū Umayyah helped their allies with weapons and food and so Khuzā'ah asked the Messenger of Allah ﷺ for help. This *āyah* was revealed and the Prophet ﷺ was commanded to help his allies as already stated.

Al-Bukhārī reports that Zayd ibn Wahb said, 'We were with Ḥudhayfah and he said, "Of those referred to in this *āyah*, '*Fight the leaders of unbelief*', there are only three or four of the hypocrites left." A Bedouin said, "You are the Companions of Muḥammad and report to us matters which we do not know! You claim that there are only four hypocrites. What about those who break into our homes and steal our valuables?" He replied, "Those are the deviants. Only four of them remain. One is an old man who, if he drank cold water, would not feel its coldness."'

'*So that hopefully they will stop*' their disbelief, falsehood and abuse of the Muslims. That means that the goal in fighting them is to prevent the harm they cause so that they stop fighting us and enter our *dīn*.

أَلَا تُقَٰتِلُونَ قَوْمًا نَّكَثُوٓا۟ أَيْمَٰنَهُمْ وَهَمُّوا۟ بِإِخْرَاجِ ٱلرَّسُولِ
وَهُم بَدَءُوكُمْ أَوَّلَ مَرَّةٍ ۚ أَتَخْشَوْنَهُمْ ۚ فَٱللَّهُ أَحَقُّ أَن
تَخْشَوْهُ إِن كُنتُم مُّؤْمِنِينَ ﴿١٣﴾

13 Will you not fight a people who have broken their oaths and resolved to expel the Messenger, and who initiated hostilities against you in the first place? Is it them you fear? Allah has more right to your fear if you are believers.

This is rebuke which contains encouragement. It was revealed about the unbelievers of Makkah. '*They have resolved to expel the Messenger*': some of them wanted to do so and therefore it is attributed to them as a whole. It is said that they brought out the Messenger ﷺ from Madīnah to fight the people of Makkah for breaking their treaty. Al-Ḥasan said that.

'Initiated' means they started the fighting and the phrase *'in the first place'* refers to their breaking the treaty and helping the Banū Bakr against Khuzā'ah. It is said that it refers to their starting the fighting in the Battle of Badr, because the Prophet ﷺ went out to the caravan and after they had protected their caravan, they could have left, but they insisted on going to Badr and drinking wine there. *'Allah has more right to your fear'* and you should fear His punishment for not fighting them more than you fear something disliked happening to you in fighting them. It is said that it is their preventing the Messenger ﷺ from performing *ḥajj*, *'umrah* and *ṭawāf*. Allah knows best.

قَٰتِلُوهُمۡ يُعَذِّبۡهُمُ ٱللَّهُ بِأَيۡدِيكُمۡ وَيُخۡزِهِمۡ وَيَنصُرۡكُمۡ عَلَيۡهِمۡ وَيَشۡفِ
صُدُورَ قَوۡمٖ مُّؤۡمِنِينَ ١٤ وَيُذۡهِبۡ غَيۡظَ قُلُوبِهِمۡۗ وَيَتُوبُ ٱللَّهُ عَلَىٰ مَن
يَشَآءُۗ وَٱللَّهُ عَلِيمٌ حَكِيمٌ ١٥

> **14-15 Fight them! Allah will punish them at your hands, and disgrace them and help you against them, and heal the hearts of those who believe. He will remove the rage from their hearts. Allah turns to anyone He wills. Allah is All-Knowing, All-Wise.**

Fight them! Allah will punish them at your hands, and disgrace them

'Fight them!' is a command and its apodosis is *'Allah will punish them at your hands.'* It is in the jussive with a meaning of requital. It implies: 'If you fight them, Allah will punish them at your hands, abase them and help you against them and heal the hearts of a believing people.'

He will remove the rage from their hearts.

This indicates that their rage was intense. Mujāhid said that it refers to Khuzā'ah, the allies of the Prophet ﷺ. All of it is added and all of it can end in *ḍammah*, added to what came first. It is also possible that it ends in *fatḥah* by an implied *in*. That is its inflection with the Kufans. [POEM-GRAM]

As was said, it refers to the Banū Khuzā'ah. Quraysh helped the Banū Bakr against them. Khuzā'ah were allies of the Prophet ﷺ. One of the Banū Bakr composed satire about the Messenger of Allah ﷺ and one of Khuzā'ah told him, 'If you do it again, I will smash your mouth.' He did it again and he smashed his mouth. Then fighting broke out between them and some of Khuzā'ah were killed. 'Amr ibn Salim al-Khuzā'ī went to the Prophet ﷺ with a group and told him what had happened. He then entered Maymūnah's house and said, 'Pour out some water for me.' He had a *ghusl*, saying, 'I will not be helped if I do not help the Banū Ka'b.' Then the Messenger of Allah ﷺ commanded preparations to be made for setting out for Makkah and the Conquest occurred.

Allah turns to anyone He wills.

It is read with a *ḍammah* on the verb as a new sentence because it is not directly connected to the first. This is why Allah does not say *'yatub'* in the jussive because fighting does not oblige Allah to turn. It obliges punishment and disgrace for them, the healing of the hearts of the believers, and the removal of rage from their hearts. It is similar to: *'If Allah willed, He could seal up (yakhtub) your heart'* using the jussive. His words end there and He then says: *'Allah wipes out (yamhu) the false.'* (42:24) Those to whom Allah turned were those like Abū Sufyān, 'Ikrimah ibn Abī Jahl and Sulaym ibn Abī 'Amr who became Muslim.

Ibn Abī Isḥāq recited *'yatūba'*. That is how it is related from 'Īsā ath-Thaqafī and al-A'raj. According to this *tawbah* (turning) is included in the apodosis of the precondition because it means: 'If you fight them, Allah will punish them.' *'Allah turns'* if you fight them. So He combined their being punished at your hands, healing your hearts, removing rage from your hearts and turning to you. The *ḍammah* is better because turning is not the result of fighting since it can exist without fighting for whomever Allah wishes to turn to in any case.

أم حسبتم أن تتركوا ولما يعلم الله الذين جاهدوا منكم ولم يتخذوا من دون
الله ولا رسوله ولا المؤمنين وليجة والله خبير بما تعملون ﴿١٦﴾

16 Or did you suppose that you would be left without Allah knowing those of you who have done *jihād* and who have not taken anyone as their intimate friends besides Allah and His Messenger and the believers? Allah is aware of what you do.

This moves from one topic to another. The verb *'would be left'* is in the position of two objects according to Sībawayh, and according to al-Mubarrad, the second is elided. It means: 'Did you suppose that you would be left without being tested by a test that distinguishes believers from hypocrites?' This distinguishing is the criterion by which reward and punishment are merited and has already been discussed elsewhere (2:214, 3:142).

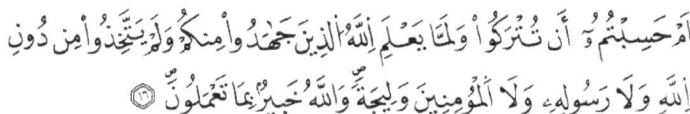

'Without Allah knowing' is jussive by *lammā*, though the *mā* is redundant. According to Sībawayh, it is normally the apodosis of the verb in the past tense, and the *mīm* has a *kasrah* (*ya'lami*) because of the meeting of two silent letters.

The word '*intimate friends*' (*walījah*) refers to people who are close and visit one another and the word derives from *wulūj* which means entering. From it comes *tawlaj* which is used for a covert in which wild animals take refuge. *Walaja* means to enter. It means entering with affection towards others to the exclusion of Allah and His Messenger. Abū 'Ubaydah said, 'Anything that enters into something which is not part of it is *walījah*. A man who is with a people while not one of them is *walījah*.' Ibn Zayd said that *walījah* is a confidant and *wulajā'* are confidants. A confidant of a man is one who is closely involved with his business to the exclusion of other people. *Walījah* can be for both the singular and plural. Abān ibn Taghlib said:

An evil intimate (*walījah*) for those who flee,
those who rely and the people of doubt.

It said that *walījah* are close intimates as we find in the *āyah*: *'Do not take any outside yourselves as intimates.'* (3:118) Al-Farrā' said that *walījah* is taking close friends from the idolaters and disclosing secrets to them and informing them of their affairs.

مَا كَانَ لِلْمُشْرِكِينَ أَن يَعْمُرُوا مَسَٰجِدَ ٱللَّهِ شَٰهِدِينَ عَلَىٰٓ أَنفُسِهِم
بِٱلْكُفْرِ أُوْلَٰٓئِكَ حَبِطَتْ أَعْمَٰلُهُمْ وَفِى ٱلنَّارِ هُمْ
خَٰلِدُونَ ﴿١٧﴾

17 It is not for the idolaters to frequent the mosques of Allah, bearing witness against themselves of their unbelief. They are the ones whose actions will come to nothing. They will be in the Fire timelessly, for ever.

It is not for the idolaters to frequent the mosques of Allah,

The phrase '*to frequent*' is in the nominative as the noun of *kāna* and '*bearing witness*' is an adverbial *ḥāl*. Scholars disagree about the interpretation of this *āyah*. It is said that it means that they are not to perform the *ḥajj* after what they did in terms of denying access to the *Masjid al-Ḥarām*. The business of the House were things like being its doorkeeper, bringing water and providing food for the idolaters. He made it clear that they do not merit that. It is the believers who merit that.

It is said that when al-'Abbās was captured and blamed for unbelief and cutting off ties of kinship, he said, 'You mention our bad qualities but not our good qualities.' 'Alī asked, 'Do you have good qualities?' He answered, 'Yes, we frequent the Sacred Mosque, act as doorkeepers to the Ka'bah, give water to pilgrims and relieve those in distress.' This *āyah* was revealed to refute him. So it is obligatory for the Muslims to observe the rulings governing mosques and prevent the idolaters from entering them.

Most recite *'ya'murū'* (*frequent*) from *'amara, ya'muru.* Ibn as-Samayfa' recited *'yu'mirū'*, meaning make it thrive or help in its upkeep. *'Mosques'* can be recited as *'masjid'* in the singular, referring to the *Masjid al-Ḥarām* in particular. It is the reading of Ibn 'Abbās, Sa'īd ibn Jubayr, 'Aṭā' ibn Abī Rabāḥ, Mujāhid, Ibn Kathīr, Abū 'Amr, Ibn Muḥayṣin and Ya'qūb. The rest recite *'masājid'* to make it universal. That is the choice of Abū 'Ubayd because it is more general, and the specific is included under the general. It is possible that the plural here means the *Masjid al-Ḥarām* in particular. This is permissible with generic nouns, as when you say, 'He rides horses,' when he only ever rides one horse. The plural reading is more correct because it will support both meanings. They agree that it is plural as an-Naḥḥās said. Al-Ḥasan said that *'mosques'* means the *Masjid al-Ḥarām* because it is the *qiblah* and chief of all mosques.

bearing witness against themselves of their unbelief.

It is said that it means: 'they bear witness' and when 'they' is removed, it is in the accusative. Ibn 'Abbās said that their bearing witness against themselves of their unbelief is their prostrating to their idols and admitting that they are created. As-Suddī said, 'Their bearing witness to unbelief is when you ask a Christian, "What is your religion?" and he says, "Christian", or a Jew says he is, "Jewish", or a Sabaean says he is, "Sabaean," or an idolater, says he is an, "idolater".

إِنَّمَا يَعْمُرُ مَسَٰجِدَ ٱللَّهِ مَنْ ءَامَنَ بِٱللَّهِ وَٱلْيَوْمِ ٱلْءَاخِرِ وَأَقَامَ ٱلصَّلَوٰةَ
وَءَاتَى ٱلزَّكَوٰةَ وَلَمْ يَخْشَ إِلَّا ٱللَّهَ فَعَسَىٰٓ أُو۟لَٰٓئِكَ أَن يَكُونُوا۟ مِنَ
ٱلْمُهْتَدِينَ ١٨

18 The mosques of Allah should only be frequented by those who believe in Allah and the Last Day and establish the prayer and pay *zakāt*, and fear no one but Allah. They are the ones most likely to be guided.

The mosques of Allah should only be frequented

This indicates that the testimony of the faith of those who frequent the mosques is sound because Allah connected it to them and reported that it is binding for them. One of the early generations said, 'When you see a man frequenting the mosque, have a good opinion of him.' At-Tirmidhī related from Abū Sa'īd al-Khudrī that the Messenger of Allah ﷺ said, 'When you see a man frequenting the mosque, testify that he has faith. Allah Almighty says: "*The mosques of Allah should only be frequented by those who believe in Allah and the Last Day.*"' One variant has: 'frequent mosques'. He said that it is a *gharīb ḥasan ḥadīth.*

Ibn al-'Arabī said, 'This is apparent righteousness which is not found in someone who breaks his oaths. Testimony has different states according to those who provide it. Some witnesses are intelligent and have a full grasp of things based on their knowledge of creed and reports, and some are gullible. Each of them is in his station and assessed according to his description.'

and fear no one but Allah.

This means they fear only Allah in respect of the *dīn*. The believers and Prophets continue to fear other enemies. It is said to him, 'The meaning is that only Allah is feared with regard to worship. The idolaters worshipped idols and feared them and had hopes of them.' A second answer is that only Allah is feared in the area of the *dīn*.

If it is said that faith is confirmed in this *āyah* for those who frequent the mosques to pray in them, clean them and put them in order and believe in Allah but that Allah did not mention belief in the Messenger here nor the belief of someone who does not believe in the Messenger, the response is that the Messenger is indicated by the mention of establishing the prayer and other things because it is part of what he brought. Establishing the prayer and paying *zakāt* are only possible from someone who believes in the Messenger. That is why he is not singled out for mention. When *"asā'* (which normally refers to something that might happen) is used in respect of Allah it means that it is definite, as Ibn 'Abbās and others said. It is also said that *'asā* can mean 'appropriate'.

أَجَعَلْتُمْ سِقَايَةَ الْحَاجِّ وَعِمَارَةَ الْمَسْجِدِ الْحَرَامِ كَمَنْ ءَامَنَ
بِاللَّهِ وَالْيَوْمِ الْآخِرِ وَجَٰهَدَ فِي سَبِيلِ اللَّهِ لَا يَسْتَوُۥنَ عِندَ اللَّهِ
وَاللَّهُ لَا يَهْدِي الْقَوْمَ الظَّٰلِمِينَ ﴿١٩﴾

19 Do you make the giving of water to the pilgrims and looking after the *Masjid al-Ḥarām* the same as believing in Allah and the Last Day and doing *jihād* in the Way of Allah? They are not equal in the sight of Allah. Allah does not guide wrongdoing people.

Do you make the giving of water to the pilgrims

This implies in Arabic: 'Do you make the people who give water to the pilgrims equal to those who believe in Allah and strive in His Cause?' It is sound for there to be something implied in 'believing': i.e., 'do you make the action of giving water to the pilgrims like the action of those who believe?' It implies: 'like the faith of those who believe'.

Siqāyah (giving water) is a verbal noun like *si'ayah* and *ḥimāyah*. The noun is used in the position of a verbal noun since the meaning is known. It is like saying 'Generosity is Ḥātim' and 'Poetry is Zuhayr'. Looking after the *Masjid al-Ḥarām* is like '*ask the city*'. (12:82) Abū Wajzah recited, '*suqāta-l-ḥājji wa 'amarati-l-Masjidi-l-Ḥarām.*' *Suqāh* is the plural of *sāqī* (water-giver). The root is *suqyah*. Similarly, Ibn az-Zubayr and Sa'īd ibn Jubayr recited '*suqāh*' and '*amarah*. Ibn Jubayr has '*masjid*' in the accusative from the intention of the *tanwīn* in '*amarah*. Aḍ-Ḍaḥḥāk said *suqāyah*, which is a dialect. *Al-Ḥājj* is generic for pilgrims. The phrase '*looking after* ('*imārah*) *the Masjid al-Ḥarām*' means having responsibility for it and undertaking its best interests.

The evident meaning of this *āyah* is that the words of the idolaters who boast about giving water to the pilgrims and looking after the *Masjid al-Ḥarām* are baseless as as-Suddī mentioned. He said, "Abbās boasted of giving water, Shaybah of looking after the Mosque, and 'Alī of Islam and *jihād*. Allah says that 'Alī is telling the truth and other two are lying and informs us that '*imārah* is not by unbelief, but by faith, worship and performing acts of obedience. This is clear and indisputable.'

It is said that the idolaters asked the Jews and said, 'We give water to the pilgrims and look after the *Masjid al-Ḥarām*. Who is better: us or Muḥammad and his Companions?' The Jews told them out of obstinacy towards the Messenger of Allah ﷺ, 'You are better.'

Here there is an ambiguity which is what is reported in *Ṣaḥīḥ Muslim*. An-Nu'mān ibn Bashīr said, 'I was by the *minbar* of the Messenger of Allah ﷺ when a man said, "I am not concerned about doing anything after Islam except giving water to the pilgrims." Another said, "I am not concerned about doing anything after Islam except looking after the *Masjid al-Ḥarām*." Yet another said, "*Jihād* in the Cause of Allah is better than what you have said." 'Umar rebuked them and said, "Do not raise your voices by the *minbar* of the Messenger of Allah ﷺ. (It was the day of *Jumu'ah*.) When *Jumu'ah* has been performed, I will go in and ask for a decision about your disagreement." Allah revealed: *"Do you make the giving of water to the pilgrims and looking after the Masjid al-Harām the same as believing in Allah and the Last Day?..."*'

This suggests that it must have been revealed when the Muslims disagreed about what actions are best. Were that the case, it would not be proper to say to them at the end of the *āyah*: *'Allah does not guide wrongdoing people.'* So the lack of clarity is specific and it is removed by saying that some transmitters leave out the words 'Allah revealed', meaning that the Prophet ﷺ just recited the *āyah* to 'Umar when he asked him and the transmitter thought that it had been revealed then. The Prophet ﷺ cited it as evidence that *jihād* is better than what those whom 'Umar heard had mentioned. He asked for a decision on their behalf and he ﷺ recited to him what had been revealed to him, and it was not that it had been revealed about those men. Allah knows best.

If it is said that according to this it is possible to deduce something for Muslims from what was actually revealed about the unbelievers, when it is known that their rulings are different, the answer is that it is not impossible that one can derive rulings which apply to the Muslims from what Allah revealed about the idolaters. 'Umar said, 'If we had wished, we could have had boiled and roasted food and have one plate put down and another removed, but we heard the words of Allah Almighty: *"You dissipated the good things you had in your worldly life and enjoyed yourself in it."* (46:20)' This *āyah* is a text about the unbelievers and nevertheless 'Umar understood it to convey reprimand for being somewhat like them and none of the Companions objected to him doing that. So it is possible that this *āyah* is similar to that. This is precious and removes ambiguity and doubt. Allah knows best.

ٱلَّذِينَ ءَامَنُواْ وَهَاجَرُواْ وَجَٰهَدُواْ فِے سَبِيلِ ٱللَّهِ بِأَمْوَٰلِهِمْ وَأَنفُسِهِمْ أَعْظَمُ
دَرَجَةً عِندَ ٱللَّهِ وَأُوْلَٰٓئِكَ هُمُ ٱلْفَآئِزُونَ ٢٠

20 Those who believe and make *hijrah* and do *jihād* in the Way of Allah with their wealth and themselves have a higher rank with Allah. They are the ones who are victorious.

'Those who believe' is in the position of the nominative by the inceptive whose predicate is *'have a higher rank'*. The noun *'darajah'* (rank) is in the accusative for clarification. It implies: 'than those who boast of giving water and looking after the House'. The unbelievers do not have any rank with Allah so that it could be

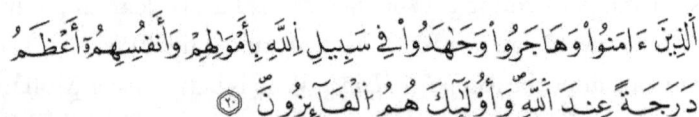

said, "The believer has a higher rank.' What is meant is that they assign a rank for themselves by giving water and looking after the House and Allah addresses them according to their own estimate of themselves, even though that estimation is an error, as in His words elsewhere: *'The Companions of the Garden on that Day will have better lodging.'* (25:24) '*A higher rank*' means they have superiority and high rank. They are made victorious by that.

يُبَشِّرُهُمْ رَبُّهُم بِرَحْمَةٍ مِّنْهُ وَرِضْوَانٍ وَجَنَّاتٍ لَّهُمْ فِيهَا نَعِيمٌ
مُّقِيمٌ ﴿٢١﴾ خَالِدِينَ فِيهَا أَبَدًا ۚ إِنَّ اللَّهَ عِندَهُ أَجْرٌ عَظِيمٌ ﴿٢٢﴾

21-22 Their Lord gives them the good news of His mercy and good pleasure and Gardens where they will enjoy everlasting delight, remaining in them timelessly, for ever and ever. Truly there is an immense reward with Allah.

Allah informs them in this world of the ample reward and abiding bliss that they will have in the Next World. '*Everlasting delight*' is an easy and comfortable life. The word '*khālidīn*' is in the accusative as an adverbial *ḥāl*. *Khalūd* means abiding. He has prepared for them that reward in the Abode of Honour.

يَا أَيُّهَا الَّذِينَ آمَنُوا لَا تَتَّخِذُوا آبَاءَكُمْ وَإِخْوَانَكُمْ أَوْلِيَاءَ إِنِ اسْتَحَبُّوا
الْكُفْرَ عَلَى الْإِيمَانِ ۚ وَمَن يَتَوَلَّهُم مِّنكُمْ فَأُولَٰئِكَ هُمُ الظَّالِمُونَ ﴿٢٣﴾

23 You who believe, do not befriend your fathers and brothers if they prefer unbelief to faith. Those among you who do befriend them are wrongdoers.

The literal meaning of the *āyah* is that it is addressed to all the believers and that its judgment in terms of cutting off friendship between the believers and unbelievers will remain until the Day of Rising. One group related that this *āyah* was revealed about encouraging emigration and leaving the lands of unbelief. According to this, it is addressed to the believers in Makkah and other Arab lands. They are told not to take their fathers and brothers as friends and allies and therefore follow them by dwelling in the lands of unbelief. The verb *istiḥabba* '*prefer*' has the same meaning as *aḥabba*, as is the case with *istijāba* and *ajāba* (respond). It means: 'Do not obey them or single them out.' Allah singled out fathers and brothers since they have the closest kinship. The negation of mutual friendship between them is the same as Allah's negation of it between people in His words: *'O you who believe, do not take the Jews and Christians as friends'* (5:51) to make it clear that true closeness is that of religion, not that of bodies. The Sufis composed about this:

They tell me: 'The house of the lovers is near
    and it is extraordinary that you are sad.'
I replied, 'Close houses are not enough
    when there is no closeness between hearts.
'How many a distant house obtains its desire
    while the next door neighbour dies in sorrow.'

Allah does not mention sons in this *āyah* since usually sons follow fathers.

Charity and gifts are exceptions in this matter of befriending. Asmā' said, 'Messenger of Allah, my mother has come wanting to see me and she is an idolatress, shall I give [something] to her?' 'Give to your mother,' he said. Al-Bukhārī transmitted it.

Those among you who do befriend them are wrongdoers.

Ibn 'Abbās said that if someone befriends them, he is an idolater like them. His contentment with *shirk* makes him an idolater.'

قُلْ إِن كَانَ ءَابَآؤُكُمْ وَأَبْنَآؤُكُمْ وَإِخْوَٰنُكُمْ وَأَزْوَٰجُكُمْ
وَعَشِيرَتُكُمْ وَأَمْوَٰلٌ ٱقْتَرَفْتُمُوهَا وَتِجَٰرَةٌ تَخْشَوْنَ كَسَادَهَا وَمَسَٰكِنُ
تَرْضَوْنَهَآ أَحَبَّ إِلَيْكُم مِّنَ ٱللَّهِ وَرَسُولِهِۦ وَجِهَادٍ فِى سَبِيلِهِۦ
فَتَرَبَّصُوا۟ حَتَّىٰ يَأْتِىَ ٱللَّهُ بِأَمْرِهِۦ ۗ وَٱللَّهُ لَا يَهْدِى ٱلْقَوْمَ
ٱلْفَٰسِقِينَ ﴿٢٤﴾

24 Say: 'If your fathers or your sons or your brothers or your wives or your tribe, or any wealth you have acquired, or any business you fear may slump, or any house which pleases you, are dearer to you than Allah and His Messenger and doing *jihād* in His Way, then wait until Allah brings about His command. Allah does not guide people who are deviators.'

When the Messenger of Allah ﷺ was commanded to emigrate from Makkah to Madīnah, a man began to say to his son, a father to his son, a brother to his brother and a man to his wife, 'We are commanded to emigrate.' Some of them hurried to do so and some of them refused to emigrate. Those emigrating would say, 'By Allah, if you do not leave for the Abode of *Hijrah*, I will not help you or spend anything on you ever.' Some of them had ties with a wife and children who would say to them in response, 'I beseech you by Allah! Do not go. We will be lost after you go!' Some of them were kind-hearted and so did not emigrate and remained with those who refused to go. So Allah's words refer to their preferring to stay with unbelief in Makkah over faith and emigrating to Madīnah after He had said: '*Those among who do befriend them are wrongdoers*'. So He revealed this about those who stayed behind and did not make *hijrah*. The term used here for tribe (*'ashīrah*) refers to a single group like a group of ten or more. Connected to that is the term *mu'āsharah*, which is people gathering together around something they have in common.

The phrase '*any wealth you may have acquired*' means in Makkah. The root of *iqtirāf* is removing a thing from one place to another. Ibn al-Mubārak said that the word '*business*' here refers to daughters and sisters if they remain in their houses and fail to find any suitor. A poet said:

They [the women] were stagnant in poverty among their people,
and my position increases their lack of market.

'*Any house which pleases you*' are houses in which you would like to live. '*Dearer to you than Allah and His Messenger*' means you prefer them to emigrating to Allah and His Messenger in Madīnah. The word '*aḥabba*' is the predicate of *kāna*. It is permitted outside of the Qur'an for '*aḥabb*' to be in the nominative as a predicate and predicate where the noun is implied in it. Sībawayh quotes verses illustrating this. [POEMS]

The *āyah* contains evidence of the obligatory nature of love for Allah and His Messenger. There is no disagreement that the *āyah* makes that clear. They take precedence over every other loved one. The meaning of love of Allah and love of His Messenger was discussed in *Āl 'Imrān* (3:21).

The verb '*wait*' is in the imperative and it is a threat: 'Wait and see!' What is meant by '*His command*' is fighting and the Conquest of Makkah, as Mujāhid says. Al-Ḥasan said that it refers to punishment, sooner or later. '*Doing jihād in His Way*' is evidence of the excellence of *jihād* and its being preferred over someone's leisure and his attachment to family and wealth. The excellence of *jihād* will be discussed at the end of the *sūrah*. The rulings concerning *hijrah* were adequately discussed in *an-Nisā'* (4:25). Praise belongs to Allah.

We find in a sound *ḥadīth*: 'Shayṭān sits in wait in three places for the son of Ādam. He sits in wait for him on the path to Islam and says, "Why have you left your religion and the religion of your fathers?" When the person opposes him and becomes Muslim, he sits in wait for him on the path to *hijrah* and says to him, "Will you leave your property and family?" When he opposes him and emigrates, he sits in wait on the path to *jihād* and says, "You will go off to *jihād* and be killed and then your wife will re-marry and your wealth be divided up." When he opposes him and does *jihād*, it is right for Allah to admit him to the Garden.' An-Nasā'ī transmitted it from Sabarah ibn Abī Fākih who said that he heard the Messenger of Allah ﷺ say that. Al-Bukhārī said 'Ibn Fākih' and did not mention any disagreement about it. Ibn Abī 'Adī said, 'Both Ibn Fākih and Ibn Abī Fākih are narrated.'

لَقَدْ نَصَرَكُمُ اللَّهُ فِي مَوَاطِنَ كَثِيرَةٍ وَيَوْمَ حُنَيْنٍ إِذْ
أَعْجَبَتْكُمْ كَثْرَتُكُمْ فَلَمْ تُغْنِ عَنكُمْ شَيْئًا وَضَاقَتْ عَلَيْكُمُ
الْأَرْضُ بِمَا رَحُبَتْ ثُمَّ وَلَّيْتُم مُّدْبِرِينَ ﴿٢٥﴾ ثُمَّ أَنزَلَ اللَّهُ سَكِينَتَهُ
عَلَىٰ رَسُولِهِ وَعَلَى الْمُؤْمِنِينَ وَأَنزَلَ جُنُودًا لَّمْ تَرَوْهَا وَعَذَّبَ الَّذِينَ
كَفَرُوا وَذَٰلِكَ جَزَاءُ الْكَافِرِينَ ﴿٢٦﴾ ثُمَّ يَتُوبُ اللَّهُ مِن بَعْدِ
ذَٰلِكَ عَلَىٰ مَن يَشَاءُ وَاللَّهُ غَفُورٌ رَّحِيمٌ ﴿٢٧﴾

25-27 Allah has helped you on many occasions, including the Day of Ḥunayn when your great numbers delighted you but did not help you in any way, and the earth seemed narrow to you for all its great breadth, and you turned your backs. Then Allah sent down His serenity on His Messenger and on the believers, and sent down troops you could not see, and punished those who disbelieved. That is how the unbelievers are repaid. Then after that Allah will turn to anyone He wills. Allah is Ever-Forgiving, Most Merciful.

Allah has helped you on many occasions, including the Day of Ḥunayn

When Hawāzin heard about the conquest of Makkah, Mālik ibn 'Awf an-Naṣrī from the Banū Naṣr ibn Mālik gathered them together. He was given overall leadership of the army and, along with their army, they sent their property, livestock, women and children. He claimed that that was to encourage their souls and make them strong in fighting. They numbered eight thousand according to al-Ḥasan and Mujāhid. It is said that there were four thousand of Hawāzin and Thaqīf. Mālik ibn 'Awf was in charge of Hawāzin and Kinānah ibn 'Abd in charge of Thaqīf. They stopped at Awṭās.

The Messenger of Allah ﷺ sent out 'Abdullāh ibn Abī Ḥadrad al-Aslamī as a spy. He went to him and reported to him what he had seen of them. The Messenger of Allah ﷺ resolved to proceed towards them. He borrowed some armour from Ṣafwān ibn Umayyah ibn Khalaf al-Jumaḥī. It is said that it was a hundred pieces of armour. It is said that it was four hundred. He borrowed thirty or forty thousand dirhams from ['Abdullāh ibn Abī] Rabī'ah al-Makzūmī, a debt he settled when he came back. Then the Prophet ﷺ said to him, 'May Allah bless you in your family and property. The reward for lending is repayment and words of praise.' Ibn Mājah transmitted it in *as-Sunan*.

The Messenger of Allah ﷺ went out with twelve thousand Muslims, ten thousand who had accompanied him from Madīnah and two thousand of those who became Muslim at the Conquest, who are called the 'freed' (*ṭulaqā'*), as well as some of the desert Arabs from [the tribes of] Sulaym, the Banū Kilāb, 'Abs and Dhubyān. He put 'Attāb ibn Usayd in charge of Makkah. When he set out, some of the ignorant Arabs saw a green tree. In the Jāhiliyyah they had a tree known as Dhāt Anwāṭ to which the unbelievers went on a certain day of the year in order to esteem it. They said, 'Messenger of Allah, make a Dhāt Anwāṭ for us!' The Prophet ﷺ said, 'Allah is greater! By the One Who has my soul in His hand, this is the same as what the people of Mūsā said! "Give us a god as they have gods!" You are an ignorant people! You would follow the customs of those before you exactly to the point that if they were to enter a lizard hole, you too would enter it!'

The Messenger of Allah ﷺ continued on until they reached the wadi of Ḥunayn which was one of the wadis of Tihāmah. Hawāzin had concealed themselves in the sides of the wadi. That was in the darkness before sunrise. They attacked the Muslims all at once and most of the Muslims retreated, no one paying any attention to anyone else. The Messenger of Allah ﷺ remained firm, and Abū Bakr and 'Umar remained with him together with, from among the people of his house, 'Alī, al-'Abbās, Abū Sufyān ibn al-Ḥārith ibn 'Abd al-Muṭṭalib and his son Ja'far, Usāmah ibn Zayd, Ayman ibn 'Ubayd (who is Ayman ibn Umm Ayman who was killed at Ḥunayn), Rabī'ah ibn al-Ḥārith and al-Faḍl ibn 'Abbās. Some have Qutham ibn al-'Abbās in place of Ja'far ibn al-Ḥārith. There were ten men.

That is why al-'Abbās said:

We helped the Messenger of Allah, nine men,
  when those who fled did so and dispersed.
The tenth of us met fate itself
  with what he experienced for Allah and did not complain.

Umm Sulaym remained firm in the group who remained firm. She was girded while holding the camel of Abū Ṭalḥah with a dagger in her hand. Neither the Messenger of Allah ﷺ nor any of these people retreated. The Messenger of Allah ﷺ was riding his white mule called Duldul.

We find in *Ṣaḥīḥ Muslim* from Kathīr ibn 'Abbās that al-'Abbās said, 'I was holding the reins of the mule of the Messenger of Allah ﷺ, holding it back from going swiftly, while Abū Sufyān was holding the stirrup of the Messenger of Allah ﷺ. The Messenger of Allah ﷺ said, "'Abbās! Call the people of the acacia!" ('Abbas was a man with a loud voice and the force of his voice was such that it is reported that one day in Makkah he shouted, "Morning!" and every pregnant woman who heard his voice miscarried.) I called out in my loudest voice, "People of the acacia!" By Allah, it was as if I awakened in them, when I called, affection such as cows have for their calves. They said, "At your service! At your service!" Then they and the unbelievers fought … Then the Messenger of Allah ﷺ took some pebbles and threw them in the faces of the unbelievers. Then he said, "They are defeated, by the Lord of Muḥammad!" I went to look and the fighting was as it had been. By Allah, he only threw pebbles at them. And then I continued to see them weaken and they began to retreat.'

Abū 'Umar said, 'We related by various paths from one of the idolaters who became Muslim and was present at Ḥunayn that when he was asked about Ḥunayn, he said, "We met the Muslims and quickly overcame them. We pursued them until we reached a man riding a white mule. When he saw us, he rebuked us and scolded us. He took a handful of pebbles and earth and threw it, saying, 'The faces are disgraced!' There was no eye that it did not enter. We could not stop ourselves from turning on our heels."'

Sa'īd ibn Jubayr said, 'One of the idolaters on the day of Ḥunayn told us, "When we met the Companions of the Messenger of Allah ﷺ, they did not stand against us for the length of time it takes to milk a sheep. We reached the man with the white mule (i.e. the Messenger of Allah ﷺ) and some men with handsome white faces met us and said to us, 'The faces are disgraced! Go back!' We returned with them at our shoulders," i.e. the angels.'

There is no contradiction. It is possible that both he ﷺ and the angels said, 'The faces are disgraced!' This indicates that angels fought in the Battle of Ḥunayn. Allah knows best. In the Battle of Ḥunayn 'Alī killed forty men with his own hand and the Messenger of Allah ﷺ captured four thousand prisoners. It is also said that it was six thousand. He also captured twelve thousand camels, in addition to unknown amounts of booty.

Scholars say that the Prophet ﷺ said during this expedition, 'Whoever kills someone and has evidence of it has his personal spoils.' This was discussed in *al-Anfāl* (8:41). Ibn al-'Arabī said that those who deal with the rulings connected to this expedition include this point and others in their rulings. They also include permission to borrow weapons and use what has been borrowed in the way it is normally used, and permission for the ruler to borrow money when that is needed and to return it to its owner. The *ḥadīth* of Ṣafwān forms the basis of this. On this expedition the Messenger of Allah ﷺ also gave an order (concerning captured women): 'There should be no sexual intercourse with a pregnant woman until she gives birth nor with a married woman until she has had one menstrual period.' This indicates that capture severs the bond of marriage as was made clear in *Sūrat an-Nisā'* (4:24)

We find in the *ḥadīth* of Mālik that Ṣafwān, while he was an unbeliever, went out with the Messenger of Allah ﷺ. He was present at Ḥunayn and Ṭā'if. His wife was a Muslim. Mālik said, 'That was not at the command of the Messenger of Allah ﷺ and I do not think that idolaters are asked to help against idolaters except as servants or sailors. Abū Ḥanīfah, ash-Shāfi'ī, ath-Thawrī and al-Awzā'ī said that there is nothing wrong with that happening when the rule of Islam is dominant, but it is disliked to ask for their assistance when the rule of *shirk* is dominant. The sharing out of booty was discussed in *al-Anfāl* (8:41).

Ḥunayn is a wadi between Makkah and Ṭā'if. It is declined in the Qur'an as a masculine noun. Some Arabs do not decline it and make it a noun of place. It is quoted [from Ḥassān ibn Thābit]:

> They helped their Prophet and gave him support
> at Ḥunayn [undeclined] on the day when the heroes attacked.

The word '*Day*' is an adverb of time and is in the accusative here meaning: 'He helped you on the Day of Ḥunayn.' Al-Farrā' said that the word '*occasions*' (*mawāṭin*) is not declined because it has no like in the singular and it is not plural unless a poet needs to make it so. Not everything permitted in poetry is permitted in normal speech. [POEM] An-Naḥḥās said, 'I saw that Abū Isḥāq was surprised at this and said, "He took the position of al-Khalīl and erred in it because al-Khalīl said that it is not declined because it has a plural which has no like in the singular and not a broken plural. It is not forbidden for it to have a definite article.'

when your great numbers delighted you but did not help you in any way,

It is said that they were twelve thousand and it is said they were sixteen thousand. Some of them said, 'We will not be defeated today for lack of numbers.' They relied on this statement and so what we mentioned concerning their being overcome at the beginning occurred until they regrouped and there was victory and success by the *barakah* of the Master of the Messengers ﷺ and Allah made it clear in this *āyah* that victory was gained through the help of Allah not by means of their great number. Allah says: *'If He forsakes you, who can help you after that?'* (3:160)

and the earth seemed narrow to you for all its great breadth

This was due to fear. It was as is said:

Even though the land of Allah is wide,
for the fearful who are pursued it is the hunter's snare.

Ruḥb is expanse, as in a broad chest, and *raḥb* is wide, as when describing the earth. The verb is *raḥuba*. It is said that *bā'* means 'with' and so it is 'in spite of'. It is said that it means *"alā'*, and it is said that it means 'with its breadth' and *mā* acts like a verbal noun.

and you turned your backs.

Muslim related that Abū Isḥāq says, 'A man came to al-Barā' and said, "You turned your backs in the Battle of Ḥunayn, Abū 'Umārah." He replied, "I testify that the Prophet of Allah ﷺ did not turn his back. Some people went too quickly and were exposed to a section of Hawāzin who were archers. They shot a volley of arrows like a swarm of locusts and they were exposed. The people turned to the Messenger of Allah ﷺ while Abū Sufyān was leading his mule. He dismounted and made supplication, saying, 'I am the Prophet and it is no lie. I am the son of 'Abd al-Muṭṭalib. O Allah, send down Your help!' By Allah, when the fighting was fierce, we would seek protection by proximity to him. The brave one among us was the one who confronted [the enemy],"' referring to what the Prophet ﷺ did.

Then Allah sent down His serenity on His Messenger and on the believers,

He sent down on them that which would make them tranquil and removed their fear so that they were emboldened to fight the idolaters after they had turned back.

and sent down troops you could not see,

They were the angels who reinforced the believers by the thoughts and confidence they cast into their hearts and by making them firm, while they weakened the unbelievers by making them cowardly from out of nowhere. Without fighting, however, because the angels only fought in the Battle of Badr. It is related that a man of the Banū Naṣr said to the believers after the fighting, 'Where are the piebald horses and the white men on them? We were only like a mole among them and we were only killed by their hands.' They told the Prophet ﷺ that and he said, 'Those were the angels.'

and punished those who disbelieved.

Allah punished them with your swords.

Then after that Allah will turn to anyone He wills.

He will turn towards those who were defeated and guide them to Islam, like Mālik ibn 'Awf an-Naṣrī, the leader of Ḥunayn, and those of his people who became Muslim. When the Messenger of Allah ﷺ divided the spoils of Ḥunayn at al-Ji'rānah, the delegation of Hawāzin came asking for him to be kind and good to them. They said, 'Messenger of Allah, you are the best and kindest of people. You have taken our sons, our women and our property.' He told them, 'I have waited for you and the division has occurred. I have what you see. The best words are those which are most truthful. Choose between your dependents or your wealth.' They said, 'We think nothing is equal to lineage.' So the Prophet ﷺ stood up and spoke: 'These people have come to us as Muslims. We have given them a choice and they do not consider anything to be equal to lineage. They are content with the return of their dependents. What has gone to me and the Banū 'Abd al-Muṭṭalib and Banū Hāshim is returned to them.' The *Muhājirūn* and *Anṣār* said, 'What we have is for the Messenger of Allah ﷺ.' Al-Aqra' ibn Ḥābis and 'Uyaynah ibn Ḥisn and their people refused to return any of their share as did al-'Abbās ibn Mirdās as-Sulamī. He wanted his people to support him as al-Aqra' and 'Uyaynah had been supported by their people, but the Banū Sulaym refused and said, 'Rather what we have is for the Messenger of Allah ﷺ.' The Messenger of Allah ﷺ said, 'We will compensate any of you who are niggardly with what is in their possession.' So the Messenger of Allah ﷺ returned their women and children to them and compensated those who were not content to forego their share with a compensation with which they were satisfied.

Qatādah said, 'It was mentioned to us that the foster-sister of the Prophet ﷺ with whom he had been suckled among the Banū Sa'd came to him after the Battle of Ḥunayn and asked on behalf of the captives of Ḥunayn. The Prophet ﷺ said, "I only control those of them which have gone to me. Come to me tomorrow and ask me while the people are with me. When I give you my share, the people will give theirs to you." She came the next day and he spread out his garment for her and she sat on it. Then she asked him and he gave her his share and when the people saw that, they gave her theirs.'

According to Sa'īd ibn al-Musayyab, the number of the captives of Hawāzin was six thousand. It is also said that it was four thousand. Abū 'Umar said, 'One of them was ash-Shaymā', the milk-sister of the Prophet ﷺ. She was the daughter of al-Ḥārith ibn 'Abd al-'Uzzā of the Banū Sa'd ibn Bakr and daughter of Ḥalīmah as-Sa'diyyah. The Messenger of Allah ﷺ honoured her, gave to her and was good to her. She returned happy to her land with her *dīn* and what Allah had given her.'

Ibn 'Abbās said, 'On the day of Awṭās, the Messenger of Allah ﷺ saw a woman shouting who would not stay still. He asked about her and was told, "She is missing her young son." Then he saw her when she had found her son, kissing him and holding him near. He called her and said to his Companions, "Would this woman throw her child in the fire?" "No," they answered. "Why?" he asked. They replied, "Because of her compassion." He said, "Allah is more merciful to you than she is (to her child)."' Praise belongs to Allah.

يَٰٓأَيُّهَا ٱلَّذِينَ ءَامَنُوٓا۟ إِنَّمَا ٱلْمُشْرِكُونَ نَجَسٌ فَلَا يَقْرَبُوا۟ ٱلْمَسْجِدَ
ٱلْحَرَامَ بَعْدَ عَامِهِمْ هَٰذَا ۚ وَإِنْ خِفْتُمْ عَيْلَةً فَسَوْفَ يُغْنِيكُمُ
ٱللَّهُ مِن فَضْلِهِۦٓ إِن شَآءَ ۚ إِنَّ ٱللَّهَ عَلِيمٌ حَكِيمٌ ٢٨

28 You who believe! the idolaters are unclean, so after this year they should not come near the *Masjid al-Ḥarām*. If you fear impoverishment, Allah will enrich you from His bounty if He wills. Allah is All-Knowing, All-Wise.

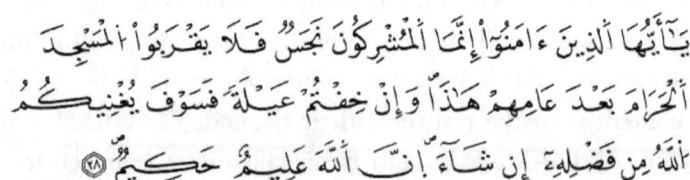

You who believe! the idolaters are unclean,

Scholars disagree about why the idolaters are described as unclean. Qatādah, Ma'mar ibn Rāshid and others said that that was because they were in *janābah* and did not wash on account of it, not that they were unwashed. Ibn 'Abbās and others said that it is their *shirk* which makes them unclean. Al-Ḥasan al-Baṣrī said, 'Anyone who shakes hands with an idolater should perform *wuḍū'*.'

The entire Madhhab believes that a *ghusl* is mandatory for an unbeliever when he becomes Muslim except for Ibn 'Abd al-Ḥakam who says that it is not mandatory because Islam wipes out what came before it. Abū Thawr and Aḥmad said that a *ghusl* is mandatory. Ash-Shāfi'ī dropped it and said, 'I prefer that he has a *ghusl*.' Ibn al-Qāsim states the like. Mālik has one view in which he does not acknowledge the need for the *ghusl* and that is related from him by Ibn Wahb and Ibn Abī Uways. The *ḥadīth* of Thumāmah and Qays ibn 'Aṣim refutes these positions.

Abū Ḥātim al-Bustī related in his sound *isnād* that the Prophet ﷺ passed by Thumāmah one day and Thumāmah became Muslim, so he sent him to the garden of Abū Ṭalḥah and commanded him to have a *ghusl*. He had a *ghusl* and prayed two *rak'ahs*. The Messenger of Allah ﷺ said, 'The Islam of your companion is good.' Muslim transmitted the account. It says that when the Prophet ﷺ freed him, he went to some palm trees near the mosque and had a *ghusl*. He ﷺ also told Qays ibn 'Āṣim to have a *ghusl* with water and lote-leaves. He became Muslim shortly before puberty and so his *ghusl* was only recommended. If someone becomes Muslim after puberty, he intends purification from *janābah* by his *ghusl*. This is the position of our scholars and is a summary of the School. Ibn al-Qāsim permits an unbeliever to have a *ghusl* before he presents himself for the testimony on his tongue when he believes in Islam with his heart. It is a weak view and contrary to Tradition. That is because one is not a Muslim by mere intention without articulation. This is the position of a group of the people of the Sunnah regarding faith since words are on the tongue and their affirmation is in the heart and purification is by action. The Almighty says: *'All good words rise to Him and He elevates all virtuous deeds.'* (35:10)

they should not come near the *Masjid al-Ḥarām*

This is a prohibition. That is why the *nūn* is elided from 'come near'. 'The *Masjid al-Ḥarām*' is an expression applied to the entire *Ḥaram*. That is the position of 'Aṭā'. There is a consensus that it is forbidden for idolaters to enter the *Ḥaram*. When a messenger comes to us from some unbelievers, the ruler should go out of the *Ḥaram* to hear what he has to say. If an idolater enters the *Ḥaram* in concealment and dies, his bones are disinterred and removed. They are not allowed to reside there or to pass through.

As for the Arabian peninsula, which is Makkah, Madīnah, Yamāmah, Yemen and its districts, Mālik said that anyone (living there) who is not following Islam should be removed from these places, but they are not forbidden to frequent it as travellers. That is what ash-Shāfi'ī said, but he excluded Yemen from that. He allowed them three days as 'Umar had done when he exiled them. They are not buried there, but are taken out of the *Ḥaram*.

Scholars disagree about unbelievers entering mosques and the *Masjid al-Ḥarām*. There are five views. The people of Madīnah say that the *āyah* is general to all idolaters and all mosques. That is what 'Umar ibn 'Abd al-'Azīz wrote to his governors and adopted in his letters based on this *āyah*. That is supported by the words of the Almighty: *'In houses which Allah has permitted to be built and in which His Name is remembered'"* (24:36). Unbelievers entering them is contrary to this.

We find in *Ṣaḥīḥ Muslim* and elsewhere: 'These mosques are not places for any urine or filth.' Unbelievers are not free of that. The Prophet ﷺ said, 'This mosque is not lawful for a menstruating woman or anyone in *janābah*.' An unbeliever is automatically in a state of *janābah*. The Almighty says: *'The idolaters are unclean'* and so that is what they are. It must refer to the actual uncleanness of the individual or be based on a legal judgement. In any case, it is mandatory to forbid them from entering mosques because the cause, which is uncleanness, exists in them and purity is demanded in the mosque. The word *najas* (unclean) is used for a man, a woman, two men, two women, and several men or women. It has no plural because it is a verbal noun. *Nijs* is not used except with *rijs*. If it is singular, it is *najis* and *najus*.

Ash-Shāfi'ī said that the *āyah* is general to all idolaters, and is specific to the *Masjid al-Ḥarām*, and they are not prevented from entering other mosques. Jews and Christians are allowed to enter other mosques. Ibn al-'Arabī said, 'This is him inflexibly clinging to the literal text because the words of Allah: *"The idolaters are unclean"* calls attention to the reason found in their *shirk* and uncleanness.'

If it is observed that the Prophet ﷺ bound Thumāmah in the mosque while he was still an idolater, scholars have several responses to this *ḥadīth* if it is sound. One is that it was before the revelation of the *āyah*. The second is that the Prophet ﷺ knew that he would become Muslim and that is why he tied him up. The third is that the case is a specific one and so it is not necessary to defend it with the proofs we mentioned since its specificity means that the general ruling is not applicable in this case. So it is possible to say that he tied him in the mosque so that he could see the excellence of the prayer and gathering of the Muslims and their good manners in sitting in the mosque so that he would feel at ease with that and become Muslim. That is what happened. It is possible that they had no other place to bind him except the mosque. Allah knows best.

Abū Ḥanīfah and his people said that Christians and Jews are not forbidden to enter the *Masjid al-Ḥarām* or any other mosque. Only idolaters and idol-worshippers are forbidden to enter the *Masjid al-Ḥarām*. This position is refuted by all that we mentioned from the *āyah* and other things. Aṭ-Ṭabarī said, 'According to Abū Ḥanīfah a *dhimmī* is permitted to enter all mosques without any need. Ash-Shāfi'ī said that need is considered and even with need, he is not permitted to enter the *Masjid al-Ḥarām*.' 'Aṭā' ibn Abī Rabāḥ said, 'All of the *Ḥaram* is a mosque and a *qiblah* and therefore they are forbidden to enter the *Ḥaram* by the words of Allah: *"Glory be to Him who took His slave on a journey by night from the Masjid al-Ḥarām to the Masjid al-Aqṣā."* (17:1) He travelled from the house of Umm Hāni'.'

Qatādah said, 'An idolater may not approach the *Masjid al-Ḥarām* except in order to pay *jizyah*, nor may an unbelieving slave belonging to a Muslim.' Ismā'īl ibn Isḥāq related from Jābir that the Prophet ﷺ said, 'No idolater should come near the mosque except for a slave or slave-girl who enters for a need.' Because of this Jābir ibn 'Abdullāh said that idolaters in general are forbidden to approach the *Masjid al-Ḥarām*, but it is specific about slaves.

so after this year they should not come near the *Masjid al-Ḥarām*.

There are two positions about *'after this year'*. One is that the year referred to is 9 AH, the year in which Abū Bakr led the *ḥajj*. Then second is that it is 10 AH, as Qatādah stated. Ibn al-'Arabī said, 'That is the sound position that the words stipulate. It is extraordinary to suggest that it is 9 AH, which was the year in which the announcement occurred. If a man's slave had entered his house one day and his master said to him, "You will not enter this house after today," he would not mean the day he entered.'

If you fear impoverishment, Allah will enrich you

'Amr ibn Fā'id said that it means 'When you fear.' That is barbaric [grammatically]. What is correct is that it means *'if'*. When the Muslims forbade the idolaters to attend the Festival, and they were the ones who normally brought food and goods, Shayṭān cast fear of poverty into their hearts and they said, 'But how will we live?' So Allah promised them that He would enrich them from His bounty. Aḍ-Ḍaḥḥāk said, 'Allah opened for them the gate of *jizyah* from the people of the *dhimmah* when He said: *"Fight those of the people who were given the Book who do not believe in Allah and the Last Day…".* (9:29)' 'Ikrimah said, 'Allah made them rich with abundant rain, plants and fertility of soil so it flourished with herbs and grain. Food, produce and much good were brought to Makkah and Allah further enriched them through *jihād* and the conquest of other nations.'

'Aylah means poverty. The verb *'āla* means to be poor. A poet says:

A poor man does not know when he will be enriched
and a rich man does not know when he will be impoverished (*ya'īl*).

'Alqamah and some of the companions of Ibn Mas'ūd recited '*'ā'ilah'* which is a verbal noun like *qā'ilah* and *'āfiyah.* It is possible that it describes something elided implying: 'a state of poverty'. It means a difficult state. One uses the verb to mean that something was hard on a person. Aṭ-Ṭabarī related that the verb *'āla* means to be poor.

This *āyah* contains evidence that it is permitted for the heart to be attached to means of provision. That is not contrary to trust in Allah. Even though provision is determined and the command and allotment of Allah are carried out, it is still connected to secondary causes by a wisdom so that the hearts which are connected to secondary causes can be distinguished from the hearts which are imbued with total reliance on the Lord of lords. It has already been stated that secondary means are not incompatible with trust in Allah. (5:3) The Prophet ﷺ said, 'If you truly relied on Allah, He would provide for you as He provides for the birds. They go out hungry in the morning and return full at night.' Al-Bukhārī transmitted it. He reported that true trust is not contrary to going out morning and evening seeking provision.

Ibn al-'Arabī said, 'The Sufi shaykhs say, "They go out in the morning and return in the evening with acts of obedience to Allah. That is the cause of their provision." They said, "Two things provide evidence for it. One is the words of the Almighty: *'Instruct your family to do the prayer, and be constant in it. We do not ask you for provision. We provide for you'* (30:132) and the second is His words: *'All good words rise to Him and He elevates all virtuous deeds.'* (35:10) So He only sends down provision from its place, which is heaven, by what rises, which is good *dhikr* and righteous actions. It is not by striving in the earth: there is no provision in that."'

According to the *fuqahā'* who deal with the outward, the sound position is the judgment of the Sunnah: it is acting by worldly means, such as farming, trading in markets, cultivating wealth and planting fruits. The Companions used to do that while the Prophet ﷺ was among them. Abū al-Ḥasan ibn Baṭṭāl said, 'Allah commanded His slaves to spend of the good things which they earn.' There are other *āyahs* about that, as when Allah says: *'But anyone who is forced to eat it – without desiring it or going to excess in it – commits no crime.'* (2:183). So when someone is forced by dire need, what was unlawful for him becomes lawful in the absence of the food which he was commanded to earn and nourish himself with. He is not commanded to wait until food descends to him from heaven. If he were to abandon striving for what would nourish himself, he would kill himself. The stomach of the Messenger of Allah ﷺ writhed from hunger when he could not find anything to eat and food from heaven did not descend to him. He used to store a year's food for his family when Allah opened conquests to him. Anas ibn Mālik related that a man brought a camel to the Prophet ﷺ and said, 'Messenger of Allah, should I hobble it and rely on Allah or leave it unhobbled and rely on Allah?' He answered, 'Hobble it and rely on Allah.'

They have no argument in the People of the Ṣuffah. They were poor people who sat in the mosque without engaging in agriculture of trade. They had no earnings or money. They were the guests of Islam in the time of constriction before things opened up. Nonetheless, they used to gather firewood in the day and bring it to the house of the Messenger of Allah ﷺ. They recited the Qur'an and prayed at night. This is how al-Bukhārī and others describe them. So they used secondary means. When the Prophet ﷺ was given a gift, he ate it with them. If it was *ṣadaqah,* he gave it to them. When the Conquest occurred and Islam spread, they went out and assumed command, as Abū Hurayrah did, and did not remain sedentary.

Then it is said that there are six categories of means by which provision is correctly obtained. The highest category is the earning of our Prophet Muḥammad ﷺ. He said, 'My provision was put under the shadow of my spear and humiliation and degradation was placed on those who oppose my command.' At-Tirmidhī transmitted it and said that it is sound. Allah placed the provision of His Prophet ﷺ in his earning by his excellence and He singled him out for the best type of provision, which is taking spoils and conquering because of the honour it entails.

The second category is a man eating from the work of his own hand. The Prophet ﷺ said, 'The best of what a man eats is from the work of his own hand. The Prophet Dāwūd ate from the work of his own hand.' Al-Bukhārī transmitted it. It says in the Revelation: *'We taught him the art of making garments for you…'* (21:80) It is related that 'Īsā ate from his spinning.

The third is trade and it was the work of most of the Companions, may Allah be pleased with them, especially the *Muhājirūn.* The Revelation indicates that in more than one place.

The fourth category is agriculture and planting which was dealt with *Sūrat al-Baqarah* (2:205)

The fifth is the Qur'an, teaching it and making talismans from it, which was dealt with in the *Fātiḥah.*

The sixth category is, when there is need, borrowing it with the intention of repaying it. The Prophet ﷺ said, 'If someone borrows people's property intending to repay it, Allah will repay it for him. If someone takes it wanting to destroy it, Allah will destroy him.' Abū Hurayrah related it.

if He wills

This is evidence that provision is not obtained through striving; it comes from the bounty of Allah who distributes it between His slaves. That is clear in His words: '*We have allocated their livelihood among them in the life of this world.*' (43:32)

قَٰتِلُوا۟ ٱلَّذِينَ لَا يُؤْمِنُونَ بِٱللَّهِ وَلَا بِٱلْيَوْمِ ٱلْءَاخِرِ وَلَا يُحَرِّمُونَ
مَا حَرَّمَ ٱللَّهُ وَرَسُولُهُۥ وَلَا يَدِينُونَ دِينَ ٱلْحَقِّ مِنَ ٱلَّذِينَ
أُوتُوا۟ ٱلْكِتَٰبَ حَتَّىٰ يُعْطُوا۟ ٱلْجِزْيَةَ عَن يَدٍ وَهُمْ صَٰغِرُونَ ﴿٢٩﴾

29 Fight those of the people who were given the Book who do not believe in Allah and the Last Day and who do not make unlawful what Allah and His Messenger have made unlawful and do not take as their *dīn* the *dīn* of Truth, until they pay the *jizyah* with their own hands in a state of complete abasement.

When Allah forbade the unbelievers to approach the *Masjid al-Ḥarām*, the Muslims felt that trade, which the idolaters used to bring, had been cut off from them and Allah said, '*If you fear impoverishment…*' as we said. Then, in this *āyah*, Allah made *jizyah* lawful. It had not been taken before that. He made it replace the commerce that the idolaters had brought which they had now been denied. He says: '*Fight those of the people…*'. Allah Almighty commands that all the unbelievers be fought because they all share in this description. He singled out the People of the Book to honour their Scripture and the fact that they have knowledge of *tawḥīd*, the Messengers, Divine Laws and religions, especially the mention (in their books) of Muḥammad ﷺ, his nation and religion. When they denied him, the proof was reinforced against them and the heinousness of their crime revealed. Allah calls attention to their position and then sets an end to the fighting: that is the payment of *jizyah* instead of killing. That is sound.

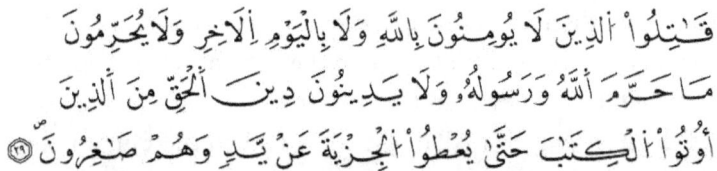

Ibn al-'Arabī said, 'I heard Abū al-Wafā' 'Alī ibn 'Aqīl in a debate reciting it and using it as evidence. He said, "The word '*fight*' is a command to punish. Then Allah says: '*those who do not believe*' which explains the wrong action for which there is punishment."' The words "*and the Last Day*" stress that the crime has to do with creed. Then Allah says: "*who do not make unlawful what Allah and His Messenger have made unlawful*" which is an additional wrong action in opposition to right action. He then says: "*...do not take as their dīn the dīn of Truth,*" and this indicates that their disobedience is in deviation, obstinacy and refusing to submit. Allah then says: "*the people who were given the Book*" to stress the argument because they found it written with them in the Torah and Gospel. Then He says: "*until they pay the jizyah with their own hands*" stipulating the end of the punishment and specifying the alternative by which it is removed.'

Scholars disagree about those from whom *jizyah* should be taken. Ash-Shāfi'ī said, 'Based on this *āyah, jizyah* is only accepted from the People of the Book, Arab or non-Arab. They are those singled out for mention and so the ruling is directed to them as opposed to others based on Allah's words: "*kill the idolaters wherever you find them.*" (9:5) He does not say: "except when they pay *jizyah*" as He says about the People of the Book.' He said, 'It is accepted from the Magians based on the Sunnah.' That is also the position of Aḥmad and Abū Thawr, and it is that of ath-Thawrī and Abū Ḥanīfah and his people.

Al-Awzā'ī said, '*Jizyah* is taken from every idol-worshipper, fire-worshipper, denier or contester.' That is also the position of Mālik. He thought that *jizyah* should be taken from all categories of *shirk* and denial, Arab or non-Arab, Taghlibī or Qurashī, whoever it is, except for apostates. Ibn al-Qāsim, Ashhab and Saḥnūn said that '*Jizyah* should be taken from Magians, Arabs and all nations. As for idol-worshippers among the Arabs, Allah did not institute *jizyah* for them and none of them remain on the earth. They had a choice between being fought or becoming Muslims.' It is found that Ibn al-Qāsim said, '*Jizyah* is taken from them, as Mālik says.' That is also found in *at-Tafrīq* by Ibn al-Jallāb and it is a possibility, not a text.

Ibn Wahb said, '*Jizyah* is not accepted from Magian Arabs, but is accepted from other Magians.' He added, 'That is because there are no Magians among the Arabs. All of them have become Muslim. Any of them who is other than Muslim is an apostate who is killed in every instance if he does not become Muslim. *Jizyah* is not accepted from him.' Ibn al-Jahm said, '*Jizyah* is accepted from everyone who has a religion other than Islam except for what is agreed upon about the unbelievers of Quraysh.' He mentioned in respect of the reason for that, their being honoured above abasement and belittlement due to their position in respect of the Messenger of Allah ﷺ. Someone else said, 'That is because all of them became Muslim on the day Makkah was conquered.' Allah knows best.

As for the Magians, Ibn al-Mundhir said, 'I do not know of any disagreement that *jizyah* should be taken from them.' In the *Muwaṭṭā'*, Mālik reported from Ja'far ibn Muḥammad from his father that 'Umar ibn al-Khaṭṭāb mentioned the Magians and said, 'I do not know what to do about them.' 'Abd ar-Raḥmān ibn 'Awf said, 'I testify that I heard the Messenger of Allah ﷺ say, "Follow the *sunnah* of the People of the Book with them."' Abū 'Umar said that he was referring specifically to *jizyah*. The words of the Messenger of Allah ﷺ here indicate that they are not People of the Book. This is the position of most *fuqahā'*. It is related from ash-Shāfi'ī that they were People of the Book and then made alterations. I think that he believed something which is related from 'Alī ibn Abī Ṭālib, through a path of transmission centred on Abū Sa'īd al-Baqqāl that has some weakness in it. 'Abd ar-Razzāq and others mentioned it. Ibn 'Aṭiyyah related that a Prophet called Zoroaster was sent to the Magians. Allah knows best.

Allah Almighty did not mention in His Book the amount of the *jizyah* to be taken from them and scholars disagree about the amount. 'Aṭā' ibn Abī Rabāḥ said the amount of *jizyah* is not fixed. It is set according to the treaty they are given. That is what Yaḥyā ibn Ādam and aṭ-Ṭabarī said, although aṭ-Ṭabarī said that its minimum is one dinar and there is no limit to its maximum. They use as evidence what is related by the people of the *Ṣaḥīḥ* from 'Amr ibn 'Awf about the Messenger of Allah ﷺ making peace with the people of Baḥrayn in exchange for the *jizyah*.

Ash-Shāfi'ī said, 'It is a dinar for both the wealthy and poor free adult males and is not decreased at all.' He used as evidence what Abū Dāwūd and others related from Mu'ādh that the Messenger of Allah ﷺ sent him to Yemen and commanded him to take a dinar from every adult male for *jizyah*.' Ash-Shāfi'ī said, 'That makes it clear what Allah means.' It is the position of Abū Thawr. Ash-Shāfi'ī said, 'It is allowed to conclude a treaty for payment of more than a dinar. If it is more and they are content with it, it is accepted from them. If they make peace in exchange for giving hospitality for three days, that is allowed when the level of hospitality is known in terms of bread, barley, straw and condiments.' He mentioned the medium amount of that and what the wealthy owe. He also mentioned welcome and protection from heat and cold.

Mālik said in what Ibn al-Qāsim, Ashhab and Muḥammad ibn al-Ḥārith ibn Zanjawayh related from him that it is four dinars for the people who use gold and forty dirhams for the people who use silver. It is the same for both rich and poor. In the case of a Magian, it is not increased or decreased as 'Umar stipulated and it is not taken from anyone else.

It is said that it may be lessened for someone weak according to what the ruler thinks best. Ibn al-Qāsim said, 'The obligation is not lessened due to difficulty and not increased for the wealthy.' Abū 'Umar said, 'It is taken from their poor according to what they can bear, even if it is only a dirham.' Mālik ended up with that position. Abū Ḥanīfah and his people, Muḥammad ibn al-Ḥasan and Aḥmad ibn Ḥanbal said, 'Twelve, twenty-four and forty.' Ath-Thawrī said, 'Different amounts have come from 'Umar ibn al-Khaṭṭāb regarding that. One can take whichever of them he wishes if they are *dhimmīs*. If they are people with a treaty, it is solely on the basis of the treaty they made.'

Our scholars said that what is indicated by the Qur'an is that *jizyah* is taken from fighting men in that Allah says: *'Fight those … until they pay the jizyah.'* That shows that it is mandatory for those who fight. It also indicates that it is not imposed on a slave, even if he fights, because he has no wealth and because the Almighty says: *'until they pay'* and that is not said about someone who does not own anything that would enable them to pay. So there is a consensus among scholars that the *jizyah* is imposed on adult free men. They are those who can fight. Not on women, children, slaves, the insane, or feeble old men. There is disagreement about monks. Ibn Wahb related from Mālik that it should not be taken from them. Muṭarrif ibn al-Mājishūn said, 'As long as he does not become a monk after its imposition. If he becomes a monk after it has been imposed, it is not cancelled for him.'

When the people of *jizyah* have paid *jizyah*, none of their fruits, goods or crops may be taken from them unless they trade in lands other than those in which they normally reside and with which there is a truce. When they leave as merchants from the lands where they live to other lands, a tenth is taken from them when they sell and have the cash they received in their hands, even if that happens several times a year, unless they are carrying food, wheat and oil to Madīnah and Makkah. From them only half of the tenth is taken based on what 'Umar did. Some of the people of Madīnah think that the tenth should only be taken from the people of the *Dhimmah* in their trading once in a year, as is the case with the Muslims. That is the position of 'Umar ibn 'Abd al-'Azīz and a group of the imams of the *fuqahā'*. The former is the position of Mālik and his people.

When the people of *jizyah* have paid the *jizyah* which was imposed on them, or on the basis of which they have concluded peace treaties, they are left with their property, vines and pressing as long as they conceal their wines and they are not openly sold to a Muslim. They are forbidden to openly display wine or pork in Muslim markets. If a Muslim pours it away without their having openly displayed it, he has transgressed and is liable for its value. It is also said that he does not have to pay it. If he wrongfully seizes it, he is obliged to return it.

They are not opposed in respect of any rulings and trade between themselves which involve usury. When they ask us to make a ruling, the judge can choose: he can render his ruling based on what Allah has revealed or decline to make judgment. It is said that he should judge between them where there are injustices in any case and take from their strong to give to their weak because that is an aspect of defending them. The ruler must fight their enemy for them and support them in their fight. They have no portion of *fay'* spoils. The churches they made a treaty to preserve may not be increased in size. They are not prevented from repairing them but may not build new ones. They should wear clothing and have an appearance which distinguishes them from Muslims. They are forbidden to take on the appearance of the people of Islam. There is nothing wrong in buying the children of the enemy from them when those are not subject to the *Dhimmah*. Someone who refuses to pay *jizyah* is disciplined for that and it should be taken from him while he is abased.

Scholars disagree about what *jizyah* obliges. Mālikī scholars say that payment of *jizyah* prevents the payee from being killed on account of unbelief. Ash-Shāfi'ī said that it prevents one's blood being shed and also allows the payee to live in the land [of Islam]. The point of the legal disagreement is that if we say that *jizyah* just prevents killing and then the non-Muslim becomes Muslim, *jizyah* is cancelled for him for the past [period for which it is owed], even if he becomes Muslim a day before the end of the year or after the completion of a year according to Mālik. According to ash-Shāfi'ī, it is a debt established by the status of a being a *dhimmī* which becoming Muslim does not cancel, like the rent for living in a house. Some Ḥanafīs hold to our view and some of them say that it is imposed instead of having to provide military support and fighting in *jihād*. Qāḍī Abū Zayd preferred that and claimed that it was Allah's underlying reason with regard to this matter.

The position of Mālik is sounder according to the words of the Prophet ﷺ: 'A Muslim does not owe *jizyah*.' Sufyān said that it means that when a *dhimmī* becomes Muslim after the *jizyah* is obliged for him, it no longer applies. At-Tirmidhī and Abū Dāwūd transmitted it. Our scholars said that that is indicated by Allah's words: *'until they pay the* jizyah *with their own hands in a state of complete abasement'* because Islam removes the need to do this. There is no disagreement about the fact that when people become Muslim, they do not pay *jizyah* with their own hands in abasement. Ash-Shāfi'ī said, 'When someone becomes Muslim *jizyah* is not taken from them in the manner described by Allah.' He said that *jizyah* is a debt which is obliged on him from the past, which entailed living in the land of Islam or protection from being killed, and it is like any other debt.

If a ruler makes a treaty with a town or fortress and then they break their treaty and refuse to pay the *jizyah* obligatory on them and refuse the ruling of Islam without being wronged and without the ruler being unjust towards them, then the Muslims, under their leader, must attack them and fight them. If they fight and are defeated, their ruling is the same as people in the Abode of War. It is said that they and their women are *fay'* and there is no fifth on it. That is the position of the School.

If they go out as thieves and highwaymen, while not refusing to pay *jizyah,* they are in the same position as Muslim *muḥāribs*. If they go out on account of injustice being done to them, then their case is examined and they are restored to the *dhimmah* and given justice by the one who wronged them. None of them are enslaved. They are free. If some of them break the terms of *dhimmah* but not others, those who have not broken the treaty are not punished for the others' violation of it. Their remaining with the treaty is known by their objecting to those who break it.

Jizyah is the grammatical form *fi'lah* from the verb *jazā, yajzī*, when someone gives compensation for what he has been given. So it is as if they give it as repayment for the gift of security. Part of this idea is seen in the poem:

He repays (*yujzīka*) you or praises you.
The one who praises you for what you did is like someone who repays (*jazā*).

Muslim related that Hishām ibn Ḥakīm ibn Ḥizām passed by some Nabateans in Syria who were standing in the sun (one variant has 'with oil poured on their heads'). He asked, 'What is happening here?' They answered, 'They are being held to make them pay the *jizyah*.' Hishām said, 'I testify that I heard the Messenger of Allah ﷺ say, "Allah will torture those who tortured people in this world."' One variant has that the leader [of those who did this] was 'Umayr ibn Sa'd who was in charge of Palestine at that time. Hishām went to him and informed him and he then ordered that they be released. Our scholars say, 'It is permitted to punish them if they refuse to pay *jizyah* when they are able to pay it. If it is clear that they are unable to pay, they are not punished because if someone is unable to pay *jizyah*, it is cancelled for him and the rich are not obliged to pay for the poor.'

Abu Dāwūd related from Ṣafwān ibn Sulaym from several sons of Companions of the Messenger of Allah ﷺ from their fathers that the Messenger of Allah ﷺ said, 'If someone wrongs someone with a treaty, degrades him, imposes on him that which is beyond his power or takes from him something he is not happy with, I will argue against him on the Day of Rising.'

with their own hands

Ibn 'Abbās said, 'He pays it himself rather than by the agency of a deputy.' Abū al-Bakhtarī related that Salmān said, 'being blameworthy'. Ma'mar related from Qatādah: 'by force'. It is said that '*with their own hands*' means by your blessing to them because when *jizyah* is taken from them, they are blessing themselves by doing that. 'Ikrimah said that they pay it while standing and the one who receives it is sitting. Sa'īd ibn Jubayr said that. Ibn al-'Arabī said, 'This is not from Allah's words: "*with their own hands*", but from His words: "*in a state of abasement*".' The *imāms* related from 'Abdullāh ibn 'Umar that the Messenger of Allah ﷺ said, 'The upper hand is better than the lower hand. The upper hand is the giving one and the lower hand is the begging one.' It is also related: 'The upper hand is the giving one.' He made the hand of the giver of *ṣadaqah* the upper one, and He made the hand of the giver of *jizyah* the lower one while the hand of its taker is the upper one. That is because Allah is One Who raises and lowers. He raises whomever He wishes and lowers whomever He wishes. There is no god but Him.

Ḥabīb ibn Abī Thābit reported that a man came to Ibn 'Abbās and said, 'The people of the *kharāj* land are unable to pay. Should I cultivate it, plant it and pay its *kharāj*?' 'No,' he answered. Another man came and he also gave him a negative answer. He recited the words of Allah: *'Fight those of the people who were given the Book who do not believe in Allah and the Last Day…'* to the end. He said, 'Does one of you take up abasement on the neck of one of them, remove it and place it on his own neck?' Kulayb ibn Wā'il said, 'I said to Ibn 'Umar, "I have purchased some land." "Purchase is good," he replied. I said, "I will give a dirham and a *qafīz* of food for every *jarīb* of land." He answered, "Do not place abasement on your neck."' Maymūn ibn Mihrān related that Ibn 'Umar said, 'I would not be happy to have the entire earth in exchange for a *jizyah* of five dirhams by which I affirm abasement for myself.'

وَقَالَتِ ٱلْيَهُودُ عُزَيْرُ ٱبْنُ ٱللَّهِ وَقَالَتِ ٱلنَّصَٰرَى ٱلْمَسِيحُ
ٱبْنُ ٱللَّهِ ذَٰلِكَ قَوْلُهُم بِأَفْوَٰهِهِمْ يُضَٰهِـُٔونَ قَوْلَ ٱلَّذِينَ
كَفَرُوا۟ مِن قَبْلُ قَٰتَلَهُمُ ٱللَّهُ أَنَّىٰ يُؤْفَكُونَ ٣٠

30 The Jews say, "Uzayr is the son of Allah,' and the Christians say, 'The Messiah is the son of Allah.' That is what they say with their mouths, copying the words of those who disbelieved before. Allah fight them! How perverted they are!

'Āṣim and al-Kisā'ī recited "Uzayrun' with *tanwīn*. It means that '*ibna*' is the predicate of the inceptive from 'Uzayr. 'Uzayr is declined, whether non-Arabic or Arabic. Ibn Kathīr, Nāfi', Abū 'Amr and Ibn 'Āmir recited *"Uzayru-bnu'* without *tanwīn* because of the meeting of two silent letters. This happens elsewhere in the Qur'an and frequently in poetry. An example of that is the reading: '*qul huwa-llāhu aḥadu, Allāhu-ṣ-ṣamad*' (112:1-2). Abū 'Alī said that it is frequently used in poetry. [POEM]

'*The Jews say...*' is an expression which is undefined, while what is meant is particular because not all of them said that. This is like the words of the Almighty: '*those to whom people said*' (3:173) when not all people said that. It is said that those who said what is related from the Jews were Sallām ibn Mishkam, Nu'mān ibn Abī Awfā, Shāsh ibn Qays and Mālik ibn aṣ-Ṣayf. They said that to the Prophet ﷺ.

An-Naqqāsh said, 'No Jew who said it remains. They have died out. Since one of them said it, it is assumed that the community hold to the ugliness of the statement because of the high position that the speaker held among them. The statements of notable men are always well-known among the people and taken as authoritative. This is why it is valid for a group to take the position of their notable man.' Allah knows best.

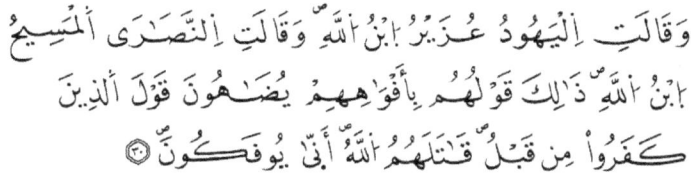

It is related that the reason for that statement was that the Jews killed Prophets after Mūsā ﷺ and so the Torah was taken from them and effaced from their hearts. 'Uzayr went out to wander in the land and Jibrīl came to him and said, 'Where are you going?' He answered, 'I am seeking knowledge.' So he taught him all of the Torah. Then 'Uzayr brought the Torah back to the tribe of Israel and taught it to them. It is said that Allah had 'Uzayr memorise it to honour him. He told the tribe of Israel, 'Allah had me memorise the Torah.' They began to learn it from him. The Torah was buried as their scholars buried it when they were afflicted by trial, expulsion and disease and killing by Nebuchadnezzar. Then the buried Torah was found and it was the same that 'Uzayr taught and they were misled by that and said, "Uzayr was only able to this because he is the son of Allah.' Aṭ-Ṭabarī said that.

The apparent meaning of the words of the Christians is that 'the son of God' means a son by lineage as the Arabs say about the angels. That is demanded by what aḍ-Ḍaḥḥāk and aṭ-Ṭabarī said. This is the worst kind of unbelief. Abū al-Ma'ālī said, 'The Christians agree that the Messiah is God and that he is the son of God.' Ibn 'Aṭiyyah said, 'It is said that some of them believe in sonship by way of kindness and mercy. This idea also cannot be applied to him. It is unbelief.'

Ibn al-'Arabī said, 'This contains evidence for the statement that our Lord is blessed and exalted so that if one reports about the disbelief of others which no one is permitted to originate, he incurs no harm because he speaks by way of exalting Him and refuting it. Had our Lord so willed, no one would say it. When He allowed the tongues to speak, He gave permission to report it so that it is denied in the heart and on the tongue and in order to refute it by proof and evidence.'

That is what they say with their mouths

This is a repetition for the purpose of emphasis as He says: *'they write the Book with their own hands'* (2:79); *'flying creature, flying on its wings'* (6:38); and *'When the Trumpet is blown with a single blast.'* (69:13) There are many examples of this.

It is said that it means that it is a simple statement lacking any clarification or proof. It is a statement made with the mouth, a simple claim with no sound meaning underlying it because they acknowledge that Allah has not taken a consort, so how can they claim that He has a son? It is a lie and a mere verbal assertion as opposed to a sound statement supported by proofs and on which proofs may be based. The people of meanings say that Allah only mentions statements connected to the mention of mouths and tongues when it is a false statement, as in: *'saying with their mouths what was not in their hearts'* (3:167); and: *'It is a monstrous utterance which has issued from their mouths. What they say is nothing but a lie'* (18:5); and: *'They say with their tongues what is not in their hearts.'* (48:11)

copying the words of those who disbelieved before

'*Copying*' means resembling. The Arabs use *ḍahī* for a woman in menopause, a woman who does not menstruate, or a woman who has no breasts since such women resemble men. Scholars say three things about the phrase: *'the words of those who disbelieved before.'* The first is that it refers to those who worshipped the idols, al-Lāt, al-'Uzzā and Manāt the third. The second is that it is the statement of the unbelievers that the angels are the daughters of Allah. The third that it is the statement of their ancestors whom they imitated in falsehood and followed in unbelief, as is reported about them when the Almighty says: *'We found our fathers following a religion.'* (43:23)

Scholars disagree about whether *'ḍahī'* has a *maddah* or not. Ibn Wallād said 'a woman who is *ḍahya'* is one who does not menstruate, having it with a *hamzah* and no *maddah*. Some of them, like Sībawayh, have a *maddah* and say that the *hamzah* in it is extra because the plural is *ḍuhā* and the *hamzah* is elided. Abū al-Ḥasan said that an-Najīramī said *ḍahyā'ah* with a *maddah* and a *hā'*. He related it from Abū 'Amr ash-Shaybānī in *an-Nawādir.* [POEM] Ibn 'Aṭiyyah said. 'Those who recite "*yuḍāhi'ūna*" take it from a woman who is *ḍahya'*. This is an error because the *hamzah* in *ḍāha'a* is part of the root as Abū 'Alī said, because the *hamzah* in "*ḍāha'a*" is part of the root while in "*ḍahyā*"' it is extra, as it is in "*ḥamrā*"'.

Allah fight them!

It means 'May Allah curse them!' referring to the Jews and Christians because someone who is cursed is like someone who is killed. Ibn Jurayj said that it is an expression of astonishment. Ibn 'Abbās said, 'Every mention of killing in the Qur'an is cursing.' An example of that is the words of Abān ibn Taghlib:

May Allah fight her! She insulted me
and knew that I can corrupt myself or put myself right.

An-Naqqāsh related that the words *'May Allah fight them!'* constitute a supplication whose usage became so widespread that it was used for astonishment in both good and evil so that the actual supplication is not intended. Al-Aṣma'ī quoted:

May Allah fight Laylā! How she astonishes me!
Tell people that I do not care about her.

ٱتَّخَذُوٓا۟ أَحْبَارَهُمْ وَرُهْبَٰنَهُمْ أَرْبَابًا مِّن دُونِ ٱللَّهِ
وَٱلْمَسِيحَ ٱبْنَ مَرْيَمَ وَمَآ أُمِرُوٓا۟ إِلَّا لِيَعْبُدُوٓا۟ إِلَٰهًا وَٰحِدًا لَّآ
إِلَٰهَ إِلَّا هُوَ سُبْحَٰنَهُۥ عَمَّا يُشْرِكُونَ ﴿٣١﴾

31 They have taken their rabbis and monks as lords besides Allah, and also the Messiah, son of Maryam. Yet they were commanded to worship only one God. There is no god but Him! Glory be to Him above anything they associate with Him!

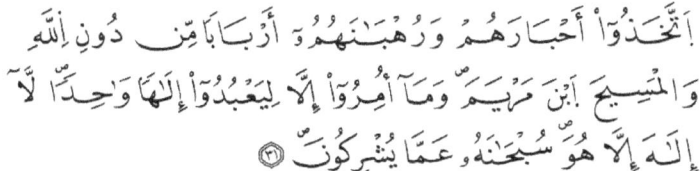

They have taken their rabbis and monks as lords besides Allah,

Aḥbār (rabbis) is the plural of *ḥibr* and it is someone who speaks well and orders his words and makes them very clear. *Muḥabbir* describes a garment which has much embellishment. It is said that *ḥibr* is the singular of *aḥbār*. Commentators say that it is written *ḥabr* while language experts say that it is *ḥibr*. Yūnus said, 'I have only heard it is *ḥibr*, and the evidence for that is the expression, the ink of a *ḥibr*, meaning a scholar's ink. Then it was used so much that they called ink itself *ḥibr*.'

Al-Farrā' said that it can be either *ḥabr* or *ḥibr*, which are two dialectical forms. Ibn as-Sikkīt said that *ḥibr* is ink and *ḥabr* is a scholar. *Ruhbān* (monks) is the plural of *rāhib*, taken from *rahbah* (awe). Such a man is one who is impelled by fear of Allah to make his intention sincere beyond the wont of other people. He is someone who devotes his time and actions to Allah and is close to Him. The people of meanings say that they made their rabbis and monks like lords when they obeyed them in everything. Exemplifying that are the words of Allah: *'He said, "Blow!" and when he had made it a red hot fire…'* (18:96), i.e. like fire. 'Abdullāh ibn al-Mubārak said:

Is it other than kings, bad rabbis and monks who corrupt the *dīn*?

Al-A'mash and Sufyān reported that Abū al-Bakhtarī said that Ḥudhayfah was questioned about these words and asked, 'Did they worship them?' He answered, 'No, but they made the unlawful lawful for them and so they considered it to be lawful and they made the lawful unlawful for them and so they considered it to be unlawful.'

At-Tirmidhī related that 'Adī ibn Ḥātim said, 'I went to the Prophet ﷺ wearing a gold cross on my neck and he said, "What is this, 'Adī? Remove this idol from yourself." I heard him recite in *Sūrat Barā'ah*: *"They have taken their rabbis and monks as lords besides Allah and also the Messiah, son of Maryam."* Then he said, "They did not worship them, but they made the unlawful lawful for them and so they considered it to be lawful and they made the lawful unlawful for them and so they considered it to be unlawful."' He said that it is a *gharīb ḥadīth* only known from 'Abd as-Salām ibn Ḥarb. Ghuṭayf ibn A'yan is not known in the *ḥadīth*.

the Messiah, son of Maryam

The derivation of *masīḥ* was discussed in *Āl 'Imrān* (3:45-46) *Masīḥ* (Messiah) is the sweat which pours down the brow. One of the later scholars spoke well and said:

Rejoice! Sorrows will become habitual
    when you witness the Gathering and Balance

And sweat (*masīḥ*) pours from your brow,
like flowing brooks.

The reason he is ascribed to Maryam was discussed in *an-Nisā'* (4:171).

يُرِيدُونَ أَن يُطْفِـُٔوا۟ نُورَ ٱللَّهِ بِأَفْوَٰهِهِمْ وَيَأْبَى ٱللَّهُ إِلَّآ أَن يُتِمَّ نُورَهُۥ وَلَوْ كَرِهَ ٱلْكَٰفِرُونَ ۝٣٢

32 They desire to extinguish Allah's Light with their mouths. But Allah refuses to do other than perfect His Light, even though the unbelievers detest it.

Allah's Light is the proof and evidence of His Unity. Proofs are put in the position of light since they provide clarification. It is said that it means the light of Islam, in other words they try to extinguish the *dīn* of Allah by their denial. *Afwāh* (mouths) is the plural of *fam* because the root of *fam* is *fāwh.*

But Allah refuses to do other than perfect His Light,

If it is asked how *illā* can be included in the words: *'Allah refuses to do other than perfect His Light'* when there is no negative in the words. Al-Farrā' says that *illā* is included because denial is the aim in the words, while az-Zajjāj stated that denial and affirmation are not expressed in this way; the verbal instruments of denial are: *mā*, *lā*, *lam* and *laysa*. These have no specific sequel. If the matter had been as he meant, it would be permitted to say 'I hate only (*illā*) Zayd', but the fact is that the Arabs elide with the verb *abā* (refuse). It implies: 'Allah refuses everything except perfecting His Light.' 'Alī ibn Sulaymān said, 'This is permitted with *abā* because it is forbidding or denial and so it is similar to negation. An-Naḥḥās said that this is good as the poet says:

Do I have any other mother if she abandons me?
Allah refuses (*abā*) that I be other than her son.

هُوَ ٱلَّذِىٓ أَرْسَلَ رَسُولَهُۥ بِٱلْهُدَىٰ وَدِينِ ٱلْحَقِّ لِيُظْهِرَهُۥ عَلَى ٱلدِّينِ كُلِّهِۦ وَلَوْ كَرِهَ ٱلْمُشْرِكُونَ ۝٣٣

33 It is He who sent His Messenger with guidance and the *Dīn* of Truth to exalt it over every other *dīn*, even though the idolaters detest it.

'His Messenger' means Muḥammad and *'guidance'* is the *Furqān. 'To exalt it over every other dīn'* is achieved by the evidence and proofs. It is exalted over the Laws of the *Dīn* so that none of them are hidden from it. Ibn 'Abbās and others said that. It is said that it means to exalt the *dīn* of Islam over every other *dīn*. Abū Hurayrah and aḍ-Ḍaḥḥāk said that this will occur when 'Īsā descends. As-Suddī said, 'That will be when the Mahdī emerges. There will be no one who has not entered Islam or paid *jizyah*.'

It is said that the Mahdī is 'Īsā alone, but this is not sound since there are sound reports by multiple transmission that the Mahdī is from the family of the Messenger of Allah ﷺ and so it is not permitted to apply the term to 'Īsā. The *ḥadīth* which states: 'There is no Mahdī except 'Īsā' is not sound. Al-Bayhaqī said in the *Book of the Resurrection* that that is because its transmitter was Muḥammad ibn Khālid al-Janadī who is unknown, and he related from Abān ibn Abī 'Abbās who is abandoned, from al-Ḥasan from the Prophet ﷺ. The chain is broken. The *ḥadīths* which were in previous texts about the emergence of the Mahdī and his being from the family of the Messenger of Allah ﷺ have a sounder *isnād*.

We have mentioned this and there is further clarification in our book, *Kitāb at-Tadhkirah* where we mentioned the reports about the Mahdī. *'To exalt it over every other dīn'* is in the Arabian peninsula, which has happened.

يَٰٓأَيُّهَا ٱلَّذِينَ ءَامَنُوٓا۟ إِنَّ كَثِيرًا مِّنَ ٱلْأَحْبَارِ وَٱلرُّهْبَانِ لَيَأْكُلُونَ
أَمْوَٰلَ ٱلنَّاسِ بِٱلْبَٰطِلِ وَيَصُدُّونَ عَن سَبِيلِ ٱللَّهِ ۗ وَٱلَّذِينَ
يَكْنِزُونَ ٱلذَّهَبَ وَٱلْفِضَّةَ وَلَا يُنفِقُونَهَا فِى سَبِيلِ ٱللَّهِ
فَبَشِّرْهُم بِعَذَابٍ أَلِيمٍ ﴿٣٤﴾

34 You who believe! many of the rabbis and monks devour people's property under false pretences and bar people from access to the Way of Allah. As for those who hoard up gold and silver and do not spend it in the Way of Allah, give them the news of a painful punishment

many of the rabbis and monks devour people's property under false pretences and bar people from access to the Way of Allah.

The *lām* is added to the imperfect verb, not the perfect because of the similarity of the action of nouns. *Rabbis* (*aḥbār*) are Jewish scholars and *monks* are Christians who strive in worship.

'False pretences': it is said that they used to take taxes from the property of their followers as well as loans in the name of the churches and synagogues and other things and they imagined that the expenditure was part of the Law and drawing close to Allah. In doing that they used to conceal that wealth as Salmān al-Fārisī mentioned about the monk whose vast hoarded wealth was exposed. Ibn Isḥāq mentioned that in the *Sīrah*. It is said that they used to take taxes from their revenue and wealth in the name of protecting religion and establishing the Law. It is said that they used to take bribes for giving judgments as many governors and judges do today. *'False pretences'* includes all of that.

The phrase *'bar people from access to the Way of Allah'* means that they stop the people of their religion from entering the *dīn* of Islam and following Muḥammad ﷺ.

As for those who hoard up gold and silver

The linguistic root meaning of *kanz* is to accumulate and gather and that is not restricted to gold and silver. Do you not see that the Prophet ﷺ said, 'Shall I tell you the best of what a man stores up (*yaknizu*)? A righteous woman.' It means what he collects to himself. A poet said:

> You did not provision yourself with all treasure (*kanz*)
> other than threads and threadbare linen.

Another said:

> May my wealth not become great if I feed the guest
> with gruel when I have wheat stored up (*maknūz*).

Gold and silver are singled out for mention because they are not part of what is open to view like other forms of wealth. Aṭ-Ṭabarī said that *kanz* is everything which is gathered together inside the earth or on top of it. Gold is called '*dhahab*' because it departs. Silver is called '*fiḍḍah*' because it breaks up and separates. Illustrating that are the words of Allah: *'they scatter off (infaḍḍū) to it'* (62:11) and '*they would have scattered (infaḍḍū) from around you.*' (3:259) This idea was discussed in *Āl 'Imrān* in connection with that.

The Companions disagreed about what is meant by this *āyah*. Mu'āwiyah believed that what is meant by it are the People of the Book. Al-Aṣamm believed that because *'those who hoard'* are mentioned after *'Many of the rabbis and monks'*. Abū Dharr and others said that what is meant by it are the People of the Book and Muslims as well. That is sound because if it had been only the People of the

Book who are meant, Allah would not have said *'alladhīna'* but just 'who'. When Allah says *'those'* (*alladhīna*), He is starting another idea and it is clear that it is one sentence added to another. So the words *'those who hoard up'* start a new sentence and it is nominative as the inceptive. As-Suddī said that it means the people of the *qiblah*. These are three views.

According to what the Companions said about it, it is evidence that the unbelievers with them are also addressed by the secondary rulings of the *Sharī'ah*. Al-Bukhārī related that Zayd ibn Wahb said, 'I passed through Rabadhah. When I saw Abū Dharr, I asked him, "What has put you in this place?" He answered. "I was in Syria and Mu'āwiyah and I disagreed about *'...those who hoard up gold and silver and do not spend it in the Way of Allah.'* Mu'āwiyah said, "It was revealed about the People of the Book," and I said, "It was revealed about both us and them." That was between us. He wrote to 'Uthmān to complain about me and 'Uthmān wrote for me to come to Madīnah. I went there and the people were too much for me – it was as if they had not seen me before. I mentioned that to 'Uthmān and he said, 'If you wish, you can withdraw while still remaining near [to us].' That is why he put me in this place. If they had put an Abyssinian in command over me, I would have obeyed him."'

Ibn Khuwayzimandād said, 'This *āyah* includes *zakāt* on money which is mandatory when five conditions are met: being free, Muslim, possessing it for a year, the *niṣāb* and being free of debt.' The *niṣāb* is two hundred dirhams or twenty dinars, or when that sum is made up by one category being added to the other. Two and a half per cent is paid from each. We say that freedom is a condition because a slave's ownership is deficient. Islam is a condition because *zakāt* is purification and purification does not apply to unbelievers and because the Almighty says: *'establish the prayer and pay zakāt'* (2:43) so *zakāt* is enjoined on those on whom the prayer is enjoined. We say that the year is a precondition because the Prophet ﷺ said, 'There is no *zakāt* on wealth until it has been owned for a year.'

We say that the *niṣāb* is a condition because the Prophet ﷺ said, 'There is no *zakāt* on less than 200 dirhams.' It is agreed that the *niṣāb* is not counted at the beginning of the year, but at the end of it because profit has the same ruling as capital. This indicates that if someone has 200 dirhams and goes into business with it and it becomes a thousand at the end of the year, he should pay *zakāt* on the thousand and the profit does not start a new year. That being the case, then the ruling on profit does not differ whether it is more or less than the *niṣāb*. They agree that if someone has forty sheep and they produce at the beginning of the year and then their mothers die except for one and the lambs complete the *niṣāb*, *zakāt* must be paid on them.

Scholars disagree about whether or not the wealth on which *zakāt* has been paid is called *kanz*. Some people said that it is. Abū aḍ-Ḍuḥā related from Ja'dah ibn Hubayrah that 'Alī said, 'Four thousand or less constitutes legitimate maintenance. What is more is hoarded wealth, even if *zakāt* has been paid on it.' It is not sound. Other people say that what *zakāt* is paid on or a person's other property is not hoarded wealth. Ibn 'Umar said, 'Wealth on which *zakāt* has been paid is not hoarded wealth, even if it is buried under seven earths, and all wealth on which *zakāt* has not been paid is hoarded, even if it is sitting on top of the earth.' Something similar is reported from Jābir. It is sound.

Al-Bukhārī related from Abū Hurayrah that the Messenger of Allah ﷺ said, 'If someone is given wealth and does not pay *zakāt* on it, it will come on the Day of Rising like a bald snake with two dots on its head and will wrap itself around him and then take hold of his jaws and say, "I am your property. I am your hoarded wealth."' Then he recited: *'Those who are tight-fisted with the bounty Allah has given them should not suppose...'* (3:180) It is also reported that Abū Dharr said, 'I went to the Prophet ﷺ who said, "By the One Who has my soul in His hand (or "By Him and there is no god but Him" or a similar oath), there is no man who has camels, cattle or sheep whose *zakāt* he has not paid but that they will be brought on the Day of Rising in their largest and fattest form and they will trample him with their hooves and gore him with their horns. Whenever the last of them passes him the first will returned until judgment has been carried out on him."' These two *ḥadīth*s indicate the soundness of what we mentioned. Ibn 'Umar made this clear in *Ṣaḥīḥ Bukhārī*. A Bedouin asked him, 'Tell me about the words of the Almighty: "*...those who hoard up gold and silver.*"' Ibn 'Umar said, 'It refers to anyone who hoards it up without paying *zakāt* on it. Woe to him!' This was before *zakāt* was revealed. When it was revealed, it was made the purification of wealth.

It is said that hoarded wealth is what exceeds your needs. That is related from Abū Dharr and it is part of what is related from his position, his hardships and what he alone was content with. It is possible to explain what is related from Abū Dharr regarding this. He related that the *āyah* was revealed at a time of need about the weakness of the *Muhājirūn*, when the Messenger of Allah ﷺ did not have the ability to suffice them and the treasury did not contain enough to take care of them. Years of need afflicted them and so they were forbidden to hold back any wealth that was over and above their needs. It was not permitted to store up gold and silver at such times. When Allah opened lands to the Muslims and expanded things for them, the Prophet ﷺ obliged them to pay five dirhams on two hundred and half a dinar on twenty. He did not make it obligatory for them to give all of it. It is considered a period of growth. That was clarification of his part. It is said that hoarded wealth is that whose rights have not been discharged, rights such as freeing captives, feeding the hungry, and other things. It is said that hoarded wealth is a term which specifies gold and silver, and that other forms of wealth are referred to as such by analogy. It includes all gold and silver except for jewellery because jewellery can be used without any right due on it. The sound position is what we first mentioned. All of that is called 'treasure' in language and *Sharī'ah.*

Scholars disagree about *zakāt* on jewellery. Mālik and his people, Aḥmad, Isḥāq, Abū Thawr and Abū 'Ubayd believed that there is no *zakāt* on jewellery. That was the position of ash-Shāfi'ī in Iraq, but he came to another conclusion later in Egypt and said, 'I did *istikhārah* about it.' Ath-Thawrī, Abū Ḥanīfah and his people and al-Awzā'ī said that there is *zakāt* on all of it. The evidence of the first is that the aim of bringing about increase is what makes *zakāt* on goods obligatory and (since that is not the case with jewellery) it is not something on which *zakāt* should be paid. So stopping growth on gold and silver by making it into jewellery cancels out the *zakāt* on it. Abū Ḥanīfah cited as evidence the general nature of the words making *zakāt* on gold and silver obligatory and said that there was no difference between jewellery and any other form of gold and silver. Al-Layth ibn Sa'd differentiates and makes *zakāt* obligatory on jewellery made to evade *zakāt* but says that someone who wears it or lends it does not have to pay it. Details about *zakāt* on jewellery in the School can be found in the books of secondary rulings.

Abū Dāwūd related that Ibn 'Abbās said, 'When the *āyah, "those who hoard up gold and silver,"* was revealed, it was hard on the Muslims and 'Umar said, "I will gain relief for you." He went and said, "Prophet of Allah, this *āyah* is hard for your Companions." He answered, "Allah made *zakāt* obligatory on you in order to make your remaining wealth pure and clean. He obliged shares of inheritance (which he particularly mentioned) so that that wealth could go to those after you." 'Umar said, "Allah is greater!" Then the Messenger of Allah ﷺ said to him, "Shall I inform you of the best treasure of a man? A righteous woman. When he looks at her, she delights him. When he commands her, she obeys him. When he is absent, she protects his interests."'

At-Tirmidhī and others related from Thawbān that the Companions of the Messenger of Allah ﷺ said, 'Allah has censured gold and silver. If we knew of any better kind of wealth we would seek it.' 'Umar said, 'I will ask the Messenger of Allah ﷺ for you.' He asked him and he said, "A remembering tongue, a thankful heart and a wife who helps her spouse in his *dīn*.' [At-Tirmidhī says] it is a *ḥasan ḥadīth*.

and do not spend it in the Way of Allah

Allah does not use the dual pronoun [referring to gold and silver] here. There are six reasons given for that. The first is that Ibn al-Anbārī said, 'What is aimed at is the most usually used, which is silver. It is like His words: *'Seek help in steadfastness and the prayer. But that is a very hard thing.'* (2:45) which picks out the prayer because it is more universal. And like His words: *'When they see a chance of trade or entertainment they scatter off to it,'* (62:11) in which the pronoun '*it*' refers to the word '*trade*' because it is more important and entertainment is not referred to. Many commentators said that although some have rejected it and said that it is not the same because the conjunction '*or*' separates trade from entertainment and it is good to have the pronoun refer to one of them. The second is the reverse of that, which is that the pronoun refers to gold and the second is added to it. Gold is feminine when the Arabs call it red gold. It can be masculine, although the feminine is better known. The third is that the pronoun refers to hoards. The fourth is that it refers to hoarded wealth. The fifth is that it refers to *zakāt* since it implies: 'they do not spend the *zakāt* on hoarded wealth.' The sixth is that using the pronoun for one noun spares the need for the other since the meaning is understood. That is frequent in Arabic as Sībawayh illustrates:

We are pleased (singular) with what we have
and you have although we have different opinions.

He uses '*rāḍi*' rather than '*rāḍūn*'. Someone else said:

He accused me of a matter of which I and my father
are innocent (singular), and he accused me because of hunger.

He used '*barī*'' rather than '*barī'īn*'. There is a similar example in what Ḥassān ibn Thābit said:

If the prime of youth and black hair do not
contend (singular), it is cowardice.

He did not use the dual.

If it is asked if the ruling governing someone who does not hoard or spend in the Way of Allah but spends in acts of disobedience is the same as that governing someone who hoards and does not spend in the Way of Allah, the answer is that it is more severe. Someone who squanders his wealth in acts of disobedience disobeys Allah in two ways: by both spending and consuming, like buying wine and then drinking it. Indeed, there are even more aspects to it since disobedience is in itself wrongdoing. The one who hoards disobeys in two ways: by refusing to pay *zakāt* and by holding on to wealth, and he is not concerned about holding on to wealth. Allah knows best.

give them the good news of a painful punishment

This idea was already mentioned (2:25). The Messenger of Allah ﷺ explained what the punishment was when he said, 'Give good news to the hoarders of branding on their backs which will go through to their sides and branding on their necks which will go through to their foreheads.' Muslim transmitted it. Abū Dharr related in his version, 'Give good news to the hoarders of a hot stone heated in the fire of Hell which will be placed on their nipples until it comes through their shoulder bones and then placed on their shoulder bones until it comes out through their nipples, going back and forth.' Our scholars said that it will go from their nipples to their shoulders to punish their hearts inside since they were filled with joy at having much wealth and joy in this world. So they are punished in the Next World by anxiety and punishment.

Our scholars say that the literal meaning of the *āyah* connects the threat to those who hoard wealth and do not spend it in the Way of Allah and do not undertake the obligation [due on it] and other things. However it is not only the quality of hoarding that should be taken into consideration. If someone does not hoard but refuses to spend in the Way of Allah, he also merits that description. Someone who conceals his wealth, refusing to spend it in the way that is obligatory for him: he is the one who is singled out for the threat. Allah knows best.

يَوْمَ يُحْمَىٰ عَلَيْهَا فِي نَارِ جَهَنَّمَ فَتُكْوَىٰ بِهَا جِبَاهُهُمْ وَجُنُوبُهُمْ
وَظُهُورُهُمْ هَٰذَا مَا كَنَزْتُمْ لِأَنفُسِكُمْ فَذُوقُوا مَا كُنتُمْ
تَكْنِزُونَ ٣٥

35 on the Day it is heated up in the fire of Hell and their foreheads, sides and backs are branded with it: 'This is what you hoarded for yourselves, so taste what you were hoarding!'

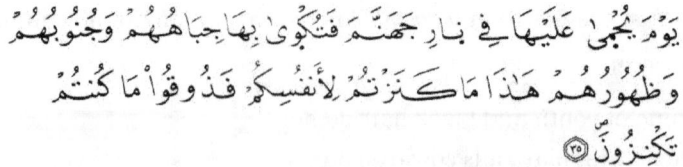

on the Day it is heated up in the fire of Hell

The noun '*Day*' is used adverbially. It implies: 'they will be punished on the Day it is heated up.' It is not valid for it to imply: 'give good news to them on the Day it is heated up' because there is no good news then. One says that iron is heated in the fire, i.e. made red hot in it. Here the verb *aḥmā* is used with a direct object, not the predicate *'alā*. Heating up here means putting it into the fire so that it can be used for branding. Branding (*kayy*) entails placing red hot iron onto a limb to the point that the skin becomes burned.

Jibāh (*foreheads*) is the plural of *jibhah*. It is the open area of the face between the eyebrows and the front of the hairline. The verb *jabaha* is to confront someone and hit his brow. *Junūb* (sides) is the plural of *janb*. Branding on the face is better known and more infamous, and it is more painful on the back and side. That is why these are singled out for mention among the other limbs.

Sufi scholars said, 'Allah will disgrace them because they sought wealth and rank. Their sides are branded because they withhold their wealth from the poor when they sit beside them. Their backs are branded because they lean back on their wealth, trusting and relying on it.' Scholars of the outward have said that these limbs are singled out because when someone wealthy sees someone poor, his eyes contract and he frowns. It is as is said:

He continued to turn his glance down away from me,
    as if he were knitting his eyebrows against me.
What is contracted of your eyes is not released
    and he only meets me with disdain.

When a poor man asks him for something, he frowns, and when he continues to ask, he turns his back on him. So Allah punishes him according to the state of his disobedience.

Traditions disagree about how the branding will be carried out. We find in *Ṣaḥīḥ Muslim* the description of the hot stone reported from Abū Dharr. It also contains the *ḥadīth* of Abū Hurayrah in which the Messenger of Allah ﷺ said, 'If someone owns gold or silver on which he has not paid *zakāt*, on the Day of Rising it will be turned into leaves of fire which will be heated in the fire of Hell and then his sides, forehead and back will be branded with them. Whenever they cool, they will be restored on a day whose length is five thousand years until people are judged and he sees whether he will go to the Garden or the Fire.'

We find in *al-Bukhārī* that: '...his hoard will take the form of a bald serpent.' It has already been mentioned from other than the *Ṣaḥīḥ* that 'Abdullāh ibn Mas'ūd said, 'If someone has wealth on which he has not paid *zakāt*, it will turn into a bald serpent and encircle his neck.' This may refer to different places: there is one place where wealth takes the form of a serpent, another place where it appears as leaves, and yet another place where it takes the form of a stone. The forms change while the physical reality is the same. The serpent is a body and wealth is a body. This example is real in contrast to his words ﷺ, 'Death will be brought like a white and black ram' which is more metaphorical. Allah Almighty can do whatever He wishes. The serpent is singled out for mention because it is the second enemy of creation.

Shijāʿ is a male snake which attacks riders and walkers. It stands on its tail and sometimes reaches as high as someone riding. It is found in deserts. It is also said that it is the *thuʿbān*. Al-Laḥyātī said, 'A snake is called *shijāʿ*. The plural is *ashjaʿa* and *shujʿān*.' *Al-Aqraʿ* is a name of a snake with a smooth head which is white from poison. It says in the *Muwaṭṭā'* that it has two protuberant spots on the sides of its jaws. That is also seen in people when they are angry and speak a lot. Umm Ghaylān bint Jarīr said, 'Sometimes my father became so angry that raisins formed on his jaws.' A *shijā'* is used as an example because it contains a lot of venom. Wealth takes on the form of that creature and directs anger towards the person who has it. Ibn Darīd said, 'It has two black spots over its eyes.' One variant has 'the form of *shijāʿ* which follows him and harms him and he gives his hand to it and it gnaws it like a foal gnaws.' Ibn Masʿūd said, 'By Allah, Allah will not punish anyone for hoarding and touch him with it dirham by dirham or dinar by dinar, but He will expand his skin so that every dirham and dinar can be placed on it.' That is true for the unbeliever, as is reported in *ḥadīth*, but not the believer. Allah knows best.

Aṭ-Ṭabarī said that Abū Umāmah al-Bāhilī said, 'A man of the Ṣuffah died and a dinar was found in his cloak. The Messenger of Allah ﷺ said, "A brand." Then another died and was found to have two dinars. The Messenger of Allah ﷺ said, "Two brands."' This is either because they were living off *ṣadaqah* while they had gold or because it was at the beginning of Islam. Then the *Sharīʿah* confirmed the possession of property and paying its due. If keeping property had been forbidden, its due would be to give all of it. There is no one in the community who obliges that. Enough for you is the state of the Companions and their property. May Allah be pleased with them.

As for what is mentioned from Abū Dharr, it was his position. Mūsā ibn ʿUbaydah related from ʿImrān ibn Abī Anas from Mālik ibn Aws ibn al-Ḥadathān from Abū Dharr that the Messenger of Allah ﷺ said, 'If someone amasses a dinar or dirham, gold or silver, which is not counted for a creditor or spent in the Cause of Allah, it is a hoard with which he will be branded on the Day of Rising.' This is in keeping with the position of Abu Dharr. What is beyond one's needs is not considered to be hoarded when it is used in the Way of Allah. Abū Umāmah said, 'Anyone who leaves silver or gold will be branded with it, forgiven or not forgiven, unless it is the adornment of a sword.' Thawbān related that the Messenger of Allah ﷺ said, 'Any man who dies in possession of gold or silver, Allah will make for a him a plate from every *qīrāṭ* by which he will be branded from his head to his feet, forgiven after that or punished.' This may be about that on which *zakāt* has not been paid as indicated by what we mentioned about the *āyah* before this. So it implies: 'He has gold or silver on which he has not paid *zakāt*. That is how it is related from Abū Hurayrah: 'If someone leaves ten thousand, it will be made into plates by which the person will be punished on the Day of Rising,' i.e. if he has not paid *zakāt* on it, so that the *ḥadīth*s do not contradict one another. Allah knows best.

This is what you hoarded for yourselves

They will be told, 'This is what you hoarded' and there is some elision. You will receive a punishment for what you hoarded.

إِنَّ عِدَّةَ ٱلشُّهُورِ عِندَ ٱللَّهِ ٱثْنَا عَشَرَ شَهْرًا فِى كِتَٰبِ ٱللَّهِ يَوْمَ
خَلَقَ ٱلسَّمَٰوَٰتِ وَٱلْأَرْضَ مِنْهَآ أَرْبَعَةٌ حُرُمٌ ذَٰلِكَ ٱلدِّينُ ٱلْقَيِّمُ
فَلَا تَظْلِمُوا۟ فِيهِنَّ أَنفُسَكُمْ وَقَٰتِلُوا۟ ٱلْمُشْرِكِينَ كَآفَّةً كَمَا
يُقَٰتِلُونَكُمْ كَآفَّةً وَٱعْلَمُوٓا۟ أَنَّ ٱللَّهَ مَعَ ٱلْمُتَّقِينَ ﴿٣٦﴾

36 The number of months with Allah in the Book of Allah has been twelve since the day He first created the heavens and earth. Four of them are sacred. That is the True *Dīn*. So do not wrong one another during them. However, fight the idolaters totally just as they fight you totally, and know that Allah is with those who are godfearing.

The number of months with Allah in the Book of Allah has been twelve,

Shuhūr is the plural of *shahr*. If a man says to his brother, 'I will not speak to you for months,' and swears an oath to that effect, he should not speak to him for a year. Some scholars say that. Some say that he must never speak to him. Ibn al-'Arabī said, 'I think that if he does not have a specific intention, three months are demanded because it is the minimum of the plural which the form *fu'ūl* demands as the plural of *fa'l*.' *'With Allah'* means in Allah's judgment and in what is recorded on the Protected Tablet. *'Twelve months'* is declined without any likes because it contains the letter of syntax and its proof. Most recite *"ashhar'* while Abū Ja'far recites *"ashr'*. *'The Book of Allah'* here means the Protected Tablet. He repeats it after He says *'with Allah'* because many things are described as being 'with Allah' while they are not said to be written in the Book of Allah. An example is His words: *'Allah has knowledge of the Hour.'* (31:34)

from the day He first created the heavens and the earth

This makes it clear that Allah's Decree and determination came before that and that He set out these months and named them according to the order He gave them on the day He created the heavens and the earth and He revealed that to His Prophets in His revealed Books. That is the meaning of His words here. Their ruling will continue as it was and the idolaters' changing of their names or putting one ahead of another does not change the reality of their fixed order. What is meant by that is following the command of Allah regarding them and negating what the people of the Jāhiliyyah did in delaying and advancing the names of these months and connecting judgments to the names according to the order they put them in. That is why the Prophet ﷺ said in his *khuṭbah* in the Farewell Ḥajj: 'O people! Time revolves in the manner in which it revolved on the day Allah created the heavens and the earth.' The explanation of this will come in due course. What the people of the Jāhiliyyah did by way of changing Muḥarram for Ṣafar and Ṣafar for Muḥarram does not alter what Allah states here.

The regent in '*day*' is a verbal noun which is 'Book of Allah'. It does not mean one of the Books. It implies: 'in what Allah wrote on the day He created the heavens and the earth.' The preposition '*with*' is connected to the verbal noun in the number, which is its regent. The preposition '*in*' in His words, '*in the Book of Allah*' is connected to something elided, which is the description of His word '*twelve*'. It implies: Twelve months are counted or written in the Book of Allah. It is not permitted for it to be connected to 'number' because of the separation between the conjunction and that to which it is connected by the predicate of *inna* [which is 'twelve'.]

This *āyah* indicates that the obligation is connected to acts of worship as well as other things. It is connected to the months and years which the Arabs knew rather than the months which the Persians, Romans and Copts used. Nothing is added to twelve months because it is a difference in numbers, including what is more than thirty and what is less. The months of the Arabs are not more than thirty days, even though some of them can be less. Those which are less are not specific months but vary in being less or more according to the reckoning of the passage of the moon through its phases.

Four of them are sacred

The sacred months mentioned in this *āyah* are Dhu-l-Qa'dah, Dhu-l-Ḥijjah, Muḥarram, and Rajab which is between Jumāda-l-Ākhirah and Sha'bān. It is Rajab of Muḍar. It is called that because Rabī'ah ibn Nizār used to esteem the month of Ramaḍān and called it Rajab. Muḍar respected Rajab itself. That is why the Prophet ﷺ said about it, 'That which is between Jumāda-l-Ākhirah and Sha'bān.' That removes the disagreement about the name. The Arabs also used to call it *Munṣil al-Asinnah* (the dropper of arrows).

Al-Bukhārī related from Abū Rajā' al-'Uṭāridī, whose name is 'Imrān ibn Malḥān or 'Imrān ibn Taym, 'We used to worship stones. When we found a better stone, we threw the first away and adopted the other one. When we did not find a stone, we collected a pile of dirt and brought a sheep and milked it on it and then went around it in a circle. When the month of Rajab began, we said, "The Dropper of arrows," and we threw away every spear with an iron point and every arrow with an iron point.'

That is the True *Dīn*.

It is the sound reckoning and full number. Ibn 'Abbās said, 'That is the Decree.' Muqātil said that it is the Truth. Ibn 'Aṭiyyah said, 'What I consider to be correct is that the *dīn* here means its best known aspect, in other words "That is the *Sharī'ah* and obedience."' 'True' means upright and straight. The root of *qayyim* is *qayūm*.

So do not wrong one another during them.

According to Ibn 'Abbās, this refers to all the months and, according to some people, it refers to the sacred months in particular, because it is closer to them and they have the special quality in making wrongdoing worse during them by the words of Allah: *'There must be no sexual intercourse, no wrongdoing nor any quarrelling during ḥajj.'* (2:197) It does not mean that wrongdoing in other months is permitted as we will make clear.

Two things are said about the wrongdoing referred to. One is that they wronged themselves in them by fighting and then that was abrogated by allowing fighting in all months. Qatādah, 'Aṭā' al-Khurāsānī, az-Zuhrī and Sufyān ath-Thawrī said that. Ibn Jurayj said, "Aṭā' ibn Abī Rabāḥ swore by Allah that it is not lawful for people to attack in the *Haram* or in the sacred months unless fighting is initiated against them in them, and that is not abrogated.' The first is what is sound because the Prophet ﷺ attacked Hawāzin at Ḥunayn and Thaqīf at Ṭā'if and they besieged them in Shawwāl and some of Dhu-l-Qa'dah. This was already discussed in *al-Baqarah* (2:217-218).

The second is that it means: 'Do not wrong yourselves in them by committing any wrong actions because when Allah gives esteem to something for one particular reason, it has a single sanctity. When it is given esteem for two or more reasons, its sanctity is multiple and so the punishment is doubled in it for someone who commits an evil action, in the same way that the reward is doubled for a righteous action.' If someone obeys Allah in a sacred month in the sacred land, his reward is not like that of someone who obeys Him in a non-sacred month in non-sacred land. Allah indicated that when He says: *'Wives of the Prophet, if any of you commits an obvious act of indecency she will receive double the punishment.'* (33:30)

Scholars disagree about this in respect of someone who kills accidentally in a sacred month, about whether the blood-money is made greater for him or not? Al-Awzā'ī said, 'According to what has reached us, killing in a sacred month or in the *Ḥaram* brings about an increase of the blood money. It is made a third more and there is an increase in the ages of camels that must be given in the case of semi-deliberate killing.' Ash-Shāfi'ī said, 'The blood-money is increased for taking a life or wounding in a sacred month, in sacred land, or for blood relatives.' It is related from al-Qāsim ibn Muḥammad, Sālim ibn 'Abdullāh, Ibn Shihāb and Abān ibn 'Uthmān that if someone kills in a sacred month or in the *Ḥaram*, the blood-money is increased by about a third. That was also related from 'Uthmān ibn 'Affān.

Mālik, Abū Ḥanīfah and his people and Ibn Abī Laylā said that it is the same whether the killing is in the *Ḥaram* or outside of it, in a sacred month or outside of it. That is the position of a group of the *Tābi'ūn*. It is sound because the Prophet ﷺ made blood money a *sunnah*, and he did not mention the *Ḥaram* or sacred months with regard to it. They agree that the *kaffārah* for accidental killing in or out of a sacred month is the same. The analogy makes it the same for blood-money. Allah knows best.

Allah singled out the four months and forbade wrongdoing in them to honour them, even though wrongdoing is forbidden at all times, as borne out by His words: *'There must be no sexual intercourse, no wrongdoing nor any quarrelling during ḥajj.'*

(2:198) This is the position of most of the people of interpretation. It means: 'Do not wrong yourselves in the four sacred months.' Ḥammād ibn Salamah related from 'Alī ibn Zayd from Yūsuf ibn Mihran that Ibn 'Abbās said, 'Do not wrong yourselves' in the twelve. Qays ibn Muslim related that Muḥammad ibn al-Ḥanafiyyah said, 'In any of them.'

If the position taken is the first view, why did Allah use the pronoun '*hunna*' and not '*hā*'? The answer is that it is because the Arabs use '*hunna*' and *hā'ulā'* for numbers between three and ten. When it is more than ten, they say *hiya* and *hādhihi*. This is so that you recognise the designation of few from many. It is related that al-Kisā'ī said, 'I am surprised at what the Arabs do in that respect.' Similarly when there are less than ten nights, they say *khalawn* and for more than that *khalat*. If it is asked why some times are given more sanctity than others, we say that the Creator can do whatever He wishes and singles out for superiority whatever He wishes. There is no cause or limitation on His action, He does what He wishes by His wisdom and that wisdom may be evident or hidden.

However, fight the idolaters totally just as they fight you totally

The imperative verb '*fight*' is a command to fight. *Kāffah* means 'all' and it is a verbal noun used adverbially, implying 'surround them and gather together'. Az-Zajjāj said, 'Similar to this in verbal nouns are: *'āfāhu* – He granted him *'āfiyah*, and *'āqabahu* – He punished him with an *'āqibah*. They have a dual case and no plural. It is like that with the general and the particular.

Some scholars say that these *āyah*s made fighting an individual obligation and then that was abrogated and it became a communal obligation. Ibn 'Aṭiyyah said, 'What he said is not known at all in the *Sharī'ah* of the Prophet ﷺ, namely that he obliged the entire nation to go out to fight. The meaning of this *āyah* is to encourage fighting the enemy, forming parties against them and being unified.' Then He defines it and says, '*just as they fight you totally*' and so their fighting and gathering against us makes it an obligation for us to gather against them. Allah knows best.

إِنَّمَا ٱلنَّسِىٓءُ زِيَادَةٌ فِى ٱلْكُفْرِ يُضَلُّ بِهِ ٱلَّذِينَ كَفَرُوا۟ يُحِلُّونَهُۥ
عَامًا وَيُحَرِّمُونَهُۥ عَامًا لِّيُوَاطِـُٔوا۟ عِدَّةَ مَا حَرَّمَ ٱللَّهُ فَيُحِلُّوا۟
مَا حَرَّمَ ٱللَّهُ زُيِّنَ لَهُمْ سُوٓءُ أَعْمَٰلِهِمْ وَٱللَّهُ لَا يَهْدِى
ٱلْقَوْمَ ٱلْكَٰفِرِينَ ﴿٣٧﴾

37 Deferring a sacred month is an increase in unbelief by which the unbelievers are led astray. One year they make it profane and another sacred to tally with the number Allah has made sacred. In that way they profane what Allah has made sacred. Their bad actions are made to seem good to them. Allah does not guide unbelieving people.

Deferring a sacred month is an increase in unbelief

Nasīʾu is how most imams read it. An-Naḥḥās said, 'As far as we know, no one recites *nasīʾu* without a *hamzah* from Nāfiʿ except Warsh alone [who gives *nasiyyu*]. It is derived from the verb *nasaʾa* and *ansaʾa* which means to defer. Al-Kisāʾī related both dialects. Al-Jawharī said, '*Nasī*'' is the nominal form *faʿīl* with a passive meaning from the verb *nasaʾa* which is used for something which is delayed, which is *mansūʾ* and then *mansūʾ* is changed to *nasīʾ* as *maqtūl* is changed to *qatīl*. A man is *nāsiʾ* and people are *nasaʾah* as with *fāsiq* and *fasaqah*.' Aṭ-Ṭabarī said that *nasīʾ* with a *hamzah* means to add and he said that the *hamzah* is only omitted in *nisyān* as Allah says in 9:67. He rejected Nāfiʿ's reading and used as evidence the fact that it is transitive with a genitive particle, saying *nasaʾa fī* as you say '*zāda fī*' (add to). This is seen in the words of the Prophet ﷺ: 'Whoever is happy to have his provision expanded and his life-span lengthened (*nusaʾu fī atharihi*) should maintain ties of kinship.' Al-Azharī said that the noun is put in the place of a real verbal noun.

They used to make fighting unlawful in Muḥarram, but when they needed to, they made Ṣafar sacred instead and fought in Muḥarram. The reason for that was that the Arabs were a people engaged in wars and excursions and it was hard for them to remain for three months in a row without making an attack. They said, 'If we go for three months without getting anything we will be finished!' So when they went out from Minā, someone from the Banū Kinānah would stand and then a man from the Banū Fuqaym called al-Qalammas would stand and say, 'I am the one whose decision is not rejected.' They would say, 'Defer a month for us,' meaning defer the sanctity of Muḥarram for us and put it in Ṣafar. So Muḥarram became a non-sacred month for them. They did the same month by month until the sanctity was applied to the entire year. Islam came and Muḥarram was returned to the place where Allah had put it. This is the meaning of the words of the Prophet ﷺ: 'Time revolves in the manner in which it revolved on the day Allah created the heavens and the earth.'

Mujāhid said, 'The idolaters used to perform *ḥajj* in every month for two years. They performed *ḥajj* in Dhu-l-Ḥijjah for two years, then they performed *ḥajj* in Muḥarram for two years and then performed *ḥajj* in Ṣafar for two years. It was like that in all the months until the *ḥajj* of Abū Bakr in the year before the Farewell Ḥajj, which fell in Dhu-l-Qa'dah in 9 AH. Then the Messenger of Allah ﷺ performed *ḥajj* the following year in the Farewell Ḥajj and it fell in Dhu-l-Ḥijjah. That is why he said in his *khuṭbah*, 'Time revolves in the manner in which it revolved.' By that he meant the months of *ḥajj* had returned to their proper place. The *ḥajj* returned to Dhu-l-Ḥijjah and the deferring was made invalid.

A third position was stated by Iyās ibn Mu'āwiyah: 'The idolaters used to reckon the year as twelve months and fifteen days. So the *ḥajj* was in Ramadān, in Dhu-l-Qa'dah, and in every month of the year according to the revolving of the months by an extra fifteen days. Abū Bakr performed *ḥajj* in Dhu-l-Qa'dah in 9 AH by the principle of revolving and the Messenger of Allah ﷺ did not perform *ḥajj*. The following year the *ḥajj* coincided with Dhu-l-Ḥijjah in 10 AH and that agreed with the new moons. This statement most accords with the words of the Prophet ﷺ: 'Time revolves in the manner in which it revolved,' meaning that the time of *ḥajj* has reverted to its original time which Allah set for it on the Day He created the heavens and the earth by the basis of the legislation which He already knew and His ruling was carried out. Then He said that the year is twelve months and negated that addition of fifteen days which they added to the year arbitrarily. He specified the original time and made the ignorant judgment void.

Imām al-Māzinī related from al-Khawārizmī that the first thing that Allah created was the sun which He made travel in Aries. The time which the Prophet ﷺ indicated coincided with the sun being in Aries. This requires a source of information. It is only reached by the transmission from the Prophets and there is no sound transmission from them about that and whoever claims it must provide its *isnād*. Then the intellect allows a different view to what he said: that Allah created the sun before the constellations. It is also possible that He created that all at once. Then the scholars who deal with measurement have tested that and found that the sun was in Pisces at the time the Prophet ﷺ said that and there are twenty degrees between it and Aries. Some of them say ten degrees. Allah knows best.

The scholars of interpretation disagree about who was the first to postpone the month. Ibn 'Abbās, Qatādah and aḍ-Ḍaḥḥāk said that it was the sons of Mālik ibn Kinānah. They were three. Juwaybir related from aḍ-Ḍaḥḥāk that Ibn 'Abbās said that the first to do that was 'Amr ibn Luḥayy ibn Qam'ah ibn Khindif. Al-Kalbī said that the first to do that was a man of the Banū Kinānah called Junādah ibn 'Awf. He is the one who met the Messenger of Allah ﷺ. Az-Zuhrī said, 'It was a branch of the Banū Kinānah and then from the Banū Fuqaym in the form of one of their men called al-Qalammas. His name was Ḥudhayfah ibn 'Ubayd.' One variant has Mālik ibn Kinānah. He was the one who dealt with the postponing, displaying the leadership the Arabs gave him. Their poet said:

From us is the one who postponed the mouth, al-Qalammas.

Al-Kumayt said:

We are not those who postponed the lawful months for Ma'add,
making them sacred.

The expression *'an increase in unbelief'* explains that what the Arabs did of combining them is one of the categories of unbelief and it denies the existence of the Creator and so they said, *'What is the All-Merciful?'* (25:10) They denied the Resurrection and said, *'Who will give life to the bones when they are decayed?'* (36:78) They denied the sending of the Messengers and said, *'Are we to follow a human being, one of us?'* (54:24) They claimed that they could make things lawful or unlawful and innovated that on their own initiative because of their desires and so they made lawful what Allah had forbidden. There is no changing His words, even if the idolaters dislike it.

by which the unbelievers are led astray

There are three readings of this. The people of Makkah and Madīnah and Abū 'Amr read it as *'yaḍillu* – go astray'. The Kufans read it as *'yuḍallu* – are led astray' making it a passive verb. Al-Ḥasan and Abū Rajā' recited it as *'yuḍillu* – lead astray'. All three meanings come from the same idea except that the third implies an elided object. It implies: those who disbelieved misguided by it those who accepted that from them. The word *'alladhīna'* is in the nominative, and it is also permitted for the pronoun [in *yuḍillu*] to refer to Allah. It implies: 'by it Allah misguides those who disbelieve,' as in His words: *'He misguides whomever He wishes'* (11:27) and His words at the end of the *āyah*: *'Allah does not guide unbelieving people.'* The second reading means that they are charged with it. Abū 'Ubayd preferred this reading going by Allah's words: *'Their bad actions are made to seem good to them.'* Abū Ḥātim preferred the first reading because they were misguided by it, in other words by deferring, because they calculated it and were misguided in it. The *hā'* in *'make it profane'* refers to deferring. It is related from Abū Rajā' as *yaḍallū*, which is a dialectical form.

'To tally' is in the accusative by the *lām* meaning 'in order to', signifying that they agree on it. This means that they do not deem one month non-sacred without making another sacred [in place of it] so that there are still four sacred months. This is sound. It is not mentioned that they made five sacred months. Qatādah said, 'They added Ṣafar to the sacred months and joined it to Muḥarram in sacredness.' Quṭrub and aṭ-Ṭabarī said that.

يَٰٓأَيُّهَا ٱلَّذِينَ ءَامَنُوا۟ مَا لَكُمْ إِذَا قِيلَ لَكُمُ ٱنفِرُوا۟ فِى سَبِيلِ
ٱللَّهِ ٱثَّاقَلْتُمْ إِلَى ٱلْأَرْضِ ۚ أَرَضِيتُم بِٱلْحَيَوٰةِ ٱلدُّنْيَا مِنَ ٱلْءَاخِرَةِ ۚ
فَمَا مَتَٰعُ ٱلْحَيَوٰةِ ٱلدُّنْيَا فِى ٱلْءَاخِرَةِ إِلَّا قَلِيلٌ ﴿٣٨﴾

38 You who believe! what is the matter with you that when you are told, 'Go out and fight in the way of Allah,' you sink down heavily to the earth? Are you happier with this world than the Next World? Yet the enjoyment of this world is very small compared to that of the Next World.

You who believe! what is the matter with you that when you are told, 'Go out and fight in the way of Allah,'

Mā is an interrogative pronoun that indicates affirmation and rebuke. It implies: 'What will keep you from that?' There is no disagreement that this was revealed to censure those who did not go with the Prophet ﷺ on the Tabūk expedition in 9 AH, a year after the Conquest of Makkah. That will be discussed at the end of the *āyah*, Allah willing.

Nafr is moving quickly from a place because of something that has happened. The verb *nafara* means to hasten to something. People are described as *nufūr*, exemplified in the words of Allah: *'They turn their backs and run away (nufūr).'* (17:46) The verb is used of an animal which shies away and the noun is *nifār*. It is used to describe those on *ḥajj* coming from Minā.

you sink down heavily to the earth?

Commentators say that the meaning of *'you sink down heavily to the earth'* is to sink down heavily to the comfort of the land or to stay in the land. It is a rebuke for abandoning *jihād* and censure for sitting down and not going out quickly. It is like *akhlada*, for inclining to the earth. The root of the word is *tathāqaltum* and the *tā'* has been incorporated into the *thā'* because they are similar and the *alif* of the connection is needed to connect to articulating it with a *sukūn*. There are other instances of this in different words in the Qur'an (7:38, 2:72, 27:47, 10:24). [POEM] Al-A'mash recited *'tathāqaltum'*, making it a basic root. Al-Mahdawī related that.

People were called on to go out to Tabūk when the midday heat was intense and when the fruit was ripe and the shade was cool, as we find in sound *ḥadīths* in al-Bukhārī and Muslim. Laziness overcame the people and they did not want to go and felt indolent and so Allah rebuked them by saying this, censuring them for preferring this world to the Next World.

Are you happier with this world than the Next World?

This means 'rather than it'. It implies: 'Are you content with the blessing of this world rather than that of the Next World?' So *min* contains the meaning of substitution, as in Allah's words: *'If We wished We could appoint angels in exchange for you to succeed you in the earth'* (43:60), meaning 'in your place'. A poet said:

Would that we had, in place of Zamzam water,
    a cool drink that had spent the night on a stand.

'Stand' (*ṭahyān*) is a stick set up in an area of the house exposed to the air on which water is hung so that it can cool. Allah censured them for preferring rest in this world to rest in the Next World since rest in the Next World is only obtained by effort expended in this world. The Prophet ﷺ said to 'A'ishah when she did *ṭawāf* mounted, 'Your reward is according to your effort.' Al-Bukhārī transmitted it.

إِلَّا تَنفِرُوا۟ يُعَذِّبْكُمْ عَذَابًا أَلِيمًا وَيَسْتَبْدِلْ قَوْمًا
غَيْرَكُمْ وَلَا تَضُرُّوهُ شَيْـًٔا ۗ وَٱللَّهُ عَلَىٰ كُلِّ شَىْءٍ قَدِيرٌ ﴿٣٩﴾

39 If you do not go out to fight, He will punish you with a painful punishment and substitute another people in your place. You will not harm Him in any way. Allah has power over all things.

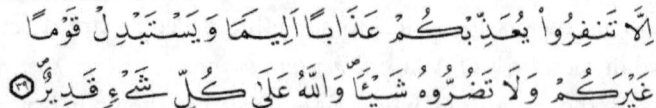

'If you do not go out to fight' is a precondition which is why the *nūn* is elided from it. The apodosis is *'He will punish you.'* This is a strong threat and definite warning about not going out. Ibn al-'Arabī said, 'It is one of the undoubted basic principles that when the command comes, nothing further is needed to promote action.' As for the punishment for not doing it, that is not taken from the command itself and not demanded by it. The punishment is when it is reported as when it is said, "If you do not do this, I will punish you in such-and-such a manner." That is what comes in this *āyah*.' Accordingly, it is mandatory to go out to *jihād* and go out against the unbelievers to fight them in order that the Word of Allah may be uppermost.

Abū Dāwūd reported that Ibn 'Abbās said that this and the following *āyah*s up to 9:120 were abrogated by the *āyah* after it: *'It is not necessary for the believers to go out all together.'* (9:122) That is the view of aḍ-Ḍaḥḥāk, al-Ḥasan and 'Ikrimah. Regarding the words *'He will punish you'*, Ibn 'Abbās said that the punishment is withholding rain. Ibn al-'Arabī said, 'If that is sound, he knows better than the One Who said it. The painful punishment in this world is by being overcome by the enemy and it is by the Fire in the Next World.' What Ibn 'Abbās said is transmitted by Abū Dāwūd in the *Sunan* from Ibn Nufay'. He said, 'I asked Ibn 'Abbās about this *āyah*: *"If you do not go out to fight, He will punish you,"* and he said, "He will withhold rain from you. That is your punishment."' Imām Abū Muḥammad ibn 'Aṭiyyah mentioned it *marfū'* from Ibn 'Abbās. He said, 'The Messenger of Allah ﷺ asked one of the tribes to come out to fight and they stayed behind, so Allah kept the water from them and punished them by it.' *Alīm* (painful) means causing pain. It was already mentioned (2:103).

'He will substitute another people in your place' is a threat that He will give His Messenger to another people who do not stay behind when asked to fight. It is said that it is the people of Persia and it is also said that it is the people of Yemen.

You will not harm Him in any way.

This is added to what is before it. The *hā'* (him) is said to refer to Allah and it is also said to refer to the Prophet ﷺ. Sinking down heavily in respect of going out on *jihād*, while showing dislike for it, is forbidden for everyone. If there is no dislike but it is something that the Prophet ﷺ has mentioned specifically, it is forbidden for him to sink heavily. If there is security from both of those things, then it is a *farḍ kifāyah*. Al-Qushayrī mentioned it.

It is said that what is meant by this *āyah* is the obligation to go out when there is need, when the unbelievers appear and when their force is great. The literal meaning of the *āyah* indicates that that happens by way of summoning. According to this, it should not be taken to mean the time of the actual appearance of the idolaters. That obligation is not specific to being summoned because it is an individual duty. When that is confirmed, then summoning and asking for forgiveness are unlikely to make anything obligatory that was not obligatory before. However, when the ruler specifies certain people and he calls them to *jihād*, they are not permitted to sink down heavily when they have specifically been called. Specification makes it an obligation for the one specified, not by virtue of it being *jihād*, but in order to obey the ruler. Allah knows best.

إِلَّا تَنصُرُوهُ فَقَدْ نَصَرَهُ ٱللَّهُ إِذْ أَخْرَجَهُ ٱلَّذِينَ كَفَرُوا۟
ثَانِىَ ٱثْنَيْنِ إِذْ هُمَا فِى ٱلْغَارِ إِذْ يَقُولُ لِصَٰحِبِهِۦ لَا تَحْزَنْ إِنَّ
ٱللَّهَ مَعَنَا ۖ فَأَنزَلَ ٱللَّهُ سَكِينَتَهُۥ عَلَيْهِ وَأَيَّدَهُۥ بِجُنُودٍ
لَّمْ تَرَوْهَا وَجَعَلَ كَلِمَةَ ٱلَّذِينَ كَفَرُوا۟ ٱلسُّفْلَىٰ ۗ وَكَلِمَةُ
ٱللَّهِ هِىَ ٱلْعُلْيَا ۗ وَٱللَّهُ عَزِيزٌ حَكِيمٌ ﴿٤٠﴾

40 If you do not help him, Allah did help him when the unbelievers drove him out and there were two of them in the Cave. He said to his companion, 'Do not be despondent, Allah is with us.' Then Allah sent down His serenity upon him and reinforced him with troops you could not see. He made the word of the unbelievers undermost. It is the word of Allah that is uppermost. Allah is Almighty, All-Wise.

If you do not help him, Allah did help him

In other words, if you do not help him by going out in the Tabūk expedition. Allah censured them after His Prophet ﷺ returned from Tabūk. An-Naqqās said, 'This was the first *āyah* of *at-Tawbah* that was revealed.' It means: if you failed to help him, Allah is responsible for him since Allah helped him in situations where the numbers were less and gave him victory over his enemy by conquest and might.

It is said that Allah helped him with his companion in the cave by that companion heartening him and supporting him, and through his fidelity to him and protection of him by means of his person and his wealth. Al-Layth ibn Sa'd said, 'None of the Prophets had a companion like Abū Bakr.' Sufyān ibn 'Uyaynah said, 'By this *āyah* Abū Bakr is removed from the criticism inherent in Allah's words: *"If you do not help him."*'

when the unbelievers drove him out,

He had to flee, but it was because they compelled him to do that, and the action was attributed to them and judgment regarding it was against them. That is why the one who forces someone else to kill is also killed and is liable for the property destroyed by compulsion since the killer and the one who destroyed were forced to do it.

and there were two of them

'There were two of them' is literally 'the second of two', and that is a form used in Arabic for numbers, like the third of three and the fourth of four. The phrase can differ and so one can say, 'the third of four' and 'the fourth of five' which means that he made three into four and four into five. It is in the accusative for the adverbial *ḥāl*. It means: they drove him out alone from all people except Abū Bakr. The regent in it is *'Allah did help him'*, i.e. He helped him alone and helped him with one of the two. 'Alī ibn Sulaymān said that it implies: 'He went, being the second of two' which is the same Arabic usage as in Allah's words: *'Allah caused you to grow from the earth.'* (71:17)[5]

The majority of people recited *'thāniyya'* with a *fatḥah* on the *yā'*. Abū Ḥātim said, 'Only this is known.' Another group recited *thānī* with a *sukūn* on the *yā'*. Ibn Jinnī said, 'Abū 'Amr ibn al-'Alā' related it, and the point is that the *yā'* has a *sukūn* because it is like *alif*.' Ibn 'Aṭiyyah said, 'It is like the reading of al-Ḥasan: "*mā baqī mina-r-ribā*".' The same usage in found in a verse by Jarīr. [POEM]

in the Cave

A cave is a hole in a mountainside, and here refers to the cave of Thawr. When Quraysh saw that the Muslims had gone to Madīnah, they said, 'This is an evil, a matter of serious concern which cannot be tolerated.' They agreed to kill the Messenger of Allah ﷺ and spent the night lying in ambush at the door of his house throughout the night to kill him when he came out. The Prophet ﷺ instructed 'Alī ibn Abī Ṭālib to sleep in his bed and prayed to Allah to hide his tracks from them. Allah covered their eyes. The Prophet ﷺ went out and they had fallen asleep. He put dust on their heads and left. In the morning, 'Alī came out to them and told them that there was no one in the house. They knew that the Messenger of Allah ﷺ had escaped.

5 This reflects the repetition of the verb in the Arabic. Here *'nabātan'* is the verbal noun of *anbata* (make grow).

The Messenger of Allah ﷺ had arranged to emigrate with Abū Bakr aṣ-Ṣiddīq and sent their camels to 'Abdullāh ibn Arqaṭ or Urayqiṭ. He was an unbeliever, but they trusted him. He was a guide and so they hired him to guide to them Madīnah. The Messenger of Allah ﷺ went out through a window in the back of the house of Abū Bakr which was among the Banū Jumaḥ. They went up to the cave in Mount Thawr. Abū Bakr ordered his son 'Abdullāh to listen out for what Quraysh were saying and instructed his client, 'Āmir ibn Fuhayrah, to herd his sheep and bring them to them in the evening so that they could take what they needed from them. Then they went up and entered the cave. 'Āmir ibn Fuhayrah followed them with the sheep to wipe out their tracks. Asma', the daughter of Abū Bakr aṣ-Ṣiddīq, used to bring them food and 'Abdullāh ibn Abī Bakr used to bring them news.

When Quraysh realised that he was missing, they began to search for him with a tracker known for following tracks until he stood at the cave and said, 'The tracks end here.' They looked and a spider had spun a web over the mouth of the cave. This is why the Prophet ﷺ forbade killing it. When they saw the spider-web, they were certain that there was no one there and so they went back. They offered a hundred she-camels to the person who returned the Prophet ﷺ to them. The report is well known and the story of Surāqah ibn Mālik ibn Ju'sham was mentioned. It is related from Abū ad-Dardā' and Thawbān that Allah commanded a dove to stay above the spider-web and it sat on its eggs. When the unbelievers saw it, they turned away from the cave.

Al-Bukhārī related that 'Ā'ishah said, 'The Messenger of Allah ﷺ and Abū Bakr hired a man from the Banū ad-Dīl as a skilled guide. He was following the religion of the unbelievers of Quraysh. They gave him their camels and arranged to meet him at the cave of Thawr after three nights. He brought their camels on the morning of the third day and they set out and 'Āmir ibn Fuhayrah and the Dīlī man guided travelled with them. The guide took them by the coastal route. Al-Muhallab said, 'It incorporates the *fiqh* of entrusting the people of *shirk* with secrets and property when it is known that they are trustworthy and possess integrity as the Prophet ﷺ trusted this idolater with his secret in leaving Makkah and with the two camels.' Ibn al-Mundhir said, 'It encompasses the fact that the Muslims can hire idolaters as guides.'

Al-Bukhārī has 'Chapter on hiring idolaters in a time of need or when the people of Islam are not available.' Ibn Baṭṭāl said that al-Bukhārī explains it as being 'when the people of Islam are not available'. For instance, the Prophet ﷺ hired the people of Khaybar to work on its land since there were no Muslims to undertake work on the land until Islam became strong and there was no need of them: then 'Umar expelled them. Most scholars permit hiring them in necessity and at other times.

It also shows that two men can hire one man for one job for both of them. It also provides proof that it is permitted in the *dīn* to flee out of fear of the enemy and to hide in caves and the like, unless a man surrenders to the enemy trusting in Allah and submitting to him. If your Lord wished, He could have protected him while he was among them. But that is the *sunna* of Allah with the Prophets and others. You will not find any change to the *sunna* of Allah. This is the clearest evidence of the falsity of the one who forbids that and said, 'If someone fears other than Allah, that is a shortcoming in his trust in Allah and he does not believe in the Decree.' All of this is found in the meaning of the *āyah*. Praise belongs to Allah and He is the Guide.

He said to his companion, 'Do not be despondent. Allah is with us.'

This *āyah* contains some of the virtues of Abū Bakr aṣ-Ṣiddīq. Aṣbagh and Abū Zayd related from Ibn al-Qāsim from Mālik that the companion here is the Ṣiddīq. Allah fulfilled what he said to him in His speech and described him as a Companion in His Book. Some scholars said, 'Those who deny that 'Umar, 'Uthmān, or any of the Companions was not a Companion of the Messenger of Allah ﷺ is an innovating liar. Anyone, however, who denies that Abū Bakr was the Companion of the Messenger of Allah ﷺ is an unbeliever because of the text of the Qur'an.'

Allah is with us

'Allah is with us' through His help, preservation, protection and safe-keeping. At-Tirmidhī and al-Ḥārith ibn Abī Usāmah related from Anas that Abū Bakr told him, 'I said to the Prophet ﷺ while we were in the cave, "If one of them were to look at his feet, he would see us under his feet." He said, "Abū Bakr, what do you think of two when Allah is their third?"' Al-Muḥāsibī said, 'Allah means that He is with them by means of help and defence, not with the meaning of what is common to people as when He says: *"Three men cannot confer together secretly without Him being the fourth of them,"* (58:7) whose general meaning is that He hears and sees the unbelievers and believers.'

Ibn al-'Arabī said, 'The Imāmī Shī'ah – may Allah make them ugly! – say that the sorrow of Abū Bakr in the cave indicates his ignorance and deficiency, the weakness of his heart and his foolishness. Our scholars answer that by saying that ascribing sorrow to him is not a deficiency, just as it is not said that Ibrāhīm was deficient when it is said about him: *'He suspected them and felt afraid of them. They said, "Have no fear!"'* (11:70) Mūsā was not deficient when it is said: *'Mūsā experienced in himself a feeling of alarm. We said, "Have no fear."'* (20:67-68) It is said about Lūṭ: *'Do not fear and do not grieve. We are going to rescue you and your family.'* (29:33) According to the text, those great men experienced fear but that did not detract from them or describe them as being deficient in any way. The same is true of Abū Bakr. Then the Ṣiddīq had fortitude. He said, 'If one of them were to look at his feet, he would see us under his feet.' The second answer is that the sorrow of the Ṣiddīq was fear that some harm might touch the Prophet ﷺ and that the Prophet ﷺ was not protected at that moment. The words: *'Allah will protect you from people'* (5:67) were revealed in Madīnah.

Ibn al-'Arabī said, 'Abū al-Faḍā'il said to us, quoting from the Shaykh al-Islam, Abu-l-Qāsim [al-Qushayrī]: 'Mūsā said: *"Never! My Lord is with me and He will guide me,"* (26:62) and Allah says about Muḥammad ﷺ [and his companion]: *"Do not be despondent. Allah is with us."* There is no doubt that when Mūsā was alone with his Lord, his companions reverted while he was away, and when he returned from his Lord, he found them worshipping the Calf. When He says in reference to Muhammad: *"Do not be despondent. Allah is with us,"* Abū Bakr remained a guided unifier with resolve and knowledge, acting correctly without leaving anything out.'

At-Tirmidhī transmitted from Nubayṭ ibn Shurayṭ that Sālim ibn 'Ubayd, who was a Companion, said, 'The Messenger of Allah ﷺ fainted…' It says in it: 'The *Muhājirūn* gathered to consult one another and said, "Let us go to our brothers of the *Anṣār* so that we can bring them into this business with us." The *Anṣār* said, "A ruler from us and a ruler from you." 'Umar said, "Who possesses the like of these three: '*There were two of them in the Cave. He said to his companion, "Do not be despondent, Allah is with us."'* Who were the two of them?" Then he stretched out his hand and gave allegiance to him and the people did so as well.'

This is why some scholars say that *'There were two of them in the Cave'* indicates that the successor after the Prophet ﷺ was Abū Bakr aṣ-Ṣiddīq because the caliph is always the second. I heard our shaykh, Abū al-'Abbās Ahmad ibn 'Umar say, 'The Ṣiddīq deserves to be called "*the second of two*" since he established the matter after the Prophet ﷺ as the Prophet ﷺ first established it. That was because when the Prophet ﷺ died, all the Arabs apostasised and Islam remained in Madīnah, Makkah and Juwāthā alone. Abū Bakr rose to call the people to Islam and fought them to make them enter the *dīn* as the Prophet ﷺ had done. This is the one who deserves to be called the "*second of two.*"'

Sound *ḥadīth*s have come in the Sunnah whose apparent meaning indicates that he is the caliph after him ﷺ and there is a consensus on that and no one disagrees about it. The one who detracts from his caliphate is cut off by his error and deviance. There is disagreement about whether such a person is an unbeliever and the most apparent position is that he is an unbeliever. This will be further discussed in *Sūrat al-Fatḥ*, Allah willing. He is cut off by the Book and Sunnah and the statements of the scholars of the Community. It is obligatory for hearts to believe in the excellence of the Ṣiddīq over all the Companions. One does not pay any attention to the statements of the Shī'ah or people of innovation. They are either deniers whose heads should be struck off or deviant innovators whose word is not accepted.

After the Ṣiddīq came the Fārūq and after him 'Uthmān. Al-Bukhārī related that Ibn 'Umar said, "We used to compare people in the time of the Messenger of Allah ﷺ and the best was Abū Bakr, then 'Umar and then 'Uthmān." The *imāms* of the early generations disagreed about 'Uthmān and 'Alī and most of them put 'Uthmān first. It is related that Mālik hesitated about that, but it is also related from him that he took the position of the majority. That is sounder, Allah willing.

Then Allah sent down His serenity upon him.

There are two positions about this. One is that it refers to the Prophet ﷺ. The second is that it refers to Abū Bakr. Ibn al-'Arabī said, 'Our scholars say that that is the stronger position, because he feared harm coming to the Prophet ﷺ from other people. So Allah sent down His Serenity on him to reassure him that the Prophet ﷺ would be safe. So his anxiety was calmed, his fear left and he felt secure. Allah made some grass grow, inspired a dove to build a nest there and sent the spider to spin its web. How weak this army was outwardly yet how strong in the inward meaning! This is why the Prophet ﷺ said to 'Umar when he quarrelled with the Ṣiddīq, "Will you leave me my companion? Everyone said, 'You lied' while Abū Bakr said, 'You spoke the truth.'"' Abū ad-Dardā' related it.

and reinforced him with troops

Allah reinforced him with troops of angels. The pronoun in '*reinforced him*' refers to the Prophet ﷺ. So the two pronouns refer to different people. This occurs often in the Qur'an and in Arabic in general.

He made the word of the unbelievers undermost. It is the word of Allah which is uppermost.

Their '*word*' is *shirk*. '*The word of Allah*' is said to be 'There is no god but Allah' and it is said to be the promise of help. Al-A'mash and Ya'qūb recited the second '*kalimata*' in the accusative by 'made" while the rest recite it as '*kalimatu*' as a new sentence. Al-Farrā' claimed that the accusative reading is unlikely. Abū Ḥātim said something similar. An-Naḥḥās said, 'That which al-Farrā' mentioned does not resemble the *āyah*, but resembles what Sībawayh quoted:

I do not see anything outstripping death. Nothing outstrips death.
Death chokes both rich and poor.

This is good and excellent without any ambiguity. Indeed, expert grammarians say that there is a point in repeating the mention in similar instances, which is that it conveys great emphasis. Allah says: '*When the earth is convulsed with its shaking and the earth then disgorges its charges.*' (99:1-2) There is no ambiguity in this.

The plural of *kalimah* is *kalim*. Tamīm say that it is *kilmah*. Al-Farrā' related three dialectical possibilities in it: *kalimah*, *kilmah* and *kalmah*, like *kabid*, *kibd* and *kabd*, and *wariq*, *wirq* and *warq*. A '*kalimah*' is also a full ode as al-Jawharī said.

انفِرُوا۟ خِفَافًا وَثِقَالًا وَجَٰهِدُوا۟ بِأَمْوَٰلِكُمْ وَأَنفُسِكُمْ فِى سَبِيلِ
ٱللَّهِ ۚ ذَٰلِكُمْ خَيْرٌ لَّكُمْ إِن كُنتُمْ تَعْلَمُونَ ﴿٤١﴾

41 Go out to fight, whatever your circumstances or desires, and do *jihād* with your wealth and yourselves in the Way of Allah. That is better for you if you only knew.

Sufyān related from Ḥuṣayn ibn 'Abd ar-Raḥmān that Abū Mālik al-Ghifārī said, 'The first *āyah* of *Sūrat Barā'ah* to be revealed was '*Go out to fightt, whatever your circumstances or desires…*' Abū aḍ-Ḍaḥḥāk said the same and then said, 'Then later the first and last of it was revealed.'

Go out to fight, whatever your circumstances or desires,

The literal meaning of '*whatever your circumstances*' is 'light and heavy'. '*Khifāfan wa thaqālan*' is in the accusative for the adverbial *ḥāl*. There are ten statements about it. The first is mentioned from Ibn 'Abbās: '*Go out to fight in separate groups*' (4:71) means on different expeditions. The second is also related from Ibn 'Abbās and Qatādah that it means whether or not you have the energy for it. The third is that 'light' means wealthy and 'heavy' means poor. Mujāhid said that. The fourth is that 'light' means young and 'heavy' means old. Al-Ḥasan said that. The fifth is that it refers to being busy and not busy. Zayd ibn 'Alī and al-Ḥakam ibn 'Utbah said that. The sixth is that 'heavy' refers to someone with dependents and 'light' to someone without dependents. Zayd ibn Aslam said that. The seventh is that 'heavy' means someone with a property he does not want to leave and 'light' means someone without such a property. Ibn Zayd said that. The eighth is that the 'light' are foot soldiers and the 'heavy' cavalry. Al-Awzā'ī said that. The ninth is that the 'light' are those who go out first as the vanguard and the 'heavy' are the main body of the army. The tenth is that the 'light' are the brave and the 'heavy' are the cowardly. An-Naqqāsh related it.

What is sound about the meaning of the *āyah* is that people are commanded as a whole: 'Go out whether doing so is difficult or easy for you.' It is related that Ibn Umm Maktūm went to the Messenger of Allah ﷺ and asked him, 'Do I have to go out?' 'Yes,' he answered, until Allah revealed: '*There is no objection to the blind.*' (26:61) These statements are examples of what is meant by heaviness and lightness.

There is disagreement about whether this *āyah* is abrogated by Allah's words: '*Nothing is held against the weak and sick...*' (9:91) It is also said that it is abrogated by His words: '*If a party from each group of them were to go out...*' (9:122) The sound position is that it is not abrogated. Ibn 'Abbās related from Abū Ṭalḥah about this is that it refers to young men and mature men. Allah does not excuse anyone. So he went to Syria and engaged in *jihād* until he died. Ḥammād ibn Thābit and 'Alī ibn Zayd related that Abū Ṭalḥah recited *Sūrat at-Tawbah* and came to this *āyah* and said, 'My sons! Get me ready! Get me ready!' His sons said, 'May Allah have mercy on you! You went on expeditions with the Prophet ﷺ until his death and then with Abū Bakr until his death, and then with 'Umar until his death. We will go on expeditions on your behalf.' He answered, 'No. Get me ready!' He went on a sea expedition and died at sea and they did not find an island on which to bury him until seven days later. They buried him and his corpse had not changed.

Aṭ-Ṭabarī reported with an *isnād* from someone who saw al-Miqdād ibn al-Aswad at Ḥomṣ at the stall of a money-changer. He was leaning on the stall because of his corpulence while preparing for an expedition. He was told, 'Allah has excused you.' He answered, 'The *Sūrah* of Expeditions came to us: "*Go out to fight, whatever your circumstances.*"' Az-Zuhrī said, 'Sa'īd ibn al-Musayyab went on an expedition after he had lost an eye. He was told, 'You are ill.' He replied, 'I ask for Allah's forgiveness. "*Whatever your circumstances.*" If I am unable to fight, I will make up the numbers and guard the baggage.' It is related that some people saw a man in the expeditions of Syria whose eyebrows drooped over his eyes due to his old age. It was said to him, 'Uncle, Allah has excused you.' He replied, 'Nephew, we were commanded to go out to fight "*whatever our circumstances.*"'

Ibn Umm Maktūm, whose name was 'Amr, said during the Battle of Uḥud, 'I am a blind man. Give me the banner. When the banner-bearer retreats, the army retreats. I will not know if someone is coming at me with a sword, so I will remain where I am.' Muṣ'ab ibn 'Umayr took the banner on that day as was already mentioned in *Āl 'Imrān*. This and similar stories are related from the Companions and *Tābi'ūn*. We said that it is not correct to say it has been abrogated.

There may be situations that actually require everyone to go out. Such a case – when *jihād* becomes an individual duty for every Muslim – is when the enemy occupies a region or alights in one's land. Then it is obligatory for all of the people of that place to go out against them, light or heavy, young or old, each according to his ability. A father's permission is not then required and someone with no father should also go. No one who is able to go out may stay behind, whether he can fight or just make up the numbers. If the people of that land are unable to withstand their enemy, then it is incumbent on those near them and their neighbours to go out (in their support), according to the needs of the people of that land, until they know that they have the power to withstand them and repel them. The same is true of everyone who knows that some people are too weak to resist the enemy and knows that he can reach them and has the power to help them: he must go out to them. The Muslims are a single limb where fighting others is concerned, so that when the people of one region rise to resist an enemy who has come, the obligation is cancelled for the rest.

If the enemy approaches the land of Islam but has not yet entered it, it is also obligatory for people to go out to fight them so that the *dīn* of Allah may be victorious, the territory defended, the land preserved and the enemy humiliated. There is no disagreement about that.

A second category of the obligation of *jihād* is the obligation for the ruler to send out a group against the enemy once a year, either going out with them himself or sending someone he trusts to call them to Islam, encourage them, restrict their harm and make the *dīn* of Allah victorious until they enter Islam or pay *jizyah* with their own hands. There is also a supererogatory aspect of *jihād* and that is when the ruler sends out group after group and sends out expeditions at times of surprise and opportunity in order to lay in ambush for the enemy in *ribāṭs* in places where there is fear of them and in order to make a show of strength.

If it asked how can one do this when all fall short, the answer is that one should ransom a captured fighter. If someone ransoms one, he has performed for that one person more than is obliged on the community as a whole. If the wealthy were to divide up the ransom of captives, not every one of them would do it except at the least expense possible.

A person should go on a military expedition himself if he has the power to do so. Otherwise, he should equip a fighter to go. The Prophet ﷺ said, 'Anyone who equips someone else to go on an expedition has gone on it. And anyone who takes someone's place in taking proper care of his family has also gone on expedition.' This is transmitted in the *Ṣaḥīḥ*. That is because his position is not independent and his wealth may not be sufficient.

It is related that a certain king made a treaty with the unbelievers that they would not detain prisoners. One of the Muslims entered their land and passed by a locked house. A woman called out to him, 'I am a prisoner! Give news of me to your leader.' When he met with him and ate with him and they began to talk, he told him about this captive woman. He had not even finished his account before the ruler rose up and went out to attack. He went to the frontier and fought until he had the woman prisoner released and occupied the place. May Allah be pleased with him.

Ibn al-'Arabī mentioned this and said, 'The enemy – may Allah destroy them completely! – came on us in 527 and stormed our houses and imprisoned the best of us and occupied our land in such numbers that it terrified the people. They were numerous and it was not known how many of them there were. I said to the governor, who was in charge of it, "This is the enemy of Allah who has snares and traps. You should gain blessing by helping the *dīn*. It is incumbent on you to have all the people go out against the enemy so that none of the enemy remains in the entire land. You must surround the enemy. They must be destroyed if Allah makes it easy for you. Sins have become dominant and hearts are unsettled owing to their acts of disobedience; every person has become a fox seeking refuge in its own den, even if they see harm done to their neighbour. We belong to Allah and to Him We return. Allah is enough for us and the Best Guardian.'

Do *jihād* with your wealth and yourselves

This is a command to do *jihād*. The word is derived from *jahd* (effort). *'With your wealth and yourselves'*: Abū Dāwūd related from Anas that the Messenger of Allah ﷺ said, 'Strive against the idolaters with your wealth, lives and tongues.' This is the most comprehensive description of *jihād* and the most beneficial in the sight of

Allah. He ﷺ encouraged the perfection of noble qualities. He mentioned wealth first since it is the first to be used at the time of preparation. He puts the matter in the order that it usually occurs.

لَوْ كَانَ عَرَضًا قَرِيبًا وَسَفَرًا قَاصِدًا لَّاتَّبَعُوكَ وَلَٰكِن بَعُدَتْ
عَلَيْهِمُ الشُّقَّةُ وَسَيَحْلِفُونَ بِاللَّهِ لَوِ اسْتَطَعْنَا لَخَرَجْنَا مَعَكُمْ
يُهْلِكُونَ أَنفُسَهُمْ وَاللَّهُ يَعْلَمُ إِنَّهُمْ لَكَاذِبُونَ ﴿٤٢﴾

42 If it had been a case of easy gains and a short journey, they would have followed you, but the distance was too great for them. They will swear by Allah: 'Had we been able to, we would have gone out with you.' They are destroying their own selves. Allah knows that they are lying.

When the Prophet ﷺ returned from Tabūk, Allah revealed people's hypocrisy. *"Araḍ'* (*easy gains*) is what is present of the benefits of this world. The meaning is: booty which is at-hand. He is saying that had they been called to booty, they would have followed. *"Araḍ'* is the predicate of *kāna* and *qarīb* (easy) is its adjective. *'And a short journey'* was added to it and the noun is elided since the words indicate it. It implies: 'if it had been worldly goods that are at-hand and a short journey – meaning easy to obtain on a known route – they would have followed you.'

This alludes to the hypocrites because they are included in the sum total of those who are told to go out to fight. This usage exists in Arabic. They mention the sum total and then bring something implied which refers to just some of them, as is the case in Allah's words: *'There is not one of you who will not come to it'* (19:71) where '*it*' is the Day of Resurrection. He then says: *'Then We will rescue those who are godfearing and We will leave the wrongdoers in it on their knees.'* (19:72) Here '*it*' means Hellfire.

The like of this *āyah* is found in the Sunnah when the Prophet ﷺ said, 'If one of them had known that he would find a meaty bone or two good legs of lamb, he would attend *'Ishā'*.'' He also said ﷺ, 'If one of them knew that he would find something there he could take away, he would come to the mosque for it.'

but the distance was too great for them

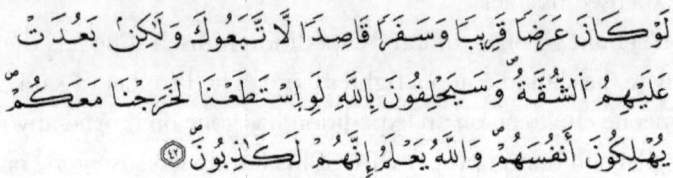

Abū 'Ubaydah and others related that the word *shuqqah* designates a journey to a distant land. What is meant by all of that is the Tabūk expedition. Al-Kisā'ī related that it can be *shuqqah* or *shiqqah*. Al-Jawharī said, '*Shuqqah* has to do with clothes (a cut piece of a garment) and it is also a distant journey. Sometimes they said *shiqqah*. *Shiqq* is a splinter of a tablet or piece of wood. One says about an angry person, "He became furious and it was as if a splinter (*shiqq*) flew from him."'

'Had we been able to' means 'If we had the necessary mounts and wealth.' *'We would have gone out with you'* is like *'Ḥajj to the House is a duty owed to Allah by all mankind – those who find a way (are able) to do it.'* (3:97) The Prophet ﷺ explained it and said that that refers to provision and a ride. *'They are destroying their own selves'* by lying and hypocrisy. *'Allah knows they are lying'* in their excuses.

عَفَا ٱللَّهُ عَنكَ لِمَ أَذِنتَ لَهُمْ حَتَّىٰ يَتَبَيَّنَ لَكَ ٱلَّذِينَ صَدَقُوا۟ وَتَعْلَمَ
ٱلْكَٰذِبِينَ ﴿٤٣﴾

43 Allah pardon you! Why did you excuse them until it was clear to you which of them were telling the truth and until you knew the liars?

Allah pardon you!

This is something said at the beginning of words, as you might say, 'May Allah put you right!' or 'May Allah exalt you!' or 'May Allah have mercy on you!' According to this interpretation, it is good to stop after 'Allah pardon you!' Makkī, al-Mahdawī and an-Naḥḥās related that. Allah spoke to him ﷺ about pardon before the wrong action so that his heart would not be overcome by fear. It is said that it means: 'May Allah pardon you for your sin in excusing them,' and so it is not good to stop at His words: *'Allah pardon you!'* This is what is applied and al-Mahdawī related it and an-Naḥḥās chose it.

Why did you excuse them

Two things are said about this excusing. The first is *'Why did you excuse them'*, allowing them to go out with you when their going out without preparation or true intention is without merit? The second is that it is about excusing them for staying behind when they offered their excuses. Al-Qushayrī mentioned it and said, 'This is a gentle rebuke since Allah says,: "*Allah pardon you!*" The Prophet ﷺ had excused them without any revelation about the matter.' Qatādah and 'Amr ibn Maymūn said, 'The Prophet ﷺ did two things without being commanded to do them. He gave permission to a group of hypocrites to stay behind, when normally he did not do things without receiving revelation. He also accepted ransom for the captives [of Badr]. So Allah censured him as you hear.' Some scholars said that the normal manner of expression is not adhered to: Allah put pardon first before addressing him in a manner which is in the form of rebuke.

until it was clear to you which of them were telling the truth and until you knew the liars.

It means: 'until it was clear to you who was telling the truth and who were the hypocrites.' Ibn 'Abbās said, 'That was because until that day the Messenger of Allah ﷺ did not recognise the hypocrites; he recognised them by the revelation of *Sūrat at-Tawbah*.' Mujāhid said, 'Those are people who said, "We will ask him for permission to stay. If he gives us permission, we will stay, and if he does not give us permission, we will still stay."' Qatādah said that this *āyah* was abrogated by what Allah says in *Sūrat an-Nūr*: *'If they ask your permission to attend to their own affairs, give permission to any of them you please.'* (24:62) An-Naḥḥās mentioned it in *Ma'ānī al-Qur'an*.

لَا يَسْتَـْٔذِنُكَ ٱلَّذِينَ يُؤْمِنُونَ بِٱللَّهِ وَٱلْيَوْمِ ٱلْءَاخِرِ أَن يُجَٰهِدُوا۟ بِأَمْوَٰلِهِمْ
وَأَنفُسِهِمْ ۗ وَٱللَّهُ عَلِيمٌۢ بِٱلْمُتَّقِينَ ﴿٤٤﴾ إِنَّمَا يَسْتَـْٔذِنُكَ ٱلَّذِينَ لَا
يُؤْمِنُونَ بِٱللَّهِ وَٱلْيَوْمِ ٱلْءَاخِرِ وَٱرْتَابَتْ قُلُوبُهُمْ فَهُمْ فِى رَيْبِهِمْ
يَتَرَدَّدُونَ ﴿٤٥﴾

44-45 Those who believe in Allah and the Last Day do not ask you to excuse them from doing *jihād* with their wealth and themselves. Allah knows the people who are godfearing. Only those who do not believe in Allah and the Last Day ask you to excuse them. Their hearts are full of doubt and in their doubt they waver to and fro.

'Those who believe in Allah and the Last Day do not ask you to excuse them,' they do not request you to allow them to stay behind and not go out. On the contrary, when you command something to be done, they hurry [to carry it out]. Therefore asking for permission at that moment, without a valid excuse for doing so, is one of the signs of hypocrisy. That is why Allah says that. Abū Dāwūd related that Ibn 'Abbās said that this is abrogated by 24:62.

The phrase *'from doing jihād'* is in the accusative by an implied elision, as az-Zajjāj said. It is said that it implies: 'out of dislike for doing *jihād*' as in Allah's words: *'Allah makes them clear to you so that you will not go astray.'* (4:186)

'Their hearts are full of doubt' about the *dīn*. *'In their doubt they waver to and fro'* means: they come and go in their doubt.

وَلَوْ أَرَادُوا۟ ٱلْخُرُوجَ لَأَعَدُّوا۟ لَهُۥ عُدَّةً وَلَٰكِن كَرِهَ ٱللَّهُ
ٱنۢبِعَاثَهُمْ فَثَبَّطَهُمْ وَقِيلَ ٱقْعُدُوا۟ مَعَ ٱلْقَٰعِدِينَ ﴿٤٦﴾

46 If they had really desired to go out, they would have made proper preparations for it, but Allah was averse to their setting out so He held them back and they were told: 'Stay behind with those who stay behind.'

If they had really desired to go out, they would have made proper preparations for it,

If they had truly desired to do *jihād*, they would have made the necessary preparations to travel, and the fact that they did not make any preparations is proof of their desire to stay behind. *'Allah was averse to their setting out'* with you, *'so He held them back'* from you and disappointed them because they said, 'If he does not give us permission to stay behind, we will cause corruption and encourage people against the believers.' This is indicated by what comes after it: *'If they had gone out among you, they would have added nothing to you but confusion.'*

'They were told: "Stay behind with those who stay behind."' It is said that they said this to one another. It is said that the Prophet ﷺ said it. This is referring to the permission they were given which was already mentioned. It is said that the Prophet ﷺ said that in anger. They took his words literally and said, 'He has excused us.' It is said that it is an expression of disapprobation, implying that Allah cast it into their hearts to stay behind. The people meant by '*those who stay behind*' are those with an impairment, the chronically ill, old, women and children.

لَوْ خَرَجُوا۟ فِيكُم مَّا زَادُوكُمْ إِلَّا خَبَالًا وَلَأَوْضَعُوا۟ خِلَٰلَكُمْ يَبْغُونَكُمُ ٱلْفِتْنَةَ وَفِيكُمْ سَمَّٰعُونَ لَهُمْ ۗ وَٱللَّهُ عَلِيمٌۢ بِٱلظَّٰلِمِينَ ﴿٤٧﴾

47 If they had gone out among you, they would have added nothing to you but confusion. They would have scurried about amongst you seeking to cause conflict between you, and among you there are some who would have listened to them. Allah knows the wrongdoers.

If they had gone out among you,

This is solace for the believers in the face of the hypocrites staying behind. The word *khabāl* covers corruption, backbiting, causing dissension and spreading false rumours. This is a separated exception. It means: they would not have increased you in strength but only have sought to create confusion. That is why the exception is separate.

they would have added nothing to you but confusion.

This means: they would have hastened to cause dissension between you. The verb *īḍā'* means to travel quickly. The poet says:

Would that there was a stump in it
against which I could surge and hasten to (*aḍa'*).

The verb *waḍa'a* is used for a camel when it goes fast and *awḍa'a* means to make it go fast. *Īḍā'* is travelling at a trotting pace. *Khalal* is a gap between two things and the plural is *khilāl*. It means: the gaps between the ranks. They would hurry between you with slander and trying to foster disunity.

seeking to cause conflict between you

This is a second object and means: seeking to cause corruption and encouraging it. It is said that *fitnah* here means *shirk*.

and among you there are some who would have listened to them

This means that they would have helped them and given them information about you. Qatādah said, 'Among you are those who would accept what they say and obey them.' An-Naḥḥās Said, 'The first position is more appropriate because it is the more predominant of the two meanings. *Sammā'* means listening to words, like *'who listen to lies'* (4:41). The second view is that as soon as they speak, they are heard.

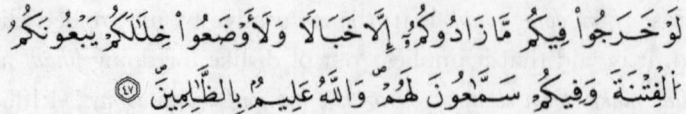

لَقَدِ ابْتَغَوُا الْفِتْنَةَ مِن قَبْلُ وَقَلَّبُوا لَكَ الْأُمُورَ حَتَّىٰ جَاءَ الْحَقُّ
وَظَهَرَ أَمْرُ اللَّهِ وَهُمْ كَارِهُونَ ﴿٤٨﴾

48 They have already tried to cause conflict before, and turned things completely upside down for you, until the truth came and Allah's command prevailed even though they detested it.

They have already tried to cause corruption and confusion before their affair was made clear and the Revelation descended with what they were concealing and what they were going to do. Ibn Jurayj said, 'Allah is referring to twelve of the hypocrites who stood at Thaniyyah al-Wadā' on the night of 'Aqabah with the intention of assassinating the Prophet ﷺ.' The words: *'turned things upside down for you'* means that they changed them, hoping to invalidate what you brought. *'Allah's command'* is His *dīn*.

وَمِنْهُم مَّن يَقُولُ ائْذَن لِّي وَلَا تَفْتِنِّي أَلَا فِي الْفِتْنَةِ سَقَطُوا وَإِنَّ
جَهَنَّمَ لَمُحِيطَةٌ بِالْكَافِرِينَ ﴿٤٩﴾ إِن تُصِبْكَ حَسَنَةٌ تَسُؤْهُمْ وَإِن
تُصِبْكَ مُصِيبَةٌ يَقُولُوا قَدْ أَخَذْنَا أَمْرَنَا مِن قَبْلُ وَيَتَوَلَّوا
وَّهُمْ فَرِحُونَ ﴿٥٠﴾

49-50 Among them there are some who say, 'Give me permission to stay. Do not put temptation in my way.' Have they not fallen into that very temptation? Hell hems in the unbelievers. If good happens to you it galls them. If a mishap occurs to you, they say, 'We made our preparations in advance,' and they turn away rejoicing.

The verb for 'give permission' is *adhina, ya'dhanu*. When it is a command, a *hamzah* with a *kasrah* is added and the *hamzah* after it is the *fā'* of the verb. Two *hamzah*s may not be joined together, thus the second is changed to the *yā'* by the *kasrah* before it and so it becomes *īdhan*. When it is connected, the reason for the combination of the two *hamzah*s is removed and then the *hamzah* is used and you say, *'wa minhum man yaqūlu'dhan'*. Warsh related from Nāfi': *'wa minhum man yaqūl-ūdhan'* and the *hamzah* is lightened.

An-Naḥḥās said that one says *'īdhan li-fulān, thumma i'dhan li-fulān.'* The manner of the first and second is the same with the *alif* and *yā'* before the *dhāl* when it is written. If you say, *'īdhan li-fulān wa udhan li-ghayrihi,'* the second does not have a *yā'*. The same is true if there is a *fā'* (so). The difference between *thumma*, *wāw* and *fā'* is that there can be a stop at *thumma* or it can be connected while there cannot be a stop at either *wāw* and *fā'* and they are not separated.

Muḥammad ibn Isḥāq said, 'The Messenger of Allah ﷺ said to al-Jadd ibn Qays, one of the Banū Salamah, when they wanted to go to Tabūk, "Jadd! Won't you attack the Greeks (Banū al-Aṣfar) and take captives and servants from them?" Al-Jadd said, "My people know that I love women and I fear that if I see the Greeks I will not be able to do without them. Do not tempt me. Give me permission to stay behind and I will help you with my wealth." The Messenger of Allah ﷺ turned from him and said, "I have given you permission."' Then this *āyah* was revealed. He meant, 'Do not tempt me by the beauty of their faces.' There is no reason for it except hypocrisy.

Al-Mahdawī said, 'Al-Aṣfar was a man from Abyssinia who had daughters who were the most beautiful women of their time. He was in the land of the Greeks.' It is said that they were called that because the Abyssinians defeated the Romans and they had daughters who had some of the whiteness of the Romans and the darkness of the Abyssinians. So they were yellowish and red-lipped. Ibn 'Aṭiyyah said that there are gaps in what Ibn Abī Isḥāq said.

Aṭ-Ṭabarī reported with an *isnād* that the Messenger of Allah ﷺ said, 'Attack and take the daughters of al-Aṣfar as booty.' Al-Jadd said to him, 'Give me permission and do not tempt me with women.' This is a different kind of behaviour from the first and more like hypocrisy and opposition. When it was revealed, the Prophet ﷺ said to the Banū Salamah, of which al-Jadd ibn Qays was one, 'Who is your master, Banū Salamah?' They answered, 'Jadd ibn Qays even though he is a cowardly hypocrite.' The Prophet ﷺ said, 'What disease is worse than miserliness? Rather your master is the white youth, Bishr ibn al-Barā' ibn Ma'rūr.' Hassān ibn Thābit al-Anṣārī said:

Bishr ibn al-Barā' is a master because of his generosity.
 It is right for Bishr ibn al-Barā' to be a master
When the delegation came to him, he got rid of his wealth
 and said, 'Take it. I will return tomorrow.'

Have they not fallen into that very temptation

This means into that sin and disobedience, which is hypocrisy and staying behind the Prophet ﷺ.

Hell hems in the unbelievers

This means that they will end up in the Fire and so it encircles them.

If good happens to you, it galls them.

It is precondition and apodosis as is the following phrase which is added to it. '*Good*' here is booty and victory, and '*mishap*' is defeat. The meaning of their words, '*We made our preparations in advance*' means: 'We protected ourselves and made a firm resolution and did not go out to fight.' '*They turn away*' from faith, thinking highly of that attitude.

قُل لَّن يُصِيبَنَآ إِلَّا مَا كَتَبَ ٱللَّهُ لَنَا هُوَ مَوْلَىٰنَا ۚ وَعَلَى ٱللَّهِ
فَلْيَتَوَكَّلِ ٱلْمُؤْمِنُونَ ﴿٥١﴾

51 Say: 'Nothing can happen to us except what Allah has ordained for us. He is Our Master. It is in Allah that the believers should put their trust.'

'*What Allah has ordained for us*' is what is in the Preserved Tablet. It is said that it is reported to us in His Book: 'Either we will be victorious and have the best or we will be killed and martyrdom is a greater good for us.' It means: 'Everything is by a decree and determination.' It was already mentioned in *al-A'rāf* (7:37) that knowledge, the Decree and the Book are the same. '*He is Our Master*' means 'Our Helper'. *Tawakkul* is entrusting the matter to Him.

The majority recite '*yuṣībanā*' and Abū 'Ubaydah related that some Arabs put it in the jussive. Ṭalḥah ibn Muṣarrif recited '*yuṣībunā*'. It is related that A'yan, the Qāḍī of Rayy, recited '*yuṣabīnna*' which is erroneous. A report in the third person may not have a double *nūn*. Had this been in the reading of Ṭalḥah, it would have been permitted. Allah says: '*Let him see whether his stratagem gets rid (yudhhibanna) of what enrages him!*' (22:15)

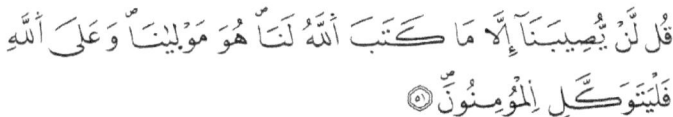

قُلْ هَلْ تَرَبَّصُونَ بِنَآ إِلَّآ إِحْدَى ٱلْحُسْنَيَيْنِ وَنَحْنُ نَتَرَبَّصُ بِكُمْ أَن يُصِيبَكُمُ ٱللَّهُ بِعَذَابٍ مِّنْ عِندِهِۦٓ أَوْ بِأَيْدِينَا فَتَرَبَّصُوٓا۟ إِنَّا مَعَكُم مُّتَرَبِّصُونَ ﴿٥٢﴾

52 Say: 'What do you await for us except for one of the two best things? But what we await for you is for Allah to inflict a punishment on you either directly from Himself or at our hands. So wait, we are waiting with you!'

'Hal tarabbaṣūna': the Kufans assimilate the *lām* into the *tā'*. In the case of the *lām* of the definite article, it must be assimilated as in *'at-ta'būn'* (9:111) and because the *lām* of the definite article is used frequently. It is not permitted to assimilate it in *'qul ta'ālū'* (6:151) because *'qul'* is a weak verb and two deficiencies are not combined. *Tarabbuṣ* means waiting. The verb is used for waiting to sell food until the time prices are high. *Ḥusnā* (best) is the feminine of *ḥasan*. The singular of *ḥusnayan'* is *'ḥusnā'* and the plural is *'ḥusan'*. It is only used with a definite article.

What is meant by *'the two best things'* is booty and martyrdom according to Ibn 'Abbās, Mujāhid and others. The expression is in the form of a question while what is meant by it is rebuke. *'A punishment on you'* is by Allah destroying you as He smote the past nations before you. *'At our hands'* is allowing us to fight you. *'Wait'* is a threat. *'We are waiting with you'* means: while you await the promises of *Shayṭān*, we are awaiting the promises of Allah.

قُلْ أَنفِقُوا۟ طَوْعًا أَوْ كَرْهًا لَّن يُتَقَبَّلَ مِنكُمْ ۖ إِنَّكُمْ كُنتُمْ قَوْمًا فَٰسِقِينَ ﴿٥٣﴾

53 Say: 'Whether you give readily or reluctantly, it will not be accepted from you. You are people who are deviators.'

Ibn 'Abbās said, 'This was revealed about al-Jadd ibn Qays when he said, "Give me permission to stay behind and here is my money to help you."' *'Give'* is a command and it means the precondition and apodosis. That is how the Arabs use it in this sort of case and *'or'* is used as in the poem:

Whether you are bad to us or good to us, there is no blame
with us and no hatred if you hate.

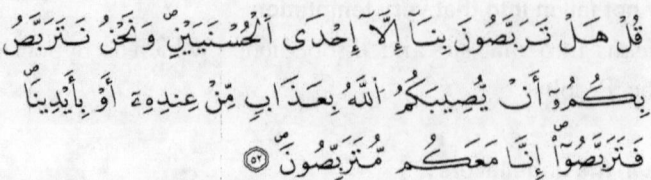

It means: 'whether you are bad or good, we remain as you know us to be.' The *āyah* means: whether you spend willingly or unwillingly, it will not be accepted from you. Then Allah makes clear those from whom it will not be accepted in the following *āyah.*

This is the greatest indication that when the actions of an unbeliever are good – such as maintaining ties with relatives or helping someone in distress – he will not be rewarded for them and they will not help him in the Next World. He is fed by them in this world. Its proof is what Muslim related from 'Ā'ishah: 'I said, "Messenger of Allah, in the Jāhiliyyah, Ibn Jud'ān used to give to relatives and feed the poor. Will that help him?" He answered, "No, that will not help him. He did not say on any day, 'Lord, forgive me my errors on the Day of Rising.'"'

It is related from Anas that the Messenger of Allah ﷺ said, 'Allah will not wrong a believer in respect of any good deed which he did: He gives to him on account of it in this world and will reward him for it in the Next World. As for an unbeliever, he enjoys in this world all the fruits of the good deeds he does altruistically so that when he goes to the Next World, he has no good deeds left for which to be rewarded.' This is a text.

Then it is asked: 'By the principle of this true promise, is it mandatory for the unbeliever to be fed and given to by his good actions in this world, or is that limited by the Will of Allah mentioned in His words: *"We hasten in it whatever We will to whomever We want."* (17:18)?' This is sound on both accounts. Allah knows best. Calling what an unbeliever does 'a good deed' is in respect of what the unbeliever thinks. An action by which he might draw near to Allah is not applicable to him since he lacks the precondition which would make it applicable, which is faith. It also may be called 'a good deed' because it outwardly resembles the good action of the believer.

If it is said that Muslim related that Ḥakīm ibn Ḥizām asked the Messenger of Allah ﷺ, 'Messenger of Allah, do you think that I will have a reward for the acts of devotion of *ṣadaqah*, emancipation, and gifts to relatives that I performed in the Jāhiliyyah?" and the Messenger of Allah ﷺ said, 'You became Muslim with your prior good,' we say that the literal meaning of the words 'You became Muslim with your prior good' differ from the basic principles because, in the case of an unbeliever, drawing near to Allah, thus being rewarded for his obedience, is not applicable, since knowledge that he is drawing near to Allah by what he does is a precondition for that occurring. If the precondition is lacking, the result is negated. Therefore the *ḥadīth* means: 'You gained good character in the Jāhiliyyah which brought you to good behaviour in Islam.' That is because Ḥakīm lived to the age of a hundred and twenty: sixty in Islam and sixty in the Jāhiliyyah. In the Jāhiliyyah he freed a hundred slaves and gave a hundred camels for people to ride. That is also what he did in Islam. This is clear.

It is said that it is not unlikely that Allah, by His generosity, rewarded him with Islam for that as He cancelled for him the sins he committed while an unbeliever. He does not reward the one who does not become Muslim nor turn to him and dies as an unbeliever. This is the apparent meaning of the *ḥadīth*, and it is sound, Allah willing. The absence of the precondition of faith is not about the absence of reward for the good he does, and when he becomes Muslim and dies Muslim the precondition is not changed. Allah is too generous to waste his actions when he is a good Muslim. Al-Ḥarbī interpreted the *ḥadīth* in this way and said that it means: 'You became Muslim with your prior good deeds, as you say, "I became Muslim with a thousand dirhams," i.e. with what he stored up for himself.' Allah knows best.

Someone may observe that Muslim related that al-'Abbās said, 'I said, "Messenger of Allah, Abū Ṭālib protected and helped you, will that help him?' He said, 'Yes, I found him in the depths of the Fire and I brought him to the shallow part."' The person who said that is told, 'It is not unlikely that some of the punishment may be lightened for an unbeliever because of the good he did, but only with the addition of intercession, as has come about Abū Ṭālib. As for others, the Revelation says: *"The intercession of interceders will not help them"* (74:48) and Allah reports about the unbelievers that they will say: *"And now we have no one to intercede for us; we do not have a single loyal friend."* (26:100-101)' Muslim related from Abū Sa'īd al-Khudrī that the uncle of the Messenger of Allah ﷺ, Abū Ṭālib, was mentioned in his presence and he said, 'Perhaps my intercession will help him on the Day of Rising and He will be put in the shallows of the Fire which reach his ankles by which his brains boil.' We find in the *ḥadīth* of al-'Abbās: 'Were it not for me, he would be in the lowest level of the Fire.' The '*deviators*' here are the unbelievers.

وَمَا مَنَعَهُمْ أَن تُقْبَلَ مِنْهُمْ نَفَقَٰتُهُمْ إِلَّآ أَنَّهُمْ كَفَرُوا۟ بِٱللَّهِ
وَبِرَسُولِهِۦ وَلَا يَأْتُونَ ٱلصَّلَوٰةَ إِلَّا وَهُمْ كُسَالَىٰ وَلَا يُنفِقُونَ إِلَّا
وَهُمْ كَٰرِهُونَ ٥٤

54 Nothing prevents what they give from being accepted from them but the fact that they have rejected Allah and His Messenger, and that they only come to the prayer lethargically, and that they only give reluctantly.

Nothing prevents what they give from being accepted from them but the fact that they have rejected Allah and His Messenger,

The first *an* is in the accusative and the second is nominative. It means: 'What prevents their charity being accepted other than their disbelief?' The Kufans recite '*yuqbalu*' because *nafaqāt* and *infāq* (spending) mean the same.

and that they only come to the prayer lethargically,

Ibn 'Abbās said about their '*lethargy*' in the prayer that it means that when they are in a group, they pray, but when they are alone, they do not. Such people neither hope for a reward for their prayer nor do they fear a punishment for abandoning it. Hypocrisy inevitably results in laziness in worship. This was all discussed in *an-Nisā'* (4:142) where we mentioned the *ḥadīth* of al-'Alā'.

and that they only give reluctantly.

This is because they consider it to be a fine and their refusal to pay to be a blessing for them. When that is the case, it is not accepted from them and there is no reward for it.

فَلَا تُعْجِبْكَ أَمْوَٰلُهُمْ وَلَآ أَوْلَٰدُهُمْ ۚ إِنَّمَا يُرِيدُ ٱللَّهُ لِيُعَذِّبَهُم بِهَا فِى ٱلْحَيَوٰةِ
ٱلدُّنْيَا وَتَزْهَقَ أَنفُسُهُمْ وَهُمْ كَٰفِرُونَ ﴿٥٥﴾ وَيَحْلِفُونَ بِٱللَّهِ إِنَّهُمْ لَمِنكُمْ
وَمَا هُم مِّنكُمْ وَلَٰكِنَّهُمْ قَوْمٌ يَفْرَقُونَ ﴿٥٦﴾

55-56 Do not let their wealth and children impress you. Allah merely wants to punish them by them during their life in this world and for them to expire while they are unbelievers. They swear by Allah that they are of your number, but they are not of your number. Rather, they are people who are scared.

Do not think that what they have given you is good and do not incline towards it. It just draws them on. In respect of the words: '*Allah merely wants to punish them by them,*' al-Ḥasan said that they mean their payment of *zakāt* and spending in the Way of Allah. This was preferred by aṭ-Ṭabarī. Ibn 'Abbās and Qatādah said that there is a change of order in the words and they mean: 'Do not admire their wealth and children *in the life of this world. Allah merely wants to punish them by them* in the Next World.' This is the position of most of the scholars of Arabic. An-Naḥḥās mentioned it. Allah punishes them by making them fatigued by everything they do. According to the first position and what al-Ḥasan said, there is change in the normal order. That is good. It is also said that the meaning is: 'Do not admire their wealth and children. Allah desires to punish them by them in this world because they are hypocrites, so they spend unwillingly and are punished by what they spend.'

The words: *'for them to expire while they are unbelievers'* constitute a text stating that Allah wants them to die while they are unbelievers as He already decreed, and by the words: *'They swear by Allah that they are of your number'* Allah makes it clear that one of the qualities of the hypocrites is that they swear falsely that they are believers. *Faraq* is fear, which means that they are afraid that they will be exposed and killed.

لَوْ يَجِدُونَ مَلْجَـًٔا أَوْ مَغَـٰرَٰتٍ أَوْ مُدَّخَلًا لَّوَلَّوْا۟ إِلَيْهِ وَهُمْ يَجْمَحُونَ ﴿٥٧﴾

57 If they could find a bolt-hole, cave or burrow, they would turn and scurry away into it.

If they could find a bolt-hole,

That is how it is. When written with two *alifs maljaʾan* (bolt-hole), the first is for the *hamzah* and the second replaces the *tanwīn*. *Maljaʾ* (bolt-hole) is a fortress. Qatādah and others said that. Ibn 'Abbās said that it is a fortified place. The verb is *lajaʾa*. The place is called both *lajaʾ* and *maljaʾ*. *Taljiʾah* is forcing. *Aljaʾa* is to commit one's affairs to something. It is also to commit one's affair to Allah, relying on Him. Al-Jawharī said that 'Amr ibn Lajaʾ at-Taymī is a poet.

cave or burrow,

Maghārāt (caves) is the plural of *maghārah* from the verb *ghāra*. Al-Akhfash said that it is possible that it is from Form IV, *aghāra, yughīru* as the poet said:

Praise be to Allah in our evening (*mumsānā*) and morning (*muṣbaḥanā*).

Ibn al-'Abbās said that caves are caverns and vaults, which are places in which one hides. *Ghāra* is also used for water seeping away or a spring drying up. *Muddakhal* is form *mufta'al* from entering (*dukhūl*). It is a path by which one seeks to hide by entering in on it. The repetition is because of the use of different words. An-Naḥḥās said that the root in it is *mudtakhal* and the *tāʾ* has become a *dāl*. It is also said that the root is *mutadakhkhal* from Form V as in the reading of Ubayy. It means: entering after entering, i.e. people enter with them. Al-Mahdawī said, 'It is *mutakhkhal* from Form V when someone seeks to enter. Ubayy also has *mundakhal* from Form IX. It is aberrant because, according to Sībawayh and his people, the tripartite form is not transitive. Al-Ḥasan, Ibn Abī Isḥāq, and Ibn Muḥayṣin recite '*madkhal*'. Az-Zajjāj said that it is recited as '*mudkhal*'. The first is from Form I and the second from Form IV. That is like *maṣdar*, *makān* and *zamān*. [POEM] It is related from Qatādah, 'Īsā and al-A'mash as '*muddakhkhal*'. The majority only double the *dāl*. So there are six readings.

they would turn and scurry away into it.

They would return to it and go quickly without looking back, fleeing from the Muslims. It comes from the verb *jamaḥa* when a horse overpowers its rider. A poet said:

Running swiftly, uncontrolled (*jamūḥ*), ready,
like a burning bough.

It means: if they had found any of these things that were mentioned, they would turn and hurry away from the Muslims to it.

وَمِنْهُم مَّن يَلْمِزُكَ فِي الصَّدَقَاتِ فَإِنْ أُعْطُوا مِنْهَا رَضُوا وَإِن لَّمْ
يُعْطَوْا مِنْهَا إِذَا هُمْ يَسْخَطُونَ ﴿٥٨﴾

58 Among them there are some who find fault with you concerning the *zakāt*. If they are given some of it, they are pleased but if they are not given any, they are angry.

Among them there are some who find fault with you concerning the *zakāt*.

'*Find fault with you*' here means 'attack you' according to Qatādah. Al-Ḥasan said that it means 'criticise you'. Mujāhid said: 'entreat you and ask of you'. An-Naḥḥās said, 'Scholars of language say that the proper position is that of Qatādah and al-Ḥasan. *Lamz* is to criticise.' *Lamz* linguistically is to criticise in secret. Al-Jawharī said that it is criticism and its root is to indicate with the eye and the like. The verb usually has a direct object but sometimes takes the preposition *bā'*. A man who criticises is called *lammāz*. The verb *lamaza* is to push and prod and so it is like *hamz*. *Hāmiz* and *hammāz* also mean that, as does *humazah*. The verb *hamaza* is to goad and push someone. It is also said that *lamz* is done to one's face while *hamz* is done behind one's back.

Allah is here describing some of the hypocrites who criticised the Prophet ﷺ concerning the distribution of *ṣadaqah*. They claimed that they were poor so that he would give some to them. Abū Sa'īd al-Khudrī said, 'When the Messenger of Allah ﷺ was distributing some wealth, Ḥarqūṣ ibn Zuhayr, the leader of the Kharijites, came. He was called Dhu-l-Khuwayṣirah at-Tamīmī. He said, "Be fair, Messenger of Allah!" He ﷺ responded, "Bother you! Who will be fair if I am not fair?" So the *āyah* was revealed.' It is a sound *ḥadīth* and Muslim transmitted something similar. In it 'Umar ibn al-Khaṭṭāb said, 'Let me kill this hypocrite, Messenger of Allah!' He said, 'I seek refuge with Allah from people saying that I kill my Companions! This one and his fellows recite the Qur'an, but it does not go beyond their throats. It passes through them as arrows pass through game.'

وَلَوْ أَنَّهُمْ رَضُوا۟ مَآ ءَاتَىٰهُمُ ٱللَّهُ وَرَسُولُهُۥ وَقَالُوا۟ حَسْبُنَا ٱللَّهُ سَيُؤْتِينَا
ٱللَّهُ مِن فَضْلِهِۦ وَرَسُولُهُۥٓ إِنَّآ إِلَى ٱللَّهِ رَٰغِبُونَ ٥٩

59 If only they had been pleased with what Allah and His Messenger had given them and had said, 'Allah is enough for us. Allah will give us of His bounty as will His Messenger. It is to Allah that we make our plea.'

The apodosis of *law* (*if*) is elided and what is implied is: 'it would have been better for them.'

إِنَّمَا ٱلصَّدَقَٰتُ لِلْفُقَرَآءِ وَٱلْمَسَٰكِينِ وَٱلْعَٰمِلِينَ عَلَيْهَا وَٱلْمُؤَلَّفَةِ
قُلُوبُهُمْ وَفِى ٱلرِّقَابِ وَٱلْغَٰرِمِينَ وَفِى سَبِيلِ ٱللَّهِ وَٱبْنِ
ٱلسَّبِيلِ فَرِيضَةً مِّنَ ٱللَّهِ وَٱللَّهُ عَلِيمٌ حَكِيمٌ ٦٠

60 *Zakāt* is for: the poor, the destitute, those who collect it, reconciling people's hearts, freeing slaves, those in debt, spending in the Way of Allah, and travellers. It is a legal obligation from Allah. Allah is All-Knowing, All-Wise.

***Zakāt* is for: the poor,**

Allah singled out some people for wealth rather than others as a blessing from Him to them. As thankfulness for that, He made them give a share of it to those who have no wealth, representing Him in what He guaranteed in His words: *'There is no creature on the earth which is not dependent upon Allah for its provision.'* (11:6)

Allah's words, '*for the poor...*' to the end of the *āyah*, explain how *zakāt* is to be spent and where, so that it is not spent outside of these people. Then there is a choice between those of them who have a share. This is the position of Mālik and Abū Ḥanīfah and his people. So for them the *lām* in *li-l-fuqara* is as it is said, 'The saddle is for the mount and the door is for the house.' Ash-Shāfi'ī said that the *lām* is the *lām* of conveying ownership as when you say, 'The property belongs to (*li*) Zayd, 'Amr and Bakr.' So it must be equally divided between them. Ash-Shāfi'ī and his people said, 'This is like when someone makes final instructions to specific categories or specific people.' They use for evidence the word '*innamā*' which demands that *zakāt* be confined to the eight categories.

They support this with the *ḥadīth* of Ziyād ibn al-Ḥārith aṣ-Ṣuddā'ī. He said, 'I went to the Messenger of Allah ﷺ as he was sending out an army to fight my people. I said, "Keep your army back. I will deal with their Islam and obedience for you." I wrote to my people and they became Muslim and obeyed. The Messenger of Allah ﷺ said, "Brother of Ṣuddā' who is obeyed among his people!" I said, "Rather Allah has been gracious to them and guided them." Then a man came to ask him for *zakāt* and the Messenger of Allah ﷺ said to him, "Allah is not pleased with a ruling of a Prophet or anyone else regarding *zakāt* so He has divided it into eight parts. If you are one of those parts, I will give to you."' Abū Dāwūd and ad-Dāraquṭnī related it and the wording is that of ad-Dāraquṭnī. It is related that Zayn al-'Ābidīn said, 'Allah Almighty taught us the amount of *zakāt* to be paid and what is enough for these categories [and made it mandatory for them], and He made it a right for all of them. Whoever refuses to pay that wrongs them in their provision.'

Our scholars hold to the words of the Almighty: '*If you make your ṣadaqah public, that is good. But if you conceal it and give it to the poor, that is better for you.*' (2:271) When the term *ṣadaqah* is used in the Qur'an, it means the obligatory *zakāt*. The Prophet ﷺ said, 'I am commanded to take *ṣadaqah* (*zakāt*) from your rich and return it to your poor.' This is a text about mentioning one of the eight categories in the Qur'an and Sunnah. That is the position of 'Umar ibn al-Khaṭṭāb, 'Alī, Ibn 'Abbās and Ḥudhayfah, and a group of the *Tābi'ūn* also said that. They said that it is permitted to give it to the eight categories and to any category among them. Al-Minhāl ibn 'Amr related from Zirr ibn Ḥubaysh from Ḥudhayfah about this *āyah*: 'Allah mentioned these categories so that they are known. Any category among them satisfies the requirement.' Sa'īd ibn Jubayr related about this *āyah* from Ibn 'Abbās, 'Paying it to any of the categories satisfies it.' That is the position of al-Ḥasan, Ibrāhīm and others. Aṭ-Ṭabarī said, 'It was such that Mālik claimed that there was a consensus regarding it.' He means a consensus of the Companions. It is not known that any of them opposed it according to what Abū 'Amr said. Allah knows best. Ibn al-'Arabī said, 'The distinction we make between us and them is that the community agreed that if every category is given its share, it is not mandatory to include them all. It is like that with including all the categories. Allah knows best.'

the destitute,

Scholars of language and the people of fiqh disagree about the difference between *faqīr* and *miskīn*. There are nine views. Ya'qūb ibn as-Sikkīt, al-Qutabī and Yūnus ibn Ḥabīb believe that a *faqīr* has a better state than a *miskīn*. They said that the *faqīr* is the one who has some of what will suffice and sustain him while a *miskīn* has nothing. They cited as evidence the words of the shepherd:

A *faqīr* is the one whose milking is according to his dependents
and does not leave anything after that.

Some of the people of language and *ḥadīth*, including Abū Ḥanīfah and Qāḍī 'Abd al-Wahhāb, believed this. 'According to' (*wafq*) comes from the word meaning a correspondence between two things as if they were interjoined. 'Milking according to his dependents' means that they have just enough milk sufficient for them and no more. Al-Jawharī stated that.

Others take the reverse position and make a *miskīn* better than a *faqīr*. They use as evidence the words of Allah, *'As for the boat, it belonged to some poor people (*masākīn*) who worked on the sea.'* (18:79) So Allah tells us that they had a boat which is usually worth something. They reinforced that opinion with what is related about when the Prophet ﷺ sought refuge from poverty (*faqr*), it being related that he said, 'O Allah, let me live *miskīn* and die *miskīn*.' Had a *miskīn* had a worse state than a *faqīr*, the two reports would conflict since it is impossible to seek refuge from *faqr* and then ask for a worse state than it. Allah answered his supplication and when he died, Allah had given him booty but it was not sufficient for him which is why he had to pawn his armour. They said that the verse of the shepherd is not an authoritative proof because he had a sheep to milk in spite of his poverty. They said that the meaning of *faqīr* in Arabic is someone who has had a vertebrae of his back broken due to the intensity of his poverty. There is no worse state than this. Allah reported about them: *'they are unable to travel in the land.'* (2:273) A poet said:

When Lubad [the old eagle of Luqmān] saw the vultures flying away,
he raised his feathers like a defenceless poor person (*faqīr*).

It was unable to fly, so it is in the position of someone whose back is broken and sticks to the ground. Al-Aṣma'ī and others believe this, and aṭ-Ṭaḥāwī related it from the Kufans. That is one of the positions of ash-Shāfi'ī and most of his people. Ash-Shāfi'ī has another position that the *faqīr* and *miskīn* are the same and there is no difference between them in the idea, but only in the word. That is a third view, and Ibn al-Qāsim and the rest of Mālik's adherents believe this. It is the position of Abū Yūsuf.

The apparent meaning of the word indicates that a *miskīn* is not the same as a *faqīr*. They are two categories, and one of the two categories has greater need than the other. This position is close to the one who makes them a single category. Allah knows best. There is no evidence in the position of someone who uses as evidence: *'As for the boat, it belonged to some poor people (*masākīn*) who worked on the sea'* (18:79) because it is possible that they had hired it, as you say that it is so-and-so's house when he lives there, even if it belongs to someone else. The Almighty says about the people of the Fire: *'they will be beaten with cudgels made of iron'* (22:21) and they are ascribed to them, and: *'Do not hand over to the simple-minded any property of theirs'* (4:5). The Prophet ﷺ said, 'Whoever sells a slave who has (*li*) property…' Something is often ascribed to someone by *li* when he does not own it. It is as they say, 'The house's door,' 'the horse's saddle' and like. It is possible that they are called 'poor (*masākīn*)' out of mercy and kindness, as is said to someone suffering a calamity or affliction: 'poor you.' We also find in a *ḥadīth*, 'the poor (*masākīn*) of the people of the Fire.' A poet says:

The poor (*masākīn*) of the people of love, right until the earth of abasement
covers their graves among the cemeteries, …

As for the interpretation of the words of the Prophet ﷺ related by Anas: 'O Allah, make me live poor (*miskīn*)', it is not like that. The meaning here is humility to Allah which contains no arrogance, haughtiness, pride, vanity, hubris, cockiness or insolence. How excellent is what Abū al-'Atāhiyyah said!

When you want the noble of all the people,
look at a king in the garb of the poor (*masākīn*).
That is the one whose desire for Allah is great
and that is the one who is fit for this world and the *dīn*.

He is not a beggar because the Prophet ﷺ disliked begging and forbade it. He said about a black woman who refused to move from the road, 'Leave her. She is proud.' As for Allah's words: *'It is for the poor* (fuqarā') *held back in the Way of Allah, unable to travel in the land'* (2:273), that does not prevent them having something. Allah knows best.

What the people of Mālik and ash-Shāfi'ī believed about them being the same is good. Close to that is what Mālik said in the book of Ibn Saḥnūn: 'A *faqīr* is in need but refrains from asking while a *miskīn* is someone who asks.' That is related from Ibn 'Abbās and az-Zuhrī said it. Ibn Sha'bān preferred it and it is the fourth view.

The fifth view was stated by Muḥammad ibn Maslamah: a *faqīr* is the one who has a house, servant or less than that. A *miskīn* has nothing. This is the opposite of what is confirmed in *Ṣaḥīḥ Muslim* from 'Abdullāh ibn 'Amr. A man asked him [for something] and he said, 'Are we not among the poor *Muhājirūn*?' 'Abdullāh said to him, 'Do you not have a woman to whom you go?' 'Yes,' he answered. He said, 'Do you not have a house in which you live?' 'Yes,' he answered. He said, 'You are one of the wealthy.' He added, 'I have a servant.' He said, 'Then you are one of the kings.'

The sixth position is related from Ibn 'Abbās who said, 'The poor (*fuqarā'*) are from the *Muhājirūn* and the *masākīn* are from the desert Arabs who have not emigrated.' Aḍ-Ḍaḥḥāk said that.

The seventh position is that a *miskīn* is the one who is humble and concealed, even if he does not ask. A *faqīr* is the one who endures and accepts the things secretly and is not humble. 'Ubaydullāh ibn al-Ḥasan said that.

An eighth view is stated by Mujāhid, 'Ikrimah and az-Zuhrī. It is that the *masākīn* are servants (*ṭawwāfūn*) and the *fuqarā'* are the poor Muslims.

'Ikrimah has a ninth view which is that the *fuqarā'* are the poor Muslims and *masākīn* are the poor of the People of the Book.

The point of the disagreement about the *fuqarā'* and *masākīn* being a single category appears when someone makes a will and leaves a third of his wealth to a certain person and to the *fuqarā'* and *masākīn*. If someone says that they are one category, he gives half of the third to the individual named and half of the third to the poor. If someone says that they are different categories, then the third is divided into three parts between them.

Scholars disagree about the definition of the degree of poverty needed for it to be permitted to take *zakāt*. The consensus of most of those who have taken from the people of knowledge is that someone who has a house and servant which he cannot do without can take from the *zakāt* and the payer can give to him. Mālik said, 'If he has nothing beyond the price of the house and servant he needs, he is permitted to take it. Otherwise he is not permitted.' Ibn al-Mundhir mentioned that. Mālik said that and an-Nakha'ī and ath-Thawrī also said that. Abū Ḥanīfah said that anyone who has twenty dinars or two hundred dirhams may not take *zakāt* because they possess the *niṣāb,* since the Prophet ﷺ said, 'I was commanded to take *zakāt* from your rich and return it to your poor.' This is clear. Al-Mughīrah related it from Mālik.

Ath-Thawrī, Aḥmad, Isḥāq and others said that someone who has fifty dirhams or that amount in gold should not take it, and that no one is given more than fifty dirhams of it unless he is a debtor. Aḥmād and Isḥāq said that. The evidence for this view is what ad-Dāraquṭnī related from 'Abdullāh ibn Mas'ūd that the Prophet ﷺ said, '*Zakāt* is not lawful for a person who has fifty dirhams.' Its *isnād* contains 'Abd ar-Raḥmān ibn Isḥāq, who is weak, and Bukayr ibn Khunays, who relates from him, is also weak. Ḥakīm ibn Jubayr related the like of it from Muḥammad ibn 'Abd ar-Raḥmān ibn Yazīd from his father from 'Abdullāh from the Prophet ﷺ. He said, 'Fifty dirhams'. Ḥakīm ibn Jubayr is weak and was abandoned by Shu'bah and others as ad-Dāraquṭnī said. Abū 'Umar said, 'This *ḥadīth* depends on Ḥakīm ibn Jubayr who is abandoned.'

'Alī and 'Abdullāh said, '*Zakāt* is not lawful for someone who has fifty dirhams or its equivalent in gold.' Ad-Dāraquṭnī mentioned it. Al-Ḥasan al-Baṣrī said, 'It is not taken by someone who has forty dirhams.' Al-Wāqidī related it from Mālik. The evidence for this position is what ad-Dāraquṭnī related from 'Abdullāh ibn Mas'ūd. He said that he heard the Prophet ﷺ say, 'If someone begs from people while he is rich, he will come on the Day of Rising with scratches and abrasions on his face.' It was asked, 'Messenger of Allah, what is his wealth?' 'Forty dirhams,' he answered. We find in the *ḥadīth* of Mālik from Zayd ibn Aslam from 'Aṭā' ibn Yasār from a man of the Banū Asad that the Messenger of Allah ﷺ said, 'If someone asks from me while he has an *ūqiyyah* or its equivalent, he has importuned. The *ūqiyyah* is forty dirhams.' What is well-known from Mālik is what Ibn al-Qāsim related. He was asked, 'Can someone who has forty dirhams receive something from the *zakāt*?' 'Yes,' he answered. Abū 'Umar said, 'It is possible that the first man was strong enough to work and earn in a good manner and the second was too weak to work or had dependents. Allah knows best.'

The position of ash-Shāfi'ī and Abū Thawr is that if someone is strong enough to work and has a skill in addition to his strength and is able to properly manage his affairs so that he is able to enrich himself from people, *zakāt* is unlawful for him. For proof, he used the *ḥadīth* of the Prophet ﷺ: '*Ṣadaqah* [*zakāt*] is not lawful for a wealthy person nor one with sufficient health and strength.' 'Abdullāh ibn 'Umar related it and Abū Dāwūd, at-Tirmidhī and ad-Dāraqutnī transmitted it.

Jābir related: '*Zakāt* came to the Messenger of Allah ﷺ and people gathered to receive it. He said, "It is not proper for a wealthy man nor a healthy person nor a worker."' Ad-Dāraqutnī transmitted it.

Abū Dāwūd related from 'Ubaydullāh ibn 'Adī ibn al-Khiyār that two men went to the Prophet ﷺ during the Farewell Ḥajj while he was distributing *zakāt* and they asked for it. He raised his eyes towards us and then lowered them. We saw two sturdy men. He said, 'If you wish, I will give to you. Neither the wealthy nor strong people who can earn have a portion of it.' That is because they can become wealthy by their work and become like someone who is wealthy with his own wealth. Neither of them has any need to ask. Ibn Khuwayzimandād said that. He related it from the School. There is no need to rely on it. That the Prophet ﷺ gave it to the poor and stopped it going to the chronically ill is false.

Abū 'Īsā at-Tirmidhī said in his *Collection*, 'When a man is strong but in need and has nothing and is given *zakāt*, he satisfies the requirement of the giver according to the people of knowledge.' Aṭ-Ṭabarī said, 'The literal meaning stipulates that it is permitted because he is poor in spite of his strength and physical health.' Abū Ḥanīfah and his people said that. 'Ubaydullāh ibn al-Ḥasan said, 'Anyone who does not have sufficient to sustain him for a year can be given *zakāt*.' His proof is what Ibn Shihāb related from Mālik ibn Aws ibn al-Ḥadathān from 'Umar ibn al-Khaṭṭāb that the Messenger of Allah ﷺ used to store up food for a year from the *fay'* Allah gave him. Then he used the rest of it for animals and weapons as Allah said: *'Did He not find you impoverished and enrich you?'* (93:8) One of the people of knowledge said, 'Each can take from the *zakāt* what is essential for him.'

Some people say that someone who has enough for his evening meal is wealthy. That is related from 'Alī. They use as evidence the *ḥadīth* that 'Alī reported that the Prophet ﷺ said, 'Anyone who asks for something when he is wealthy will have many of the hot stones of Hell.' They asked, 'Messenger of Allah, what is wealth then?' He replied, 'The evening meal.' Ad-Dāraqutnī transmitted it and said that 'Amr ibn Khālid is in its *isnād*. He is abandoned. Abū Dāwūd transmitted it from Sahl ibn al-Ḥanẓaliyyah from the Prophet ﷺ. In it is: 'If someone asks when he has what will be enough for him, he is asking for a lot of the Fire.' An-Nufaylī said in another place, 'the coal of Hell'. They asked, 'Messenger of Allah, what is enough for him?' An-Nufaylī said in another place, 'What is the wealth with which one should not ask?' He answered, 'The amount needed for his midday and evening meal.' An-Nufaylī said in another place, 'That he does not have enough to satisfy his hunger for a day and a night.'

This is a clarification of the scale of poverty which permits the taking of *zakāt*. The general term *fuqarā'* does not specify Muslims rather than the people of the *dhimmah* but multiple reports state that *zakāt* is taken from wealthy Muslims and given to their poor. 'Ikrimah said, 'The *fuqarā'* here are the poor Muslims and the *masākīn* are the poor of the People of the Book.' Abū Bakr al-'Absī said, "Umar ibn al-Khaṭṭāb saw a blind *dhimmī* prostrate at the gate of Madīnah. 'Umar asked, 'What is the matter with you?' He answered, 'They made me work for the *jizyah* until I went blind and then left me and I have no one to bring me anything.' 'Umar said, 'You have not been fairly treated then.' He commanded that he be given food and what would rectify his situation.' Then he said, 'This one is from those about whom Allah says, "*Zakāt is for: the poor, the destitute...*" They are those of the Book who are chronically ill.'

Allah says: '*Zakāt is for: the poor, the destitute...*' and one phrase follows another: the phrase '*aṣ-ṣadaqāt* [*zakāt*]' is followed by words expressing how it is spent which the Prophet ﷺ made clear. When he sent Mu'ādh to Yemen, he said, 'Tell them that Allah has obliged *zakāt* for them which is taken from their rich and returned to their poor.' He singled out the people of every land for the *zakāt* of their land.

Abū Dāwūd related that Ziyād, or one of the governors, sent 'Imrān ibn Ḥuṣayn to collect *zakāt*. When he returned, he asked 'Imrān, 'Where is the wealth?' He said, 'Did you send me to bring wealth? We took it from where we used to take it in the time of the Messenger of Allah ﷺ and placed it where we used to place it in the time of the Messenger of Allah ﷺ.' Ad-Dāraquṭnī and at-Tirmidhī related from 'Awn ibn Abī Juḥayfah that his father said, 'The *zakāt* collector of the Messenger of Allah ﷺ came to us and took *zakāt* from our wealthy and gave it to our poor. I was an orphan boy and he gave me a young she-camel from it.' At-Tirmidhī said, 'The *ḥadīth* of Ibn Abī Juḥayfah is a good *ḥadīth* in the chapter of Ibn 'Abbās.'

Scholars disagree about transferring *zakāt* from the place where it is collected. There are three positions. One is that it may not be transferred, and Saḥnūn and Ibn al-Qāsim stated that. It is the sound one based on what we have mentioned. Ibn al-Qāsim also said that some of it can be moved if there is need, and I think that it is correct. It is related that Saḥnūn said, 'If the ruler learns that there is great need in one land, he is permitted to transfer to it part of the *zakāt* collected in another land. When the need arises, then it is obliged to put that need before those who are not in need. "A Muslim is the brother of another Muslim, He does not surrender him nor wrong him."'

The second view is that it may be transferred. Mālik also said that. The evidence for this position is what is related that Muʿādh said to the people of Yemen, 'Give me *khamīs* cloth or garments taken in *zakāt* which I can take from you in place of millet and barley. It is easier for you and more beneficial for the *Muhājirūn* in Madīnah." Ad-Dāraquṭnī and others transmitted it. *Khamīs* is a name of several things. Here it means a cloth which is five spans in length. It is said that it is called that because the first to make it was al-Khims, one of the kings of Yemen. Ibn Fāris mentioned it in *al-Mujmal* as did al-Jawharī. This *ḥadīth* provides evidence for two things. One is what we mentioned about transferring *zakāt* from Yemen to Madīnah where the Prophet ﷺ could distribute it. This is supported by the words of Allah: *'Zakāt is for the poor,'* and He did not distinguish between a poor person in one place rather than another. Allah knows best. The second is that he can take the price in *zakāt*.

Transmission from Mālik varies about paying the price in *zakāt*. Sometimes he permits it and sometimes he forbids it. The reason for the permission, which is the position of Abū Ḥanīfah, is this *ḥadīth*. It is confirmed in *Ṣaḥīḥ Bukhārī* from the *ḥadīth* of Anas that the Prophet ﷺ said, 'If someone owes a *jidhʿah* (four-year-old-female) in his *zakāt* and does not have a *jidhʿah* but has a *ḥiqqah* (three-year-old female), it is taken from him and what is feasible of either two sheep or twenty dirhams.'

The Prophet ﷺ said, 'Spare them from the begging on this day,' referring to the *'Īd* of *Fiṭr*. He means to give them enough to satisfy their need and whatever will satisfy their need is permitted. The Almighty says: '*Take zakāt from their wealth*' (9:103) and did not single out one thing rather than another.

According to Abū Ḥanīfah, lodging in a house is not permitted as a replacement for *zakāt*, as when someone owes five dirhams and gives lodging to a poor person for a month. This is not permitted. He said that that is because lodging is not wealth. The reason for his words, 'the value is not permitted,' which is the apparent position of the school, is because the Prophet ﷺ said, 'There is a sheep due on five camels and a sheep on every forty sheep.' The text states a sheep. If he does not bring it, he does not bring what he is commanded and if he does not bring what he is commanded, the command remains outstanding for him.

The third position is that the share of the poor and destitute is distributed in the place where it was collected and the rest of the shares can be transferred as the ruler thinks best. The first view is sounder, and Allah knows best.

Does one consider the place where the property is at the time that the year is completed and divide out the *zakāt* there, or the place where the owner is, since he is the one whose duty it is to pay it? There are two views. Abū 'Abdullāh

Muḥammad ibn Khuwayzimandād preferred the second view in *al-Aḥkām*. He said, 'That is because it is the human being who is charged with producing it and so the property follows him and the ruling on it is where the person is. It is like a traveller. He may be wealthy in his land but poor in another land, and so his ruling is according to where he is.'

Point. Transmissions from Mālik vary about someone who thinks he is giving to a poor Muslim and then discovers that the person to whom he gave was a slave, an unbeliever, or wealthy. Sometimes he says that it satisfies the requirement and sometimes he says that it does not. The reason for allowing it, which is sounder, is what is related by Muslim from Abū Hurayrah who said that the Prophet ﷺ said, 'A man was going to give his *ṣadaqah* in the night and he went out with it and put it in the hand of a fornicatress. In the morning people talked about some *ṣadaqah* that had been given to a fornicatress. He said, "O Allah, praise is Yours! I gave *ṣadaqah* to a fornicatress!" So he took out his *ṣadaqah* and placed it in the hand a rich man. In the morning they talked about some *ṣadaqah* that had been given to a rich man. He said, "O Allah, praise is Yours! I gave *ṣadaqah* to a rich man!" So he took out his *ṣadaqah* and placed it in the hand a thief. In the morning they talked about *ṣadaqah* that had been given to a thief. He said, "O Allah, praise is Yours! I gave to a fornicatress, a rich man and a thief!" He was told, "Your *ṣadaqah* has been accepted. Perhaps the fornicatress will use it to abstain from fornication. Perhaps the rich man will reflect and spend from what Allah has given him. Perhaps the thief will use it to refrain from stealing."'

It is related that a man took the *zakāt* due on his wealth and gave it to his father. In the morning he learned of that and asked the Prophet ﷺ who said to him, 'The reward for your *zakāt* has been written for you as well as the reward for gifts to kin. You have two rewards.' Part of the meaning is that the giver has discretion. When he makes an effort and gives to someone who thinks is entitled to it, he has performed his obligation. The reason for not allowing it is that he has not given it to the one entitled to it and because deliberateness and error is the same in property liability. So he must ensure that what is meant for the poor reaches the poor.

If he pays the *zakāt* in the right place and it is destroyed without negligence on his part, he is not liable because he is a trustee for the poor. If he produces it sometime after that and it is destroyed, he is liable since he kept it from its proper place. Then it was lost while he was responsible for it and so he is liable. Allah knows best.

When the ruler is fair in taking and distribution, the owner cannot undertake the distribution himself in cash or anything else. It is also said that the distribution of cash is done by its owners. Ibn al-Mājishūn said, 'That is when distribution is just for the poor and destitute. When it needs to be given to other than these two categories, that requires a ruler to distribute it.' There are many secondary points in this topic: these are the primary points.

those who collect it,

This means the collectors and taxmen whom the ruler sends out to collect *zakāt* and entrusts with that task. Al-Bukhārī related that Abū Ḥumayd as-Sā'idī said, 'The Messenger of Allah ﷺ appointed a man from Asad called Ibn al-Lutbiyyah to collect the *zakāt* from the Banū Sulaym. When he came, he asked him about what he had collected.'

Scholars disagree about the amount which they may take, and there are three positions about it. Mujāhid and ash-Shāfi'ī said that it is according to the value [of what he collected]. Ibn 'Umar and Mālik said that they are given a wage commensurate with their work, and that is the position of Abū Ḥanīfah and his people. They said, 'That is because he stopped his work for the benefit of the poor. So he and his helpers are paid for their task. It is like a woman who does not work because of her due to her husband: her husband owes her maintenance and that of a servant or two. The value is not determined, but one takes account of the value of the task or more, like the wages of a *qāḍī*.' In our time one does not consider the task of the helpers because that is pure extravagance.

The third view is that they are paid by the Treasury. Ibn al-'Arabī said, 'This is a sound view from Mālik ibn Anas as related by Ibn Abī Uways and Dāwūd ibn Sa'īd ibn Abī Zanbar. The evidence for it is weak. Allah speaks about their share in a text, so how can they differ from it in investigation and examination? What is sound is that there is discretion in the amount of the wage because the explanation of the categories are for the place [where it is dispersed], not the one entitled.'

There is disagreement about what happens when the collector is a Hāshimī. Abū Ḥanīfah forbade it since the Prophet ﷺ said, '*Ṣadaqah* is not lawful for the family of Muḥammad. It is people's detritus.' This is *ṣadaqah* from one aspect and so it is connected to *ṣadaqah* in all aspects out of honour and keeping pure the kinship of the Messenger of Allah ﷺ from people's leavings. Mālik and ash-Shāfi'ī allowed them to do it and to be given the wage for their work because the Prophet ﷺ sent out 'Alī ibn Abī Ṭālib as a *zakāt* collector and sent him to collect it in Yemen. He appointed a group of the Banū Hāshim, and the caliphs after him did the same. Because he was hired for a permissible action and so it is obliged that a Hāshimī should be equal with others in respect to different types of work. The Ḥanafīs say that 'Alī's *ḥadīth* does not say that he ﷺ allotted him any of the *zakāt*. If he allots him something from other sources, that is permitted. It is related from Mālik.

Allah's words: *'those who collect it'* refer to all those who have a task connected with it, such as the messenger, the scribe, the distributor, the collector and others: those who undertake such duties receive a wage for it. Part of that is the imamate. Even if the prayer is directed at all creation, some of them are advanced to it as a *farḍ kifāyah* and so they are not permitted to take a wage for it. This is the basic principle in respect of the matter. The Prophet ﷺ indicated it by his words, 'What I leave after the maintenance of my wives and provision of my agent is *ṣadaqah*.' Ibn al-'Arabī said it.

reconciling people's hearts

There is no mention of reconciling hearts in the Revelation outside of the distribution of *zakāt*. They are people at the beginning of Islam who made a show of Islam who were reconciled by giving them a share of the *zakāt* because of the weakness of their certainty. Az-Zuhrī said, 'Those who are reconciled are those Jews or Christians who became Muslim, even if they were rich.'

Some of the later people disagree about who they were. It is said that they are a group of unbelievers who are given to in order to reconcile them to Islam. They did not become Muslim by force or the sword, but became Muslim through giving and being treated well. It is said that they are people who had become Muslim outwardly but their hearts were not certain and so they were given to so that Islam might be made firm in their hearts. It is said that they were some of the great idolaters who had followers who were to given to so as to reconcile their followers to Islam. These positions are similar: the aim in all of them is giving to those whose Islam is only made truly firm by such giving and so it is like a form of *jihād*.

There are three categories of idolaters: one group who become Muslim by the establishment of the proof, one group by force, and one group by charity. The leader who oversees the Muslims uses with each group what will deliver them from unbelief. We find in *Ṣaḥīḥ Muslim* from the *ḥadīth* of Anas that the Messenger of Allah ﷺ said (to the *Anṣār*), 'I give to men who were recently unbelievers to reconcile them.' Ibn Isḥāq said, 'He gave to them to reconcile them, and through them their people were reconciled. They were nobles. He gave a hundred camels to Abū Sufyān ibn Ḥarb and gave his son a hundred camels. He gave Ḥakīm ibn

Ḥizām a hundred camels. He gave al-Ḥārith ibn Hishām a hundred camels and gave Suhayl ibn 'Amr a hundred camels. He gave Ḥuwayṭib ibn 'Abd al-'Uzzā a hundred camels. He gave a hundred camels to Ṣafwān ibn Umayyah.' He also gave to Mālik ibn 'Awf and al-'Alā' ibn Jāriyah. He said, 'Those are the people of the hundreds.' He gave some men of Quraysh less than a hundred, including Makhramah ibn Nawfal az-Zuhrī, 'Umayr ibn Wahb al-Jumaḥī, and Hishām ibn 'Amr al-'Āmirī.' Ibn Isḥāq said, 'I do not know what he gave to those.' He gave fifty camels to Sa'īd ibn Yarbū'. He gave a few camels to 'Abbās ibn Mirdās and that made him angry so he said:

'It was spoils I took
    when I charged on my filly on the sandy ground
And woke the people lest they sleep.
    When they slept, I did not sleep.
My spoils and those of my horse al-'Ubayd
    are shared by 'Uyaynah and al-Aqra'.
I fought fiercely in battle
    but am not given anything and not protected –
Except for a few small camels,
    the number of their four legs!
Neither Ḥiṣn or Ḥābis
    surpass Mirdās in the assembly,
And I am not inferior to either of them.
    Him who you demean today will not be elevated.'

The Messenger of Allah ﷺ said. 'Go and cut off his tongue from insulting me.' So they gave to him until he was satisfied. That stopped his tongue.

Abū 'Umar said, 'Among those mentioned whose hearts were reconciled were: an-Naḍīr ibn al-Ḥārith ibn 'Alqamah ibn Kaladah, the brother of an-Naḍr ibn al-Ḥārith who was executed at Badr. Others mentioned that he was one of those who emigrated to Abyssinia. If he was one of them, it is impossible for him to be one of those who hearts were reconciled. Whoever emigrated to Abyssinia was one of the first *Muhājirūn* whose faith was firm in it and fought for it, not one of those whose hearts were reconciled.'

Abū 'Umar said, 'The Messenger of Allah ﷺ appointed Mālik ibn 'Awf ibn Sa'd ibn Yarbū' an-Naṣrī over those of his people who had become Muslim from the tribes of Qays and put him in command of attacking Thaqīf. He did that and constricted things for them. He was a good Muslim as were those whose hearts were reconciled, except 'Uyaynah ibn Ḥiṣn to whom he continued to be very generous. The rest of those whose hearts were reconciled vary in excellence: some were good and excellent and there is agreement about their excellence, like al-Ḥārith ibn Hisham, Ḥakīm ibn Ḥizām, 'Ikrimah ibn Abī Jahl, and Suhayl ibn 'Amr. Others were less than these. Allah has preferred some of the Prophets and believers over others. He has the best knowledge of them.'

Mālik said, 'I heard that Ḥakīm ibn Ḥizām spent what the Messenger of Allah ﷺ gave him for reconciling hearts and gave it away as *ṣadaqah* after that.' Ḥakīm ibn Ḥizām and Ḥuwayṭib ibn 'Abd al-'Uzzā each lived to the age of one hundred and twenty: sixty years in the Jāhiliyyah and sixty in Islam. I heard our shaykh, Imām Abū Muḥammad 'Abd al-'Aẓīm say, 'Two of the Companions lived for sixty years in the Jāhiliyyah and sixty in Islam and died in Madīnah in 54 AH. One of them was Ḥakīm ibn Ḥizām. He was born inside the Ka'bah thirteen years before The Elephant. The second was Ḥassān ibn Thābit ibn al-Mundhir ibn Ḥarām al-Anṣārī.' This was also mentioned by Abū 'Umar and 'Uthmān ash-Shahrzurī in *Kitāb ma'rifah anwā' 'ilm al-ḥadīth.* He only mentioned the two of them. Abū al-Faraj al-Jawzī mentioned Ḥuwayṭib ibn 'Abd al-'Uzzā in *Kitāb al-Wafā.* Abū 'Umar mentioned in the *Book of the Companions* that Islam came when he was sixty years old and he died when he was one hundred and twenty. He also mentioned Ḥamnan ibn 'Awf, the brother of 'Abd ar-Raḥmān ibn 'Awf, who lived sixty years in Islam and sixty years in the Jāhiliyyah.

Mu'āwiyah and his father Abū Sufyān are also counted among those whose hearts were reconciled. As for Mu'āwiyah, it is unlikely that he should be one of them. How could he be one of them when the Prophet ﷺ entrusted him with the Revelation of Allah and its reading and socialised with him? His state in the time of Abū Bakr is still more famous. There is no discussion about his father being one of them. There is disagreement about their number. In general, all of them were believers, and none of them were unbelievers. Allah knows best.

Scholars disagree about whether this share still remains. 'Umar, al-Ḥasan, ash-Sha'bī and others said that this category ceased to exist when Islam became powerful and victorious. This is the well-known position in the school of Mālik and the People of Opinion. Some of the Ḥanafīs say that when Islam and its people became powerful and the rest of the unbelievers were cut off, the Companions all agreed in the caliphate of Abū Bakr that the reconciliation share of *zakāt* was dropped. One group of scholars said that it remains because the ruler may need to renew Islam. 'Umar stopped it when he saw that the *dīn* was strong.

Yūnus said, 'I asked az-Zuhrī about them and he said, "I do not know of any abrogation in respect of that."' Abū Ja'far an-Naḥḥās said, 'According to this, the ruling regarding them remains if anyone needs to renew it and fears that some calamity may afflict the Muslims or hopes to make their Islam good after being given it.' Qāḍī 'Abd al-Wahhāb said, 'If it is needed at some times, they are given some of the *zakāt*.' Qāḍī Ibn al-'Arabī said, 'What I believe is that if it strengthens Islam, it remains. If they need it, they are given their share, as the Messenger of Allah ﷺ gave to them. We find in the *Ṣaḥīḥ*: "Islam began as a stranger and will revert to how it began."'

When it is decided that their share is not given to them, it reverts to the other categories or how the ruler thinks best. Az-Zuhrī said that half of their share is given to make mosques flourish. This is part of what indicates that the eight categories do not have equal entitlement. If there are those who are entitled, then this share is cancelled when the people to whom it would go do not exist and it does not go to anyone else, as when someone makes a bequest to particular people and then one of them dies: his share does not go to those who remain. Allah knows best.

freeing slaves,

Ibn 'Abbās and Ibn 'Umar said that it means simply that and it is the position of Mālik and others. The ruler is permitted to purchase slaves with the *zakāt* money and free them on behalf of the Muslims. They are then *mawlā*s of the Muslim community. It is permitted for the one who pays the *zakāt* to buy them and also set them free. This is the gist of the school of Mālik. It is related from Ibn 'Abbās and al-Ḥasan. Aḥmad, Isḥāq and Abū 'Ubayd also said that. Abū Thawr said, 'The payer of *zakāt* does not actually buy a slave himself with it whom he frees in exchange for the *walā'*.' That is the position of ash-Shāfi'ī and the People of Opinion and also one transmission from Mālik. The sound position is the first because Allah says, 'Necks'. Therefore it is the neck of the slave which receives a share of *zakāt*. He can therefore buy the slave and set him free. There is no disagreement between the people of knowledge that a man can buy a horse and let it be used in the Way of Allah. If he can buy a horse in full from the *zakāt*, he can buy a slave in whole. There is no difference in that. Messenger of Allah knows best.

The root is about the *walā'*. Mālik said that it is the slave that is freed and the *walā'* goes to the Muslims. The same is true if the ruler sets him free. The Prophet ﷺ forbade selling or giving away the *walā'*. He ﷺ said, 'The *walā'* is flesh like the flesh of lineage. It is neither sold nor given away.' The Prophet ﷺ said, 'The *walā'* belongs to the one who sets free.' Women do not inherit any of the *walā'* since the Prophet ﷺ said, 'Women do not inherit any of the *walā'* unless they were the ones who freed or freed the one who set free.' The Prophet ﷺ gave the daughter of Ḥamzah the inheritance of a *mawlā*: she had half and her daughter had half. If the emancipator leaves children, male and female, the *walā'* goes to the male children rather than the female. That is the consensus of the Companions. The *walā'* is inherited by pure *'aṣabah* and women do not partake in that and so they do not inherit any of the *walā'*. Understand and you will be correct.

They disagree about whether a *mukātab* can be helped [to pay his contract] from the *zakāt*. It is said that he may not be, and that is related from Mālik because Allah mentioned the 'neck' and that indicates that He means full emancipation. But a *mukātab* is included in the category of debtors because he owes the debt of the *kitābah*. He is not included under the category of slaves. Allah knows best. It is related from Mālik from the transmission of the Madinans with an addition that a *mukātab* can be helped with the end of his *kitābah* with the amount necessary to free him. Most scholars take this view in interpreting the words of the Almighty, '*riqāb*' (literally "necks", meaning "slaves"). That is what Ibn Wahb, ash-Shāfi'ī, al-Layth, an-Nakha'ī and others said.

'Alī ibn Mūsā al-Qummī al-Ḥanafī said in *al-Aḥkām*: 'There is a consensus that the *mukātab* is meant.' However, there is disagreement about *riqāb*. Aṭ-Ṭabarī said, 'He mentioned the logic behind forbidding that and said, "Freeing is the invalidation of ownership but not transferring ownership, and what is given to the *mukātab* is transfer of ownership (*tamlīk*)." Part of the right of *zakāt* is only satisfied when there is a transfer of ownership. That is strengthened by the fact that if the *zakāt* is used to settle the debt of a debtor without his instruction it does not satisfy the obligation to pay it since there was no ownership. Therefore it is more likely to apply to emancipation. He mentioned that in emancipation *walā'* goes to the one who frees, and that is not achieved when it is paid to the *mukātab*. He mentioned that when the price for a slave is paid to a slave, the slave does not own it. If it is given to his master, he owns the emancipation. If it is given to him after buying and emancipation, it settles a debt. That does not satisfy *zakāt*.'

There is a *ḥadīth* which provides a text for what we have mentioned about both freeing a slave and helping a *mukātab* which ad-Dāraquṭnī transmitted from al-Barā'. He said, 'A man came to the Prophet ﷺ and said, "Direct me to an action which will bring me close to the Garden and put me far from the Fire." He said ﷺ, "Although you are lacking in the preamble [in your words], you have presented the question. Free a person and release a slave." He asked, "Messenger of Allah, are they not the same?" He answered, "No. Freeing a person is simply by setting him free and releasing a slave is by helping him with his price."'

There is disagreement about freeing captives using *zakāt*. Aṣbagh said that it is not allowed and that is the position of Ibn al-Qāsim. Ibn Ḥabīb said that it is allowed because the 'neck' (*riqāb*) is owned by owning the slave and so it emerges from enslavement to emancipation. That is better than releasing the slaves in our hands because it is a Muslim being released from being enslaved to a Muslim and that satisfies *zakāt*, so it is better to release a Muslim from enslavement and their consequent abasement to an unbeliever.

those in debt,

'Those in debt' are those burdened by debts that they cannot pay. There is no disagreement about it, O Allah, unless the debts are incurred as a result of foolishness. In that case, the debtor is not given any of it nor anything else until he repents. Someone can be given some of it if he has wealth but wealth that would be totally taken up by what is needed to settle the debt. If he has no wealth and has debts, he is both *faqīr* and a debtor and so he can be a recipient based on both counts. Muslim related that Abū Sa'īd al-Khudrī said, 'In the time of the Messenger of Allah ﷺ, a man suffered a loss in respect of some fruit that he had purchased and his debt was large. The Messenger of Allah ﷺ said, "Give *ṣadaqah* to him." People gave *ṣadaqah* to him but it was not enough to settle his debts. The Messenger of Allah ﷺ said to his creditors, "Take what you find. You cannot have any more than that."'

It is permitted for someone who accepts financial responsibility properly and correctly to be given some of the *zakāt* which will settle the liability he accepted as mandatory for him, even if he is wealthy, since he incurs harm in respect of his wealth, just like a debtor. This is the position of ash-Shāfi'ī and his people, Aḥmad ibn Ḥanbal and others. Those who take this position use as evidence the *ḥadīth* of Qabīṣah ibn Mukhāriq who said, 'I accepted a financial liability and went to the Prophet ﷺ to beg of him regarding settling it. He said, "Stay until the *zakāt* arrives and we will order some to be given to you." Then he said, "Qabīṣah, asking is only lawful for three: a man who accepts financial liability and he can ask until he gets it and then he must refrain; a man afflicted by a disaster which destroys his property, and he is allowed to ask until he reaches sustenance from his livelihood; and a man who is afflicted by poverty so that three intelligent men of his people testify that he is afflicted by poverty, and he is allowed to ask until he reaches sustenance from his livelihood. Qabīṣah, any asking beyond these three is ill-gotten gains which the person consumes illegally.' His words, 'must refrain' indicate that he is wealthy because a poor person does not have to refrain. Allah knows best.

It is related that the Prophet ﷺ said, 'Asking is only lawful from one of three: someone in wretched poverty, with a large debt or a difficult blood payment.' It is related that he ﷺ said, '*Ṣadaqah* is only lawful for five...'

They disagree about whether the debts of a dead person can be settled from *zakāt*. Abū Ḥanīfah said that the debts of a dead person may not be paid from *zakāt*. That is the position of Ibn al-Mawwāz. Abū Ḥanīfah said that he is not given any of it to pay for *kaffārah* and similar rights owed to Allah. The debtor is someone with a debt for which he can be imprisoned.

Our scholars and others said. 'The debts of a dead person can be settled because he comes under the category of debtors.' The Prophet ﷺ said, 'I am more entitled to every believer than himself. If someone leaves wealth, it is for his family. If someone leaves debts or loss, it is for me and against me.'

spending in the Way of Allah,

They are those who go on expeditions and stay in *ribāṭs*. They are given what they spend in their expedition, whether they are rich or poor. That is the position of most scholars and that is the gist of the school of Mālik. Ibn 'Umar said that it refers to those performing *ḥajj* and *'umrah*. It is reported that Aḥmad and Isḥāq said that 'the Way of Allah' is *ḥajj*. Al-Bukhārī mentioned from Abū Lās: 'The Prophet ﷺ let us ride *zakāt* camels for *ḥajj*.' It is mentioned from Ibn 'Abbās that he set slaves free from the *zakāt* on his wealth and gave for *ḥajj*.

Abū Muḥammad 'Abd al-Ghanī transmitted from Muḥammad ibn Muḥammad al-Khayāsh from Abū Ghassān Mālik ibn Yaḥyā from Yazīd ibn Hārūn from Mahdī ibn Maymūn from Muḥammad ibn Abī Ya'qūb that Abū al-Ḥakam 'Abd ar-Raḥmān ibn Abī Nu'm said, 'I was sitting with 'Abdullāh ibn 'Umar when a woman came to him and said, "Abu 'Abd ar-Raḥmān, my husband left his property as a bequest in the Way of Allah." Ibn 'Umar said, "It is according to Allah's words: *'in the Way of Allah.'*" I said to him, "You have increased her sorrow at what she asked about." He asked, "What do you command me to say, Ibn Abī Nu'm? Should I command her to give it to those armies going out in the Way of Allah and corrupting the land and cutting off the roads?" I asked, "So what do you command her to do?" He said, "Tell her to give it to righteous people, to those making *ḥajj* to the Sacred House of Allah. Those are the delegation of the All-Merciful. Those are the delegation of the All-Merciful. Those are the delegation of the All-Merciful. They are not like the delegation of Shayṭān." He also repeated that three times. I asked, "Abū 'Abd ar-Raḥmān, what is the delegation of Shayṭān?" He answered, "People who visit these rulers and pass on conversations and lie about Muslims. They are given rewards and gifts."'

Muḥammad ibn 'Abd al-Ḥakam said, 'Mounts and weapons are given from the *zakāt*, as well as implements of war which are required for defending territory from the enemy, because all of that is part of the Way of expeditions and its benefit. The Prophet ﷺ gave a hundred camels in the event spoken of by Sahl ibn Abī Ḥathmah to calm feelings.' Abū Dāwūd transmitted from Bishr ibn Yasār that a man of the *Anṣār* called Sahl ibn Abī Ḥathmah told him that the Messenger of Allah ﷺ paid the blood money of a hundred camels for the Anṣārī who was killed at Khaybar.

'Īsā ibn Dīnār said, '*Zakāt* is lawful for someone who goes on an expedition in the Way of Allah and has needs during his expedition when his wealth is not present with him.' He added, 'It is not lawful for someone who has with him wealth from the expedition. It is only lawful for someone whose wealth is absent.' This is the school of ash-Shāfi'ī, Aḥmad, Isḥāq and a group of the people of knowledge.

Abū Ḥanīfah and his two companions said that someone on an expedition is only given *zakāt* if he is poor and cut off. This is an addition to the text and he considered an addition to the text to be abrogation, and abrogation can only be by the Qur'an or *mutawātir* report. That is lacking here. There is something different from that in the sound Sunnah by the words of the Prophet ﷺ: '*Ṣadaqah* (*zakāt*) is not lawful for someone who is not in need except in five cases: someone fighting in the Way of Allah, someone who collects it, a debtor, someone who buys it with his wealth, and a man who has a poor neighbour who is given *zakāt* and then that poor person then gives a gift to the rich person.' Mālik related it *mursal* from Zayd ibn Aslam from 'Aṭā' ibn Yasār. Ma'mar has it *marfū'* from Zayd ibn Aslam from 'Aṭā' ibn Yasār from Abū Sa'īd al-Khudrī from the Prophet ﷺ.

This *ḥadīth* explains the meaning of the *āyah* and that it is permitted for some wealthy people to receive it. It explains the words of the Prophet ﷺ: '*Zakāt* is not lawful for a wealthy person or for someone fit and healthy' because this statement is undefined and its general meaning is not indicated by the proof of the five wealthy people who are mentioned. Ibn al-Qāsim used to say, 'A rich person is not permitted to take from the *zakāt* what he can use to help in *jihād* and spends in the Way of Allah. That is permitted for a poor person.' He said, 'That is also the case with a debtor: he is not permitted, as long as he still has wealth, to take from the *zakāt* and pay his debts with it if his wealth is sufficient to pay them.' He says, 'When a fighter in an expedition is in need and he is wealthy but does not have his wealth with him, he should not take any of the *zakāt*, but may borrow from it and then when he arrives home, repay it from his wealth.'

Ibn Ḥabīb mentioned all of this from Ibn al-Qāsim. He claimed that Ibn Nāfi' and others disagreed with him about it. Abū Zayd and others related that Ibn al-Qāsim said that a fighter can receive some of the *zakāt*, even if he has sufficient wealth with him in the expedition and is wealthy in his homeland. This is sound based on the literal meaning of the *ḥadīth*, '*Zakāt* is not lawful for someone who is not in need except in five cases...' Ibn Wahb related that Mālik gave some of it to fighters and places of *ribāṭ*, whether they were poor or rich.

and travellers.

Sabīl is a path. A traveller is attributed to it (lit. 'son of the road') because he stays on it and passes on it as the poet says:

> If you ask about passion, I am passion,
> and the son of passion, and the brother and father of passion.

What is meant are those whose means to continue the journey to their land, residence and property are cut off. Such a person can be given some of the *zakāt*, even if he is rich in his homeland. He is not obliged to take it as a loan. Mālik said in the Book of Saḥnūn, 'If he finds someone to borrow from, he should not be given it.' The first position is sounder. He is not obliged to be beholden to anyone when the favour of Allah exists. If he has what will be sufficient for him, there are two transmissions about whether it is permitted for him to take it as a traveller. The well-known position is that he is not given it. If he does take it, he is not obliged to repay it when he reaches his home.

When someone comes and claims to be one of those described, does one accept his word or not? Should he be asked for confirmation of what he says? He must establish himself in terms of his *dīn* but with regard to other qualities, his apparent state will testify on his behalf and there is enough in that. The evidence for that is found in two sound *ḥadīth*s transmitted by the people of the *Ṣaḥīḥ* and it is the literal meaning of the Qur'an. Muslim related from Jarīr that his father said, 'We were with the Prophet ﷺ at the beginning of the day when some people came who were barefooted, clearly destitute, wrapped in striped or plain cloaks, with swords girded on [around their necks]. Most of them were from Muḍar – or all of them were from Muḍar. The face of the Messenger of Allah ﷺ changed when he saw their poverty. He went inside and then came out and ordered Bilāl to give the *adhān* and *iqāmah* and prayed. Then he addressed them, saying, *"O mankind, have taqwā of your Lord who created …* (to the end)" (4:1) and then the *āyah* in *al-Ḥashr*: *"Let each self look to what it has sent forward for Tomorrow."* (59:18) Then people gave *ṣadaqah* in the form of dinars, clothing, a *ṣāʿ* of wheat (until he said) or even half a date." Then one of the *Anṣār* came with a bag which he could barely lift. Indeed, he could not lift it. The people came one after another until I saw two heaps of food and clothing, and I saw the face of the Messenger of Allah ﷺ shining as if it were gold. The Messenger of Allah ﷺ said, "Whoever establishes a good *sunnah* in Islam has its reward and the reward of those who act on it after him without that decreasing their rewards in any way. Whoever establishes a bad *sunnah* in Islam has its burden and the burden of those who act on it after him without that decreasing their burdens in any way."' Enough for the Prophet ﷺ was their outward state and so he encouraged *ṣadaqah* and did not ask for any proof nor investigate whether they had wealth or not.

It is like the *ḥadīth* about the leper, the bald man, and the blind man which Muslim and others transmitted. Abū Hurayrah reported that he heard the Messenger of Allah ﷺ say, 'Among the Banū Israel were a leper, a bald man and a blind man. Allah wanted to test them. He therefore sent an angel to them. He went to the leper and asked him what he would like best. He replied, "A good colour, a good complexion and to be rid of what makes people find me impure." The angel stroked him and his impurity vanished and he was given a good colour and a good complexion. He then asked him, "What type of property do you like best?" The leper answered, "Camels (or cattle)." (Between the leper and bald man, one said camels and the other cattle.) He gave him a pregnant she-camel. He said, "May Allah bless you in them."

'Then the angel went to the bald man and asked him what he would like best. He replied, "Good hair and to be rid of what makes me repellent to people." The angel stroked him and took away what made him repellent and gave him good hair. He then asked him, "What type of property do you like best?" The bald man answered, "Cattle." He gave him a pregnant cow. He said, "May Allah bless you in them."

'Then he went to the blind man and asked him what he would like best. He replied, "I wish that Allah restore my sight to me so that I may see people." He stroked him and Allah restored his sight to him. He then asked him, "What type of property do you like best?" "Sheep," he replied and he was given a pregnant ewe. Flocks and herds were produced for the three men, the first having a valley full of camels, the second one a valley full of cows, and the third one full of sheep.

'Then the angel came in the form of a leper to the one who had been a leper, and said: "I am a poor man and my resources have been exhausted on my journey. My only means of arrival are dependent on Allah and then on you, so I ask you by Him Who gave you your good colour, good complexion and wealth, for a camel by which I may get to my destination." He told him, "I have many obligations." The angel said: "I think I recognise you. Were you not a leper whom people found impure and a poor man to whom Allah gave wealth?" He replied: "I inherited this property through generations." The angel said, "If you are telling a lie, may Allah return you to your former condition."

'The angel then went in the form of a bald man to the one who had been bald, and said the same as he had said to the former and received a similar reply. So he said: "If you are telling a lie, may Allah return you to your former condition." The angel then went to the one who had been blind and said, "I am a poor man and my resources have been exhausted in my journey. My only means of arrival are dependent on Allah and then on you, so I ask you by Him Who restored your eyesight for a sheep by which I may get to my destination." He said, "Yes, I was blind. Allah restored my eyesight, so take what you wish and leave what you wish. I swear by Allah that I shall not argue with you today to return anything you take, as I give it for Allah's sake." The angel said: "Keep your property. You have all simply been put to a test, and Allah is pleased with you and displeased with both of your companions."'

This is the clearest evidence that if someone claims additional poverty in the form of dependents or something else it is not investigated, contrary to someone who is investigated if possible. We find in the *ḥadīth*: 'A poor man and a traveller said: I ask you for a sheep.' He did not oblige him to prove he was travelling. As for a *mukātab*, he is obliged to confirm his *kitābah* because enslavement is his basic state unless freedom is established.

It is not permitted to give *zakāt* to those one is obliged to support: parents, children and spouses. If the ruler gives a man's *zakāt* to his children, parents or wife, it is permitted, but he is not permitted to do that himself because he would be using it to remove his duty [to support them]. Abū Ḥanīfah said, 'He should not give it to a grandchild nor to his *mukātab*, *mudabbar*, *umm walad* or a slave when he has freed half of him because he is commanded to pay it to Allah by means of the hand of the poor person. The benefits of ownership are shared between him and those people, and that is why their testimony is not accepted against one another.'

He said, 'A *mukātab* is a slave as long as he still owes a single dirham. Perhaps he will lose his strength so that the earnings will revert to him.' According to Abū Ḥanīfah, a partially-freed slave is in the position of a *mukātab*, but his companions, Abū Yūsuf and Muḥammad, say that he is in the position of a free person and so *zakāt* may be paid to him.

There is disagreement about when a person pays *zakāt* to someone whom he is not obliged to support. Some of them allow it and some dislike it. Mālik said, 'Fear of praise.' It is related that Muṭarrif said, 'I saw Mālik giving his *zakāt* to his relatives.' Al-Wāqidī said that Mālik said, 'The best place to give your *zakāt* is to your relatives who are not your dependents.' The Prophet ﷺ said to the wife of 'Abdullāh ibn Mas'ūd, 'You have two rewards: the reward for relatives and the reward for *ṣadaqah*.'

There is also disagreement about a woman giving her *zakāt* to her husband. It is mentioned from Ibn Ḥabīb that he can use what she gave him to help with his maintenance of her. Abū Ḥanīfah said that it is not permitted, but his two companions disagreed with him and said that it is permitted. That is sounder because of what is established about Zaynab, the wife of 'Abdullāh, coming to the Messenger of Allah ﷺ and saying, 'I want to give *ṣadaqah* to my husband? Am I allowed to do so?' He answered, 'Yes, and you will have two rewards: the reward for relatives and the reward for *ṣadaqah*.' When the term *ṣadaqah* is undefined, it means *zakāt*. Because she does not have to financially support her husband, he is in the position of a non-relative in respect of her. The reasoning of Abū Ḥanīfah is that the benefits of ownership are shared between them so that the testimony of one of them is not accepted against the other. The *ḥadīth* is therefore taken to mean voluntary *ṣadaqah*. Ash-Shāfi'ī, Abū Thawr and Ashhab believed that it is permitted when he does not pay it to her to discharge part of his obligation. He spends what he took from her on his own maintenance and clothing and spends on her from his own property.

There is also disagreement about the amount that may be given. A debtor is given the amount of his debt, and the poor and destitute are given what will be enough for them and their dependents. There is disagreement about whether it is permitted to give the *niṣāb* or less than it which is based on the previous disagreement about the definition of what constitutes the poor who are permitted to take it. It is related from 'Alī ibn Ziyād and Ibn Nāfi' that there is no defined amount with regard to that, it being up to the discretion of the ruler. There may be few poor people and a great deal of *zakāt* and so a poor person is given the food for a year. Al-Mughīrah related, 'He is given less than the *niṣāb* and the amount given should not reach that.'

Some later scholars said that if there are two *zakāts* in a place: cash and crops, he can take what will make him reach the other.' Ibn al-'Arabī said, 'I think that he can be given the *niṣāb* if there are two or more *zakāts* in the place. The aim is to enrich the poor so that they are not in need. If they take that and there is another *zakāt* collected and they already have what will be enough for them, it should be given to someone else.' This is the position of the People of Opinion about giving the *niṣāb*. Abū Ḥanīfah mentioned that it is permitted. Abū Yūsuf allowed it and said, 'Some of it is for his need and will be consumed immediately and what is left after his immediate need should be less than two hundred dirhams. If he is given more than two hundred altogether, and two hundred is more than his immediate needs is, it is not permitted.'

Some later Ḥanafīs say, 'This is when he has no dependents and no debts. If he has debts, there is nothing wrong in giving him two hundred dirhams or more according to what will settle his debts and leave him with less than two hundred. If he has dependents, there is nothing wrong in giving him an amount which, if divided between his dependents, would mean that each of them got less than two hundred because giving *zakāt* to him means giving it to him and his dependents.' This is a good position.

The words of the Almighty, *'the poor'* is undefined and there is no precondition or limitation on it. It provides evidence that it is permitted to give it to the group who constitute the poor, whether they are from the Banū Hāshim or not. However, the Sunnah reports preconditions. One of them is that it may not go to the Banū Hāshim and that it should not go to those whom the payer is obliged to financially support. There is no disagreement about this. A third precondition is that the recipient should not be strong enough to earn since the Prophet ﷺ said, '*Zakāt* is not lawful for a rich person nor someone fit and healthy.'

There is no disagreement among Muslim scholars that obligatory *zakāt* was not lawful for the Prophet ﷺ or the Banū Hāshim or their clients. It is related that Abū Yūsuf permitted a Hāshimī to give his *ṣadaqah* to another Hāshimī. Aṭ-Ṭabarī related that. Some of the people of knowledge take an aberrant position and say that no *zakāt* is unlawful to the clients of the Banū Hāshim. This is contrary to a firm report from the Prophet ﷺ to his freedman, Abū Rāfi', 'A freedman (*mawlā*) of a people is one of them.'

They disagree about giving voluntary *ṣadaqah* to the Banū Hāshim. That which the majority of scholars believe – and it is sound – is that there is nothing wrong with voluntary *ṣadaqah* given to the Banū Hāshim and their clients because 'Alī, al-'Abbās and Fāṭima were given *ṣadaqah* and *waqf*s were established for a group of the Banū Hāshim. Their *ṣadaqah* comes from well-known famous *waqfs*. Ibn al-Mājishūn, Muṭarrif, Aṣbagh and Ibn Ḥabīb said, 'The Banū Hāshim should not be given obligatory or voluntary *ṣadaqah*.' Ibn al-Qāsim said that the Banū Hāshim may be given voluntary *ṣadaqah*.

Ibn al-Qāsim said, 'The *ḥadīth* from the Prophet ﷺ which says, "*Ṣadaqah* is not lawful for the family of Muḥammad" is about *zakāt*, not voluntary *ṣadaqah*.' Ibn Khuwayzimandād preferred this position, and it is also the position of Abū Yūsuf and Muḥammad. Ibn al-Qāsim said, 'Their clients can receive both kinds of *ṣadaqah*.' Mālik said in *al-Wāḍiḥah*: 'Voluntary *ṣadaqah* is not given to the family of Muḥammad.' Ibn al-Qāsim said, 'It was asked, "And their clients?" He said, "I do not know what their clients are."' He cited as evidence the words of the Prophet ﷺ, 'A freedman of a people is one of them.' He said that he said, 'The nephew of a people is one of them.' Aṣbagh said, 'That is in respect of kindness and sanctity.'

A legal obligation from Allah

This is in the accusative case based on the verbal noun according to Sībawayh. It means that Allah has prescribed it as an obligation. It is permitted for it to be in the nominative for the severance in the words of al-Kisā'ī, i.e. 'It is an obligation.' Az-Zajjāj said, 'I do not know of anyone who recited it.' But, in fact, it was recited by Ibrāhīm ibn Abī 'Aqlah. He made it a predicate.

وَمِنْهُمُ ٱلَّذِينَ يُؤْذُونَ ٱلنَّبِىَّ وَيَقُولُونَ هُوَ أُذُنٌ قُلْ أُذُنُ
خَيْرٍ لَّكُمْ يُؤْمِنُ بِٱللَّهِ وَيُؤْمِنُ لِلْمُؤْمِنِينَ وَرَحْمَةٌ لِّلَّذِينَ
ءَامَنُوا۟ مِنكُمْ وَٱلَّذِينَ يُؤْذُونَ رَسُولَ ٱللَّهِ لَهُمْ عَذَابٌ أَلِيمٌ ﴿٦١﴾

61 Among them are some who insult the Prophet, saying he is only an ear. Say, 'An ear of good for you, believing in Allah and believing in the believers, and a mercy for those among you who believe.' As for those who insult the Messenger of Allah, they will have a painful punishment.

Allah made it clear that the among the hypocrites are some who let their tongues loose in abusing the Prophet ﷺ and said, 'If he blames me, I will swear that I did not do it, and he will accept it. He is an ear which listens.' Al-Jawharī said, 'A man is called "an ear" when he listens to the words of everyone and a single person and many are the same in that.' 'Alī ibn Abī Ṭalḥah related from Ibn 'Abbas that 'an ear' is hearing and accepting.

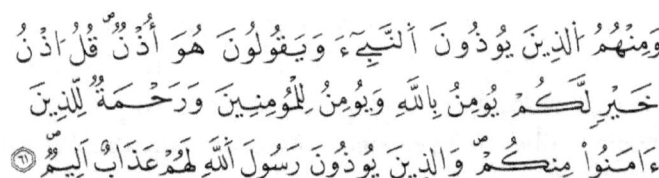

This *āyah* was revealed about 'Attāb ibn Qushayr. He said, 'Muḥammad is an ear. He accepts what is said to him.' It is said that it was Nabtal ibn al-Ḥārith as Ibn Isḥāq said. Nabtal was a corpulent man with long, flowing hair and beard, dark skin, inflamed red eyes, brown discoloured cheeks and ugly character. He is the one about whom the Prophet ﷺ said, 'Whoever wants to look at Shayṭān should look at Nabtal ibn al-Ḥārith.' 'Brown discoloured cheeks' is *suf'ah* which is black mixed with red and a man is calle *'asfa'*. Al-Jawharī said that.

It (*ear*) is recited as *udhun* and *udhn*. *'An ear of good for you'* means: 'an ear of good, not evil.' This means that he listens to good, not to evil. Al-Ḥasan and 'Āṣim in the transmission of Abū Bakr recited *'udhunun khayrun'* while the rest recite it with *iḍāfah*: *'udhunu khayrin'*. Ḥamzah recited *'raḥmatin'* in the genitive while the rest recite *'raḥmatun'* in the nominative as added to *'udhun'*. It implies: 'Say: "He is an ear of good and he is a mercy,"' i.e. he listens to good and not to evil. He listens to what he likes to hear, which is mercy.

If it is read in the genitive, it is added to 'good'. An-Naḥḥās said, 'This is unlikely with the scholars of Arabic because of the distance between the two nouns and it is ugly in the case of the genitive.' Al-Mahdawī said, 'If someone puts "mercy" in the genitive case, it is added to "good" and means "listening to good and listening to mercy" because mercy is part of good. It is not valid to add "mercy" to "believers" because the meaning is: "affirming Allah and affirming the believers."'

The *lām* is extra in the position of the Kufans. It is like *'who feared their Lord (li-rabbihim)'* (7:154). Abū 'Alī said that it is like *'right behind you (lakum)'* (27:72). According to al-Mubarrad, it is connected to a verbal noun indicated by the verb. It implies: 'he believes the believers,' i.e. believes that the believers are telling the truth rather than the unbelievers. Or it implies the meaning as 'believe' means to 'affirm'. So it is transitive with the *lām* as it is transitive in *'affirming what came before it.'* (5:46)

يَحْلِفُونَ بِاللَّهِ لَكُمْ لِيُرْضُوكُمْ وَاللَّهُ وَرَسُولُهُ أَحَقُّ أَن يُرْضُوهُ
إِن كَانُوا مُؤْمِنِينَ ﴿٦٢﴾

62 They swear to you by Allah in order to please you, but it would be more fitting for them to please Allah and His Messenger if they are believers.

They swear to you by Allah in order to please you,

It is related that some of the hypocrites met, among them al-Julās ibn Suwayd and Wadī'ah ibn Thābit. With them was a lad of the *Anṣār* called 'Āmir ibn Qays.

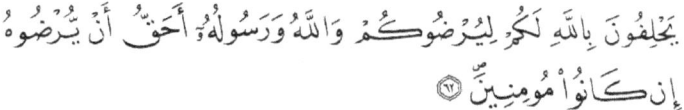

They spoke disparaging of the Prophet ﷺ and said, 'If what Muḥammad says is true, then we are worse than donkeys.' The boy became angry and said, 'By Allah, what he says is true and you are worse than donkeys!' He informed the Prophet ﷺ about what they said and they swore that 'Āmir was lying. 'Āmir said, 'They are the liars!' He swore to that and said, 'O Allah, so not let us part until it is clear who is lying and who is telling the truth!' Then Allah revealed this *āyah.*

but it would be more fitting for them to please Allah and His Messenger if they are believers.

This is an inceptive and predicate. The position of Sībawayh is that it implies: 'It is more fitting to please Allah and more fitting to please His Messenger.' Then there is some elision. It is as one of them said:

We are pleased with what we have and you are pleased with what you have.
Opinions differ.

Muḥammad ibn Yazīd said, 'There is no elision in the words. It implies: "It is more fitting to please Allah and His Messenger" with a change in the normal word order.' Al-Farrā' said that it means that it is more fitting to please His Messenger. Allah began the words as you might say, 'What Allah wills, and you will.' An-Naḥḥās said that the position of Sībawayh is better because there is a sound transmission that the Prophet ﷺ forbade that one say, 'What Allah wills, and you will.' It is not assumed then that there is any change in the word order. Its meaning is sound.

It is said that Allah put His own pleasure in his pleasure ﷺ. Do you not see that He says: *'Whoever obeys the Messenger has obeyed Allah'* (4:80)? When ar-Rabī' ibn Khuthaym recited this *āyah*, he would stop and then say, 'A particle and what a particle! He entrusted to him and he only commanded us good.'

Our scholars said that this *āyah* entails acceptance of an oath sworn by someone, even if the one against whom it is sworn is not pleased. The oath is the right of the claimant. It contains the fact that an oath by Allah is according to what was mentioned. The Prophet ﷺ said, 'Whoever swears an oath should swear by Allah or be silent. Whoever is sworn to should believe it.' Oaths were already discussed and the exception in them in *al-Mā'idah* (5:89).

أَلَمْ يَعْلَمُوٓا۟ أَنَّهُۥ مَن يُحَادِدِ ٱللَّهَ وَرَسُولَهُۥ فَأَنَّ لَهُۥ نَارَ جَهَنَّمَ
خَٰلِدًا فِيهَا ۚ ذَٰلِكَ ٱلْخِزْىُ ٱلْعَظِيمُ ٦٣

63 Do they not know that whoever opposes Allah and His Messenger, will have the Fire of Hell, remaining in it timelessly, for ever? That is the great disgrace.

'*They*' are the hypocrites. Ibn Hurmuz and al-Ḥasan recited 'you know' (*ta'lamū*) with a *tā'* in the second person. '*Innahu*' is in the accusative by the effect of 'know' and the pronoun *hā'* alludes to the opposing speech. '*Whoever opposes Allah and His Messengers*' is in the nominative by the inceptive. *Maḥāddah* (opposing) means opposition where one party is on one edge (*ḥadd*) while the other party is on another edge, like a split. The verb is *ḥādda*, to be on an edge other than that of another.

The phrase '*will have the Fire of Hell*' is preceded by *fā'*, and it is said that what is after the *fā'* in a precondition is inchoative as the subject of a nominal sentence. Therefore it is obliged for it to be read as *inna*. Al-Khalīl and Sībawayh allow *inna*. Sībawayh said that it is excellent and cited a verse in support of it. Most, however, recite it as *anna*. Al-Khalīl and Sībawayh also said that the second *anna* is an appositive for the first. Al-Mubarrad claimed that this is rejected and that what is sound was what al-Jarmī said. He said that the second is repeated for stress since the words are long. It is like: '*They will be the greatest losers in the Next World*' (27:5) [literally: 'They, they will be] and like "*The final fate of both of them is that they will be forever in the Fire*" (59:17) [in which the pronouns are repeated.]

Al-Akhfash said, 'It means that the Fire is obliged for him.' Al-Mubarrad objected to that and said, 'This is an error since, when *inna* has a *fatḥah* and double *nūn*, one does not begin with it or imply the predicate.' 'Alī ibn Sulaymān said, 'It means that he will have the Fire of Hell. If the second is a predicate, the inceptive is elided.' It is said that it implies: 'He will have the Fire of Hell.' '*Anna*' is nominative by the implication of a word governed by the preposition between the *fā'* and *anna*.

يَحْذَرُ ٱلْمُنَٰفِقُونَ أَن تُنَزَّلَ عَلَيْهِمْ سُورَةٌ تُنَبِّئُهُم بِمَا فِى
قُلُوبِهِمْ ۚ قُلِ ٱسْتَهْزِءُوٓا۟ إِنَّ ٱللَّهَ مُخْرِجٌ مَّا تَحْذَرُونَ ٦٤

64 The hypocrites are afraid that a *sūrah* may be sent down about them, informing them of what is in their hearts. Say: 'Go on mocking! Allah will expose everything you are afraid of.'

The hypocrites are afraid

This is a report and not a command. It indicates that it is the predicate of the *'anna'* after it: *'Allah will expose everything you are afraid of'* because they obstinately disbelieved. As-Suddī said, 'By Allah, one of the hypocrites said, "I would prefer to be brought and flogged a hundred times than that something should be revealed to disgrace us." Then the *āyah* was revealed.'

'Yaḥdharu' means to be wary and on guard. Az-Zajjāj said that it means: 'they should be on guard'. It is a command, as it is said, 'He should do that.'

that a *sūrah* may be sent down about them,

In the words *'may be sent down about them' an* is in the accusative, i.e. 'that there may be revealed.' According to the position of Sībawayh, it can be in the genitive based on the elision of *min*. It is permitted for it to be in the accusative as the object of *'are afraid'* because Sībawayh permitted one to say *'ḥadhirtu Zaydan'*. [POEM] Al-Mubarrad does not permit it because *ḥidhr* (being afraid) is not transitive.

The meaning of *'alayhim* (*about them*: the hypocrites) can also mean 'to them' (to the believers) [about the hypocrites]. The hypocrites are afraid that something will be revealed about them, speaking about their shameful doings, evils and shortcomings. This is why the *sūrah* is called: the Disgracer, the Provoker and the Scatterer as was mentioned at the beginning of the *sūrah*. Al-Ḥasan said, 'The Muslims called this *sūrah* "the Digger" because it digs into what is in the hearts of the hypocrites and displays it.'

Say: 'Go on mocking! Allah will expose everything you are afraid of.'

This is a command which is a threat. *'Allah will expose…'* and bring it to light. Ibn 'Abbās said, 'Allah revealed the names of the hypocrites. There were seventy of them. Then Allah left the mention of those names out of the Qur'an out of compassion and mercy because their children were Muslims. People criticised one another.' According to this, Allah carried out His threat and made that known. It is said that He acquainted His Prophet ﷺ with their states and names, not that He revealed them in the Qur'an. Allah Almighty says: *'…and know them by their ambivalent speech.'* (47:30) This is a type of inspiration. Some hypocrites hesitated and neither denied or affirmed Muhammad ﷺ and there were also some of them who recognised his truthfulness, but were obstinate.

وَلَئِن سَأَلْتَهُمْ لَيَقُولُنَّ إِنَّمَا كُنَّا نَخُوضُ وَنَلْعَبُ قُلْ أَبِاللَّهِ وَءَايَٰتِهِۦ
وَرَسُولِهِۦ كُنتُمْ تَسْتَهْزِءُونَ ﴿٦٥﴾

65 If you ask them they will say, 'We were only joking and playing around.' Say: 'Would you make a mockery of Allah and of His Signs and of His Messenger?

This *āyah* was revealed about the Tabūk expedition. Aṭ-Ṭabarī and others said that Qatādah said, 'While the Prophet ﷺ was travelling in the Tabūk expedition, some riders of the hypocrites were traveling in front of him and said, "Wait for this man to conquer the fortresses of Syria and take the forts of the Greeks!" Allah acquainted him with what was in their hearts and what they were talking about. He said, "Hold the riders for me." Then he went to them and said, "You said such-and-such." They swore an oath and said, "We were only joking and playing around."' They meant that they were not serious.

Aṭ-Ṭabarī mentioned that 'Abdullāh ibn 'Umar said, 'I think that the one who said that was Wadī'ah ibn Thābit while holding on to the girth of the she-camel of the Messenger of Allah ﷺ while he was walking with it and he was saying, "We were only joking and playing around." The Prophet ﷺ then said, *"Would you make a mockery of Allah and of His Signs and of His Messenger?"*' An-Naqqāsh said that the one hanging onto it was 'Abdullāh ibn Ubayy ibn Salūl. That is what al-Qushayrī mentioned from Ibn 'Umar. Ibn 'Aṭiyyah said, 'That is an error because he was not present at Tabūk.' Al-Qushayrī said, 'It is said that the Prophet ﷺ said this to Wadī'ah ibn Thābit who was one of the hypocrites on the expedition to Tabūk.'

Khawḍ (joking) is to dive into water and then it is used metaphorically for every entry into something which contains soiling and abuse. Qāḍī Abū Bakr ibn al-'Arabī said, 'What they said must be either serious or a jest. Whichever it was is unbelief. Joking with unbelief is unbelief. Seriously expressing unbelief is unbelief without any disagreement in the community. Realisation is the brother of knowledge and the truth. Jesting is the brother of falsehood and ignorance.' Our scholars say, 'Look at Allah's words: *"They said, 'What! Are you making a mockery of us?' He said, 'I seek refuge with Allah from being one of the ignorant!'"* (2:67)'

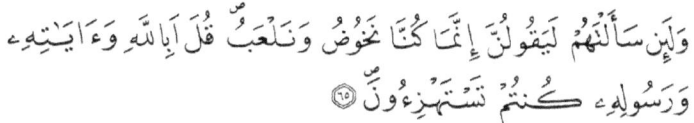

Scholars disagree about jesting in respect of other rulings, such as those applying to buying, marriage and divorce, and there are three positions. One is that it is not binding in general, another that it is generally binding, and another that makes a distinction between selling and other things. It is binding in cases of marriage and divorce. That is the position of ash-Shāfiʿī about divorce. It is not binding where sales are concerned.

Mālik said in the Book of Muḥammad that a jest made with regard to marrying someone is binding. Abū Zayd said from Ibn al-Qāsim in *al-ʿUtbiyyah* that it is not binding. ʿAlī ibn Ziyād said that it is nullified both before and after. Ash-Shāfiʿī said that there are two views about the one who jokes and two views are also transmitted from our scholars. Ibn al-Mundhir related the consensus that jests and serious statements are the same in respect of divorce. Some of our later people said, 'There is agreement that jesting in respect of marriage and selling are not binding. If they disagree, seriousness takes precedence over jest.'

Abū Dāwūd, at-Tirmidhī and ad-Dāraquṭnī related from Abū Hurayrah that the Messenger of Allah ﷺ said, 'There are three areas in which seriousness and jest are both the same: marriage, divorce, and taking back a wife.' At-Tirmidhī said that it is a *gharīb ḥasan ḥadīth.* This was the basis of the practice of the people of knowledge among the Companions of the Prophet ﷺ and others. 'Taking back a wife' is found in the *ḥadīth.* We find in the *Muwaṭṭā'* from Yaḥyā ibn Saʿīd that Saʿīd ibn al-Musayyab said, 'There are three matters in which there can be no playing about: marriage, divorce and emancipation.' That is how it is related from ʿAlī ibn Abī Ṭālib, ʿAbdullāh ibn Masʿūd and Abū ad-Dardā'. He said, 'There are three matters in which there can be no playing about or retraction, and someone who does play about regarding them is considered serious: marriage, divorce and emancipation.' Saʿīd ibn al-Musayyab related that ʿUmar said, 'Four are legal in every case: emancipation, divorce, marriage and vows.' Aḍ-Ḍaḥḥāk said, 'There are three instances in which there can be no playing about: marriage, divorce and vows.'

لَا تَعْتَذِرُوا۟ قَدْ كَفَرْتُم بَعْدَ إِيمَٰنِكُمْ ۚ إِن يُعْفَ عَن طَآئِفَةٍ مِّنكُمْ
تُعَذَّبْ طَآئِفَةٌۢ بِأَنَّهُمْ كَانُوا۟ مُجْرِمِينَ ٦٦

66 Do not try to excuse yourselves. You have disbelieved after having believed. If one group of you is pardoned, another group will be punished for being evildoers.'

'Do not try to excuse yourselves. You have disbelieved after having believed.' This is rebuke. It is as if Allah is saying, 'Do not do that which is of no use.' Then He judged that they are unbelievers and there is no excuse for the wrong action. *Iʿtidhara* means *aʿdhara*, i.e. to become someone with an excuse. Using *iʿtidhara*, Labīd said:

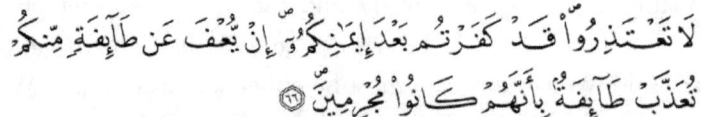

Anyone who weeps for an entire year is excused.

Excusing is to wipe out the effect of an outburst. *I'tidhar* describes the effacement of dwellings. *I'tidhar* is obliteration. A poet said:

Did you recognise signs made by
the ruins of the walls of your friend effaced by oil?

Ibn al-A'rābī said, 'Its root meaning is cutting off. When you apologise to someone, you cut off the feelings in his heart. An example of this is the use of the word for the circumcision (*'adhrah*) of a boy and what is cut from him in circumcision. There is also the virginity (*'udhrah*) of a girl because the seal of her virginity is cut by sexual intercourse.'

If one group of you is pardoned, another group will be punished for being evildoers.'

It is said that there were three groups. Two of them mocked and one laughed. The one who was pardoned was the one who laughed and did not speak. *Ṭā'ifah* is a group. It is used in the singular, meaning 'the very group'. Ibn al-Anbārī said, 'The plural word is used for one person as you say, "So-and-so went out on mules."' He said that it is permitted for it to be *ṭā'ifah* when you mean one and the *hā'* in it is for stress.

There is disagreement about the name of this man who was pardoned for the words. It is said that it was Makhshī ibn Ḥumayyir as Ibn Isḥāq stated. Ibn Hishām said that it was Ibn Makhshī. Khalīfah ibn Khayyāṭ said in his *History* that his name was Mukhāshin ibn Ḥumayyir. Ibn 'Abd al-Barr mentioned Mukhāshin al-Ḥimyarī and as-Suhaylī mentioned Mukhashshin ibn Ḥumayyir.

They all mentioned that he was martyred at Yamāmah. He repented and was called 'Abd ar-Raḥmān. He prayed to Allah to make him a martyr. His grave is unknown. They disagree about whether he was a hypocrite or a sincere Muslim. It is said that he was a hypocrite and then repented sincerely. It is said that he was a sincere Muslim, but he listened to the hypocrites and laughed with them and did not object to them.

ٱلْمُنَٰفِقُونَ وَٱلْمُنَٰفِقَٰتُ بَعْضُهُم مِّنۢ بَعْضٍ يَأْمُرُونَ بِٱلْمُنكَرِ وَيَنْهَوْنَ
عَنِ ٱلْمَعْرُوفِ وَيَقْبِضُونَ أَيْدِيَهُمْ نَسُوا۟ ٱللَّهَ فَنَسِيَهُمْ إِنَّ
ٱلْمُنَٰفِقِينَ هُمُ ٱلْفَٰسِقُونَ ﴿٦٧﴾

67 The men and women of the hypocrites are as bad as one another. They command what is wrong and forbid what is right and keep their fists tightly closed. They have forgotten Allah, so He has forgotten them. The hypocrites are deviators.

'The men and women of the hypocrites' is the inceptive and '*ba'ḍuhum*' is the predicate. It is permitted that it is an appositive and the predicate is '*min ba'ḍ*'. *'The hypocrites are as bad as one another'* means that they are like a single thing in being outside the *dīn*. Az-Zajjāj said that this is connected to Allah's words: *'They swear by Allah that they are of your number, but they are not of your number.'* (9:55) This means that they are not believers. They resemble one another in commanding what is wrong and forbidding what is right. *'Keeping their fists tightly closed'* means in abandoning *jihād* and the due which is mandatory for them.

Nisyān (forgetting) here means failing to do. In other words they abandoned what Allah commanded them to do and so He left them in doubt. It is said that they abandoned His command so that He became like something forgotten and so they were in the position of being forgotten in respect of reward. Qatādah said that *'He has forgotten them'* means in respect of any good. He has not forgotten them in respect of evil. *Fisq* (deviance) is leaving obedience and the *dīn*. It was already mentioned (2:27).

وَعَدَ ٱللَّهُ ٱلْمُنَٰفِقِينَ وَٱلْمُنَٰفِقَٰتِ وَٱلْكُفَّارَ نَارَ جَهَنَّمَ
خَٰلِدِينَ فِيهَا هِىَ حَسْبُهُمْ وَلَعَنَهُمُ ٱللَّهُ وَلَهُمْ عَذَابٌ
مُّقِيمٌ ﴿٦٨﴾

68 Allah has promised the men and women of the hypocrites and unbelievers the Fire of Hell, remaining in it timelessly, for ever. It will suffice them. Allah has cursed them. They will have everlasting punishment.

It is said that Allah's promise of good is designated by the word *wa'd* and His threat of evil by *wa'īd*. *'Khālidīn'* is in the accusative for the adverbial *ḥāl* and the regent is elided. It means: they will roast in it forever. *'It will suffice them'* is an inceptive and predicate, meaning that it is enough for them and an ample repayment for their actions. The word for curse (*la'n*) denotes distance, implying that they are far from Allah's mercy. This was already mentioned (2:88) *'Everlasting'* means constant and continuous.

كَالَّذِينَ مِن قَبْلِكُمْ كَانُوٓا۟ أَشَدَّ مِنكُمْ قُوَّةً وَأَكْثَرَ أَمْوَٰلًا وَأَوْلَٰدًا
فَٱسْتَمْتَعُوا۟ بِخَلَٰقِهِمْ فَٱسْتَمْتَعْتُم بِخَلَٰقِكُمْ كَمَا ٱسْتَمْتَعَ ٱلَّذِينَ
مِن قَبْلِكُم بِخَلَٰقِهِمْ وَخُضْتُمْ كَٱلَّذِى خَاضُوٓا۟ أُو۟لَٰٓئِكَ حَبِطَتْ
أَعْمَٰلُهُمْ فِى ٱلدُّنْيَا وَٱلْءَاخِرَةِ وَأُو۟لَٰٓئِكَ هُمُ ٱلْخَٰسِرُونَ ٦٩

69 Like those before you who had greater strength than you and more wealth and children. They enjoyed their portion; and you enjoyed your portion as those before you enjoyed theirs. You have plunged into defamation as they plunged into it. The actions of such people come to nothing in this world or the Next World. They are the lost.

Like those before you

Az-Zajjāj said that the *kāf* is in the position of the accusative. It means: 'Allah has promised the unbelievers the Fire of Hell as He promised those before them.' It is said that it means: 'you performed actions like those before you in commanding the bad and forbidding the good.' The *muḍāf* is elided. It is said that it means: 'you are like those before you,' and so the *kāf* is in the nominative because it is the predicate of an elided inceptive. *'Ashadd'* (greater) is not inflected because it is the comparative of an adjective and its root is *ashdad*, i.e. they were stronger than you and that did not enable them to remove Allah's punishment.

Sa'īd related from Abū Hurayrah that the Prophet ﷺ said, 'You will take on what the nations before you took on arm by arm, hand and by hand, and fathom by fathom until if one of them were to enter a lizard's hole, you would also enter it.' Abū Hurayrah said, 'If you wish, you can recite: *"Like those before you who had greater strength than you and more wealth and children. They enjoyed their portion* (and Abū Hurayrah said that *khalāq* is the *dīn*), *so enjoy your portion as those before you enjoyed their portion…"*' They said, 'Prophet of Allah, does that refer to the Jews and Christians?' He answered, 'Who are the people but them?' We find from him in the *Ṣaḥīḥ* that the Prophet ﷺ said, 'You will follow the customs of those before you hand by hand and arm by arm until if they were to enter a lizard's hole, you would also enter it.' They asked, 'Messenger of Allah, the Jews and Christians?' 'Who else then?' he replied. Ibn 'Abbās said, 'How similar today is to yesterday! We resemble those of the tribe of Israel!' Ibn Mas'ūd said something similar.

They enjoyed their portion;

This means that they benefited from their portion of the *dīn* as those before them did.

You have plunged into defamation as they plunged into it.

'*You have plunged*' means by moving from slander to direct address. In '*as they plunged into it*' the *kāf* is in the position of the accusative as describing the adjective of an elided verbal noun. It means: 'you plunged as those ones plunged.' '*Alladhī*' is an imperfect noun like '*man*' which can be used for the singular or the plural, and it was discussed in *al-Baqarah* (2:114).

The verb *khāḍa* is used for plunging into water. The verbal noun is *khawḍ* or *khiyāḍ* and the place is *makhāḍah* (ford) through which riders and animals cross. The plural is also *makhāḍ* and *makhāwiḍ*, as Abū Zayd said. *Akhāḍa* is used for making an animal ford through water. *Khāḍa* is used for plunging into floods of ignorance and moving a sword about in someone you have struck with it. *Khawwaḍa* is used for wallowing in spilled blood – this is an intensive form used for stress. *Mikhwaḍ* is an instrument in which drink is mixed as a *mijda'* is used for stirring pottage. *Khāḍa* is used for people entering into discourse and Form VI is used for people involved in talk.

So it means: 'You have plunged into the ways of this world through jest and playing. It is said to mean plunging into the business of Muḥammad by denial. '*Come to nothing*' means to be null and void. This was already discussed (2:217-218). '*Actions*' means their good deeds. '*Lost*' was already discussed (2:27).

أَلَمْ يَأْتِهِمْ نَبَأُ ٱلَّذِينَ مِن قَبْلِهِمْ قَوْمِ نُوحٍ وَعَادٍ وَثَمُودَ وَقَوْمِ
إِبْرَٰهِيمَ وَأَصْحَٰبِ مَدْيَنَ وَٱلْمُؤْتَفِكَٰتِ أَتَتْهُمْ رُسُلُهُم بِٱلْبَيِّنَٰتِ
فَمَا كَانَ ٱللَّهُ لِيَظْلِمَهُمْ وَلَٰكِن كَانُوٓا۟ أَنفُسَهُمْ يَظْلِمُونَ ٧٠

70 Has the news of those who came before them not reached them, the people of Nūḥ and 'Ād and Thamūd, the people of Ibrāhīm and the inhabitants of Madyan and the overturned

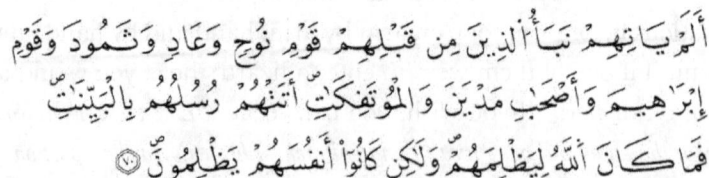

cities? Their Messengers brought them the Clear Signs. Allah did not wrong them; rather they wronged themselves.

'Not reached them' is a predicate. The *alif* at the beginning is for confirmation and warning, i.e. 'Have you not heard of Our destroying the unbelievers before you?' *'The people of Nūḥ and 'Ād and Thamūd'* is an appositive for *'those'*. *'The people of Ibrāhīm'* were Nimrod ibn Kan'ān and his people. Madyan is the name of the land where Shu'ayb was located. They were destroyed by the punishment of the Day of the Shadow. *'The overturned cities'* refers to the people of Lūṭ because their land was overturned with them on it. Qatādah said that. It is said that it is used for all who are destroyed as it is said, 'This world was overturned on them.'

'The Messengers' means all the Prophets. It is said that their Messengers came to the people of the overturned cities. According to this, their Messenger was Lūṭ alone, but a Messenger was sent to every city, and there were three cities – or four. In another place He uses *'overturned cities'* (53:53) generically. It is also said that it means one Messenger, like *'Messengers, eat of the good things'* (23:51) when he was the only one in his generation. This is debatable based on the sound *ḥadīth* reported from the Prophet ﷺ: 'Allah addressed the believers with what he commanded the Messengers.' It was already mentioned in *al-Baqarah* (2:172), What is meant are all Messengers. Allah knows best.

'Allah did not wrong them' since He did not destroy them until He had sent Prophets to them. *'They wronged themselves'* after the proof had been established against them.

وَالْمُؤْمِنُونَ وَالْمُؤْمِنَٰتُ بَعْضُهُمْ أَوْلِيَآءُ بَعْضٍ يَأْمُرُونَ بِالْمَعْرُوفِ
وَيَنْهَوْنَ عَنِ الْمُنكَرِ وَيُقِيمُونَ الصَّلَوٰةَ وَيُؤْتُونَ الزَّكَوٰةَ وَيُطِيعُونَ
اللَّهَ وَرَسُولَهُۥٓ أُوْلَٰٓئِكَ سَيَرْحَمُهُمُ اللَّهُ إِنَّ اللَّهَ عَزِيزٌ حَكِيمٌ ﴿٧١﴾

71 The men and women of the believers are friends of one another. They command what is right and forbid what is wrong, and establish the prayer and pay *zakāt*, and obey Allah and His Messenger. They are the people on whom Allah will have mercy. Allah is Almighty, All-Wise.

The men and women of the believers are friends of one another.

Their hearts are united in affection, love and friendship. Allah says that the hypocrites are *'as bad as one another'* because their hearts are in disagreement, but they are added together in the ruling.

They command what is right and forbid what is wrong,

Commanding what is right refers to worship of Allah and His *tawḥīd* and all that that entails. Forbidding what is wrong refers to worshipping idols and all that that entails. Aṭ-Ṭabarī mentioned that Abū al-'Āliyah said, 'All that Allah mentions in the Qur'an about commanding what is right [which is inviting people from *shirk* to Islam] and [all that He mentions about] forbidding what is wrong is about forbidding the worship of idols and *shaytāns*.' Commanding the good and forbidding the wrong was already discussed in *Sūrat al-Mā'idah* (5:79) and *Āl 'Imrān* (3:21-22). Praise be to Allah.

and establish the prayer and pay *zakāt*,

'Establish the prayer' was already mentioned in *al-Baqarah* (2:3). Ibn 'Abbās said that it is the five prayers, and *zakāt* here is the obligatory *zakāt*. Ibn 'Aṭiyyah said, 'I consider the praise entailed by supererogatory prayers to be more effective since it is more fitting for those who perform the supererogatory than those who perform the obligatory.'

and obey Allah and His Messenger.

They *'obey Allah'* by fulfilling obligations and *'His Messenger'* by following the Sunnah. The future use of the *sīn* in *'will have mercy'* means that souls will enjoy hope of it and Allah's bounty.

وَعَدَ ٱللَّهُ ٱلْمُؤْمِنِينَ وَٱلْمُؤْمِنَٰتِ جَنَّٰتٍ تَجْرِى مِن تَحْتِهَا ٱلْأَنْهَٰرُ
خَٰلِدِينَ فِيهَا وَمَسَٰكِنَ طَيِّبَةً فِى جَنَّٰتِ عَدْنٍ وَرِضْوَٰنٌ مِّنَ
ٱللَّهِ أَكْبَرُ ذَٰلِكَ هُوَ ٱلْفَوْزُ ٱلْعَظِيمُ ﴿٧٢﴾

72 Allah has promised the men and women of the believers Gardens with rivers flowing under them, remaining in them timelessly, for ever, and fine dwellings in the Gardens of Eden. And Allah's good pleasure is even greater. That is the great victory.

'Rivers flowing under them' are rivers under the trees and houses of the Gardens. It was already mentioned in *al-Baqarah* (2:25) that their flow is constrained by Divine Power without banks. *'Fine dwellings'* are castles built of emeralds, pearls and rubies whose scent spreads a distance of five hundred years.

'Gardens of Eden' is in the Abode of Permanence. A place is called *'adn* when one abides in it. The word for mine *(ma'din)* derives from it. 'Aṭā' al-Khurāsānī said, 'The Gardens of Eden are the very pinnacle of the Garden and their roof is the Throne of the All-Merciful.' Ibn Mas'ūd said, 'It is in the middle of the Garden.' Al-Ḥasan said, 'It is a gold castle which is only entered by a Prophet, true man, martyr or just judge.' Something similar is related from aḍ-Ḍaḥḥāk. Muqātil and al-Kalbī said, 'Eden is the highest degree in the Garden. In it is the Spring of Tasnīm. There are gardens around it encircling it which are hidden until the Prophets, true, martyrs, righteous and whomever Allah wishes alight in them.' Allah's good pleasure is even greater than that.

يَٰٓأَيُّهَا ٱلنَّبِيُّ جَٰهِدِ ٱلْكُفَّارَ وَٱلْمُنَٰفِقِينَ وَٱغْلُظْ عَلَيْهِمْ ۚ وَمَأْوَىٰهُمْ
جَهَنَّمُ ۖ وَبِئْسَ ٱلْمَصِيرُ ﴿٧٣﴾

73 O Prophet, do *jihād* against the unbelievers and hypocrites and be harsh with them. Their shelter will be Hell. What an evil destination!

O Prophet, do *jihād* against the unbelievers and hypocrites

This is addressed to the Prophet ﷺ and it includes his community after him. It is said that it means: 'Do *jihād* against the unbelievers together with the believers.' Ibn 'Abbās said, 'Allah orders *jihād* against the unbelievers with the sword, and with the tongue, and by strong reprimand and harshness against the hypocrites.' It is related that Ibn Mas'ūd said, 'Strive against the hypocrites with your own hand. If you cannot do so, then with your tongue. If you cannot do that, then frown to their faces.' Al-Ḥasan said, 'Strive against the hypocrites by carrying out the *ḥudūd* punishments on them and with the tongue (Qatādah preferred that). They are the ones who most frequently violate the *ḥudūd*.'

Ibn al-'Arabī said, 'As for establishing evidence against them with the tongue, it is constant. As for the *ḥudūd* because they are those who most frequently violate the *ḥudūd*, that is a claim without any proof. Someone who is disobedient is not a hypocrite. The hypocrite is the one who has hypocrisy hidden in his heart, and it may not appear on the limbs. The context of the reports about those who violated the *ḥudūd* testify that they were not hypocrites.'

and be harsh with them.

Ghilaẓ is the opposite of gentleness. It is the hardness of the heart in bringing about something against a person and that is not by the tongue. The Prophet ﷺ said, 'When a person's slave-girl commits fornication, flog her with the *ḥadd* punishment and do not blame her.' Indicating that are the words of Allah: *'If you had been rough or hard of heart (ghalīẓ), they would have scattered from around you.'* (3:159) There is also what the women said to 'Umar, 'You are coarser and rougher (*aghlaẓ*) than the Messenger of Allah ﷺ.' The meaning of *ghilaẓ* is to have a hard side. It is the opposite of the words of the Almighty: *'Take the believers who follow you under your wing'* (26:215) and: *'Take them under your wing, out of mercy.'*(17:24) This *āyah* abrogates everything regarding pardon, truce and overlooking.

يَحْلِفُونَ بِاللَّهِ مَا قَالُوا وَلَقَدْ قَالُوا كَلِمَةَ الْكُفْرِ وَكَفَرُوا بَعْدَ
إِسْلَامِهِمْ وَهَمُّوا بِمَا لَمْ يَنَالُوا وَمَا نَقَمُوا إِلَّا أَنْ أَغْنَاهُمُ اللَّهُ
وَرَسُولُهُ مِنْ فَضْلِهِ فَإِنْ يَتُوبُوا يَكُ خَيْرًا لَهُمْ وَإِنْ يَتَوَلَّوْا
يُعَذِّبْهُمُ اللَّهُ عَذَابًا أَلِيمًا فِي الدُّنْيَا وَالْآخِرَةِ وَمَا لَهُمْ فِي الْأَرْضِ
مِنْ وَلِيٍّ وَلَا نَصِيرٍ ﴿٧٤﴾

74 They swear by Allah that they said nothing, but they definitely spoke the word of unbelief and returned to unbelief after their Islam. They planned something which they did not achieve and they were vindictive for no other reason than that Allah and His Messenger had enriched them from His bounty. If they were to repent, it would be better for them. But if they turn away, Allah will punish them with a painful punishment in this world and the Next World, and they will not find any protector or helper on the earth.

They swear by Allah that they said nothing,

It is related that this *āyah* was revealed about al-Julās ibn Suwayd ibn aṣ-Ṣāmit and Wadī'ah ibn Thabit who attacked the Prophet ﷺ and said, 'If Muḥammad is telling the truth about our brethren who are our masters and leaders, then we are worse than donkeys.' 'Āmir ibn Qays said to him, 'Yes, by Allah! Muḥammad speaks the truth and is affirmed and you are worse than monkeys!' 'Āmir reported that to the Prophet ﷺ and al-Julās came and swore by Allah at the minbar of the Prophet ﷺ that 'Āmir was lying and 'Āmir swore that he had indeed said that. He added, 'O Allah, send down something to Your truthful Prophet!' and this was revealed.

It is also said that the one who heard that was 'Āṣim ibn 'Adī. It is said that it was Ḥudhayfah. It is also said that his wife's son heard it: his name was 'Umayr ibn Sa'd. Ibn Isḥāq said that. Others said that his name was Muṣ'ab. Al-Julās wanted to kill him so that he would not inform on them and so Allah revealed: *'They planned something which they did not achieve.'* Mujāhid said, 'When al-Julās's companion said to him, "I will tell the Messenger of Allah ﷺ what you said," he wanted to kill him but was unable to do so.' He said, 'That indicates His words: "*They planned something which they did not achieve.*"'

It is said that it was revealed about 'Abdullāh ibn Ubayy who saw a man of Ghifār fighting with a man of Juhaynah. Juhaynah were the allies of the *Anṣār.* The Ghifārī got the better of the Juhanī and Ibn Ubayy said, 'Banū Aws and Khazraj! Help your brother! By Allah, the metaphor of us and Muḥammad is only as saying goes: "Fatten your dog and it will eat you." When we return to Madīnah, the mightier will expel the inferior from it!' The Prophet ﷺ was informed about that and 'Abdullāh ibn Ubayy came to him and swore that he had not said it. Qatādah said that.

There is a third position that it is what all the hypocrites say. Al-Ḥasan said that. Ibn al-'Arabī said, 'That is sound because of the universality of the words and the meaning applies to both him and them. The basis of that is their belief that he was not a Prophet.'

they definitely spoke the word of unbelief

An-Naqqāsh said, 'It is their denial of the victory which Allah promised.' It is said that the '*word of unbelief*' is al-Julās's statement: 'If what Muḥammad brought is the truth, we are worse than donkeys' and the words of Ibn Ubayy, 'When we return to Madīnah, the mightier will expel the inferior from it!' Al-Qushayrī said, '"*The word of unbelief*" is insulting the Prophet ﷺ and attacking Islam.'

and returned to unbelief

They returned to unbelief after being judged to be Muslims. This indicates that the hypocrites are unbelievers. Allah says elsewhere: *'That is because they have believed and then returned to unbelief.'* (63:3) The *āyah* also indicates that unbelief entails all that contradicts affirmation and recognition. Faith requires only: 'There is no god but Allah' and not any other words or actions except that of the prayer. Isḥāq ibn Rāhawayh said, 'They agree about the prayer while there is not agreement about other Divine ordinances, all of them saying, "If someone is thought to be an unbeliever and then is seen praying the prayers at their proper times for several prayers in succession when it is not known if he has affirmed it with his tongue, it is judged that he believes." This is not the case with the fast, *zakāt* or other things.'

They planned something which they did not achieve

This refers to what the hypocrites wanted to do in respect of killing the Prophet ﷺ on the night of 'Aqabah in the Tabūk expedition. There were twelve men. Ḥudhayfah said, 'The Messenger of Allah ﷺ named them, listing every one of them. I asked, "Why not send for them and kill them?" He answered, "I do not want the Arabs to say, 'When he got his Companions, he went and killed them.' Allah will let the *dubaylah* deal with them." Someone asked, "Messenger of Allah, what is the *dubaylah*?" He answered, "A blaze from Hell which Allah puts on the aorta of the heart of someone until he expires." That was what happened.' Muslim transmitted the gist of it. It is said that they had wanted to crown Ibn Ubayy so that they could agree on him as leader. What Mujāhid said about this was already discussed. [see above]

They were vindictive for no other reason than that Allah and His Messenger had enriched them

There was no reason for their vindictiveness as an-Nābighah says:

There is no criticism of them other than the fact that their swords
are blunted by the blows of the squadrons.

The verb is *naqama, yanqimu* and *naqima, yanqamu*. The poet says:

They were only vindictive to the Umayyads
because they were forbearing when they usurped.

Zuhayr said:

He defers and puts it in a book so that it is stored up
for the Day of Reckoning or He advances it and takes revenge.

It is recited as *yanqimu* and *yanqamu*.

Ash-Sha'bī said, 'They used to ask for blood money and the Messenger of Allah ﷺ judged that they should have it and so they were enriched.' 'Ikrimah mentioned that there were twelve men. It is said that the one killed was the client of al-Julās. Al-Kalbī said, 'Before the Prophet ﷺ came, they were in straightened circumstances, not riding horses or obtaining booty. When the Prophet ﷺ came to them, they became wealthy through booty.' The saying is famous: 'Fear the evil of someone you are good to.'

Abū Naṣr al-Qushayrī said, 'Al-Bajalī was asked, "Do you find in the Book of Allah: 'Fear the evil of someone you are good to'?" He answered, "Yes: '*They were vindictive for no other reason than that Allah and His Messenger had enriched them.*'"'

If they were to repent it would be better for them

It is related that when the *āyah* was revealed, al-Julās stood and asked for forgiveness and repented. This is the repentance of an unbeliever who conceals unbelief and makes a show of faith. It is someone whom *fuqahā'* call a '*zindīq*'. Scholars disagree about that. Ash-Shāfi'ī said that his repentance is accepted. Mālik said, 'The repentance of a *zindīq* is not recognised because he makes a show of faith while concealing unbelief. His faith is only known by his words. That is what is now done all the time: he says, "I am a believer," while concealing the opposite of what he displays. When he is discovered and says, "I repent," his state does not change at all. When someone comes to us in repentance without being exposed, then his repentance is accepted. That is what is meant by the *āyah*.' Allah knows best.

'*If they turn away*' from faith and repentance, '*Allah will punish them*' in this world with killing and in the Hereafter with the Fire. They will not find anyone to protect or help them. This has already been discussed (2:48).

وَمِنْهُم مَّنْ عَٰهَدَ ٱللَّهَ لَئِنْ ءَاتَىٰنَا مِن فَضْلِهِۦ لَنَصَّدَّقَنَّ وَلَنَكُونَنَّ مِنَ
ٱلصَّٰلِحِينَ ﴿٧٥﴾ فَلَمَّآ ءَاتَىٰهُم مِّن فَضْلِهِۦ بَخِلُوا۟ بِهِۦ وَتَوَلَّوا۟ وَّهُم مُّعْرِضُونَ ﴿٧٦﴾
فَأَعْقَبَهُمْ نِفَاقًا فِى قُلُوبِهِمْ إِلَىٰ يَوْمِ يَلْقَوْنَهُۥ بِمَآ أَخْلَفُوا۟ ٱللَّهَ مَا وَعَدُوهُ
وَبِمَا كَانُوا۟ يَكْذِبُونَ ﴿٧٧﴾ أَلَمْ يَعْلَمُوٓا۟ أَنَّ ٱللَّهَ يَعْلَمُ سِرَّهُمْ
وَنَجْوَىٰهُمْ وَأَنَّ ٱللَّهَ عَلَّٰمُ ٱلْغُيُوبِ ﴿٧٨﴾

75-78 Among them there were some who made an agreement with Allah: 'If He gives us of His bounty we will definitely give *ṣadaqah* and be among the righteous.' But when He does give them of His bounty they are tight-fisted with it and turn away, so He has punished them by putting hypocrisy in their hearts until the day they meet Him because they failed Allah in what they promised Him and because they lied. Do they not know that Allah knows their secrets and their private talk, and that Allah is the Knower of all unseen things?

Among them there were some who made an agreement with Allah:

Qatādah said, 'This is about a man from the *Anṣār* who said, "If Allah provides me with anything, I will pay His due on it and pay *zakāt*." But when Allah gave him something, he did what the text tells us. They are warned about lying and that it leads to iniquity.'

'Alī ibn Yazīd related from al-Qāsim from Abū Umāmah al-Bāhilī that Tha'labah ibn Ḥāṭib al-Anṣārī (whom he named) asked the Prophet ﷺ, 'Pray to Allah to provide me with wealth.' The Prophet ﷺ said, 'Woe to you, Tha'labah! A little for which one shows gratitude is better than a great amount which one is incapable of dealing with.' He returned a second time and the Prophet ﷺ said, 'Are you not content to be like the Prophet of Allah? If I had wished to have mountains of gold, I could have had them.' He said, 'By the One Who sent you with the Truth, if you pray to Allah and He gives me wealth, I will give everyone with a right his right!' So the Prophet ﷺ made supplication for him and he got sheep and they bred like rabbits [lit. worms]. Madīnah was too small for him and so he moved away from it and settled in one of the wadis until he began to pray only *Ẓuhr* and *'Aṣr* in congregation and leave the rest of the congregational prayers. Then his flocks grew and increased until he left all the prayers except *Jumu'ah*. They then continued to grow until he abandoned *Jumu'ah* as well. The Prophet ﷺ said, 'Woe to you, Tha'labah' three times. Then it was revealed: *'Take zakāt from their wealth.'* (9:103) The Prophet ﷺ sent two men to collect *zakāt* and told them, 'Go to Tha'labah and to so-and-so (naming a man of the Banū Sulaym) and collect their *zakāt*.' They went to Tha'labah and read him the letter of the Messenger of Allah ﷺ and he said, 'This is nothing but the brother of *jizyah*!' They went on and finished what they were doing and then returned. The story is famous.

It is said that the reason for Tha'labah's wealth was that he inherited from a nephew of his. Ibn 'Abd al-Barr said: 'It is said that Tha'labah ibn Ḥāṭib is the one about whom it was revealed when he refused to pay *zakāt*. Allah knows best.' What has come about the one who was present at Badr is incompatible with the words of the Almighty in the *āyah*: *'He has punished them by putting hypocrisy in their hearts…'*

It is mentioned that Ibn 'Abbās said that the reason for the revelation of the *āyah* was that Ḥāṭib ibn Abī Balta'ah's wealth was slow in coming to him from Syria and he swore in one of the gatherings of the *Anṣār* that if that was safe, he would give *ṣadaqah* from it and give to kin from it. When it was safe, he was miserly about that and so this was revealed. Ḥāṭib was a Badri Anṣārī, and one of those about whose faith Allah and His Messenger attested and so what is related about him is not sound. Abū 'Umar said, 'Perhaps the statement of the one who spoke saying that Tha'labah refusing to pay *zakāt* was the one about whom the *āyah* was revealed is not sound. Allah knows best.'

Aḍ-Ḍaḥḥāk said, 'The *āyah* was revealed about some of the hypocrites: Nabtal ibn al-Ḥārith, Jadd ibn Qays, and Mu'attib ibn Qushayr. It is more likely to have been revealed about them, although Allah's words: *'He has punished them by putting hypocrisy...'* indicate that the one who made the agreement was not a hypocrite before that, unless it means that He increased them in hypocrisy on which they remained until they died. That is expressed in His words: *'until the day they meet Him.'*

Our scholars say that when Allah says: *'Among them there were some who made an agreement with Allah,'* it is possible that it is about someone who made an agreement with Allah with his tongue while not believing it in his heart, and it is possible that it was with both of them. Then he met with an evil seal [to his actions/life] because actions are according to their seals and days according to their ends. The pronoun *'man'* is in the nominative by the inceptive and the predicate is in the word governed by the preposition.

The word 'oath' comes in the *ḥadīth* but not in the literal text of the Qur'an. It is an oath merely by the connection and obligation in the form of what has the meaning of an oath. The *lām* indicates it, and there are two *lām*s: the first is for the oath and the second of the *lām* of the apodosis. Both are for stress. Some people say that they are both *lām*s of the oath. The first is clearer, and Allah knows best.

Agreements, divorce and everything which a person is alone judge of and which he does not require anyone else to ratify are binding on him if he makes them binding by his aim, even if he does not articulate it. Our scholars said that. Ash-Shāfi'ī and Abū Ḥanīfah said, 'A ruling is not binding on someone until he has articulated it.' That is another position of our scholars.

Ibn al-'Arabī said, 'The proof for the validity of what we believe is in what Ashhab related from Mālik. He was asked, "What if a man intends divorce with his heart but does not articulate it on his tongue?" He answered, "It is binding on him, as when someone believes with his heart or disbelieves with his heart."' Ibn al-'Arabī said, 'This is an extraordinary principle. Its exact formulation is that it is said that a man does not require anyone else to make a contract binding. It becomes binding on him by his intention.' Its root is faith and unbelief.

The argument for the second position is what Muslim related from Abū Hurayrah. He said that the Prophet ﷺ said, 'Allah overlooks for my community what their selves say to them as long as they do not act on it or articulate it.'

At-Tirmidhī related it and said that it is a sound *ḥasan ḥadīth.* One acts on that according to the people of knowledge. When his self tells him to divorce, there is nothing until he speaks it. Abū 'Umar said, 'If someone makes divorce in his heart but his tongue does not speak it, it is nothing. That is the most famous position from Mālik.' It is related from him that divorce is obliged for him if his heart intends it, in the same way that he disbelieves with his heart even if his tongue does not articulate it. The first is sounder on the basis of research and by the path of traditions since the Messenger of Allah ﷺ said, 'Allah overlooks for my community what their selves whisper to as long as their tongues do not speak or their hands act on it.'

If it is a vow, the fulfilment of vows is mandatory without disagreement and not doing that is an act of disobedience to Allah. If it is an oath, the fulfilment of oaths is not mandatory by agreement. However, the meaning here is that when a man is poor, the obligation of *zakāt* is not incumbent on him. If he then asks Allah for money so that he will have a level of wealth on which *zakāt* is due and on which he will then pay the *zakāt* due but then, when Allah gives him what he has asked for, he refuses to do what is obligatory for him, that is tantamount to reneging on a debt. The pursuit of wealth to settle obligations gets you into difficulties if you seek it from Allah without a sincere intention or even with an intention if ultimate wretchedness has already been decreed for you. We seek refuge with Allah from that.

Corroborating this, the Prophet ﷺ said, 'When one of you hankers for something, he should look to what he hankers for. He does not know what is written in Allah's Unseen about his hopes.' This means what their result will be. Many desires result in trials or transgression and thus become a reason for destruction in this world and the Next because the ends of the affairs of this world are unclear and very dangerous. Hopes for the matters of the *dīn* and the Next World are praiseworthy and are encouraged and recommended.

If He gives us of His bounty we will definitely give *ṣadaqah*

This is evidence that if someone says, 'If I get this or that, it is *ṣadaqah*,' that is binding on him. Abū Ḥanīfah said that. Ash-Shāfi'ī said that it is not binding. There is a similar disagreement about divorce and emancipation. Aḥmad ibn Ḥanbal said, 'It is binding in emancipation but not in divorce, because emancipation is an act of devotion and it is confirmed as being made binding by a vow which is not the case with divorce. Divorce applies to a particular person and so such an oath does not entail bindingness.'

Ash-Shāfi'ī uses as evidence what Abū Dāwūd, at-Tirmidhī and others related from 'Amr ibn Shu'ayb from his father that his grandfather said that the Messenger of Allah ﷺ said, 'The son of Ādam cannot make a vow regarding something that is not his nor any act of emancipation regarding what is not his and nor any divorce regarding what is not his.' The wording is that of at-Tirmidhī. He mentioned regarding the topic from 'Alī, Mu'ādh Jābir, Ibn 'Abbās and 'Ā'ishah the *ḥadīth* of 'Abdullāh ibn 'Amr, a good *ḥadīth*, which is the best thing related in this area. It is stated by most of the people of knowledge among the Companions of the Prophet ﷺ and others. Ibn al-'Arabī said, 'The people of ash-Shafi'ī quote many *ḥadīths* regarding this topic, but none of them are sound or can be relied on. All that remains is the apparent meaning of the *āyah*.'

But when He goes give them of His bounty, they are tight-fisted with it and turn away.

They are tight-fisted in the matter of giving *ṣadaqah*, spending wealth in good, and fulfilling what they are responsible for and obliged to do. Miserliness was discussed in *Āl 'Imrān* (3:180) *'They turn away'* from obeying Allah and they turn from Islam, meaning they display their turning away from it.

He has punished them by putting hypocrisy in their hearts

There are two objects in the sentence. It is said that He punished miserliness with hypocrisy. This is why He says: *'they are tight-fisted with it'*.

'The day they meet Him' is in the genitive, meaning they meet with their miserliness, in other words the repayment for their miserliness. This indicates that the person concerned will die a hypocrite and so it is unlikely that it was revealed about Tha'labah or Ḥāṭib because the Prophet ﷺ said to 'Umar, 'How do you know? Perhaps Allah has looked on the people of Badr and said, "Do what you wish. I have forgiven you."' Tha'labah and Ḥāṭib were among those who were present at Badr.

because they failed Allah in what they promised Him and because they lied.

Allah says that they lied and broke their agreement and failed to perform what they were obliged to do in that. If hypocrisy is found in the heart, it is unbelief. If it is found in actions, it is disobedience. The Prophet ﷺ said, 'If anyone has four characteristics, he is [like] a pure hypocrite, and if anyone has one of them, he has an aspect of hypocrisy until he gives it up: when he is trusted, he betrays his trust; when he speaks, he lies; when he makes an agreement, he breaks it; and when he quarrels, he deviates from the truth and speaks falsely.' Al-Bukhārī transmitted it. The derivation of *nifāq* was mentioned in *al-Baqarah* (2:8) and there is no need to repeat it.

People disagree about the interpretation of this *ḥadīth*. One group said that it describes someone who says something knowing that he is lying, makes an agreement he does not intend to keep to, and intends to betray his trust. They explain it by a *ḥadīth* with a weak *isnād* in which 'Alī ibn Abī Ṭālib met Abū Bakr and 'Umar who had just left the Messenger of Allah ﷺ and appeared to be downcast. 'Alī asked, 'Why do I see you downcast?' They answered, 'Because of a *ḥadīth* which we heard from the Messenger of Allah ﷺ about the qualities of a hypocrite: "When he speaks, he lies, when he makes an agreement, he breaks it, when he is trusted, he betrays his trust, and when he makes a promise, he breaks it."' 'Alī asked, 'Did you not question him?' They replied, 'We are too in awe of the Messenger of Allah ﷺ.' He said, 'Then I will ask him.' He went to the Messenger of Allah ﷺ and said, 'Messenger of Allah, Abū Bakr and 'Umar have emerged downcast,' and he mentioned what they had said. He said, 'I said it to them but I do not take it the way they took it. The hypocrite is the one who, when he speaks, tells himself that he is lying; when he makes a promise, he tells himself that he will break it; and when he is trusted, he tells himself that he will betray it.'

Ibn al-'Arabī said, 'The clear proof is established that someone who has these qualities is not an unbeliever. Someone is an unbeliever by a belief founded on ignorance of Allah and His attributes or by denying Allah, Who is pure of and exalted above the creed of the ignorant and the deviance of deviators.' One group said that it applies specifically to the hypocrites in the time of the Messenger of Allah ﷺ. What they related is explained by Muqātil ibn Ḥayyān from Sa'īd ibn Jubayr that Ibn 'Umar and Ibn 'Abbās said, 'We went to the Messenger of Allah ﷺ with some of his Companions and said, "Messenger of Allah, you said: 'Three have it concealed in them that they are hypocrites, even if they pray and fast and state that they are believers: when they speak they lie, when they make a promise, they break it, and when they are trusted, they betray it. If someone has one of these qualities, he has a third of hypocrisy.' We think that we are not safe from them or from some of them and indeed most people are not safe from them." The Messenger of Allah ﷺ laughed and said, "What do you have to do with those qualities? They are assigned to the hypocrites as Allah singled them out in His Book. I said, 'When they speak they lie' and that is from the words of Allah, *'When the hypocrites come to you…'* (63:1) Are you like that?" "No," we answered. He said, "It is not about you. You are free of that. I said, 'When they make a promise they break it,' and that is about what Allah revealed to me: *'Among them there were some who made an agreement with Allah: "If He gives us of His bounty…"'"* Are you like that?" "No," we answered, "when we make any promise to Allah, we fulfil it." He said, "It is not about you. I said, 'When they are trusted they betray it' and that is about what Allah revealed to me: *'We offered the Trust to the heavens and the earth and the mountains…'* (33:72) Every human being is entrusted with His *dīn*. A believer has a *ghusl* on account of *janābah* publicly and in secret while a hypocrite only does that in public. Are you like that?" "No," we answered. He said, "It is not about you. You are free of that."' This is what most of the *Tābi'ūn* and *imāms* believe.

One group said that this is about someone who is dominated by these qualities. It is clear from the school of al-Bukhārī and others among the people of knowledge that if someone is described by these blameworthy qualities, he remains a hypocrite until the Day of Rising. Ibn al-'Arabī said, 'What I believe is that if someone is dominated by acts of disobedience, they do not make him an unbeliever as long as that does not affect his belief.' Our scholars said, 'The brothers of Yūsuf made an undertaking to their father and they failed to carry it out. They spoke to him and lied to him. He trusted them with Yūsuf and they betrayed him. But they were not hypocrites.' 'Aṭā' ibn Abī Rabāḥ said, 'The brothers of Yūsuf did these things and were not hypocrites. They were Prophets.'

Al-Ḥasan ibn Abī al-Ḥasan al-Baṣrī said, 'There are two types of hypocrisy: the hypocrisy of lying and the hypocrisy of action. Hypocrisy of lying was in the time of the Messenger of Allah ﷺ and hypocrisy of action will not end until the Day of Rising.' Al-Bukhārī related from Ḥudhayfah that hypocrisy was in the time of Messenger of Allah ﷺ and today it is unbelief after belief.

'Do they do not know…' is a rebuke. Allah knows and will repay them.

ٱلَّذِينَ يَلْمِزُونَ ٱلْمُطَّوِّعِينَ مِنَ ٱلْمُؤْمِنِينَ فِي ٱلصَّدَقَٰتِ وَٱلَّذِينَ لَا
يَجِدُونَ إِلَّا جُهْدَهُمْ فَيَسْخَرُونَ مِنْهُمْ سَخِرَ ٱللَّهُ مِنْهُمْ وَلَهُمْ
عَذَابٌ أَلِيمٌ ﴿٧٩﴾

79 As for the people who find fault with those believers who give *ṣadaqah* spontaneously, and with those who can find nothing to give but their own effort, and deride them, Allah derides them. They will have a painful punishment.

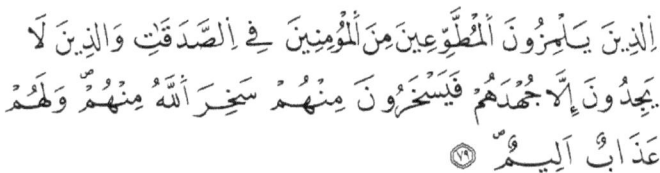

As for the people who find fault with those believers who give *ṣadaqah* spontaneously,

This is also an aspect of the qualities of the hypocrites. Qatādah said that finding fault is to criticise. He said, 'That was because 'Abd ar-Raḥmān ibn 'Awf gave away half of his wealth in *ṣadaqah.* He had 80,000 and gave away 40,000 as *ṣadaqah.* Some people said, "Look at how he shows off!" Then Allah revealed: *"As for the people who find fault with those believers who give ṣadaqah…"* A man of the *Anṣār* came and gave half a basket of dates and they said, "Allah has no need of this!" Then Allah revealed, *"those who can find nothing to give but their own effort."'*

Muslim transmitted that Abū Mas'ūd said, 'Allah ordered us to give *ṣadaqah.*' He said, 'We used to carry loads on our backs.' He said, 'Abū 'Aqīl gave half a *ṣā'* in *ṣadaqah,*' and he said that another man came with a little more. The hypocrites said, 'Allah has no need of the *ṣadaqah* of this person! What the other person did is only showing-off!' Then this *āyah* was revealed. It refers to Abū 'Aqīl whose name was al-Ḥabḥāb.

Juhd is something small on which one with only a little can live. *Juhd* and *jahd* mean the same. *Yalmizūna* means to criticise. The root of *muṭṭawwi'īna* is *mutaṭawwi'īna* and the *tā'* is elided into the *ṭā'*. They are those who give something as a gift without being obliged to. '*Those*' is in the genitive as added to '*believers*' and it is not permitted to add something to a noun when it has not been completed. '*Deride*' is added to '*find fault*'. *'Allah derides them'* is the predicate of the inceptive and it is an invocation against them. Ibn 'Abbās said that it is a predicate, implying He derides them when they go to the Fire. His derision of them is to repay them for their deriding the believers. This was dealt with in *al-Baqarah* (2:212).

اسْتَغْفِرْ لَهُمْ أَوْ لَا تَسْتَغْفِرْ لَهُمْ إِن تَسْتَغْفِرْ لَهُمْ سَبْعِينَ
مَرَّةً فَلَن يَغْفِرَ اللَّهُ لَهُمْ ذَٰلِكَ بِأَنَّهُمْ كَفَرُوا بِاللَّهِ وَرَسُولِهِ وَاللَّهُ
لَا يَهْدِي الْقَوْمَ الْفَاسِقِينَ ﴿٨٠﴾

80 You can ask forgiveness for them, or not ask forgiveness for them. Even if you asked forgiveness for them seventy times, Allah still would not forgive them. That is because they have rejected Allah and His Messenger. Allah does not guide deviant people.

This is explained in connection with Allah's words: *'Never pray over any of them who die.'* (9:84)

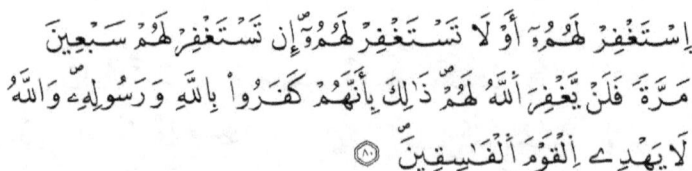

فَرِحَ ٱلْمُخَلَّفُونَ بِمَقْعَدِهِمْ خِلَٰفَ رَسُولِ ٱللَّهِ وَكَرِهُوٓا۟ أَن يُجَٰهِدُوا۟
بِأَمْوَٰلِهِمْ وَأَنفُسِهِمْ فِى سَبِيلِ ٱللَّهِ وَقَالُوا۟ لَا تَنفِرُوا۟ فِى ٱلْحَرِّ قُلْ
نَارُ جَهَنَّمَ أَشَدُّ حَرًّا لَّوْ كَانُوا۟ يَفْقَهُونَ ﴿٨١﴾

81 Those who were left behind were glad to stay behind the Messenger of Allah. They did not want to do *jihād* with their wealth and themselves in the Way of Allah. They said, 'Do not go out to fight in the heat.' Say: 'The Fire of Hell is much hotter, if they only understood.'

Those who were left behind were glad to stay behind

Qa'ada means 'to sit' and *aq'ada* is to make others sit, as al-Jawharī said. Someone who is left behind is abandoned, meaning that Allah abandoned them and made them lazy, or the Messenger of Allah ﷺ and believers left them behind since they knew that they were too sluggish to do *jihād*. These are two positions. This was in reference to the Tabūk expedition. *'Stay behind the Messenger of Allah'* is a direct object or a verbal noun. *Khilāf* means opposition. If someone recites *khilf* instead, it means to delay *jihād*.

'They said, "Do not go out to fight in the heat."' Allah is reporting about what some of them said to one another. *'The Fire of Hell is much hotter.'* It means: 'Tell them, Muḥammad, this.' *'If they only understood'* that the one who abandons Allah's command will be exposed to that Fire. *'Ḥarr'* is in the accusative for clarification.

فَلْيَضْحَكُوا۟ قَلِيلًا وَلْيَبْكُوا۟ كَثِيرًا جَزَآءًۢ بِمَا كَانُوا۟ يَكْسِبُونَ ﴿٨٢﴾

82 Let them laugh little and weep much, in repayment for what they have earned.

'Let them laugh little' is a command which is a threat. It is not ordering them to laugh. The root is that the *lām* has a *kasrah* which is elided since that is heavy. Al-Ḥasan said that it means: '"*Let them laugh little*" in this world and "*weep much*" in Hell."' It is also said that it is a command which is a report, which means: they will laugh little and weep much. *Jazā'* is a direct object.

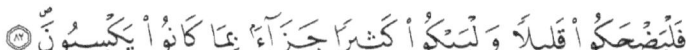

There are some people who, because of the intensity of their fear, do not laugh out of concern for themselves and belief in the venality of their own state, even if they are righteous slaves of Allah. The Prophet ﷺ said, 'By Allah, if you knew what I know, you would laugh little and weep much and you would go out to the hills seeking refuge with Allah Almighty. I wish that I could be a tree lopped off.' At-Tirmidhī transmitted it.

Al-Ḥasan al-Baṣrī was one of those who was dominated by sorrow and did not laugh. Ibn Sīrīn used to laugh and argue with al-Ḥasan, saying, 'It is Allah who makes one laugh and weep.' The Companions used to laugh but laughing a lot and persisting on it until it dominates a person is blameworthy and forbidden. It is the action of fools and the idle. We find in a report: 'Too much of it kills the heart.'

Weeping out of fear of Allah, His punishment and the severity of His punishment is praiseworthy. The Prophet ﷺ said, 'Weep. And if you do not weep, then imitate weeping. The people of the Fire will weep until their tears flow on their faces like streams until the tears cut grooves and blood flows and the eyes are wounded. If there had been boats to travel in it, they would travel."' Ibn al-Mubārak transmitted it from Anas as did Ibn Mājah.

فَإِن رَّجَعَكَ ٱللَّهُ إِلَىٰ طَآئِفَةٍ مِّنْهُمْ فَٱسْتَـْٔذَنُوكَ لِلْخُرُوجِ فَقُل لَّن تَخْرُجُوا۟ مَعِىَ أَبَدًا وَلَن تُقَـٰتِلُوا۟ مَعِىَ عَدُوًّا ۖ إِنَّكُمْ رَضِيتُم بِٱلْقُعُودِ أَوَّلَ مَرَّةٍ فَٱقْعُدُوا۟ مَعَ ٱلْخَـٰلِفِينَ ٨٣

83 If Allah returns you to a group of them, and they ask you for permission to go out, say, 'You will never go out with me, nor will you ever fight an enemy with me. You were happy to stay behind the first time, so stay behind with those who are left behind.'

'A group of them' is of the hypocrites. Allah says: *'to a group of them'* because not all of those who stayed in Madīnah were hypocrites. Among them were those who were excused as well as those who had no excuse. Then He pardoned them and turned to them, like the three who remained behind and who will be discussed. The words: *'You will never go out with me'* mean that Allah punished them by their never being allowed to accompany him again. It is similar to what He says in *Sūrat al-Fatḥ*: *'Say: "You may not follow us."'* (48:15)

Khālifīn is the plural of *khālif.* It is as if they stayed behind those who went out. Ibn 'Abbās said, 'Those who were left behind were those hypocrites who stayed behind.' Al-Ḥasan added, 'with the women and weak men,' and so the masculine is used. It is said that it means: 'Stay with the corrupters.' They say that someone is the '*khālifah*' of the people of a house when he corrupts them. That comes from *khulūf*, which is the change in the smell of the breath of someone who is fasting. It also describes milk when it goes off by being left for a long time in its container. This indicates that it is not permitted for someone who has been abandoned to accompany expeditions.

وَلَا تُصَلِّ عَلَىٰٓ أَحَدٖ مِّنۡهُم مَّاتَ أَبَدٗا وَلَا تَقُمۡ عَلَىٰ قَبۡرِهِۦٓۖ
إِنَّهُمۡ كَفَرُواْ بِٱللَّهِ وَرَسُولِهِۦ وَمَاتُواْ وَهُمۡ فَٰسِقُونَ ٨٤

84 Never pray over any of them who die or stand at their graves. They rejected Allah and His Messenger and died as deviators.

It is related that this *āyah* was revealed about what happened with 'Abdullāh ibn Ubayy ibn Salūl and the Prophet ﷺ praying over him. It is confirmed in the two *Ṣaḥīḥ* collections and elsewhere, with transmissions supporting one another, that the Prophet ﷺ prayed over him and the *āyah* was revealed after that. It is related from Anas ibn Mālik that when the Prophet ﷺ went forward to pray over him, Jibrīl came to him and tugged on his garment and he recited to him, *'Never pray over any of them who die.'* The Messenger of Allah ﷺ left without praying over him. The firm transmissions are different. We find in al-Bukhārī that Ibn 'Abbās said, 'The Messenger of Allah ﷺ prayed over him and then left. It was only a short time later that the two *āyah*s of *at-Tawbah* were revealed: *"Never pray over any of them who die."*'

Something similar is reported from Ibn 'Umar which Muslim transmitted. Ibn 'Umar said, 'When 'Abdullāh ibn Ubayy ibn Salūl died, his son 'Abdullāh went to the Messenger of Allah ﷺ and asked him to give him a shirt in which to shroud his father and he gave it to him. Then he asked him to pray over him and the Messenger of Allah ﷺ rose to pray over him and 'Umar rose and took hold of the garment of the Messenger of Allah ﷺ and said, "Messenger of Allah! Will you pray over him when Allah has forbidden you to pray over him?" The Messenger of Allah ﷺ said, "Allah Almighty has given me a choice when He said, *'You can ask forgiveness for them, or not ask forgiveness for them. Even if you asked forgiveness for them seventy times…'* (9:80) and I will do more than seventy!" 'Umar said, "He is a hypocrite." The Messenger of Allah ﷺ prayed over him and then Allah revealed: *"Never pray over any of them who die…"* So he stopped praying over them.' Some scholars said that the Prophet ﷺ prayed over 'Abdullāh ibn Ubayy based on the outward appearance of his Islam. Then he did not do that when he was forbidden to.

If someone asks how ‘Umar could say, ‘Will you pray over him when Allah has forbidden you to pray over him?’ when there was no prior prohibition against praying over him, he should be told that it is possible that it occurred to his mind and that came from the inspiration and prompting which the Prophet ﷺ witnessed concerning it and that the Qur’an was revealed according to what he wanted as he said, ‘My Lord agreed with me in three (or four),’ as was mentioned in *al-Baqarah* (2:102). This may be an aspect of that. It is possible that he understood that from His words: *‘You can ask forgiveness for them, or not ask forgiveness for them’* (9:80), not that there already was a prohibition according to what is indicated by the *ḥadīth* of al-Bukhārī and Muslim. Allah knows best. It is possible that ‘Umar understood it from His words: *‘It is not right for the Prophet and those who believe to ask forgiveness for the idolaters’* (9:113) because it was revealed in Makkah as will be discussed.

In the *āyah*, *‘You can ask forgiveness for them…,’* Allah makes it clear that even if he ﷺ asks forgiveness for them, that will not help them, even if he does it often. Al-Qushayrī said, ‘It is not confirmed that he said: “I will do more than seventy.”’ This is a disagreement about what is affirmed in the *ḥadīth* of Ibn ‘Umar: ‘I will do more than seventy’ when he says in that of Ibn ‘Abbās: ‘Had I known that they would be forgiven if I did more than seventy, I would have done more.’ He said that the Messenger of Allah ﷺ prayed over him. Al-Bukhāri transmitted it.

Scholars disagree about the interpretation of ‘*You can ask forgiveness for them*’ and whether it is despair or choice. One group said about the interpretation of ‘*You can ask forgiveness for them*’ that what is meant by it is despair because of the words of the Almighty: *‘Allah still would not forgive them.’* (9:80) Seventy may be mentioned in the normal way, or may be a number expressing many and the utmost limit. If someone says, ‘I will not speak to him for seventy years,’ that is like saying, ‘I will never speak to him.’ An example of it indicating the utmost limit is found in Allah’s words: *‘in a chain which is seventy cubits long”* (69:32) and in the words of the Prophet ﷺ: ‘If someone fasts a day in the Way of Allah, Allah will put his face far from the Fire at a distance of seventy years.’

One group, including al-Ḥasan, Qatādah and ‘Urwah, say that it implies a choice: ‘If you wish, you may ask forgiveness for them, and if you wish, you may not ask for forgiveness for them.’ This is why, when he wanted to pray over Ibn Ubayy, ‘Umar said, ‘Are you going to pray over the enemy of Allah who said such-and-such on such-and-such a day?’ He ﷺ said, ‘I was given a choice and I chose.’ They said that that was then abrogated when Allah revealed: *‘It makes no difference whether you ask forgiveness for them or do not ask forgiveness for them’* (63:6) and:

'That is because they have rejected.' (9:80) It means: Allah will not forgive them because of their unbelief.

Allah says: *'It is not right for the Prophet and those who believe to ask forgiveness for the idolaters'* (9:113). This *āyah* was revealed in Makkah when Abū Ṭālib died as will be explained. From this one can understand the prohibition against asking forgiveness for those who die unbelievers. It was already stated that this *āyah* conveys the understanding of a choice as he said, 'Allah gave me a choice.' This is problematic. It is said that his aim in asking forgiveness for his uncle was that he hoped for acceptance so that he would be forgiven. In this prayer for forgiveness he ﷺ was asking his Lord for permission for his mother and he was not given permission for it. As for asking for forgiveness for the hypocrites about which he had a choice, it is a prayer for forgiveness on the tongue which is of no use. His goal was to give cheer to the hearts of the some of the living relatives of the man for whom forgiveness was asked. Allah knows best.

They disagree about the Prophet ﷺ giving his shirt to 'Abdullāh. It is said that he gave it to him because 'Abdullāh gave al-'Abbās, the uncle of the Prophet ﷺ, his shirt on the day of the Battle of Badr. That was when al-'Abbās was captured at Badr as was mentioned. His shirt had been taken as spoils and the Prophet ﷺ saw him and felt compassion for him. He looked for a shirt for him and did not find any shirt which was adequate for him except for 'Abdullāh's because they were similar in stature. The Prophet ﷺ wanted give him the shirt to remove any sense of being beholden to him in this world so that he would not meet him in the Next World owing him compensation for it. It is said that he gave him the shirt to honour his son, humour him in his request and cheer his heart.

The first is sounder. Al-Bukhārī transmitted that Jābir ibn 'Abdullāh said, 'On the Day of Badr, the prisoners were brought and al-'Abbās was brought and he had no garment. The Prophet ﷺ looked for a shirt for him and found that the shirt of 'Abdullāh ibn Ubayy fitted him and the Prophet ﷺ gave it to him to wear. That is why the Prophet ﷺ removed the shirt he was wearing.' We find in a *ḥadīth* that the Prophet ﷺ said, 'My shirt will not help him against Allah in any way. I hope that by this action of mine a thousand men of my people will be made safe.' This is found in some variants: 'my people' and he means the hypocrites of the Arabs. The sound version is that he said, 'men from my people.' It is found in *al-Maghāzī* of Ibn Isḥāq and some books of *tafsīr*: 'A thousand men of Khazraj became Muslim because of this action of the Messenger of Allah ﷺ.'

Our scholars have said that the words of Allah: *'Never pray over any of them who die,'* is a text forbidding praying over unbelievers. There is no evidence in it regarding praying over believers. There is disagreement about whether it gives the understanding that it is obligatory to pray over the Muslims. There are two views. It is taken that the reason for the prohibition against praying over the unbelievers is their unbelief because Allah says: '*They rejected Allah and His Messenger.*' If there is no unbelief, there is an obligation to pray. This is like the words of the Almighty: '*No indeed! Rather that Day they will be veiled from their Lord.*' (83:15) He means the unbelievers. This indicates that people other than the unbelievers will see Him: they are the believers. So this is like that, and Allah knows best.

Thus the origin of the funeral prayer derives from evidence outside of this *āyah*: the *ḥadīth*s reported on the topic and the consensus about it. The disagreement [about its obligation] comes from the use of the direct address in the *āyah* about not doing it [over unbelievers]. Muslim related that Jābir ibn 'Abdullāh said that the Messenger of Allah ﷺ said, 'A brother of yours has died, so rise and pray over him.' He said, 'We got up and formed rows.' It was for the Negus. Abū Hurayrah reported that the Messenger of Allah ﷺ announced the death of the Negus on the day he died and took them to the place of prayer and did four *takbīr*s. The Muslims agree that it is not permitted to abandon the funeral prayer over Muslims, whether they are people of serious wrong actions or righteous heirs of their Prophet ﷺ in word and deed. Praise belongs to Allah. Scholars agree on that except in the case of a martyr as was mentioned (3:169-170), or the people of innovation and rebels.

Most scholars say that there are four *takbīr*s. Ibn Sīrīn said that there are three *takbīr*s and one was added. One group say that there are five. That is related from Ibn Mas'ūd and Zayd ibn Arqam. Six is related from 'Alī. Ibn 'Abbās, Anas ibn Mālik and Jābir ibn Zayd said, 'Three *takbīr*s and four is what is relied on.' Ad-Dāraquṭnī related from Ubayy ibn Ka'b that the Messenger of Allah ﷺ said, 'The angels prayed over Ādam and said four *takbīr*s over him, saying, "This is your custom, sons of Ādam."' In the well-known position from Mālik there is no recitation in this prayer, which is also the case with Abū Ḥanīfah and ath-Thawī. That is based on the words of the Prophet ﷺ: 'When you pray for the dead person, make sincere supplication for him.' Abū Dāwūd related it from Abū Hurayrah. Ash-Shāfi'ī, Aḥmad, Isḥāq, Muḥammad ibn Maslamah, Ashhab among our scholars, and Dāwūd believe that the *Fātiḥah* is recited because of the words of the Prophet ﷺ, 'There is no prayer without the *Fātiḥah* of the Book', which they take with its non-specific meaning, and what al-Bukhārī transmitted from Ibn 'Abbās: 'He prayed a funeral prayer and recited the *Fātiḥah* of the Book and said, "You should know that it is six."'

An-Nasā'ī transmitted from the *ḥadīth* of Abū Umāmah: 'The *sunnah* in the funeral prayer is that the *Umm al-Qur'ān* is recited silently after the first *takbīr*. Then there are three *takbīr*s and the *taslīm* at the end.' Muḥammad ibn Naṣr al-Marwazī mentioned also from Abū Umāmah: 'The *sunnah* in the funeral prayer is that you say the *takbīr*, then recite the *Umm al-Qur'ān*, then the prayer on the Prophet ﷺ, and then sincere supplication for the dead person. There is only recitation after the first *takbīr*. Then say the *taslīm*.' Our shaykh Abū al-'Abbās said, 'These two *ḥadīth*s are sound and they are connected by the *isnād* according to the people of fundamentals. It is more proper to act on the *ḥadīth* of Abū Umāmah since it combines the words of the Prophet ﷺ, 'There is no prayer…' and sincere supplication for the deceased. The recitation of the *Fātiḥah* in it is the beginning of the supplication. Allah knows best.

The *sunnah* for the *imām* is to stand at the head of a man and at the hips of a woman based on what Abū Dāwūd related from Anas. He performed the funeral prayer and al-'Alā' ibn Ziyād asked him, 'Abū Ḥamzah, was the funeral prayer performed by the Messenger of Allah ﷺ like your prayer? Is it four *takbīr*s and standing at the head of a man and at the hips of a woman?' 'Yes,' he replied. Muslim related that Samurah ibn Jundub said, 'I prayed behind the Prophet ﷺ when he prayed over the mother of Ka'b who had died after childbirth. The Messenger of Allah ﷺ stood at her waist to pray over her.'

'Or stand at their graves'. When the dead were buried, the Messenger of Allah ﷺ used to stand at the grave and make supplication for being firm as we made clear in *at-Tadhkirah*. Praise belongs to Allah.

وَلَا تُعْجِبْكَ أَمْوَٰلُهُمْ وَأَوْلَٰدُهُمْ إِنَّمَا يُرِيدُ ٱللَّهُ أَن يُعَذِّبَهُم
بِهَا فِى ٱلدُّنْيَا وَتَزْهَقَ أَنفُسُهُمْ وَهُمْ كَٰفِرُونَ ﴿٨٥﴾

85 Do not let their wealth and their children impress you. Allah merely wants to punish them by them in this world, and for them to expire while they are unbelievers.

This is repeated for stress and was already discussed earlier (9:56).

وَإِذَآ أُنزِلَتْ سُورَةٌ أَنْ ءَامِنُوا۟ بِٱللَّهِ وَجَٰهِدُوا۟ مَعَ رَسُولِهِ
ٱسْتَـْٔذَنَكَ أُو۟لُوا۟ ٱلطَّوْلِ مِنْهُمْ وَقَالُوا۟ ذَرْنَا نَكُن مَّعَ ٱلْقَٰعِدِينَ ﴿٨٦﴾

86 When a *sūrah* is sent down saying: 'Believe in Allah and do *jihād* together with His Messenger,' those among them with wealth will ask you to excuse them, saying, 'Let us remain with those who stay behind.'

The believers responded readily and the hypocrites made excuses and so the believers are commanded to continue to believe and the hypocrites to begin to believe. *'An'* is in the accusative. *Ṭawl* means wealth. It was already discussed (4:25). He singled out the wealthy for mention because someone without wealth does not need an excuse because he is already excused. *'Those who stay behind'* means those who were unable to go out.

وَطُبِعَ عَلَىٰ قُلُوبِهِمْ فَهُمْ لَا يَفْقَهُونَ ﴿٨٧﴾ لَٰكِنِ ٱلرَّسُولُ
وَٱلَّذِينَ ءَامَنُوا۟ مَعَهُۥ جَٰهَدُوا۟ بِأَمْوَٰلِهِمْ وَأَنفُسِهِمْ ۚ وَأُو۟لَٰٓئِكَ لَهُمُ
ٱلْخَيْرَٰتُ ۖ وَأُو۟لَٰٓئِكَ هُمُ ٱلْمُفْلِحُونَ ﴿٨٨﴾ أَعَدَّ ٱللَّهُ لَهُمْ جَنَّٰتٍ تَجْرِى
مِن تَحْتِهَا ٱلْأَنْهَٰرُ خَٰلِدِينَ فِيهَا ۚ ذَٰلِكَ ٱلْفَوْزُ ٱلْعَظِيمُ ﴿٨٩﴾

87-89 They are pleased to be with those who stay behind. Their hearts have been stamped so they do not understand. But the Messenger and those who believe along with him have done *jihād* with their wealth and with themselves. They are the people who will have the good things. They are the ones who are successful. Allah has prepared Gardens for them with rivers flowing under them, remaining in them timelessly, forever. That is the great victory.

They are pleased to be with those who stay behind.

Khawālif is the plural of *khālifah* and '*those who stay behind*' are the women, children and men with valid excuses. A man can be referred to as both *khālifah* and *khālif* when he is not a noble. Someone is described as *khālifah* in relation to his people when he is lower than them. An-Naḥḥās said that its root is the verb *khalafa*, which is used for milk which has changed and curdled because of remaining in a container. *Khalafa* is used for the changed smell of the mouth of someone fasting.

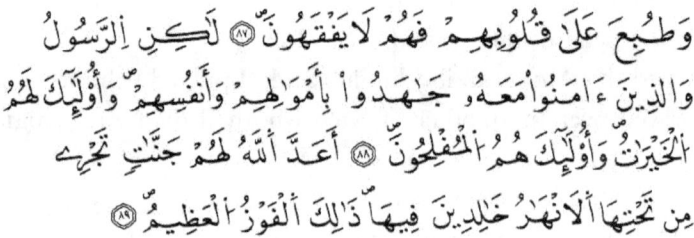

It is used in *khalafa saw'*. The form *fawā'il* is the plural of *fā'ilah* and is only used as a plural for *fā'il* in poetry, except for two cases: *fāris* and *hālik*.

Allah says about those who do *jihād*: *'They are the people who will have the good things.'* '*Good things*' is said by al-Ḥasan to mean beautiful women. His evidence is the words of Allah: *'In them are sweet, lovely maidens (khayrāt).'* (55:70) It is said that it is good women and the root is *khayyarah* and has been lightened, and it is said that it is the plural of *khayrah*. It means that they will have the benefits of both worlds. The meaning of *falāḥ* (success) was discussed in 2:5. *Jannāt* are gardens and were already discussed as well (2:25).

وَجَآءَ ٱلْمُعَذِّرُونَ مِنَ ٱلْأَعْرَابِ لِيُؤْذَنَ لَهُمْ وَقَعَدَ ٱلَّذِينَ
كَذَبُوا۟ ٱللَّهَ وَرَسُولَهُۥ ۚ سَيُصِيبُ ٱلَّذِينَ كَفَرُوا۟ مِنْهُمْ عَذَابٌ
أَلِيمٌ ﴿٩٠﴾

90 The desert Arabs came with their excuses asking for permission to stay, and those who lied to Allah and His Messenger stayed behind. A painful punishment will afflict those among them who disbelieve.

The desert Arabs came with their excuses

Al-A'raj and aḍ-Ḍaḥḥāk recited *'al-mu'dhirūn'*. Abū Kurayb related it from Abū Bakr from 'Āṣim, and the people of readings from Ibn 'Abbās. Al-Jawharī said that Ibn 'Abbās used to recite *'al-mu'dhirūn'* from *a'dhara*. He said, 'By Allah, that is how it was revealed.' An-Naḥḥās said, 'Its central point is reported from al-Kalbī. It is from *a'dhara*. Exemplifying that is the saying, "He who warns is excused," meaning that someone who came and warned you has a sufficient excuse.' There are two positions about the reading of *'al-mu'adhdhirūn'* with a *shaddah* on the *dhāl*. One is that it is true and means the one who makes excuses because he has an excuse and it retains its primary meaning (*mu'tadhirūn*) but the *tā'* has taken the *dhāl* and been assimilated into it and its vowel is on the *'ayn*, as it is recited: *'yakhaṣṣimūna'* (36:49) with a *fatḥah* on the *khā'*. It is possible that it can be *'al-mu'idhdhirūn'* with a *kasrah* on the *'ayn* because of the joining of two silent letters. It is also possible that it can be read with a *ḍammah* following the *mīm*. Al-Jawharī and an-Naḥḥās mentioned that. However, an-Naḥḥās mentioned it from al-Akhfash, al-Farrā', Abū Ḥātim and Abū 'Ubayd. It is possible that the root is *'mu'tadhirūn'* and the *tā'* is assimilated into the *dhāl*, and they are those who have an excuse. Labīd said:

For a year, and then the name of peace be upon you both.
Someone who weeps for an entire year has an excuse (*iʿtadhara*).

The second view is that it denotes those who do not have true excuses and ask to be excused when they have no excuse. Al-Jawharī said *'muʿadhdhir'* is someone who makes an excuse because he is ill or lacks the means and apologises without an excuse. Another said that *'adhdhara* is used for a business, i.e. he falls short and does not reach it. The meaning is that they lied in their excuses. Al-Jawharī said, 'Ibn 'Abbās said, "Allah cursed those who made excuses."' It is as if the business with him is that a *'muʿadhdhir'* is someone who displays an excuse as a pretext without any shred of truth in it.

An-Naḥḥās said that Abū al-'Abbās Muḥammad ibn Yazīd said, 'It is not permitted for the root in it to be "*muʿtadhirūn*", and *idghām* is not permitted so that there is confusion. Ismā'īl ibn Isḥāq mentioned that *idghām* is avoided according to al-Khalīl and Sībawayh after the context of the words indicates that they are blamed and have no real excuse because they came to ask for permission. If they had truly been among the weak and ill and those who do not have the means to spend, they would not need to ask for permission.' An-Naḥḥās said that the root of all these is the same, and it is about what is hard and difficult. The Arabs say, 'Who will excuse (*'adhīr*) me if I requite so-and-so?', meaning that he has done something terrible for which I am entitled to punish him, even if people do not know it. So who will excuse me if I punish him?

According to the first reading, Ibn 'Abbās said, 'They are those who stayed behind with an excuse and the Prophet ﷺ gave them permission.' It is said that they are the group of 'Āmir ibn aṭ-Ṭufayl who said, 'Messenger of Allah! If we go out with you, the Arabs of Ṭayy' will attack our wives, children and livestock.' So the Messenger of Allah ﷺ excused them. According to the second reading and the second view, they are some people of Ghifār who offered excuses and the Prophet ﷺ did not excuse them because he knew that the excuses were not real. Allah knows best. Some people stayed behind without an excuse and did that out of boldness towards the Messenger of Allah ﷺ. They are those about whom Allah is talking when He says: *'those who lied,'* and what is meant is their lying about saying that they were believers.

لَّيْسَ عَلَى ٱلضُّعَفَآءِ وَلَا عَلَى ٱلْمَرْضَىٰ وَلَا عَلَى ٱلَّذِينَ لَا يَجِدُونَ
مَا يُنفِقُونَ حَرَجٌ إِذَا نَصَحُوا۟ لِلَّهِ وَرَسُولِهِۦ مَا عَلَى ٱلْمُحْسِنِينَ مِن سَبِيلٍ
وَٱللَّهُ غَفُورٌ رَّحِيمٌ ﴿٩١﴾ وَلَا عَلَى ٱلَّذِينَ إِذَا مَآ أَتَوْكَ لِتَحْمِلَهُمْ قُلْتَ لَآ أَجِدُ
مَآ أَحْمِلُكُمْ عَلَيْهِ تَوَلَّوا۟ وَّأَعْيُنُهُمْ تَفِيضُ مِنَ ٱلدَّمْعِ حَزَنًا أَلَّا يَجِدُوا۟ مَا
يُنفِقُونَ ﴿٩٢﴾

91-92 Nothing is held against the weak and the sick or against those who find nothing to spend, provided they are true to Allah and His Messenger – there is no way open against good-doers, Allah is Ever-Forgiving, Most Merciful – nor is anything held against those who, when they came to you for you to provide them with mounts and you said, 'I cannot find anything on which to mount you,' turned away with their eyes overflowing with tears, overcome by grief at having nothing to give.

Nothing is held against the weak and the sick

The basis of cancelling the obligation from someone who is unable is that if anyone is unable to do something, it is cancelled for him, sometimes to be replaced by a substitute in terms of action, and sometimes by a substitute which is resolve. There is no difference between inability due to lack of strength and inability due to lack of money. This *āyah* is similar to the words of the Almighty: *'Allah does not impose on any self any more than it can stand.'* (2:286) He also says: *'There is no objection to the blind, no objection to the lame, no objection to the sick…'* (24:61)

Abū Dāwūd related from Anas that the Messenger of Allah ﷺ said, 'You left in Madīnah people who are such that you have not travelled any distance nor spent anything nor crossed any valley but that they are with you in it.' They asked, 'Messenger of Allah, how can they be with us when they are still in Madīnah?' He said, 'A valid excuse kept them back.' This *āyah* makes it clear that there is nothing held against those with valid excuses, who are those whose excuses are acknowledged, like those who are elderly, senile, blind and lame, and people who do not find the wherewithal to spend. There is nothing held against such people.

provided they are true to Allah and His Messenger –

This is when they acknowledge the Truth and love His friends and hate His enemies. Scholars said that Allah excused the people with excuses but their hearts could still not bear it. Ibn Umm Maktūm went to Uḥud and asked to be given the banner. Muṣ'ab ibn 'Umayr took it and a man of the unbelievers came and struck his hand which was holding the banner and cut it off. He took it with the other hand and the other hand was struck off. He held it to his chest and recited, *'Muḥammad is only a Messenger and he has been preceded by other Messengers.'* (3:144) This is the resolve of the people. Allah says: *'There is no objection to the blind,'* and it is the first, *'and no objection to the lame.'* (24:61) 'Amr ibn al-Jamūḥ, one of the leaders of the *Anṣār*, was lame and he was in the front of the army. The Messenger of Allah ﷺ told him, 'Allah has discussed your case.' He said, 'By Allah, I will dig with this lameness of mine in the Garden.' There are other examples of what is in this *sūrah* which are mentioned. 'Abdullāh ibn Mas'ūd said, 'A man came (to the prayer) being led between two men until he stood in the row.'

Naṣḥ (true) is sincere action free of any dissimulation. One aspect of that is sincere (*naṣūḥ*) repentance. Nifṭawayh said, 'Something is described with *naṣaḥa* when it is pure and the term is also used of words which are sincere.' We find in *Ṣaḥīḥ Muslim* that Tamīm ad-Dārī said, 'The Prophet ﷺ said, "The *dīn* is good counsel" three times. We asked, "For whom?" He answered, "For Allah, His Book, His Messenger and the leaders of the Muslim and their common people."' Scholars have said, 'Good counsel to Allah is sincere belief in His Unity and describing Him with the attributes of Divinity and His freedom from any imperfection and having desire for things He loves and distance from what He hates.'

Good counsel for His Messenger is affirmation of his Prophethood, obedience to him in his commands and prohibitions, taking as friends those he takes as friends and being hostile to those to whom he is hostile, respect for him, loving him, loving the people of his house, esteem for him and esteem for his *Sunnah* and reviving it after his death by researching it and learning its *fiqh*, defending it and spreading it and calling to it and taking on his noble character.

Good counsel for the Book of Allah is reading it, defending it and teaching it and honouring it and taking on its character.

Good counsel for the leaders of the Muslims is not going out against them, guiding them to the Truth, calling attention to what they have neglected regarding the affairs of the Muslims, obliging others to obey them and undertaking the obligation due to them.

Good counsel for the common people is not to be hostile to them, guide them, love the righteous among them, supplicate for all of them and desire good for all of them. We find in a sound *ḥadīth*: 'The metaphor of the believers in their mutual love, mercy and kindness is that of the body. When one limb of it complains, the rest of the body prays for it with sleeplessness and fever.'

there is no way open against the good-doers

'Min sabīl' is in the nominative as the noun of *mā*, i.e. there is no way to punish them. This *āyah* stipulates the fundamental principle of the removal of punishment from everyone who does good. This is why our scholars say that if someone who seeks retaliation against another person for the severing of his hand carries that out and that leads to the death of that person, he owes no blood money because he was acting rightly in taking retaliation for the aggression against him. Abū Ḥanīfah, however, said that blood money is obliged. That is also the case when someone attacks a man and the man kills the attacker in self-defence: he has no liability. Ash-Shāfi'ī said that. Abū Ḥanīfah said that [if the person killed is a slave] then he must pay his price to his owner. Ibn al-'Arabī said, 'That is the case with all the cases in the *Sharī'ah*.'

nor is anything held against those who, when they come to you for you to provide them with mounts

It is related that this *āyah* was revealed about 'Irbāḍ ibn Sāriyah. It is said that it was revealed about 'Ā'idh ibn 'Amr, and it is also said that it was revealed about the sons of Muqarrin. The latter is the position of most commentators. They were seven brothers, all of whom were Companions of the Prophet ﷺ. They are the only seven brothers among the Companions of the Prophet ﷺ. They were: an-Nu'mān, 'Aqīl, Ma'qil, Suwayd, Sinān and the others are not named. The sons of Muqarrin were seven brothers who were Muzanīs and emigrated and were Companions of the Messenger of Allah ﷺ. According to Ibn 'Abd al-Barr and others, no one else shared with them in this honour. It is said that they were all present at the Battle of the Ditch.

It is also said that it was revealed about seven men of various tribes who went to the Messenger of Allah ﷺ at the time of the Tabūk expedition to ask for rides and he did not find any mounts for them, so they *'turned away with their eyes overflowing with tears, overcome by grief at having nothing to give.'* For this reason they were called 'the weepers'. They were: Sālim ibn 'Umayr from the Banū 'Amr ibn 'Awf, 'Ulbah ibn Zayd, one of the Banū Ḥārithah, Abū Laylā 'Abd ar-Raḥmān ibn Ka'b of the Banū Māzin ibn an-Najjār, 'Amr ibn al-Ḥumān of the Banū Salamah, 'Abdullāh ibn al-Mughaffal al-Muzanī, who is also said to be 'Abdullāh ibn 'Amr al-Muzanī, Haramī ibn 'Abdullāh, one of the Banū Wāqif, and 'Irbāḍ ibn Sāriyah al-Fazārī. This is how they are named by Abū 'Umar in *Kitāb ad-durar.*

There is some disagreement about them. Al-Qushayrī said: Ma'qil ibn Yasār, Ṣakhr ibn Khansā', Abdullāh ibn Ka'b al-Anṣāri, Sālim ibn 'Umayr, Tha'labah ibn Ghanamah, 'Abdullāh ibn al-Mughaffal and another. They said, 'Prophet of

Allah, we are tasked with going out with you, so give us some quick mounts to carry us and some sandals of palm leaves so that we can fight with you.' He said, 'I do not find any mounts for you,' and they turned away weeping. Ibn 'Abbās said, 'They asked him to provide mounts for them. A man needed two camels: one to ride and one to carry his water and provision because the way was long.'

Al-Ḥasan said, 'It was revealed about Abū Mūsā and his companions who went to the Messenger of Allah ﷺ to ask for mounts and that happened to coincide with a moment when he was angry. He said, "By Allah, I will not give you mounts and I do not have anything for you to ride!" They turned away weeping and then the Messenger of Allah ﷺ called them back and gave them some she-camels. Abū Mūsā said, "Did you not make an oath, Messenger of Allah?" He said, "If Allah wishes, I never make an oath and then find something better than it but that I do what is better and expiate my oath."' This is a sound *ḥadīth* which al-Bukhārī and Muslim transmitted. In the Muslim variant: 'He called us and gave us five she-camels…' He said at the end of it: 'Go. Allah has given you mounts.' Al-Ḥasan and Bakr ibn 'Abdullāh said: 'it was revealed about 'Abdullāh ibn Mughaffal al-Muzanī who went to the Prophet ﷺ to ask him for mounts.'

Al-Jurjānī said, 'What is implied is: 'nor is anything held against those who, when they came to you for you to provide them with mounts and you said, 'I cannot find anything.''' So it is a subject of a nominal sentence added to what is before it without a *wāw* and the apodosis is *"turned away"*.'

with their eyes overflowing with tears

This is a sentence in the accusative as an adverbial *ḥāl*. *'Ḥazan'* is a verbal noun. *'On which to mount you'* is in the accusative by *an*. An-Naḥḥās said that al-Farrā' said that it permitted to say: *'lā yajidūna'* and *lā* means *laysa*. The Basrans say that it means the negative *lā*.

Most scholars say that if someone does not have the means to go on an expedition, it is not mandatory for him to do so. Our scholars said, 'If it is his custom to beg, then he must do so, as is the case with *ḥajj*. He goes according to his normal habit since his situation does not cease with respect to his obligation just as it applies to someone with the means.' Allah knows best.

'Eyes overflowing with tears' is used as evidence of context. Then part of that is what gives a priori knowledge and there is hesitation about another part. The first is when someone passes by a house in which death is announced, cheeks are scratched, hair is shaved, voices are released, and shirts torn, and they are calling out about the death of the owner. It is known from that that he has died. The

second case is like the tears of orphans at the doors of judges. Allah reports about the brothers of Yūsuf: *'That night they came back to their father in tears.'* (12:16) They were lying. Allah says of them: *'They then produced his shirt with false blood on it.'* (12:17) Furthermore circumstances indicate what is normal. So testimony is based on it as is the case with normal outward appearance. A poet said:

When the tears joined together on the cheeks,
it was clear that the one who wept was one of those who shams weeping.

This will be discussed in full in *Yūsuf*, Allah willing (12:18).

إِنَّمَا ٱلسَّبِيلُ عَلَى ٱلَّذِينَ يَسْتَـٰذِنُونَكَ وَهُمُۥٓ أَغْنِيَآءُۖ رَضُواْ بِأَن يَّكُونُواْ مَعَ
ٱلْخَوَالِفِۖ وَطَبَعَ ٱللَّهُ عَلَىٰ قُلُوبِهِمْ فَهُمْ لَا يَعْلَمُونَ ﴿٩٣﴾

93 There are only grounds against those who ask you for permission to stay when they are rich. They were pleased to be among those who were left behind. Allah has sealed up their hearts so they do not know.

The *'grounds'* here refer to sin and punishment. Those who are *'rich'* here are the hypocrites. '*They do not know*' is repeated to emphasise the warning about their evil actions.

يَعْتَذِرُونَ إِلَيْكُمُۥٓ إِذَا رَجَعْتُمُۥٓ إِلَيْهِمْۖ قُل لَّا تَعْتَذِرُواْ لَن نُّومِنَ لَكُمْۖ قَدْ نَبَّأَنَا ٱللَّهُ
مِنَ اَخْبَارِكُمْۖ وَسَيَرَى ٱللَّهُ عَمَلَكُمْ وَرَسُولُهُۥۖ ثُمَّ تُرَدُّونَ إِلَىٰ عَٰلِمِ ٱلْغَيْبِ
وَٱلشَّهَٰدَةِ فَيُنَبِّئُكُم بِمَا كُنتُمْ تَعْمَلُونَ ﴿٩٤﴾

94 They will make excuses to you when you return to them. Say: 'Do not make excuses, we will not believe you. Allah has already informed us about you. Allah will see your actions, as will His Messenger. Then you will be returned to the Knower of the Unseen and the Visible, and He will inform you regarding what you did.'

'*They*' here are the hypocrites. *'We will not believe'* that you are telling the truth. *'Allah has already informed us'* about your secrets and He sees your future actions. Allah will repay you for what you did. All of this has already been discussed.

سَيَحْلِفُونَ بِٱللَّهِ لَكُمْ إِذَا ٱنقَلَبْتُمْ إِلَيْهِمْ لِتُعْرِضُوا۟ عَنْهُمْ ۖ فَأَعْرِضُوا۟
عَنْهُمْ ۖ إِنَّهُمْ رِجْسٌ ۖ وَمَأْوَىٰهُمْ جَهَنَّمُ جَزَآءًۢ بِمَا كَانُوا۟ يَكْسِبُونَ ﴿٩٥﴾

95 They will swear to you by Allah when you return to them, so that you leave them alone. Leave them alone, then! They are filth. Their shelter will be Hell as repayment for what they did.

'When you return to them' from Tabūk. There is something elided, i.e. they will swear that they were unable to go out with you. *'So that you leave them alone'*, i.e. so that you will overlook blaming them. Ibn 'Abbās said the meaning was, 'So that you will not speak to them.' There is a report that the Prophet ﷺ said when he came from Tabūk, 'Do not sit with them and do not talk with them.' *'They are filth'* means that their actions are filth, meaning ugly. *'Their shelter will be Hell'*: that will be their abode and place of refuge. Al-Jawharī said, '*Ma'wā* is any place where something seeks refuge day or night. The verb is *awā, ya'wī.* One usage of that is found in the words of the Almighty: *'I will take refuge on a mountain. It will protect me from the water.'* (11:43) *Āwā* and *awā* both mean give shelter to someone. Ibn Zayd said that. *Ma'wī* is another form of the word *ma'wā,* which is camel pen, but that form of the word is an unusual form.

يَحْلِفُونَ لَكُمْ لِتَرْضَوْا۟ عَنْهُمْ ۖ فَإِن تَرْضَوْا۟ عَنْهُمْ فَإِنَّ ٱللَّهَ لَا يَرْضَىٰ عَنِ
ٱلْقَوْمِ ٱلْفَٰسِقِينَ ﴿٩٦﴾

96 They will swear to you to make you pleased with them, but even if you are pleased with them, Allah is certainly not pleased with deviant people.

'Abdullāh ibn Ubayy swore that he would never again stay behind the Messenger of Allah ﷺ and sought to please him.

ٱلْأَعْرَابُ أَشَدُّ كُفْرًا وَنِفَاقًا وَأَجْدَرُ أَلَّا يَعْلَمُوا۟ حُدُودَ مَآ أَنزَلَ ٱللَّهُ عَلَىٰ
رَسُولِهِۦ ۗ وَٱللَّهُ عَلِيمٌ حَكِيمٌ ﴿٩٧﴾

97 The desert Arabs are more obdurate in unbelief and hypocrisy and more likely not to know the limits which Allah has sent down to His Messenger. Allah is All-Knowing, All-Wise.

After the Almighty has mentioned the states of hypocrites in Madīnah, He then mentions those outside of it and the Arabs at some distance from it. He says that their unbelief is greater because their hearts are harder, their words coarser and grosser and they are furthest away from hearing the Revelation. That is why Allah says this about them. *'Ajdar'* means more likely. In the phrase '*not to know the limits*,' *an* is in the accusative by the elision of *bā'*. It is correct to use it with *an* and other particles. You say. 'It is proper for you to stand' as (*jadīr an taqūm*) as (*jadīr bi-l-qiyām*). If you said, '*jadīr al-qiyām*', it would be wrong. It is proper with *an* to indicate the future and so it is as if it replaces what is elided.

'Not to know the limits' means be ignorant of the obligations of the *Sharī'ah*. It is also said that it refers to their failing, due to their lack of investigation, to know the proofs of Allah regarding His being the Lord and sending Messengers. Since that is the case and indicates their falling short and being incomplete in their faith, there are three rulings based on that.

The first is that they have no share in *fay'* spoils and booty as the Prophet ﷺ said in the *ḥadīth* of Buraydah in *Ṣaḥīḥ Muslim*. He says in it, 'Then call them to move from their abode to the abode of the *Muhājirūn* and inform them that if they do that, they will have what the *Muhājirūn* have and owe what the *Muhājirūn* owe. If they refuse to move from it, tell them that they will be like the desert Arabs of the Muslims on whom the ruling of Allah is carried out as it is carried out on the believers, but they will not have anything of the *fay'* spoils and booty unless they do *jihād* together with the Muslims.'

The second ruling is that the testimony of a desert Arab against a town resident is not counted since they are automatically suspect. Abū Ḥanīfah, however, allowed their testimony and said, 'Because not every suspicion is acted on,' and he considers all the Muslims to be just. Ash-Shāfi'ī allows it when the witness is a pleasing upright person. That is the sound position based on what we explained in *al-Baqarah* (2:282)

Allah Almighty describes the desert Arabs as falling into three categories. One is those subject to unbelief and hypocrisy. The second is those who take what they spend as an imposition and are waiting for you to have a reversal of fortunes in their favour. The third is those who believe in Allah and the Last Day, and take what they spend as something that will bring them near to Allah and the prayers of the Prophet. Someone whose description this is then it is improbable that his testimony should not be accepted, and he should not be attached to the first two categories. That is false. This was discussed in *an-Nisā'* (4:135).

The third ruling is that it is forbidden for them to act as *imāms* for townspeople because of their ignorance of the Sunnah and failure to attend Jumu'ah. Abu Miljah mentioned a desert Arab acting as *imām*. Mālik said that they should not act as *imām* even if they know more of Qur'an than others. Sufyān ath-Thawrī, ash-Shāfi'ī, Isḥāq and the People of Opinion say that it is permitted to pray behind a desert Arab. Ibn al-Mundhir preferred that as long as the limits of the prayer are observed.

The root of '*ashadd*' (more obdurate) is *ashdad* and it was already mentioned. '*Kufr'* is in the accusative case for clarification and '*nifāq'* is added to it. '*Ajdar'* is added to *ashadd*. It means 'more likely' as we said. One can use *jadīr* and *khalīq* interchangeably. The plural is *judarā'* and *jadīrūn*. Its root comes from the *jadr* (wall) of a garden which is raised up around it. *Jadīr* is used for something one is closer to and more entitled to. '*Not to know'* means that they do not know.

The '*arab* are a nation of people. One ascribed to them is called an '*arabī* whose Arab nature is clear. They are the people of cities. The *a'rāb* are the desert Arabs in particular. Eloquent Arabic used *a'ārīb* and the relative form is *a'rābī* because there is no singular. *A'rāb* is not the plural *of 'arab* as *anbāṭ* is not the plural of *nabaṭ*. '*Arab* is a generic noun and '*arab a'rab* are singled out from them. It is taken from the word and stresses it, like *layl lā'il*. Sometimes they said: "'*arab 'urabā*'". The verb *ta'arraba* means to resemble the Arabs. When *ta'arraba* describes someone after his emigration, it means that he became an *a'rābī*. Arabs described as *musta'rib* are those who are not pure Arabs and the same is true of *muta'arrib*. '*Arabiyyah* is the language. Ya'rub ibn Qaḥṭān was the first to speak Arabic. He is the father of all Yemen. '*Urb* and '*arab* are the same, like '*ujm* and '*ajam*. '*Urayb* is the diminutive. A poet said:

> Lizards' eggs are the food of the desert Arabs ('*urayb*).
> The Persians do not like them.

He uses the diminutive out of esteem as happens in Arabic. Al-Qushayrī related that the plural of '*arabī* is '*arab* and the plural of *a'rābī* is *a'rāb* and *a'ārīb*. When it is said to an *a'rābī*, 'O 'Arabī,' he rejoices, but when an '*arabī* is called an *a'rābī*, he becomes angry. The Muhājiūn and *Anṣār* are '*arab*, not *a'rāb*. The Arabs are called Arabs because the children of Ismā'īl grew from 'Arabah, which is part of Tihāmah, and they are ascribed to it. Quraysh resided at 'Arabah, which is Makkah, and the rest of the Arabs spread through its peninsula.

وَمِنَ الْأَعْرَابِ مَن يَتَّخِذُ مَا يُنفِقُ مَغْرَمًا وَيَتَرَبَّصُ بِكُمُ الدَّوَائِرَ عَلَيْهِمْ دَائِرَةُ
السَّوْءِ وَاللَّهُ سَمِيعٌ عَلِيمٌ ﴿٩٨﴾

98 Among the desert Arabs there are some who regard what they give as an imposition and are waiting for your fortunes to change. The evil turn of fortune will be theirs! Allah is All-Hearing, All-Knowing.

Among the desert Arabs there are some who regard what they give as an imposition

The preposition '*min*' here is in the position of the nominative by the inceptive. '*Regard what they give as an imposition*' has two objects. It implies: 'spends it' and the *hā'* is elided because the noun is long. '*Maghram*' means something imposed and a loss. Its root is to make a thing mandatory. An example of that is: '*Its punishment is inescapable pain* (gharām).' (25:65) It means that it is bound to happen. They think that what they spend in *jihād* and *ṣadaqah* is an imposition and they do not expect any reward for it.

and are waiting for your fortunes to change.

Tarabbuṣ is waiting. It was already mentioned (2:226-227) *Dawā'ir* is the plural of *dā'irah*, and it is a state which moves from blessing to affliction. So they combine ignorance about spending with a bad intention and foul heart.

The evil turn of fortune will be theirs!

Ibn Kathīr and Abū 'Amr recited this with a *ḍammah* on the *sīn* (*sū'*) and the rest with a *fatḥah* (*saw'*). They agree on the *fatḥah* in '*Your father was not an evil man* (saw').' (19:28) The difference between them is that *sū'* is what is disliked. Al-Afkhas said, 'They will have their turn of defeat and misfortune.' Al-Farrā' said, 'They will have their turn of punishment and affliction.' They both said that it is not permitted to describe an evil person as *sū'*. It is related from Muḥammad ibn Yazīd that *saw'* is badness. Sībawayh said, 'I passed by a man of truthfulness (*ṣidq*)' when he means a man of righteousness. That is not a reference to truthfulness of the tongue. If he had meant the truthfulness of the tongue, he would have said 'a garment of truthfulness'. 'An evil man' is not one characterised by evil, but one who has been corrupted. Al-Farrā' said that *saw'* is a verbal noun of *sā'a*. Other ones are *masā'ah* and *sawā'īyah*. *Sū'* is a noun, not a verbal noun. It is like saying, 'They will experience the turn of affliction and what is disliked.'

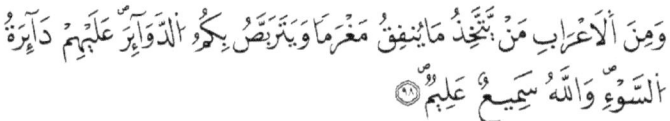

وَمِنَ ٱلْأَعْرَابِ مَن يُؤْمِنُ بِٱللَّهِ وَٱلْيَوْمِ ٱلْآخِرِ وَيَتَّخِذُ مَا يُنفِقُ قُرُبَٰتٍ عِندَ
ٱللَّهِ وَصَلَوَٰتِ ٱلرَّسُولِ ۚ أَلَآ إِنَّهَا قُرْبَةٌ لَّهُمْ ۚ سَيُدْخِلُهُمُ ٱللَّهُ فِى رَحْمَتِهِۦٓ ۗ
إِنَّ ٱللَّهَ غَفُورٌ رَّحِيمٌ ﴿٩٩﴾

99 And among the desert Arabs there are some who believe in Allah and the Last Day and regard what they give as something which will bring them nearer to Allah and to the prayers of the Messenger. It does indeed bring them near. Allah will admit them into His mercy. Allah is Ever-Forgiving, Most Merciful.

'And among the desert Arabs there are some who believe' and affirm. What is meant are the sons of Muqarrin ibn Muzaynah. Al-Mahdawī mentioned it. The noun *'qurubāt'* is the plural of *qurbah* and it is something which is given to draw closer to Allah. The plural is *qurab*, *qurubāt*, *qarabāt* and *qurbāt*. An-Naḥḥās related it. *Qurubāt* are actions that bring one closer to Allah. *Qurbān* (sacrifice) is something that brings one near to Allah and is offered to Allah. *Qirbah* is a container in which one gets water. The plural for a small number is *qirbāt*, *qirabāt* and *qiribāt*. *Qirab* is the plural for many. That is the plural for all of the form *fi'lah*, like *sidrah* and *fiqrah*. The middle letter can take a *fatḥah*, *kasrah* or *sukūn*. Al-Jawharī related it. Nāfi', in the recension of Warsh, has *qurubah*, which is the root, and the rest have it as *qurbah*. There is no disagreement about *qurubāt*. Ibn Sa'dān related that Yazīd ibn al-Qa'qā' recited *'qurbah'*.

'The prayers of the Messenger' refer to his asking for forgiveness and his supplication. The word for prayer, *'ṣalāt'*, is applied in various ways. 'Prayer' from Allah is mercy, good and blessing. Allah says: *'It is He Who calls down blessing (yuṣallī) on you, as do his angels.'* (33:43) Prayer from the angels is supplication and that is also what it is from the Prophet ﷺ as Allah says: *'Your prayers bring relief to them.'* (9:103) Your supplication makes them firm and gives them tranquillity. *'It does indeed bring them near'* to the mercy of Allah, meaning that their spending does that.

وَٱلسَّٰبِقُونَ ٱلْأَوَّلُونَ مِنَ ٱلْمُهَٰجِرِينَ وَٱلْأَنصَارِ وَٱلَّذِينَ ٱتَّبَعُوهُم
بِإِحْسَٰنٍ رَّضِىَ ٱللَّهُ عَنْهُمْ وَرَضُوا۟ عَنْهُ وَأَعَدَّ لَهُمْ جَنَّٰتٍ تَجْرِى تَحْتَهَا
ٱلْأَنْهَٰرُ خَٰلِدِينَ فِيهَآ أَبَدًا ۚ ذَٰلِكَ ٱلْفَوْزُ ٱلْعَظِيمُ ﴿١٠٠﴾

100 The Forerunners – the first of the *Muhājirūn* and the *Anṣār* – and those who have followed them in doing good: Allah is pleased

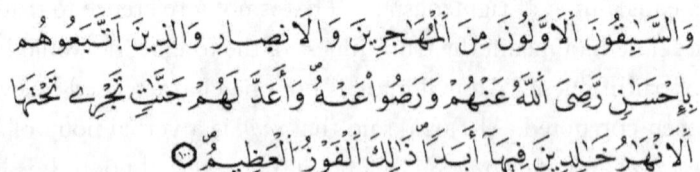

with them and they are pleased with Him. He has prepared Gardens for them with rivers flowing under them, remaining in them timelessly, for ever and ever. That is the great victory.

When Allah speaks of the categories of Arabs, he also mentions the *Muhājirūn* and *Anṣār* and makes it clear that some of them were forerunners in terms of emigration and some of them followed later. He praises them. There is disagreement about the number of groups and categories they fall into. We will clarify all of that, Allah willing. 'Umar ibn al-Khaṭṭāb related that *Anṣār* is recited in the nominative case, added to 'the Forerunners'. Al-Afkhas said, '*Anṣār* being in the genitive is correct because the Forerunners come from both groups.' *Anṣār* is a term belonging to Islam. Anas ibn Mālik was asked, 'Do you think that the name *Anṣār*, which people give you, is a name by which Allah named you or were you called that in the Jāhiliyyah?' He answered, 'It is a name by which Allah named us in the Qur'an.' Abū 'Umar mentioned it in *al-Istidhkār*.

The Qur'an provides a text about the excellence of the first Forerunners among the *Muhājirūn* and *Anṣār*. They are those who prayed to the two *qiblahs* according to Sa'īd ibn al-Musayyab and one group of scholars. In the view of the people of ash-Shāfi'ī, they are those who were present at the Pledge of Riḍwān, which is the Pledge of al-Ḥudaybīyah. Ash-Sha'bī said that. Muḥammad ibn Ka'b and 'Aṭā' ibn Yasār said that they are the people of Badr. There is general consensus that those who emigrated before the change of *qiblah* are among the first *Muhājirūn*.

As for the best of them, Abū Manṣūr al-Baghdādī at-Tamīmī said, 'Our companions agreed that the best of them are the four Rightly-Guided Caliphs and then the remaining six who make up the ten (Companions promised the Garden), then the people who fought at Badr, then the people who fought at Uḥud, and then the people of the Pledge of Riḍwān at al-Ḥudaybīyah, and then every Muslim who saw the Messenger of Allah ﷺ and was one of his Companions.'

As for the first of them to become Muslim, Mujālid related that ash-Sha'bī said, 'I asked Ibn 'Abbās about the first person to become Muslim and he answered that it was Abū Bakr. It is as I heard Ḥassān say:

When you mention grief for a trustworthy brother,
    remember your brother Abū Bakr and what he did:
The best of people, the most godfearing and justest
    after the Prophet, and the most faithful to what he bore.
The second whose grave is praised
    and the first of people to affirm the Messengers.

Abū al-Faraj al-Jawzī mentioned that Yūsuf ibn Ya'qūb ibn al-Mājishūn said, 'I met my father, and our shaykh Muḥammad ibn al-Munkadir, Rabī'ah ibn Abī 'Abd ar-Raḥmān, Ṣāliḥ ibn Kaysan, Sa'd ibn Ibrāhīm and 'Uthmān ibn Muḥammad al-Akhnasī who did not doubt that the first person to become Muslim was Abū Bakr. That was stated by Ibn 'Abbās, Ḥassān, and Asmā' bint Abī Bakr. That was also stated by Ibrāhīm an-Nakha'ī.'

It is also said that the first to become Muslim was 'Alī and that was related from Zayd ibn Arqam, Abū Dharr, al-Miqdād and others. Al-Ḥākim Abū 'Abdullāh said, 'I do not know of any disagreement between the authors of histories that 'Alī was the first to become Muslim.' It is also said that the first to become Muslim was Zayd ibn Ḥārithah. Ma'mar mentioned the like of that from az-Zuhrī and it is the position of Sulaymān ibn Yasār, 'Urwah ibn az-Zubayr and 'Imrān ibn Abī Anas. It is said, as well, that the first to become Muslim was Khadījah, the *Umm al-Mu'minīn*. That is related by various paths from az-Zuhrī. It is the view of Qatādah, Muḥammad ibn Isḥāq ibn Yasār and a group. It is also related from Ibn 'Abbas. Ath-Tha'labī, the Qur'anic commentator, claimed that scholars agreed that Khadījah was the first to become Muslim and that the disagreement is about who was the first to become Muslim after her.

Isḥāq ibn Ibrāhīm ibn Rāhawayh al-Ḥanẓalī combined these reports and used to say: 'The first man to become Muslim was Abū Bakr. The first woman was Khadījah. The first child was 'Alī. The first *mawlā* was Zayd ibn Ḥārithah and the first slave was Bilāl. Allah knows best.' Muḥammad ibn Sa'd mentioned that Abū al-Aswad Muḥammad ibn 'Abd ar-Raḥmān ibn Nawfal said, 'Az-Zubayr became Muslim after Abū Bakr, and he was the fourth or fifth.' He also said, 'Az-Zubayr became Muslim when he was eight.' It is related that 'Alī became Muslim when he was seven. It is also said that he was ten.

What is known by way of the people of *ḥadīth* is that every Muslim who saw the Messenger of Allah ﷺ is one of his Companions. Al-Bukhārī said in the *Ṣaḥīḥ*, 'Any Muslim who kept the company of a Prophet ﷺ or saw him was one of his Companions.' It is related from Sa'īd ibn al-Musayyab that the only one who is counted as a Companion is someone who stayed with the Messenger of Allah ﷺ for one or two years and went on one or two expeditions with him. If this statement attributed to Sa'īd ibn al-Musayyab were true, then Jarīr ibn 'Abdullāh al-Bajalī would not be counted as a Companion, nor those like him, because he did not meet the literal conditions of what was stipulated, but we know of no disagreement that he was a Companion.

There is no disagreement that Abū Bakr aṣ-Ṣiddīq was the first of the Forerunners of the *Muhājirūn*. Ibn al-'Arabī said, 'Being a Forerunner is based on three things: the quality, which is faith, the time and the place. The best of these aspects is going first in terms of quality.' The evidence for that is found in the words of the Prophet ﷺ in the *Ṣaḥīḥ*: 'We are the first in spite of the fact that they were given the Book before us and we were given it after them. This is their day about which they disagreed. Allah guided us to it. The Jews have the next day and the Christians the day after it.' So the Prophet ﷺ reported that although some nations came before us in time, we got ahead of them by faith and obeying the command of Allah Almighty and following it and submitting to His command and pleasure which He imposed and bearing its duties. We do not oppose Him and do not exercise choice where He is concerned. We do not change His *Sharī'ah* by opinion as the People of the Book did. That was by the success of Allah which He decreed and made easy for those with whom He is pleased. We would not have been guided if Allah had not guided us.

Ibn Khuwayzimandād said, 'This *āyah* contains the details of the excellence of the Forerunners with all their virtues found in the noble *Sharī'ah* in terms of knowledge, *dīn*, courage or other things involving the giving of wealth and attaining rank in nobility.' In this regard there is a difference between Abū Bakr and 'Umar. Scholars disagree about the levels of excellence of the Forerunners in the light of the stipend paid to them rather than others. It is related that Abū Bakr aṣ-Ṣiddīq did not prefer anyone over anyone else in the amount of stipend paid to them on the basis of their precedence in Islam. 'Umar said to him, 'Do you make the one with precedence like the one without it?' Abū Bakr said, 'They acted for Allah and He will reward them for it.' 'Umar, however, used to give them preference when he was caliph, although he said when he was dying, 'If I were to live until tomorrow, I would join the lowest of the people to the highest,' but he died that night. This disagreement has continued until today.

those who have followed them in doing good

'Umar recited *'wa al-anṣāru'* in the nominative and dropped the *wāw* before 'those' so that it describes the *Anṣār*. Zayd ibn Thābit differed with him about it and 'Umar asked Ubayy ibn Ka'b who confirmed Zayd and so 'Umar relied on that. He said, 'We only think that it is in the nominative and it is nothing else in our view.' Ubayy said, 'I found the confirmation of that in the Book of Allah at the beginning of *Sūrat al-Jumu'ah*: *"And others of them who have not yet joined them"* (62:3), in *Sūrat al-Ḥashr*: *"Those who have come after them say, 'Our Lord forgive us and our brothers who preceded us in faith'"* (59:10), and in *Sūrat al-Anfāl*: *"Those who believe and make hijrah later on and accompany you in doing jihād, they are also of your number."* (8:75)'

So he affirmed the reading with the *wāw*. Allah makes it clear by His words: '*in doing good*' in the actions and words which follow it, not in any slips and mistakes they may make since they are protected from that. May Allah be pleased with them.

Scholars disagree about who the *Tābi'ūn*, or Followers, are and their ranks. Al-Khaṭīb al-Ḥāfiẓ said that a Follower is whoever kept the company of a Companion. One of them is called a *Tābi'* or *Tābi'ī*. Al-Ḥākim Abū 'Abdullāh and others said that it conveys the fact that it is enough to have listened to a Companion or met him, even if that is not keeping known company. It is said that the term *Tābi'ūn* is applied to those who became Muslim after al-Ḥudaybīyah, such as Khālid ibn al-Walīd and 'Amr ibn al-'Āṣ and those close to them who became Muslim at the Conquest of Makkah. That is because it is confirmed that 'Abd ar-Raḥmān ibn 'Awf complained to the Prophet ﷺ about Khālid ibn al-Walīd and the Prophet ﷺ said to Khālid, 'Leave my Companions alone. By the One Who has my soul in His hand, if one of you were to spend the like of Uḥud in gold every day, it would not reach the *mudd* of one of them, nor even half a *mudd*.'

It is extraordinary that al-Ḥākim Abū 'Abdullāh counted an-Nu'mān and Suwayd, the sons of Muqarrin al-Muzanī, among the *Tābi'ūn* when he mentioned them as being among the *Tābi'ūn*! They are two known Companions who are mentioned among the Companions and were present at the Battle of the Ditch. Allah knows best. The greatest of the *Tābi'ūn* are the seven *fuqahā'* of Madīnah: Sa'īd ibn al-Musayyab, al-Qāsim ibn Muḥammad, 'Urwah ibn Hisham, Khārijah ibn Zayd, Abū Salamah ibn 'Abd ar-Raḥmān, 'Abdullāh ibn 'Utbah ibn Mas'ūd, and Sulaymān ibn Yasār. One of the esteemed scholars put them together in a single verse:

Take them: 'Abdullah, 'Urwah, Qāsim,
Sa'īd, Abū Bakr, Sulaymān, Khārijah.

Aḥmad ibn Ḥanbal said, 'The best of the *Tābi'ūn* was Sa'īd ibn al-Musayyab.' It was said to him, "Alqamah and al-Aswad.' He replied, 'Sa'īd ibn al-Musayyab, 'Alqamah and al-Aswad.' He also said, 'The best of the *Tābi'ūn* were Qays, Abū 'Uthmān, 'Alqamah, and Masrūq. Those are excellent and the highest of the *Tābi'ūn*.' He also said, "Aṭā' was the Muftī of Makkah and al-Ḥasan was the Muftī of Basra. People gained much from them.' It is related that Abū Bakr ibn Abī Dāwūd said, 'The greatest of the *Tābi'ūn* among women were Ḥafṣah bint Sīrīn and 'Amrah bint 'Abd ar-Raḥmān. The third, who does not reach their level, was Umm ad-Dardā'.'

It is related that al-Ḥākim Abū 'Abdullāh said, 'A group are counted among the *Tābi'ūn* even if it is not true that any of them listened to the Companions. They include Ibrāhīm ibn Suwayd an-Nakha'ī – not Ibrāhīm ibn Yazīd an-Nakha'ī the *faqīh* – Bukayr ibn Abī as-Samīṭ, Bukayr ibn 'Abdullāh al-Ashajj and others.' He said, 'A group of people count them among the *Tābi'ūn*. Some of them met the Companions, including Abū az-Zinād 'Abdullah ibn Dhakwān who met 'Abdullāh ibn 'Umar and Anas. Hishām ibn 'Urwah visited 'Abdullah ibn 'Umar, Jābir ibn 'Abdullāh and Mūsā ibn 'Uqbah. He met Anas ibn Mālik and Umm Khālid bint Khālid ibn Sa'īd.'

The *Tābi'ūn* also include a group called the *Mukhaḍramūn*. They are those who were alive in both the Jāhiliyyah and in the lifetime of the Messenger of Allah ﷺ and became Muslims but were not Companions (because they never met the Prophet ﷺ). One of them is called a *Mukhaḍram*, as if they are cut off (*khuḍrima*) from their peers who were Companions. Muslim mentioned them, and there were twenty of them, including Abū 'Amr ash-Shaybānī, Suwayd ibn Ghafalah al-Kindī, 'Amr ibn Maymūn al-Awdī, Abū 'Uthmān an-Nahdī, 'Abd Khayr ibn Yazīd al-Khayrānī (a tribe of Hamdān), 'Abd ar-Raḥmān ibn Mull, Abū al-Ḥilāl al-'Utakī and Rabī'ah ibn Zurārah. Muslim did not mention some of them, including Abū Muslim al-Khawlānī, 'Abdullāh ibn Thuwab, and al-Aḥnaf ibn Qays.

This is a small sample of the knowledge concerning the Companions and *Tābi'ūn* whose excellence was mentioned in the Noble Qur'an: may Allah be pleased with all of them. Enough for us are the words of the Almighty: *'You are the best nation ever to be produced before mankind'* (2:110) and: *'In this way We have made you a middlemost community'* (2:143). The Messenger of Allah ﷺ said, 'I wish that we had seen our brothers…' (Aḥmad) He made us his brothers if we are godfearing and follow in his footsteps. May Allah gather us in his company!

وَمِمَّنْ حَوْلَكُم مِّنَ ٱلْأَعْرَابِ مُنَٰفِقُونَ ۖ وَمِنْ أَهْلِ ٱلْمَدِينَةِ ۙ مَرَدُوا۟ عَلَى
ٱلنِّفَاقِ لَا تَعْلَمُهُمْ ۖ نَحْنُ نَعْلَمُهُمْ ۚ سَنُعَذِّبُهُم مَّرَّتَيْنِ ثُمَّ يُرَدُّونَ إِلَىٰ
عَذَابٍ عَظِيمٍ ﴿١٠١﴾

101 Some of the desert Arabs around you are hypocrites and some of the people of Madīnah are obdurate in their hypocrisy. You do not know them but We know them. We will punish them twice over and then they will be returned to a terrible punishment.

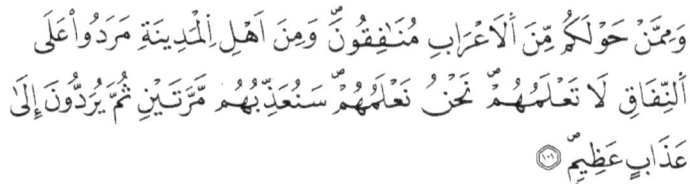

Some of the desert Arabs around you are hypocrites

This is an inceptive and predicate. They are a people who are hypocrites: this refers to the tribes of Muzaynah, Juhaynah, Aslam, Ghifār and Ashja'.

and some of the people of Madīnah are obdurate in their hypocrisy.

'Obdurate in their hypocrisy' means that some people remained stubbornly hypocrites. *'Maradū'* describes the hypocrites and so there is some change in the normal order of the words. It means: 'Around you are some desert Arabs who are hypocrites and are stubborn in their hypocrisy. Some of the people of Madīnah are also like that.' *'Maradū'* means: they remained in that state and did not repent. Ibn Zayd said that. Others said: they persisted in it and refused anything else. The meanings are similar.

The root of '*maradū*' means: softness, flexibility and stripping. It is as if they divested themselves for hypocrisy. Sand is described as bare (*mardā'*) when it has no plants on it. A bare (*amrad*) branch has no leaves on it. A horse which is *amrad* has no hair on its rump. A beardless boy has a clear neck and *mardā'* is not used for a girl. *Marrada* is to plaster a building. An example of its use is: *'a courtyard paved with glass'* (27:44) and *marrada* is used for stripping a branch of leaves. The verb is *marada*, *yamrudu*, *murūd* and *marādah*.

You do not know them but We know them

This is similar to the words: *'...whom you do not know. Allah knows them.'* (8:60) It means: 'You, Muḥammad, do not know the end of their affairs. It is We who know that.' This forbids making a judgment about whether someone will go to the Fire or the Garden.

We will punish them twice over and then they will be returned to a terrible punishment.

Ibn 'Abbās said that the punishment is by illnesses in this world and torment in the Next World. The illness of a believer is expiation and that of an unbeliever is a punishment. It is said that the first punishment is their disgrace through the Prophet ﷺ being informed about them and the second is the punishment of the grave. Al-Ḥasan and Qatādah said that it is the punishment of this world and the punishment of the grave. Ibn Zayd said that the first is by disasters in respect of their property and children and the second is the punishment of the grave. Mujāhid said that it is by hunger and killing. Al-Farrā' said that it is killing and the punishment of the grave. It is said that it is capture and killing. It is also said that the first punishment is by *zakāt* being taken from their wealth and by the carrying out of the *ḥudūd* punishments on them, and the second is the punishment of the grave. It is said that it is one of the two punishments as the Almighty says: *'Do not let their wealth and children impress you. Allah merely wants to punish them by you in the life of this world.'* (9:55) The import of the *āyah* is that punishment will follow or the punishment will be doubled for them.

وَءَاخَرُونَ ٱعْتَرَفُوا۟ بِذُنُوبِهِمْ خَلَطُوا۟ عَمَلًا صَٰلِحًا وَءَاخَرَ سَيِّئًا عَسَى ٱللَّهُ أَن
يَتُوبَ عَلَيْهِمْ ۚ إِنَّ ٱللَّهَ غَفُورٌ رَّحِيمٌ ﴿١٠٢﴾

102 But others have acknowledged their wrong actions and mixed a right action with another which is wrong. It may well be that Allah will turn towards them. Allah is Ever-Forgiving, Most Merciful.

But others have acknowledged their wrong actions and mixed a right action with another which is wrong.

'Others' means those from the people of Madīnah and those around are people who have admitted their wrong actions, while others hope for the command of Allah to give whatever judgment on them that He wishes. The first class can be hypocrites, but not obdurate in hypocrisy. It is also possible that they were believers. Ibn 'Abbās said that it was revealed about the ten who stayed behind the Tabūk expedition. Seven of them chained themselves to the pillars of the mosque. Qatādah said the same, adding, '*"Take zakāt from their wealth"* (9:103) was revealed about them:' Al-Mahdawī mentioned it. Zayd ibn Aslam said that they were eight. It is also said that they were six or five.

Mujāhid said, 'The *āyah* was revealed about Abu Lubābah al-Anṣārī particularly about what happened between him and the Banū Qurayẓah. That was when they spoke to him about coming down to face the judgment of Allah and His Messenger ﷺ and he pointed at his throat, indicating that the Messenger of Allah ﷺ would kill them if they came down. When he was disgraced, he repented and regretted what he had done and tied himself to the pillars of the mosque and swore that he would not eat or drink until Allah pardoned him or he died. He remained like that until Allah pardoned him and the *āyah* was revealed and the Messenger of Allah ﷺ commanded that he be released. Aṭ-Ṭabarī mentioned it from Mujāhid, and Ibn Isḥāq mentioned it in greater detail in the *Sīrah.*

Ashhab said that Mālik said, 'The word "*others*" was revealed about Abu Lubābah and his companions. When he committed the wrong action, he said,

"Messenger of Allah, should I stay in your company and forfeit my property?" He said, "A third will be enough for you when the Almighty says: '*Take zakāt from their wealth to purify and cleanse them.*' (9:103)"' Ibn al-Qāsim and Ibn Wahb related it from Mālik.

Most believe that the *āyah* was revealed about those who failed to go on the Tabūk expedition. They tied themselves to the pillars of the mosque as Abū Lubābah had done. They made a covenant with Allah that they would not release themselves until the Messenger of Allah ﷺ was the one to release them and was pleased with them. The Messenger of Allah ﷺ said, 'I swear by Allah that I will not release them or excuse them until I am commanded to release them. They were loath to go with me and stayed behind the expedition with the Muslims.' Then Allah revealed this *āyah*. When it was revealed, the Prophet ﷺ sent for them and released and excused them. They said, 'Messenger of Allah, this is our wealth which kept us behind you. Take it as *ṣadaqah* for us, purify us, and ask forgiveness for us.' He answered, 'I was not commanded to take anything from your wealth and so Allah revealed, *"take zakāt from their wealth."* (9:103)'

Ibn 'Abbās said that they were ten men and Abū Lubābah was one of them. He ﷺ took a third of their wealth and it was expiation for the wrong actions they had committed. Their evil deed was that of staying behind and there is a consensus on that among the people who say that.

They disagree about the right action. Aṭ-Ṭabarī and others said that it is admission, repentance and regret. It is said that it was the righteous actions which they performed: they joined the Messenger of Allah ﷺ and tied themselves to the pillars of the mosque and said, 'We will not go near our wives or children until Allah sends down our pardon.' Another group said that the righteous action was past expeditions with the Prophet ﷺ. Even if this *āyah* was revealed about the desert Arabs, it remains general until the Day of Rising about those with righteous and evil actions. It gives hope. Aṭ-Ṭabarī mentioned that Ḥajjāj ibn Abī Zaynab said that he heard Abū 'Uthmān say, 'There is no *āyah* in the Qur'an which I consider more hopeful for this community than the words of the Almighty: "*But others have acknowledged their wrong actions and mixed a right action with another which is wrong.*"'

We find in al-Bukhārī from Samurah ibn Jundub, 'The Messenger of Allah ﷺ said to us, "Two people came to me in the night and took me and we reached a city built of gold and silver bricks. Some men met us, half of whose form was the most beautiful that anyone has seen and the other half the ugliest anyone has seen. They said to them, 'Go into that river.' They went into it and then returned to us and that evil had departed from them and they left in the most beautiful form. The two said to me, 'This is the Garden of Eden and this is your dwelling.' They said, 'The people who were half beautiful and half ugly mixed right actions with wrong actions and Allah pardoned them.''''

Al-Bayhaqī mentioned the *ḥadīth* of the Night Journey from ar-Rabī' ibn Anas from Abū Hurayrah from the Prophet ﷺ. In it he said, 'I was taken up to heaven...' In it he mentioned ascending to the seventh heaven where they said: '"Allah greets a brother and caliph! An excellent brother! An excellent caliph! An excellent arrival!" There was a grey-haired man sitting on a throne at the gate of the Garden and with him were some people with white faces and some people with black faces. There was something off about their colour. They went to a river and entered it and washed and some of their colour was washed off. Then they went to another river and entered it and washed and some more of their colour was washed off. Then they went to a third river and entered it and washed and yet more of their colour was washed off and their colour became like that of their companions. They went and sat with their companions. I asked, "Jibril, who are these with white faces and those with something off about their colour who entered a river and then emerged with their colour purified?" He said, "This is your father Ibrāhīm. He was the first one with grey hair on the surface of the earth. Those with white faces are those who did not mix with faith any wrongdoing. Those with something off about their colour are those who mixed righteous actions with evil actions and repented, and so Allah turned to them. The first river was Allah's mercy; the second was the blessing of Allah; and the third river is *'a pure draught which their Lord gave them to drink.'* (76:22)"'

The *wāw* in *'with another which is wrong'* is said to have the meaning of *bā'* and also to have the meaning of *ma'* (with), as when one says, 'The water is level with (*wa*) the wood.' The Kufans object to that usage and say it is not permitted to put wood before water, and *'ākhar'* in the *āyah* can be put before the first and it is in the position of: 'I mixed water with (*wa*) milk.'

خُذْ مِنْ أَمْوَٰلِهِمْ صَدَقَةً تُطَهِّرُهُمْ وَتُزَكِّيهِم بِهَا وَصَلِّ عَلَيْهِمْ إِنَّ
صَلَوٰتَكَ سَكَنٌ لَّهُمْ وَٱللَّهُ سَمِيعٌ عَلِيمٌ ١٠٣

103 Take *zakāt* from their wealth to purify and cleanse them and pray for them. Your prayers bring relief to them. Allah is All-Hearing, All-Knowing.

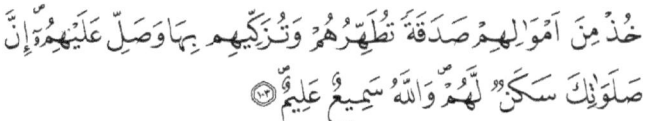

Take *zakāt* from their wealth to purify and cleanse them

This is *sadaqah* in the Arabic, and there is disagreement about the *ṣaqadah* commanded in this *āyah*. It is said that this *ṣadaqah* is the obligatory *zakāt*. Juwaybir quoted that from Ibn 'Abbās and it is the position of 'Ikrimah according to what al-Qushayrī said. It is specifically about those about whom the *āyah* was revealed. The Prophet ﷺ took a third of their property. That is not anything to do with obligatory *zakāt*. This is why Mālik said, 'When a man says he will give away all his property as *ṣadaqah*, that is satisfied by giving away a third of it, based on the *hadīth* of Abū Lubābah.'

According to the first view, it is addressed to the Prophet ﷺ as demanded by the literal text and confined to him, so no one but him takes it. According to this, it would necessarily be annulled and removed by his death. This is the explanation presented by those who refused to pay *zakāt* to Abū Bakr aṣ-Ṣiddīq. They said, 'He gave us purification and the prayer for us in exchange for it. No one else can do that for us.' Their poet said:

We obeyed the Messenger of Allah as long as he was among us.
How extraordinary! What is the kingdom of Abu Bakr?
You refused what they asked of you
and it is like dates or sweeter still with them.
We will refuse them as long as any nobles remain
with us against harm in hardship and ease.

This is a category who stood against Abū Bakr and Abū Bakr said about them, 'By Allah, I will fight those who make a distinction between the prayer and *zakāt*!'

Ibn al-'Arabī said, 'As for what they say about this being addressed to the Prophet ﷺ, no one else connected it to him exclusively and so these are the words of someone who is ignorant of the Qur'an, heedless of the source of the *Sharī'ah*, and who toys with the *dīn*. The use of the second person in the Qur'an does not have a single implication. It means different things in different places. Sometimes the entire Community is addressed as when Allah says: *"O you who believe, when you get up to do the prayer..."* (5:6) and *"O you who believe, fasting is prescribed for you..."* (2:183) and similar cases. Sometimes he ﷺ in particular is addressed in words and no one else shares with him in it, as when Allah says: *"And stay awake for prayer during part of the night as a supererogatory action for yourself"* (17:79) and: *"exclusively for you."* (33:50) Sometimes he ﷺ in particular is addressed in words and all of the Community share with him in the meaning, as when Allah says: *"Establish the prayer from the time the sun declines"* (17:78): *"Whenever you recite the Qur'an, seek refuge from the accursed Shayṭān"* (16:98) and: *"When you are with them and leading the prayer."*

(4:102) Anyone for whom the sun declines is instructed to pray, just as anyone who recites the Qur'an is instructed to seek refuge, and anyone who is in a state of fear performs the prayer in this manner. Another example of this is Allah's words: *"Take zakāt from their wealth to purify and cleanse them."* This is also the case in His words: *"O Prophet, have taqwā of Allah"* (33:1) and *"O Prophet, when you divorce women…"* (65:1)'

As for the term wealth (*māl*), some Arabs, namely Daws, believe that *māl* is clothing, household utensils and goods, and do not call money '*māl*'. There is some corroboration of this in the firm Sunnah from Mālik from Thawr ibn Zayd ad-Dīlī from Abū al-Ghayth Sālim, the client of Ibn Muṭi', that Abū Hurayrah said, 'We went out with the Messenger of Allah ﷺ in the year of Khaybar. We did not take any booty of gold or silver, but only some clothing and household goods (*amwāl*).'

Others believe that 'silent *māl*' is gold and silver. It is also said that it is camels in particular, as they say, 'Wealth (*māl*) is camels.' It is said that it is all livestock. Ibn al-Anbārī said that Aḥmad ibn Yaḥyā Tha'lab an-Naḥawī said, 'That which falls short of reaching the level of *zakāt* in gold and silver is not wealth.' He recited a poem, saying:

By Allah, my livestock has not reached the limit
nor *zakāt* nor camels nor wealth (*māl*).

Abū 'Umar said, 'What is known in the language of the Arabs is that all that is wealth and owned is *māl* by the words of the Prophet ﷺ, "The son of Ādam says, 'My wealth! My wealth!' All that he has of his wealth is what he eats and is consumed, or wears and is worn out, or gives away as *ṣadaqah* and is carried out."' Abū Qatādah said, 'He gave me a coat of mail. I sold it and with the proceeds bought a garden at the Banū Salimah, and it was the first wealth (*māl*) I got in Islam.' If someone swears that he will give all his wealth as *ṣadaqah*, that applies to every category of his wealth, whether it is something on which *zakāt* is obliged or not, unless he intends something specific and then it is as he intends. It is said that that only applies to all the types of wealth subject to *zakāt*. Knowledge is comprehensive and the tongue bears witness to what he owns is called *māl*. Allah knows best.

The sentence, '*Take zakāt from their wealth,*' is undefined and does not specify any precondition about what is taken and what it is taken from. The amount taken is not made clear nor what it is taken from. The clarification of that is found in the *Sunnah* and consensus as we will mention. *Zakāt* is taken from all wealth. The

Prophet ﷺ obliged *zakāt* on livestock, grains and money. There is no dispute about that. They disagree about other things such as horses and other goods. Horses and honey will be mentioned in *an-Naḥl* (16:8, 69), Allah willing. The *imāms* related from Abū Sa'īd that the Prophet ﷺ said, 'There is no *zakāt* on less than five *wasqs* of dates. There is no *zakāt* on what is less than five *ūqiyyahs* of silver. There is no *zakāt* on less than five camels." The *zakāt* on grains was adequately discussed in *al-An'ām* (6:141), mines in *al-Baqarah* (2:267), and jewellery in this *sūrah* (9:34). Scholars agree that an *ūqiyyah* is forty dirhams. When a free Muslim man owns 200 dirhams of minted silver, which is the five *ūqiyyahs* mentioned in the *ḥadīth*, for a full year, he is obliged to pay *zakāt* on it. That is 2.5% or five dirhams. The passage of a year is a precondition since the Prophet ﷺ said, 'There is no *zakāt* until a person has had it in his possession for a year.' At-Tirmidhī transmitted it.

When there is more silver than 200, then 2.5% is calculated on it, great or small. This is the position of Mālik, al-Layth, ash-Shāfi'ī, most of the adherents of Abū Ḥanīfah, Ibn Abī Laylā, ath-Thawrī, al-Awzā'ī, Aḥmad ibn Ḥanbal, Abū Thawr, Isḥāq and Abū 'Ubayd. That is related from 'Alī and Ibn 'Umar. One group said that there is nothing on more than 200 dirhams until it reaches forty more dirhams. When it reaches that, there is a dirham owed on it and that is 2.5%. That is the position of Sa'īd ibn al-Musayyab, al-Ḥasan, 'Aṭā', Ṭāwūs, ash-Sha'bī, az-Zuhrī, Makḥūl, 'Amr ibn Dīnār and Abū Ḥanīfah.

As for *zakāt* on gold, most scholars believe that when there are twenty dinars, which is the price of 200 dirhams, or more, *zakāt* is mandatory on it based on the *ḥadīth* of 'Alī. At-Tirmidhī transmitted it from Ḍamrah and al-Ḥārith from 'Alī. At-Tirmidhī said, 'I asked Muḥammad ibn Ismā'īl about this *ḥadīth* and he said, "I think that both of them are sound from Abu Isḥāq. It is possible that both of them are from him."'

Al-Bājī said in *al-Muntaqā*: 'This *ḥadīth* does not have an *isnād* here, although the agreement of the scholars to use it is an indication of the soundness of the ruling. Allah knows best.' It is related from al-Ḥasan and ath-Thawrī – and it is a view that some of the adherents of Dāwūd ibn 'Alī inclined to – that there is no *zakāt* on gold until it reaches forty dinars. This is refuted by the *ḥadīth* of 'Alī and that of Ibn 'Umar and 'Ā'ishah that the Prophet ﷺ used to take half a dinar from every twenty dinars and a dinar from forty dinars. This is the position of the people of knowledge except for what was mentioned.

The Community agree that if there are less than five camels, there is no *zakāt* due on them. When there are five, one sheep (*shāh*) is due. *Shāh* is one of *ghanam* which includes both sheep as well as goats. There is also agreement among scholars that there is only one sheep due on five. It is the obligation. The *zakāt* due on livestock is explained in the letter which Abū Bakr aṣ-Ṣiddīq wrote to Anas when he sent him to Baḥrayn. Al-Bukhārī, Abū Dāwūd, ad-Dāraquṭnī, an-Nasā'ī, Ibn Mājah and others transmitted it.

All agree on it, although there is disagreement on two matters in it. One is the *zakāt* on camels when there are 121 camels. Mālik said that the collector has a choice: he can take three *bint labūns* or two *ḥiqqahs*. Ibn al-Qāsim said that Ibn Shihāb said that there are three *bint labūns* until the number reaches 130, and then there is a *ḥiqqah* and two *bint labūns*. Ibn al-Qāsim said, 'My opinion is that of Ibn Shihāb.' Ibn Ḥabīb mentioned that 'Abd al-'Azīz ibn Abī Salamah, 'Abd al-'Azīz ibn Abī Ḥāzim and Ibn Dīnār say what Mālik says.

The second matter concerns the *zakāt* of sheep when there are more than 201 of them. Al-Ḥasan ibn Ṣāliḥ ibn Ḥayy said that four sheep are due. When the number of sheep reaches 401, five sheep are due. That is how it is with every increase for every hundred sheep. Something similar is related from Ibrāhīm an-Nakha'ī. Most say that three sheep are due on 201 sheep, and then there is nothing until 400 when four sheep are due, and one sheep is due on every further hundred. There is consensus and agreement on that. Ibn 'Abd al-Barr said, 'Ibn al-Mundhir is weak in respect of this matter and related errors from scholars and is muddled and has many errors.'

Neither al-Bukhārī or Muslim mentioned the details of the *zakāt* on cattle in their *Ṣaḥīḥ*. Abū Dāwūd, at-Tirmidhī, an-Nasā'ī, ad-Dāraquṭnī and Mālik in the *Muwaṭṭā'* transmitted that as *mursal*, cut and *mawqūf*. Abū 'Umar said, 'Some people related it from Ṭāwūs from Mu'ādh although they make the *mursal* firmer than that with an *isnād*. The rest give it an *isnād* from al-Mas'ūdī from al-Ḥakam from Ṭāwūs. They disagree about what the rest have by single transmission from reliable men. Al-Ḥasan ibn 'Umārah related it from al-Ḥakam as the rest related it from al-Mas'ūdī from al-Ḥakam and al-Ḥasan [ibn 'Umārah] who is agreed to be weak. This report is transmitted [from Mu'ādh] with a sound firm connected *isnād* from other than Ṭāwūs. 'Abd ar-Razzāq said that Ma'mar and ath-Thawrī reported from al-A'mash from Abū Wā'il from Masrūq that Mu'ādh ibn Jabal said, 'The Messenger of Allah ﷺ sent me to Yemen and commanded me to take a cow from every thirty: a *tabī'* or *tabī'ah*, and a *musinnah* from forty, and a dinar from every adult [non-Muslim] male or its equivalent in clothes.' Ad-Dāraquṭnī and Abū 'Īṣā at-Tirmidhī mentioned it and said that it is sound.

Abū 'Umar said, 'There is no disagreement between scholars that the *zakāt* due on cattle from the Prophet ﷺ and his Companions is what Mu'ādh ibn Jabal transmitted that there is a *tabīʿ* on thirty cattle and a *musinnah* on forty cattle, except for something related from Saʿīd ibn al-Musayyab, Abū Qilābah, az-Zuhrī and Qatādah. They oblige a sheep on every five head of cattle up to thirty.' These are the particulars of the fundamentals and secondary rulings of *zakāt* in the books of *fiqh*. Mixing together will be mentioned in *Sūrah Ṣād*, Allah willing.

Ṣadaqah is derived from *ṣidq* since it indicates the soundness of faith and inward and outward sincerity and that the person concerned is not one of the hypocrites who criticise those believers who voluntarily give *ṣadaqah*.

The phrase *'to purify and cleanse them'* connects to the one who is addressed. It implies: 'Take it in order to purify them and cleanse them by it.' It is permitted to make them two adjectives modifying *ṣadaqah*, meaning that *ṣadaqah* purifies and cleanses them and the subject of purifying them is the second person and the pronoun in '*bihā*' refers to what is described and undefined. An-Naḥḥās and Makkī related that '*purify them*' describes *ṣadaqah* and '*cleanse them by it*' is a *ḥāl* modifying the pronoun in '*Take*', which refers to the Prophet ﷺ. It is possible that it is a *ḥāl* describing *ṣadaqah*, but that is weak because it is a *ḥāl* describing something indefinite.

Az-Zajjāj said, 'The best that is said is that it is addressed to the Prophet ﷺ, meaning 'you purify and cleanse them,' as a separate and new sentence. It is possible for it to be in the jussive as the apodosis of the command. It means: 'You take *ṣadaqah* from their wealth to purify and cleanse them.' Imru al-Qays said:

Stand and let us weep at the memory of the beloved and a house.

Al-Ḥasan recited '*purify*' with a *sukūn* on the *ṭā'*. It is transmitted with a *hamzah* from *ṭahara*, *aṭhara*.

pray for them.

The basic principle is that every leader who takes *zakāt* prays for blessings for the one who pays it. Muslim related from 'Abdullāh ibn Abī Awfā: 'When some people paid their *zakāt*, the Messenger of Allah ﷺ used to say, "O Allah, send blessings on them!"' Ibn Abī Awfā brought his *zakāt* to him and he ﷺ said, 'O Allah, send blessings for Ibn Abī Awfā.' Some people believe this and others believe that it is abrogated by the words of Allah: *'Never pray over any of them who die.'* (9:84) Therefore they said, 'It is only permitted for the Prophet ﷺ alone to pray for anyone because he was singled out for that. They cite as evidence the words of Allah: *"Do not make the Messenger's summoning of you the same as your summoning one another."* (24:63)' They also cite the fact that Ibn 'Abbās used to say, 'Praying over someone is only for the Prophet ﷺ.' The first is sounder. The address was not confined to him as was already stated and will be mentioned in the next *āyah.*

It is mandatory to imitate the Messenger of Allah ﷺ and take him as a model in his obedience to Allah's words: '*Pray for them. Your prayers bring relief to them.*' It means: 'When you pray for them when they bring their *zakāt*, it brings relief to their hearts and makes them rejoice in doing it.' It is related that Jābir ibn 'Abdullāh said, 'The Prophet ﷺ came to me and I said to my wife, "Do not ask the Messenger of Allah ﷺ for anything." She said, "Is the Messenger of Allah ﷺ to leave us without us asking him for anything!" She said, "Messenger of Allah, pray for my husband." The Messenger of Allah ﷺ said, "May Allah bless you and your husband!"' *Ṣalāt* here is mercy and asking for mercy.

An-Naḥḥās said, 'All the people of language, as far as we know, say that *ṣalāt* in Arabic is supplication and an aspect of that is the prayer said in funerals.' Ḥafṣ, Ḥamzah and al-Kisā'ī recite '*ṣalātaka*' in the singular while the rest have it in the plural. The same difference about the recitation of the word is found in 11:87. *Sakan* is also recited as *sakn.* Qatādah said that it means gravity for them. *Sakan* is that which makes souls tranquil and puts hearts at rest.

أَلَمْ يَعْلَمُوٓا۟ أَنَّ ٱللَّهَ هُوَ يَقْبَلُ ٱلتَّوْبَةَ عَنْ عِبَادِهِۦ وَيَأْخُذُ ٱلصَّدَقَٰتِ وَأَنَّ
ٱللَّهَ هُوَ ٱلتَّوَّابُ ٱلرَّحِيمُ ١٠٤

104 Do they not know that Allah accepts repentance from His slaves and acknowledges their *zakāt*, and that Allah is the Ever-Returning, the Most Merciful?

Do they not know that Allah accepts repentance from His slaves

It is said that that those who did not repent among those who stayed behind said, 'Those people were with us yesterday, but now they do not speak to us or sit with us. Why are they doing this now? What special thing do they have that we do not have?' So it was revealed: '*Do they not know...*' The pronoun '*they*' refers to those who did not repent among those who stayed behind. Ibn Zayd said something along those lines. It is possible that it refers to those who repented and tied themselves to the columns. Allah's use of the word *huwa* [*Do they not know that Allah* He *accepts...*] here is to stress that Allah alone has control of these matters. That is verified by the fact that if He had said, 'Allah accepts repentance' without the *huwa*, it would be possible for His Messenger to accept it on His behalf. The *āyah* makes it clear that it is something which no Prophet or angel can do.

and acknowledges their *zakāt*,

This is a clear text that Allah takes it and rewards it and that the right is His and the Prophet ﷺ is the means. If he dies, then his agent is the one who becomes the means after him. Allah is the Living Who does not die. Allah thus makes it clear that His words: *'Take zakāt from them'* are not confined to the Prophet ﷺ. At-Tirmidhī related from Abū Hurayrah that the Messenger of Allah ﷺ said, 'Allah accepts *ṣadaqah* and takes it in His right hand and makes it grow for one of you as one of you raises his colt, so that a morsel becomes like Uḥud. The confirmation of that is in the Book of Allah: "*[He] accepts repentance from His slaves and acknowledges their zakāt.*" (9:104) "*Allah obliterates ribā but makes ṣadaqah grow in value.*" (2:276)' He says that it is a sound *ḥasan ḥadīth*. We find in *Ṣaḥīḥ Muslim*: 'No one gives a date as *ṣadaqah* from good earnings but that Allah takes it with His right hand,' and one variant adds, 'it grows in the hand of the All-Merciful until it becomes bigger than a mountain.' It is also related: '*Ṣadaqah* falls into the hand of the All-Merciful before it falls into the hand of the asker and He makes it grow as one of you makes his foal or colt grow. Allah doubles it for whomever He wishes.'

Our scholars say in the interpretation of these *ḥadīth*s: 'This alludes to acceptance and reward for it, in the same way that Allah alludes to Himself in the case of the sick person as kindness to Him when He said, "Son of Ādam, I was ill and you did not visit Me."' This was discussed in *al-Baqarah* (2:245). He singles out mention of the right hand and palm since everyone who accepts something takes it in his palm or right hand or it is placed there. Allah uses that language because it is something people will understand. Allah is exalted and, of course, far above having a limb! This was already mentioned (5:64). The term 'right hand' in Arabic is often used without actually meaning the limb as a poet says:

If there is a banner raised for glory
    then 'Arābah will take it in his right hand.

meaning that he is someone worthy of glory and honour. He did not mean the physical right hand because glory is an idea and the right hand which takes its banner is similarly an idea. That is also the case when 'right hand' is used in reference to Allah Almighty. It is said that the meaning of 'grows in the hand of the All-Merciful' designates the scale of the balance in which actions are weighed and so there is elision of the *muḍāf*. It is as if He were saying, 'The scale of the balance of the All-Merciful grows.'

It is related that Mālik, ath-Thawrī and Ibn al-Mubārak said about the interpretation of these *ḥadīth*s and their like, 'Use them without asking "how".'

At-Tirmidhī and others said that this is what is said by the people of knowledge among the people of the Sunnah and the Community.

وَقُلِ ٱعْمَلُوا۟ فَسَيَرَى ٱللَّهُ عَمَلَكُمْ وَرَسُولُهُۥ وَٱلْمُؤْمِنُونَ ۖ وَسَتُرَدُّونَ إِلَىٰ
عَٰلِمِ ٱلْغَيْبِ وَٱلشَّهَٰدَةِ فَيُنَبِّئُكُم بِمَا كُنتُمْ تَعْمَلُونَ ﴿١٠٥﴾

105 Say: 'Act, for Allah will see your actions, and so will His Messenger and the believers. You will be returned to the Knower of the Unseen and the Visible and He will inform you regarding what you did.'

'Say: "Act."' This is addressed to everyone. *'...for Allah will see your actions, and so will His Messenger and the believers'* by His giving them knowledge of your actions. We find in a report: 'If a man did actions inside a rock with no door or window, his actions would go out to people, whatever they were.'

وَءَاخَرُونَ مُرْجَوْنَ لِأَمْرِ ٱللَّهِ إِمَّا يُعَذِّبُهُمْ وَإِمَّا يَتُوبُ عَلَيْهِمْ ۗ وَٱللَّهُ
عَلِيمٌ حَكِيمٌ ﴿١٠٦﴾

106 And others are left awaiting Allah's command as to whether He will punish them or turn to them. Allah is All-Knowing, All-Wise.

This was revealed about the three who were made to repent: Ka'b ibn Mālik, Hilāl ibn Umayyah of the Banū Wāqif and Murārah ibn ar-Rabī'. It is said that it was Ibn Rib'ī al-'Amrī. Al-Mahdawī said that. They stayed behind the Tabūk expedition although they were wealthy. It implies: 'Among them are others who are hopeful,' meaning deferred. Part of that is the Murji'ah (Murji'ites) because they postponed actions. Ḥamzah and al-Kisā'ī recited *'murjawna'* without a *hamzah*. It is said that it is from *arja'a*, to delay. Al-Mubarrad said that *arja'a* is not used with the meaning of simply postponed, but it contains hope.

'Whether He will punish them or turn to them...' In Arabic *immā* is used for one of two alternatives. Allah knows what will happen to things, but it is addressed to His slaves according to what they know, meaning that their business with you will be based on hope because His slaves do not have more than that.

الَّذِينَ اتَّخَذُوا مَسْجِدًا ضِرَارًا وَكُفْرًا وَتَفْرِيقًا بَيْنَ الْمُؤْمِنِينَ وَإِرْصَادًا لِّمَنْ
حَارَبَ اللَّهَ وَرَسُولَهُ مِن قَبْلُ وَلَيَحْلِفُنَّ إِنْ أَرَدْنَا إِلَّا الْحُسْنَىٰ
وَاللَّهُ يَشْهَدُ إِنَّهُمْ لَكَاذِبُونَ ﴿١٠٧﴾

107 As for those who have set up a mosque, causing harm and out of unbelief, to create division between the believers, and in readiness for those who previously made war on Allah and His Messenger, they will swear, 'We only desired the best.' But Allah bears witness that they are truly liars.

As for those who have set up a mosque,

'As for those who have set up a mosque' is conjoined, meaning that some of them have set up a mosque, and one sentence is conjoined to another. It can be in the nominative as the inceptive while its predicate is elided as if it is 'they will be punished' or the like. Some recite it without *wāw* before '*those*': it is the reading of the Madinans, and they consider it to be in the nominative by the inceptive and the predicate is '*Do not ever stand in it.*' It implies: 'Do not ever stand in the mosque those people have set up.' Al-Kisā'ī said that. An-Naḥḥās said that the predicate of the inceptive is '*The buildings they have built will not cease to be a bone of contention in their hearts.*' (9:110) It is said that the predicate is 'they will be punished', as was already said.

The *āyah* was revealed regarding what was related about Abū 'Āmir ar-Rāhib because he went to Caesar and became a Christian and Caesar promised that he would come to them. Therefore they built the Mosque of Harm to wait for him to come to it. Ibn 'Abbās, Mujāhid, Qatādah and others stated that. The story was already given in *al-A'rāf* (7:175).

Commentators say that the Banū 'Amr ibn 'Awf set up a mosque at Qubā' and sent to the Prophet ﷺ asking him to come to them and pray in it. The Banū Ghanam ibn 'Awf envied their brothers and said, 'We will also build a mosque,' and they sent for the Prophet ﷺ asking him to come to them and pray for them as he had for the mosque of their brothers. Abū 'Āmir prayed in it when he went to Syria. They went to the Prophet ﷺ while he was preparing to go to Tabūk. They said, 'Messenger of Allah, we built a mosque for those in need and ill and for rainy nights. We would like you to pray in it and pray for blessing.' The Prophet ﷺ said, 'I am travelling and busy. When we come back, we will go and pray for you in it.'

When the Prophet ﷺ came from Tabūk, they went to him. They had finished it, and they prayed Friday, Saturday and Sunday in it. He called for his shirt so that he could put it on and go to them and then the Qur'an was revealed with the report about the Mosque of Harm. The Prophet ﷺ summoned Mālik ibn ad-Dukhshum, Ma'n ibn 'Adī, 'Āmir ibn as-Sakan and Waḥshī, the killer of Ḥamzah, and said, 'Go to this mosque whose people are wrongdoers and destroy and burn it.' They set out straight away. Mālik brought a brand of fire from his house. They pulled it down, burned it and destroyed it.

There were twelve men who built the mosque: Khidhām ibn Khālid of the Banū 'Ubayd ibn Zayd, one of the Banū 'Amr ibn 'Awf – and the Mosque of Harm was built out from his house – Mu'attib ibn Qushayr, Abū Ḥabīb ibn al-Az'ar, 'Abbād ibn Ḥunayf, the brother of Sahl ibn Ḥunayf of the Banū 'Amr ibn 'Awf, Jāriyah ibn 'Āmir and his sons, Mujammi' and Zayd, Nabtal ibn al-Ḥārith, Baḥzaj, Bijād ibn 'Uthmān, and Wadī'ah ibn Thabit. Tha'labah ibn Ḥāṭib is mentioned among them. Abū 'Umar ibn 'Abd al-Barr said that that is debatable because he had been present at Badr.

'Ikrimah said, "Umar ibn al-Khaṭṭāb asked a man among them about the assistance he gave to this mosque. He said, "I helped with a pillar in it." He said, "Good news to you! A pillar of the fire of Hell on your neck!""

causing harm and out of unbelief, to creation division between the believers,

Ḍirār is a verbal noun that is the causative object, and *'out of unbelief, to create division between the believer, and in readiness'* is all added. The people of interpretation said that it is harm through the mosque and not that the mosque itself was harm. The harm belonged to its people. Ad-Dāraquṭnī related from Abū Sa'īd al-Khudrī that the Prophet ﷺ said, 'No harm or causing harm. If someone does harm, Allah will harm him. If someone causes hardship, Allah will cause hardship to him.' Some scholars said that '*ḍarar*' (harm) is something that contains benefit for you and harm for your neighbour. *Ḍirār* is that which has no benefit for you and harm for your neighbour. It is said that they mean the same and both are used by way of emphasis.

Our scholars have said that it is not permitted to build a mosque next to another mosque and it is mandatory to destroy the new mosque. It is forbidden to build it to prevent the people of the first mosque from being diverted so that the first becomes vacant, unless the district is large and one mosque is not enough for all of them. In this case, another mosque may be built. It is not correct to build two or three Jumu'ah mosques in one city. If that is done it is mandatory to forbid the second one and if someone prays Jumu'ah in it, the prayer is not accepted. The Prophet ﷺ burned the Mosque of Harm and destroyed it.

Aṭ-Ṭabarī has an *isnād* that Shaqīq came to pray in the mosque of the Banū Ghāḍirah and found that he had missed the prayer. He was told, 'The mosque of the Banū so-and-so have not prayed yet.' He said, 'I do not want to pray in it since it was built on harm.' Our scholars said that every mosque which is built on harm or for showing off and reputation has the same ruling as the Mosque of Harm, and it is not permitted to pray in it. An-Naqqāsh said, 'This makes it forbidden to pray in a church or the like because it was built on evil.' This does not necessarily follow because the church was not built to harm someone, even if the basis of its building was evil. Christians set up churches and the Jews synagogues as places for worship according to their claims as we set up mosques and so they are different. There is, in fact, a consensus among scholars that if someone does the prayer in a church or synagogue in a pure place, his prayer is sound and allowed. Al-Bukhārī mentioned that Ibn 'Abbās used to pray in a synagogue when there were no images in it. Abū Dāwūd mentioned from 'Uthmān ibn Abī al-'Aṣ that the Prophet ﷺ commanded him to establish the mosque of Ṭā'if in a place where their idols had been located.

Scholars have said that if someone acts as *imām* for a tyrant, you should not pray behind him unless his excuse is clear or he repents. The Banū 'Amr ibn 'Awf who built the Qubā' mosque asked 'Umar ibn al-Khaṭṭāb when he was caliph to ask for permission for Mujammi' ibn Jāriyah to lead them in the prayer in their mosque. He said, 'No, there is certainly no blessing in that! Was he not the *imām* of the Mosque of Harm!' Mujammi' said, 'Do not be too quick in judging me! By Allah, I did pray in it but I did not know what they were doing there. If I had known, I would not have led them in the prayer in it. I was a lad who recited the Qur'an and they were old men who lived according to their Jāhiliyyah ways. They did not recite any of the Qur'an. I prayed and did not think that what I did was a sin. I did not know what was inside them.' So 'Umar excused him, believed him, and put him in charge of the prayers in Qubā'.

Our scholars have said that if that mosque, which was set up for worship and whose building the *Sharī'ah* encourages – for the Prophet ﷺ said, 'If someone builds a mosque for Allah, even like the nest of a sand-grouse, Allah will build a house for him in the Garden,' – was destroyed and removed because it contained harm for others, what do you think of other [mosques which cause harm]? It is more fitting that they be removed and destroyed so that harm does not come to an older mosque. That is also true when someone builds a baking oven or mill, or digs a well or something else which brings harm to others.

The ruling regarding this is that it is forbidden for someone to bring harm to another person. If he brings harm to his brother by something he does in respect of his own property which harms his neighbour or someone other than his neighbour, that action is examined. If not doing it causes more harm than the harm resulting from doing it, the more harmful of the two harms is prevented. An example of that is when a man puts a window in his house which overlooks his brother's house where his wife and children live. When they are in their houses and attending to their needs, women normally remove some of their garments and it is known that violating their privacy is forbidden and its prohibition has been reported. Since it is forbidden to look at private areas, scholars think that the one who made the door or window should be made to block up what he had opened for the sake of benefit and relaxation. Closing it may contain some harm for him, but they aim to stop the worse of the two harms since one of them must be stopped. That is the ruling in this case.

The people of ash-Shāfi'ī say that if a man digs a well on his property and then another man digs a well on his property in such a way as to steal water from the first well, it is allowed because each of them dug in his own property and that is not forbidden. Similar in their view is when he digs a lavatory beside that of his neighbour which will ruin it for him, he is not forbidden because he is disposing of his own property. The Qur'an and Sunnah refute this position. Success is by Allah.

There are other similar forms of harm which scholars forbid, like the smoke from an oven and bath-house, the dust of threshing, and maggots generated by rubbish spread out in squares and similar things: the harm caused must be stopped when it is feared that it will continue. As for something short-lived, like shaking clothing and mats at the door, it is something people are not concerned with and nothing need be done about it. The harm entailed by forbidding such things is greater and more deleterious than putting up with it for a short time. Part of the proper manners of the Sunnah is that someone should endure his neighbour's annoyance as much as he can, just as that neighbour should not annoy him and should be good to him.

Connected to this matter is what Ismā'īl ibn Abī Uways mentioned from Mālik. He was asked about a woman who was affected by the jinn and when her husband came to her, was near her or beside her, that was terrible for her. Mālik said, 'I do not think that he should go near her and I think that the ruler should separate them.'

The word '*unbelief*' is used here because they disbelieved by believing that the Qubā' mosque or the mosque of the Prophet ﷺ was not deserving of respect. Ibn al-'Arabī said that. It is also said that it is *'unbelief'* in the Prophet ﷺ and what he brought. Al-Qushayrī and others said that. The phrase *'create division between the believers'* means to break up their consensus causing some people not to go out with the Prophet ﷺ. This shows that the greatest aim and most apparent goal in establishing the community is to bring the hearts together and to unite people in obedience and consolidate the contract of mutual protection and respect for religion so that people will mingle together and their hearts be purified of any rancour.

Mālik understood from this *āyah* that two communal prayers may not be performed in the same mosque under two different *imāms*. This differs from some other scholars. It is related from ash-Shāfi'ī that it is forbidden since it breaks up unity and undermines it and is a means of allowing someone who wants to be on his own and separate from the group to find an excuse to do that. So he then has his group stand separately for the prayer and puts his own *imām* forward. This creates disharmony and the social order is broken while that is concealed from them. Ibn al-'Arabī said, 'This was his concern with them. He has a firmer position in wisdom than they and has better knowledge of the sections of the *Sharī'ah*.'

and in readiness for those who previously made war on Allah and His Messenger

This refers to Abū 'Āmir ar-Rāhib. He was called the monk (*rāhib*) because he used to worship and pursue knowledge and he died in Qinnasrin as an unbeliever following the supplication of the Prophet ﷺ. He had said to the Prophet ﷺ, 'If I find any people who are fighting you, I will fight you with them.' He continued to fight until the Battle of Ḥunayn. When Hawāzin were defeated, he left to join the Greeks and became Christian. He sent word to the hypocrites: 'Prepare whatever strength and arms you can and build a mosque. I will go to Caesar and bring a Byzantine army to expel Muḥammad from Madīnah.' They built the Mosque of Harm. This Abū 'Āmir was a son of Ḥanẓalah who was washed by the angels.

Irṣād means waiting. The verb *arṣada* is to prepare for something in anticipation of it happening. Abū Zayd said that when it is used with a direct object, it is used for waiting for good, and when it is used with *li*, it is used for waiting for evil. Ibn al-A'rābī said that one does not say *'arṣadtu'* to mean 'I expected it'. *'Previously'* means before the Mosque of Harm was built. The words: '*They will swear, "We only desired the best*"' mean, 'We only wanted to do the best kind of action,' which is an act of kindness towards the Muslims, as they mentioned to those in need. This indicates that actions differ according to intention and desire. That is why Allah says this. *'Allah bears witness that they are truly liars.'* He knows their bad consciences and their lies in respect of what they are swearing to.

لَا تَقُمْ فِيهِ أَبَدًا ۚ لَّمَسْجِدٌ أُسِّسَ عَلَى ٱلتَّقْوَىٰ مِنْ أَوَّلِ يَوْمٍ أَحَقُّ أَن تَقُومَ
فِيهِ ۚ فِيهِ رِجَالٌ يُحِبُّونَ أَن يَتَطَهَّرُوا۟ ۚ وَٱللَّهُ يُحِبُّ ٱلْمُطَّهِّرِينَ ١٠٨

108 Do not ever stand in it. A mosque founded on *taqwā* from the first day has a greater right for you to stand in it. In it there are men who love to purify themselves. Allah loves those who purify themselves.

Do not ever stand in it.

This means the Mosque of Harm, i.e. 'Do not stand to pray in it.' 'Standing' designates the prayer. Indicating that is the sound *ḥadīth*: 'Whoever stands [in prayer] in Ramaḍān in faith and in expectation of a reward will have his prior wrong actions forgiven.' Al-Bukhārī transmitted it from Abū Hurayrah from the Prophet ﷺ. It is related that after this *āyah* was revealed, the Messenger of Allah ﷺ never went on the road where the mosque had been and ordered that it should be used as a rubbish heap on which corpses, filth and rubbish should be thrown.

'Ever' is an adverb of time. There are two types of adverbs of time: one which is determinate, like 'day', and one which is indeterminate like *ḥīn* and *waqt*. *Abad* is part of this sort, as is *dahr*. A question concerning fundamentals arises here. It is that even though *abadan* is an indeterminate adverb which is not universal, when it is connected to the negative *lā*, it becomes universal. If Allah had said, 'Do not stand,' the general restriction is enough. When He adds *abadan*, it is as if He means at any time whatsoever. As for the indefinite in the affirmation, if it reports about an event, it is not universal and that is understood by the people who know language and that is the judgment made by the *fuqahā'* of Islam. They said, 'If a man says to his wife, "You are divorced *abadan*," it is a single divorce.'

A mosque founded on *taqwā* from the first day

'A mosque founded on taqwā' means one whose foundations were laid and whose walls were built. *Uss* is the foundation of a building. The same is true of *asās* and the plural of *asās* is *usus*. *Asas* is a shortened version and its plural is *asās*. The verb *assasa* is to lay the foundation for a building. People say, 'in ancient times' as *'alā uss ad-dahr*, *ass ad-dahr* or *iss ad-dahr*, which are three dialectical usages i.e. on the base of time.

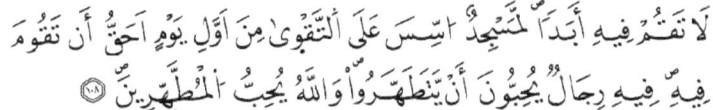

The *lām* connected to 'mosque' is the *lām* of the oath. It is also said that it is the *lām* of the inceptive as you say, 'Zayd (*la-Zayd*) is the best of people in action.' It imposes emphasis. *'Founded on taqwā'* is an adjective describing '*mosque*'. *'Has a greater right'* is the predicate of the inceptive which is '*mosque*'. Here *taqwā* means the qualities by which punishment is averted. It is the form *fa'lā* from the verb *waqā*.

Scholars disagree about the mosque which was founded on *taqwā*. One group said that it is the mosque of Qubā', and that is related from Ibn 'Abbās, aḍ-Ḍaḥḥāk and al-Ḥasan. They connected it to the words '*from the first day*,' and the mosque of Qubā' was founded in Madīnah on the first day. It was built before the Mosque of the Prophet ﷺ. Ibn 'Umar, Ibn al-Musayyab and Mālik said that in what Ibn Wahb, Ashhab and Ibn al-Qāsim related from them.

At-Tirmidhī related from Abū Sa'īd al-Khudrī, 'Two men argued about the mosque which was '*founded on taqwā from the first day*' and one man said, "It is the mosque of Qubā'." The other said, "It is the mosque of the Prophet ﷺ." The Messenger of Allah ﷺ said, "It is this mosque of mine!"' It is a sound *ḥadīth*.

The first view is appropriate to the story since He says '*in it*' and the pronoun of the adverb connects with '*men who love to purify themselves*' and that relates to the Qubā' Mosque. Evidence for that is found in the *ḥadīth* of Abū Hurayrah who said, 'This *āyah* was revealed about the people of Qubā': "*In it there are men who love to purify themselves.*"' He added, 'They used to do *istinjā'* with water and Allah revealed this *āyah* about them.' Ash-Sha'bī said, 'They are the people of the Qubā' Mosque. This was revealed about them.' Qatādah said, 'When this *āyah* was revealed, the Messenger of Allah ﷺ said to the people of Qubā': "Allah has praised you for your purification of yourselves. What is it that do you do?" They answered, "We wash away any traces of faeces and urine with water."' Abū Dāwūd related it. Ad-Dāraquṭnī related that Ṭalḥah ibn Nāfi' said that Abū Ayyūb, Jābir ibn 'Abdullāh, and Anas ibn Mālik al-Anṣārī said about this *āyah* that he ﷺ said, 'Company of *Anṣār*! Allah has praised you for your purity. What is this purity of yours?' They answered, 'Messenger of Allah, we do *wuḍū'* for the prayer and do *ghusl* on account of *janābah*.' The Messenger of Allah ﷺ asked, 'Is there anything else?' They replied, 'Only that when one of us leaves the lavatory, he cleans himself with water.' He said, 'It is that. You should do that.'

This *ḥadīth* means that the mosque mentioned in the *āyah* is the Mosque of Qubā' while the *ḥadīth* of Abū Sa'īd al-Khudrī is a text from the Prophet ﷺ indicating that it is his mosque without debate. Abū Kurayb related that 'Abdullāh ibn Buraydah said about the words of the Almighty: *'In houses which Allah has permitted to be built and in which His Name is remembered'* (24:36): 'They are four mosques which were all built by Prophets: the Ka'bah which was built by Ibrāhīm and Ismā'īl, the house of Jericho, Jerusalem, built by Dāwūd and Sulaymān, the mosques of Madīnah and Qubā' which were founded on *taqwā*, built by the Messenger of Allah ﷺ.'

In the phrase '*from the first day*' grammarians say that '*min*' means 'since'. *Mundhu* in time is in the position of *min* in place. It is said that here it means 'since'. It implies: 'since the first day it started to be built.' It is added to the verbal noun of the verb which is '*founded*'. It is as is said:

Whose are the abodes at the summit of al-Ḥijr,
desolate for (*min*) years and ages?

This calls attention to the fact that one of the principles of grammarians is that *min* does not make the noun genitive where times are concerned: *mundhu* does that with times. You say, 'I have not seen him for (*mundhu*) a month or a day.' You do not use *min*. When it occurs in language and is followed by a time, then it implies something elided to make it genitive with *min*. I think that it is good to spare the need of implication in this *āyah*: '*min*' takes the genitive from the word '*first*' because it means the beginning, as you say, 'From the beginning of days.'

has a greater right for you to stand in it.

The verb '*taqūma*' has a *fatḥah*, and '*aḥaqq*' is the comparative from *ḥaqq*. The comparative only comes between two shared things when one of them has a prerogative over the other in the aspect in which they share. Even if the Mosque of Harm was false with no right in it, they share in the right in respect of their builders' belief or in respect of the opinion of everyone who thinks that standing in it was permitted since it is a mosque, but one of the two beliefs was false inwardly in the sight of Allah and the other is true inwardly and outwardly. Similar to this are the words of the Almighty: '*The Companions of the Garden on that Day will have better lodging and a better resting-place.*' (25:24) It is known that the quality of the lodging being '*better*' in comparison with the Fire is huge. But it is according to the belief of each group that it is better and that what it will go to is better since each group rejoices in what it has. A different sort of comparison is seen in, 'Honey is sweeter than vinegar.' Even if honey is sweet, every agreeable thing is also sweet. Do you not see that some people put vinegar ahead of honey on a one-to-one basis and any ascription to something else is relative?

'*In it*' may refer to the mosque of the Prophet ﷺ or to the mosque of Qubā'. The *hā'* in '*in it*' would be the same in both cases. If someone says that it is the Qubā' Mosque, the pronoun in '*in it*' refers to it according to the previous disagreement.

In this *āyah* Allah praises those who love purity and cleanliness. It is human decency and a legal duty. At-Tirmidhī reports from 'Ā'ishah: 'Command your wives to clean themselves with water. I am too shy to say that to them.' He said that it is a sound *ḥadīth*. It is confirmed that the Prophet ﷺ used to carry water with him for cleansing himself in the lavatory. He used stones to start with and then water to purify. Ibn al-'Arabī said, 'The scholars of Qayrawān used to put stones on the ground in their lavatories in order to clean themselves with them and then they would perform *istinjā'* with water.'

It is mandatory to lessen impurity which emerges and purification from impurity is necessary for the rest of the body and clothing. That is an allowance from Allah for His slaves both when there is water and in its absence. That is what most scholars say while Ibn Ḥabīb has an aberrant view that *istijmār* with stones may only done in the absence of water. Firm reports about *istijmār* with stones when there is water refutes him. Although there is agreement that the blood of fleas may be overlooked as long as it is not excessive, scholars disagree about the removal of impurity from bodies and clothing, taking three views:

The first is that it is a mandatory obligation and the prayer of someone who is wearing an impure garment is not valid, whether he knows that or forgets about it. That is related from Ibn 'Abbās, al-Ḥasan, and Ibn Sīrīn. It is the position of ash-Shāfi'ī, Aḥmad and Abū Thawr. Ibn Wahb related it from Mālik. It is also the position of Abū al-Faraj al-Mālikī and aṭ-Ṭabarī. However aṭ-Ṭabarī said, 'If the impurity covers the size of a dirham or more, he should repeat the prayer.' That is the position of Abū Ḥanīfah and Abū Yūsuf seeing the size of a dirham as analogous to that of the anus.

One group said that removing impurity from clothes and the body is made mandatory by the Sunnah. It is mandatory (*wājib*) by the *Sunnah* and not obligatory (*farḍ*). They said that if someone prays in an impure garment, he should repeat the prayer inside the time. If the time has passed, he owes nothing. This is the position of Mālik and his people except for Abū al-Faraj, and it is transmitted from him by Ibn Wahb. Malik said in the case of flowing blood that he does not have to repeat the prayer in the time or after it, but someone with even a small amount of urine or faeces must repeat it. The position of al-Layth is similar to all of this in the school of Mālik. Ibn al-Qāsim said that it is obliged to remove it if someone remembers it but not if they forget about it. It is one of his individual points.

The first view is sounder, Allah willing, because the Prophet ﷺ passed by two graves and said, 'They are being punished, and they are not being punished for anything great. One of them used to carry tales and the other did not protect himself from urine.' Al-Bukhārī and Muslim transmitted it. It is enough for you. That will be mentioned in *al-Isrā'* (17:44). They have said, 'A human being is only punished for omitting something mandatory.' This is clear. Abū Bakr ibn Abī Shaybah related from Abū Hurayrah that the Prophet ﷺ said, 'Most of the punishment in the grave is due to urine.'

Others use as evidence the fact that the Prophet ﷺ removed his sandals in the prayer when Jibrīl informed him that there was impurity on them. Abū Dāwūd and others transmitted it from Abū Sa'īd al-Khudrī. It will come in *Ṭaha*, Allah willing. They said, 'Since he did not repeat what he had prayed, that indicates that removing it is *sunnah* and his prayer is sound. He can repeat it within the time seeking perfection.' Allah knows best.

Qāḍī Abū Bakr ibn al-'Arabī said, 'As for the difference between a little and a lot going by the size of a Baghlī dirham – meaning the large dirhams which have the same circumference as a dinar – that is a false analogy in two ways. One is that sizes are not established by analogy, so this is not accepted. The second is that this is lightened for him by reason of need and need is not a basis for analogy.'

أَفَمَنُ اُسِّسَ بُنْيَٰنُهُۥ عَلَىٰ تَقْوَىٰ مِنَ اَ۬للَّهِ وَرِضْوَٰنٍ خَيْرٌ اَم مَّنُ اُسِّسَ
بُنْيَٰنُهُۥ عَلَىٰ شَفَا جُرُفٍ هَارٍ فَانْهَارَ بِهِۦ فِے نَارِ جَهَنَّمَ وَاللَّهُ
لَا يَهْدِے اِ۬لْقَوْمَ اَ۬لظَّٰلِمِينَ ۝١٠٩

109 Who is better: someone who founds his building on *taqwā* of Allah and His good pleasure, or someone who founds his building on the brink of a crumbling precipice so that it collapses with him into the Fire of Hell? Allah does not love wrongdoers.

someone who founds his building

The words: '*someone who founds his building*' refer to what he bases it on. This is a question which implies affirmation. '*Man*' means 'who' and it is in the nominative by the inceptive and its predicate is '*khayr*'. Nāfi', Ibn 'Āmir and a group recite '*ussasa bunyānuhu*' on the basis that '*founds*' is passive and '*building*' is in the nominative in both places. Ibn Kathīr, Abū 'Amr, Ḥamzah, al-Kisā'ī and a group recite '*assasa bunyānahu*' with the verb being active and '*building*' is accusative with them. It is preferred by Abū 'Ubayd since many recite it and because the subject is named in it. Naṣr ibn ʿĀṣim ibn ʿAlī recited *'ususu'* with a final *ḍammah* and *'bunyānihi'* in the genitive. He also has *'asāsu'* and *'ussu'*, both taking the genitive after them. What is meant are the foundations of the building. Abū Ḥātim related a sixth reading, which is *'asāsu bunyanihi'*. An-Naḥḥās said that it is the plural of *uss*, like *khuff* and *akhfāf*. Many have *isās* like the form of *khifāf*. A poet said:

The kingdom is firmly founded (*āsās*)
among the masters of the Banū 'l-'Abbās.

on *taqwā* of Allah

According to Sībawayh, ʿĪsā ibn ʿUmar recited it with *tanwīn* and the *alif* is the *alif* of affixion. [POEM] Sībawayh objected to the *tanwīn* and said that it has no basis.

or someone who founds his building on the brink of a crumbling precipice

Shafā (brink) is the edge and limit of something. It was mentioned in *Āl 'Imrān* (3:103). It is recited as *'juruf'* while Abu Bakr and Ḥamzah recite it as *jurf*. A precipice (*juruf*) is the edge formed by floods in wadis. They are the sides which are gouged out by water. It derives from *jarf* and *ijtirāf* and it is wresting a thing from its root. *Hāri* means falling. *Tahawwara* is used for the collapse of a building. Its root is *hā'ir*. There is reversal in it and one can say *hāri* or *hā'ir*. Az-Zajjāj said that. It is like *lātha*, to turn round a thing, and so it becomes *lāthi*, i.e. *lā'ith* (tangled) and as one says *shākī* and *shā'ik* for bristling with weapons. Al-'Ajjāj said:

Palm-trees and lote trees surrounded (*lāthin*) him.

Abū Ḥātim claimed that its root is *hāwir* and then one says *hā'ir*, like *ṣā'im* (fasting), and then there is a reversal of letters, and it becomes *hāri*. Al-Kisā'ī said that it is both from the root *wāw* and the root *yā'* and one can say *tahawwur* and *tahayyur*. I say that this is why it has *imālah* and takes a *fatḥah*.

so that it collapses with him into the Fire of Hell?

'The brink collapses,' so it is as if the brink falls with the building into the Fire because 'brink' is masculine. It is also possible that the pronoun (*bihi*) refers to *'man'*, the builder. It implies: the one who founds his building on other than *taqwā* collapses. This *āyah* is a sort of metaphor for them, meaning who is good, the one who bases his building on Islam or the one who bases his building on *shirk* and hypocrisy? It is clear that the building of an unbeliever is like a building on the edge of Hell which is on the point of falling into it with its people. *Shafā* is the edge from the verb *ashfā* which means 'to be close'.

This *āyah* contains evidence that those things whose formation begins with *taqwā* of Allah Almighty and desire for His Noble Face are those which abide, and those by which a person will be truly fortunate, and rise and ascend to Allah, as evinced by His words: *'But the face of your Lord will remain, Master of Majesty and Generosity'* (55:27) according to one of two meanings. Allah speaks of it when He says: *'right actions which are lasting'* (18:46) and that will be explained in its place, Allah willing.

Scholars disagree about whether the phrase *'It collapses with him into the Fire of Hell'* is what actually happens or is metaphorical. The first view is that it is actual and when the Prophet ﷺ sent to have it destroyed, smoke was seen issuing from it. That is according to Sa'īd ibn Jubayr. One of them said that a man put a palm branch in it and it came out black and burned. Commentators say they excavated the place where it collapsed and smoke came out. 'Āṣim ibn Abī an-Nujūd related from Zirr ibn Ḥubaysh that Ibn Mas'ūd said, 'Hell is inside the earth,' and he recited: *'so that it collapses with him into the Fire of Hell.'* Jābir ibn 'Abdullāh said, 'I saw smoke issuing from it in the time of the Messenger of Allah ﷺ.' The second view is that it is metaphorical and that the builder will go to Hell, and so it is as if it collapses with him into it. This is like Allah's words: *'His mother is Hāwiyah.'* (101:9) What is apparent is the first view since there is no transfer in that. Allah knows best.

لَا يَزَالُ بُنْيَٰنُهُمُ ٱلَّذِى بَنَوْا۟ رِيبَةً فِى قُلُوبِهِمْ إِلَّآ أَن تُقَطَّعَ قُلُوبُهُمْ
وَٱللَّهُ عَلِيمٌ حَكِيمٌ ﴿١١٠﴾

110 The buildings they have built will not cease to be a bone of contention in their hearts, until their hearts are cut to shreds. Allah is All-Knowing, All-Wise.

The buildings they have built will not cease to be a bone of contention in their hearts,

This refers to the Mosque of Harm. The phrase: *'a bone of contention in their hearts'* is doubt in their hearts, as Ibn 'Abbās, Qatādah and aḍ-Ḍaḥḥāk said. An-Nābighah said:

I swore, and left you with no doubt,
and a man has nowhere to go to except Allah.

Al-Kalbī said that it signifies regret and remorse because they regretted building it. As-Suddī, Ḥabīb and al-Mubarrad said that it means hatred and rancour.

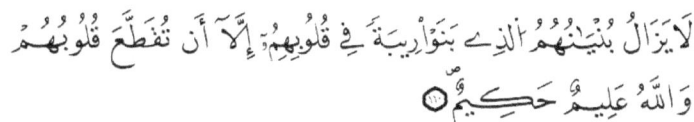

until their hearts are cut to shreds.

This means that their hearts burst and they die according to Ibn 'Abbās. It is like Allah's words: *'We would have cut off their life-blood'* (69:46), because life ends when it is cut off. Qatādah, aḍ-Ḍaḥḥāk and Mujāhid said that. Sufyān said, 'until they repent.' 'Ikrimah said, 'until their hearts are cut to shreds in their graves.' The companions of Ibn Mas'ūd used to recite it as: *'walaw taqaṭṭa'a'*. Al-Ḥasan, Ya'qūb and Abū Ḥātim recited: *'ilā an taqaṭṭa'a'* until the end, in other words they will continue to be in doubt about it until they die and then they will have certainty and clarity.

Reciters disagree about *taqaṭṭa'a*. Most have *tuqaṭṭa'a* in the passive. Ibn 'Āmir, Ḥafṣ and Ya'qūb have a *fatḥah* on the *tā'*. It is also related from Ya'qūb and Abū 'Abd ar-Raḥmān as *tuqṭa'* in the passive. It is related from Shibl and Ibn Kathīr as *'taqṭa''* with *qulūbahum* in the accusative, implying 'you do that to them'. We already mentioned the readings of Ibn Mas'ūd's people. The words *'Allah is All-Knowing, All-Wise'* were explained earlier (2:32).

إِنَّ ٱللَّهَ ٱشْتَرَىٰ مِنَ ٱلْمُؤْمِنِينَ أَنفُسَهُمْ وَأَمْوَٰلَهُم بِأَنَّ
لَهُمُ ٱلْجَنَّةَ يُقَٰتِلُونَ فِى سَبِيلِ ٱللَّهِ فَيَقْتُلُونَ وَيُقْتَلُونَ وَعْدًا
عَلَيْهِ حَقًّا فِى ٱلتَّوْرَىٰةِ وَٱلْإِنجِيلِ وَٱلْقُرْءَانِ وَمَنْ أَوْفَىٰ بِعَهْدِهِۦ
مِنَ ٱللَّهِ فَٱسْتَبْشِرُوا۟ بِبَيْعِكُمُ ٱلَّذِى بَايَعْتُم بِهِۦ وَذَٰلِكَ هُوَ ٱلْفَوْزُ
ٱلْعَظِيمُ ١١١

111 Allah has bought from the believers their selves and their wealth in return for the Garden. They fight in the Way of Allah and they kill and are killed. It is a promise binding on Him in the Torah, the Gospel and the Qur'an, and who is truer to his contract than Allah? Rejoice then in the bargain you have made. That is the great victory.

Allah has bought from the believers their selves

It is said that is a metaphor, like Allah's words: *'Those are the people who have sold guidance for misguidance.'* (2:16) The *āyah* was revealed about the second oath of Allegiance, which was the Greater 'Aqabah. It is that in which the men of the *Anṣār* attending exceeded seventy in number. The youngest of them was 'Uqbah ibn 'Amr. It was when they met with the Messenger of Allah ﷺ at 'Aqabah. 'Abdullāh ibn Rawāḥah said to the Prophet ﷺ, 'Stipulate for your Lord and for yourself what you wish.' The Prophet ﷺ said, 'I stipulate for my Lord that you worship Him and do not associate anything with Him. I stipulate for myself that you defend me from the same as what you defend yourselves and your property from.' They asked, 'If we do that, what do we have in return?' He answered, 'The Garden.' They said, 'A profitable sale! We will not cancel nor ask for it to be annulled!' Then Allah revealed this. After that it was general to everyone from the community of Muḥammad ﷺ who strives in the Cause of Allah until the Day of Rising.

This *āyah* is evidence for the permission of a master to carry out a transaction with his slave. Even though all belongs to the master, when he gives him control, he deals with him in what he appointed him over. What is permitted between a master and his slave is not permitted between him and someone else because the property belongs to him and he can remove it.

The basis of buying and selling between people is that they receive something more beneficial for them in exchange for what leaves their possession than it, or what is the same in benefit. Allah has bought from the slaves the destruction of themselves and their property in obedience to Him and He gives them the Garden in exchange when they do that. It is a tremendously profitable exchange to which nothing else is comparable. That is conveyed by means of a metaphor of buying and selling which is easily understood by them. The slave surrenders his person and property and Allah grants the reward. So this is called a purchase.

Al-Ḥasan related that the Messenger of Allah ﷺ said, 'Above every kind of goodness (*birr*) is another kind up until the slave gives up his lifeblood. If he does that, there is no act of goodness beyond that.' A poet said about this:

Being generous with water is generosity which contains nobility.
    But generosity with one's life is the utmost generosity.

Al-Aṣma'ī composed for Ja'far aṣ-Ṣādiq:

I discuss the price for the precious life with its Lord
    when nothing can be compared with it in all creation.
The Garden is purchased by it. If I were to sell it
    for something else, that would be fraud.
If my life is loss for some of this world which I obtain,
    then my life is gone and so is the price.

Al-Ḥasan said, 'A Bedouin passed by the Prophet ﷺ while he was reciting: *"Allah has bought from the believers their selves."* He asked, "Whose words are these?" He answered,

"The words of Allah." He said, "A sale, by Allah, which is profitable which we will not cancel or ask to be cancelled." He went out to fight and was martyred.'

Scholars say that in the same way that Allah buys from adult believers who possess responsibility, He also buys from children through giving them pain and illness since there is benefit in that and it contains a lesson for the adults. They do not have anything with greater benefit and less loss for them than the pain of children and the reward which parents gain for the worry they experience through it and the increase in support it engenders in them. Then He gives their children something in exchange when they suffer it. It is the same when you hire someone to build and move earth: doing that will cause him pain and some harm, but he will have a benefit from his work and the wage he receives for it.

They fight in the Way of Allah

This explains what they are fighting for and against.

and they kill and are killed.

An-Nakhaʿī, al-Aʿmash, Ḥamzah, al-Kisāʾī and Khalaf recite it with the passive first ('are killed and kill'). An example of that is in the words of ʿImru al-Qays:

If you kill us, we will fight you.

It means: 'If you kill some of us, some of us will fight you.' The rest put the active form first.

It is a promise binding on Him in the Torah, the Gospel and the Qur'an

This is a report from Allah that this was in those Books and that the basis of *jihād* and confronting the enemy comes from the time of Mūsā. *Waʿd* and *ḥaqq* are two verbal nouns used for emphasis.

who is truer to his contract than Allah?

No one is truer to his contract than Allah. He guarantees that His promise and threat will be carried out. This is not for all: His promise is for all but His threat is specific to some wrongdoers and some wrong actions and in some situations. This has already been adequately discussed (4:93).

Rejoice then in the bargain you have made.

This means be happy about it. The verb of *bashārah* means to display happiness in the skin. It was already mentioned (2:25). Al-Ḥasan said, 'By Allah, there is no believer on the earth who is not included in this sale.' '*That is the great victory,*' which is gaining the Garden and being in it forever.

ٱلتَّٰٓئِبُونَ ٱلۡعَٰبِدُونَ ٱلۡحَٰمِدُونَ ٱلسَّٰٓئِحُونَ ٱلرَّٰكِعُونَ ٱلسَّٰجِدُونَ
ٱلۡأٓمِرُونَ بِٱلۡمَعۡرُوفِ وَٱلنَّاهُونَ عَنِ ٱلۡمُنكَرِ وَٱلۡحَٰفِظُونَ
لِحُدُودِ ٱللَّهِۗ وَبَشِّرِ ٱلۡمُؤۡمِنِينَ ١١٢

112 Those who repent, those who worship, those who praise, those who fast, those who bow, those who prostrate, those who command what is right, those who forbid the wrong, those who preserve the limits of Allah: give good news to the believers.

Those who repent

They are those who return from the blameworthy state of disobedience to Allah to the praiseworthy state of obedience to Allah. The one who repents (*tā'ib*) is the one who returns. The one who returns to obedience is better than the one who merely returns from disobedience because he combines the two.

those who worship, those who praise,

'Those who worship' are the obedient who aim to obey Allah. 'Those who praise' are those who are pleased with His Decree and spend His blessing to them in obeying Him. They are those who praise Allah in every state.

those who fast,

Sā'iḥūn are those who fast, as Ibn Mas'ūd, Ibn 'Abbās and others said. Corroborating that are Allah's words: '*women who worship, women who fast much (sā'iḥāt).*' (66:5) Sufyān ibn 'Uyaynah said that someone who fasts is called *sā'iḥ* because he leaves the pleasures of food, drink and sex. Abū Ṭālib said:

The fasters (*sā'iḥūn*) who do not taste a drop for their Lord,
and the women who remember and act.

Another said:

You see him pray at night, and in the day
he continues to fast (*sā'iḥ*) and remember Allah often.

It is related that 'Ā'ishah said, 'The *siyāḥah* of this community is fasting.' Aṭ-Ṭabarī gave its *isnād*. Abū Hurayrah related it *marfū'* that the Prophet ﷺ said, 'The *siyāḥah* of my community is fasting.' Az-Zajjāj said, 'The position of al-Ḥasan is that they are those who fast the obligatory fast.' It has been said that they are the ones who fast constantly.

'Aṭā' said that it means those who strive in *jihād*. Abū Umāmah related that a man asked permission of the Messenger of Allah ﷺ to do *siyāḥah*. He said, 'The *siyāḥah* of my community is *jihād* in the Cause of Allah.' Abū Muḥammad 'Abd al-Ḥaqq said that it is sound. 'Abd ar-Raḥmān ibn Zayd said that it means people who make *hijrah*. It is also said that it is those who travel to seek *ḥadīth* and knowledge, as 'Ikrimah said. It is said that they are those who travel inwardly with their thoughts in the *tawḥīd* of their Lord and His domains and what He created of lessons and Signs which indicate His *tawḥīd* and immensity. An-Naqqāsh related it.

It is related that one of those who worship took a goblet with which to perform *wuḍū'* for the night prayers and put his finger in the handle of the goblet and then sat reflecting until dawn. He was asked about that and said, 'I put my finger in the handle of the goblet and thought about the words of Allah: *"they have shackles and chains around their necks"* (40:71). I remembered how I might receive the shackle and spent the entire night thinking about that.'

The root *'s-y-ḥ'* indicates the soundness of these statements. The root of *siyāḥa* is moving on the surface of the earth like water. The faster continues to obey by leaving food and other things and so he is in the position of the *sā'iḥ*. The hearts of those who reflect move around what they reflect on. We find in a *ḥadīth*, 'Allah has angels who go around (*sayyāḥīna*) through the horizons conveying to me the prayers of my community.' The word is also read with a *ṣād*.

those who bow, those who prostrate,

This means in the obligatory prayers and other prayers.

those who command what is right, those who forbid the wrong,

'Those who command what is right' refers to the Sunnah or faith. *'Those who forbid the wrong'* refers to innovation or unbelief. It is said that it is general to everything which is right or wrong.

those who preserve the limits of Allah

These are those who undertake what Allah has commanded and refrain from what He has forbidden.

The people of interpretation disagree about this *āyah* and whether it is connected to what was before it or separate. One group say that the first *āyah* is independent: every unifier who fights in the Cause of Allah so that the Word of Allah will be uppermost falls under that contract, even if he is not described by these qualities mentioned in the second *āyah* or more. Another group say that these qualities come as a precondition and the two *āyahs* are connected. Therefore only the believers who have these qualities and spend themselves in the Way of Allah partake in this contract. Aḍ-Ḍaḥḥāk said that. Ibn 'Aṭiyyah said, 'This position is too narrow and constrictive. The *āyah,* according to what the statements of scholars and the *Sharī'ah* demand, describes the qualities of the perfect believers. Allah mentioned it so that the people of *tawḥīd* will race to them until they reach the highest level.'

Az-Zajjāj said, 'What I believe is that "*Those who repent, those who worship...*" is in the nominative by the inceptive and its predicate is elided, meaning that the people with this description will have the Garden, even if they do not do *jihād*, since none of them are obstinate and refuse to do *jihād.* This is because some Muslims fighting spare others the need to fight *jihād*.' Al-Qushayrī preferred this view and said, 'It is good since if the description of the believers had been in *"Allah has bought from the believers,"* the promise would have been specific to those who do *jihād* alone.'

We find in the copy of the Qur'an of 'Abdullah: *'at-tā'bīna al-'ābidīn...'* There are two points in this. One is that the description of the believers follows and the second is that it is in the accusative as praise. Scholars disagree about the *wāw* in *'and those who forbid the wrong.'* It is also said that it is included in the description of those who forbid, as we find in the first three *āyahs* of *Ghāfir* where some qualities are added with a *wāw* and some are not. This is allowed and customary in language and no wisdom or cause is looked for in its use.

It is said that it is included since the one who forbids the wrong accompanies the one who commands what is right and so neither of them should be mentioned alone, as in *'previously married women as well as virgins'* (66:5). It is included in *'those who preserve'* since it is close to the conjunction. It is said that it is redundant, but this is weak and without sense.

It is also said that it is the *wāw* of eight because seven with the Arabs is a perfect sound number. That is also what they say about Allah's words: *'previously married women as well as virgins'* (66:5) and His words about the gates of the Garden: *'finding its gates open'* (39:73) and His words: *'They will say, 'There were seven of them, their dog being the eighth.''* (18:22) Ibn Khālawayh mentioned it in his debates with Abū 'Alī al-Fārisī regarding the meaning of *'finding its gates open'* (39:73). Abū 'Alī objected to it.

Ibn 'Aṭiyyah said, 'My father related to me that the grammar master Abū 'Abdullāh al-Kafīf al-Māliqī, who lived in Granada and recited in it at the time of Ibn Ḥabūs, said, 'It is eloquent language used by some Arabs. Their habit is to say when they count: "one, two, three, four, five, six, seven, and eight, nine, ten." That is how it is in their language. So when "eight" is used, they add the *wāw*.' I say that it is the dialect of Quraysh. It will be explained in *Sūrat al-Kahf*, Allah willing, and in *az-Zumar*.

مَا كَانَ لِلنَّبِيِّ وَالَّذِينَ ءَامَنُوٓاْ أَن يَسْتَغْفِرُواْ لِلْمُشْرِكِينَ وَلَوْ كَانُوٓاْ
أُوْلِى قُرْبَىٰ مِنۢ بَعْدِ مَا تَبَيَّنَ لَهُمْ أَنَّهُمْ أَصْحَٰبُ ٱلْجَحِيمِ ﴿١١٣﴾

113 It is not right for the Prophet and those who believe to ask forgiveness for the idolaters – even if they are close relatives – after it has become clear to them that they are the Companions of the Blazing Fire.

Muslim related from Sa'īd ibn al-Musayyab that his father said, 'When Abū Ṭālib was dying, the Messenger of Allah ﷺ went to him and found Abū Jahl and 'Abdullāh ibn Abī Umayyah ibn al-Mughīrah with him. The Messenger of Allah ﷺ said, "Uncle! Say 'There is no god but Allah,' a statement by which I will testify for you in the presence of Allah." Abū Jahl and 'Abdullāh ibn Abī Umayyah said, "Abū Ṭālib! Will you turn from the religion of 'Abd al-Muṭṭalib?" The Messenger of Allah ﷺ continued to offer it to him and repeated what he said to him until the last words which Abū Ṭālib said were that he was following the religion of 'Abd al-Muṭṭalib. He refused to say, "There is no god but Allah." The Messenger of Allah ﷺ said, "By Allah, I will ask forgiveness for you as long as I am not forbidden to do so." Then Allah revealed this. Allah revealed about Abū Ṭālib and said to the Messenger of Allah ﷺ: *"You cannot guide those you would like to but Allah guides those He wills. He has the best knowledge of the guided."* (28:56)' The *āyah*, according to this, abrogates the Prophet ﷺ asking for forgiveness for his uncle. It is asking forgiveness for him after his death according to what is related from other than the *Ṣaḥīḥ*. Al-Ḥusayn ibn al-Faḍl said that this is unlikely because the *sūrah* was one of the last parts of the Qur'an to be revealed whereas Abū Ṭālib died while Islam was still young and the Prophet ﷺ was in Makkah.

This *āyah* entails cutting off friendship (*muwālāh*) with unbelievers, alive and dead. Allah did not task the believers with asking forgiveness for idolaters. Seeking forgiveness for an idolater is not permitted. If it is said that it is sound that the

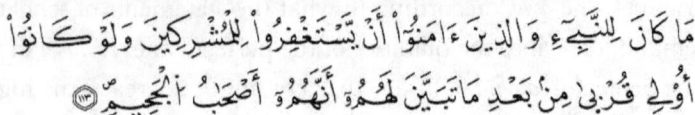

Prophet ﷺ said on the Day of the Battle of Uḥud, when his tooth was broken and face lacerated: 'O Allah, forgive my people. They do not know', so how can this be combined with Allah forbidding His Messenger and the believers to ask for forgiveness for the idolaters? The answer is that statement made by the Prophet ﷺ was repeating what the Prophets before him had said. The evidence for that is what Muslim related from 'Abdullāh: 'I can visualise the Prophet ﷺ reporting about one of the Prophets whose people struck him on the head and while he was wiping the blood from his face, he was saying, "Lord, forgive my people. They do not know."' We find in al-Bukhārī that the Prophet ﷺ mentioned a Prophet before him whose people cut his skull and he said, 'O Allah, forgive my people. They do not know.' He was clearly recounting what those before him had said, not saying it for the first time as some of them claim. Allah knows best. The Prophet who said that was Nūḥ as will come in *Sūrat Hūd*, Allah willing. (11:41-42)

It is said that what is meant by asking forgiveness in the *āyah* is the prayer (*ṣalāt*). One of them said, 'I do not fail to pray over any of the people of the *qiblah*, even an Abyssinian woman pregnant from adultery, because I heard from Allah that He only stopped the prayer from being done for idolaters when He said, *"It is not right for the Prophet and those who believe to ask forgiveness or the idolaters…"*' 'Aṭā' ibn Abī Rabāḥ said, 'The *āyah* is about the prohibition against praying over the idolaters and asking for forgiveness here means the prayer.'

A third response is that it is permitted to ask for forgiveness for the living because it is still hoped that they will believe and it is possible that eloquent words will make them amenable and encourage them to the *dīn*. Many scholars say that there is no harm in a man making supplication for his unbelieving parents and asking forgiveness for them as long as they are alive. When they die, then hope for them is cut off and you should not make supplication for them. Ibn 'Abbās said, 'They used to pray for forgiveness for their dead and then this was revealed and they stopped asking for forgiveness for them. They were not forbidden to pray for forgiveness for the living before they had died.'

The people of meanings say that in the Qur'an '*mā kāna*' is used in two ways. One is in a negative sense, as in Allah's words: *'You could never make their trees grow'* (27:60) and: *'No self can die except with Allah's permission.'* (3:145) The other is as a prohibition as in the words: *'It is not right for you to cause annoyance to the Messenger of Allah'* (33:53) and: *'It is not right for the Prophet and those who believe to ask forgiveness for the idolaters.'*

وَمَا كَانَ ٱسْتِغْفَارُ إِبْرَٰهِيمَ لِأَبِيهِ إِلَّا عَن مَّوْعِدَةٍ وَعَدَهَآ إِيَّاهُ
فَلَمَّا تَبَيَّنَ لَهُۥٓ أَنَّهُۥ عَدُوٌّ لِّلَّهِ تَبَرَّأَ مِنْهُ ۚ إِنَّ إِبْرَٰهِيمَ لَأَوَّٰهٌ حَلِيمٌ ﴿١١٤﴾

114 Ibrāhīm would not have asked forgiveness for his father but for a promise he made to him, and when it became clear to him that he was an enemy of Allah, he renounced him. Ibrāhīm was tender-hearted and forbearing.

An-Nasā'ī related that 'Alī ibn Abī Ṭālib said, 'I heard a man asking forgiveness for his parents who were idolaters. I said, "Do you ask forgiveness for them when they are idolaters?" He answered, "Did not Ibrāhīm ask forgiveness for his father?" I went to the Prophet ﷺ and mentioned that to him, and the revelation came: "*Ibrāhīm would not have asked forgiveness for his father but for a promise he made to him.*"' The meaning is: There is no evidence for you, believers, in Ibrāhīm the Friend asking for forgiveness for his father. That was only because of a promise he had made.'

Ibn 'Abbās said, 'Ibrāhīm's father used to promise Ibrāhīm the Friend that he would believe in Allah and cast aside others. Then when he died in unbelief, he knew that he was an enemy of Allah and stopped praying for him.' His word '*iyyāhu*' alludes to Ibrāhīm and the one making the promise was his father. It is also said that the one making the promise was Ibrāhīm, implying that he promised his father that he would ask forgiveness for him. When he died an idolater, he was free of him. He indicated this promise in Allah's words: *'I will ask my Lord to forgive you.'* (19:47)

Qāḍī Abū Bakr ibn al-'Arabī said, 'The Prophet ﷺ connected asking for forgiveness for Abū Ṭālib to the words of Allah: *"I will ask my Lord to forgive you."* (9:47) Allah Almighty then states that Ibrāhīm's asking for forgiveness for his father was on account of a promise he had made before his unbelief became clear. When his unbelief was clear, he declared himself free of him, so how could he, Muḥammad, ask forgiveness for his uncle when he witnessed his death as an unbeliever?'

A person is judged according to his apparent state when he dies. If he dies in faith, that is the judgment made about him. If he dies in unbelief, he is judged to be an unbeliever and his Lord knows best what his inner state is, although al-'Abbās asked the Prophet ﷺ, 'Messenger of Allah, did you help your uncle at all?' 'Yes,' he replied. This intercession was in lightening the punishment, not leaving the Fire, as we made clear in *Kitāb at-tadhkirah.*

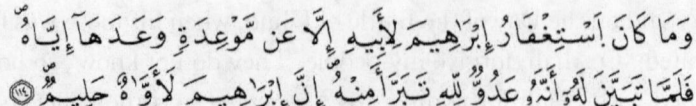

Ibrāhīm was tender-hearted and forbearing.

Scholars disagree about the word *awwāh* (tender-hearted) and say fifteen things about it. The first is that the *awwāh* is someone who makes a lot of supplication as Ibn Mas'ūd and 'Ubayd ibn 'Umar said. The second is that it is someone who is merciful to Allah's servants. Al-Ḥasan and Qatādah said that. It is also related from Ibn Mas'ūd. The first has a sounder *isnād* from Ibn Mas'ūd. An-Naḥḥās said that. The third is that it is the one who knows with certainty. 'Aṭā' and 'Ikrimah said that. Abū Zubyān related it from Ibn 'Abbās. The fourth is that it means 'believer' in Abyssinian. Ibn 'Abbās said that. The fifth is that it is the glorifier who remembers Allah on earth in desolate poverty. Al-Kalbī and Sa'īd ibn al-Musayyab said that. The sixth is that it is someone who remembers Allah often. 'Uqbah ibn 'Āmir said that. A man who used to remember Allah and glorify was mentioned in the presence of the Prophet ﷺ and he said, 'He is *awwāh*.' The seventh is that he recites the Qur'an a lot. This is related from Ibn 'Abbās. These views run into each other. The recitation of the Qur'an combines them.

The eighth is that it is the one who sighs. Abū Dharr said that. Ibrāhīm used to say, 'Ah for the Fire before "Ah" is of no use.' Abū Dharr said that it is a man who does a lot of *ṭawāf* of the House and says in his supplication, 'Awh! Awh!' Abū Dharr complained about such a man to the Prophet ﷺ and he said, 'Leave him. He is *awwāh*.' He said, 'I went out that night and the Prophet ﷺ was burying that man at night and had a light with him.' The ninth is that it means a *faqīh*. Mujāhid and an-Nakha'ī said that. The tenth is that it is the one who makes humble supplication. 'Abdullāh ibn Shaddād ibn al-Hād related it from the Prophet ﷺ. Anas said, A woman said something to the Prophet ﷺ which he disliked and 'Umar forbade her. The Prophet ﷺ said, 'Leave her. She is *awwāhah*.' It was asked, 'What is *awwāhah*, Messenger of Allah?' 'Humble,' he answered.

The eleventh is that he is one who, when he remembers his errors, asks forgiveness for them. Abū Ayyūb said that. The twelfth is that it is someone who sighs a lot for wrong actions. Al-Farrā' said it. The thirteenth is that he is distinguished by good. Sa'īd ibn Jubayr said that. The fourteenth is that he is compassionate. 'Abd al-'Azīz ibn Yaḥyā said that. Abū Bakr aṣ-Ṣiddīq was called *awwāh* because of his compassion and kindness. The fifteenth is that he is the one who turns away from all that Allah Almighty dislikes. 'Aṭā' said that.

The root of the word is *ta'awwuh*. It is what is heard from a breast when breathing on an ascent. Ka'b said, 'When Ibrāhīm remembered the Fire, he sighed.' Al-Jawharī said, 'They say in complaint, "Awh!" It is pain.' A poet said:

A sigh at her remembrance when remembering her
when the distance between us is what between the heaven and earth.

Sometimes they change the *wāw* for an *alif* and say, *'Āh*!' Sometimes they double the *wāw* and have a *sukūn* on the *hā'* and say *'Awwih*!' Sometimes the *hā'* is elided and there is a *shaddah* and one says, *'Awwi*!' without extension. Some say *'Āwwah*!' with extension and doubling and a *fatḥah* on the *wāw* with a silent *hā'* to make the sound of complaint long. Sometimes they add a *tā'* and say, *'Awwatāh'*, both extended and not extended. The verb is *awwaha* with the verbal noun *ta'wīh* and *ta'awwaha* with the verbal noun *ta'awwuh*. The noun for sigh is *āhah*. Al-Muthaqqib al-'Abdī said:

When I rose to make it move at night,
it gave the sigh (*āhah*) of a sorrowful man.

The adjective *ḥalīm* means having a lot of forbearance. Someone who is *ḥalīm* is the one who pardons wrong actions and endures harm. It is said that it is the one who does not punish anyone except for the sake of Allah and does not help anyone except for the sake of Allah. Ibrāhīm was like that. When he stood to pray, he was heard for miles and his heart answered.

وَمَا كَانَ ٱللَّهُ لِيُضِلَّ قَوْمًۢا بَعْدَ إِذْ هَدَىٰهُمْ حَتَّىٰ يُبَيِّنَ لَهُم مَّا
يَتَّقُونَ ۚ إِنَّ ٱللَّهَ بِكُلِّ شَىْءٍ عَلِيمٌ ﴿١١٥﴾ إِنَّ ٱللَّهَ لَهُۥ مُلْكُ
ٱلسَّمَٰوَٰتِ وَٱلْأَرْضِ ۖ يُحْىِۦ وَيُمِيتُ ۚ وَمَا لَكُم مِّن دُونِ ٱللَّهِ
مِن وَلِىٍّ وَلَا نَصِيرٍ ﴿١١٦﴾

115-16 Allah would never misguide a people after guiding them until He had made it clear to them how to be godfearing. Allah has knowledge of all things. Allah is He to Whom the kingdom of the heavens and earth belongs. He gives life and causes to die. You have no protector or helper besides Allah.

Allah would never misguide a people after guiding them

Allah would not make misguidance fall into their hearts after guidance until it was clear to them how to be godfearing and they were not godfearing. At that point they merit misguidance. That gives the clearest evidence that when acts of disobedience are committed and they are exposed, that is a reason for misguidance and ruin and a ladder to abandoning right direction and guidance. We ask Allah for correctness, success and right guidance by His favour!

Abū 'Amr ibn al-'Alā' said that the words: *'until He had made it clear to them'* mean after He has sent them His command as in His words: *'When We desire to destroy a city, We send a command to the affluent in it.'* (17:16) Mujāhid said that the words *'until He had made it clear to them'* refer to what Allah had said to Ibrāhīm. They should not ask for forgiveness for the idolaters in particular, and He made it clear to them that obedience and rebellion are general.

It is related that when the prohibition of wine was revealed and it was made binding, they asked the Prophet ﷺ about those who had died while drinking it and so Allah revealed this. This *āyah* refutes the Mu'tazilites and others who say that guidance and faith are created, as we already mentioned in *al-Fātiḥah.*

Allah is He to Whom the kingdom of the heavens and earth belongs. He gives life and causes to die. You have no protector or helper besides Allah.

This has already been discussed in more than one place, as in 2:28.

لَّقَد تَّابَ ٱللَّهُ عَلَى ٱلنَّبِيٓءِ وَٱلْمُهَٰجِرِينَ وَٱلْأَنصَارِ ٱلَّذِينَ ٱتَّبَعُوهُ فِي
سَاعَةِ ٱلْعُسْرَةِ مِنۢ بَعْدِ مَا كَادَ تَزِيغُ قُلُوبُ فَرِيقٍ مِّنْهُمْ ثُمَّ
تَابَ عَلَيْهِمْ إِنَّهُۥ بِهِمْ رَءُوفٌ رَّحِيمٌ ﴿١١٧﴾

117 Allah has turned towards the Prophet, and the *Muhājirūn* and the *Anṣār*, those who followed him at the 'time of difficulty', after the hearts of a group of them had almost deviated. Then He turned towards them – He is All-Gentle, Most Merciful to them –

At-Tirmidhī related from 'Abd ibn Ḥumayd from 'Abd ar-Razzāq from Ma'mar from az-Zuhrī from 'Abd ar-Raḥmān ibn Ka'b ibn Mālik that his father said, 'I did not stay behind any expedition the Prophet ﷺ went on until Tabūk except for Badr. The Prophet ﷺ did not blame anyone who did not go to Badr. He went out making for the caravan and Quraysh came out to protect their caravan and they met without prior arrangement, as Allah says. By my life, the noblest of the battles of the Messenger of Allah ﷺ in people's eyes was Badr. I would love to have been present at it even more than at my oath of allegiance on the night of 'Aqabah when we made a contract for Islam. After that I did not fail to go on any expedition with the Prophet ﷺ until Tabūk, which was the last expedition he made. The

Prophet ﷺ announced that they would set out… (the *ḥadīth* continues in length and in it he says) I went to the Prophet ﷺ while he was sitting in the mosque with the Muslims around him. He was shining like the full moon. When he was happy about something, he shone. I went and sat before him and he said, "Good news, Ka'b ibn Mālik, of the best day to come to you since your mother bore you!" I said, "Prophet of Allah, is it from Allah or from you?" "It is from Allah," he answered, and recited this verse: *"Allah has turned towards the Prophet, and the Muhājirūn and Anṣār…"* The following was also revealed about us: *"Have taqwā of Allah and be with the truly sincere."* (9:119)' The full story is found in the *ḥadīth* in *Ṣaḥīḥ Muslim*.

Scholars have different views about this 'turning' of Allah towards the *Muhājirūn* and *Anṣār*. Ibn 'Abbās said, 'Turning towards the Prophet is on account of him giving permission to remain behind. The evidence is His words: *"Allah pardon you! Why did you excuse them?"* (9:42) He turned towards the believers because the hearts of some of them inclined to staying behind him.'

It is said that Allah's turning to them is delivering them from the severity of hardship. It is said that it is their being delivered from the harm of the enemy. That is designated as '*tawbah*', even if it is outside of what they recognised of the meaning of *tawbah* in it which is returning to the first state.

The people who know meanings say, 'The Prophet ﷺ was mentioned in *tawbah* because since he was the reason for their repentance, he is mentioned with them, as in *"a fifth of it belongs to Allah and to the Messenger."* (8:41)'

those who followed him at the 'time of difficulty'

'Moment' (*waqt*) means in the time of difficulty. What is meant are all the times of those expeditions, and does not mean a particular moment. It is said that the '*time of difficulty*' was the harshest of the moments which they experienced in that fighting. '*Usrah* is the difficulty of the business. Jābir said, 'The difficulty they had was in respect of their mounts, the difficulty in finding provision and the difficulty in finding water.'

Al-Ḥasan said, 'The difficulty for the Muslims was that they went out on camels which they had to ride on by turns. Their provision was rotten dates, barley that had gone off and rancid fat. Some people had only some dates they passed around between them. When someone's hunger became extreme, he would take a date and chew it until he experienced its taste and then his companion would take it until he took a drink of water. That continued until it reached the last of them and only the stone of the date was left. They went with the Prophet ﷺ based on their sincerity and certainty. May Allah be pleased with them.'

'Umar was asked about '*the time of difficulty*' and said, 'We set out in intense heat and camped while afflicted by such severe thirst that we thought our necks would be cut off due to thirst and a man would slaughter his camel and squeeze the contents of its stomach and drink it and put what was left on his stomach. Abū Bakr said, "Messenger of Allah, Allah is good to you, so make supplication." He asked, "Would you like that?" "Yes," he said. So he raised his hands and he had not lowered his hands before the sky clouded over and then it poured with rain and they filled the containers they had. When we left, we looked and the rain had not gone beyond the place where the army was.'

Abū Hurayrah and Abū Sa'īd said, 'We were on the Tabūk expedition and people were afflicted by hunger and said, "Messenger of Allah, if you would permit us to slaughter our camels, we could eat them and have oil." The Messenger of Allah ﷺ said, "Do it." 'Umar came and said, "Messenger of Allah, if they do that, there will be few mounts. Tell them to bring their excess provisions and pray to Allah for blessing over them. Perhaps Allah will put blessing in that." "Yes," he said. Then he called for an ox-skin to be spread out and called for the excess provisions. One man would bring a handful of sorghum, another a handful of dates and yet another a piece of bread until something insignificant was collected on the mat. I assessed it and it was about the size of a goat. The Messenger of Allah ﷺ prayed for blessing and then said, "Bring your containers." They started to put it in their containers until, by the One – there is no god but Him! – there did not remain in the army any container that was not filled. The people ate until they were full and there was some left over. The Prophet ﷺ said, "I testify that there is no god but Allah and I am the Messenger of Allah. Any slave who meets Allah without any doubt about this [the double testimony] will not be barred from the Garden."' Muslim transmitted it in his *Ṣaḥīḥ*. Praise is due to Allah.

Ibn 'Arafah said that the Army of Tabūk is called the Army of Hardship because the Messenger of Allah ﷺ encouraged people to go on the expedition in the heat of midsummer and it was harsh and difficult for them. It was the time of selling dates. An example is made of the Army of Hardship because the Messenger of Allah ﷺ had not gone on an expedition with such numbers before. On the Day of Badr, he had about 310 men, at Uḥud 700, at Khaybar 1500, at the Conquest of Makkah 10,000, and at Ḥunayn 12,000. His army in the Tabūk expedition was over 30,000. It was the last expedition of the Prophet ﷺ. The Messenger of Allah ﷺ set out in the month of Rajab and stayed at Tabūk through Sha'bān and some days of Ramaḍān. He sent out expeditions and made peace with some people in exchange for *jizyah*.

During this expedition, he left 'Alī in charge of Madīnah and the hypocrites said, 'He left him behind because of something he dislikes in him.' He went out after the Prophet ﷺ and informed him. The Prophet ﷺ said, 'Are you not content to be in the position of Hārūn to Mūsā?' He made it clear that his staying at his command was equal in reward to going out with him because the fulcrum is the command of the Lawgiver.

It is called the Tabūk expedition because the Prophet ﷺ saw some of his Companions putting their cups (*yabūkūna*) in the sand of Tabūk and moving them to bring out water. He said, 'You will continue to seek it (*tabākūna*).' That is why that expedition was called Tabūk. '*Ḥisiyy*' is water which sinks through the sand and remains when it reaches the hard surface under it. The sand can be dug out over it and the water extracted. The action is called *iḥtisā'*. Al-Jawharī said that.

after the hearts of a group of them had almost deviated

'Hearts' is in the nominative by '*deviated*' according to Sībawayh and it is concealed in '*kāda*' and so it is like *kāna* because the report obliges it as *kāna* obliges it. If you wish, you can say that it is in the nominative by *kāda*. It implies: 'after the hearts of a group of them almost deviated.' Al-A'mash, Ḥamzah and Ḥafṣ recited *yazīghu* with *yā'*. Abū Ḥātim claimed that if it is recited with *yā'*, then it is not permitted to have 'hearts' in the nominative by *kāda*. An-Naḥḥās said, 'The one who does allow it allows it with others when the plural is masculine.' Al-Farrā' related *raḥuba* for breadth of land which is the dialect of the Hijaz.

There is disagreement about the meaning of 'deviate'. It means that they were broken by effort, hardship and difficulty. Ibn 'Abbās said that it means to turn away from the Truth by their resistance and [refusal] to help. It is said that it is after a group of them wanted to stay behind and disobey and then joined them. It is said that they wanted to travel and so Allah turned to them and commanded them to do that.

Then He turned towards them

It is said that His turning to them is by taking hold of their hearts so that they do not deviate. That is the *sunnah* of Allah with His friends when they look at destruction and fear destruction: He causes the clouds of generosity to rain on them and gives life to their hearts. It is said:

I have hopes of You and I do not recognize another lord
from whom I hope for what I hope for from You.

When hardships are harsh in the earth for people,
    they ask for help and implore.
You tested the slaves with fear and hunger
    and yet they persisted in wrong actions.
I have no refuge but You, my Lord,
    and I am certain that I will be saved by You.

He said about the three: *'He turned to them so that they might turn to Him.'* It is said that the meaning of 'He turned to them', is that gave them success in repenting so that they repented. It is said that it means: *'He turned to them,'* by giving them more time and did not hasten their punishment so that they could repent. It is said that He turned to them so that they would remain firm in repentance. It is said that it means He turned to them so that their repentance brought them to a state when He was pleased with them. In general, if Allah had not already known that repentance had been decreed for them, they would not have repented, as in the words of the Prophet ﷺ: 'Act: everyone is eased to what they are created for.'

وَعَلَى ٱلثَّلَٰثَةِ ٱلَّذِينَ خُلِّفُواْ حَتَّىٰٓ إِذَا ضَاقَتۡ عَلَيۡهِمُ ٱلۡأَرۡضُ بِمَا
رَحُبَتۡ وَضَاقَتۡ عَلَيۡهِمۡ أَنفُسُهُمۡ وَظَنُّوٓاْ أَن لَّا مَلۡجَأَ مِنَ ٱللَّهِ إِلَّآ
إِلَيۡهِ ثُمَّ تَابَ عَلَيۡهِمۡ لِيَتُوبُوٓاْ إِنَّ ٱللَّهَ هُوَ ٱلتَّوَّابُ ٱلرَّحِيمُ ١١٨

118 and also towards the three who were left behind, so that when the earth became narrow for them, for all its great breadth, and their own selves became constricted for them and they realised that there was no refuge from Allah except in Him, He turned to them so that they might turn to Him. Allah is the Ever-Returning, the Most Merciful.

and also towards the three who were left behind,

It is said that it is '*left behind*' in terms of repentance. Mujāhid and Abū Mālik said that. Qatādah said that it refers to staying behind the Tabūk expedition. It is related from Muḥammad ibn Zayd that '*left behind*' means 'abandoned', because 'when you leave someone behind' it means that you parted from him and failed to do what he encouraged you to do. 'Ikrimah ibn Khālid recited '*khalafū*', meaning that they stayed behind the Messenger of Allah ﷺ. It is related that Ja'far ibn Muḥammad recited *khālifū*.

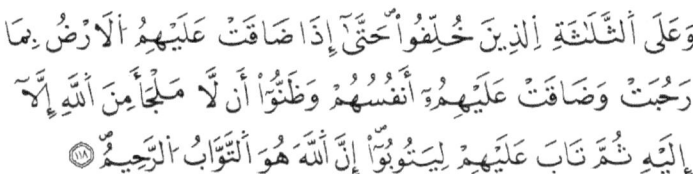

It is said that *khullifū* means deferred and delayed behind the hypocrites and no judgement was made about them. That is because the repentance of the hypocrites was not accepted. Some people made excuses and their excuses were accepted and the Prophet ﷺ deferred those three until the Qur'an was revealed about them. This is sound based on what Muslim, al-Bukhārī and others related. Ka'b said, 'We, the three, were excluded from the business of those whose excuse the Messenger of Allah ﷺ accepted when they swore to him and he accepted their allegiance and asked for forgiveness for them. The Messenger of Allah ﷺ delayed our business until Allah judged it. That is why Allah said, *"Towards the three who were left behind"*. When He said "*khullifū*", it was not about our failing to go on the expedition, but it was about his holding us back and delaying our affair after those who had sworn oaths and made excuses to him which he accepted.' It is a long *ḥadīth* and this is the end of it.

The three who stayed behind were Ka'b ibn Mālik, Murārah ibn Rabī'ah al-'Āmirī and Hilāl ibn Umayyah al-Wāqifī. All of them were from the *Anṣār.* Al-Bukhārī and Muslim transmitted their *ḥadīth.* Muslim related that Ka'b ibn Mālik said, 'I did not stay behind any expedition which the Prophet ﷺ made until Tabūk although I had stayed behind Badr. He did not blame anyone who had not gone to it. The Messenger of Allah ﷺ and the Muslims went out making for the caravan of Quraysh and Allah had them meet their enemy without prior arrangement. I was present with the Messenger of Allah ﷺ on the night of 'Aqabah when we made a contract for Islam. I would have preferred to exchange it for having been present at Badr. Nothing is remembered among people more than Badr. Then I stayed behind the Messenger of Allah ﷺ on the Tabūk expedition. I had never been stronger or wealthier than I was when I failed to go out with the Messenger of Allah ﷺ on that expedition. By Allah, never before had I owned two camels until that expedition. The Messenger of Allah ﷺ went out in great heat, facing a long journey, the desert and a very numerous enemy. He made it clear to the Muslims so that they could made adequate preparations for their expedition and informed them of the direction he intended to take. The number of Muslims was too numerous to be put into a register. The rare person who wanted to be absent thought that that would be hidden as long as no revelation from Allah Almighty was revealed. The Messenger of Allah ﷺ went on that expedition when the fruits were ripe and there was shade. I inclined towards that. The Messenger of Allah ﷺ and the Muslims made preparations and I kept intending to make preparations with them, but went home without doing anything, saying to myself, "I can do that when I want." I kept procrastinating until the Messenger of Allah ﷺ set out on the expedition with the Muslims while I still had not made any preparations. Again I went home without doing anything. That continued until they left swiftly and I missed the battle. I still intended to travel and catch them up, and how I wish that I had done so! But that was not decreed for me.

'After the Messenger of Allah ﷺ had left and I walked around the people, it saddened me that all that I saw were men thought to be hypocrites or weak men whom Allah had given an excuse. The Messenger of Allah ﷺ did not remember me until he reached Tabūk. While he was sitting among the people at Tabūk, he asked, "What happened to Ka'b ibn Mālik?" One of the Banū Salimah said, "Messenger of Allah, he has been stopped by his cloaks and looking at his flanks." Mu'ādh ibn Jabal said to him, "Evil is what you have said! By Allah, we only know good of him!" The Messenger of Allah ﷺ was silent. While he was sitting, a man appeared who was white in the mirage. The Messenger of Allah ﷺ said, "Let it be Abū Khaythamah," and indeed it was Abū Khaythamah al-Anṣārī. He was the one whom the hypocrites criticised when he gave a *ṣā'* of dates as *ṣadaqah*."

Ka'b continued: 'When I heard that the Messenger of Allah ﷺ was on his way back from Tabūk, I was grieved and began to think of lying to the Messenger of Allah ﷺ and said, "How can I escape his anger tomorrow?" I asked the views of all of my family about that. When I was told, "The Messenger of Allah ﷺ is coming, all falsehood left me and I knew that nothing would save me from him. So I resolved to tell him the truth." The Messenger of Allah ﷺ arrived in the morning. When he arrived from a journey, he first went to the mosque and prayed two *rak'ah*s in it and then sat down for the people. When he did that, those who had stayed behind went to him and began to offer him their excuses and swear to it. There were about eighty men. The Messenger of Allah ﷺ accepted their outward excuses, accepted their allegiance and asked for forgiveness for them, entrusting their secrets to Allah. I went and when I greeted him, he smiled the smile of someone who is angry. He said, "Come." I went forward until I sat before him. He asked me, "What made you stay behind? Had you not purchased your mount?" I answered, "Messenger of Allah, by Allah, if I had sat with anyone but you among the people of this world, I think that I would have tried to escape his anger by making an excuse. I have been given the skill of debate. But, by Allah, I know that if I tell you a lie today in order to please you, it will not be long before Allah makes you angry with me. If I tell you the truth, you will be angry with me, but I hope that Allah will reward me for it in the end. By Allah, I have no excuse. By Allah, I have never been stronger or wealthier than I was at the moment I stayed behind you." The Messenger of Allah ﷺ said, "This one has spoken the truth. Get up until Allah judges regarding you."

'I got up and some of the Banū Salimah rushed after me and said, "By Allah, we have never seen you commit a wrong action before this! Were you unable to make an excuse to the Messenger of Allah ﷺ as the others who stayed behind did? The prayer of the Messenger of Allah ﷺ for forgiveness would have been enough for your wrong action!" By Allah, they kept at me until I wanted to go back to the Messenger of Allah ﷺ and say that I had lied, but then I asked them, "Has anyone else met with what I have met?" "Yes," they answered, "two men said the like of what you said and were told the like of what you were told." "Who are they?" I asked. They replied, "Murārah ibn Rabī'ah al-'Āmirī and Hilāl ibn Umayyah al-Wāqifī." They mentioned two righteous men who had been present at Badr and who were a model for me. I continued when they mentioned them to me.

'The Messenger of Allah ﷺ forbade the Muslims to speak to us three among those who had stayed behind and people avoided us and changed their demeanour towards us until the earth seemed alienated for me and there was nothing in the earth which I recognised. We remained like that for forty days. My two companions were humiliated and remained in their houses weeping. I was the youngest and firmest of the people and so I continued to go out and attend the prayer and go around in the markets while no one spoke to me. I would go to the Messenger of Allah ﷺ while he was seated after the prayer and greet him and would ask myself whether his lips moved in reply or not. Then I would pray near him and steal a glance at him. When I turned to my prayer, he would look at me, and when I turned towards him, he would turn away from me.

'When the harshness of the Muslims had gone on for a long time, I went and climbed over the garden wall of Abū Qatādah. He was my cousin and the dearest of people to me. I greeted him and, by Allah, he did not return the greeting. I said to him, "Abū Qatādah, I ask you by Allah, do you know that I love Allah and His Messenger?" He was silent. I repeated it and implored him, but he was still silent. I repeated it again and implored him and he said, "Allah and His Messenger know best." My eyes flowed with tears and I turned around and climbed back over the wall. While I was walking in the market of Madīnah, one of the Nabateans of Syria who had come to sell food in Madīnah, said, "Who will direct me to Ka'b ibn Mālik?" The people began to point me out to him and he came up to me and handed me a letter from the king of Ghassan. I knew how to read and write. I read it and it said: "We have heard that your companion is harsh to you. Allah has not made you live in an abode of humiliation and constriction. Join us and we will console you." When I read it, I exclaimed, "This is also part of the affliction!" I took it to the oven and burned it.

'When forty of the fifty days had passed and no revelation had come, a messenger came to me from the Messenger of Allah ﷺ and said, "The Messenger of Allah ﷺ commands you to withdraw from your wife." I asked, "Should I divorce her or what should I do?" He answered, "No, just withdraw from her and do not go near her." He sent the same instruction to my two companions. I told my wife, "Go to your family and stay with them until Allah gives judgement in the matter." The wife of Hilāl ibn Umayyah went to the Messenger of Allah ﷺ and said, "Messenger of Allah, Hilāl is an old weak man who does not have a servant. Would you dislike it if I served him?" "No," he answered, "but he should not approach you." She said, "By Allah, he does not move for anything! By Allah, he has continued to weep since his business started until today." Some of my family said, "You should have asked permission from the Messenger of Allah ﷺ for your wife to stay. The wife of Hilāl ibn Umayyah was given permission to serve him." I answered, "I will not ask the Messenger of Allah ﷺ for permission for her. How do I know what the Messenger of Allah ﷺ would do if I asked him for permission for her when I am a young man!"

'It continued like that for another ten days and so the fifty were completed for us from the time when it was forbidden to speak to us. When I finished the *fajr* prayer on the morning of the fiftieth day on the roof of one of our houses and I was sitting in the manner which Allah mentioned about us, my soul felt constricted and the earth seemed narrow for me in spite of its spaciousness. I heard a voice shouting on top of Sal' in his loudest voice, "Ka'b ibn Mālik! Good news!" I fell down in prostration and recognised that relief had come. After he had prayed the *fajr* prayer, the Messenger of Allah ﷺ announced to the people that Allah had turned to us.

'The people came to give us the good news. Some had gone to give my two companions the good news. One man galloped his horse to me while a runner of the Aslam went up the mountain and his voice was swifter than the horse. When I heard his voice giving me the good news, I removed my two garments and gave them to the one who had given me the good news. By Allah, those were the only two garments I owned on that day. I borrowed two garments to wear. Then I set off for the Messenger of Allah ﷺ and people met him in batches to congratulate me for my repentance being accepted. They said, "Congratulations that Allah has turned to you." I entered the mosque and the Messenger of Allah ﷺ was sitting in the mosque with the people around him. Ṭalḥah ibn 'Ubaydullāh rose and rushed to shake my hand and congratulate me. By Allah, none of the *Muhājirūn* but him got up. (Ka'b did not forget Ṭalḥah doing that.) When I greeted the Messenger of Allah ﷺ and his face was shining with joy. He said, "Good news of the best day for you since your mother bore you!" I asked, "Is it from Allah, Messenger of Allah, or from you?' "Rather it is from Allah," he answered. When the Messenger of Allah ﷺ was happy, his face shone as if it was a part of the full moon. We used to recognise that.

'When I sat before him, I said, "Messenger of Allah, since Allah has turned to me, part of my repentance is that I will give away my wealth as *ṣadaqah* for Allah and His Messenger." The Messenger of Allah ﷺ said, "Keep some of your wealth. That is better for you." I said, "Then I will keep my share at Khaybar." I said, "Messenger of Allah, Allah has saved me because I told the truth. Part of my repentance is that I will only speak the truth as long as I live." By Allah, I do not know of any of the Muslims whom Allah has tested in truthfulness since I mentioned that to the Messenger of Allah ﷺ until today more than how Allah has tested me. By Allah, I have not deliberately told a lie since I said that to the Messenger of Allah ﷺ until today and I hope that Allah will preserve me in what remains of my life. Allah revealed: *"Allah has turned towards the Prophet, and the Muhājirūn and the Anṣār…"*'

Ka'b added, 'Allah never gave me a greater blessing after He guided me to Islam than my telling the truth to the Messenger of Allah ﷺ so that I did not lie and fall into destruction as those who lied were destroyed. Allah said about those who lied when He sent down the Revelation the worst that can be said: *"They will swear to you by Allah … Allah is certainly not pleased with a deviant people."* (9:95)'

Ka'b said, 'We three differed from those whose excuses the Messenger of Allah ﷺ accepted when he swore to them, and he accepted their allegiance and asked for forgiveness for them. The Messenger of Allah ﷺ deferred our business until Allah judged it. That is why Allah said: "*and also towards the three…*" When He said "*khullifū*", it was not about our failing to go on the expedition, but it was about his holding us back and delaying our affair after those who had sworn oaths and made excuses to him which he accepted.'

when the earth became narrow for them, for all its great breadth,

In spite of its expanse. A spacious house is called *raḥb*, *raḥīb*, and *ruḥāb*. The *mā* has the nature of a verbal noun. The earth felt constricted for them even though it is spacious because they were shunned and could not interact or speak with people. This is evidence for shunning the people who are involved in acts of disobedience until they repent.

and their own selves became constricted for them and they realised that there was no refuge from Allah except in Him

This means that they were constricted by worry, alienation and the harshness they met with from the Companions. They were certain that there was no refuge for pardoning them and accepting their repentance except in Allah. Abu Bakr al-Warrāq said, 'True repentance is when the earth seems narrow to the one who repents in spite of its spaciousness and is constricted for him, as was the case in the repentance of Ka'b and his two companions.'

He turned to them so that they might turn to Him. Allah is the Ever-Returning, the Most Merciful.

Allah begins with turning on His part. Abū Zayd said, 'I erred in four things in the beginning with Allah. I thought that I loved Him when in fact He loved me. Allah Almighty says: *"whom He loves and who love Him"* (5:54). I thought that I was pleased with Him when He was pleased with me. Allah Almighty says: *"Allah is pleased with them and they are pleased with Him"* (5:119). I thought that I remembered Him when He remembered me. Allah Almighty says: *"The remembrance of Allah is greater."* I thought that I turned in repentance to Him while He turned to me. The Almighty says: *"He turned to them so that they might turn to Him."'*

It is said that it means: then He turned to them so that they would be firm in repentance as the Almighty says: *'O you who believe, believe…'* (4:136) It is said that He gave them more time and did not hasten their punishment as He did with others. Allah says: *'Because of wrongdoing on the part of the Jews, We made unlawful for them some good things which has previously been lawful for them.'* (4:160)

يَـٰٓأَيُّهَا ٱلَّذِينَ ءَامَنُوا۟ ٱتَّقُوا۟ ٱللَّهَ وَكُونُوا۟ مَعَ ٱلصَّـٰدِقِينَ ١١٩

119 You who believe! have *taqwā* of Allah and be with the truly sincere.

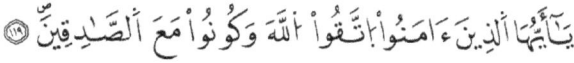

This command to the people of sincerity is good after the story of the three since their sincerity helped them and removed them from the ranks of the hypocrites. Muṭarrif said, 'I heard Mālik ibn Anas say, "When a man is truthful and does not lie he is given the full use of his mind and is not afflicted by the senility and dotage that others are afflicted by."'

They have different positions regarding who is meant here by the believers and truly sincere. It is said that it is addressed to those of the People of the Book who believe. It is said that it is addressed to all the believers, with the meaning 'Fear opposing Allah's command.' *'Be with the truly sincere'* means be with those who went out with the Prophet ﷺ, not with the hypocrites, in other words follow the school and path of the truly sincere. It is said that it refers to the Prophets and means be with them in the Garden through righteous actions. It is said that *'the truly sincere'* are the ones who are meant by Allah's words: *'Goodness does not lie in turning your faces … Those are the people who are true.'* (2:177) It is said that they are those who fulfil their contract, indicated by the words of Allah: *'…men who were true to the contract they made with Allah.'* It is said that they are the *Muhājirūn* based on the words of Abū Bakr on the Day of the Verandah: 'Allah named us the truly sincere and He said, *"It is for the poor Muhājirūn …"* (59:8) and then He named you the successful in His words, *"Those who were already settled in the abode and in faith"* (59:9).' It is said that they are those who are the same outwardly and inwardly.

Ibn al-'Arabī said, 'This statement is the truth and the end which is aspired to. This is the quality which removes hypocrisy in belief and difference in action. Someone who possesses that quality is called *ṣiddīq* as were Abū Bakr, 'Umar, 'Uthmān and those less than them in their degrees and times. As for those who say that they – "*the truly sincere*" – are those who are meant by the *āyah* in *al-Baqarah* (2:177) which shows a high degree of sincerity, that high degree necessarily contains the lesser degree, which is the meaning of the *āyah* in *al-Aḥzāb* (33:23). As for the explanation of Abū Bakr, it is general to all the views because all those qualities exist in them.'

The duty of the one who has understanding from Allah and grasps what is meant is that he should cling to truthfulness in his speech, sincerity in his actions and purity in his states. Anyone who is like that will join the good and achieve the pleasure of the Ever-Forgiving. The Prophet ﷺ said, 'You must have truthfulness (*ṣidq*). Truthfulness guides to piety and piety guides to the Garden. A man continues to be truthful and pursues truthfulness until he is written with Allah as truthful.' Lying is the opposite of that. The Prophet ﷺ said, 'Beware of lying. Lying leads to impiety and impiety leads to the Fire. A man continues to lie and pursues lying until he is written with Allah as a liar.' Muslim transmitted it.

Lying is a source of shame and its people are stripped of the permission to testify. The Prophet ﷺ rejected the testimony of a man because of a lie which he told.

Ma'mar said, 'I do not know whether he lied to Allah or lied to His Messenger or lied to someone else.' Shurayk ibn 'Abdullāh was asked, 'Abū 'Abdullāh, I heard a man lying deliberately. Should I pray behind him?' 'No,' he answered. Ibn Mas'ūd said, 'Lying is not acceptable, whether serious or in jest, and none of you should make a promise and then not fulfil it. Recite, if you wish: *"O you who believe, have taqwā of Allah and be with the truly sincere."* Do you see any indulgence there for lying?'

Mālik said, "The report of a liar is not accepted about the words of other people, even if he is truthful in transmitting the *ḥadīth* of the Prophet ﷺ.' Others said that their testimony is accepted. The sound position is that neither the testimony nor the report of a liar should be accepted based on what we mentioned. Being worthy of acceptance is a great rank and noble appointment. It is only for someone whose qualities are perfect. There is no quality worse than lying and so it results in dismissal from appointments and invalidation of testimony.

مَا كَانَ لِأَهْلِ الْمَدِينَةِ وَمَنْ حَوْلَهُم مِّنَ الْأَعْرَابِ أَن يَتَخَلَّفُوا
عَن رَّسُولِ اللَّهِ وَلَا يَرْغَبُوا بِأَنفُسِهِمْ عَن نَّفْسِهِ ذَٰلِكَ بِأَنَّهُمْ
لَا يُصِيبُهُمْ ظَمَأٌ وَلَا نَصَبٌ وَلَا مَخْمَصَةٌ فِي سَبِيلِ اللَّهِ وَلَا يَطَئُونَ
مَوْطِئًا يَغِيظُ الْكُفَّارَ وَلَا يَنَالُونَ مِنْ عَدُوٍّ نَّيْلًا إِلَّا كُتِبَ لَهُم بِهِ
عَمَلٌ صَالِحٌ إِنَّ اللَّهَ لَا يُضِيعُ أَجْرَ الْمُحْسِنِينَ ﴿١٢٠﴾ وَلَا يُنفِقُونَ نَفَقَةً
صَغِيرَةً وَلَا كَبِيرَةً وَلَا يَقْطَعُونَ وَادِيًا إِلَّا كُتِبَ لَهُمْ لِيَجْزِيَهُمُ
اللَّهُ أَحْسَنَ مَا كَانُوا يَعْمَلُونَ ﴿١٢١﴾

120-121 It was not for people of Madīnah, and the desert Arabs around them, to remain behind the Messenger of Allah nor to prefer themselves to him. That is because no thirst or weariness or hunger will afflict them in the Way of Allah, nor will they take a single step to infuriate the unbelievers, nor secure any gain from the enemy, without a right action being written down for them because of it. Allah does not let the wage of the good-doers go to waste. Nor will they give away any amount, whether large or small, nor will they cross any valley, without it being written down for them so that Allah can recompense them for the best of what they did.

It was not for people of Madīnah, and the desert Arabs around them, to remain behind the Messenger of Allah

This looks in literal terms to be a report whereas it is actually a command as in Allah's words: *'It is not right for you to cause annoyance to the Messenger of Allah...'* (33:53) *'To remain behind'* is in the nominative as the subject of *kāna*. It is a rebuke directed at the believers of the people of Yathrib and the neighbouring Arab tribes, such as Muzaynah, Juhaynah, Ashja', Ghifār and Aslam, for failing to go out with the Messenger of Allah ﷺ on the Tabūk expedition.

The meaning is: those mentioned should not have stayed behind. The call to arms was to them but not others, who were not called on to come out. But it is possible that the call applies to every Muslim. Those are the people singled out for criticism because of their nearness and proximity so they were more blameworthy than others.

nor to prefer themselves to him.

They should not be pleased with ease and tranquillity for themselves when the Messenger of Allah ﷺ is suffering hardship. The expression *'raghiba 'an'* means to deem oneself above something.

That is because no thirst or weariness or hunger will afflict them in the Way of Allah,

Ẓama' means thirst. 'Ubayd ibn 'Umayr recited *'ẓamā''* wih a *maddah*. They are two dialectical forms. The word *'weariness'* is added, and means tiredness and *'walā'* is added for stress. The same is true of *'hunger'*. The root of *makhmaṣah* is the emaciation of the belly. A man who has an empty belly is described as *khamīṣ* and a woman as *khumṣānah*. This was already mentioned (5:3). The phrase *'in the Way of Allah'* means in obedience to Him.

nor will they take a single step to infuriate the unbelievers, nor secure any gain from the enemy,

The phrase *'take a single step to infuriate the unbelievers'* means to march on the ground towards them and *'secure any gain from the enemy'* refers to killing and defeating them. The root is *nayl* from the verb *nāla* is to get hold of a thing. Al-Kisā'ī said that *manīl* describes a matter which is achieved. It is not derived from *tanāwul* which is obtaining a gift. Others have said that it comes from *nāla, yanūlu*, to give a gift. *Nāla yanīlu*, is to receive it.

nor will they cross any valley

The Arabs say *wādī*, *awdiyah* for valley. An-Naḥḥās said, 'It is not known as far as I know that the form *fā'il* has the plural *af'ilah* in other than this instance. This plural is necessary to avoid heaviness in combining two *wāws* so that they say *'uqqitat'* for *'wuqqitat'*. Al-Khalīl and Sībawayh related *Uwayṣil* for the diminutive of the man's name, *Wāṣil*. No one else says that. Al-Farrā' related that the plural of *wādi* is *awdā'*. The plural is actually *'awdāh'* as can be seen in a verse of Jarīr. [POEM]

without it being written down for them.

Ibn 'Abbās said, 'Every moment of fear which anyone endures in the Way of Allah is equivalent to seventy thousand good deeds.' We find in the *Ṣaḥīḥ*: 'Horses are for three purposes,' and in it there is: 'As for the one who has a reward, that is the man who tethers them in the Way of Allah, giving them a long tether in pasture or meadow. He will have good deeds for whatever the horse gets from the pasture or the meadow for the extent of its tether. If it breaks its tether and crosses a hill or two, then he has good deeds for its tracks and dung.' If that is in the case in those places, then what about when he enters enemy territory mounted on it?

Some scholars use this *āyah* as evidence for the fact that entitlement to booty is gained on the basis of going into enemy territory and being in the land of the enemy. If someone dies after that, they are entitled to a share. That is the position of Ashhab, 'Abd al-Malik and one of the two positions of ash-Shāfi'ī. Mālik and Ibn al-Qāsim said, 'He has no right to anything because Allah mentions the reward in this *āyah* but does not mention the share.'

The words of the Almighty indicate that the first position is sounder in that He makes entering into the houses of the unbelievers the same as obtaining some of their wealth and bringing them out of their houses. This is what exasperates them and brings humiliation to them by way of obtaining booty, killing and taking prisoners. Since that is the case, entitlement to booty is earned by entering enemy territory, not by obtaining it. That is what 'Alī said: 'The abasement of people comes about when other people walk through their land.' Allah knows best.

This *āyah* was abrogated by the words of the Almighty: *'It is not necessary for the believers to go out all together.'* (9:122) Its ruling applies to the time when the Muslims were few in number. When they became numerous, then it was abrogated and whoever wished was allowed to stay behind. Ibn Zayd said that. Mujāhid said, 'The Prophet ﷺ sent people to the Bedouin to teach them. When this *āyah* was revealed, they were afraid and returned. So Allah revealed: *"It is not necessary for the believers to go out all together."'*

Qatādah said, 'This applies specifically to when the Prophet ﷺ himself went on an expedition. In such a case, no one could stay behind unless he had a valid excuse. In the case of other leaders and governors, any Muslim who wishes can stay behind when there is no need or necessity for the people as a whole to go.' A third view is that its judgment remains in force. Al-Walīd ibn Muslim said, 'I heard that al-Awzā'ī, Ibn al-Mubārak, al-Fazārī, as-Sabī'ī and Sa'īd ibn 'Abd al-'Azīz said that this *āyah* is for the first and the last of the Community.' What Qatādah said is good as is indicated by what happened with the Tabūk expedition. Allah knows best.

Abū Dāwūd related from Anas ibn Mālik that the Messenger of Allah ﷺ said, 'I left behind in Madīnah people who have not traversed any distance nor spent any outlay nor crossed any valley but they are with you.' They asked, 'Messenger of Allah, how can they be with us when they are in Madīnah?' He answered, 'They were kept back by a valid excuse.' Muslim transmitted it from Jābir. He said, 'We were with the Messenger of Allah ﷺ on an expedition when he said, "There are men in Madīnah who are with you wherever you travel and whatever valley you cross. Illness kept them back.' The Prophet ﷺ gave the person with an excuse the same reward that he gave the strong person who acted.

Some people say that the reward for someone with a valid excuse is not doubled, but the reward of the person who actually takes part is doubled. Ibn al-'Arabī said, 'This is an arbitrary judgment about Allah Almighty and constricts the vast span of His mercy.' He went on to criticise those people and said, "They can be given the reward absolutely doubled. We do not restrict doubling to a particular situation. It is based on intentions and this is something which is not seen. The one who is given it doubled receives that because your Lord knows best who deserves it."'

What is apparent from the *ḥadīth*s and *āyah*s is that there is equality in the reward. That is reflected in the words of the Prophet ﷺ: 'Whoever directs to good has the same reward as the one who does it.' He said ﷺ, 'If someone performs *wuḍū'* and goes out to the prayer and finds that the people have already prayed, Allah will give him a similar reward to those who attended and prayed it.' That is the apparent meaning of the words of the Almighty: *'If anyone leaves his home, making hijrah to Allah and his Messenger, and death catches up with him, it is Allah who will reward him.'* (4:100) The evidence is that sincere intention is the basis of actions. When there is a sound intention to obey Allah in a deed and the person is then unable to do it because of some impediment which stops him, it is not impossible that the reward for that person who lacked the power to achieve it is the same as the reward of the one who was able to do it, and more, since the Prophet ﷺ said, 'The intention of a believer is better than his action.' Allah knows best.

وَمَا كَانَ ٱلْمُؤْمِنُونَ لِيَنفِرُوا۟ كَآفَّةً ۚ فَلَوْلَا نَفَرَ مِن كُلِّ فِرْقَةٍ مِّنْهُمْ
طَآئِفَةٌ لِّيَتَفَقَّهُوا۟ فِى ٱلدِّينِ وَلِيُنذِرُوا۟ قَوْمَهُمْ إِذَا رَجَعُوٓا۟ إِلَيْهِمْ
لَعَلَّهُمْ يَحْذَرُونَ ﴿١٢٢﴾

122 It is not necessary for the believers to go out all together. If a party from each group of them were to go out so they could increase their knowledge of the *dīn* they would be able to notify their people when they returned to them so that hopefully they would take warning!

It is not necessary for the believers to go out all together.

Jihād is not an obligation for every individual. It is a *farḍ kifāyah.* That is because if everyone had gone out, then their dependents left behind them would perish. One group should go out on *jihād* and one group should study *fiqh* of the *dīn* and guard the women and children so that when those who go out return, those who remained at home can inform them about what they have learned of the rules of the *Sharīʿah* and any new revelation of the Prophet ﷺ. This abrogates 9:38-39 according to Mujāhid and Ibn Zayd.

This *āyah* is the basis of the obligation to seek knowledge because the meaning is: 'It is not necessary for the believers to go out all together when the Prophet ﷺ is staying and not going out, so that he would not be left alone.'

If a party from each group of them were to go out

So after they knew that the going out did not include all of them, the rest of them remained with the Prophet ﷺ to take the *dīn* and *fiqh* from him. Then when those who went out return to them, they will tell them what they heard and teach it to them. This obliges learning *fiqh* of the Book and *Sunnah* and establishes the fact that it is a *farḍ kifāyah* and not an individual obligation. It also indicated Allah's words: *'Ask the people of remembrance if you do not know.'* (16:43) This includes those who do not know the Book and *sunnah*. Instead of *'falawlā nafara'* al-Akhfash says *'fa-hallā nafara'*.

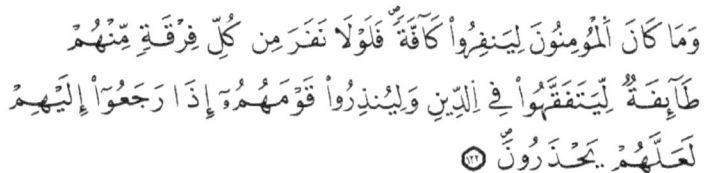

The noun *ṭā'ifah* linguistically means a group. It can be applied to less than that down to two men, and even to one with the meaning of a group. This was already mentioned under His words: *'If one group of you is pardoned another group will be punished.'* (9:66), where one man is meant.

There is no doubt that what is meant here is a group for two reasons: one logical and one linguistic. Logically, it is because knowledge is not usually achieved by a single person. Linguistically, it is because Allah says: *'so they could increase their knowledge of the dīn and they would be able to notify their people'* in which the plural pronoun is used. Ibn al-'Arabī said, 'Qāḍī Abū Bakr and Shaykh Abū al-Ḥasan before him related that *ṭā'ifah* here is referring to one person, and their position is based on the fact that it is obligatory to act on the report of a single person. That is sound, not because the word *ṭā'ifah* can be applied to one person, but because the report of a single person or various persons constitutes one report. Opposite that is the *mutawātir* report which is not limited in the number who transmit it.

A text which indicates that one person can be called a '*ṭā'ifah'* is found in the words of the Almighty: *'If two parties of the believers fight…'* (49:9), meaning two people, backed up by the words of the Almighty: *'Make peace between your brothers'* (49:9) where the dual is used. Even if the pronoun in '*fight*' is plural, the minimum of the plural is two according to one of two positions scholars take.

so that they could increase their knowledge of the *dīn*

The pronoun 'they' here refers to those who stayed with the Prophet ﷺ. Qatādah and Mujāhid said that. Al-Ḥasan said, 'They are the group who go out.' Aṭ-Ṭabarī preferred that. The words '*increase their knowledge of the dīn'* mean to have more insight and certainty about what Allah shows them in victory over the idolaters and supporting the *dīn.*

they would be able to notify their people when they returned to them.

In that case the words *'to notify their people'* refer to notifying them about the unbelievers, and the words *'when they returned to them'* refer to when they returned from *jihād* to inform them of Allah granting victory to His Prophet ﷺ and believers and to inform the unbelievers that they will not defeat them by fighting them and fighting the Prophet ﷺ and that what happened to their fellow unbelievers will also happen to them.

What Mujāhid and Qatādah said is clearer, meaning that the reference is to the group who stayed behind with the Messenger of Allah ﷺ rather than going on the expedition so that they might increase their understanding of the *dīn.* This makes it an encouragement to seek knowledge and a recommendation to do it rather than making it an obligation and mandatory since that is not what is demanded by these words. However, seeking knowledge is obliged by various proofs. Abū Bakr ibn al-'Arabī said that.

There are two categories of seeking knowledge. One is obligatory for individuals, such as knowledge of the prayer, *zakāt* and fasting. There is a *ḥadīth* related about this: 'Seeking knowledge is an obligation.' 'Abd al-Quddūs ibn Ḥabīb related that Ibrāhīm an-Nakha'ī said that he heard Anas ibn Mālik say, 'I heard the Messenger of Allah ﷺ say, "Seeking knowledge is an obligation for every Muslim."' Ibrāhīm added, 'I only heard this *ḥadīth* from Anas ibn Mālik.'

Another category of knowledge seeking is *farḍ kifāyah*, such as knowledge pertaining to obtaining people's rights, establishing the *ḥudūd*, resolving disputes and the like, since it is not necessary for all people to learn that, because that would result in their circumstances and that of others being impaired and their ability to earn a living being inadequate or non-existent. So the difference between the two cases is that some undertake it without that being a specific obligation. That is according to what Allah made easy for His slaves and distributed between them of His mercy and wisdom by His prior decree.

Seeking knowledge is a great virtue and has a noble rank to which no other action is equal. At-Tirmidhī related that Abū ad-Dardā' said, 'I heard the Messenger of Allah ﷺ say, "If someone travels a path seeking knowledge by it, Allah has made him travel a path to the Garden by it. The angels lower their wings out of pleasure with the one who seeks knowledge and the scholar so that those in the heavens and those in the earth and the fish in the sea ask forgiveness for him. The superiority of a scholar over a worshipper is like the superiority of the full moon over other planets. The scholars are the heirs of the Prophets. Prophets do not bequeath a dinar or dirham. They leave knowledge. Anyone who takes it has taken an immense portion."'

Abū Muḥammad ad-Dārimī relates in his *Musnad* from Abū al-Mughīrah from al-Awzā'ī that al-Ḥasan said, 'The Messenger of Allah ﷺ was asked about two men from the tribe of Israel: one was a scholar who prayed the obligatory prayer and then sat and taught people while the other fasted in the day and prayed at night. Which of them was better? The Messenger of Allah ﷺ said, "The superiority of the one who prayed the obligatory prayer and then sat and taught people over the one who fasted in the day and prayed at night is like my superiority over the least of you."' Abū 'Umar gave its *isnād* in the 'Book of the Clarification of Knowledge' from Abū Sa'īd al-Khudrī where the Messenger of Allah ﷺ said, 'The superiority of a scholar over a worshipper is like my superiority over my community.'

Ibn 'Abbās said, 'The best *jihād* is that of someone who builds a mosque in which he teaches the Qur'an, *fiqh* and the Sunnah.' Shurayk related it from Layth ibn Abī Sulaym. 'Alī al-Azdī said, 'I wanted to do *jihād* and Ibn 'Abbās said to me, "Shall I direct you to something which will be better for you than *jihād*? Go to a mosque and recite the Qur'an in it and teach *fiqh* in it."' Ar-Rabī' said, 'I heard ash-Shāfi'ī say, "Seeking knowledge is more obligatory than voluntary prayer."'

The statement in the *ḥadīth* that the angels lower their wings can be explained in two ways. One is that they are kind to him and show him mercy as the Almighty instructs children about being good to parents when He says: *'Take them under your wing, out of mercy, with due humility.'* (17:24) It means: be humble to them. The other is that what is meant is spreading their wings because some variants have, 'the angels spread their wings,' which would imply that when the angels see a seeker of knowledge, seeking it properly and desiring the pleasure of Allah – and the rest of his condition is consistent with the quest for knowledge – they spread out their wings for him on his journey and carry him on them, ensuring his safety. He is not barefoot if he is walking and does not get tired. They shorten the long road for him and keep him from suffering the types of harm which so often befall travellers, such as illness, loss of money and getting lost. Something along these lines was discussed in *Āl 'Imrān* when Allah says, *'Allah bears witness that…'* (3:18)

'Imrān ibn Ḥuṣayn related that the Messenger of Allah ﷺ said, 'A group of my Community will continue to know the truth until the Final Hour comes.' Yazīd ibn Hārūn said, 'If they are not the people of *ḥadīth*, I do not know who they are.' This is the position of 'Abd ar-Razzāq in the interpretation of the *āyah*: that they are the people of *ḥadīth*. Ath-Tha'labī mentioned it.

I heard al-Muqri', the grammarian and *ḥadīth* scholar, say about the words of the Prophet ﷺ: 'The people of the West will continue to know the truth until the Final Hour comes' that scholars say that the word *'gharb'* (West) is a noun with various meanings, and it means a large bucket and the place where the sun sets. It is also used for an overflow of tears. So it can mean, 'The people whose tears overflow from fear of Allah will continue to have knowledge of Him and His judgments.' Allah says, *'Only those of His slaves with knowledge fear Allah.'* (35:28)

This interpretation is supported by the words of the Prophet ﷺ in *Ṣaḥīḥ Muslim*: 'If Allah desires good for a person, He gives him understanding of the *dīn*. A group of Muslims will continue to fight for the truth and overcome those far from them until the Day of Rising.'

يَٰٓأَيُّهَا ٱلَّذِينَ ءَامَنُواْ قَٰتِلُواْ ٱلَّذِينَ يَلُونَكُم مِّنَ ٱلۡكُفَّارِ
وَلۡيَجِدُواْ فِيكُمۡ غِلۡظَةٗۚ وَٱعۡلَمُوٓاْ أَنَّ ٱللَّهَ مَعَ ٱلۡمُتَّقِينَ ١٢٣

123 You who believe! fight those of the unbelievers who are near to you and let them find you implacable. Know that Allah is with those who are godfearing.

There is one point of instruction in this. Allah is telling the believers how to carry out *jihād* and to begin with the closest enemy and then the next closest. That is why the Messenger of Allah ﷺ began with the Arabs. When he had done that, he turned to the Byzantines who were in Syria. Al-Ḥasan said, 'This was revealed before the Messenger of Allah ﷺ was commanded to fight the idolaters as a whole and so it is part of the gradual advance of Islam.' Ibn Zayd said, 'What was meant by this *āyah* at the moment of its revelation was the Arabs. When he finished with them, revelation came about the Byzantines and others in the words: *"Fight those who do not believe in Allah."* (9:29)'

It was related from Ibn 'Umar that what was meant were the Persians. It is related that he was asked whether one should begin with the Byzantines or the Persians. He answered, 'The Byzantines." Al-Ḥasan said, 'It is about fighting the Persians and leaving the Byzantines.' Qatādah said, 'The *āyah* has a general meaning about fighting the closest to you and then the next closest.'

The statement of Qatādah is the apparent meaning of the *āyah*. Ibn al-'Arabī preferred that one begin with the Byzantines before the Persians according to Ibn 'Umar for three reasons. One is that they are the People of the Book and the argument against them is more emphasised. The second is that they were closer to them, i.e. to the people of Madīnah. The third is that the land of the Prophets is in their land and so it is more obligatory to deliver it from them. Allah knows best.

'Implacable' (*ghilẓah*) is fierce, strong and zealous. Al-Faḍl related from al-A'mash and 'Āṣim '*ghalẓah*'. Al-Farrā' said that it is the language of the people of the Hijaz, and the Banū Asad read it as *ghilẓah*. The dialect of Tamīm has it as *ghulẓah*.

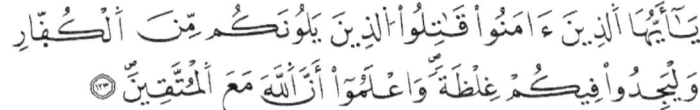

وَإِذَا مَآ أُنزِلَتْ سُورَةٌ فَمِنْهُم مَّن يَقُولُ أَيُّكُمْ زَادَتْهُ
هَٰذِهِۦٓ إِيمَٰنًا فَأَمَّا ٱلَّذِينَ ءَامَنُوا۟ فَزَادَتْهُمْ إِيمَٰنًا وَهُمْ
يَسْتَبْشِرُونَ ﴿١٢٤﴾

124 Each time a *sūrah* is sent down there are some among them who say, 'Which of you has this increased in faith?' As for those who believe, it increases them in faith and they rejoice at it.

'Mā' is connective, and what is meant by '*some among them*' are the hypocrites. Increase and decrease in faith was already discussed in *Sūrat Āl 'Imrān* (3:173) and was already mentioned in the introduction to the book. Al-Ḥasan wrote to 'Umar ibn 'Abd al-'Azīz: 'Faith has *sunnah*s and obligatory elements. If someone has all of them, he has complete faith. If someone does not have all of them he does not have complete faith.' 'Umar ibn 'Abd al-'Azīz said, 'If I live, I will make it clear to you. If I die, I am not eager for your company.' Al-Bukhārī mentioned it. Ibn al-Mubārak said, 'I did not find any alternative to saying that faith increases without refuting the Qur'an.'

وَأَمَّا ٱلَّذِينَ فِى قُلُوبِهِم مَّرَضٌ فَزَادَتْهُمْ رِجْسًا إِلَىٰ رِجْسِهِمْ
وَمَاتُوا۟ وَهُمْ كَٰفِرُونَ ﴿١٢٥﴾

125 But as for those with sickness in their hearts, it adds defilement to their defilement, and they die unbelievers.

'Sickness' here is doubt, uncertainty and hypocrisy. It has already been mentioned (2:10). '*Defilement to their defilement*' is doubt on top of their doubt and unbelief on top of their unbelief. Muqātil said, 'Sin on top of sin.' The meanings are similar.

أَوَلَا يَرَوْنَ أَنَّهُمْ يُفْتَنُونَ فِى كُلِّ عَامٍ مَّرَّةً أَوْ مَرَّتَيْنِ ثُمَّ لَا يَتُوبُونَ
وَلَا هُمْ يَذَّكَّرُونَ ﴿١٢٦﴾

126 Do they not see that they are tried once or twice in every year? But still they do not turn back. They do not pay heed.

Most people read this with *yā'* (*yarawna*) (do they not see) referring to the hypocrites while Ḥamzah and Ya'qūb read it with *tā'* (*tarawna*) (do you not see) reporting about them and addressed to the believers. Al-A'mash reads *'aw lam yaraw* (or do they not see?)'. Ṭalḥah ibn Muṣarraf read '*law tarā* (if only you see)', which is the reading of Ibn Mas'ūd, as addressed to the Messenger of Allah ﷺ.

Aṭ-Ṭabarī said that *'yuftanūna'* means: 'they are tested'. Mujāhid said that they are tried by drought and hardship. Ibn 'Aṭiyyah said that it is by illness and pain, which are the harbingers of death. Qatādah, al-Ḥasan and Mujāhid said that it is by expeditions and *jihād* with the Prophet ﷺ and seeing what Allah has promised of victory. 'Then they do not turn back' at that and do not remember.

وَإِذَا مَآ أُنزِلَتْ سُورَةٌ نَّظَرَ بَعْضُهُمْ إِلَىٰ بَعْضٍ هَلْ يَرَىٰكُم
مِّنْ أَحَدٍ ثُمَّ ٱنصَرَفُوا۟ صَرَفَ ٱللَّهُ قُلُوبَهُم بِأَنَّهُمْ قَوْمٌ لَّا
يَفْقَهُونَ ﴿١٢٧﴾

127 Each time a *sūrah* is sent down, they look at one another, implying, 'Can anyone see you?' Then they turn away. Allah has turned their hearts away because they are people who do not understand.

In the phrase *'Each time a sūrah is sent down,'* the *mā* is connective. What is being referred to are the hypocrites, meaning when they are present with the Messenger while he is reciting the Qur'an, there might be a revelation to him that will disgrace them or one of them. They began to look at one another with fear that their hypocrisy would be confirmed, saying, 'Can anyone see you when you say this who would then convey it to Muḥammad?' That is ignorance on their part about his Prophethood ﷺ and the fact that Allah will acquaint him with whatever He wishes of His Unseen.

It is said that *'naẓara'* in this *āyah* means to report. Aṭ-Ṭabarī related from some of them that *'naẓara'* in this *āyah* is in the position of 'He said'.

Then they turn away.

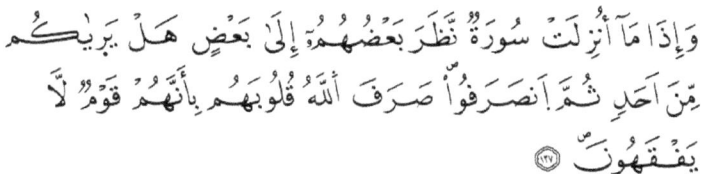

They turn away from the path of guidance. That was when it was clear to them that their secrets were disclosed and hidden things made public, then there must be wonder, stopping and looking. If they had been guided, that would have been a likely moment for them to come to belief. However, they persisted in their unbelief and committed what they did as if they were turning away from that state in which sound investigation and guidance is likely to happen. They did not hear the recitation of the Prophet ﷺ in the manner of someone who reflects and looks into its Signs: *'The worst of beasts in Allah's sight are those who are deaf and dumb and have no intellect.'* (8:22) And: *'Will they not then ponder the Qur'an or are there locks on their hearts?'* (47:24)

Allah has turned their hearts away

This is a supplication against them, implying, 'Say this to them'. It may also be that it speaks about those whose turning away from good was actually their requital for what they had done. It is a statement used as an imprecation, like *'May Allah fight them!'* (9:30) The *bā'* after 'hearts' is connected to 'turned'.

Ibn 'Abbās said that it is disliked to use this verb in reference to the prayer (*inṣarafnā mina'ṣ-ṣalāh*, 'We left the prayer') because some people turned away and so Allah turned their hearts away. Rather one should say, 'We completed (*qaḍaynā*) the prayer.' Aṭ-Ṭabarī has it from him. Ibn al-'Arabī said, 'This is debatable but I do not think that it is sound. The structure of the words is that it is said, "No one says, 'We left (*inṣarafnā*) the prayer.'" It was said about some people: *"Then they turn away. Allah has turned their hearts away."*" Muḥammad ibn 'Abd al-Malik al-Qaysī al-Wā'iẓ reported that he heard Abū al-Faḍl al-Jawharī say, 'We were at a funeral and he said to warn about it, "Turn away, may Allah have mercy on you!" He said, "No one says, 'Turn away (*inṣarafū*).' Allah says to censure some people, *'Then they turn away. Allah has turned their hearts away.'* Rather say, 'Return (*inqalabū* (instead of *inṣarafū*).' Allah Almighty said in praise of some people: *'They returned* (inqalabū) *with blessings and bounty from Allah and no evil touched them.'* (3:174)"'

Allah is saying in this *āyah* that He is the One Who directs the hearts and disposes of them and turns them over and reverses them. This refutes the Qadariyyah who believe that people's hearts are under their own control, as are their limbs, to dispose of as they wish and to decide according to what they want and choose. That is why Mālik said in what Ashhab related from him, 'How clear this is in refuting the Qadariyyah! *"The buildings they have built will not cease to be a bone of contention in their hearts"* (9:110) as well as what He said to Nūḥ: *"None of your people are going to believe except for those who have already believed."* (11:36). This is always the case and will not change or cease to be the case.'

لَقَدْ جَآءَكُمْ رَسُولٌ مِّنَ اَنفُسِكُمْ عَزِيزٌ عَلَيْهِ مَا
عَنِتُّمْ حَرِيصٌ عَلَيْكُم بِالْمُؤْمِنِينَ رَءُوفٌ رَّحِيمٌ ﴿١٢٨﴾ فَإِن تَوَلَّوْاْ
فَقُلْ حَسْبِيَ اللَّهُ لَآ إِلَٰهَ إِلَّا هُوَ عَلَيْهِ تَوَكَّلْتُ وَهُوَ رَبُّ
الْعَرْشِ الْعَظِيمِ ﴿١٢٩﴾

128-129 A Messenger has come to you from among yourselves. Your suffering is distressing to him; he is deeply concerned for you; he is gentle and merciful to the believers. But if they turn away, say, 'Allah is enough for me. There is no god but Him. I have put my trust in Him. He is the Lord of the Mighty Throne.'

According to Ubayy these two *āyah*s were the last *āyah*s of the Qur'an to be revealed. According to Sa'īd ibn Jubayr, the last of the Qur'an to be revealed was: *'Have fear of a Day when you will be returned to Allah.'* (2:281) It is possible that Ubayy means they were last of the Qur'an after the *āyah* in *al-Baqarah* (2:281). Allah knows best.

This is addressed to the Arabs to underline the blessings to them in it, in that the Message has come in their language that they understand and is something that will ennoble them for all time. Az-Zajjāj said, 'It is addressed to the entire world, and it means, "A Messenger of mankind has come to you."' The first is more correct. Ibn 'Abbās said, 'There is no Arab tribe that could not genuinely claim that the Prophet ﷺ was descended from them. So it is as if it is saying: "Company of Arabs! A Messenger from the descendants of Ismā'īl has come to you."' The second view is more generally substantiated in that he is a human being like themselves so they understand him and feel secure with him.

from among yourselves.

This is praise for the lineage of the Prophet ﷺ, saying that he is a genuine and pure Arab. We find in *Ṣaḥīḥ Muslim* that Wāthilah ibn al-Asqa' says that he heard the Messenger of Allah ﷺ say, 'Allah chose Kinānah from the sons of Ismā'īl, and He chose Quraysh from Kinānah, and He chose the Banū Hāshim from Quraysh and He chose me from the Banū Hāshim.' It is related that he ﷺ said, 'I came from marriage, not fornication.' It means that his lineage back to Ādam ﷺ is only through lawful marriage, never fornication.

'Abdullāh ibn Qusayt al-Makkī related *'min anfasikum'* from *nafāsah*. It is related from the Prophet ﷺ and from Fāṭimah. It means: 'A Messenger has come to you from the noblest and best of you.' It is as you call a thing 'precious' (*nafīs*) when it is desirable. It is said that it means that he is the greatest of you in obedience.

Your suffering is distressing to him;

Your hardship distresses him. *'Anat* means hardship. A hill is described as *'anūt* when it is difficult and dangerous. Ibn al-Anbārī said, 'The root of *ta'annut* is making things difficult. When the Arabs use the verb in relation to a person, it means that someone is causing difficulties to someone and obliging him to do something which is hard for him to do.' It was mentioned in *al-Baqarah* (2:221).

The *mā* has the nature of a verbal noun. It is the inceptive and '*distressing*' is the predicate. It is also possible that *'mā 'anittum'* is the subject of '*distressing*' and 'distressing' describes the Messenger. That is more correct. It is the same with '*he is deeply concerned with you*'. Similarly '*gentle and merciful*' is nominative as an adjective. Al-Farrā' said, 'If it is recited as *"azīzan'* and with '*gentle and merciful*' also in the accusative for the adverbial *ḥāl*, that is permitted.

Abū Ja'far an-Naḥḥās said, 'The best of what is said about its meaning, which concords with Arab linguistic usage, is what Aḥmad ibn Muḥammad al-Azdī related from 'Abdullāh ibn Muḥammad al-Khuzā'ī who heard 'Amr ibn 'Alī say that he heard 'Abdullāh ibn Dāwūd al-Khuraybī say about Allah's words: *'Your suffering is distressing to him'*: 'It is distressing to him that you might enter the Fire and he is eager for you to enter the Garden.' It is said that the words '*he is deeply concerned for you;*' mean that he is eager for you to believe. Al-Farrā' said: 'It means he wants as few of you as possible to enter the Fire.' *Ḥarīs* in relation to a thing is to want as little of it as possible to be lost and destroyed.

He is gentle and merciful to the believers.

The adjective *ra'ūf* means possessing extreme kindness and compassion. This was already fully discussed in *al-Baqarah* (2:143). Al-Ḥusayn ibn al-Faḍl said, 'Allah did not combine two of His names to describe any of His Prophets except the Prophet Muḥammad ﷺ. Allah says: *'He is gentle (ra'ūf) and merciful (raḥīm) to the believers'* and He says: *'Allah is All-Gentle (ra'ūf), Most Merciful (raḥīm) to mankind.'* (1:143)

'Abd al-'Azīz ibn Yaḥyā said: 'What this *āyah* says is: 'A Messenger has come to you from among yourselves, distressed and deeply concerned for the believers, gentle, merciful. Your suffering is distressing to him and he is only concerned with your affairs. He undertakes to intercede for you, so do not be concerned with what you suffer in holding to his *Sunnah*. The only thing he wants is for you to enter the Garden.'

But if they turn away, say, 'Allah is enough for me.'

It means: If the unbelievers turn away, Muḥammad, after these blessings which Allah has bestowed on them, *say, 'Allah is enough for me.'*

There is no god but Him. I have put my trust in Him.

This means 'I have relied on Him and entrusted all my affairs to Him.'

He is the Lord of the Mighty Throne.

The Throne is singled out for mention because it is the greatest of created things and includes everything below it. Most recite *'al-'aẓīmi'* in the genitive describing the Throne. It is also recited in the nominative *(al-'aẓīmu)* to describe the Lord. That is related from Ibn Kathīr and it is the reading of Ibn Muḥayṣin.

We find in the book of Abū Dāwūd that Abū ad-Dardā' said, 'If someone says seven times in the morning and evening: "*Allah is enough for me. There is no god but Him. I have put my trust in Him. He is the Lord of the Mighty Throne,*" Allah will relieve him of what worries him, whether he is truthful or lying in what he says.' We find in *Nawādir al-Uṣūl* that Buraydah said that the Messenger of Allah ﷺ said, 'If someone says ten phrases after every prayer, he will find them adequate and sufficient with Allah: five are for this world and five for the Next World. They are: "Allah is enough for me regarding my *dīn*;" "Allah is enough for me regarding my worldly portion;" "Allah is enough for me regarding what concerns me;" "Allah is enough for me against anyone who transgresses against me;" "Allah is enough for me against anyone who envies me;" "Allah is enough for me against anyone who plots evil against me;" "Allah is enough for me regarding my death;" "Allah is enough for regarding the questioning in the grave;" "Allah is enough for me at the Balance;" "Allah is enough for me at the *Ṣirāṭ*;" "Allah is enough for me. There is no god but Him. I have put my trust in Him and to Him I repent."'

An-Naqqāsh related that Ubayy ibn Ka'b said, 'The last of the Qur'an to come from Allah are these two *āyahs*, "*A Messenger has come to you from among yourselves...*" to the end of the *sūrah*. We have already talked about that. Yūsuf ibn Mihrān related from Ibn 'Abbās that the last of the Qur'an to be revealed was this. Al-Māwardī mentioned it. We mentioned something different from Ibn 'Abbās about *al-Baqarah* which is sounder. Muqātil said that it was revealed in Makkah. This is unlikely because the *sūrah* is Madinan. Allah knows best.

Yaḥyā ibn Ja'dah said, "Umar ibn al-Khattāb did not confirm an *āyah* in the written copy of the Qur'an until two men had testified to it. A man of the *Anṣār* brought the end of at-*Tawbah*, "*A Messenger as come to from among yourselves...*" *and* 'Umar said, "By Allah, I will not ask you for evidence for these two *āyahs*. That is how the Prophet ﷺ was." He confirmed them.' Our scholars said, 'His name was Khuzaymah ibn Thābit and 'Umar confirmed them based on his testimony alone since the proof was established of its soundness in the quality of the Prophet ﷺ. It was a situation in which the need for another witness was spared as opposed to the *āyah* of *al-Aḥzāb* (33:23) Praise be to Allah.

10. Sūrah Yūnus – Jonah

Sūrat Yūnus is a Makkan *sūrah* according to al-Ḥasan, 'Ikrimah, 'Aṭā' and Jābir. Ibn 'Abbās said 'except for three *āyahs*', from *'If you are in doubt'* (10:94) to the end. Muqātil said that it is Makkan except for two *āyahs*: *'If you are in doubt'* (10:94) which were revealed in Madīnah. Al-Kalbī said except for *āyah* 40 which was revealed in Madīnah about the Jews. Another group said that the first forty *āyahs* were revealed in Makkah and the rest in Madīnah.

الٓر تِلْكَ ءَايَٰتُ ٱلْكِتَٰبِ ٱلْحَكِيمِ ①

Alif Lām Rā'. Those are the Signs of the Wise Book.

Alif Lām Rā'

An-Nāḥḥās said, 'Abū Ja'far Aḥmad ibn Shu'ayb ibn 'Alī ibn al-Ḥusayn ibn Ḥurayth related from his father from Yazīd that 'Ikrimah related to him from Ibn 'Abbās: "*Alif, Lām, Rā', Ḥā, Mīm* and *Nūn* are letters of *ar-Raḥmān* which are separated." I related that to al-A'mash and he said, "You have knowledge of these things and do not inform me?"' Ibn 'Abbās also said, *'Alif Lām Rā'* is: "I am Allah. I see (*anā Allāh arā*)."' An-Naḥḥās said, 'I saw that Abū Isḥāq inclined to this view because Sībawayh related the like of it from the Arabs.' He quoted:

Good things are by good, but evil is not.
I do not intend evil unless you wish it.

Al-Ḥasan and 'Ikrimah said that *'Alif Lām Rā'* is an oath. Sa'īd said that Qatādah said that it is the name of the *sūrah*. He said, 'That is the case with every use of the letters at the beginning of the *sūrahs* in the Qur'an.' Mujāhid said that they are the openings of *sūrahs*. Muḥammad ibn Yazīd said, 'It is notification and that is the case with other isolated letters.' *Alif Lām Rā'* is read without *imālah*. And it is read with *imālah* so that it will not resemble *mā* and *lā* of the particles.

Those are the Signs of the Wise Book.

This is an inceptive and predicate. It means those which We mentioned are the Signs of the Wise Book. Mujāhid and Qatādah said that it is a reference to the Torah and Gospel and earlier Books and '*those*' indicates something absent which is in the feminine. It is said that '*those*' means 'these', i.e. 'these are the *āyahs* of the Wise Qur'an.' We see this in poetry as well. [POEM] What is meant here is the Qur'an. That is more appropriate and correct because earlier books were not mentioned and because the adjective '*Wise*' is used to describe the Qur'an. The evidence for that is in the words of the Almighty: '*Alif Lām Rā'. A Book whose āyahs are perfectly constructed.*' (11:1) This was discussed at the beginning of *al-Baqarah* (2:2).

The word '*Wise*' (*hakīm*) means that which renders judgement regarding the lawful and unlawful, and judges between people with the truth. The form *fa'īl* has the meaning of an active participle and the evidence is the words of the Almighty: '*With them He sent down the Book with truth, to decide between people regarding their differences.*' (2:213) It is also said that *hakīm* means that which is determined, meaning that in it Allah determines that there should be justice, doing good, and giving to relatives, and in it He determines that outrage and the objectionable should be forbidden, and He determines the Garden for those who obey Him and the Fire for those who disobey Him. So the form *fa'īl* has the meaning of the passive participle. Al-Ḥasan and others said that. Muqātil says that it is fortified against falsehood. There is no lying or disagreement in it and *fa'īl* has the meaning of *maf'al*. [POEM]

أَكَانَ لِلنَّاسِ عَجَبًا أَنْ أَوْحَيْنَآ إِلَىٰ رَجُلٍ مِّنْهُمْ أَنْ أَنذِرِ ٱلنَّاسَ وَبَشِّرِ
ٱلَّذِينَ ءَامَنُوٓا۟ أَنَّ لَهُمْ قَدَمَ صِدْقٍ عِندَ رَبِّهِمْ قَالَ ٱلْكَٰفِرُونَ إِنَّ هَٰذَا
لَسِحْرٌ مُّبِينٌ ②

2 Do people find it so surprising that We should reveal to a man among them: 'Warn mankind and give good news to those who believe that they are on a sure footing with their Lord'? The unbelievers say, 'This is downright magic!'

Do people find it so surprising that We should reveal to a man among them:

This is a question which implies confirmation and rebuke. The word '*surprising*' is the predicate of *kāna* and its noun is '*that We should reveal*'. It is in the position of the nominative implying, 'Is Our granting Revelation surprising to people?'

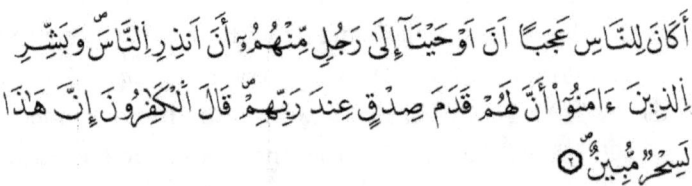

The reading of 'Abdullāh is *'ajab* as the noun of *kāna* and the predicate is 'that We should reveal.' *'To a man among them'* is recited also as *rajl* (instead of *rajul*).

The reason for the revelation of the *āyah*, according to Ibn 'Abbās, is that when Muḥammad ﷺ was sent, the unbelievers said, 'Allah is too great to have sent a human being as a Messenger.' They said, 'Did Allah find no one else to send except the orphan of Abū Ṭālib?' So this was revealed and the noun *'mankind'* here means the people of Makkah. It is said that they were amazed by the mention of resurrection.

Warn mankind and give good news to those who believe

The phrase '*Warn mankind and give good news to those who believe*' is in the position of the accusative by the omission of the genitive (*bi-an*). That is also the case with the phrase *'that they are on a sure footing with their Lord.'* The meaning of warning, good news and other things in this *āyah* were already mentioned (2:6&25). There is disagreement about the meaning of *'sure footing'* (*qadama ṣidqin*). Ibn 'Abbās said that 'a sure footing' is a secure station. His evidence is the words of the Almighty: *'Say, "My Lord, make my entry secure."'* (17:80) He also said that it is a good reward after the good actions they sent ahead. He also said that it means the happiness already written for them [on the Preserved Tablet]. Mujāhid also said that. Az-Zajjāj said that it is a high degree. Dhū ar-Rummah said:

> You have a footing such that people do not deny that
> in addition to high lineage it overflows the sea.

Qatādah said that it is a footing of truthfulness. Ar-Rabī' said that it is the reward for truthfulness. 'Aṭā' said that it is a station of truthfulness. It is sincere belief. It is said that it is the supplication of the angels. It is said that it is a righteous child they send ahead. Al-Māwardī said that it is when the sincere obedience coincides with sincere reward.

Al-Ḥasan and Qatādah said that it refers to Muḥammad ﷺ. He is the obeyed intercessor who goes before them as he said, 'I am your forerunner to the Basin.' He ﷺ was asked and said, 'It refers to my intercession by which you seek mediation with your Lord by me.' At-Tirmidhī al-Ḥakīm said, 'Allah put him ﷺ forward in the Praiseworthy Station.' Al-Ḥasan also said, 'Their calamity in [the loss of] the Prophet ﷺ.' 'Abd al-'Azīz ibn Yaḥyā said, ' The meaning of "*a sure footing*" is in the words of the Almighty: "*Those for whom the Best from Us was preordained.*" (31:101)' Muqātil said that they are actions they sent ahead. Aṭ-Ṭabarī preferred it. Al-Waḍḍāḥ said:

Pray to the Master of the Throne and take a footing by which
you will be saved from slipping on the Day of stumbling and slipping.

It is said that it is Allah putting this community first in the gathering from the graves in entering the Garden as he said, 'We are the last but will be the foremost on the Day of Rising being judged before all the others.'

Its reality is that it alludes to striving in righteous actions, and it is alluded to by the word 'foot' as giving blessing is alluded to by the hand and praise to the tongue. Ḥassan composed:

We have the upper foot over you
and we followed the first of us obeying Allah.

He means being the first to sincerely obey. Allah knows best. Abū 'Ubaydah and al-Kisā'ī said, 'Everyone who is the first to good or evil is called "a foot" by the Arabs. One says, "He had a foot in Islam, and he has a foot of truthfulness, or a foot in good or evil."' *Qadam* is feminine although it can be masculine. Ibn al-A'rābī said, 'The foot is precedence in honour.' Al-'Ajjāj said:

The Banū al-'Awwām slipped from the Banū 'l-Ḥakam, and
left the kingdom to the kingdom of those with precedence (*qadam*).

We find in *aṣ-Ṣiḥāḥ* that the Prophet ﷺ said, 'I have five names. I am Muḥammad and Aḥmad, and I am al-Māḥī, and by me Allah effaces the unbelief. I am al-Ḥāshir and people will be gathered at my foot (*qadam*). And I am al-'Āqib,' i.e. the last of the Prophets as the Almighty says, *'The seal of the Prophets.'* (33:40)

downright magic

Ibn Muḥayṣin, Ibn Kathīr, the Kufans, 'Āṣim, Ḥamzah, al-Kisā'ī, Khalaf, and al-A'mash recite *'sāḥir,'* describing the Messenger of Allah ﷺ while the rest recited *'siḥr'* to describe the Qur'an. Magic was already discussed in *al-Baqarah* (2:102).

إِنَّ رَبَّكُمُ ٱللَّهُ ٱلَّذِى خَلَقَ ٱلسَّمَٰوَٰتِ وَٱلْأَرْضَ فِى سِتَّةِ أَيَّامٍ ثُمَّ ٱسْتَوَىٰ عَلَى
ٱلْعَرْشِ يُدَبِّرُ ٱلْأَمْرَ مَا مِن شَفِيعٍ إِلَّا مِنۢ بَعْدِ إِذْنِهِۦ ذَٰلِكُمُ ٱللَّهُ رَبُّكُمْ
فَٱعْبُدُوهُ أَفَلَا تَذَكَّرُونَ ③

3 Your Lord is Allah, Who created the heavens and the earth in six days and then established Himself firmly on the Throne. He directs the whole affair. No one can intercede except with His

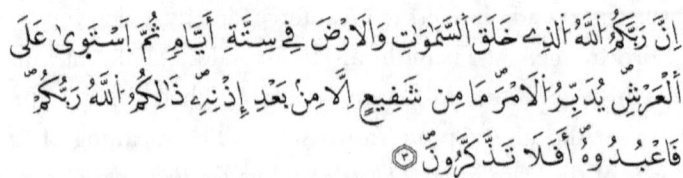

permission. That is Allah your Lord, so worship Him. Will you not pay heed?

'Your Lord is Allah, Who created...' was spoken about in *al-A'rāf* (7:54).

He directs the whole affair.

Mujāhid said, 'He alone decrees and determines.' Ibn 'Abbās said, 'No one shares with Him in the management of His creation.' It is said that He brings about the business. It is said that He sends it down. It is said that He commands it and carries it out. The meanings are similar. Jibrīl is in charge of revelation, Mīkā'īl in charge of rain, Isrāfīl in charge of the Horn, and 'Azrā'īl in charge of taking souls. Its reality is that he put down matters in their ranks according to the determinations of their ends. Direction or management (*tadbīr*) is derived from the root *dubur*. *Amr* is a generic term for all affairs.

The words *'No one can intercede'* are in the nominative and mean that there is no intercessor *'except with His permission.'* The meaning of intercession was mentioned in *al-Baqarah* (2:255). No one, Prophet or anyone else, intercedes except with the permission of the Almighty. This refutes the unbelievers who say about what they worship other than Allah: *'These are our intercessors with Allah.'* (10:18) Allah informed them that no one can intercede for anyone else except with His permission, so how could idols lacking in sentience possibly intercede?

That is Allah your Lord, so worship Him.

This means: 'He is the One Who did these things in creating the heavens and the earth. He is your Lord. You have no Lord but Him.' *'Worship Him'* means proclaim Him one and be sincere in your worship. *'Will you not pay heed?'* O creatures, will you not use this as evidence of Him?

إِلَيْهِ مَرْجِعُكُمْ جَمِيعًا وَعْدَ ٱللَّهِ حَقًّا إِنَّهُۥ يَبْدَؤُا۟ ٱلْخَلْقَ ثُمَّ يُعِيدُهُۥ لِيَجْزِىَ
ٱلَّذِينَ ءَامَنُوا۟ وَعَمِلُوا۟ ٱلصَّٰلِحَٰتِ بِٱلْقِسْطِ وَٱلَّذِينَ كَفَرُوا۟ لَهُمْ شَرَابٌ
مِّنْ حَمِيمٍ وَعَذَابٌ أَلِيمٌۢ بِمَا كَانُوا۟ يَكْفُرُونَ ﴿٤﴾

4 Each and every one of you will return to Him. Allah's promise is true. He brings creation out of nothing and then regenerates it so that He can repay with justice those who believed and did right actions. Those who disbelieved will have scalding water to drink and a painful punishment because of their unbelief.

The verb *'you will return to Him'* is in the nominative by the inceptive. *'Each and every one'* is in the accusative for the adverbial *ḥāl*. Returning to Allah is returning to His repayment of you.

Allah's promise is true.

Allah's promise of that will come about and it is true without dispute. Ibrāhīm ibn Abī 'Ablah recited *'ḥaqqun'* as a new sentence.

He brings creation out of nothing and then regenerates it

'He brings creation' from the earth and then returns it back to it. Mujāhid said, 'He makes them grow and then makes them die and then brings them to life for the Resurrection, or produces them from water and then changes them from state to state.' Yazīd ibn al-Qa'qā' recited *'annahu'*, and *anna* is in the accusative, meaning 'He promises you that He originates creation.' It is possible that it implies: 'He originates creation' as is said, 'At Your service. All praise and blessing is Yours.' It is better with a *kasrah*. Al-Farrā' said that *an* is in the nominative and so it is a noun. Aḥmad ibn Yaḥyā said, 'It implies: "It is true that He originated creation."'

Those who disbelieved will have scalding water to drink

Scalding water is extremely hot water. *Ḥamīmah* is the same. The verb *ḥamma* is to heat water after which it is *ḥamīm*, heated. The form *fa'īl* denotes the passive. The Arabs call anything which is heated is *ḥamīm*.

a painful punishment

A *painful punishment* is one whose pain reaches their hearts. Most of Quraysh acknowledged that Allah was their Creator and this is used as an argument against them and He is saying, 'The One Who is able to initiate a thing is also able to regenerate it after it is gone or after its constituents are broken up.'

هُوَ ٱلَّذِے جَعَلَ ٱلشَّمْسَ ضِيَآءً وَٱلْقَمَرَ نُورًا وَقَدَّرَهُۥ مَنَازِلَ لِتَعْلَمُواْ عَدَدَ
ٱلسِّنِينَ وَٱلْحِسَابَ مَا خَلَقَ ٱللَّهُ ذَٰلِكَ إِلَّا بِٱلْحَقِّ نُفَصِّلُ ٱلْآيَٰتِ لِقَوْمٍ
يَعْلَمُونَ ٥

5 It is He who appointed the sun to give radiance, and the moon to give light, assigning it phases so you would know the number of years and the reckoning of time. Allah did not create these things except with truth. We make the Signs clear for people who know.

It is He who appointed the sun to give radiance, and the moon to give light,

The verb has two objects [sun and moon]. He made the sun give radiance or be intrinsically luminous. *Ḍiyā'* is not feminine because it is a verbal noun. The phrase *'and the moon to give light'* is added, meaning the moon gives light or has light. So *ḍiyā'* is what illuminates things and *nūr* is an apparent light which can disappear because it is from *nār* (fire) and has the same root. *Ḍiyā'* is the plural of *ḍaw'* as *siyāṭ* is the plural of *sawṭ* and *ḥiyāḍ* is the plural of *ḥawḍ*. Qunbul recited *ḍi'ā'an* from Ibn Kathīr with a *hamzah* on the *yā'* and this is not correct because its *yā'* was a *wāw* with a *fatḥah* which is the root of the verb. Its root is *ḍaw'* and it has been changed and made a *yā'* as happens in the words *ṣiyām* and *qiyām*. Al-Mahdawī said, 'Whoever recites *ḍi'ā'an* with a *hamzah* reverses and puts the *hamzah* which is after the *alif* before it and then it becomes *ḍi'āyan* and then changes the *yā'* into a *hamzah* since it is redundant after the *alif*. It is said that the sun and moon give light and their fronts are for the people of the seven heavens and backs are for the people of the seven earths.

assigning it phases

This means that the moon has phases (*manāzil*) or phases are calculated for it. It is said that it means Allah assigned both of them and only one is mentioned for the sake of brevity as when He says: *'But when they see a chance of trade or entertainment they scatter off to it'* (62:11) or as the poem has it:

> We are content with what we have and you have
> what you have while opinions differ.

It is said that this is speaking about the moon alone since the months are calculated by it on the basis of which transactions and other things are carried out as was mentioned in *al-Baqarah* (2:189). We read in *Sūrah Yāsin*: *'We have decreed set phases for the moon,'* (36:39) This accords with the days of the months. There are twenty-eight phases and two days for shortening and waning. This will be explained.

so that you would know the number of years and the reckoning of time

Know the number of years and the reckoning of months. Ibn 'Abbās said, 'If Allah had made two suns: one for the day and one for the night, there would be neither darkness nor night in them and the number of years and reckoning of months would not be known.' The singular of *sinīn* (years) is *sannah*. Some Arabs used *sanawāt* for the plural while some use *sanahāt*. The diminutive is *sunayyah* and *sunayhah*.

Allah did not create these things except with truth.

By the creation of that Allah only desired wisdom and what is correct and to display His work and wisdom and to indicate His power and knowledge, and to repay every soul for what it has earned. This is the truth.

We make the Signs clear for people who know.

Tafṣīl in respect of Signs is to make them clear so as to indicate His power since He singled out the night for darkness and the day for light without any merit or necessity for them, and so this is a proof that it is by the will of Someone. Ibn Kathīr, Abū 'Amr and Ya'qūb recited *yufaṣṣilu* and Abū 'Ubayd and Abū Ḥātim preferred it because He said, *'Allah did not create'* and after it *'What Allah created in the heavens…'* and so it follows it. Ibn as-Sumayfa' recited *tufaṣṣalu* with 'Signs' in the nominative. The rest recite *nufaṣṣilu* with the Divine 'We'.

إِنَّ فِي اخْتِلَافِ اللَّيْلِ وَالنَّهَارِ وَمَا خَلَقَ اللَّهُ فِي السَّمَاوَاتِ وَالْأَرْضِ لَآيَاتٍ
لِّقَوْمٍ يَتَّقُونَ ۝٦

6 In the alternation of night and day and what Allah has created in the heavens and the earth there are Signs for people who are godfearing.

This was already mentioned in *al-Baqarah* (2:164) and elsewhere. It is said that the reason for its revelation was that the people of Makkah asked for a sign and the reply was that they should reflect on what Allah has fashioned and examine that. Ibn 'Abbās said that. A '*people who are godfearing*' means that they fear *shirk*. As for someone who is an idolater and does not follow the evidence, it is not a sign for him.

إِنَّ الَّذِينَ لَا يَرْجُونَ لِقَاءَنَا وَرَضُوا بِالْحَيَاةِ الدُّنْيَا وَاطْمَأَنُّوا بِهَا وَالَّذِينَ هُمْ
عَنْ آيَاتِنَا غَافِلُونَ ۝٧ أُولَٰئِكَ مَأْوَاهُمُ النَّارُ بِمَا كَانُوا يَكْسِبُونَ ۝٨

7-8 As for those who do not expect to meet Us and are content with the life of this world and at rest in it, and those who are heedless of Our Signs, their shelter will be the Fire because of what they earned.

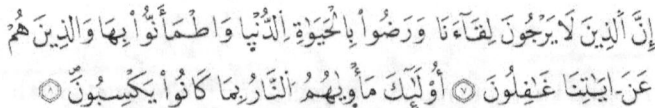

As for those who do not expect to meet Us

'*Yarjūna*' (expect) can mean 'fear' as a poet said:

If a bee stings him, he does not fear (*yarjū*) its sting,
contending with it in a house with worker-bees.

It is also said that it means 'desire' as another said:

Do the Banū Marwān desire (*yarjū*) to listen and obey me?
My people are Tamīm, and the desert is beyond.

Thus *rajā'* can mean both fear and desire and so it means: they do not fear the punishment or hope for a reward. He made meeting the punishment and reward tantamount to meeting Allah, showing respect for them both. It is said that the meeting is literal, which is seeing, implying 'they do not desire to see Us.' Some scholars say that *rajā'* only means fear when there is denial, as in Allah's words: '*Why do you not hope for honour from Allah?*' (71:14) Some say that whenever it is used, its context indicates its meaning.

content with the life of this world and at rest in it

They are content with this world rather than the Next World and they work for this world. The expression '*at rest in it*' means that they are happy with it and rely on it. The root of *iṭma'anna* is *ṭa'mana, ṭuma'nīnah.* Its *mīm* was brought forward and a *nūn* was added and an *alif waṣl*. Al-Ghaznawī mentioned it.

Those who are heedless of Our signs

'Our Signs' are 'Our proofs' which they take no note of and do not reflect on. '*Their shelter*' is their dwelling and where they will stay. What they earned is unbelief and denial.

إِنَّ ٱلَّذِينَ ءَامَنُوا۟ وَعَمِلُوا۟ ٱلصَّٰلِحَٰتِ يَهْدِيهِمْ رَبُّهُم بِإِيمَٰنِهِمْ ۖ تَجْرِى
مِن تَحْتِهِمُ ٱلْأَنْهَٰرُ فِى جَنَّٰتِ ٱلنَّعِيمِ ۝٩

9 But as for those who believe and do right actions, their Lord will guide them by their faith. Rivers will flow under them in Gardens of Delight.

But as for those who believe and do right actions, their Lord will guide them by their faith.

The verb '*believe*' means affirm. The phrase '*their Lord will guide them by their faith*' implies that their Lord will increase them in guidance as He says elsewhere: '*He increases in guidance those who are already guided.*' (47:17) It is said that their Lord will guide them by their faith to a place under which rivers will flow. Abū Rawq said, 'He will guide them by their faith to the Garden.' 'Aṭiyyah said that it means He will reward and repay them.

Mujāhid said that '*their Lord will guide them by their faith*' means by light on the *Ṣirāṭ* to the Garden. He will give them a light to walk by. It is related that the Prophet ﷺ said, 'The believer's actions will meet him in the most beautiful form and be friendly to him and guide him. The unbeliever's actions will meet him in the ugliest form and make him alienated and misguide him.' This is the meaning of the *ḥadīth*. Ibn Jurayj said, 'He makes their actions a guide for them.' Al-Ḥasan said that '*guide them*' means 'show mercy to them.

Rivers will flow under them

It is said that there is a *wāw* elided in the words before 'flow', so it means: 'and' rivers will flow under their gardens, or under their seats. This is better in terms of relaxation and relief.

دَعْوَىٰهُمْ فِيهَا سُبْحَٰنَكَ ٱللَّهُمَّ وَتَحِيَّتُهُمْ فِيهَا سَلَٰمٌ ۚ وَءَاخِرُ
دَعْوَىٰهُمْ أَنِ ٱلْحَمْدُ لِلَّهِ رَبِّ ٱلْعَٰلَمِينَ ١٠

10 Their call there is: 'Glory be to You, O Allah!' Their greeting there is: 'Peace!' The end of their call is: 'Praise be to Allah, the Lord of all the worlds!'

Their call there is: 'Glory be to You, O Allah!'

Their call in the Garden is this. *Da'wā* is the verbal noun of *da'ā* as *shakwā* is the verbal noun of *shakā*. It means: their call in the Garden is: 'Glory be to You, O Allah.' It is said that when they want to ask for something, they produce the request in an expression of glorification and end it with praise. It is said that they call for servants to bring them what they wish and then glorify. It is said that the call means wishing. Allah says: '*You will have there everything you demand*' (41:31), in other words what you wish for. Allah knows best.

Their greeting there is: 'Peace!'

The greeting to them is from Allah or from the angel or it is to one another. This was discussed adequately in *an-Nisā'* (4:86). Praise be to Allah.

The end of their call is: 'Praise be to Allah, the Lord of all the worlds!'

There are four points in this. The first is that it is said that when a bird passes by them in the Garden and they desire it, they say, 'Glory be to You, O Allah!' and an angel brings what they desire and they eat it and praise Allah. Their request is in the form of glorification and it ends with praise.

Abū 'Ubayd only related *an* and the nominative after it. He said, 'We think that they chose this and differentiated between it and the words of the Almighty: *"Indeed (anna) the curse of Allah"* and: *"Indeed (anna) the anger of Allah"* because they want to recount when it is said, *"Praise be to Allah."*' An-Naḥḥās said, 'The position of al-Khalīl and Sībawayh is that this '*an*' is a lightened form. It means: "It is praise be to Allah."' Muḥammad ibn Yazīd said, 'It is permitted that "*Praise be to Allah*" is given the light form *an* when the action is heavy. The nominative is closer to the form.' An-Naḥḥās said, 'Abū Ḥātim related that Bilāl ibn Abī Burdah recited "*anna*".' This is the reading of Ibn Muḥayṣin. Al-Ghaznawī related it because it is related from him.

Saying '*Subḥānallāh,*' '*al-ḥamdu lillāh*' and '*lā ilaha illā'llāh*' can be called supplication. Muslim and al-Bukhārī related from Ibn 'Abbās that the Prophet ﷺ used to say in times of distress, 'There is no god but Allah, the Immense, the Forbearing. There is no god but Allah, the Lord of the Immense Throne. There is no god but Allah, the Lord of the heavens and Lord of the earth and Lord of the Noble Throne.' Aṭ-Ṭabarī said, 'The early generations used to use this supplication and they called it "the supplication of distress".' Ibn 'Uyaynah was asked about this and said, 'I know that Allah Almighty says, "When praising Me distracts My servant from asking Me, I give him better than what I give those who ask."' That which will end any dispute about it is that this is called supplication, even though it does not contain the meaning of supplication as a prayer requesting something. It is exaltation of Allah and praising him as an-Nasā'ī related from Sa'd ibn Abī Waqqāṣ that the Messenger of Allah ﷺ said, 'The supplication of Dhu-n-Nūn which he made in the belly of the Fish was: "*There is no god but You. Glory be to You. I am one of the wrongdoers.*" No Muslim uses it in any situation without being answered.'

Part of the Sunnah is that you begin by naming Allah when you eat and drink and praise Him when you finish to imitate the people of the Garden. We find in *Ṣaḥīḥ Muslim* from Anas ibn Mālik that the Messenger of Allah ﷺ said, 'Allah is pleased for a servant to eat and praise Him for it or drink and praise Him for it.' It is recommended for someone making supplication to say at the end of his supplication what the people of the Garden say: '*the end of their call is, "Praise be to Allah, the Lord of all the worlds."*' It is good to recite the end of *aṣ-Ṣāffāt*. It contains disconnection of the Creator from what is ascribed to Him, greeting the Messengers, and ends with praise be to Allah, the Lord of the Worlds.

وَلَوْ يُعَجِّلُ ٱللَّهُ لِلنَّاسِ ٱلشَّرَّ ٱسْتِعْجَالَهُم بِٱلْخَيْرِ لَقُضِىَ إِلَيْهِمْ أَجَلُهُمْ
فَنَذَرُ ٱلَّذِينَ لَا يَرْجُونَ لِقَآءَنَا فِى طُغْيَٰنِهِمْ يَعْمَهُونَ ۝١١

11 If Allah were to hasten evil for people the way they try to hasten good, their term would already have been completed for them. We abandon those who do not expect to meet Us to wander blindly in their excessive insolence.

If Allah were to hasten evil for people

It is said that it means: if Allah were to hasten the punishment for people in the same way that they ask for the reward and good to be hastened, they would have died because in this world they have been created weak; but they will not be like that on the Day of Rising because on the Day of Rising they will be created to go on forever. It is said that it means: if Allah were to deal with people by responding when they ask for something evil as they want Him to respond to them when they ask for good, then He would have destroyed them. That is the meaning of: '*their term would already have been completed for them.*' It is said that it is specifically about unbelievers and so it means: If Allah were to hasten the punishment of unbelievers for their unbelief as He hastens the good in this world for them in the form of wealth and children, He would have hastened their predestined death so as to hasten for them the punishment of the Next World. Ibn Isḥāq said that.

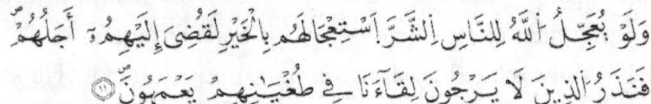

Muqātil said, 'It refers to the statement of an-Naḍr ibn al-Ḥārith: "O Allah, if this is the truth from You, then rain down stones from heaven on us." If He had hastened this for them, they would have been destroyed.' Mujāhid said, 'It was revealed about a man who prayed against himself or his property or children when he was angry, "O Allah, destroy them! O Allah, do not bless him in it. Curse him!" or the like. If they had been granted that in the same way that good is granted, their lives would have ended.' The *āyah* was revealed to censure the blameworthy behaviour of some people who pray for good and want the answer to be hastened. Sometimes that impels them to bad character in calling for evil. If it had been hastened for them, they would have been destroyed.

They disagree about the response to this supplication. It is related that the Prophet ﷺ said, 'I have asked Allah not to answer the imprecation of someone against someone he loves.' Shahr ibn Ḥawshab said, 'I read in a book that Allah Almighty says to the guardian angels of a person: "Do not record anything against My slave when he is exasperated" out of kindness on the part of Allah Almighty to him.'

One of them said that such a supplication might be answered. He cited as evidence the *ḥadīth* of Jābir which Muslim related at the end of his *Ṣaḥīḥ*. Jābir said, 'We were travelling with the Messenger of Allah ﷺ on the expedition of the Valley of Buwāṭ when he was in pursuit of al-Majdī ibn 'Amr al-Juhanī. Five, six and seven of us took turns on a water-camel. When it was the turn of an Anṣārī man to ride the camel, he made it kneel and mounted it. Then he tried to make it get up, and it delayed somewhat. He said to it, "Pah! May Allah curse you!" The Messenger of Allah ﷺ asked, 'Who cursed his camel?" "I did, Messenger of Allah," he answered. He said, "Dismount from it. Let us not have a cursed one in our company. Do not invoke against yourselves. Do not invoke against your children. Do not invoke against your property. It may coincide with a moment in which Allah will give what is asked for and so your invocation will be answered."' We find in other than the book of Muslim that the Prophet ﷺ was on a journey and a man cursed his she-camel and he said, 'Where is the one who cursed the she-camel?' A man said, 'It was me, Messenger of Allah.' He said, 'Send it away from you. You have been answered in it.' Al-Ḥulaymī mentioned it in *Minhāj ad-dīn*. 'Pah!' is related as *sha'* and *sa'*. It is a rebuke to a camel, meaning 'Go!'

If Allah were to hasten

Scholars say that hastening (*ta'jīl*) is from Allah and seeking haste (*isti'jāl*) is from His slave. Abū 'Alī said, 'They are both from Allah,' and there is some elision in the words, meaning 'if Allah were to hasten evil for people in the same way that people ask for good to be hastened...' Then he elided 'hastening' and put its attribute in its place and elided the attribute and put the *muḍāf ilayhi* in its place. This is the position of al-Khalīl and Sībawayh. According to the position of al-Akhfash and al-Farrā' it is like Form X. Then the *kāf* is elided and it is in the accusative. Al-Farrā' said, 'It is as you might say, 'You hit Zayd with your hitting," meaning you hit him.' Ibn 'Āmir recited, '*lā qaḍā ilayhim ajaluhum*'. It is a good reading because it is connected to the prior words.

We abandon those who do not expect to meet Us

This means 'We do not hasten evil for them because of the possibility that one of them might repent or a believer arise from his children.' '*Wander blindly*' means that they are bewildered. *Ṭughyān* is arrogance and insolence. It was mentioned in *al-Baqarah* (2:15). It is said that those referred to in this *āyah* are the people of Makkah and it was revealed when they said: '*Allah, if this really is the truth from You…*" (8:32) as we already mentioned. Allah knows best.

وَإِذَا مَسَّ ٱلْإِنسَٰنَ ٱلضُّرُّ دَعَانَا لِجَنۢبِهِۦٓ أَوْ قَاعِدًا أَوْ قَآئِمًا فَلَمَّا كَشَفْنَا عَنْهُ ضُرَّهُۥ
مَرَّ كَأَن لَّمْ يَدْعُنَآ إِلَىٰ ضُرٍّ مَّسَّهُۥ كَذَٰلِكَ زُيِّنَ لِلْمُسْرِفِينَ مَا كَانُوا۟
يَعْمَلُونَ ﴿١٢﴾

12 When harm touches man, he calls on Us, lying on his side or sitting down or standing up. Then when We remove the harm from him he carries on as if he had never called on Us when the harm first touched him. In that way We make what they have done appear good to the profligate.

When harm touches man, he calls on Us,

What is meant by '*man*' here is an unbeliever. It is said that it was Abū Ḥudhayfah ibn al-Mughīrah, the idolater who was afflicted by hardship, difficulty and stress. '*He calls on Us, lying on his side,*' meaning lying on his side as *li* means 'on' here. He describes all of his states because a human being must be in one of these three positions: lying down, sitting or standing. Some of them said that Allah begins with lying down because it is the position people are usually in when they are suffering most and so there is more supplication in that state and their imploring is more intense. Then comes the one sitting down and then the one standing up.

Then when We remove the harm from him he carries on as if he had never called on Us

This means: he continues in his unbelief and is not thankful or chastened. This describes many confused people of weak belief. When they enjoy well-being again, they go back to the same acts of disobedience they were doing before. The *āyah* includes both unbelievers and others. Al-Akhfash says that '*as if*' (*ka-anna*) is a heavy form which has been lightened. [POEM]

In that way We make what they have done appear good

This means that as We make this supplication when undergoing trial and turning away in times of ease seem good to the idolaters, so their actions of unbelief and rebellion also seem good to them. This appearance of good can come from Allah but it can also come from Shaytān and then his misleading him will bring him to unbelief.

وَلَقَدَ اَهۡلَكۡنَا اَ۬لۡقُرُونَ مِن قَبۡلِكُمۡ لَمَّا ظَلَمُواْ وَجَآءَتۡهُمۡ رُسُلُهُم بِالۡبَيِّنَٰتِ
وَمَا كَانُواْ لِيُومِنُواْۖ كَذَٰلِكَ نَجۡزِے اِ۬لۡقَوۡمَ اَ۬لۡمُجۡرِمِينَ ﴿١٣﴾

13 We destroyed generations before you when they did wrong. Their Messengers brought them the Clear Signs, but they were never going to believe. That is how We repay evildoers.

'We destroyed past nations before you people of Makkah when they disbelieved and associated others with Allah.' *'Their Messengers brought them the Clear Signs,'* – clear miracles and luminous proofs – '*but they were never going to believe.*' 'We destroyed them since We knew that they would not believe.' This is to threaten and frighten the unbelievers of Makkah with the punishment of past nations. It means: 'We are able to destroy these people for their denial of Muḥammad ﷺ, but we can also grant them a deferral since we know that among them are some who believe or will produce those who believe.' This *āyah* refutes those people of misguidance who say that people's guidance and faith are created [by themselves]. It is said that He will repay them for their unbelief by sealing up their hearts. This is indicated by His words.

ثُمَّ جَعَلۡنَٰكُمۡ خَلَٰٓئِفَ فِے اِ۬لۡأَرۡضِ مِنۢ بَعۡدِهِمۡ لِنَنظُرَ كَيۡفَ تَعۡمَلُونَ ﴿١٤﴾

14 Then We appointed you after them to be caliphs on the earth so We might observe how you would act.

Then We appointed you after them to be caliphs on the earth

This has two objects. *Khalā'if* (caliphs) is the plural of *khalīfah* which was mentioned at the end of *al-An'ām* (6:165-166). It means: 'We made you dwell on the earth.' *'After them'* is after the generations who have been destroyed. '*So that We might observe*' has a *fatḥah* because of the *lām* which means 'in order to'. It means: 'so that you would act and do that which merits the reward or punishment,' while

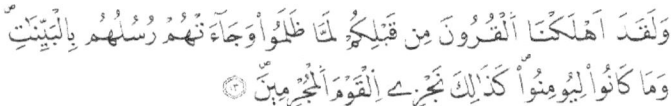

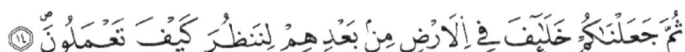

He always knows that in the unseen. It is said that it is so that He might deal with you after testing you to demonstrate His justice to you. It is said that the verb '*observe*' refers to the Messengers, meaning that Allah's observation is of how His Messengers and friends act. *Kayfa* is in the accusative by the verb 'act' because there is a question at the beginning of the words and so it does not act on what is before it.

وَإِذَا تُتْلَىٰ عَلَيْهِمْ ءَايَاتُنَا بَيِّنَٰتٍ قَالَ ٱلَّذِينَ لَا يَرْجُونَ لِقَآءَنَا ٱئْتِ
بِقُرْءَانٍ غَيْرِ هَٰذَآ أَوْ بَدِّلْهُ قُلْ مَا يَكُونُ لِىٓ أَنْ أُبَدِّلَهُۥ مِن تِلْقَآئِ نَفْسِىٓ
إِنْ أَتَّبِعُ إِلَّا مَا يُوحَىٰٓ إِلَىَّ إِنِّىٓ أَخَافُ إِنْ عَصَيْتُ رَبِّى عَذَابَ يَوْمٍ عَظِيمٍ ﴿١٥﴾

15 When Our Clear Signs are recited to them, those who do not expect to meet Us say, 'Bring a Qur'an other than this one or change it.' Say: 'It is not for me to change it of my own accord. I follow nothing except what is revealed to me. I fear, were I to disobey my Lord, the punishment of a Dreadful Day.'

When Our Clear Signs are recited to them,

Tutlā means 'recite' and '*bayyanāt*' is in the accusative for the adverbial *ḥāl*. '*Clear Signs*' are clear with no confusion or ambiguity in them. *'Those who do not expect to meet Us'* means that they have no fear of the Day of Resurrection or of any reckoning and no hope of any reward. Qatādah said that this refers to the idolaters of the people of Makka.

'Bring a Qur'an other than this one or change it.'

The difference between changing and bringing one other than it is that changing implies that only it exists while bringing another would imply the existence of another.. There are three aspects to what they said.

One is that they asked him to change the promise into a threat and the threat into a promise and the lawful to the unlawful and the unlawful to the lawful. Aṭ-Ṭabarī said that.

The second is that they asked him to remove what was in the Qur'an which blames their gods and denigrates them. Ibn 'Īsā said that.

The third is that they asked him to remove what it mentioned about the Resurrection as az-Zajjāj said.

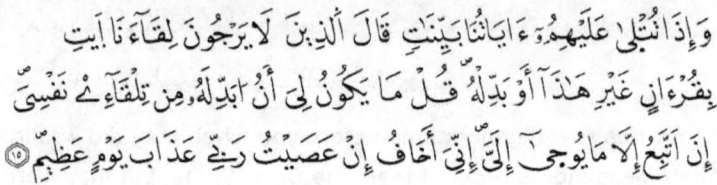

Say: 'It is not for me to change it of my own accord.

'Say, Muḥammad: "It is not up to me to reject or deny any of it."' *'I follow nothing except what is revealed to me'*: 'I only follow what I recite to you in respect of warning and promise, making lawful or unlawful, and command and prohibition.' This is used as evidence by those who forbid abrogation of the Book by the Sunnah because of what the Almighty says here. This does not necessarily follow, however, because the *āyah* is about the idolaters demanding something like the Qur'an to be produced and the Messenger ﷺ was unable to do that. They did not ask him to change a ruling nor the words. It is also because the Messenger ﷺ uttered it as revelation, and it did not come from him but from Allah Almighty.

I fear, were I to disobey my Lord, the punishment of a Dreadful Day.

The disobedience here would be by opposing Allah by altering and changing it or not acting on it. The Dreadful Day is the Day of Rising.

قُل لَّوْ شَآءَ ٱللَّهُ مَا تَلَوْتُهُۥ عَلَيْكُمْ وَلَآ أَدْرَىٰكُم بِهِۦ ۖ فَقَدْ لَبِثْتُ فِيكُمْ عُمُرًا
مِّن قَبْلِهِۦٓ ۚ أَفَلَا تَعْقِلُونَ ﴿١٦﴾

16 Say: 'Had Allah so wished, I would not have recited it to you nor would He have made it known to you. I lived among you for many years before it came. Will you not use your intellect?'

If Allah had wished, He would not have sent me to you to recite the Qur'an to you and He would not have taught you or informed you of it. The verb for *'made known'* is *darā* and *adrā*. *Darā* sometimes take a direct object and sometimes has the particle *bā'*. *Dirāyah* can mean deception and the verb is used for deceiving someone. That is why *Dārī* is not used as a name for Allah Almighty. Ibn Kathīr recited *'wala adrākum bihi'* without an *alif* between the *lām* and *hamzah*. It means: 'If Allah had wished, He would have made it known to you without me reciting it to you.' So the *lām* of stress is added to the *alif* of the first person present verb. Ibn 'Abbās and al-Ḥasan recited *'walā adra'tukum'*, changing the *yā'* into an *alif*, based on the dialect of Banū 'Uqayl.

Abū Ḥātim said, 'I heard al-Aṣma'ī say, "I asked Abū 'Amr ibn al-'Alā' whether there was any logic behind this reading of Ibn 'Abbās. He answered, "No." Abū 'Ubayd said, 'There is no logic to the reading of al-Ḥasan. It is only an error.' An-Naḥḥās said, 'The meaning of the statement of Abū 'Ubayd, "no logic" means, Allah willing, that it is an error because one says, "*daraytu*" (I knew) and "*adraytu*"

(I informed someone else). One says, "*dara'tu*" (I repelled) and so the error arises in confounding *daraytu* and *dara'tu.*' Abū Ḥātim said, 'I think that when al-Ḥasan recited "*walā adra'tukum*", changing the *yā'* into an *alif,* it is based on the dialect of the Banū al-Ḥārith ibn Ka'b. They change the *yā'* into an *alif* when there is a *fatḥah* before it.'

Al-Mahdawī said, 'If someone recites "*adra'tukum*", it is because the root of the *hamzah* is a *yā'* and so the root is "*adraytukum*" and so the *yā'* becomes an *alif,* even if it is silent as one says "*yābas*" for "*yaybas*" and "*ṭāyi'*" for "*ṭayyi'*". Then the *alif* becomes a *hamzah* in the dialect of those who say "'*a'lim*" for "'*ālim*" and "*kha'tim*" for "*khātim*".' An-Naḥḥās said that it is an error and the reading from al-Ḥasan is with a *hamzah* whereas Abū Ḥātim and others have it without *hamzah.* It is possible that it comes from *dara'a*, to repel, and therefore means: 'nor would I have commanded you to repel and abandon unbelief by the Qur'an.'

I lived among you for many years before it came.

This describes a period of time, which is forty years, '*before it came'*, before the Qur'an was revealed. You knew me to be truthful and trustworthy and that I did not read or write. Then I brought you miracles. '*Will you not use your intellect*' and know that this is only from Allah, not from me?' It is said that it means: 'I remained among you for the period of my youth in which I did not disobey Allah, and then you want me now, when I have reached the age of forty, to oppose Allah's command and change what He has revealed to me?' Qatādah said, 'He remained among them for forty years and then for two years experienced Prophetic vision. He ﷺ died at the age of sixty-two.' [The general view is that he ﷺ was sixty-three when he died.]

فَمَنْ أَظْلَمُ مِمَّنِ افْتَرَىٰ عَلَى اللَّهِ كَذِبًا أَوْ كَذَّبَ بِآيَاتِهِ ۚ إِنَّهُ لَا يُفْلِحُ
الْمُجْرِمُونَ ﴿١٧﴾

17 Who could do greater wrong than someone who invents lies against Allah or denies His Signs? Evildoers are certainly not successful.

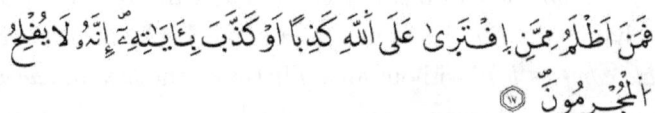

This is a question which implies denial, meaning that there is in fact no one who does greater wrong than someone who invents lies against Allah and changes His words and attributes something to Him which He did not reveal. Similarly no one does greater wrong than them when they denied the Qur'an and forged lies about Allah and said, 'This is not part of His Words.' This is part of what the Messenger ﷺ was commanded to say to them. It is said that it is Allah speaking to them directly. It is said that the inventor here is the idolater and those who deny the Signs are the People of the Book.

وَيَعْبُدُونَ مِن دُونِ ٱللَّهِ مَا لَا يَضُرُّهُمْ وَلَا يَنفَعُهُمْ وَيَقُولُونَ
هَٰٓؤُلَآءِ شُفَعَٰٓؤُنَا عِندَ ٱللَّهِ قُلْ أَتُنَبِّـُٔونَ ٱللَّهَ بِمَا لَا يَعْلَمُ فِى ٱلسَّمَٰوَٰتِ وَلَا فِى
ٱلْأَرْضِ سُبْحَٰنَهُۥ وَتَعَٰلَىٰ عَمَّا يُشْرِكُونَ ١٨

18 They worship, instead of Allah, what can neither harm them nor help them, saying, 'These are our intercessors with Allah.' Say: 'Would you inform Allah of something about which He does not know either in the heavens or on the earth?' May He be glorified and exalted above what they associate with Him!

They worship idols. Their statement: '*These are our intercessors with Allah*,' is extreme ignorance on their part since they were waiting for intercession with regard to property from those from whom there could be neither benefit nor harm in the situation. It is said that '*our intercessors*' means 'they intercede for us with Allah by putting our livelihood right in this world.'

Most recite '*Would you inform Allah of something*' as '*tunabbi'ūna*' with a *shaddah*. Abū as-Sammāl al-'Adawī recited it without the *shaddah*, from *anba'a, yunbi'u* whereas most recite it from *nabba'a, yunabbi'u, tanbī'ah*. They mean the same and the Almighty combines them in His words: "'*Who told you* (anba'aka) *of this?*" *He said, "The All-Knowing and All-Aware informed me* (nabba'anī) *of it.*"' (66:3) The meaning is: 'Would you inform Allah that He has a partner in His kingdom or an intercessor without His permission? Allah does not know of any partner with Himself in the heavens or the earth because He has no partner.' It is like His words: '*Or would you inform Him of something in the earth He does not know?*' (11:33)

Then He exalted himself above *shirk* and said that He is too great to have a partner. It is said that it means: 'Do you worship what does not intercede, help or distinguish and say, "These are our intercessors with Allah"? You lie. Would you inform Him of something He does not know?' Allah is exalted above what they associate! Ḥamzah and al-Kisā'ī recited '*you associate*' (*tushrikūna*) with a *tā'*, which Abū 'Ubayd preferred. The rest recite it with *yā'* (*yushrikūna*).

وَمَا كَانَ ٱلنَّاسُ إِلَّآ أُمَّةً وَٰحِدَةً فَٱخْتَلَفُوا۟ ۚ وَلَوْلَا كَلِمَةٌ سَبَقَتْ مِن رَّبِّكَ لَقُضِىَ بَيْنَهُمْ فِيمَا فِيهِ يَخْتَلِفُونَ ﴿١٩﴾

19 Mankind was only one community but then they differed, and had it not been for a prior Word from your Lord, they would already have been judged in respect of the differences between them.

This was already mentioned in *al-Baqarah* (2:213). Az-Zajjāj said, 'They were the Arabs who were practicing *shirk*.' It is said that every child is born on the natural form (*fitrah*) and then they differ when they reach adulthood. The verb *'they would already have been judged'* indicates the determination and the Decree, saying that if it were not for His prior wisdom, He would not have judged between them regarding what they disagreed about concerning the reward or penalty before the Rising. He would have judged between them in this world and admitted the believers to the Garden for their actions and the unbelievers to the Fire for their unbelief. But people's lifespans have already been set by Allah and He knows what they do and He made the promised time the Rising. Al-Ḥasan said that. Abū Rawq said, '*they would already have been judged*' since the Final Hour had come to them. It is said that it means: "He would have completed their destruction.'

Al-Kalbī said that the '*Word*' is that Allah has deferred this community so that they will not be destroyed by the punishment in this world until the Day of Rising. If it had not been for this delay, He would already have judged between them by the descent of the punishment or the coming of the Final Hour.

This *āyah* is solace for the Prophet ﷺ about the deferring of the punishment of those who rejected him. It is said that the '*prior Word*' is that no one will be seized except on the basis of authoritative proof which is the sending of Messengers as evinced by Allah's words: *'We never punish until We have sent a Messenger.'* (17:15) It is said that the '*Word*' is His words: 'My mercy preceded My wrath.' If it were not for that, the disobedient would not have been deferred enabling them to repent. 'Īsā reads '*qaḍā*.'

وَيَقُولُونَ لَوْلَآ أُنزِلَ عَلَيْهِ ءَايَةٌ مِّن رَّبِّهِۦ ۖ فَقُلْ إِنَّمَا ٱلْغَيْبُ لِلَّهِ فَٱنتَظِرُوٓا۟ إِنِّى مَعَكُم مِّنَ ٱلْمُنتَظِرِينَ ﴿٢٠﴾

20 They say, 'Why has a Sign not been sent down to him from his Lord?' Say: 'The Unseen belongs to Allah alone. So wait, I am waiting with you.'

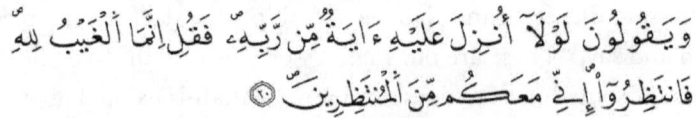

'*They*' here are the people of Makkah, who said 'Why has a miracle other than this miracle not been sent down to him so that He can make these mountains gold, have a house made of emerald and bring back to life those of our fathers who have died?' Aḍ-Ḍaḥḥāk said that they meant a staff like that of Mūsā. 'Say, Muḥammad, that the descent of the *āyah* is from the Unseen,' and *'I am waiting with you'* for its descent. It is said that it means: 'Wait for Allah to judge between us by showing the true from the false.'

وَإِذَآ أَذَقْنَا ٱلنَّاسَ رَحْمَةً مِّنۢ بَعْدِ ضَرَّآءَ مَسَّتْهُمْ إِذَا لَهُم مَّكْرٌ فِىٓ ءَايَاتِنَا ۚ
قُلِ ٱللَّهُ أَسْرَعُ مَكْرًا ۚ إِنَّ رُسُلَنَا يَكْتُبُونَ مَا تَمْكُرُونَ ﴿٢١﴾

21 When We let people taste mercy after hardship has afflicted them, immediately they plot against Our Signs. Say: 'Allah is swifter at plotting.' Your plotting is recorded by Our messengers.

The '*people*' referred to here are the unbelievers of Makkah. Mercy after hardship is ease after severity and fertility after drought. '*They plot against Our Signs*' with mockery and denial. The apodosis of '*taste mercy*' is '*idhā lahum*' according to al-Khalīl and Sībawayh. *'Say: "Allah is swifter at plotting"'* is an inceptive and predicate. '*Makr*' (plotting) is for clarification, meaning that He will hasten the repayment for their plotting and that the punishment which will come to them will destroy them more swiftly than anything they brought about through their plotting. The recording messengers or angels record what they do.

Most read it as '*tamkurūna*' in the second person while Ya'qūb in the variant of Ruways and Abū 'Amr ibn in the variant of Harūn al-'Atakī recite '*yamkurūna*' (they plot). It is said that Abū Sufyān said, 'We suffered drought by your supplication. If we are given rain, we will believe you.' They were given rain by his prayer but they did not believe. This was their plotting.

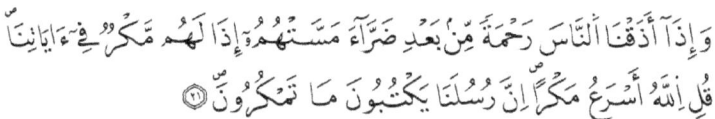

هُوَ ٱلَّذِى يُسَيِّرُكُمْ فِى ٱلْبَرِّ وَٱلْبَحْرِ ۖ حَتَّىٰٓ إِذَا كُنتُمْ فِى ٱلْفُلْكِ وَجَرَيْنَ بِهِم بِرِيحٍ طَيِّبَةٍ وَفَرِحُوا۟ بِهَا جَآءَتْهَا رِيحٌ عَاصِفٌ وَجَآءَهُمُ ٱلْمَوْجُ مِن كُلِّ مَكَانٍ وَظَنُّوٓا۟ أَنَّهُمْ أُحِيطَ بِهِمْ ۙ دَعَوُا۟ ٱللَّهَ مُخْلِصِينَ لَهُ ٱلدِّينَ لَئِنْ أَنجَيْتَنَا مِنْ هَٰذِهِۦ لَنَكُونَنَّ مِنَ ٱلشَّٰكِرِينَ ۝ فَلَمَّآ أَنجَىٰهُمْ إِذَا هُمْ يَبْغُونَ فِى ٱلْأَرْضِ بِغَيْرِ ٱلْحَقِّ ۗ يَٰٓأَيُّهَا ٱلنَّاسُ إِنَّمَا بَغْيُكُمْ عَلَىٰٓ أَنفُسِكُم ۖ مَّتَٰعَ ٱلْحَيَوٰةِ ٱلدُّنْيَا ۖ ثُمَّ إِلَيْنَا مَرْجِعُكُمْ فَنُنَبِّئُكُم بِمَا كُنتُمْ تَعْمَلُونَ ۝

22-23 It is He who conveys you on both land and sea so that when some of you are on a boat, running before a fair wind, rejoicing at it, and then a violent squall comes upon them and the waves come at them from every side and they realise there is no way of escape, they call on Allah, making their *dīn* sincerely His: 'If You rescue us from this, we will truly be among the thankful.' But then, when He does rescue them, they become rebellious in the earth without any right to do so. Mankind, your rebelliousness is only against yourselves. There is the enjoyment of the life of this world and then you will return to Us and We will inform you about what you did.

It is He who conveys you on both land and sea so that when some of you are on a boat, running before a fair wind,

Allah lets you ride animals on the land and boats on the sea. Al-Kalbī said, 'He keeps you safe on the journey.' The *āyah* contains many of the blessings people benefit from like riding on animals and boats. Travelling on the sea was already discussed in *al-Baqarah* (2:164). The verb *'conveys you'* is read by most as *'yusayyarukum'* while Ibn 'Āmir reads: *'yanshirukum,'* meaning spreads and disperses you. The noun *'fulk'* (boat) is used for both the singular and plural and can be masculine or feminine. It was already discussed (2:164). The verb *'running before'* moves from the second person to the third. This usage is often found in the Qur'an and Arab poetry. [POEM] Ibn al-Anbārī said, 'It is permitted in language to revert from the third person to the second. Allah says: *"And their Lord will give them a pure draught to drink. 'This is your reward. Your striving is fully acknowledged.'"* (76:21-22) So the *kāf* replaces the *hā*.'

before a fair wind, rejoicing at it, and then a violent squall comes upon them,

'A fair wind' was discussed in *al-Baqarah* (2:164). In the phrase *'a violent squall comes upon them* [literally, 'it]' the pronoun refers to the ship. It is also said that it refers to the fair wind. A fair wind is called *'ṭayyibah'*. *'Āṣif* is severe. The verb *'aṣifa* and *a'ṣafa* is used for the wind blowing, and the wind is *'āṣif*, *mu'ṣif* and *mu'ṣifah*, meaning strong. A poet said:

Until when the violent wind rages (*a'ṣifat*),
it contains a blunt sword and thunder whose sound rises.

'Āṣif is in the masculine because *'rīḥ'* is masculine and it is also described as *qāṣif*. The adjective *'fair'* describes a wind that is neither severe nor insufficient.

and the waves come at them from every side and they realise there is no way of escape,

'Waves' are what rises of the water. The verb *'realise'* here means that they are certain of it. Affliction surrounds them. When someone falls into affliction, it is as if it encompasses him on every side. The basis for this is that when an enemy completely surrounds a place, its people are destroyed.

they call on Allah, making their *dīn* sincerely His:

They call on Him alone and abandon anything else they were worshipping. This is proof that creation is naturally disposed to return to Allah in hardship and that someone in dire need may have his supplication answered, even if he is an unbeliever, because secondary means are cut off and he returns to the One, the Lord of lords, as will be explained later in *an-Naml*, Allah willing. Some commentators say, 'They said in their supplication, *"Ahyā sharāhiyā,"* which means "O Living, Self-Sustaining" in Persian.'

Point. This *āyah* is about travelling on the sea in general. From the *Sunnah* we find the *ḥadīth* of Abū Hurayrah: 'We travel on the sea and bring little water with us...' and the *ḥadīth* of Anas recounting the story of Umm Ḥarām which indicates the permission to travel on the sea in expeditions. This was adequately discussed in *al-Baqarah* (2:164). At the end *of al-A'rāf* (7:190) there is the ruling on someone who travels on the sea when it is turbulent and whether the ruling of someone healthy or of someone ill whose transactions are restricted applies to them. Look for it there.

'If You rescue us from this, we will truly be among the thankful.'

'If You rescue us from' these hardships and terrors – al-Kalbī said, 'From this wind' –'Then we will obey You on account of the fact that You have blessed us with deliverance.'

But then, when He does rescue them, they become rebellious in the earth without any right to do so.

But when Allah delivers them and saves them from the sea, they act on land with corruption and acts of disobedience. *Baghy* is corruption and *shirk*. The verb *baghā* is used of a wound when it festers. Its root is 'to seek', implying that they seek to be on top by means of corruption. The phrase *'without any right'* means by their denial [of Allah's blessing]. Another meaning of the root of *baghā* is when a woman looks for someone other than her husband.

your rebelliousness is only against yourselves

Its evil consequences will rebound on you. Then the words end and Allah begins a new sentence and says: *'There is the enjoyment of the life of this world…'* This is the enjoyment of the life of this world which does not last. An-Naḥḥās said, '"*Baghyukum*" is in the nominative by the inceptive and its predicate is *'enjoyment of the life of this world'*. *'Against yourselves'* is the object of the action of rebelliousness. It is also permitted that its predicate is *'against yourselves'* and its inchoative is implied: that is the goods of this world, or it is the goods of this world. There is a subtle difference between the two meanings. The noun *'enjoyment'* is in the nominative case as the predicate of *'your rebelliousness'*. It means that some of you attack others. It is like: *'greet one another'* (24:61) and: *'A Messenger has come to you from among yourselves.'* (9:128) If the predicate is *'against yourselves'*, it means that your corruption rebounds on you, as in Allah's words: *'If you do evil, you do it to your detriment'* (17:7).

It is related that Sufyān ibn 'Uyaynah said, 'Allah means that *baghy* (*rebelliousness*) is about the goods of the life of this world, implying that the punishment for it is hastened for the person in this world, as in the expression: "*Baghy* throws [its people] down."'

Ibn Abī Isḥāq recited *'matā'a'* in the accusative as a verbal noun meaning enjoying the life of this world, or it is in the genitive, implying 'for enjoyment', or a verbal noun with a passive meaning based on the *ḥāl*, implying enjoying, or it is in the accusative adverbially, implying in the enjoyment of the life of this world.

إِنَّمَا مَثَلُ ٱلْحَيَوٰةِ ٱلدُّنْيَا كَمَآءٍ أَنزَلْنَٰهُ مِنَ ٱلسَّمَآءِ فَٱخْتَلَطَ بِهِۦ نَبَاتُ
ٱلْأَرْضِ مِمَّا يَأْكُلُ ٱلنَّاسُ وَٱلْأَنْعَٰمُ حَتَّىٰٓ إِذَآ أَخَذَتِ ٱلْأَرْضُ زُخْرُفَهَا
وَٱزَّيَّنَتْ وَظَنَّ أَهْلُهَآ أَنَّهُمْ قَٰدِرُونَ عَلَيْهَآ أَتَىٰهَآ أَمْرُنَا لَيْلًا أَوْ نَهَارًا
فَجَعَلْنَٰهَا حَصِيدًا كَأَن لَّمْ تَغْنَ بِٱلْأَمْسِ كَذَٰلِكَ نُفَصِّلُ ٱلْءَايَٰتِ لِقَوْمٍ
يَتَفَكَّرُونَ ﴿٢٤﴾

24 The likeness of the life of this world is that of water which We send down from the sky, and which then mingles with the plants of the earth to provide food for both people and animals. Then, when the earth is at its loveliest and takes on its fairest guise and its people think they have it under their control, Our command comes upon it by night or day and We reduce it to dried-out stubble, as though it had not been flourishing just the day before! In this way We make Our Signs clear for people who reflect.

The likeness of the life of this world is that of water which We send down from the sky,

The aim of the *āyah* is to make a metaphor, as a description of the life of this world in respect of its vanishing, disappearance, and lack of real importance. Seeking refuge in it is like what happens with water and so the *kāf* is in the nominative. This example will be further explained in *al-Kahf.* The clause '*which We send down from the sky,*' refers back to '*water*'.

and which then mingles with the plants of the earth to provide food for both people and animals.

It is related that Nāfi' stopped after the verb '*mingles*': meaning the water mixes with the earth and then the plants of the earth grow and the earth produces various types of plants. According to this reading, the noun '*plants*' is the inceptive, but according to the one who does not stop at '*mingles*', it is nominative, meaning the plants mingle with the rain, drinking it and become tender, good and green. The verb *ikhtilāṭ* (*mingles*) means something penetrating something else. '*To provide food for people*' – grains, fruits and vegetables – '*and animals*' – pasture, straw and barley.

Then, when the earth is at its loveliest and takes on its fairest guise and its people think they have it under their control,

'At its loveliest' is in its beauty and adornment. *Zukhruf* is the perfection of the beauty of a thing, which is why gold is called *zukhruf.* The phrase *'takes on its fairest guise'* means it is adorned with grains, fruits and flowers. The root of *izzayyanat* is *tazayyanat* and the *tā'* is assimilated into the *zāyy* and there is a connective *alif* because the assimilated letter takes the place of two letters: the first is silent and one cannot begin with a silent letter. Ibn Mas'ūd and Ubayy ibn Ka'b recited it in the original unassimilated form of '*tazayyanat'*. Al-Ḥasan, al-A'raj and Abū al-'Āliyah recited '*azyanat,*' meaning that it brings its adornment onto itself, meaning its crops and produce. The verb is based on its root. If it had been made weak, one would say '*azānat'*. 'Awf ibn Abī Jamīlah al-A'rābī said, 'Our shaykhs recited *wa-zyānnat* on the measure of "*iswāddat*".' The transmission of al-Muqaddamī has *wa-zzāyanat* whose root is *tazāyanat* and there is *idghām.* Ash-Sha'bī and Qatādah recited *wa azyanat.* 'Uthmān an-Nahdī recited *azyanat* as well as *wa-zyānat* and *wa-zya'annat* with a *hamzah.* These are three readings.'

'People think' here means 'they feel certain' and the verb *'have it under their control'* means have its harvest and benefit from it. Allah speaks about the earth while He means the plants which come from it. It is said that it refers to produce and it is said that it refers to adornment.

Our command comes upon it by night or day and We reduce it to dried-out stubble, as though it had not been flourishing just the day before!

'Our command comes' means 'Our punishment', or 'We command its destruction.' *'Night or day'* are two adverbs. *'Dried-out stubble'* are two objects, implying. That it is cut and reaped with nothing in it. Allah says *'ḥaṣīd'* which is not in the feminine and is the form *fa'īl* with a passive meaning. Abū 'Ubayd said that it means completely effaced. The phrase: *'as though it had not been flourishing just the day before'* indicates that it is clearly not now flourishing at all. The verb is *ghanā*, which is to stay in a place and make it flourish. *Maghānī* are habitations. Qatādah said, 'as if they did not enjoy blessings.' Labīd said:

> I remained (*ghanītu*) for some time before [the War of] Dāḥis took place.
> If only the soul could be forever stubborn.

Most recite '*taghna'* in the feminine since *'arḍ'* (earth) is feminine while Qatādah recites *'yaghna'* referring to *zukhruf,* implying that as these fields are destroyed, so will be this world be destroyed. *Faṣṣala* is to make clear. In *'people who reflect'* their reflection is on the Signs of Allah.

وَٱللَّهُ يَدْعُوٓاْ إِلَىٰ دَارِ ٱلسَّلَٰمِ وَيَهْدِي مَن يَشَآءُ إِلَىٰ صِرَٰطٖ مُّسْتَقِيمٖ ﴿٢٥﴾

25 Allah calls to the Abode of Peace and He guides whom He wills to a straight path.

Having spoken about this abode – the abode of this world – Allah then speaks of the Next World and says: 'Allah does not call on you to amass this world. He calls on you to obey Him so that you go to the Abode of Peace which is the Garden.' Qatādah and al-Ḥasan said that '*Peace*' is Allah and His '*Abode*' is the Garden. The Garden is called the '*Abode of Peace*' because whoever enters it is free from all misfortune. One of the Divine Names is 'Peace'. We discussed that in *Kitāb al-Asnā fī sharḥ asmā' Allah al-Ḥusna*, and it will be discussed in *al-Ḥashr*, Allah willing. It is said that it means, 'Allah will call to the Abode of peace (*salāmah*).' *Salām* and *salāmah* mean the same. Az-Zajjāj said that. A poet said:

Umm Bakr greeted with peace (*salāmah*),
Do you have any peace (*salām*) after your people?

It is said that it means: Allah will call to the 'Abode of Greeting' because its people will be given the greeting and peace by Allah, and the same is true of the angels. Al-Ḥasan said, 'Peace is the constant state of the people of the Garden. It is their greeting, as Allah says: *"Their greeting in it is 'Peace'."* (10:10)' Yaḥya ibn Mu'ādh said, 'Son of Ādam, Allah called you to the Abode of Peace, so look to how you answer Him. If you respond to Him from this world, you will enter it. If you respond to Him from your grave, you are denied it.' Ibn 'Abbās said, 'There are seven Gardens: the Abode of Majesty, the Abode of Peace, the Garden of Eden. The Garden of Refuge, the Garden of Eternity, the Garden of Paradise, and the Garden of Bliss.'

He guides whom He wills to a straight path

The call is universal by demonstrating His proof and particularly to guidance as He has no need of His creation. The Straight Path is the Book of Allah. 'Alī ibn Abī Ṭālib related it and said that he heard the Messenger of Allah ﷺ say, 'The Straight Path is the Book of Allah. Almighty.' It is said to be Islam. An-Nawwās ibn Sam'ān mentioned it from the Messenger of Allah ﷺ. Mujāhid and Qatādah said that it is the Truth. It is said that it is said that it is the Messenger of Allah ﷺ and his two Companions, Abū Bakr and 'Umar.'

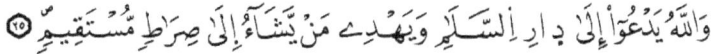

Jābir ibn 'Abdullāh said, 'The Messenger of Allah ﷺ came out one day and said, "I dreamt that Jibrīl was at my head and Mīkā'īl was at my feet. One of them said to the other, 'Make a likeness for him.' He said, 'Listen and your ears will hear. Understand and your heart will understand. The likeness of you and your community is that of a king who builds a house and then builds a room in it and in it he sets out a feast. Then he sends a messenger inviting people to eat his food. Some of them answer the messenger while others ignore him. Allah is the King. The house is Islam, the room is the Garden and you, Muḥammad, are the messenger. Whoever responds to you enters Islam. Whoever enters Islam will enter the Garden. Whoever enters the Garden will eat from what is in it.''' Then the Messenger of Allah ﷺ recited: *"He guides whom He wills to a straight path."'''* Then Qatādah and Mujāhid recited, *'Allah calls to the Abode of Peace.'*

This *āyah* is a clear refutation of the Qadariyyah because they said, 'Allah guides all creatures to a straight path,' and this *āyah* refutes them and is a text of the Qur'an.

لِّلَّذِينَ أَحْسَنُوا۟ ٱلْحُسْنَىٰ وَزِيَادَةٌ ۖ وَلَا يَرْهَقُ وُجُوهَهُمْ قَتَرٌ وَلَا ذِلَّةٌ ۚ
أُو۟لَـٰٓئِكَ أَصْحَـٰبُ ٱلْجَنَّةِ ۖ هُمْ فِيهَا خَـٰلِدُونَ ﴿٢٦﴾

26 Those who do good will have the best and more! Neither dust nor debasement will darken their faces. They are the Companions of the Garden, remaining in it timelessly, for ever.

Those who do good will have the best and more!

It is related that Anas said, 'The Messenger of Allah ﷺ was asked about the words of the Almighty: "*and more,*" and he said, "Those who do good actions in this world will have the Best, which is the Garden; '*more*' is looking at the Noble Face of Allah."' That is the position of Abū Bakr aṣ-Ṣiddīq, 'Alī ibn Abī Ṭālib in one transmission, Ḥudhayfah, 'Ubādah ibn aṣ-Ṣāmit, Ka'b ibn 'Ujrah, Abū Mūsā, Ṣuhayb, and Ibn 'Abbās in one transmission, and it is the position of a group of the *Tābi'ūn* and it is a sound understanding of this.

Muslim related in his *Ṣaḥīḥ* from Ṣuhayb that the Prophet ﷺ said, 'When the people of the Garden enter the Garden, Allah Almighty will ask, "Is there anything more that I may give you?" They will answer, "Have You not whitened our faces? Have You not admitted us to the Garden and saved us from the Fire?" The Veil will be removed and they will not be given anything they love more than looking at their Lord.' In one variant he then recited this *āyah*.

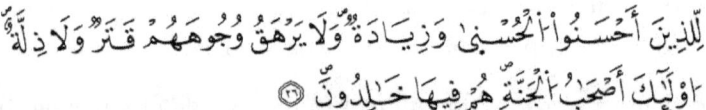

An-Nasā'ī also transmitted from Ṣuhayb that the Messenger of Allah ﷺ was asked about this and said, 'When the people of the Garden enter the Garden and the people of the Fire enter the Fire, a caller will call out, "People of the Garden! You have a promise from Allah which He wants to fulfil." They will say, "Has He not whitened our faces, made our scales heavy and saved us from the Fire?" The Veil will be lifted and they will look at Him. By Allah, Allah has not given them anything they love more than that Vision nor anything which more delights their eyes.' Ibn al-Mubārak transmitted it in *ad-Daqā'iq* from Abū Mūsā al-Ash'arī as *mawqūf*. We mentioned it in *Kitāb at-Tadhkirah* and there we also mentioned the meaning of the Veil.

At-Tirmidhī al-Ḥakīm transmitted that Ubayy ibn Ka'b said, 'I asked the Messenger of Allah ﷺ about the two increases in the Book of Allah when He says, *"Those who do good will have the best and more"* and he said, "Looking at the Face of the All-Merciful," and about *"We sent him to a hundred thousand or even more"* (37:147) and he said, "Twenty thousand."'

It is said that the increase is the multiplying of a good action ten times or more. That is related from Ibn 'Abbās. It is related from 'Alī ibn Abī Ṭālib: 'The increase is a room made of a single pearl with four thousand doors.' Mujāhid said, 'The best is one good opposite a good action and "*more*" is forgiveness from Allah and His pleasure.' 'Abd ar-Raḥmān ibn Zayd ibn Aslam said, 'The best is the Garden and "*more*" is what Allah gives them in this world of His bounty for which they will not be called to account on the Day of Rising.' 'Abd ar-Raḥmān ibn Sābiṭ said, 'The best is good news and "*more*" is looking at the Noble Face of Allah. The Almighty says: *"Faces on that Day will be radiant, gazing at their Lord."* (75:22-23)'

Yazīd ibn Shajarah said, '*More* is when the clouds pass over the people of the Garden and rain on them with every kind of rare gift they have not previously seen. He will say, "People of the Garden, do you want Me to give you rain?" They will not desire anything but for it to rain on them.' It is said that the increase is that no time passes for them equivalent to a length of a day of this world without seventy thousand angels encircling them, each angel bearing gifts from Allah which another does not have. They will never have seen the like of those gifts. Glory be to the Vast, All-Knowing, Wealthy, Praiseworthy, High, Great, Almighty, All-Powerful, Ever-Kind, Merciful, Wise Manager, Subtly Kind, the Generous whose powers are endless! It is said that to '*do good*' is in dealing with people and '*best*' is their intercession and '*more*' is the permission of Allah to enter it and His acceptance.

Neither dust nor debasement will darken their faces.

The verb for '*darken*' – *yarhaqu* – means: to attach itself. A boy who becomes a man is called *murāhiq*. It is said that it means to be above or to cover. The meanings are similar. *Qatar* is dust as it attaches to the people of the Fire. But dust does not attach itself to these people when they are gathered to Allah nor does abasement cover them. Abū 'Ubaydah recited to al-Farazdaq:

> Crowned with the king's cloak, followed by someone crowned.
> You see above him banners and dust (*qatar*).

Al-Ḥasan recited *qatr. Qatar, qatarah* and *qatr* mean the same. An-Naḥḥās said that. The singular of *qatar* is *qatarah* as Allah says, '*overcast with gloom* (*qatarah*)' (80:41), meaning dust covers them. It is said that *qatar* is calamity and eclipse. Ibn 'Abbas said that *qatar* is the darkening of faces. Ibn Baḥr said that it is the smoke of the fire as *quttār* is the smoke from a pot.

Ibn Abī Laylā said that it is the distance of their looking at their Lord. This is debatable. Allah says: *'Those for whom the Best from Us was pre-ordained will be far from it…'* (21:101) He says in another *āyah*: *'They will feel no fear and know no sorrow.'* (2:62) He also says: *'The angels descend on those who say, "Our Lord is Allah," and then go straight: "Do not fear and do not grieve."'* (41:30) This is general. So the face of the good-doer is not changed by the favour of Allah in a certain place before the Vision or after it by darkness from grief or sorrow, and none of the smoke of the Fire or from anywhere else will come over them. *'As for those whose faces are whitened, they are in Allah's mercy, remaining in it timelessly, for ever.'* (3:107)

وَالَّذِينَ كَسَبُوا۟ السَّيِّـَٔاتِ جَزَآءُ سَيِّئَةٍۭ بِمِثْلِهَا وَتَرْهَقُهُمْ ذِلَّةٌ مَّا لَهُم
مِّنَ ٱللَّهِ مِنْ عَاصِمٍ كَأَنَّمَآ أُغْشِيَتْ وُجُوهُهُمْ قِطَعًا مِّنَ ٱلَّيْلِ مُظْلِمًا أُو۟لَـٰٓئِكَ
أَصْحَـٰبُ ٱلنَّارِ هُمْ فِيهَا خَـٰلِدُونَ ۝٢٧

27 But as for those who have earned bad actions – a bad action will be repaid with one the like of it. Debasement will darken them. They will have no one to protect them from Allah. It is as if their faces were covered by dark patches of the night. Those are the Companions of the Fire, remaining in it timelessly, for ever.

But as for those who have earned bad actions – a bad action will be repaid with one the like of it.

This means they disobeyed Allah in their actions. It is said that it refers to committing *shirk*. In the phrase *'repaid with one the like of it'* the word *jazā'* is in the nominative by the inceptive and its predicate is '*the like of it*'. Ibn Kaysān said that the *bā'* [in *bi-mithlihā*] is redundant. It means: 'the repayment of a bad action is one like it.' It is said that the *bā'* along with what follows it is the predicate. It is connected to something elided in its place. It means: the repayment for a bad action is its like, as you say, 'I am for you.' It can be connected to *jazā'* and implies: 'a bad action will be repaid with its like,' and the predicate of the inchoative is elided. '*Jazā'*' is in the nominative, implying, 'they will be repaid with a bad action'. It is like *'a number of other days'* (2:184). So he owes a number and the like. According to this, the *bā'* is connected to something elided. It is as if Allah were saying to them, 'The repayment of a bad action is confirmed by its like,' or it can be for emphasis.

The meaning of this likeness is that that repayment is what is considered to be an equivalent for their wrong actions, in other words they are not wronged. The Power of the Lord is not connected to any cause. Humiliation and degradation will cover them. They have no one to defend them from Allah's punishment. *Qiṭa'* is the plural of *qaṭ'ah.* According to this, the adjective '*dark*' describes night, meaning their faces are covered with patches of the night when it is dark.

Al-Kisā'ī and Ibn Kathīr recited *'qiṭ'an'*, and so 'darken' is an adjective. It can also be a *ḥāl* modifying 'night'. *Qiṭ'* is a noun for what is cut and falls. Ibn as-Sikkīt said, '*Qiṭ'* is a period of the night.' It will be mentioned in *Hūd*, Allah willing.

وَيَوْمَ نَحْشُرُهُمْ جَمِيعًا ثُمَّ نَقُولُ لِلَّذِينَ أَشْرَكُوا مَكَانَكُمْ أَنتُمْ
وَشُرَكَاؤُكُمْ فَزَيَّلْنَا بَيْنَهُمْ وَقَالَ شُرَكَاؤُهُم مَّا كُنتُمْ إِيَّانَا تَعْبُدُونَ ﴿٢٨﴾

28 On the Day We gather them all together, We will say then to those who associated others with Allah, 'To your place, you and your partner-gods!' Then We will sift them out, and their partner-gods will say, 'It was not us you worshipped.

Ḥashr is gathering. The word *'all'* is a *ḥāl. 'Those who associated'* are those who assigned a partner to Allah. *'To your place'* means: 'stay and be firm in your place and stay in your places.' *'You and your partner-gods'* is a threat. '*Then We will sift them out'* means 'We will separate them and cut off the ties which existed between them in this world.' The verb *zayyala, tazyīl* is to separate. It is Form II. *Tazyīl* is used as the verbal noun. *Muzāyalah* is separation and *tazāyal* is difference. Al-Farrā' said that some recite '*fa-zāyalnā'* which means 'We separated.' You say, '*lā uzāyalu fulānan.*' (I will not part from so-and-so.) If you say, '*lā uzāwiluhu'*, it means 'I will not deceive him.'

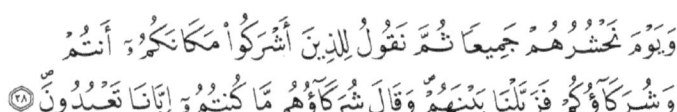

It is said that the partners here means the angels, the *shayṭāns* or the idols. Allah will make them speak and this conversation take place between them. That is because they claimed that the *shayṭāns* whom they obeyed and the idols which they worshipped ordered them to worship them by saying, 'We did not worship you until you commanded us to.' Mujāhid said, 'Allah will make them speak and they will say, "We were not aware that you worshipped us and we did not command you to worship us."' It is possible that 'partner-gods' applies to the *shayṭāns*. It means that they say this in astonishment, or they say it as a lie, trying to escape. The like of this will happen in the future and those known matters we have been informed about will definitely happen.

فَكَفَىٰ بِاللَّهِ شَهِيدًا بَيْنَنَا وَبَيْنَكُمْ إِن كُنَّا عَنْ عِبَادَتِكُمْ لَغَافِلِينَ ﴿٢٩﴾

29 Allah is a sufficient witness between us and you. We were unaware of your worship.'

The noun '*witness*' is an object. Allah is enough of a witness between us and you as to whether we commanded you to do this or we were content with it. '*We were unaware of your worship*': 'we did not hear or see or understand because we were inanimate without any living spirit.'

هُنَالِكَ تَبْلُوا كُلُّ نَفْسٍ مَّا أَسْلَفَتْ وَرُدُّوا إِلَى اللَّهِ مَوْلَاهُمُ الْحَقِّ وَضَلَّ عَنْهُم
مَّا كَانُوا يَفْتَرُونَ ﴿٣٠﴾

30 Then and there every self will be tried for what it did before. They will be returned to Allah, their Master, the Real, and what they invented will abandon them.

Then and there every self will be tried for what it did before.

'*Then and there*' is in the accusative as an adverb and means at that very moment. The verb '*tried*' means 'tested'. Al-Kalbī said: 'it will know.' Mujāhid said, 'it will be tested'. Every soul will receive the repayment for what it did before. It is said, 'having no choice but to hand over the rights it owes to their proper owners.'

Ḥamzah and al-Kisā'ī recited '*tatlū*', meaning that every soul will read its book written against it. It is said that it means 'follow', implying that every self will follow what it sent forward in this world. As-Suddī said that. A poet said:

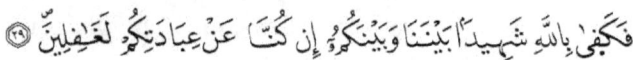

The one in doubt follows the one in doubt,
just as you see a wolf following a wolf.

They will be returned to Allah, their Master, the Real,

The noun '*Real*' is in the genitive as an appositive or an adjective. It can be in the accusative for three reasons. It implies: 'they returned in truth' and then the definite article is used. It is permitted for it to imply: 'Their Master in truth, not what they worship other than Him.' The third is that it is a kind of praise, in other words, He is the Truth. It is possible that it is in the nominative and means: 'their Lord, the Real.' Allah describes Himself as the Real because truth is from Him in the same way that He describes Himself as the Just because justice is from Him, meaning that all justice and truth is from Him. Ibn 'Abbās said, 'He repays them by the truth.'

The meaning of '*abandon them*' here reveals their nullity. '*Invented*' is in the position of nominative with the meaning of a verbal noun, meaning 'their inventing'. If it is asked why Allah says: '*they will be returned to Allah, their Master, the Real,*' when He says that the unbelievers have no master, the response is that he is not their Master in terms of inner support but is their Master terms of provision and outward blessings.

قُلْ مَن يَرْزُقُكُم مِّنَ ٱلسَّمَآءِ وَٱلْأَرْضِ أَمَّن يَمْلِكُ ٱلسَّمْعَ وَٱلْأَبْصَٰرَ
وَمَن يُخْرِجُ ٱلْحَىَّ مِنَ ٱلْمَيِّتِ وَيُخْرِجُ ٱلْمَيِّتَ مِنَ ٱلْحَىِّ وَمَن يُدَبِّرُ ٱلْأَمْرَ فَسَيَقُولُونَ
ٱللَّهُ فَقُلْ أَفَلَا تَتَّقُونَ ﴿٣١﴾

31 Say: 'Who provides for you out of heaven and earth? Who controls hearing and sight? Who brings forth the living from the dead and the dead from the living? Who directs the whole affair?' They will say, 'Allah.' Say, 'So will you not be godfearing?'

What is meant in the context of these words is the answer to the idolaters and the confirmation of the proof against them. Whoever acknowledges it among them, the proof is clear against him, and whoever does not acknowledge it, it is confirmed to him that the heavens and the earth must have a Creator. Anyone who is intelligent does not argue about this. This is close to the rank of necessary knowledge.

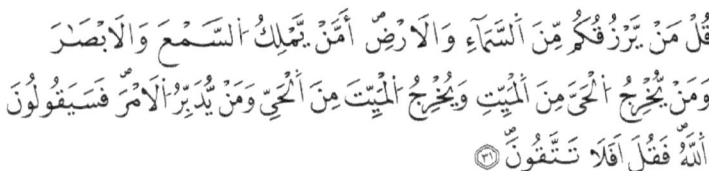

'*Out of heaven*' is through rain and '*earth*' is through plants. '*Who controls hearing and sight?*' means 'Who appointed them and gave both of them to you?' '*He brings*

forth the living from the dead' is a reference to plants growing out of the earth, a human being coming from sperm and a believer emerging from an unbeliever. *'Who directs the affair?'* Allah determines and decrees it. *'They will say, "Allah."'* This is because they believed that the Creator was Allah, or they will say that it is Allah if they reflect and are fair. The command *'Say'* is directed to Muḥammad ﷺ. *'So will you not be godfearing?'* Will you not fear His punishment and requital in this world and the Next?

فَذَٰلِكُمُ ٱللَّهُ رَبُّكُمُ ٱلْحَقُّ فَمَاذَا بَعْدَ ٱلْحَقِّ إِلَّا ٱلضَّلَٰلُ فَأَنَّىٰ تُصْرَفُونَ ﴿٣٢﴾

32 That is Allah, your Lord, the Truth, and what is there after truth except misguidance? So how have you been distracted?

That is Allah, your Lord, the Truth,

This means that the One Who does these things is your True Lord, not those you associate with Him. In *'What is there after the truth?'* *dhā* is connective, meaning 'What is there after worshipping the true God, if you abandon worshipping Him, except misguidance?' Some earlier scholars said that the apparent meaning of this *āyah* indicates that anything beyond Allah is misguidance because it begins with: '*That is Allah, your Lord, the Truth*' and ends with: '*What is there after the truth*?' This is about faith and unbelief not about actions. Some of them say that unbelief is covering up the truth. All that is other than the truth is like this. The unlawful is misguidance and the permissible is guidance. Allah is the One Who makes things clear and makes things unlawful.

The first is the sound position because before He says: *'Who provides for you out of heaven and earth?'* and then He says: *'That is Allah, your Lord, the Truth.'* He is the One Who provides for you. All of this is what He does. '*Your Lord, the Truth*': He alone Merits divinity and makes worship mandatory. Since that is the case, associating another with Him is misguidance and not truth.

Our scholars say that this *āyah* rules that there is no third position between the truth and falsehood in matters concerning the Unity of Allah. That is also the case with similar things. These are questions about the fundamental principles which only have one answer because discussion about them entails affirmation of the quality of the existence of the Divine Essence. That is different to the questions of secondary branches about which the Almighty says: *'We have appointed a law and a practice for every one of you.'* (5:48) The Prophet ﷺ said, 'The lawful is clear and the unlawful is clear. Between them are matters which are unclear.'

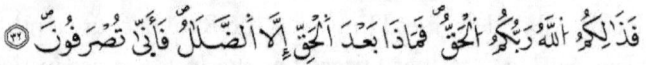

Discussion about secondary branches is about contingent rulings which apply to a confirmed essence. There is no disagreement about the confirmed essence, but there is disagreement about the secondary branches which are connected to it.

It is confirmed from 'Ā'ishah that when the Prophet ﷺ rose to pray in the middle of the night, he said, 'O Allah, praise is Yours…' He said in it: 'You are the Truth and Your promise is true. Your word is true. The meeting with You is true. The Garden is true and the Fire is true. The Final Hour is true. The Prophets are true and Muḥammad is true.' His statement: 'You are the Truth' means 'You are the One Whose existence is necessarily true.' The root of the noun *ḥaqq* derives from the verb *ḥaqqa* which is to confirm and necessitate. This description in reality belongs to Allah since He exists by Himself and non-existence did not precede Him and non-existence will never touch Him. Anything other than Him to which this term is applied was originally non-existent and may well become non-existent again and its existence comes from the One Who brought it into existence, not from itself. In respect of this meaning the most truthful word which a poet said is that of Labīd:

Every thing except Allah is false.

He indicates the words of the Almighty: *'All things are passing except His Face. Judgement returns to Him.'* (28:88)

The opposite of the truth is misguidance which is known in language and in the *Sharī'ah* as in this *āyah*. Similarly falsehood is the opposite of truth as is known in language and in the *Sharī'ah*. The Almighty says: *'That is because Allah – He is the Truth, and what you call upon besides Him is falsehood.'* (31:30) The reality of misguidance is abandoning the truth. The noun misguidance (*ḍalāl*) is taken from being misguided on a path which is turning away from the direction the path goes. Ibn 'Arafah said, 'Misguidance (*ḍalāl*) with the Arabs is travelling on a path other than the direct path.' *Ḍalla* means a thing is lost. It is specific in the *Sharī'ah* to turning away from what is correct in belief as opposed to actions. It is strange that it (*ḍalāl*) designates lack of recognition of the Truth which is equivalent to heedlessness when neither ignorance nor doubt accompanies its lack. So scholars take Allah's words: *'Did He not find you wandering and guide you?'* (93:7) to mean 'heedless' in one of the interpretations. That is corroborated by Allah's words: *'You had no idea of what the Book was, nor faith.'* (42:52)

'Abdullāh ibn 'Abd al-Ḥakam and Ashhab related that Mālik said about the words '*What is there after truth except misguidance?*' that playing chess and backgammon is part of misguidance. Yūnus related that Ibn Wahb was asked about a man who played the game 'Fourteen' in his house with his wife and Mālik said, 'How extraordinary! That is not the business of the believers. Allah says: *"What is there after truth except misguidance?"*' Yūnus related that Ashhab said that Mālik was asked about playing chess and said, 'There is no good in it. It is nothing. It is part of falsehood. All gameplaying is part of falsehood. Someone with intelligence must stop those with beards and the young from indulging in falsehood.' Az-Zuhrī said when he was asked about chess, 'It is part of falsehood and I do not like it.'

Scholars disagree about the permission to play chess and other things when there is no gambling involved. The gist of the school of Mālik and most *fuqahā'* is that if someone does not gamble on chess and plays it with his family concealed in his house once a month or once a year, and no one sees him or knows it, that is overlooked and is not forbidden or disliked for him to do that. If he is addicted to it and known for it, then he will lose his manliness and integrity and his testimony will be rejected. According to the position of his adherents, ash-Shāfi'ī did not invalidate the testimony of someone who plays chess or backgammon when he is considered by all of his companions to have integrity, and no foolishness, doubt or major wrong action appears from him, except if gambling is involved. If he gambles with it and is known for that, then his reputation falls and his foolishness is known because that is wrongful consumption of wealth. Abū Ḥanīfah said, 'The playing of chess, backgammon, Fourteen and every other game is disliked. If a major wrong action is not committed publicly by the player and his good qualities outweigh his bad qualities, his testimony is considered acceptable.' Ibn al-'Arabī said, 'The Shāfi'is say that chess is different to backgammon because it exercises the faculty of understanding and uses talent while backgammon is a game of chance and no one knows what it will produce, like drawing divining arrows.'

Our scholars said that backgammon are pieces made from boxwood and ivory and so is chess since it is its brother game. Backgammon is known for falsehood and known for dice and was known in the Jāhiliyyah as *Arun* and also as *Nardashīr.* We find in *Ṣaḥīḥ Muslim* from Sulaymān ibn Buraydah from his father that the Prophet ﷺ said, 'If someone plays *Nardashīr,* it is as if he put his hand in the flesh and blood of pigs.' Our scholars said, 'The meaning of this is like someone who puts his hand in the flesh of pigs thinking it of no significance because he eats it. It is unlawful to do this with pigs and not permitted.'

The words of the Prophet ﷺ make it clear: 'Anyone who plays backgammon has disobeyed Allah and His Messenger.' Mālik and others related it from Abū Mūsā al-Ashārī and it is a sound *ḥadīth.* He forbade playing backgammon, and the same is true of chess. He did not make an exception for one time rather than another or one state rather than another. He reported that someone who does that disobeys Allah and His Messenger. It is possible that what is meant is that it is just the playing of backgammon which is forbidden when gambling is involved, since it is related from the *Tābi'ūn* that it is permitted to play chess when no gambling is involved. It is more correct and cautious, however, to apply that in general, whether there is gambling or not, Allah willing.

Abū 'Abdullāh al-Ḥalīmī said in *Kitāb Minhāj ad-dīn*, 'Part of what is reported about chess is a *ḥadīth* in which the same is related about it as is related about backgammon in which the Messenger of Allah ﷺ said, 'Whoever plays chess has disobeyed Allah and His Messenger.' 'Alī passed by a gathering of the Banū Tamīm when they were playing chess and stood over them and said, 'By Allah, you were created for other than this! By Allah, if it were not for the *Sunnah*, I would throw it in your faces!' It is also said that he passed by some people playing chess and said, 'What are these images to which you are bowing? It would be better for one of you to touch embers that burn him than to touch them.'

Ibn 'Umar was asked about chess and said that it was worse than backgammon. Abū Mūsā al-Ash'arī said, 'Only someone in error plays chess.' Abū Ja'far was asked about chess and said, 'Keep this Magianism away from us.' There is a long *ḥadīth* in which the Prophet ﷺ said, 'Allah hates anyone who plays chess, backgammon, [the game of] walnuts and dice. Whoever sits with someone playing backgammon and chess to look at it has all his good actions erased from him and becomes one of those whom Allah hates.' All these traditions indicate the prohibition of playing it, even without gambling being involved. Allah knows best. In *al-Mā'idah* (5:90-92) we mentioned the clarification of their prohibition and that they are similar to wine in terms of prohibition because they are connected to it. Allah knows best.

Ibn al-'Arabī said in *al-Qabas*: 'Ash-Shāfi'ī allowed chess and the state of some of them led to them saying that it is recommended, to the point that they took that position in the madrasah. When a student was tired of reading, he would play it in the mosque. They had an *isnād* going back to some of the Companions and *Tābi'ūn* that they used to play it. That was not the case! By Allah, no godfearing hand touched it! They say that it sharpens the mind but eyes deny that. No man of intelligence is ever skilled in it. I heard Imām Abū al-Faḍl 'Aṭā' al-Muqaddasī say in a debate in the *Masjid al-Aqṣā* that it teaches war skills. Aṭ-Ṭurṭūshī said to him, "It corrupts war planning because the goal of war is to capture the king. One says in chess, 'Watch out for the king. Get the king out of my way.'" People laughed.' Sometimes rulers are severe about it and forbid it, saying about it: '*What is there after truth except misguidance?'* Sometimes they think a little of it does not matter. The first view is sounder and Allah knows best.

Someone may observe that it is related that 'Umar ibn al-Khaṭṭāb was asked about chess and asked, 'What is chess?' He was told, 'A woman had a son who was a king and he was wounded in a battle but not his companions. She asked, "How can I see this with my eyes?" So chess was made for her. When she saw it, she was consoled by it.' They described chess to 'Umar and he said, 'There is nothing wrong with something which is a tool of war.' The answer to this is: 'There is no evidence in this because he did not say, "There is nothing wrong with chess." He said, "There is nothing wrong with a tool of war." He said this because it was suggested to him that playing chess was used to help learn how to wage war. When he was told that, as he did not have any knowledge of it, he said, "There is nothing wrong with a tool of war." If it had been as they said, there would have been no harm in it. That is also the case with those Companions who did not forbid it. It is possible that they did not think that it was used for amusement and that it was a means to gain knowledge of fighting and an exercise, or no report with an *isnād* has reached us. Al-Ḥalīmī said, 'If the report is sound, no one has an argument in face of it. The argument in it is based on the collective view.'

Ibn Wahb mentioned with his *isnād* that 'Abdullah ibn 'Umar passed by some boys who were playing a game involving pebbles. Ibn 'Umar stopped it and forbade them to do it. Al-Hurawī mentioned in a *ḥadīth* from Ibn 'Abbās, 'There can be gambling in everything, even in children playing with pebbles.' Ibn al-A'rābī said, 'It is when a child takes a rag and rolls it up like a ball and then they gamble with it. Kujjah is the game played.'

'So how have you been distracted?'

How have you turned your minds to worshipping something that does not provide, live or die?

كَذَٰلِكَ حَقَّتْ كَلِمَتُ رَبِّكَ عَلَى ٱلَّذِينَ فَسَقُوٓا۟ أَنَّهُمْ لَا يُؤْمِنُونَ ﴿٣٣﴾

33 In that way the Word of your Lord is realised against those who are deviators, in that they do not believe.

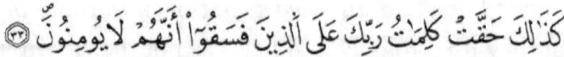

'*The Word*' is His judgment, decree and prior knowledge. '*Those who are deviators*' are those who have left obedience, disbelieved and denied. They do not affirm. This is ample evidence against the Qadariyyah. Nāfi' and Ibn 'Āmir recite '*kalimāt*' in the plural while the rest read it in the singular. In *Sūrat Ghāfir* the plural is used in three places while the rest have it in the singular. '*Anna*' is in the position of the accusative, meaning '*bi-annahum*' or '*li-annahum*'. Az-Zajjāj said, 'It is permitted for it to be nominative as an appositive for '*kalimāt*'. Al-Farrā' said that it is permitted to have '*innahum*' to begin a new sentence.

قُلْ هَلْ مِن شُرَكَآئِكُم مَّن يَبْدَؤُا۟ ٱلْخَلْقَ ثُمَّ يُعِيدُهُۥ ۚ قُلِ ٱللَّهُ يَبْدَؤُا۟ ٱلْخَلْقَ ثُمَّ
يُعِيدُهُۥ ۖ فَأَنَّىٰ تُؤْفَكُونَ ﴿٣٤﴾

34 Say: 'Can any of your partner-gods bring creation out of nothing and then regenerate it?' Say: 'Allah brings creation out of nothing and then regenerates it. So how have you been perverted?'

Their partner-gods are their deities and what they worship. It means: 'Tell them this, Muḥammad, as rebuke and confirmation.' Then if they respond… but if not then '*Say: "Allah brings creation out of nothing and then regenerates it,"*' for no one other than Him can do that. '*How have you been perverted?* How can you accept this and turn from the truth to falsehood?'

قُلْ هَلْ مِن شُرَكَآئِكُم مَّن يَهْدِىٓ إِلَى ٱلْحَقِّ ۚ قُلِ ٱللَّهُ يَهْدِى لِلْحَقِّ ۗ أَفَمَن يَهْدِىٓ
إِلَى ٱلْحَقِّ أَحَقُّ أَن يُتَّبَعَ أَمَّن لَّا يَهِدِّىٓ إِلَّآ أَن يُهْدَىٰ ۖ فَمَا لَكُمْ كَيْفَ تَحْكُمُونَ ﴿٣٥﴾

35 Say: 'Can any of your partner-gods guide to the truth?' Say: 'Allah guides to the truth. Who has more right to be followed – He who guides to the truth, or he who cannot guide unless he is guided? What is the matter with you? How do you reach your judgement?'

Say: 'Can any of your partner-gods guide to the truth?'

'Guidance to' can take the preposition *li* or *ilā*, and they mean the same. It means: 'Can any of your partners guide to the *dīn* of Islam?' If they answer 'No,' which is inevitably the case, then tell them that Allah guides to the truth. This is both a rebuke and confirmation.

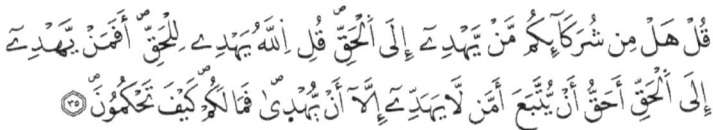

He who guides to the truth, or he who cannot guide unless he is guided?

'He Who guides to the truth' is Allah Almighty. *'He who cannot guide'* means the idols who do not guide anyone nor walk unless they are carried nor move from their place unless they are moved. A poet said:

The youth has intelligence by which he lives
when his legs guide his feet.

It is said that what are meant are the leaders and those who are misguided who do not guide themselves to guidance unless they are guided.

There are six readings of the verb 'guide':

The first is that the People of Madīnah except for Warsh recite *'yahddī* and in their reading they join two *sukūns* as they do in *ta'ddū* and *yakhṣṣimūna*. An-Naḥḥās said, 'No one is able to combine two silent letters and articulate it.' Muḥammad ibn Yazīd said, 'Someone who desires to do the like of this must use a light vowel, approaching a *kasrah*. Sībawayh calls it "filching a vowel".'

The second reading is that of Abū 'Amr and Qālūn in a transmission which is between a *fatḥah* and *sukūn*, based on the school of lowering the voice and filching.

The third is that of Ibn 'Āmir, Ibn Kathīr, Warsh and Ibn Muḥayṣin who recite *'yahaddī'*. An-Naḥḥās said that this is clear in Arabic. The root in it is *yahtadī* and the *tā'* is elided into the *dāl* and its vowel is reversed on the *hā'*.

The fourth is Ḥafṣ, Ya'qūb, and al-A'mash from Abū Bakr who have a similar reading to that of Ibn Kathīr although they have a *kasrah* on the *hā'* (*yahiddī*). They say that it is because when the jussive needs a vowel, it goes to the *kasrah*. Abū Ḥātim said that it is the dialect of Lower Egypt.

The fifth is Abū Bakr from 'Āṣim who recited *'yihiddī'*. All of that follows the *kasrah* as was already mentioned in *al-Baqarah* about *'yakhṭafu'* (2:20). It is said that it is the dialect of those who recite *'nista'īnu'* and *lan timassana-n-nār* and the like. Sībawayh does not permit *yihiddī*, but does permit *tihiddī*, *nihiddī*, and *ihiddī*. He said that it is because the *kasrah* is heavy on the *yā'*.

The sixth is that Ḥamzah, al-Kisā'ī, Khalaf, Yaḥyā ibn Abī Waththāb and al-A'mash recited *yahdī* from the verb *hadā*. An-Naḥḥās said, 'This reading has two aspects in Arabic, even if it is unlikely. One aspect is that al-Kisā'ī and al-Farrā' said that *yahdī* means *yahtadī*.' Abū al-'Abbās said, 'This is not recognised, but implies: "or he who does not guide others." Then the words end and there is a new sentence, "unless he is guided." It means that he needs to be guided and so it is a separate exception, as when you say, "So-and-so does not listen to anyone unless he is made to listen." So he needs to be made to hear."

What is the matter with you?

Abū Isḥāq said that the words are complete. It means: "What do you gain by worshipping idols?" Then Allah says to them: *'How do you reach your judgement'* for yourselves and then make a judgment which is clearly false? You worship deities which cannot do anything themselves at all. They are only acted upon. Allah does whatever He wills, so stop worshipping them. The position of 'how' is accusative by the effect of *'reach your judgement'*.

وَمَا يَتَّبِعُ أَكْثَرُهُمْ إِلَّا ظَنًّا إِنَّ الظَّنَّ لَا يُغْنِي مِنَ الْحَقِّ شَيْئًا إِنَّ اللَّهَ عَلِيمٌ بِمَا
يَفْعَلُونَ ﴿٣٦﴾

36 Most of them follow nothing but conjecture. Conjecture is of no use whatsoever against the truth. Allah most certainly knows what they are doing.

Allah is referring to those they follow, inferring that they only follow conjecture and surmise about them being deities and able to intercede on their behalf. They have no evidence. Their followers follow them in blind imitation. That is of no avail against the punishment of Allah. '*The Truth*' is Allah. It is said that the truth here is certainty, meaning that conjecture is not like truth. This *āyah* contains evidence that supposition is not adequate where matters of belief are concerned. Allah knows about their unbelief and denial and that entails a kind of threat.

وَمَا كَانَ هَٰذَا الْقُرْآنُ أَن يُفْتَرَىٰ مِن دُونِ اللَّهِ وَلَٰكِن تَصْدِيقَ الَّذِي بَيْنَ
يَدَيْهِ وَتَفْصِيلَ الْكِتَابِ لَا رَيْبَ فِيهِ مِن رَّبِّ الْعَالَمِينَ ﴿٣٧﴾

37 This Qur'an could never have been devised by any besides Allah. Rather it is confirmation of what came before it and an elucidation of the Book which contains no doubt from the Lord of all the worlds.

This Qur'an could never have been devised by any besides Allah.

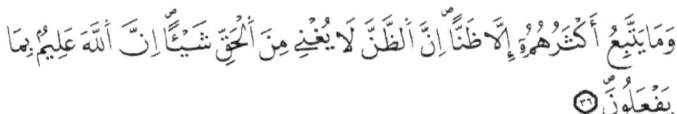

An with *yuftarā* is like a verbal noun. The meaning is: 'This Qur'an is not a forgery.' Al-Farrā' said that it means: It is not appropriate for this Qur'an to be forged. This usage is found in: *'No Prophet would ever be guilty of misappropriation'* (3:161) and *'It is not necessary for the believers to go out all together.'* (9:122) It is said that *an* means *lām*. It implies, 'The Qur'an is not forged.' It is said that it means *lā*, meaning 'it is not forged.' It is said that it means: no one is able to bring the like of the Qur'an from other than Allah and then ascribe it to Allah because of its inimitability owing to its quality, meanings and composition.

Rather it is confirmation of what came before it

Al-Kisā'ī, al-Farrā' and Muḥammad ibn Sa'dān said that it implies: but it is the confirmation of the Torah, the Gospel and other Scriptures. They gave the good news of it and it came to confirm that good news and to call to *tawḥīd* and belief in the Rising. It is said that it means that there is confirmation of the Prophet ﷺ before the Qur'an and that he is Muḥammad ﷺ because they saw him before they heard the Qur'an from him. '*Tafṣīl*' (*elucidation*) is in the nominative and accusative in the two ways mentioned about '*confirmation*'. '*Tafṣīl*' is clarification, meaning that it makes clear what was in prior Scriptures. *Kitāb* is a generic noun. It is said that it means that the Book makes clear the rulings in the Qur'an. '*There is no doubt in it*' refers to the Qur'an. There is no doubt that Allah sent it down.

أَمْ يَقُولُونَ ٱفْتَرَىٰهُ ۖ قُلْ فَأْتُوا۟ بِسُورَةٍ مِّثْلِهِۦ وَٱدْعُوا۟ مَنِ ٱسْتَطَعْتُم مِّن دُونِ
ٱللَّهِ إِن كُنتُمْ صَـٰدِقِينَ ٣٨

38 Do they say, 'He has invented it'? Say: 'Then produce a *sūrah* like it and call on anyone you can besides Allah if you are telling the truth.'

'*Am*' here is in the position of the *alif* of the question because it is connected to what is before it. It is said that it is the disjunctive *am* which implies '*bal*' and the *hamzah*, as in the words of the Almighty, '*Alif-Lām-Mīm. The Revelation of the Book, without any doubt of it, is from the Lord of the Worlds. Or do they say...*' (32:1-3) This means: 'Rather they say, "He has forged it."' Abū 'Ubaydah said that *am* means 'and' implying, 'and they say...' It is said that *mīm* is connective and implies: 'Do they say, "He has forged it"?' implying that Muḥammad forged the Qur'an on his own. It is a question which means rebuke.

Say, 'Then produce a *sūrah* like it

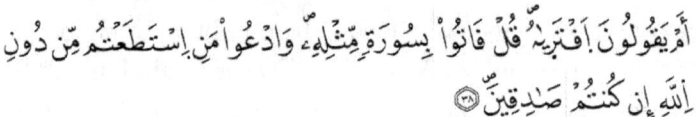

This is an answer in the form of an argument. The first *āyah* indicates that the Qur'an is from Allah because it confirms the Books before it and agrees with them without Muḥammad ﷺ learning about them from anyone. This *āyah* demands that they produce a *sūrah* like it if it is forged. The inimitability of the Qur'an and the fact that it is a miracle was already discussed in the Introduction.

بَلْ كَذَّبُوا۟ بِمَا لَمْ يُحِيطُوا۟ بِعِلْمِهِۦ وَلَمَّا يَأْتِهِمْ تَأْوِيلُهُۥ ۚ كَذَٰلِكَ كَذَّبَ ٱلَّذِينَ مِن
قَبْلِهِمْ ۖ فَٱنظُرْ كَيْفَ كَانَ عَٰقِبَةُ ٱلظَّٰلِمِينَ ﴿٣٩﴾

39 No, the fact is that they have denied something which their knowledge does not embrace and the meaning of which has not yet reached them. In the same way those before them also denied the truth. See the final fate of the wrongdoers!

They have denied the Qur'an and they are ignorant of its meanings and explanation. They must learn that by asking. This indicates that it is obliged to engage with interpretation.

and the meaning of which has not yet reached them.

This means: the reality of the ultimate end of their denial has not reached them, which will be the descent of the punishment on them. Or they denied what the Qur'an mentions about the Resurrection and the Garden and the Fire and its full explanation has not reached them, meaning the reality of what they have been promised in the Book. Aḍ-Ḍaḥḥāk said that. Al-Ḥusayn ibn al-Faḍl was asked, 'Do you find in the Qur'an, "If someone is ignorant of something, treat him as an enemy"?' 'Yes,' he answered, 'in two places: *"they have denied something which their knowledge does not embrace"* and *"Since they have not been guided to it, they are bound to say, 'This is an antiquated falsehood.'"* (46:11)'

'*Those before them*' tells us that past nations also did that in the same way and Allah seized them with destruction and punishment. The *kāf* is in the accusative. The final fate of the wrongdoers was to be seized by destruction and punishment.

وَمِنْهُم مَّن يُؤْمِنُ بِهِۦ وَمِنْهُم مَّن لَّا يُؤْمِنُ بِهِۦ ۚ وَرَبُّكَ أَعْلَمُ بِٱلْمُفْسِدِينَ ﴿٤٠﴾

40 Among them there are some who believe in it and some who do not. Your Lord best knows the corrupters.

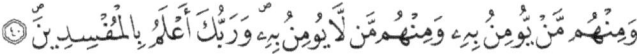

What is meant here are the people of Makkah, implying that some of them will believe in it in the future, even if they deny for a long time, since Allah already knew that they would ultimately be among the fortunate. The pronoun *'man'* (who) is nominative by the inceptive and its predicate is in the genitive. *'Some who do not'* means: some of them will persist in unbelief until they die, such as Abū Ṭālib, Abū Lahab and their like. It is said that it means the People of the Book. It is said that it is general to all unbelievers, and that is sound. It is said that the pronoun in *bihi* refers to Muḥammad ﷺ [i.e. in 'him' not 'it'] and so Allah informed him that the punishment was being delayed because some of them would come to believe. *'Your Lord best knows the corrupters'*, those who will persist in unbelief. This is a threat to them.

وَإِن كَذَّبُوكَ فَقُل لِّي عَمَلِي وَلَكُمْ عَمَلُكُمْ أَنتُم بَرِيٓـُٔونَ مِمَّآ أَعْمَلُ وَأَنَا۠ بَرِيٓءٌ مِّمَّا
تَعْمَلُونَ ﴿٤١﴾

41 If they deny you, say, 'I have my actions and you have your actions. You are not responsible for what I do and I am not responsible for what you do.'

It means: 'I have the reward for my action in conveying, warning and obeying Allah. You will have the requital for your *shirk*. No one will be punished for the wrong action of another.' This *āyah* was abrogated by the *Āyah* of the Sword according to Mujāhid, al-Kalbī, Muqātil and Ibn Zayd.

وَمِنْهُم مَّن يَسْتَمِعُونَ إِلَيْكَ أَفَأَنتَ تُسْمِعُ الصُّمَّ وَلَوْ كَانُوا۟ لَا يَعْقِلُونَ ﴿٤٢﴾
وَمِنْهُم مَّن يَنظُرُ إِلَيْكَ أَفَأَنتَ تَهْدِى الْعُمْىَ وَلَوْ كَانُوا۟ لَا يُبْصِرُونَ ﴿٤٣﴾

42-43 Among them there are some who listen to you. But can you make the deaf hear even though they cannot understand? Among them there are some who look at you. But can you guide the blind, even though they cannot see?

Some of them listen outwardly while their hearts do not retain any of the truth he says or the Qur'an he recites. This is why Allah says: *'But can you make the deaf hear even though they cannot understand?'* The words: *'they cannot understand'* mean that they do not really hear. It is literally a question while what is meant is negation. He made them like the deaf since their hearts are sealed. It means: 'you cannot guide those whom Allah has made deaf to hearing guidance.' That is the same meaning in the following *āyah*: *'But can you guide the blind, even though they cannot see?'*

Allah is saying that no one will believe unless He grants him success and guides him. This *āyah* and others like refute the Qadariyyah as we have said elsewhere.

What is intended here is consolation of the Prophet ﷺ: 'you cannot make the one deprived of hearing hear nor make the blind see so that they are guided. Similarly you cannot give those people success in believing when Allah has decreed that they will not believe.' The meaning of '*look at you*' is to continue to look at you as in the words: *'You see them looking at you, their eyes rolling like people scared to death.'* (33:19) It is said that it was revealed about the mockers. Allah knows best.

إِنَّ ٱللَّهَ لَا يَظۡلِمُ ٱلنَّاسَ شَيۡـٔٗا وَلَٰكِنَّ ٱلنَّاسَ أَنفُسَهُمۡ يَظۡلِمُونَ ﴿٤٤﴾

44 Allah does not wrong people in any way; rather it is people who wrong themselves.

When Allah mentions the people of wretchedness, He mentions that He does not wrong them. He decreed wretchedness for them and His removing the receptiveness of the heart and sight from them does not wrong them because He disposes of His kingdom as He wills and is just in all He does. They wrong themselves by unbelief, disobedience and opposing what the Creator commanded.

Ḥamzah and al-Kisā'ī recited '*walakin*' (*rather*) in the lightened form instead of *walakinna,* with '*people*' in the nominative. An-Naḥḥās said, 'A group of grammarians, including al-Farrā', claimed that when the Arabs say "*lakin*" preceded by a *wāw,* the doubled *nūn* is preferred. When the *wāw* is elided, the single form is preferred.' He says that this is faulty because when it is without *wāw*, it resembles '*bal*' so that what follows it is like what follows '*bal*'. When the *wāw* is there, it is different and so they double the *nūn* and make it have a *fatḥah* because it is '*inna*' to which is added *lām-kāf* and then becomes a single particle. He quoted a poem with that usage which has '*lakinnanī*'.

وَيَوۡمَ نَحۡشُرُهُمۡ كَأَن لَّمۡ يَلۡبَثُوٓاْ إِلَّا سَاعَةٗ مِّنَ ٱلنَّهَارِ يَتَعَارَفُونَ بَيۡنَهُمۡۚ قَدۡ خَسِرَ
ٱلَّذِينَ كَذَّبُواْ بِلِقَآءِ ٱللَّهِ وَمَا كَانُواْ مُهۡتَدِينَ ﴿٤٥﴾

45 On the day We gather them together – when it will seem as if they had tarried no more than an hour of a single day – they will recognise one another. Those who denied the meeting with Allah will have lost. They were not guided.

On the day We gather them together – when it will seem as if they had tarried no more than an hour of a single day –

It will be as if they had not lingered in their graves. *'An hour of a single day'* means that they will think that the time they remained in their graves is short because of the terror of what they see of the Resurrection. His proof is their words: *'We have been here a day or part of a day.'* (18:19) It is said that the period of their tarrying in this world is short because of the terror they face, not because of the period of remaining in the graves. Ibn 'Abbās said, 'They will see the length of their lives as like an hour in comparison with eternity.'

they will recognise one another.

This expression is in the position of the accusative as an adverbial *ḥāl* modifying '*them*'. It can also be separate and distinct as if He were saying, 'They will recognise one another.' Al-Kalbī said that when they emerge from their graves they will recognise one another in the same way they did in this world. This mutual recognition is one of rebuke and disgrace, not one of compassion, kindness and gentleness. One will say to another, 'You misled me! You made me err! You made me disbelieve!'" Then recognition will stop when they see the terrors of the Day of Rising as Allah says: *'no good friend will ask about his friend.'* (70:10)

It is said that what will remain is the mutual recognition of rebuke, and it is sound by the words of the Almighty: *'If only you could see when the wrongdoers, standing in the presence of their Lord'* to *'... round the necks of those who disbelieve.'* (34:31-33) He also says: *'Each time a nation enters, it will curse its sister nation'* (7:38) and: *"Our Lord, we obeyed our masters and great men."* (33:67) As for His words: *'no good friend will ask about his friend'* (70:10) and: *'When the Trumpet is blown, there will be no family ties between them'* (23:101), they mean that no one will ask anyone a question with mercy and compassion. Allah knows best.

It is said that there are different places in the Rising. It is said that the expression means: 'they will ask one another, "How long have you remained?"', as in Allah's words: *'Some of them will come up to others and they will question one another.'* (52:25) This is good. Aḍ-Ḍaḥḥāk said, 'That mutual recognition is the mutual affection of the believers. There will be no mutual affection between the unbelievers as Allah says: *"There will be no family ties between them"* (23:101).'

Those who denied the meeting with Allah will have lost

The meeting is being presented to Allah. Then it is said that it is possible that this is a report from Allah after indicating the Resurrection and Gathering, meaning they have lost of the reward of the Garden when they are presented before Allah.

It is said that they have lost in their meeting with Allah because the loss in that state is that in which repentance is of no use. An-Naḥḥās said, 'It is possible that the meaning is that they recognise one another.' *'They were not guided'* in Allah's foreknowledge of them.

وَإِمَّا نُرِيَنَّكَ بَعْضَ ٱلَّذِى نَعِدُهُمْ أَوْ نَتَوَفَّيَنَّكَ فَإِلَيْنَا مَرْجِعُهُمْ ثُمَّ ٱللَّهُ شَهِيدٌ
عَلَىٰ مَا يَفْعَلُونَ ﴿٤٦﴾

46 Whether We show you something of what We have promised them or take you back to Us, they will still return to Us. Then Allah will be witness against what they are doing.

What Allah promised was the victory of the *dīn* during his lifetime ﷺ. Commentators say that the '*something*' He promised them is the death of those who were killed and the imprisonment of those who were imprisoned at Badr. '*Take you back to Us*' is added to *'show you'*. It means: 'if you were to die before that.' '*They will still return to Us*' is the apodosis of '*immā*'. What is meant is: 'If We do not take revenge on them sooner, We will do later.' Allah is the Witness Who does not need another witness to their fighting against Him and denying Him. It can also mean that He is a witness there.

وَلِكُلِّ أُمَّةٍ رَّسُولٌ فَإِذَا جَآءَ رَسُولُهُمْ قُضِىَ بَيْنَهُم بِٱلْقِسْطِ وَهُمْ
لَا يُظْلَمُونَ ﴿٤٧﴾

47 Every nation has a Messenger and when their Messenger comes everything is decided between them justly. They are not wronged.

Every nation has a Messenger who is a witness for or against them. When their Messenger comes on the Day of Rising, there will be judgment between them. *'How will it be when We bring a witness from every nation?'* (4:41) Ibn 'Abbās said, 'On the Last Day the unbelievers will deny that any Messenger came to them, but the Messenger will be brought and state, "I conveyed the Message."'

It is possible that it means that they will not be punished in this world until they have a Messenger. Then whoever believes will be successful and saved, and whoever does not believe will be destroyed and punished. Its evidence is in the words of the Almighty: *'We never punish until We have sent a Messenger.'* (17:15) *Qiṣṭ* is justice. *'They are not wronged'* means they will not be punished unless there is wrong action nor will they be taken to task without evidence.

وَيَقُولُونَ مَتَىٰ هَٰذَا الْوَعْدُ إِن كُنتُمْ صَٰدِقِينَ ﴿٤٨﴾

48 They say, 'When will this promise be kept if you are telling the truth?'

'They' here are the unbelievers of Makkah because of their excessive denial of him and their hastening of punishment for themselves. It means: 'When will the punishment come?' or 'When will the Rising which Muḥammad ﷺ promises us come?' It is said that it is general to every nation who denies their Messenger.

قُل لَّا أَمْلِكُ لِنَفْسِي ضَرًّا وَلَا نَفْعًا إِلَّا مَا شَاءَ اللَّهُ لِكُلِّ أُمَّةٍ أَجَلٌ إِذَا
جَاءَ أَجَلُهُمْ فَلَا يَسْتَـْٔخِرُونَ سَاعَةً وَلَا يَسْتَقْدِمُونَ ﴿٤٩﴾

49 Say: 'I possess no power to harm or help myself except as Allah wills. Every nation has an appointed time. When their appointed time comes, they cannot delay it a single hour or bring it forward.'

When they asked the Prophet ﷺ to hasten the punishment, Allah said to him, 'Tell them, Muḥammad: "That is not up to me or anyone else. I do not have any power myself, so how can I control what you have asked to be hastened? Do not ask for it to be hastened."' *'Every nation has an appointed time.'* Their destruction and punishment has a known time in Allah's knowledge. When the decreed time comes, they will not be able to defer it for a single moment in this world nor bring it forward.

قُلْ أَرَءَيْتُمْ إِنْ أَتَىٰكُمْ عَذَابُهُۥ بَيَٰتًا أَوْ نَهَارًا مَّاذَا يَسْتَعْجِلُ مِنْهُ
الْمُجْرِمُونَ ﴿٥٠﴾

50 Say: 'What do you think? If His punishment came upon you by night or day, what part of it would the evildoers then try to hasten?'

This is the answer to their question, '*When will this promise be kept?*' Their desire to hasten the punishment is foolish. 'When the punishment comes to you, how will it benefit you? At that time faith will not help you.' This question here is meant to cause fear and show the terrible nature of the matter. It means: 'How terrible the thing you are trying to hasten is!' This as you say to someone who is seeking something, 'How unhealthy its outcome is! What are you bringing on yourself?' It is said that the pronoun in '*of it*' refers to the punishment. It is also said that it refers to Allah Almighty.

An-Naḥḥās said that if the *hā'* refers to the punishment, then two things are possible about 'what'. One is that *mā* is nominative by the inceptive and *dhā* means 'which' and is the predicate of '*mā*' while what it refers to is elided. The other possibility is that *mādhā* is a single noun in the position of the inceptive and the predicate is in the sentence. Az-Zajjāj said that. If the *hā'* refers to the name of Allah, *mā* and *dhā* are one thing and are accusative by 'hasten'. It means: 'What are the evildoers trying to hasten from Allah?'

أَثُمَّ إِذَا مَا وَقَعَ ءَامَنتُم بِهِۦٓ ءَآلْـَٔـٰنَ وَقَدْ كُنتُم بِهِۦ تَسْتَعْجِلُونَ ٥١

51 And then, when it actually comes about: 'Now do you believe in it? It was this that you were trying to hasten!'

There is some elision in these words. It implies: 'Are you safe from the punishment descending on you?' Then you will be told when it happens, 'Now do you believe in it?' This is spoken by the angels to mock them. It is also said that it is part of the words of Allah.

The *alif* of the question is added to *thumma* and means affirmation and rebuke and indicates the meaning of the second sentence after the first. It is said that *thumma* here means '*thamma*': 'then and there' and so it is adverbial. That is the position of aṭ-Ṭabarī. In this case, it does not constitute a question.

The root of '*al-ān*' is said to be [*āna*] a verb with a basic form like *ḥāna* and the *alif-lām* changes it to a noun. Al-Khalīl said that this is clear by the joining of two silent letters. The *alif-lām* is for the definite article and indicates the time. It is the limit of the two times. '*This*' refers to the punishment.

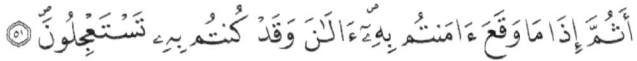

ثُمَّ قِيلَ لِلَّذِينَ ظَلَمُوا ذُوقُوا عَذَابَ الْخُلْدِ هَلْ تُجْزَوْنَ إِلَّا بِمَا كُنتُمْ
تَكْسِبُونَ ٥٢

52 Then it will be said to those who did wrong, 'Taste the punishment of eternity! Have you been repaid for anything other than what you earned?'

The guardians of Hell will say this to them. It is a punishment that will never end and it is the repayment for what they earned by their unbelief.

وَيَسْتَنبِئُونَكَ أَحَقٌّ هُوَ قُلْ إِي وَرَبِّي إِنَّهُ لَحَقٌّ وَمَا أَنتُم بِمُعْجِزِينَ ٥٣

53 They will ask you to tell them if this is true. Say: 'Yes indeed, by my Lord, it certainly is true and you can do nothing to prevent it.'

They will ask you to inform them, Muḥammad, about the punishment and the occurrence of the Final Hour. *'Aḥaqq'* is the inceptive and *huwa* takes the place of the predicate according to Sībawayh. It is is also possible that '*huwa'* is inchoative and '*aḥaqq'* is its predicate. *'Iy'* is a word which conveys realisation, necessitation and emphasis: 'Yes indeed.' *'By my Lord'* is an oath whose apodosis is something which undoubtedly must come about. *'You can do nothing to prevent it'* means 'you cannot evade His punishment and repayment.'

وَلَوْ أَنَّ لِكُلِّ نَفْسٍ ظَلَمَتْ مَا فِي الْأَرْضِ لَافْتَدَتْ بِهِ وَأَسَرُّوا
النَّدَامَةَ لَمَّا رَأَوُا الْعَذَابَ وَقُضِيَ بَيْنَهُم بِالْقِسْطِ وَهُمْ لَا يُظْلَمُونَ ٥٤

54 If every self that did wrong possessed everything on earth, it would offer it as a ransom. They will show remorse when they see the punishment. Everything will be decided between them justly. They will not be wronged.

If every self that did wrong possessed everything on earth, it would offer it as a ransom.

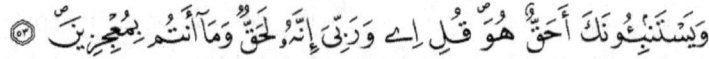

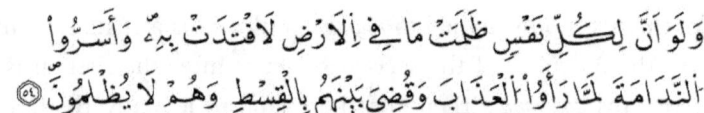

Doing wrong here is committing *shirk* and disbelieving. They would offer all their possessions to ransom themselves from the punishment of Allah, but it would not be accepted from them, as He says elsewhere: *'As for those who disbelieve and die as unbelievers, the whole earth filled with gold would not be accepted from any of them.'* (3:91)

They will show remorse when they see the punishment.

'They will show remorse' can also mean 'they concealed it' meaning that their leaders concealed their regret from their followers. *'When they see the punishment'* is before they are burned with the Fire. When they fall into the Fire, the Fire will distract them from any affectation. This is indicated by their words: *'Our Lord, our miserable destiny overpowered us.'* (23:101) It is clear that they will not conceal what they have. It is also said that *asarrū* means to show. The word is one of those with opposite meanings. It indicates that the Next World is not the abode for steadfastness and endurance. It is said that they will feel the pain of regret in their hearts because it will not be possible to show regret. Kuthayyir said:

I concealed (*asrartu*) regret on the day
the caller called for return of the camels of Ghāḍirah.

Al-Mubarrad mentioned a third aspect to the word: the features (*asirrah*) of their faces show regret. That is a furrowed brow, and the singular is *sirār*. *Nadāmah* is regret for having done something or having neglected to do something. Its root means to cling to. An aspect of that is the noun *nadīm*, a drinking companion, called that because he clings to gatherings. Someone called *nādim* and *sādim* is showing regret. *Sadam* is to be madly passionate about a thing. *Nadima* and *tanaddama* mean to be concerned with something. Al-Jawharī said that *sadam* is regret and sorrow. *Sadima* is to be worried and sad and such a person is described as *nādim* and *nadmān*. It is said that it means to follow closely, and the person doing that has no concern but that. It is said that *nadam* is a reversal of *daman* which is the urine and dung collected in a house. It is called that because it clings to it. *Dimnah* is the malice which clings to the breast and the plural is *diman*.

There will be no wronging or injustice where leaders and those under them are concerned – they will all be dealt with justly.

أَلَآ إِنَّ لِلَّهِ مَا فِي ٱلسَّمَٰوَٰتِ وَٱلْأَرْضِ ۗ أَلَآ إِنَّ وَعْدَ ٱللَّهِ حَقٌّ وَلَٰكِنَّ
أَكْثَرَهُمْ لَا يَعْلَمُونَ ٥٥

55 Yes indeed! Everything in the heavens and earth belongs to Allah. Yes indeed! Allah's promise is true but most of them do not know it.

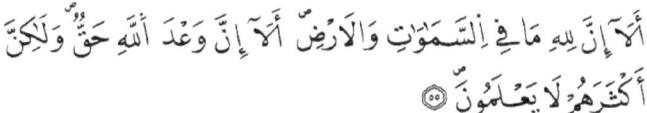

'A-lā' (*Yes indeed*) is a term used to alert a listener at the beginning of the words, meaning 'Pay attention to what I tell you.' *'The kingdom of the heavens and the earth belong to Him.'* (57:2) Nothing can prevent Allah from carrying out His promise.

هُوَ يُحۡيِۦ وَيُمِيتُ وَإِلَيۡهِ تُرۡجَعُونَ ٥٦

56 He gives life and causes to die and you will be returned to Him.

The meaning is clear and this was already discussed (2:28).

يَٰٓأَيُّهَا ٱلنَّاسُ قَدۡ جَآءَتۡكُم مَّوۡعِظَةٞ مِّن رَّبِّكُمۡ وَشِفَآءٞ لِّمَا فِي ٱلصُّدُورِ
وَهُدٗى وَرَحۡمَةٞ لِّلۡمُؤۡمِنِينَ ٥٧

57 Mankind! admonition has come to you from your Lord and also healing for what is in the breasts and guidance and mercy for the believers.

'*Mankind*' is addressed directly to Quraysh (but to all other human beings by implication). Admonition has come to you from your Lord in the Qur'an which contains warnings and wisdom. It heals what is in the breasts of doubt, hypocrisy, dispute and schism. '*Guidance*' is right guidance for those who follow it and 'mercy' is blessing. The believers are singled out because they are the ones who benefit from belief. All of the qualities enumerated here are characteristics of the Qur'an, and the use of the conjunction '*and also*' emphasises the praiseworthy nature of the Qur'an. Illustrating that usage of the conjunction, a poet said:

To the Lord King and Ibn al-Humām.[6]
Would that the squadron was in the press!

قُلۡ بِفَضۡلِ ٱللَّهِ وَبِرَحۡمَتِهِۦ فَبِذَٰلِكَ فَلۡيَفۡرَحُواْ هُوَ خَيۡرٞ مِّمَّا يَجۡمَعُونَ ٥٨

58 Say: 'It is the favour of Allah and His mercy that should be the cause of their rejoicing. That is better than anything they accumulate.'

6 'The Lord King and Ibn al-Humām,' refer to the same person.

Say: 'It is the favour of Allah and His mercy

Abū Sa'īd al-Khudrī and Ibn 'Abbās said that *'the favour of Allah'* is the Qur'an and *'His mercy'* is Islam. They also said that the favour of Allah is the Qur'an and His mercy is that He put you among its people. Al-Ḥasan, aḍ-Ḍaḥḥāk, Mujāhid and Qatādah said that the favour of Allah is belief and His mercy is the Qur'an, the reverse of the first. Other things are said.

that should be the cause of their rejoicing.

This refers to the favour and mercy. The Arabs use *'that'* for the singular, dual and plural. It is related that the Prophet ﷺ recited this with a *tā'* (you should rejoice) and this is the reading of Yazīd ibn al-Qa'qā', Ya'qūb and others. We find in a *ḥadīth*: 'take your rows.'

Faraḥ is pleasure in the heart at getting what one loves. Rejoicing is censured in places as: *'Do not gloat (tafraḥ). Allah does not love people who gloat (fariḥīn)'* (28:86) and *'He is overjoyed (fariḥ), boastful'* (11:10). But it is general. When joy is defined positively, it is not blameworthy as He says: *'Delighting (fariḥīn) in the favour Allah has bestowed on them.'* (3:170) Here Allah says that they should rejoice in the Qur'an and Islam and so here it is defined.

Hārūn said that the *ḥarf* of Ubayy has: *'fa-fraḥū'*. An-Naḥḥās said that the command comes with a *lām* so that there is a jussive participle with it, as there is a particle in the case of prohibition. However, they elide it in the imperative since it is enough to address the person. Sometimes they bring it in its normal form [with the particle].

That is better than anything they accumulate

Meaning in this world. The common reading is with a *yā'* in both verbs (rejoice and accumulate). It is related that Ibn 'Āmir recited *'rejoice'* with a *yā'* and *'accumulate'* with a *tā'* as addressed to the unbelievers. Al-Ḥasan has the reverse. Abān related from Anas that the Prophet ﷺ said, 'If Allah guides someone to Islam and teaches him the Qur'an, and then he complains of poverty, Allah will write poverty between his eyes until the Day he meets Him.' Then he recited this *āyah*.

قُلْ أَرَءَيْتُم مَّآ أَنزَلَ ٱللَّهُ لَكُم مِّن رِّزْقٍ فَجَعَلْتُم مِّنْهُ حَرَامًا وَحَلَٰلًا
قُلْ ءَآللَّهُ أَذِنَ لَكُمْ أَمْ عَلَى ٱللَّهِ تَفْتَرُونَ ﴿٥٩﴾

59 Say: 'What do you think about the things Allah has sent down to you as provision which you have then designated as lawful and unlawful?' Say: 'Has Allah given you authority to do this or are you inventing lies against Allah?'

This is addressed to the unbelievers of Makkah. In *'about' mā* is in the accusative by the effect of *'you think'*. Az-Zajjāj said that it is in the accusative by the effect of *'sent down'*. *'Sent down as provision'* here means 'created' in the same way that Allah says elsewhere: *'He sent down livestock to you – eight kinds in pairs'* (39:6) and: *'We sent down iron in which is great force.'* (57:25) So it is possible to interpret *'sent down'* as meaning 'created' because the provision in the earth exists through the rain which is sent down from heaven.

Mujāhid said that *'which you have then designated as lawful and unlawful'* is speaking about their designation of the *baḥīrah*, *sā'ibah*, *waṣīlah* and *ḥām* as being unlawful. Aḍ-Ḍaḥḥāk said that it is about the words of Allah: *'They assign to Allah a share of the crops and livestock He has created.'* (6:136) *'Has Allah given you authority'* to make things lawful or unlawful? *'Are you inventing lies'* by saying that Allah commanded them to do that.

This *āyah* is used as evidence [by some] for denying the use of deduction by analogy. This is unlikely. Deduction by analogy is based on what Allah has indicated but making things lawful and unlawful comes from Allah when Allah sets up the evidence which indicates the ruling. If there is disagreement about analogy being what Allah has indicated, it is outside of this aim and refers to something else.

وَمَا ظَنُّ ٱلَّذِينَ يَفْتَرُونَ عَلَى ٱللَّهِ ٱلْكَذِبَ يَوْمَ ٱلْقِيَٰمَةِ إِنَّ ٱللَّهَ لَذُو فَضْلٍ عَلَى
ٱلنَّاسِ وَلَٰكِنَّ أَكْثَرَهُمْ لَا يَشْكُرُونَ ﴿٦٠﴾

60 What will those who invent lies against Allah think on the Day of Rising? Allah shows favour to mankind but most of them are not thankful.

The noun *'Day'* is in the accusative as an adjective, or by the verb *'think'* as when you say, 'I think that you, Zayd…'. It means: 'Do they reckon that Allah will not take them to task for it?' *'Allah shows favour to mankind'* by deferring their requital. It is said that it means the people of Makkah since He gave them safety in the *Ḥaram*. *'Most of them'*, meaning the unbelievers, are not thankful for His blessings nor for the deferral of their punishment. It is said that *'not thankful'* is a reference to their failure to declare the unity of Allah.

وَمَا تَكُونُ فِي شَأْنٍ وَمَا تَتْلُوا مِنْهُ مِن قُرْءَانٍ وَلَا تَعْمَلُونَ مِنْ عَمَلٍ
إِلَّا كُنَّا عَلَيْكُمْ شُهُودًا إِذْ تُفِيضُونَ فِيهِ وَمَا يَعْزُبُ عَن رَّبِّكَ مِن مِّثْقَالِ
ذَرَّةٍ فِي الْأَرْضِ وَلَا فِي السَّمَاءِ وَلَا أَصْغَرَ مِن ذَٰلِكَ وَلَا أَكْبَرَ إِلَّا فِي
كِتَابٍ مُّبِينٍ ﴿٦١﴾

61 You do not engage in any matter or recite any of the Qur'an or do any action without Our witnessing you while you are occupied with it. Not even the smallest speck eludes your Lord, either on earth or in heaven. Nor is there anything smaller than that, or larger, which is not in a Clear Book.

You do not engage in any matter or recite any of the Qur'an

'Mā' is for denial: you are not involved in anything, worship or otherwise, without the Lord being aware of you. *Sha'n* is a business or matter. The plural is *shu'ūn*. Al-Akhfash said that the verb *sha'ana* is 'to do' as in the expression, 'Whatever I do' (*mā sha'ntu sha'nah*) meaning, 'Whatever action I do.'

'Or recite any of the Qur'an': al-Farrā' and az-Zajjāj said that the *hā'* in *minhu* refers to *sha'n*, i.e. 'you are engaged in something and the Qur'an is recited because of it and it informs what its judgment is, or the Qur'an is revealed about it and recited.' Aṭ-Ṭabarī said that *'minhu'* means 'from the Book of Allah' and *'of the Qur'an'* is repeated to exalt it like His words, *'I am Allah.'* (20:14)

or do any action without Our witnessing you while you are occupied with it.

'Do any action' is directed to the Prophet ﷺ and his community and *'engage in any matter'* is addressed to him while both he and his community are meant. A Messenger can be addressed while what is meant is both him and his followers. It is also said that the unbelievers of Quraysh are meant. *'Witnessing'* means that Allah knows it. Its use is similar to: *'Three men cannot confer secretly together without Him being the fourth of them.'* (58:7)

'While you are occupied with it' means being involved in it, and the pronoun 'it' refers to the action. The verb *afāḍa* is used for speaking and action when one advances into it. [POEM] Ibn 'Abbās said that it means: 'do it'. Al-Akhfash said 'speak'. Ibn Zayd said, 'delve'. Ibn Kaysān said, 'push on in words'. Aḍ-Ḍaḥḥāk said that the *hā'* refers to the Qur'an, and it means, 'When you spread lies about the Qur'an.'

Not even the smallest speck eludes your Lord, either on earth or in heaven.

Ibn 'Abbās said, 'is hidden from'. Abū Rawq said, 'is far from'. Ibn Kaysān said, 'goes'. Al-Kisā'ī recited *'ya'zibu'* while the rest recite *'ya'zubu'*. They are two sound dialectical forms like *ya'rishu, ya'rushu*. In *'min mithqāl'* the *min* is connective. It means: 'not the smallest thing eludes your Lord.' *'The smallest speck'* (*dharrah*) is the weight of a very small red ant. It was already mentioned in *an-Nisā'* (4:40). *'Either on earth...'* is added either to *mithqāl* or to *dharrah.*

nor is there anything smaller than that, or larger, which is not in a Clear Book.

Ya'qūb and Ḥamzah recite 'smaller or larger' with a *ḍammah* on the *rā'* (*asgharu, akbaru*) as added to *mithqāl* because it is an addition for emphasis. Az-Zajjāj said that it can be in the nominative for the inceptive whose predicate is *'which is not in a Clear Book'*. It means is the Preserved Tablet which is part of Allah's knowledge.

Al-Jurjānī said that *'illā'* means 'and' for order, meaning 'and it is in a Clear Book.' It is similar to Allah's words: *'In My presence the Messengers have no fear – except (illā) for one who did wrong'* (27:10), meaning 'And those who did wrong' [starting a new sentence]. Allah says: *'...so that people will have no argument against yourselves except (illā) for those among them who wrong'* (2:159), meaning and those among them who do wrong and so *illā* has the meaning of the *wāw* of succession. It implies what is after it, like in: *'Say, "Relieve us of our burdens!"'* (2:58), meaning it is relief. He said, 'Do not say, "*Three*", meaning 'They are three.' It is like what we see in the *āyah*: *'No leaf falls without His knowing it. There is no seed in the darkness of the earth, and nothing moist or dry which is not (illā) in a Clear Book.'* (6:59) It is in a Clear Book.

أَلَآ إِنَّ أَوْلِيَآءَ ٱللَّهِ لَا خَوْفٌ عَلَيْهِمْ وَلَا هُمْ يَحْزَنُونَ ﴿٦٢﴾

62 Yes, the friends of Allah will feel no fear and will know no sorrow:

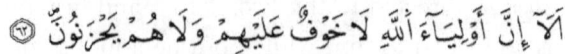

This will be in the Next World and they will not sorrow over the passing of this world. It is said that if Allah takes someone as a friend and undertakes to preserve and guard him and is pleased with him, he will feel neither fear nor sorrow on the Day of Rising. Allah says: *'Those for whom the Best was ordained … The greatest terror will not upset them.'* (21:101-103)

Sa'īd ibn Jubayr related that the Messenger of Allah ﷺ was asked, 'Who are the friends of Allah?' He said, 'Those who remind you of Allah when you see them.' 'Umar ibn al-Khaṭṭāb said about this *āyah*, 'I heard the Messenger of Allah ﷺ say, "There are among the slaves of Allah those who are not Prophets or martyrs who will be envied by the Prophets and martyrs on the Day of Rising because of their position with Allah." It was said, "Messenger of Allah, tell us who they are and what they did so that we might love them." He said, "They are people who love one another in Allah without any kinship between them nor for any property they give one another. By Allah, their faces are light. They will be on *minbars* of light and they will not fear when people are afraid and they will not sorrow when people are sad.' Then he recited: *'Yes, the friends of Allah will feel no fear and will know no sorrow.'* 'Alī ibn Abī Ṭālib said, 'The friends of Allah are people with faces yellow from sleeplessness, blear-eyed from reflection, hollow-bellied from hunger, and whose lips are dry from thirst.'

'They will feel no fear' regarding their descendants because Allah will take charge of them. *'They will know no sorrow'* for this world since Allah will replace the first and last of them because He is their Protector and Guardian.

ٱلَّذِينَ ءَامَنُوا۟ وَكَانُوا۟ يَتَّقُونَ ﴿٦٣﴾

63 those who believe and are godfearing,

This describes the friends of Allah. The pronoun *'those'* is in the position of the accusative as an appositive for the noun of *'inna'* which is 'friends'. If you wish it, is 'I mean'. It is said that it is an inceptive whose predicate is *'there is good news for them'*. So it is separate from what is before it, meaning: they fear *shirk* and acts of disobedience.

لَهُمُ ٱلْبُشْرَىٰ فِى ٱلْحَيَوٰةِ ٱلدُّنْيَا وَفِى ٱلْـَٔاخِرَةِ ۚ لَا تَبْدِيلَ لِكَلِمَـٰتِ
ٱللَّهِ ۚ ذَٰلِكَ هُوَ ٱلْفَوْزُ ٱلْعَظِيمُ ﴿٦٤﴾

64 there is good news for them in the life of this world and in the Next World. There is no changing the words of Allah. That is the great victory!

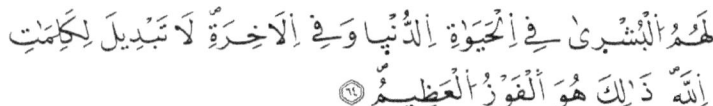

there is good news for them in the life of this world and in the Next World.

Abū ad-Dardā' said, 'I asked the Messenger of Allah ﷺ about it and he said, "No one but you has asked me about it since it was revealed. It refers to the true dream which a Muslim sees or is shown."' At-Tirmidhī transmitted it. Az-Zuhrī, 'Aṭā' and Qatādah said that it is the good news which the angels give the believer in this world as he is dying. Muḥammad ibn Ka'b al-Quraẓī said, 'When the soul of a believer is taken, the Angel of Death comes and says, "Peace be upon you, friend of Allah. Allah sends you greeting."' Then he quoted this *āyah*: '*...those the angels take in a virtuous state. They say, "Peace be upon you!"*' (16:32) Ibn al-Mubārak mentioned it.

Qatādah and aḍ-Ḍaḥḥāk said, 'It is so that a person will know where they will be before they die.' Al-Ḥasan said, 'It is those about whom Allah Almighty gives the good news of His Garden and noble reward by His words: *"Their Lord gives them the good news of His mercy and good pleasure"* (9:21) and His words: *"Give good news to those who believe and do right actions that they will have Gardens"* (2:25) and His words: *"Rejoice in the Garden you have been promised"*'(41:30).' That is why Allah says: '*There is no changing the words of Allah.*' It means that His promises are not broken. That is because His promises are known by His words. '*In the Next World*' is said to refer to the Garden when they leave their graves. It is said that when the spirit comes out of the body it is given the good news of Allah's pleasure. Abū Isḥāq ath-Tha'labī said that he heard Abū Bakr Muḥammad ibn 'Abdullāh al-Jawzaqī say, 'I saw al-Ḥāfiẓ Abū 'Abdullāh in a dream riding a mule wearing a shawl and a turban. I greeted him and said to him, "Welcome to you! We still talk of you and your good qualities." He said, "And we continue to remember you and your good qualities. Allah says: '*There is good news for them in the life of this world and in the Next World.*' This is good praise," and he pointed with his hand.'

'*There is no changing the words of Allah*' and no deviation from His promise. '*That is the great victory*' to which His friends will go.'

وَلَا يَحْزُنكَ قَوْلُهُمْ ۘ إِنَّ ٱلْعِزَّةَ لِلَّهِ جَمِيعًا ۚ هُوَ ٱلسَّمِيعُ
ٱلْعَلِيمُ ﴿٦٥﴾

65 Do not be grieved by what they say. All might belongs to Allah. He is the All-Hearing, the All-Knowing.

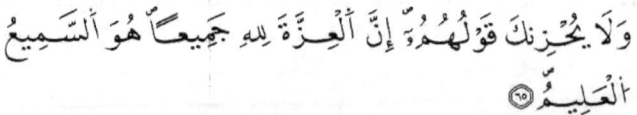

The words end with '*Do not be grieved by what they say.*' It means: 'Do not be grieved by their falsifying and denial of you.' Then Allah begins a new sentence and says: '*All might belongs to Allah.*' That is total strength, encompassing, overcoming, and absolute power which belongs to Allah alone. He is Your Helper, Supporter and Protector. The adjective *'All'* is in the accusative by the *ḥāl*. This does not contradict His words: *'All might belongs to Allah and to His Messenger and the believers.'* (63:8) All might is by Allah and so all might belongs to Allah. The Almighty says: *'Glory be to your Lord, the Lord of Might, beyond anything they describe.'* (37:180) Allah hears what they say and their voices and knows their actions, deeds and all their movements.

أَلَآ إِنَّ لِلَّهِ مَن فِي السَّمَٰوَٰتِ وَمَن فِي الْأَرْضِ وَمَا يَتَّبِعُ الَّذِينَ
يَدْعُونَ مِن دُونِ اللَّهِ شُرَكَآءَ إِن يَتَّبِعُونَ إِلَّا الظَّنَّ وَإِنْ
هُمْ إِلَّا يَخْرُصُونَ ﴿٦٦﴾

66 Yes, indeed! Everyone in the heavens and everyone on the earth belongs to Allah. Those who call on something other than Allah are not really following their partner-gods. They are only following conjecture. They are only guessing.

Allah judges them in whatever way He wills and does whatever He wishes with them. In the words: *'are not really following' mā* is negative, meaning that they do not truly follow partners but only think that they intercede for them. It is also said that *mā* may indicate a question, meaning 'What do those who call on something other than Allah follow?' This makes their action ugly. Then the answer is: they are merely guessing and denying. This has already been discussed (6:116).

هُوَ الَّذِي جَعَلَ لَكُمُ الَّيْلَ لِتَسْكُنُوا فِيهِ وَالنَّهَارَ مُبْصِرًا إِنَّ
فِي ذَٰلِكَ لَآيَٰتٍ لِّقَوْمٍ يَسْمَعُونَ ﴿٦٧﴾

67 It is He who appointed the night for you, so that you could rest in it, and the day for seeing. There are certainly Signs in that for people who listen.

It is He who appointed the night for you, so that you could rest in it,

Allah makes it clear that the One Who must be worshipped is the One Who is able to create night and day, not something which has no power to do anything. The phrase *'rest in it'* means with your wives and children to remove fatigue and stress. *Sukūn* is calmness after commotion.

and the day for seeing.

The day is illuminated so that in it you can be guided to what you need. *Mubṣir* is the one who sees and in the day one can see. It is said that *mubṣir* is metaphorical as is the linguistic habit of the Arabs as in '*layl qā'im*' and '*nahār ṣā'im*'. Jarīr said:

You blamed us, Umm Ghaylān, for travelling at night.
You slept, and the night of the riding mounts is not one of sleep.

Quṭrub said, 'One says that the night darkens since there is darkness in it, and the day gives light since it has light and allows one to see.' '*Signs*' are evidence and hallmarks and '*people who listen*' are those who listen to instruction.

قَالُوا اتَّخَذَ اللَّهُ وَلَدًا سُبْحَانَهُ هُوَ الْغَنِيُّ لَهُ مَا فِي السَّمَاوَاتِ
وَمَا فِي الْأَرْضِ إِنْ عِندَكُم مِّن سُلْطَانٍ بِهَٰذَا أَتَقُولُونَ عَلَى اللَّهِ مَا لَا
تَعْلَمُونَ ﴿٦٨﴾

68 They say, 'Allah has a son.' Glory be to Him! He is the Rich Beyond Need. Everything in the heavens and everything on the earth belongs to Him. Have you authority to say this or are you saying about Allah what you do not know?

The pronoun '*they*' here refers to the unbelievers. This was already mentioned (2:116). '*Glory be to Him*!' Allah has freed Himself from any need for a wife or children or partners or peers. He tells us that He has absolute wealth and that everything in the heavens and the earth is His as His property, creation and slaves. *'There is no one in the heavens and earth who will not come to the All-Merciful as a slave.'* (19:93) The question: *'Have you any authority…?'* means 'Do you have any proof about what you say about affirming that He has a child?' A child demands a common genus and similarity and Allah does not resemble anything.

قُلْ إِنَّ الَّذِينَ يَفْتَرُونَ عَلَى اللَّهِ الْكَذِبَ لَا يُفْلِحُونَ ﴿٦٩﴾ مَتَاعٌ فِي الدُّنْيَا
ثُمَّ إِلَيْنَا مَرْجِعُهُمْ ثُمَّ نُذِيقُهُمُ الْعَذَابَ الشَّدِيدَ بِمَا كَانُوا
يَكْفُرُونَ ﴿٧٠﴾

69-70 Say: 'People who invent lies against Allah will not be successful.' There is the enjoyment of this world. Then they will return to Us. Then We will let them taste the terrible punishment because they disbelieved.

Their lies are ineffective and they are not safe. The words end here. '*The enjoyment of this world*' means: that is enjoyment or 'that is the enjoyment of this world.' Al-Kisā'ī said that. Al-Akhfash said, 'They have enjoyment in this world.'" Abū Isḥāq said that it is permitted to use the accusative in other than the Qur'an with the meaning of enjoyment. *Marji'* is return. A terrible punishment is a harsh one, and that is on account of their unbelief.

وَٱتْلُ عَلَيْهِمْ نَبَأَ نُوحٍ إِذْ قَالَ لِقَوْمِهِۦ يَٰقَوْمِ إِن كَانَ كَبُرَ عَلَيْكُم مَّقَامِى
وَتَذْكِيرِى بِـَٔايَٰتِ ٱللَّهِ فَعَلَى ٱللَّهِ تَوَكَّلْتُ فَأَجْمِعُوٓا۟ أَمْرَكُمْ وَشُرَكَآءَكُمْ
ثُمَّ لَا يَكُنْ أَمْرُكُمْ عَلَيْكُمْ غُمَّةً ثُمَّ ٱقْضُوٓا۟ إِلَىَّ وَلَا تُنظِرُونِ ٧١

71 Recite to them the story of Nūḥ when he said to his people, 'My people, if my standing here and reminding you of Allah's Signs has become too much for you to bear, know that I have put my trust in Allah. So decide, you and your gods, on what you want to do and be open about it. Do with me whatever you decide and do not keep me waiting.

Recite to them the story of Nūḥ when he said to his people,

Allah is ordering the Prophet ﷺ to mention to them the stories of previous people and to alarm them with the painful punishment that will result from their unbelief, and the *wāw* is elided from '*wa-tlu*' because it is imperative, implying, 'Recite to them the report about Nūḥ.' '*Idh*' is in the position of the accusative.

'My people, if my standing here and reminding you of Allah's Signs has become too much for you to bear,

The verbal phrase '*has become too much*' means too great and onerous. The noun *maqām* designates the place in which someone stands and the form *muqām* means standing [which is not recited as far as we know] and so it means, 'If my remaining here among you seems so long for you that you have resolved to kill me and expel me.' '*Reminding you*' means talking to you and alarming you. 'If you resolve to kill and expel me, *"I have put my trust in Allah"*.' This is the apodosis of the precondition. He continued to put his trust in and rely on Allah in every state, but he made it clear that he put his trust in Him in this particular instance so that his people would know that Allah would spare him from dealing with them, implying, 'If you do not help me, I will rely on One Who will help me.'

So decide, you and your gods, on what you want to do and be open about it.

Most read '*fa-ajmi'ū*' with the *alif* separate and have '*shurakā'akum*' in the accusative. 'Āṣim al-Jaḥdarī reads it with the *alif* connected and a *fatḥah* on the *mīm* (*fa-jma'ū*) from the verb *jama'a* with '*shurakā'akum*' in the accusative. Al-Ḥasan, Ibn Abī Isḥāq, and Ya'qūb recited '*fa-ajmi'ū*' with the *alif* separate and '*shurakā'ukum*' in the nominative. The first reading is from *ajma'a*, to resolve on something. Al-Farrā' said that *ajma'a* means to prepare something. Al-Mu'arrij said that *ajma'a* with a direct object is more eloquent than with the particle *'alā*, [and quotes a poem illustrating this.]

An-Naḥḥās said, 'There are three reasons for *"your gods"* being in the accusative in this reading. Al-Kisā'ī and al-Farrā' said that it means: "Call on your gods to help you." They consider that it is in the accusative by the effect of an implied verb. Muḥammad ibn Yazīd said that it is added to the meaning as one says:

Would that your husband in the wild were girded with a sword and spear.

'One does not gird on a spear.' Abū Isḥāq az-Zajjāj said, 'It means with your gods in helping you, as you say that water and wood meet.'

'The second reading from *jama'a* takes into account Allah's words: *"he concocted (jama'a) his scheme and then he arrived."* (20:60) Abū Mu'ādh said that it is conceivable for *jamā'a* and *ajma'a* to mean the same. According to this reading, *"your gods"* is added to *"amrakum"*, or it has the meaning "decide on your business and collect your gods." If you wish, it can mean "with".' Abū Ja'far an-Naḥḥās said, 'I heard Abū Isḥāq allow, "*Qāma Zaydun wa 'Amra.*"'

A third reading is based on '*gods*' being added to something implied in the nominative in '*ajma'ū*'. That is good because it is a long sentence. An-Naḥḥās and others said that this meaning is unlikely because if it had been in the nominative, it would be necessary to write it with a *wāw* and that is not seen in copies of the Qur'an. Furthermore *shurakā'* means the idols, and the idols do not do anything and have no action to decide upon. Al-Mahdawī said, 'It is possible for *"idols"* to be in the nominative by the inceptive and elided predicate, meaning "and your gods should decide on their business." That is ascribed to the idols although they do not hear or see or decide, as a rebuke to those who worship idols.'

and be open about it.

This is the noun of *kāna*. In '*be open about it*' *ghummah* and *ghamm* are the same. It means covering, meaning 'let your business be open and unconcealed and do whatever you wish in it and do not be like someone whose business is hidden and cannot do what he wants.' Ṭarafah said:

> By your life, my business is not confused (*ghummah*) for me.
> Neither my day nor night are perpetual for me.

Az-Zajjāj said that *ghummah* is 'with *ghamm* (sorrow)'. *Ghamm* and *ghummah* are like *karb* and *kurbah*. It is said that *ghummah* is the constriction of the business which obliges sorrow so that the business is not clear to the person, permitting him to have relief from what grieves him. We find in *aṣ-Ṣiḥāḥ* that *ghummah* is grief. Al-'Ajjāj said:

> If you were to see people when they are wrapped in sorrow (*ghummah*),
> they would be sorrowed if you were not relieved.

A business is described as *ghummah* when it is complicated and confused as is the case in this *āyah*. Abū 'Ubaydah said that it is a metaphor for darkness and constriction. *Ghummah* also describes the bottom of a skin used for holding ghee. Someone else said that the root of all of this is derived from *ghamāmah* (clouds).

Do with me whatever you decide and do not keep me waiting.

The *alif* of '*thumma-qḍū*' is a connective *alif*. It is from the verb *qaḍā, yaqḍī*. Al-Akhfash and al-Kisā'ī said that it is like: '*the command We had decreed*' (15:66), meaning 'We made it arrive.' It is related from Ibn 'Abbās that it means: 'Decide for me and do not delay.' An-Naḥḥās said, 'This is a sound position linguistically. Part of that is *qaḍā* in respect of the dead, meaning passed away.' By this he informs them that they will not reach him. This is one of the proofs of Prophethood.

Al-Farrā' related that some reciteres have '*thumma afḍū*' with a separated *alif*, meaning 'direct yourselves'. This is Allah reporting about His Prophet Nūḥ saying that he trusted in the help of Allah and did not fear their machinations. He knew that they and their deities could not help nor harm. This is solace for His Prophet ﷺ and strengthens his heart.

فَإِن تَوَلَّيْتُمْ فَمَا سَأَلْتُكُم مِّنْ أَجْرٍ إِنْ أَجْرِيَ إِلَّا عَلَى اللَّهِ وَأُمِرْتُ أَنْ أَكُونَ
مِنَ الْمُسْلِمِينَ ﴿٧٢﴾

72 If you turn your backs, I have not asked you for any wage. My wage is the responsibility of Allah alone. I am commanded to be one of the Muslims.'

'If you turn away from what I have brought you, that is not because I asked you for a wage so that it is onerous for you to follow me. My wage for conveying His Message is up to Allah.' The Muslims are those who proclaim Allah to be One. The people of Madīnah, Abū 'Amr, Ibn 'Āmir and Ḥafṣ recite '*my wage*' with a *fatḥah* on the *yā'* wherever it occurs. The rest have a *sukūn*.

فَكَذَّبُوهُ فَنَجَّيْنَاهُ وَمَن مَّعَهُ فِي الْفُلْكِ وَجَعَلْنَاهُمْ خَلَائِفَ وَأَغْرَقْنَا
الَّذِينَ كَذَّبُوا بِآيَاتِنَا فَانظُرْ كَيْفَ كَانَ عَاقِبَةُ الْمُنذَرِينَ ﴿٧٣﴾

73 But they denied him so We rescued him, and all those with him, in the Ark and We made them the successors and We drowned the people who denied Our Signs. See the final fate of those who were warned!

They denied Nūḥ. '*Those with him*' were the believers. '*We made them the successors*' means inhabitants on the earth and successors to those who were drowned. See the end of the business of those whom the Messengers warned and did not believe after Nūḥ.

ثُمَّ بَعَثْنَا مِن بَعْدِهِ رُسُلًا إِلَىٰ قَوْمِهِمْ فَجَاءُوهُم بِالْبَيِّنَاتِ فَمَا كَانُوا لِيُؤْمِنُوا بِمَا
كَذَّبُوا بِهِ مِن قَبْلُ كَذَٰلِكَ نَطْبَعُ عَلَىٰ قُلُوبِ الْمُعْتَدِينَ ﴿٧٤﴾

74 Then after him We sent Messengers to their people, and they brought them the Clear Signs, but they were never going to believe in something which they had previously denied. That is how We seal up the hearts of those who overstep the limits.

After Nūḥ, Allah sent Messengers such as Hūd, Ṣāliḥ, Ibrāhīm, Lūṭ, Shu'ayb and others. '*Clear Signs*' means miracles. The phrase '*they were never going to believe in something*' refers to what the people of Nūḥ had earlier denied. It is also said that the adverb '*previously*' refers to the Day of '*Am I not your Lord?*' before they came into this world. It is also said that it was those who denied Him in their hearts on that Day when everyone said, '*Yes indeed you are.*'

An-Naḥḥās said that the best that has been said about this is that it was said to a specific people, as is the case in '*It makes no difference to them whether you warn them or do not warn them.*' (2:6) '*Those who overstep the limits*' are those who cross the limits in unbelief and denial and do not believe.

ثُمَّ بَعَثْنَا مِنۢ بَعْدِهِم مُّوسَىٰ وَهَٰرُونَ إِلَىٰ فِرْعَوْنَ وَمَلَإِي۟هِۦ بِـَٔايَٰتِنَا فَٱسْتَكْبَرُوا۟
وَكَانُوا۟ قَوْمًا مُّجْرِمِينَ ﴿٧٥﴾

75 Then after them We sent Mūsā and Hārūn with Our Signs to Pharaoh and his ruling circle, but they were arrogant and were a people of evildoers.

After the Messengers and previous nations. '*His ruling circle*' are the nobles of his people. The word '*Signs*' refers to the Nine Signs already mentioned (2:92; 7:133). They were arrogant about the truth and were idolaters.

فَلَمَّا جَآءَهُمُ ٱلْحَقُّ مِنْ عِندِنَا قَالُوٓا۟ إِنَّ هَٰذَا لَسِحْرٌ مُّبِينٌ ﴿٧٦﴾ قَالَ مُوسَىٰٓ
أَتَقُولُونَ لِلْحَقِّ لَمَّا جَآءَكُمْ ۖ أَسِحْرٌ هَٰذَا وَلَا يُفْلِحُ ٱلسَّٰحِرُونَ ﴿٧٧﴾

76-77 When the truth came to them from Us, they said, 'This is downright magic!' Mūsā said, 'Do you say to the truth when it comes to you, "This is magic"? Magicians are not successful.'

The pronoun '*them*' refers to Pharaoh and his people. They attributed the miracles to magic and Mūsā refuted them. It is said that there is some elision in the words: '*Do you say to the truth, "This is magic,"*' and so '*Do you say*' is denial and their words '*This is magic,*' are elided, and then there is a new sentence again denying what is before it and he says, 'Is this magic?' Elision in the first spares the need for mentioning it in the second, denying Pharaoh and his religion.

Al-Akhfash said that it is part of their words and the interrogative *alif* is added to recount their words since they said, 'Is this magic?' So they are told, 'When the truth comes to you, do you ask, "Is this magic?"' This is related from al-Ḥasan. Someone who practises magic will not have success.

قَالُوٓاْ أَجِئۡتَنَا لِتَلۡفِتَنَا عَمَّا وَجَدۡنَا عَلَيۡهِ ءَابَآءَنَا وَتَكُونَ لَكُمَا ٱلۡكِبۡرِيَآءُ فِي ٱلۡأَرۡضِ وَمَا نَحۡنُ لَكُمَا بِمُؤۡمِنِينَ ﴿٧٨﴾

78 They said, 'Have you come to us to turn us from what we found our fathers doing, and to gain greatness in the land? We do not believe you.'

'*To turn us*' means to divert us and change us. The verb *lafata*, *yalfitu, laft* means to turn away and avert. A poet said:

I turned aside (*talaffatu*) towards the tribe when I saw that
I was pained in the side of my neck from inclining in pliancy.

From this comes the verb *iltafa* which is to turn aside from the direction directly in front of a person. The phrase '*what we found our fathers doing*' refers to their worshipping idols. The noun '*greatness*' here means magnificence, sovereignty and power and '*the land*' here refers to Egypt. A king is referred to as having greatness because he is the greatest of what is sought in this world.

'*We do not believe you.*' Ibn Mas'ūd, al-Ḥasan and others recite '*yakūna*' with *yā'* because it is not a real feminine and there is a separation between them. Sībawayh related: 'Two women attended the Qāḍī today' [using the masculine particle].

وَقَالَ فِرۡعَوۡنُ ٱئۡتُونِي بِكُلِّ سَٰحِرٍ عَلِيمٖ ﴿٧٩﴾

79 Pharaoh said, 'Bring me every knowledgeable magician.'

He said that when he saw the staff and the white hand and believed that that was magic. Ḥamzah, al-Kisā'ī, Ibn Waththāb and al-A'mash recite '*saḥḥār*', and the two readings were already mentioned in *al-A'raf* (7:104-112).

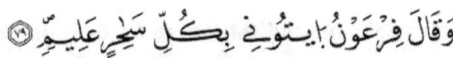

فَلَمَّا جَآءَ ٱلسَّحَرَةُ قَالَ لَهُم مُّوسَىٰٓ أَلْقُوا۟ مَآ أَنتُم مُّلْقُونَ ﴿٨٠﴾

80 When the magicians came, Mūsā said to them, 'Throw whatever you have to throw!'

'Throw on the ground the ropes and staves you have!' This was also already discussed at length in *al-A'raf* (7:112-117).

فَلَمَّآ أَلْقَوْا۟ قَالَ مُوسَىٰ مَا جِئْتُم بِهِ ٱلسِّحْرُ ۖ إِنَّ ٱللَّهَ سَيُبْطِلُهُۥٓ ۖ إِنَّ ٱللَّهَ
لَا يُصْلِحُ عَمَلَ ٱلْمُفْسِدِينَ ﴿٨١﴾

81 When they had thrown, Mūsā said, 'What you have brought is magic. Allah will certainly prove it false. Allah does not uphold the actions of corrupters.'

Mā is in the position of the nominative by the inceptive and the predicate is '*What you have brought*'. It implies: 'What thing have you brought?' and is used for rebuke and belittling the magic they brought. The reading of Abū 'Amr is *'ās-siḥr'* as a question, based on an implied inchoative. It implies: 'Is it magic?' It is possible that it is an inchoative whose predicate is elided. It implies: 'the magic you have brought'. In the reading of those who make it a question it does not mean 'which' since it has no predicate.

The rest recite *'as-siḥru'* as the predicate. The evidence for this is the reading of Ibn Mas'ūd: 'what you have brought is magic (*siḥr*),' without the definite article. The reading of Ubayy is *'mā ataytum bihi siḥr'* and *mā* means 'that which', 'you have brought' is connective, and the position of the *mā* is nominative by the inceptive with '*magic*' the predicate of the inceptive. When *mā* means 'which', it is not in the accusative because the connective does not act on what is connected.

Al-Farrā' allows for '*magic*' to be in the accusative by the action of the verb '*brought*' and it is not by a precondition and '*brought*' is in the position of the jussive by *mā* and an elided *fā'*. It implies: 'Allah will seek it out'. '*Magic*' can also be in the accusative as a verbal noun, i.e. what you brought is magic. Then the definite article is added and it is redundant. According to this, there is no need for the elision of the *fā'*. An-Naḥḥās preferred this position and said that the *fā'* is elided in condition, but many grammarians only permit that when it is required in poetry as in:

If anyone does good deeds, Allah is thankful for them.

Some of them say that it is absolutely not permitted at all. I heard 'Alī ibn Sulaymān say that Muḥammad ibn Yazīd related from al-Māzinī that he heard al-Aṣma'ī say that the grammarians changed this verse. It is:

If anyone does good, the All-Merciful is thankful for it.

[There is a '*fā'*' before 'the All-Merciful'.] I heard heard 'Alī ibn Sulaymān say that it is permitted to elide the *fā'* in the apodosis. The evidence for that is: *'Any disaster that strikes you is through what* (fa-bimā) *your own hands have earned'* (42:30) and the reading of the same verse that has it without the *fā'* and just *bimā*. Both readings are known and accepted.

Allah does not uphold the actions of corrupters.'

The action of corrupters here is magic. Ibn 'Abbās said, 'If someone goes to bed at night and then recites this *āyah*, the trickery of a magician will not harm him. It will only be written for one bewitched that Allah has repealed magic from him.'

وَيُحِقُّ ٱللَّهُ ٱلْحَقَّ بِكَلِمَٰتِهِۦ وَلَوْ كَرِهَ ٱلْمُجْرِمُونَ ﴿٨٢﴾

82 Allah confirms the Truth by His words, even though the evildoers hate it.

He makes it clear and evident. '*His words*' are His words, proofs and evidence. '*Evildoers*' refers to those among the people of Pharaoh.

فَمَآ ءَامَنَ لِمُوسَىٰٓ إِلَّا ذُرِّيَّةٌ مِّن قَوْمِهِۦ عَلَىٰ خَوْفٍ مِّن فِرْعَوْنَ وَمَلَإِيْهِمْ
أَن يَفْتِنَهُمْ ۚ وَإِنَّ فِرْعَوْنَ لَعَالٍ فِى ٱلْأَرْضِ وَإِنَّهُۥ لَمِنَ ٱلْمُسْرِفِينَ ﴿٨٣﴾

83 No one believed in Mūsā except for a few of his people out of fear that Pharaoh, and the elders, would persecute them. Pharaoh was high and mighty in the land. He was one of the profligate.

No one believed in Mūsā except for a few of his people

The *hā'* in 'his people' refers to Mūsā. Mujāhid said that it means none of them believed, but some of the children of those of the tribe of Israel to whom

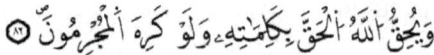

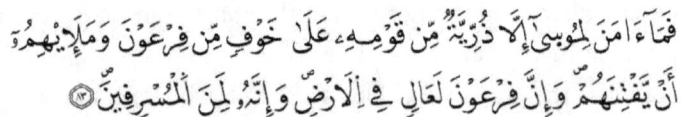

Mūsā was sent did believe after their fathers had died. This is what aṭ-Ṭabarī preferred.

Dhurriyyah are a person's descendants who may be numerous. It is said that *dhurriyyah* means the believers of the tribe of Israel. Ibn 'Abbās said that they were six hundred thousand. That was because Ya'qūb entered Egypt with seventy-two persons and they multiplied in Egypt until they reached six hundred thousand. Ibn 'Abbās said that '*his people*' means from the people of Pharaoh who included the believer of the people of Pharaoh, his treasurer, his wife, the maid of his daughter and the wife of the treasurer.

It is said that it means peoples whose fathers were among the Copts and their mothers among the tribe of Israel and so they are called *dhurriyyah* as the children of the Persians born in Yemen and the Arab lands are called *abnā'* because their mothers are not the same race as their fathers. Al-Farrā' said that. According to this, the allusion in '*his people*' refers to Mūsā because of his kinship from the maternal side and to Pharaoh since he was one of the Copts.

out of fear that Pharaoh, and the elders, would persecute them.

That was because Pharaoh controlled them harshly. There are a number of reasons given for why he said '*the elders*' [literally, 'their council' and not 'his council']. One is because Pharaoh was a tyrant who was spoken of using the plural pronoun. The second is that when Pharaoh was mentioned, he knew that there was someone else with him and so the pronoun 'them' refers to both him and them. This is one of the two views of al-Farrā'. The third is that the plural is used for Pharaoh as is the case with Thamūd. The fourth is that it implies a fear of the family of Pharaoh and so there is elision of the *muḍāf* as in '*ask the town.*' (12:81) That is the second view of al-Farrā'. According to Sībawayh and al-Khalīl, this answer is an error and they do not permit the saying of, 'Hind stood' when you mean her son. The fifth view is the position of Sa'īd al-Akhfash who has the pronoun refer to *dhurriyyah*, i.e. the gathering of offspring. Aṭ-Ṭabarī preferred that. The sixth is that the pronoun refers to '*his people*'. An-Naḥḥās says that this seems to be the most eloquent.

'*Persecute them*': This is speaking about Pharaoh. It means that he would make them turn from their *dīn* by means of punishments. It is in the position of the genitive on the basis of its being an inclusive appositive. It is also possible that it is in the position of the accusative by the action of the noun '*fear*'. Pharaoh is not declined because it is a foreign noun. It is definite.

'High and mighty' means haughty and arrogant. '*The profligate*' are those who exceed the limits in unbelief. That is because he was a slave yet claimed to be a Lord.

وَقَالَ مُوسَىٰ يَٰقَوْمِ إِن كُنتُمْ ءَامَنتُم بِٱللَّهِ فَعَلَيْهِ تَوَكَّلُوٓا۟ إِن كُنتُم مُّسْلِمِينَ ﴿٨٤﴾
فَقَالُوا۟ عَلَى ٱللَّهِ تَوَكَّلْنَا رَبَّنَا لَا تَجْعَلْنَا فِتْنَةً لِّلْقَوْمِ ٱلظَّٰلِمِينَ ﴿٨٥﴾

84-85 Mūsā said, 'My people! if you believe in Allah, then put your trust in Him, if you are Muslims.' They said, 'We have put our trust in Allah. Our Lord, do not make us a target for this wrongdoing people,

'If you affirm Allah, then rely on Allah.' The precondition is repeated for stress. Mūsā makes it clear that the perfection of faith lies in entrusting one's affairs to Allah. They said, 'We have surrendered our affairs to Allah and are content with His decree and determination. We rest with His command.'

Our Lord, do not make us a target for this wrongdoing people,

'Do not help them against us so that will tempt us to leave our *dīn* or test us by punishing us at their hands.' Mujāhid said that it means: 'Do not destroy us at the hands of our enemies nor punish us with a punishment from You so that our enemies say, "If they had had the truth, we would not have authority over them," and so they are tested.' Abū Miljāz and Abū aḍ-Ḍuḥā said that it means, 'Do not give them power over us so that they think that they are better than us and increase in transgression.'

وَنَجِّنَا بِرَحْمَتِكَ مِنَ ٱلْقَوْمِ ٱلْكَٰفِرِينَ ﴿٨٦﴾

86 and rescue us, by Your mercy, from this unbelieving people!'

'*Rescue us*' means 'deliver us'. '*This unbelieving people*' are Pharaoh and his people because they made them perform arduous tasks.

وَأَوْحَيْنَآ إِلَىٰ مُوسَىٰ وَأَخِيهِ أَن تَبَوَّءَا لِقَوْمِكُمَا بِمِصْرَ بُيُوتًا وَٱجْعَلُوا۟ بُيُوتَكُمْ
قِبْلَةً وَأَقِيمُوا۟ ٱلصَّلَوٰةَ ۗ وَبَشِّرِ ٱلْمُؤْمِنِينَ ﴿٨٧﴾

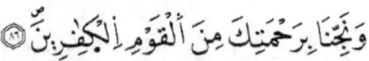

87 We revealed to Mūsā and his brother: 'Settle your people in houses in Egypt and make your houses places of worship and establish the prayer and give good news to the believers.'

We revealed to Mūsā and his brother: 'Settle your people in houses in Egypt

The verb '*Settle*' is to establish. The verb *bawwa'a* is to provide accommodation. It can be used with a direct object or with the particle *li*. *Mubawwa'* is a permanent dwelling. Illustrating this is the expression '*bawwa'ahu-llāhu manzilan*' (Allah lodged him in an abode). An example is found in the *ḥadīth*: 'Whoever lies about me should take his seat (*li-yatabawwa'*) in the Fire.' A poet said:

We are the sons of 'Adnān without doubt.
Glory and kingdom is (*tabawwa'a*) ours.

'Egypt' in this *āyah* means Alexandria according to Mujāhid. Aḍ-Ḍaḥḥāk said that it is a land called Egypt (Miṣr) and that is what is between the sea as far as Aswan. Alexandria is part of Egypt.

and make your houses places of worship

Most commentators say that the tribe of Israel used to only pray in places of worship, and synagogues were clearly places of worship. When Mūsā was sent, Pharaoh ordered all the places of worship of the tribe of Israel to be demolished and so they were unable to pray. Allah revealed to Mūsā and Hārūn to take houses (as places of prayer). It does not mean domiciles. This is the position of Ibrāhīm, Ibn Zayd, ar-Rabī', Abū Mālik, Ibn 'Abbās and others. It is related from Ibn 'Abbās and Sa'īd ibn Jubayr that it means: 'Make your houses face one another.'

The first view is sounder, i.e. make your places of prayer face the *qiblah*. It is said that this means Jerusalem, which is the *qiblah* of the Jews even today. Ibn Baḥr said that. Ibn 'Abbās said that it is the *Ka'bah*. He said, 'The *Ka'bah* was the *qiblah* of Mūsā عليه السلام and the prayer had the preconditions of purity, covering the private parts and facing *qiblah*. That is greater in terms of responsibility and fuller in terms of worship.' It is said that what is meant is: 'Pray in your houses secretly so that you are safe.' That was when Pharaoh reduced them to a state of fear. They were commanded to be patient and make places of prayer in their houses, come to the prayer and pray for Allah to carry out His promise. That is what is meant by Allah's words: '*Mūsā said to his people, "Seek help in Allah and be steadfast."*' (7:128) One aspect of their religion was that, if they were in a state of safety, they could only pray in synagogues and temples. If they were in a state of fear, they were permitted to pray in their houses. Ibn al-'Arabī said, 'The first is clearer because the second view is a claim.'

A claim, however, can be sound. We find in the *Ṣaḥīḥ* that the Prophet ﷺ said, 'The earth was made a mosque for me and a means of purification.' This is part of what was particular to him rather than other Prophets. We – may Allah be praised – can pray in mosques and houses and wherever we are when the time of prayer comes although it is better to do *nāfilah* in houses rather than in mosques – even the *rak'ahs* before *Jumu'ah* and after it – and before and after the obligatory prayers, since there can be ostentation in *nāfilah* but not in obligatory prayers. Whenever an action is free of ostentation, it is weightier with Allah Almighty.

Muslim related that 'Abdullāh ibn Shaqīq said, 'I asked 'Ā'ishah about the voluntary prayers of the Prophet ﷺ and she said, "He used to pray four *rak'ahs* in my room before *Ẓuhr* and then he would go out and lead the people in prayer. Then he would come in and pray two *rak'ahs*. He would lead the people in *Maghrib* and then come in and prayer two *rak'ahs*. He would lead the people in the *'Ishā'* prayer and then come in to my room and pray two *rak'ahs*.' Ibn 'Umar said, 'I prayed two *rak'ahs* with the Prophet ﷺ before *Ẓuhr* and after *Maghrib*. I prayed those of *Maghrib*, *'Ishā'* and *Jumu'ah* with the Prophet ﷺ in his house.' Abū Dāwūd related from Ka'b ibn 'Ujrah that the Prophet ﷺ went to the mosque of the Banū al-Ashhal and prayed *Maghrib* in it. When they finished the prayer, he saw them glorifying after it. He said, 'This is the prayer done in houses.'

Scholars disagree about night prayers in Ramaḍān and whether it is better to perform them at home or in the mosque. The position of Mālik is that it is better to do them at home for those who are strong enough to do it. Abū Yūsuf and some of the Shāfi'īs say that. Ibn 'Abd al-Ḥakam, Aḥmad and some of the people of ash-Shāfi'ī believe that it is better to do them in the group. Al-Layth said, 'If people pray in their houses and no one performs it in the mosque, then they must go out to it.'

The proof of Mālik and those who take his position is that the Prophet ﷺ said, in the *ḥadīth* reported by Zayd ibn Thābit, 'You must pray in your homes. The best prayer that a person prays is in his home except for the obligatory prayer.' Al-Bukhārī transmitted it. The one who disagrees cites as evidence the fact that the Prophet ﷺ prayed it in a group in the mosque and then said what kept him from doing that all the time: the fear that it would become obligatory for them. That is why he told them, 'You must pray in your homes.' Then the Companions used to pray it in the mosque separately until 'Umar joined them together with one reciter. So the practice was established on that and the *sunnah* confirmed.

If we accept that it is permitted for people to pray in their houses when they fear for themselves, that provides proof that someone with the excuse of fear, or something similar, is permitted to abandon the group prayer and *Jumu'ah*. Excuses which permit that are things like illness, prison, fear of aggravation of illness, or fear of the injustice of the ruler in respect of his property or an unjustified ruling against him. Too much rain and mud are also an excuse if it does not stop. The same is true if someone has a close friend who is dying and there is no one to tend to him. Ibn 'Umar did that.

Give good news to the believers

This is said to be addressed to Muḥammad ﷺ and is also said to be addressed to Mūsā, which is more apparent, i.e. 'Give good news to the tribe of Israel that Allah will give them victory over their enemy.'

وَقَالَ مُوسَىٰ رَبَّنَآ إِنَّكَ ءَاتَيْتَ فِرْعَوْنَ وَمَلَأَهُۥ زِينَةً وَأَمْوَٰلًا فِي ٱلْحَيَوٰةِ
ٱلدُّنْيَا رَبَّنَا لِيُضِلُّوا۟ عَن سَبِيلِكَ رَبَّنَا ٱطْمِسْ عَلَىٰٓ أَمْوَٰلِهِمْ وَٱشْدُدْ عَلَىٰ
قُلُوبِهِمْ فَلَا يُؤْمِنُوا۟ حَتَّىٰ يَرَوُا۟ ٱلْعَذَابَ ٱلْأَلِيمَ ﴿٨٨﴾

88 Mūsā said, 'Our Lord, You have given Pharaoh and his ruling circle finery and wealth in the life of this world, Our Lord, so that they may be misguided from Your Way. Our Lord, obliterate their wealth and harden their hearts so that they do not believe until they see the painful punishment.'

Mūsā said, 'Our Lord, You have given Pharaoh and his ruling circle finery and wealth in the life of this world,

'You have given them the wealth of this world.' They controlled the land from Fustat in Egypt to the mountains in Abyssinia where there were gold, silver, emerald, chrysolite and ruby mines.

Our Lord, so that they may be misguided from Your Way.

There is disagreement about the *lām* before '*misguided*'. The soundest of what is said about it, which is the position of al-Khalīl and Sībawayh, is that it is the *lām* of conclusion and becoming. We find in a tradition: 'Allah has an angel who calls out every day: "Be born for (*li*) death and build for (*li*) ruin."' It means: since the end of their affair is misguidance, it is as if Allah gave to them so that they would be misguided. It is also said that it is the *lām* of 'in order to' and so it means: 'You gave to them so that they would be misguided and proud and arrogant.' It is said that it is the *lām* of 'on account of', implying, 'You gave to them so that they would turn from You and not fear that You would turn from them.'

Some people claim that it means: 'You give that to them so that they will not be misguided,' and there is some elision as He says: *'Allah makes it clear to you so that you are not misguided.'* (4:176) It means: 'because you will not be misguided.' An-Naḥḥās said: 'What is clear from this answer is good, but the Arabs do not elide "*lā*" except with *an*. So those who say that mix His words, "*may be misguided*."' It is also said that it is the *lām* of invocation, meaning, 'Test them with being misguided from Your path!' because after that He says, '*Obliterate their wealth and harden their hearts*'. It is said that the verb has the meaning of a verbal noun, meaning misguide them as in Allah's words, '*so that (li) you leave them alone*' (9:95). The Kufans recite '*li-yuḍillū*' from Form IV. The rest have '*li-yaḍillū*'.

obliterate their wealth

It means: punish them for their unbelief by destroying their property. Az-Zajjāj said that to 'obliterate a thing' is to obliterate its form. Ibn 'Abbās and Muḥammad ibn Ka'b said, 'Their wealth and dirhams turned into inscribed stones, retaining their original shapes, but broken into thirds and halves. Every mine they had was obliterated by Allah to the point that no one could afterwards use it.' Qatādah said, 'We heard that their wealth and crops turned to stone.' Mujāhid and 'Aṭiyyah said, 'Allah destroyed them so that there was no visible sign of them left.' The word *maṭmūsah* is used for an obliterated eye and *ṭumisa* for a place when it is wiped out and effaced. Ibn Zayd said, 'Their dinars, dirhams, fields and everything turned to stone.'

Muḥammad ibn Ka'b said, 'A man would be with his wife in his bed and they turned into stones.' He said, "Umar ibn 'Abd al-'Azīz asked me and I mentioned that to him. He called for a leather bag obtained in Egypt and produced from it stone fruits, dinars and dirhams.' As-Suddī said, 'It was one of the nine Signs.'

harden their hearts so that they do not believe

Ibn 'Abbās said, 'Deny them the ability to believe.' It is said that it means: harden them and seal them so that they are not opened to Islam. The meaning is the same. The phrase *'so that they do not believe'* is added to *'so that they may be misguided,'* meaning: 'Give them blessings so that they are misguided and do not believe.' Az-Zajjāj and al-Mubarrad said that. According to this, it has the meaning of a supplication and '*Our Lord, obliterate … hearts*' is an interpolation.

Al-Farrā', al-Kisā'ī and Abū 'Ubaydah said that it is a supplication and is in the jussive, i.e. 'O Allah, they should not believe!' An illustration of that is found in the words of al-A'mash:

The one in front of you does not spread out what has withdrawn,
and you will meet me in spite of yourself.

It means, 'Do not spread out.' Those who say that '*so that they may be misguided*' is a supplication, implying 'test them with misguidance', say that '*so that they do not believe*' is added to it. It is said that it is in the position of the accusative as an apodosis of a command, in other words: 'harden their hearts so that they do not believe.' This is the position of al-Akhfash and al-Farrā'. {POEM]

until they see the painful punishment

Ibn 'Abbās said that the painful punishment is drowning. Some people find this *āyah* problematic and ask, 'How could Mūsā pray against them when the rule is that Messengers pray for their people to believe?' The answer is that it is not permitted for a Prophet to pray against his people except with the permission of Allah, after being informed that there was none among them who would believe nor would they give birth to any who would believe. The proof of that is the words of Nūḥ: *'None of your people are going to believe except for those who have already believed'* (11:36) and so he said, *'My Lord, do not leave a single one of the unbelievers on the earth!'* (71:26) Allah knows best.

قَالَ قَدْ أُجِيبَت دَّعْوَتُكُمَا فَاسْتَقِيمَا وَلَا تَتَّبِعَآنِّ سَبِيلَ ٱلَّذِينَ لَا يَعْلَمُونَ ﴿٨٩﴾

89 He said, 'Your request is answered, so go straight and do not follow the way of those who have no knowledge.'

He said, 'Your request is answered,

Abū al-'Āliyah said, 'This was the supplication of Mūsā.' Hārūn said, *'Āmīn,'* and so he is included in the dual pronoun. Someone who says *'Āmīn'* to a supplication is also a supplicator. *'Āmīn'* is a supplication meaning, 'Answer me.' It is also said that Hārūn made supplication together with Mūsā. Scholars say that sometimes the Arabs address a single person with the dual. [POEM ILLUSTRATING] According to this, *Āmīn* is not a supplication and Hārūn did not make one. An-Naḥḥās said that he heard 'Alī ibn Sulaymān say, 'The proof that they both made supplication is that Mūsā said, "Our Lord" and not "My Lord".' 'Alī and as-Sulamī recited *'da'wātukumā'* in the plural. Ibn as-Sumayfa' recited *'ajabtu'*, reporting from Allah, with *'request'* in the accusative.

'Āmīn' was discussed fully in connection with the *Fātiḥah*. It is something that our Prophet ﷺ, Hārūn and Mūsā were singled out for. Anas ibn Mālik related that the Messenger of Allah ﷺ said, 'Allah has given my community three things which he has not given anyone before them: the *salām* which is the greeting of the people of the Garden, the rows of the Muslims, and *Āmīn*, except what came from Mūsā and Hārūn.' At-Tirmidhī al-Ḥakīm mentioned it in *Nawādir al-Uṣūl*. It was already mentioned in the *Fātiḥah*.

so go straight

Al-Farrā' and others said that the command to go straight is a command to both of them and it is telling them to be firm in calling Pharaoh and his people to faith until what is interpreted as a response comes to them. Muḥammad ibn 'Alī and Ibn Jurayj said, 'Pharaoh and his people remained after this response for forty years and then they were destroyed.' It is said that 'going straight' here refers to the supplication and implies not seeking to hasten what is sought. Seeking to hasten is only removed from the heart by a going-straight that takes the form of being content with what happens. Such peace of mind is only experienced by those who are content with all that emerges from the Unseen.

do not follow

This has a doubled *nūn* in the jussive indicating prohibition. The *nūn* is for emphasis because the two silent letters meet and the *kasrah* is preferred for it because it resembles the *nūn* of the dual. Ibn Dhakwān recited it with a single *nūn* for negation. It is said that it is a *ḥāl* modifying *'go straight'*, implying 'go straight without following'. It means: 'Do not travel on the path of those who do not know the reality of My promise and threat.'

وَجَٰوَزْنَا بِبَنِىٓ إِسْرَٰٓءِيلَ ٱلْبَحْرَ فَأَتْبَعَهُمْ فِرْعَوْنُ وَجُنُودُهُۥ بَغْيًا وَعَدْوًا
حَتَّىٰٓ إِذَآ أَدْرَكَهُ ٱلْغَرَقُ قَالَ ءَامَنتُ أَنَّهُۥ لَآ إِلَٰهَ إِلَّا ٱلَّذِىٓ ءَامَنَتْ
بِهِۦ بَنُوٓا۟ إِسْرَٰٓءِيلَ وَأَنَا۠ مِنَ ٱلْمُسْلِمِينَ ﴿٩٠﴾

90 We brought the tribe of Israel across the sea and Pharaoh and his troops pursued them out of tyranny and enmity. Then, when he was on the point of drowning, he said, 'I believe that there is

no god but Him in whom the tribe of Israel believe. I am one of the Muslims.'

We brought the tribe of Israel across the sea

The crossing of the tribe of Israel was already mentioned in *al-Baqarah* (2:50). Al-Ḥasan recited '*wa jawwaznā*' instead of '*wa jāwaznā*'. They are two dialectical forms. *Tabi'a* and *atba'a* (pursue) mean the same. This is when they caught up with them. Al-Aṣma'ī said that *atba'a* with a separate *alif* is when someone catches up. When it is a connected *alif*, it means to follow in someone's tracks, whether they are caught up with or not. That is like what Abū Zayd said. Qatādah recited it with a connected *alif*. It is said that it is with a connected *alif* when it is a command which is followed. With a separate *alif*, it means pursuing both good and evil. This is the view of Abū 'Amr. It is said that they mean the same.

and Pharaoh and his troops pursued them out of tyranny and enmity.

Mūsā brought out the tribe of Israel, who numbered 620,000, and Pharaoh pursued them in the morning with 1,600,000 men. This was already mentioned in 2:50. *Baghy* (tyranny) is in the accusative as an adverbial *ḥāl*. *'Adw* (enmity) is added to it. So it means: 'in a state of tyranny, enmity and injustice'. The verb is *'adā, ya'dū, 'adw* like *ghazā, yaghzū, ghazw*. Al-Ḥasan recited *'uduww* like *'uluww*. Commentators say that '*baghy*' is seeking dominance without any right using words and *'adw* is doing so in action. They are in the accusative as objects.

Then, when he was on the point of drowning, he said, 'I believe that there is no god

'*On the point of drowning*' is when the water caught up to and reached him. The verb '*believe*' here means to affirm. '*Innahu*' means 'at that time'. When the genitive is elided, then the verb becomes transitive and takes the accusative. It is recited with *kasrah*, implying 'I have become a Muslim,' and then there is a new sentence. Abū Ḥātim claims that the words are elided, meaning 'I have believed and said that…' Belief is of no benefit at that time. Repentance is accepted before final despair. After it and after being directly connected to death, it is not accepted as was explained in *an-Nisā'* (4:17-18).

It is said that Pharaoh was afraid to enter the sea and he was riding a dark horse. There were no mares among the cavalry of Pharaoh. Jibrīl came on a piebald horse in the form of Hāmān and said to him, 'Go forward,' and dived into the sea and the horses of Pharaoh followed him with Mīkā'īl driving them. None of them separated from them. When the last of them entered the sea and the first wanted to leave, the sea came down on them. Drowning silenced Pharaoh and he said,

'I have believed in that which the tribe of Israel believe' and Jibrīl put water into his mouth.

At-Tirmidhī related from Ibn 'Abbās that the Prophet ﷺ said, 'When Allah drowned Pharaoh, he said, "I have believed that there is no god except the One in whom the tribe of Israel believe." Jibrīl said, "Muḥammad! If you had seen me when I took some of the sea and put it in his mouth, fearing that mercy would reach him!"' Abū 'Īsā said that it is a *ḥasan ḥadīth.* The state of the sea was the black mud which was in it. The people of language said that. Ibn 'Abbās said that the Prophet ﷺ said, 'Jibrīl stuffed mud into Pharaoh's mouth fearing that he would say, "There is no god but Allah" and Allah would show mercy to him, or he feared that He would show mercy to him.' He said that it is a sound *ḥasan gharīb ḥadīth.*

'Awn ibn 'Abdullāh said, 'I heard that Jibrīl said to the Prophet ﷺ, "Iblīs has not given birth to anyone I hate more than Pharaoh. When he was about to drown, he said, 'I have believed…' and I feared that he would say it and be shown mercy, so I stuffed earth or mud in his mouth."' It is said that he did this to punish him for the terrible things he had done.

Ka'b al-Aḥbar said, 'Allah stopped the Nile of Egypt from overflowing in his time and the Copts said to him, "If you are truly our Lord, then make the water flow for us." So he mounted his horse and commanded his armies, general by general, and they began to line up standing according to their ranks, and Pharaoh sat where they could not see him. He dismounted. He changed his shirt, prostrated and prayed to Allah and Allah made the water overflow for him. Jibrīl came to him in the form of someone asking for an opinion and said, "What does the prince say about a man who was a slave who grew up within the context of his master's blessings with no other support than his master and then the slave is ungrateful for the blessings he has received from his master and denies his master's due and claims to be a master instead of him?"' So Pharaoh wrote: "Abū al-'Abbās al-Walīd ibn Muṣ'ab ibn ar-Rayyān says that the punishment of such a man is to be drowned in the sea." So Jibrīl seized Pharaoh and proceeded and when Pharaoh was about to drown, Jibrīl handed him what he had previously written.' This was mentioned in *al-Baqarah* from 'Abdullāh ibn 'Amr ibn al-'Āṣ and Ibn 'Abbās with an *isnād.* That was on the day of 'Āshūrā' as was already explained in *al-Baqarah* (2:50).

'I am one of the Muslims' means: one of those who unify and submit to obedience.

ءَآلْـَٔنَ وَقَدْ عَصَيْتَ قَبْلُ وَكُنتَ مِنَ ٱلْمُفْسِدِينَ ٩١

91 'What, now! When previously you rebelled and were one of the corrupters?

This is part of what Allah said or part of what Jibrīl said or what Mīkā'īl or other angels said. It is also said that Pharaoh said this to himself, not on his tongue but in his heart, at a time when regret was of no use. It is like Allah's words: '*We feed you only out of desire for the Face of Allah*' (76:9) where the Lord praises them for what is in their hearts, not the words they uttered. The true words are those of the heart.

فَٱلْيَوْمَ نُنَجِّيكَ بِبَدَنِكَ لِتَكُونَ لِمَنْ خَلْفَكَ ءَايَةً وَإِنَّ كَثِيرًا مِّنَ ٱلنَّاسِ عَنْ ءَايَٰتِنَا لَغَٰفِلُونَ ٩٢

92 Today We will preserve your body so you can be a Sign for people who come after you. Surely many people are heedless of Our Signs.'

We will cast you up on higher ground (*najwah*). That was when the tribe of Israel did not believe that Pharaoh had drowned. They said, 'He is too important for that.' So Allah cast him up onto some higher land so that they could see him. Describing rain, Aws ibn Ḥajar said:

The one who is in his courtyard is not like the one on higher ground.
The one with shelter is not like one who is exposed.

Al-Yazīdī and Ibn as-Samayfa' recited: '*nunaḥḥīka*' (We will put you far away) from *tanḥīyah* (to put far away). 'Alqamah related it from Ibn Mas'ūd and it means that it was in a section (*nāḥiyah*) of the sea. Ibn Jurayj said that he was thrown up on the sea shore so that the tribe of Israel could see him. He was short and red like an ox. 'Alqamah related that 'Abdullāh recited '*bi-nadā'ika*' from *nadā'* [instead of *bi-badanika* (your body)]. Abū Bakr al-Anbārī said, 'This does not differ from the letters of our *muṣḥaf* since his method was to write a *yā'* and *kāf* after the *dāl* because the *alif* drops from *nadā'ika* in the order of writing the *muṣḥaf* as it drops from *ẓulumāt* and *samawāt*. When there is elision with it, then the form of writing *badanika* and *nadā'ika* is the same, although this reading is left since it is irregular and differs from what the Muslims as a whole have, and the *sunnah* of recitation is to take the last rather than the first. Furthermore, its meaning falls short of the explanation offered by our reading since it does not mention the armour which is a significant factor in reports about the tribe of Israel disagreeing about whether Pharaoh drowned or not. When they asked Allah to show them that he was drowned, He cast up his body and armour which he wore in battle onto higher ground. Ibn 'Abbās and Muḥammad ibn Ka'b al-Quraẓī said, 'His armour was made of strung pearls.' It is said that it was made of gold by which he was recognised. It is said that it was iron, and Abū Ṣakhr said that. It was short armour. Abū 'Ubaydah recited to al-A'shā:

White like a pond, closely linked,
with the top of a helmet above the sleeve of the body.

He also recited to 'Amr ibn Ma'dīkarīb:

Their women passed with every coat of mail,
strong breast-plates with links and bodies.

Ka'b ibn Mālik said:

You see armour with layers (*yalab*)
on heroes, and Yemenī armour.

Yalab, Yemenī armour was made of layers of leather. It is a generic term, the singular being *yalabah*. 'Amr ibn Kulthūm said:

We wear white iron and Yemeni armour (*yalab*)
and swords which are straight and bending.

It is said that '*your body*' means lifeless corpse. Mujāhid said that. Al-Akhfash said, 'As for those who say that it is "with your armour", that means nothing.' Abū Bakr said, 'That is because when they asked Allah to show them Pharaoh drowned, He brought him out to them and they saw a lifeless body. When the tribe of Israel saw him, they said, "Yes, Mūsā! This is Pharaoh and he has drowned!" Doubt left their hearts and then the sea swallowed up Pharaoh again.' According to this, the phrase '*We will preserve your body*' can have two meanings. One is: 'We will cast up your body on higher ground.' The other is: 'We will display your lifeless body.'

The meaning of the irregular reading already mentioned is the same as the normal recitation of the community because *nadā'* has two explanations. One is: 'We will cast you up by your calling out the words of repentance and your saying them after its door was closed and the moment of its acceptance passed,' and the other is, 'Today We will remove you from the depths of the sea by your claim to be the highest lord.' So saving his body was a punishment from the Lord of the Worlds for his excessive unbelief which he proclaimed and forged and lied about when he claimed power and authority and knew that he was lying about that, lacked that power and did not deserve it.

Abū Bakr al-Anbārī said, 'Our reading contains the meanings found in the irregular reading and more.'

so that you can be a Sign for people who come after you

That was so that he could be a Sign for the tribe of Israel and for the remaining people of Pharaoh who did not drown and who had not heard about this news. Many people turn away from reflecting on Allah's Signs and considering them. There is also a reading '*khalafaka*', meaning those who follow after you in your land. 'Alī ibn Abī Ṭālib recited '*khalaqaka*' with *qāf*, i.e. it is a sign of your Creator.

وَلَقَدْ بَوَّأْنَا بَنِىٓ إِسْرَٰٓءِيلَ مُبَوَّأَ صِدْقٍ وَرَزَقْنَٰهُم مِّنَ ٱلطَّيِّبَٰتِ فَمَا ٱخْتَلَفُوا۟
حَتَّىٰ جَآءَهُمُ ٱلْعِلْمُ ۚ إِنَّ رَبَّكَ يَقْضِى بَيْنَهُمْ يَوْمَ ٱلْقِيَٰمَةِ فِيمَا كَانُوا۟ فِيهِ
يَخْتَلِفُونَ ﴿٩٣﴾

93 We settled the tribe of Israel in a noble place and gave them good things as provision. They did not differ until knowledge came to them. Your Lord will decide between them on the Day of Rising regarding the things about which they differed.

We settled the tribe of Israel in a noble place and gave them good things as provision.

'*A noble place*' is a chosen, praiseworthy place, meaning Egypt. It is also said to mean Jordan and Palestine. Aḍ-Ḍaḥḥāk said that it refers to both Egypt and Syria. '*Good things*' are fruits and other things. Ibn 'Abbās said that the people referred to are Qurayẓah, an-Naḍīr and those of the tribe of Israel at the time of the Prophet ﷺ. They had believed in Muḥammad ﷺ and were waiting for him to come, but when he did come, they envied him. This is why Allah says: '*They did not differ*' about the business of Muḥammad ﷺ. '*Knowledge*' means the Qur'an and Muḥammad ﷺ. The word '*knowledge*' here is what is already known because they knew it before he emerged. Aṭ-Ṭabarī said that. '*He will decide between them,*' in other words judge between them, '*regarding the things about which they differed*' in this world and so the obedient are rewarded and the disobedient punished.

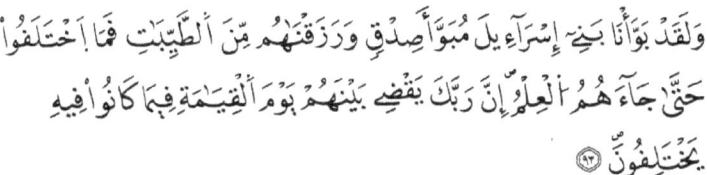

فَإِن كُنتَ فِي شَكٍّ مِّمَّا أَنزَلْنَا إِلَيْكَ فَسْـَٔلِ ٱلَّذِينَ يَقْرَءُونَ ٱلْكِتَـٰبَ
مِن قَبْلِكَ لَقَدْ جَآءَكَ ٱلْحَقُّ مِن رَّبِّكَ فَلَا تَكُونَنَّ مِنَ ٱلْمُمْتَرِينَ ﴿٩٤﴾
وَلَا تَكُونَنَّ مِنَ ٱلَّذِينَ كَذَّبُوا۟ بِـَٔايَـٰتِ ٱللَّهِ فَتَكُونَ مِنَ ٱلْخَـٰسِرِينَ ﴿٩٥﴾

94-95 If you are in any doubt about what We have sent down to you, then ask those who were reciting the Book before you. The truth has come to you from your Lord, so on no account be one of the doubters. And on no account be among those who deny Allah's Signs and so become one of the lost.

If you are in any doubt about what We have sent down to you,

This is addressed to the Prophet ﷺ while it is people other than him are meant, implying 'You are not in doubt, whereas others are in doubt.' Abū 'Umar Muḥammad ibn 'Abd al-Wāḥid az-Zāhid said, 'I heard the two *imāms*, Tha'lab and al-Mubarrad, say that the words "*If you are in any doubt*" mean: "Say, Muḥammad, to the unbelievers, 'If you are in doubt about what has been revealed to you, *"ask those who were reciting the Book before you."*'" This means: "Say: 'O idol-worshippers! If you are in doubt about the Qur'an, ask the Jews who have become Muslim,'" meaning 'Abdullāh ibn Salām and those like him, because the idol-worshippers used to affirm that the Jews had more knowledge than them because they possessed Scripture. Therefore the Messenger ﷺ called on them to ask those whom they affirmed had more knowledge than them, 'Will Allah send a Messenger after Mūsā?'""

Al-Qutabī said that this is addressed to those who did not state unequivocally that Muḥammad ﷺ was lying or that he was telling the truth, but they were in doubt either way. It is said that it is addressed to the Prophet ﷺ and no one else and means: 'If you have any doubts about what We have told you, ask the People of the Book to remove that doubt from you.' Doubt is constriction in the breast, so the meaning is, 'If your breast is constricted by the unbelief of these people, be steadfast and ask those who received the Scripture before you and they will tell you that the Prophets before you were steadfast in the face of the injury they endured from their people and what the end of their affair was.'

The linguistic root of *shakk* (doubt) implies constriction. The verb *shakka* is used of a garment when it is held together with pegs so that it is like a container. The same is true of a journey whose difficulties get worse and worse to the point that it cannot be completed. Doubt narrows the breast and tightens it so that it feels constricted. Al-Ḥusayn ibn al-Faḍl said, 'When the conjunction *fā'* is used with the particles of the precondition, it neither obliges or confirms the action. The evidence for it is what is related that the Prophet ﷺ said when this *āyah* was revealed, "By Allah, I do not doubt!'"

Then the words begin anew and Allah says: *'The truth has come...'* 'The doubters' are those who are in uncertainty and doubt. The Prophet ﷺ is addressed in these two *āyahs* while other than him are meant.

إِنَّ ٱلَّذِينَ حَقَّتْ عَلَيْهِمْ كَلِمَتُ رَبِّكَ لَا يُؤْمِنُونَ ﴿٩٦﴾ وَلَوْ جَآءَتْهُمْ
كُلُّ ءَايَةٍ حَتَّىٰ يَرَوُا۟ ٱلْعَذَابَ ٱلْأَلِيمَ ﴿٩٧﴾

96-97 Those against whom the words of your Lord are justly carried out will never believe – not even if every Sign were to come to them – until they see the painful punishment.

This was already discussed earlier in this *sūrah* (10:33). Qatādah said, 'Those referred to are the ones who merit the anger of Allah, and His anger is at their disobedience in not believing.' Even if the Signs were to come to them, they would not believe and it would not benefit them.

فَلَوْلَا كَانَتْ قَرْيَةٌ ءَامَنَتْ فَنَفَعَهَآ إِيمَٰنُهَآ إِلَّا قَوْمَ يُونُسَ لَمَّآ ءَامَنُوا۟
كَشَفْنَا عَنْهُمْ عَذَابَ ٱلْخِزْىِ فِى ٱلْحَيَوٰةِ ٱلدُّنْيَا وَمَتَّعْنَٰهُمْ إِلَىٰ حِينٍ ﴿٩٨﴾

98 How is it that there has never been a city that believed, whose faith then brought it benefit, except the people of Yūnus? When they believed We removed from them the punishment of disgrace in the life of this world and We let them have enjoyment for a time.

How is it that there has never been a city that believed,

Al-Akhfash and al-Kisā'ī said that it means: *'fa-hallā'* which is how it is found in the Qur'ans of Ubayy and Ibn Mas'ūd. The root of *'lawlā'* in language is specification or indication of the denial of a thing by the existence of another. It is understood that the *āyah* means to negate the faith of the people of cities and then makes the people of Yūnus an exception. According to the words, it is a separated exception, while according to the meaning, it is connected since it implies: no people of a city believed except for the people of Yūnus. The accusative in '*people*' is correct. Sībawayh includes it in the chapter of 'that which can only be accusative'.

An-Naḥḥās said that it is in the accusative because it is an exception which is not from the first, i.e. '*except the people of Yūnus*'. This is the position of al-Kisā'ī, al-Akhfash and al-Farrā'. It is also possible that '*except the people of Yūnus*' is in the nominative. The best of what has been stated about the nominative is what Abū Isḥāq az-Zajjāj said: 'The meaning is "other than the people of Yūnus." When the word "*illā*' is used, the noun after it takes the inflection of "*ghayr*".' [POEM]

It is related by a group of commentators that the people of Yūnus were in Nineveh in the region of Mosul. They worshipped idols and Allah sent Yūnus to them to call them to Islam and to abandon what they were doing. They refused. It was said that he remained calling them for nine years and despaired of them believing. He was told to tell them that the punishment would come to them on the third morning. He did that and they said, 'He is a man who does not lie. Watch him. If he stays among you, nothing will happen to you. If he travels away from you, there is no doubt that the punishment will arrive.' In the night, Yūnus got his provisions and left them. In the morning they did not find him and repented, prayed to Allah, donned hair-shirts, and separated the women, children and the animals from the rest of the people. They made restitution for wrongs in that state.

Ibn Mas'ūd said, 'A man would go to a stone on which he had put the foundation of his building and remove it and return it.' The punishment for them, according to what Ibn 'Abbās related, was just two-thirds of a mile away. It is also related that it was a mile away. Ibn 'Abbās related that a canopy covered them which contained heat. It continued to approach until they felt its heat between their shoulders. Ibn Jubayr said, 'The punishment covered them as a cloth covers a grave. When it was clear that their repentance was true, Allah removed the punishment from them.'

Aṭ-Ṭabarī said, 'The people of Yūnus were singled out among all nations by being turned to after the punishment was in sight.' A group of commentators said that. Az-Zajjāj said, 'The punishment did not befall them. They saw the signs indicating the imminence of the punishment. If they had seen the punishment itself, then faith would not have helped them.' The view of az-Zajjāj is good. The point at which repentance does not benefit on seeing is when one is directly touched by it as in the story of Pharaoh. That is why the story of Yūnus comes after that, because Pharaoh only believed when he saw the punishment and that did not help him, whereas the people of Yūnus repented before that. This is supported by the words of the Prophet ﷺ, 'Allah accepts a person's repentance as long as it is not at the death-rattle.' That is the state of someone in the throes of death, but that is not the case before that. Allah knows best.

The same idea was related from Ibn Mas'ūd: when Yūnus threatened them with the punishment after three days, he left them. When they did not find him in the morning, they repented and separated mothers from their children. This indicates that their repentance took place before the sign of the punishment was seen. This will be discussed clearly in *Sūrat aṣ-Ṣaffāt*, Allah willing.

We removed from them the punishment of disgrace

This was the punishment which Yūnus promised would befall them. It was not when they saw it directly or imagined it. According to this there is no problem or contradiction or specification. Allah knows best.

To sum up, Allah already knew that the people of Ninevah would be among the fortunate. It is related that 'Alī said, 'Caution does not turn back the decree. Supplication does.' That is why Allah Almighty says this. He also said that that was on 'Āshūrā'.

'For a time' is until their set term. As-Suddī said that. It is said that they will go to the Garden or the Fire. Ibn 'Abbās said that.

وَلَوْ شَآءَ رَبُّكَ لَأٓمَنَ مَن فِي الْأَرْضِ كُلُّهُمْ جَمِيعًا أَفَأَنتَ تُكْرِهُ النَّاسَ حَتَّىٰ
يَكُونُواْ مُومِنِينَ ٩٩

99 If your Lord had willed, all the people on the earth would have believed. Do you think you can force people to be believers?

Allah could have impelled all people to believe. The word *'all'* is added for emphasis and Sībawayh said that it is in the accusative for the adverbial *ḥāl*. Al-Akhfash said, '"*Jamī'*" (all) comes after "*kull*" (all) for emphasis as we see in 16:51 where "two" is repeated.' Ibn 'Abbās said that the Prophet ﷺ was eager for everyone to believe and Allah informed him that only those for whom happiness had been predetermined would believe and only those for whom misery had been predetermined would be misguided. It is said that *'people'* here means particularly Abū Ṭālib. Ibn 'Abbās also said that.

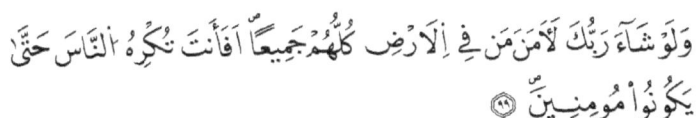

وَمَا كَانَ لِنَفْسٍ أَن تُؤْمِنَ إِلَّا بِإِذْنِ ٱللَّهِ وَيَجْعَلُ ٱلرِّجْسَ عَلَى ٱلَّذِينَ لَا
يَعْقِلُونَ ﴿١٠٠﴾

100 No self can believe except with Allah's permission. He places a blight on those who do not use their intellect.

The particle *mā* here designates the negative. No soul can believe except by Allah's decree, decision and will. Instead of *'yajʿalu'* (He places) al-Ḥasan, Abū Bakr and al-Mufaḍḍal recited *'najʿalu'* 'We place' using the Divine 'We'. 'A blight' (*rijs*) is a type of punishment and is also read as *rujs*. They are two dialectical forms. *'Those who do not use their intellect'* regarding what Allah has commanded and forbidden.

قُلِ ٱنظُرُوا۟ مَاذَا فِى ٱلسَّمَٰوَٰتِ وَٱلْأَرْضِ وَمَا تُغْنِى ٱلْءَايَٰتُ وَٱلنُّذُرُ عَن قَوْمٍ
لَّا يُؤْمِنُونَ ﴿١٠١﴾

101 Say: 'Look at what there is in the heavens and on the earth.' But Signs and warnings are of no avail to people who do not believe.

This is an instruction to the unbelievers ordering them to reflect and look at the artefacts which direct one to their Maker and to the One Who has the power to perfect them. This was discussed elsewhere (7:185). In *'mā tughnī'* the *mā* is negative. It is also said that it is interrogative, implying, 'What will be of avail?' *Signs* are evidence. *Warnings* refers to the Messengers. *Nudhur* is the plural of *nadhīr.* '*To people who do not believe*': Allah already knew that they would not believe.

فَهَلْ يَنتَظِرُونَ إِلَّا مِثْلَ أَيَّامِ ٱلَّذِينَ خَلَوْا۟ مِن قَبْلِهِمْ قُلْ
فَٱنتَظِرُوٓا۟ إِنِّى مَعَكُم مِّنَ ٱلْمُنتَظِرِينَ ﴿١٠٢﴾

102 What are they waiting for but the same fate as those who passed away before them? Say: 'Wait, I will be among the people waiting with you.'

'Days (*ayyām*)' (tr. '*same fate*') here means events. When someone is described as knowing 'the days of the Arabs' it means the history of their events. Qatādah said that it means the events of Allah which happened to the people of Nūḥ, 'Ād, Thamūd and others. The Arabs call punishment 'days' and blessing 'days'. All that passed of good or evil are 'days'. '*Wait*' is a threat. What they are waiting for is the promise of his Lord.

ثُمَّ نُنَجِّي رُسُلَنَا وَالَّذِينَ ءَامَنُواْ كَذَٰلِكَ حَقًّا عَلَيْنَا نُنجِ الْمُؤْمِنِينَ ﴿١٠٣﴾

103 Then We will rescue Our Messengers and those who believe as well. It is incumbent upon Us to rescue the believers.

This means: part of Our custom when We make a punishment descend on a people is to bring out any Messengers and believers from among them. The import of '*Then*' here is: 'Then know that We will rescue Our Messengers'. '*It is incumbent upon Us*', it is a duty because Allah has said it, and there is no disagreement about His words. Ya'qūb recited '*nunjī*'. Al-Kisā'ī, Ḥafṣ and Ya'qūb recited '*nunjī al-mu'minīn*'. The rest have it in Form II, *nunajjī*. They are sound dialectical usages *anjā, yunjī, injā'* and *najjā, yunajjī, tanjiyah* and mean the same.

قُلْ يَٰٓأَيُّهَا النَّاسُ إِن كُنتُمْ فِي شَكٍّ مِّن دِينِي فَلَآ أَعْبُدُ الَّذِينَ تَعْبُدُونَ مِن
دُونِ اللَّهِ وَلَٰكِنْ أَعْبُدُ اللَّهَ الَّذِي يَتَوَفَّىٰكُمْ وَأُمِرْتُ أَنْ أَكُونَ مِنَ
الْمُؤْمِنِينَ ﴿١٠٤﴾

104 Say: 'Mankind! if you are in any doubt about my *dīn*, I do not worship those you worship besides Allah. Rather I worship Allah who will take you back to Him and I am commanded to be one of the believers:

The appellation '*Mankind!*' here is addressed particularly to the unbelievers of Makkah. '*If you are in any doubt*' about the *dīn* of Islam to which I call you. '*Besides Allah*' means the idols which have no consciousness. '*Take you back to Him*' means that He will make you die and take your souls. '*The believers*' are those who affirm the Signs of their Lord.

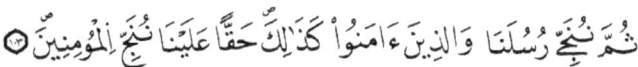

وَأَنْ أَقِمْ وَجْهَكَ لِلدِّينِ حَنِيفًا وَلَا تَكُونَنَّ مِنَ الْمُشْرِكِينَ ﴿١٠٥﴾ وَلَا تَدْعُ مِن دُونِ اللَّهِ مَا لَا يَنفَعُكَ وَلَا يَضُرُّكَ فَإِن فَعَلْتَ فَإِنَّكَ إِذًا مِّنَ الظَّالِمِينَ ﴿١٠٦﴾

105-6 Turn your face towards the *dīn* in pure natural faith, and on no account be among the idolaters. Do not call on something besides Allah which can neither help nor harm you. If you do, you will then be wrongdoers.'

'*An*' is added to '*be one of the believers*' in the preceding *āyah*, i.e. 'I am commanded to be one of the believers and to turn.' Ibn 'Abbās said that it means 'your actions', and it is also said that it means 'yourself', implying go straight on the *dīn* which Allah has commanded. A *ḥanīf* is someone who goes straight, turning away from all other religions. Ḥamzah ibn 'Abd al-Muṭṭalib said:

I praised Allah when He guided my heart
from *shirk* to the natural religion.

Its derivation was already discussed adequately in al-*An'ām* (6:89)

'On no account be among the idolaters.' This is addressed to the Prophet while others are meant by it. The same is true of '*Do not call*' which means 'do not worship'. Do not worship that whose worship cannot help you and whose disobedience will not harm you. If you worship other than Allah, you will be among those who put their worship in the wrong place.

وَإِن يَمْسَسْكَ اللَّهُ بِضُرٍّ فَلَا كَاشِفَ لَهُ إِلَّا هُوَ وَإِن يُرِدْكَ بِخَيْرٍ فَلَا رَادَّ لِفَضْلِهِ يُصِيبُ بِهِ مَن يَشَاءُ مِنْ عِبَادِهِ وَهُوَ الْغَفُورُ الرَّحِيمُ ﴿١٠٧﴾

107 If Allah afflicts you with harm, no one can remove it except Him. If He desires good for you, no one can avert His favour. He bestows it on whichever of His slaves He wills. He is Ever-Forgiving, Most Merciful.

No one can repel what Allah causes to strike you. His favour is ease and blessing. He bestows or inflicts whatever good or evil He wishes. He forgives the wrong actions and errors of His slaves. He is Merciful to His friends in the Next World.

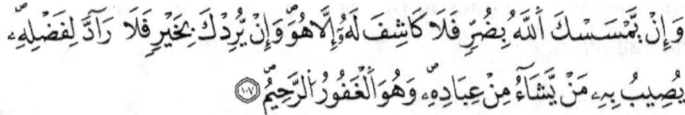

قُلْ يَٰٓأَيُّهَا ٱلنَّاسُ قَدْ جَآءَكُمُ ٱلْحَقُّ مِن رَّبِّكُمْ فَمَنِ ٱهْتَدَىٰ فَإِنَّمَا يَهْتَدِى لِنَفْسِهِۦ وَمَن
ضَلَّ فَإِنَّمَا يَضِلُّ عَلَيْهَا وَمَآ أَنَا۠ عَلَيْكُم بِوَكِيلٍ ﴿١٠٨﴾

108 Say: 'Mankind! the truth has come to you from your Lord. Whoever is guided is only guided for his own good. Whoever is misguided is only misguided to his detriment. I have not been set over you as a guardian.'

'*The truth*' is the Qur'an. It is also said that it is the Messenger ﷺ. '*Whoever is guided*' is the one who affirms Muḥammad and believes in what he brought. He is only guided to save himself. '*Whoever is misguided*' by abandoning the Messenger and the Qur'an and following idols brings on himself the bad consequences of that. '*I have not been set over you as a guardian* of your actions. I am only a Messenger.' Ibn 'Abbās said that it was abrogated by the *Āyah* of the Sword.

وَٱتَّبِعْ مَا يُوحَىٰٓ إِلَيْكَ وَٱصْبِرْ حَتَّىٰ يَحْكُمَ ٱللَّهُ وَهُوَ خَيْرُ ٱلْحَٰكِمِينَ ﴿١٠٩﴾

109 Follow what has been revealed to you and be steadfast until Allah's judgment comes. He is the Best of Judges.

This was abrogated by the *Āyah* of the Sword. It is also said that it is not abrogated. This means: be patient in obedience and in not disobeying. Ibn 'Abbās said, 'When it was revealed, the Prophet ﷺ gathered the *Anṣār* and did not gather anyone else with them. He said, "After me you will experience preference for others. Be patient until you meet me at the Basin."' Anas related the like of that. Then Anas said, 'They were not patient and so he commanded them to be patient as Allah Almighty commanded him.' 'Abd ar-Raḥmān ibn Ḥassan said:

Shall I not convey to Mu'āwiyah ibn Ḥarb,
    the Commander of the Faithful, my words?
We are patient and wait for you
    until the Day of mutual fraud and argument.

'*He is the Best of Judges*' because He only judges by the Truth.

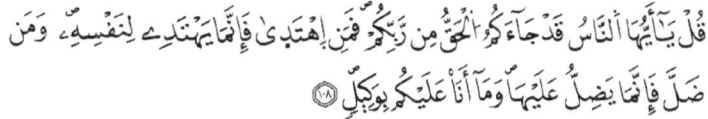

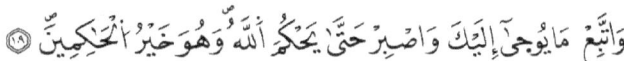

Table of Contents for Āyats

Sūrat al-Anfāl

1 They will ask you about booty. Say: 'Booty belongs to Allah... 1
2-4 The believers are those whose hearts tremble... 5
5 Just as your Lord brought you out from your house with truth... 7
6 arguing with you about the Truth after it had been made clear... 9
7-8 When Allah promised you that one of the two parties... 9
9-10 Remember when you called on your Lord for help... 10
11 And when He overcame you with sleep, making you feel secure... 12
12 And when your Lord revealed to the angels, 'I am with you... 17
13-14 This was because they were hostile to Allah and His Messenger... 19
15-16 You who believe! when you encounter those who disbelieve... 19
17-18 You did not kill them; it was Allah who killed them... 23
19 If it was a decisive victory you were seeking... 25
20 You who believe! obey Allah and His Messenger... 26
21-22 Do not be like those who say, 'We hear,' when they do not hear... 27
23 If Allah knew of any good in them, He would have made them able... 28
24 You who believe! respond to Allah and to the Messenger... 28
25 Be fearful of trials which will not afflict solely those among you... 30
26 When you were few and oppressed in the land... 33
27 You who believe! do not betray Allah and His Messenger... 33
28 Know that your wealth and children are a trial... 35
29 You who believe! if you have *taqwā* of Allah... 35
30 When those who disbelieve were plotting against you... 36
31 When Our Signs are recited to them, they say... 36
32 And they say, 'Allah, if this is really the truth from You... 37
33 Allah would not punish them while you were among them... 38
34 But why should Allah not punish them now... 39
35-37 Their prayer at the House is nothing but whistling and clapping... 39
38 Say to those who disbelieve that if they stop, they will be forgiven... 40
39-40 Fight them until there is no more *fitnah* and the *dīn* is Allah's... 43
41 Know that when you take any booty a fifth of it belongs to Allah... 43
42 when you were on the nearer slope, and they were on the further slope... 60
43 Remember when Allah showed them to you in your dream... 62

44 Remember when Allah made you see them as few... 62
45 You who believe! when you meet a troop, stand firm... 63
46 Obey Allah and His Messenger and do not quarrel... 64
47 Do not be like those who left their homes in arrogance... 65
48 when Shayṭān made their actions appear good to them... 65
49 And when the hypocrites and those with sickness in their hearts said... 67
50-51 If only you could see when the angels take back those who... 67
52 Such was the case with Pharaoh's people and those before them... 68
53 That is because Allah would never change a blessing... 69
54 Such was the case with Pharaoh's people and those before them... 69
55-56 The worst of animals in the sight of Allah are... 69
57 So if you come upon such people in war... 70
58 If you fear treachery on the part of a people, revoke your treaty... 71
59 Do not imagine that those who disbelieve have got ahead... 73
60 Arm yourselves against them with all the firepower and cavalry... 75
61 If they incline to peace, you too incline to it... 78
62-63 If they intend to deceive you, Allah is enough for you... 81
64 O Prophet! Allah is enough for you, and for the believers... 82
65-66 O Prophet! spur on the believers to fight.... 83
67 It is not fitting for a Prophet to take captives... 84
68 Were it not for a prior decree which had already proceeded... 90
70-71 O Prophet! say to those you are holding prisoner... 90
72-75 Those who believe and have made *hijrah* and done *jihād*... 94

Sūrat at-Tawbah

1 An announcement to those idolaters you have a general treaty with... 100
2 'You may travel about in the land for four months... 102
3 A proclamation from Allah and His Messenger to mankind... 107
4 except those among the idolaters you have treaties with... 109
5 Then, when the sacred months are over, kill the idolaters wherever... 110
6 If any of the idolaters ask you for protection, give them protection... 113
7 How could any of the idolaters possibly have a treaty with Allah and... 115
8 How indeed! For if they get the upper hand over you... 116
9 They have sold Allah's Signs for a paltry price... 118
10 They respect neither kinship nor treaty where a believer is concerned... 118
11 But if they repent and establish the prayer and pay *zakāt*... 118
12 If they break their oaths after making their treaty... 119
13 Will you not fight a people who have broken their oaths... 123

14-15 Fight them! Allah will punish them at your hands... 124
16 Or did you suppose that you would be left without Allah knowing... 125
17 It is not for the idolaters to frequent the mosques of Allah... 126
18 The mosques of Allah should only be frequented by those... 127
19 Do you make the giving of water to the pilgrims and looking after... 129
20 Those who believe and make *hijrah* and do *jihād*... 130
21-22 Their Lord gives them the good news of His mercy... 131
23 You who believe, do not befriend your fathers and brothers... 131
24 Say: 'If your fathers or your sons or your brothers or your wives... 132
25-27 Allah has helped you on many occasions... 134
28 You who believe! the idolaters are unclean... 140
29 Fight those of the people who were given the Book who do not believe... 146
30 The Jews say, "Uzayr is the son of Allah,' and the Christians say... 153
31 They have taken their rabbis and monks as lords besides Allah... 155
32 They desire to extinguish Allah's Light with their mouths... 157
33 It is He who sent His Messenger with guidance and the *Dīn* of Truth... 157
34 You who believe! many of the rabbis and monks devour... 158
35 on the Day it is heated up in the fire of Hell and their foreheads... 164
36 The number of months with Allah in the Book of Allah... 167
37 Deferring a sacred month is an increase in unbelief... 172
38 You who believe! what is the matter with you... 175
39 If you do not go out to fight, He will punish you... 176
40 If you do not help him, Allah did help him when the unbelievers... 178
41 Go out to fight, whatever your circumstances or desires... 184
42 If it had been a case of easy gains and a short journey... 188
43 Allah pardon you! Why did you excuse them until it was clear... 189
44-45 Those who believe in Allah and the Last Day do not ask... 190
46 If they had really desired to go out, they would have made... 191
47 If they had gone out among you, they would have added nothing... 192
48 They have already tried to cause conflict before... 193
49-50 Among them there are some who say, 'Give me permission... 193
51 Say: 'Nothing can happen to us except what Allah has ordained... 195
52 Say: 'What do you await for us except for one of the two best things?... 196
53 Say: 'Whether you give readily or reluctantly... 196
54 Nothing prevents what they give from being accepted from them but... 198
55-56 Do not let their wealth and children impress you... 199
57 If they could find a bolt-hole, cave or burrow... 200
58 Among them there are some who find fault with you... 201
59 If only they had been pleased with what Allah and His Messenger... 202

60 *Zakāt* is for: the poor, the destitute, those who collect it... 202
61 Among them are some who insult the Prophet... 226
62 They swear to you by Allah in order to please you... 227
63 Do they not know that whoever opposes Allah and His Messenger... 229
64 The hypocrites are afraid that a sūrah may be sent down... 229
65 If you ask them they will say, 'We were only joking... 231
66 Do not try to excuse yourselves. You have disbelieved after... 232
67 The men and women of the hypocrites are as bad as one another... 234
68 Allah has promised the men and women of the hypocrites... 234
69 Like those before you who had greater strength than... 235
70 Has the news of those who came before them not reached them... 236
71 The men and women of the believers are friends of one another... 237
72 Allah has promised the men and women of the believers Gardens... 238
73 O Prophet, do *jihād* against the unbelievers and hypocrites... 239
74 They swear by Allah that they said nothing, but they definitely spoke... 240
75-78 Among them there were some who made an agreement... 243
79 As for the people who find fault with those believers... 249
80 You can ask forgiveness for them, or not ask forgiveness for them... 250
81 Those who were left behind were glad to stay behind the Messenger... 251
82 Let them laugh little and weep much, in repayment... 251
83 If Allah returns you to a group of them, and they ask you... 252
84 Never pray over any of them who die or stand at their graves... 253
85 Do not let their wealth and their children impress you... 257
86 When a *sūrah* is sent down saying: 'Believe in Allah and do *jihād*... 258
87-89 They are pleased to be with those who stay behind... 258
90 The desert Arabs came with their excuses asking for permission to stay...259
91-92 Nothing is held against the weak and the sick... 261
93 There are only grounds against those who ask you for permission... 265
94 They will make excuses to you when you return to them... 265
95 They will swear to you by Allah when you return to them... 266
96 They will swear to you to make you pleased with them... 266
97 The desert Arabs are more obdurate in unbelief and hypocrisy... 266
98 Among the desert Arabs there are some... 269
99 And among the desert Arabs there are some who believe in Allah... 270
100 The Forerunners – the first of the *Muhājirūn* and the *Anṣār*... 270
101 Some of the desert Arabs around you are hypocrites... 275
102 But others have acknowledged their wrong actions... 277
103 Take *zakāt* from their wealth to purify and cleanse them... 279
104 Do they not know that Allah accepts repentance from His slaves... 285

105 Say: 'Act, for Allah will see your actions, and so will His Messenger… 287
106 And others are left awaiting Allah's command… 287
107 As for those who have set up a mosque, causing harm… 288
108 Do not ever stand in it. A mosque founded on *taqwā*… 293
109 Who is better: someone who founds his building on *taqwā* of Allah… 297
110 The buildings they have built will not cease to be a bone of contention… 299
111 Allah has bought from the believers their selves and their wealth… 300
112 Those who repent, those who worship, those who praise… 303
113 It is not right for the Prophet and those who believe… 306
114 Ibrāhīm would not have asked forgiveness for his father… 308
115-16 Allah would never misguide a people after guiding them… 310
117 Allah has turned towards the Prophet, and the *Muhājirūn*… 311
118 and also towards the three who were left behind… 315
119 You who believe! have *taqwā* of Allah and be with the truly sincere… 321
120-121 It was not for people of Madīnah, and the desert Arabs… 323
122 It is not necessary for the believers to go out all together… 327
123 You who believe! fight those of the unbelievers who are near to you… 331
124 Each time a *sūrah* is sent down there are some among them… 332
125 But as for those with sickness in their hearts… 332
126 Do they not see that they are tried once or twice in every year?… 332
127 Each time a *sūrah* is sent down, they look at one another… 333
128-129 A Messenger has come to you from among yourselves… 335

Sūrah Yūnus

Alif Lām Rā'. Those are the Signs of the Wise Book… 339
2 Do people find it so surprising that We should reveal to a man… 340
3 Your Lord is Allah, Who created the heavens and the earth… 342
4 Each and every one of you will return to Him. Allah's promise is true… 343
5 It is He who appointed the sun to give radiance… 344
6 In the alternation of night and day and what Allah has created… 346
7-8 As for those who do not expect to meet Us… 346
9 But as for those who believe and do right actions… 347
10 Their call there is: 'Glory be to You, O Allah!' Their greeting there… 348
11 If Allah were to hasten evil for people the way they try to hasten good… 350
12 When harm touches man, he calls on Us, lying on his side or sitting… 352
13 We destroyed generations before you when they did wrong… 353
14 Then We appointed you after them to be caliphs on the earth… 353
15 When Our Clear Signs are recited to them… 354
16 Say: 'Had Allah so wished, I would not have recited it to you… 355

17 Who could do greater wrong than someone who invents lies… 356
18 They worship, instead of Allah, what can neither harm them… 357
19 Mankind was only one community but then they differed… 358
20 They say, 'Why has a Sign not been sent down to him from his Lord?'… 358
21 When We let people taste mercy after hardship has afflicted them… 359
22-23 It is He who conveys you on both land and sea… 360
24 The likeness of the life of this world is that of water which We send… 363
25 Allah calls to the Abode of Peace and He guides whom He wills… 365
26 Those who do good will have the best and more!… 366
27 But as for those who have earned bad actions – a bad action… 368
28 On the Day We gather them all together, We will say then… 369
29 Allah is a sufficient witness between us and you… 370
30 Then and there every self will be tried for what it did before… 370
31 Say: 'Who provides for you out of heaven and earth?… 371
32 That is Allah, your Lord, the Truth, and what is there after truth… 372
33 In that way the Word of your Lord is realised… 376
34 Say: 'Can any of your partner-gods bring creation out of nothing… 377
35 Say: 'Can any of your partner-gods guide to the truth?'… 377
36 Most of them follow nothing but conjecture. Conjecture is of no use… 379
37 This Qur'an could never have been devised by any besides Allah… 379
38 Do they say, 'He has invented it'? Say: 'Then produce a *sūrah* like it… 380
39 No, the fact is that they have denied something… 381
40 Among them there are some who believe in it and some who do not… 381
41 If they deny you, say, 'I have my actions and you have your actions… 382
42-43 Among them there are some who listen to you… 382
44 Allah does not wrong people in any way; rather it is people who… 383
45 On the day We gather them together – when it will seem as if… 383
46 Whether We show you something of what We have promised them… 385
47 Every nation has a Messenger and when their Messenger comes… 385
48 They say, 'When will this promise be kept if you are telling the truth?'… 386
49 Say: 'I possess no power to harm or help myself except as Allah wills… 386
50 Say: 'What do you think? If His punishment came upon you by night… 386
51 And then, when it actually comes about: 'Now do you believe in it?… 387
52 Then it will be said to those who did wrong, 'Taste the punishment… 388
53 They will ask you to tell them if this is true. Say: 'Yes indeed… 388
54 If every self that did wrong possessed everything on earth… 388
55 Yes indeed! Everything in the heavens and earth belongs to Allah… 389
56 He gives life and causes to die and you will be returned to Him… 390
57 Mankind! admonition has come to you from your Lord… 390

58 Say: 'It is the favour of Allah and His mercy that should be the cause... 390
59 Say: 'What do you think about the things Allah has sent down... 392
60 What will those who invent lies against Allah think on the Day... 392
61 You do not engage in any matter or recite any of the Qur'an... 393
62 Yes, the friends of Allah will feel no fear and will know no sorrow... 394
63 those who believe and are godfearing... 395
64 there is good news for them in the life of this world and in the Next... 395
65 Do not be grieved by what they say. All might belongs to Allah... 396
66 Yes, indeed! Everyone in the heavens and everyone on the earth... 397
67 It is He who appointed the night for you, so that you could rest in it... 397
68 They say, 'Allah has a son.' Glory be to Him!... 398
69-70 Say: 'People who invent lies against Allah will not be successful.'... 399
71 Recite to them the story of Nūḥ when he said to his people... 399
72 If you turn your backs, I have not asked you for any wage... 402
73 But they denied him so We rescued him, and all those with him... 402
74 Then after him We sent Messengers to their people... 402
75 Then after them We sent Mūsā and Hārūn with Our Signs to Pharaoh... 403
76-77 When the truth came to them from Us, they said... 403
78 They said, 'Have you come to us to turn us from what we found... 404
79 Pharaoh said, 'Bring me every knowledgeable magician.'... 404
80 When the magicians came, Mūsā said to them, 'Throw whatever... 405
81 When they had thrown, Mūsā said, 'What you have brought is magic... 405
82 Allah confirms the Truth by His words... 406
83 No one believed in Mūsā except for a few of his people out of fear... 406
84-85 Mūsā said, 'My people! if you believe in Allah, then put your trust... 408
86 and rescue us, by Your mercy, from this unbelieving people!'... 408
87 We revealed to Mūsā and his brother: 'Settle your people in houses... 409
88 Mūsā said, 'Our Lord, You have given Pharaoh and his ruling circle... 411
89 He said, 'Your request is answered, so go straight... 413
90 We brought the tribe of Israel across the sea and Pharaoh... 414
91 'What, now! When previously you rebelled... 417
92 Today We will preserve your body so you can be a Sign for people... 417
93 We settled the tribe of Israel in a noble place... 419
94-95 If you are in any doubt about what We have sent down to you... 420
96-97 Those against whom the words of your Lord are justly carried out... 421
98 How is it that there has never been a city that believed... 421
99 If your Lord had willed, all the people on the earth... 423
100 No self can believe except with Allah's permission... 424
101 Say: 'Look at what there is in the heavens and on the earth.'... 424

102 What are they waiting for but the same fate as those who passed… 424
103 Then We will rescue Our Messengers and those who believe… 425
104 Say: 'Mankind! if you are in any doubt about my *dīn*… 425
105-6 Turn your face towards the *dīn* in pure natural faith… 426
107 If Allah afflicts you with harm, no one can remove it except Him… 426
108 Say: 'Mankind! the truth has come to you from your Lord… 427
109 Follow what has been revealed to you and be steadfast… 427

Glossary

'Abs: an Arab tribe that is a branch of Ghaṭafān.
Abū al-'Abbās: Muḥammad ibn Yazīd al-Mubarrad, a leading philologist and grammarian of the school of Basra. He died in Baghdad in 285/898. He wrote many books, including *al-Kāmil* and *al-Kitāb.*
Abū Ḥātim: Sahl ibn Muḥammad al-Jushanī as-Sijistānī, d. 255/869, a prominent Basran philologist.
Abū Ḥaywah: Shurayḥ ibn Yazīd al-Ḥaḍramī, the Qur'an reciter of Syria from Homs. He has a *shādhdh* reading, and died in 203/818.
Abū Isḥāq: Ibrāhīm ibn as-Sarī az-Zajjāj, author of *I'rab al-Qur'ān.*
Abū Ja'far: aṭ-Ṭabarī.
Abū Jahl: 'Amr ibn Hishām, one of the important men of Quraysh who was violently opposed to Islam.
Abū 'Ubayd: al-Qāsim ibn Sallām al-Harawī or al-Baghdādī, d. 224/838.
Abū 'Ubaydah: Ma'mar ibn al-Muthanna at-Taymī, d. 209/824, author of *Majāz al-Qur'ān*, the first book on the linguistic analysis of the Qur'an.
'Ād: an ancient people in southern Arabia to whom the Prophet Hūd was sent.
Al-Aḍbā': a very fast camel belonging to the Prophet ﷺ.
adhān: the call to prayer.
'Adn: Eden, part of Paradise.
Al-Akhfash: Abū al-Khaṭṭāb 'Abd al-Ḥamīd ibn 'Abd al-Majīd al-Akhfash al-Kabīr, a grammarian in Basra, one of the first to study Arabic poetry as well as contributing to philology and lexicography and recording Bedouin vocabulary. He revised *Kitāb*, the first book on Arabic grammar, written by his student Sībawayh. He was a client of the Qays tribe and died in 177/793.
Allāhu akbar: the Arabic expression 'God is greater.'
Āmīn: 'Ameen', a compound of verb and noun meaning 'Answer our prayer' or 'So be it'.
amīr: the one who commands; the source of authority in a situation; a military commander.
Amīr al-Mu'minīn: 'the Commander of the Believers', the caliph.

Anṣār: the "Helpers", the people of Madīnah who welcomed and aided the Prophet ﷺ.
'Aqabah, lit. the steep slope, a pass to the north of Makkah, just off the caravan route to Madīnah, where the Prophet ﷺ met with the first Muslims from Yathrīb (Madīnah) in two successive years. On the first occasion, they pledged to follow the Messenger ﷺ, and in the second or Great Pledge of 'Aqabah, to defend him and his Companions as they would their own wives and children.
'āqilah: the paternal kinsmen of an offender who are liable for the payment of blood money.
'Arafah: a plain 15 miles to the east of Makkah. One of the essential rites of the ḥajj is to stand on 'Arafah on the 9th of Dhū'l-Ḥijjah.
'arīyah: a kind of sale by which the owner of an *'arīyah* is allowed to sell fresh dates while they are still on the palms by means of estimation, in exchange for dried plucked dates.
'aṣabah: male relatives on the father's side.
Asad: a strong and famous Arab tribe.
Ashja': a sub-tribe of Ghaṭafān.
Aslam: an Arab tribe who were a branch of Khuzā'ah and allied themselves to the Prophet ﷺ early on.
Al-Aṣma'ī: Abū Sa'īd ibn 'Abd al-Malik ibn Qurayb, 122/740-213/820, an early philologist and Arabic grammarian of Basra. He also wrote on genealogy, natural science and zoology and was a scholar of Arabic poetry in the court of Hārūn ar-Rashīd. He spent a great deal of time recording the language of desert Bedouins.
'Aṣr: the mid-afternoon prayer.
Aws: along with Khazraj, one of the two major tribes of Madīnah.
Awṭās: a location between Makkah and Ta'if, about fifteen miles from Makkah, the site of a battle.
āyah: a verse of the Qur'an.
'Ayr: the second largest mountain in Madīnah after Uḥud, located to the south of Madīnah.
Ayyūb: the Prophet Job.
Badr: a place near the coast, about 95 miles to the south of Madīnah where, in 2 AH in the first battle fought by the newly established Muslim community, the 313 outnumbered Muslims led by the Messenger of Allah overwhelmingly defeated 1000 Makkan idolaters.
Baghlī dirham: a dirham minted by the assay-master, Ra's Baghl, at the command of 'Umar ibn al-Khaṭṭāb and was based on the Persian drahm.

It weighed twenty *qirāṭ*s. (There are other theories of the source of the name as well.)

baḥīrah: in the Jāhiliyyah period, a female camel which had given birth five times, the last being a male. Its ears were slit and it was let free to graze.

Bakr: a large Arab tribe in the Hijaz belonging to the larger Rabī'ah branch. They were allies of Quraysh in pre-Islamic times.

banū: lit. sons, meaning a tribe or clan.

barakah: blessing, any good which is bestowed by Allah, and especially that which increases, a subtle beneficent spiritual energy which can flow through things or people.

basmalah: the expression 'In the name of Allah, the All-Merciful, the Most Merciful'.

Al-Baydā': a hill on the way to Makkah.

bint labūn: a two-year-old female camel.

Bu'āth: a battle between Aws and Khazraj two years before the Hijrah.

Camel: Battle of the Camel, one of the major incidents of the first Civil War in which the forces of 'Alī ibn Abī Ṭālib defeated the forces under 'Ā'ishah, Ṭalha and az-Zubayr outside Basra in 36/656.

Dajjāl: the false Messiah whose appearance marks the imminent end of the world. The root in Arabic means 'to deceive, cheat, take in'.

ḍammah: the Arabic vowel 'u'.

Ḍamrah: a tribe who lived about eighty miles from Madīnah. They entered into a treaty with the Prophet in 2/632. They were a clan of the Banū Kinānah.

ḍarūrī: necessary, indispensible. In respect of the prayer, it is the time in which the prayer must be performed unless there is a valid excuse.

Dār an-Nadwah: a house built by Qusayy next to the Ka'bah where tribal meetings took place.

Dāwūd: the Prophet David.

dhikr: lit. remembrance, mention. Commonly used, it means invocation of Allah by repetition of His names or particular formulae.

dhimmah: obligation or contract, in particular a treaty of protection for non-Muslims living in Muslim territory.

dhimmī: a non-Muslim living under the protection of Muslim rule.

Dhū Amarr: also known as the Ghaṭafān expedition led by the Prophet ﷺ in 3/624.

Dhū al-Fiqār: the sword of 'Alī ibn Abī Ṭālib given to him by the Prophet ﷺ.

Dhū'l-Ḥijjah: the twelfth month of the Muslim calendar, the month of the *ḥajj*.

Dhū'l-Ḥulayfah: the *mīqāt* of the people of Madīnah.
Dhū'l-Qa'dah: the eleventh month of the Muslim calendar.
Dhubyān: the Banū Dhubyān tribe in the Hijaz., a branch of Ghaṭafān.
dihqān: landlord, one of the class of Persian landlords who administered sub-districts.
dīn: the life-transaction, lit. the debt between two parties, in this usage between the Creator and created.
Ditch: the Battle of the Ditch (or Trench), which took place in 627 CE/5 AH in which the combined forces of Quraysh and their allies unsuccessfully laid siege to Madīnah for thirty days.
Ḍuḥā: forenoon, in particular the voluntary morning prayer at that time.
Fajr: the dawn prayer.
faqīh: pl. *fuqahā'*, a man learned in knowledge of *fiqh* who by virtue of his knowledge can give a legal judgement.
farḍ: an obligatory act of worship or practice of the *dīn* as defined by the Sharī'ah.
farḍ kifāyah: a collective obligation, something which is obligatory for the community as a whole and is satisfied if one adult performs it.
al-Fārūq: a name for the second caliph, 'Umar ibn al-Khaṭṭāb, It means someone who makes a distinction between truth and falsehood, or between cases.
Al-Farrā': Abū Zakariyyā Yaḥyā ibn Ziyād, ca. 144/761- 207/882, a noted grammarian of Kufa. Al-Farrā' means 'he who skins/scrutinises language'. He wrote *Majāz al-Qur'an.*
fāsiq: pl. *fussāq*, impious, someone not meeting the legal requirements of righteousness. The evidence of such a person is inadmissible in the court.
fatḥah: the Arabic vowel 'a'.
Fātiḥah: "the Opener," the first *sūrah* of the Qur'an.
fatwā: an authoritative statement on a point of law.
fay': booty.
fiqh: the science of the application of the Sharī'ah. A practitioner or expert in *fiqh* is called a *faqīh.*
fisq: deviant behavior, leaving the correct way or abandoning the truth, disobeying Allah, immoral behavior.
fitnah: civil strife, sedition, schism, trial, temptation, also *shirk.*
Fiṭr: *see 'Īd al-Fiṭr.*
fiṭrah: the natural form on which man was created.
fuqahā': plural of *faqīh.*
Fuqaym: a branch of Mālik of Kinānah who lived in Hijaz and from

whom Qusayy came. They were said to have been entrusted in pre-Islamic times with the intercalation of an extra month in the year to make the Hajj coincide with the markets.

gharīb: a hadith which has a single reporter at some stage of the *isnād*.

Ghassān: an Arab tribe established in southern Syria, best known for the sixth century Roman client state, the Ghassānids.

Ghaṭafān: a very large tribal grouping who lived east of Madīnah and Makkah in the land between the Hijaz and the Shammar mountains.

Ghifār: an Arab tribe that lived in the Hijaz near Yathrib (Madīnah) in the Waddān valley who were known for highway robbery in pre-Islamic times.

ghusl: major ablution of the whole body with water required to regain purity after menstruation, lochia and sexual intercourse.

Hābīl: Abel.

hadith: reported speech of the Prophet ﷺ.

ḥadd: Allah's boundary limits for the lawful and unlawful. The *ḥadd* punishments are specific fixed penalties laid down by Allah for specified crimes.

ḥāfiẓ: pl. *ḥuffāẓ*, someone who has memorised the Qur'an.

ḥajj: the annual pilgrimage to Makkah which is one of the five pillars of Islam.

ḥāl: In Arabic grammar, a circumstantial adverb in the accusative case which describes something happening at the same time as the action or event mentioned in the main clause.

ḥalāl: lawful in the Sharī'ah.

ḥām: a male camel which had fathered ten females in succession which was then freed from work for the idols.

hamzah: the character in Arabic which designates a glottal stop.

ḥanīf: someone following the primordial religion of *tawḥīd* and sincerity to Allah.

Ḥanīfiyyah: the religion of the Prophet Ibrāhīm, the primordial religion of *tawḥīd* and sincerity to Allah.

harām: unlawful in the Sharī'ah.

Ḥaram: Sacred Precinct, a protected area in which certain behavior is forbidden and other behaviour necessary. The area around the Ka'bah in Makkah is a Haram, and the area around the Prophet's Mosque in Madīnah is a Haram. They are referred to together as al-*Ḥaram*ayn, 'the two *Ḥarams*'.

ḥarbī: a belligerent.

ḥarf: (plural *aḥruf*) one of the seven modes or manners of recitation in which the Qur'an was revealed.
Hārūn: the Prophet Aaron, the brother of Mūsā.
ḥasan: good, excellent, often used to describe a hadith which is reliable, but which is not as well authenticated as one which is *ṣaḥīḥ*.
Hāshim: the Banu Hāshim is a clan of the Quraysh tribe of which the Prophet ﷺ was a member, the name coming from his great-grandfather, Hāshim ibn 'Abd Manāf.
Ḥawāmīm: the seven *sūrahs* of the Qur'an that begin with *'Ḥā-Mīm'* (40-46).
Hawāzin: one of the large Arab tribes in the Hijaz who were part of the Qays tribal grouping.
Hāwiyah: the abyss, bottomless pit, Hell.
Ḥawwā': Eve, the first woman.
Hijaz: the region along the western seaboard of Arabia in which Makkah, Madīnah, Jidda and Ta'if are situated.
Hijrah: emigration in the way of Allah. Islamic dating begins with the Hijrah of the Prophet Muḥammad ﷺ from Makkah to Madīnah in 622 AD.
Ḥimyar: a major tribe in the ancient Sabaean kingdom of southwestern Arabia. They were concentrated on the coast of Yemen with their capital at Ẓafār and later at Sanā' under the Ḥimyarite kingdom.
ḥiqqah: a three-year-old she-camel.
Ḥirā': a mountain two miles north of Makkah where the Prophet ﷺ used to go into retreat before he received the Revelation.
Hūd: the Prophet sent to the people of 'Ād.
Ḥudaybīyah: a well-known place ten miles from Makkah on the way to Jiddah where the Pledge of ar-Riḍwān took place.
Hudhayl: a tribe which lived in the hills between Makka and Ṭā'if and were linked genealogically with Quraysh.
ḥudūd: plural of *ḥadd*.
ḥuffāẓ: plural of *ḥāfiẓ*.
Ḥums: an alliance in the pre-Islamic period, centred on the Ka'bah in Makkah and the religion of the Prophet Ibrāhīm ﷺ. It included the tribe of Quraysh as well as some other tribes. It was based on strictness in their religion. It came about around the year of the Elephant (522 CE).
Ḥunayn: a valley between Makkah and Ta'if where the battle took place between the Prophet ﷺ and Quraysh pagans in 8/630.

Iblīs: the personal name of the Devil. He is also called Shayṭān or the 'enemy of Allah'.
Ibn Isḥāq: Muḥammad, the author of the most famous biography of the Prophet ﷺ. He died in 150/767.
Ibrāhīm: the Prophet Abraham.
'Īd: a festival, either the festival at the end of Ramadan or at the time of the Hajj.
'Īd al-Fiṭr: the festival at the end of the month of fasting (Ramadan).
iḍāfah: a possessive construction in Arabic in which the first noun is indefinite and the second usually definite. It is used to indicate possession. The first word is called '*muḍāf*' and the second is '*muḍāf ilayhi*'.
idghām: In Qur'an recitation, to assimilate one letter into another. Thus *an-ya'bud* becomes *ay-ya'bud*, *qad rabayyan* becomes *qattabayyan*, etc.
Idrīs: a Prophet, possibly Enoch.
'ifrīt: a powerful sort of jinn.
iftitāḥ: the opening supplication of the prayer.
iḥrām: the conditions of clothing and behaviour adopted by someone on *ḥajj* or *'umrah*.
ijtihād: to exercise personal judgement in legal matters.
'illah: underlying reason, effective cause.
Ilyās: also Ilyāsīn, the Prophet Elijah or Elias.
imālah: a vowel shift in Arabic where an open vowel rises, *ā* towards *ī*, and short *a* towards *i*.
imam: Muslim religious or political leader; leader of Muslim congregational worship.
Imāmiyyah: the Twelver Shī'ah, also known as Ja'fariyyah, from Ja'far aṣ-Ṣādiq.
īmān: belief, faith.
'Īsā: the Prophet Jesus.
Isḥāq: the Prophet Isaac.
ishbā': lengthening a vowel.
Ismā'īl: the Prophet Ishmael.
isnād: a hadith's chain of transmission from individual to individual.
Isrāfīl: the archangel who will blow the Trumpet which announces the end of the world.
istinjā': cleaning oneself with water after urination or defecation.
istikhārah: a prayer performed by someone who has not decided what to do in a matter hoping to be inspired to do the right thing.
Jahannam: Hell.

Jāhiliyyah: the Time of Ignorance before the coming of Islam.
jalālah: animals that have been eating filth and impurities.
janābah: major ritual impurity requiring a ghusl: caused by sexual intercourse, sexual discharge, menstruation, childbirth.
janāzah: the dead person, the funeral bier, or the actual funeral.
jarīb: (plural *ajribah*) a grain measure of either 16, 26, or 29.5 litres; also a unit of area equal to *qaṣabah* squared, or 3,600 square cubits.
Jibrīl: the angel Gabriel.
jihad: struggle, particularly fighting in the way of Allah to establish Islam.
jinn: inhabitants of the heavens and the earth made of smokeless fire who are usually invisible.
Al-Ji'rānah: a place near Makkah where the Messenger of Allah ﷺ distributed the booty from the Battle of Ḥunayn and where he went into *iḥrām* for *'umrah.*
jizyah: a protection tax payable by non-Muslims living under Muslim rule as a tribute to the Muslim ruler.
Judhām: an Arab tribe who were agents of the Byzantines in pre-Islamic times.
Al-Juḥfah: the *mīqāt* of the people of Syria and Europe, about 183 km from Makkah.
Juhaynah: a large nomadic tribe from the Hijaz whose territory covered the routes between Syria and Makkah.
Jumādā'l-Ākhir: the sixth month of the Muslim calendar.
Jumādā'l-Ulā: the fifth month of the Muslim calendar.
Jumu'ah: the day of gathering, Friday, and particularly the Jumu'ah prayer which is performed instead of *Ẓuhr* by those who attend it.
Ka'bah: the cube-shaped building at the centre of the *Ḥaram* in Makkah, originally built by the Prophet Ibrāhīm. Also known as the House of Allah.
kaffārah: atonement, prescribed way of making amends for wrong actions, especially missed obligatory actions.
kāfir: (pl. *kāfirūn* or *kuffār*)**:** an unbeliever, a person who rejects Allah and His Messenger. The opposite is believer or *mumin.*
Kalīlah and Dimnah: a famous book containing fables originally written in Sanskrit and translated into Pahlavi in the reign of Khusrau I.
Kalīmullāh: the one to whom Allah spoke, namely the Prophet Mūsā.
kasrah: the Arabic vowel i.
Khalīl: "Friend", a title of the Prophet Ibrāhīm.
Al-Khalīl: Abū 'Abd ar-Raḥmān ibn 'Amt al-Farāhidī, 110/718-170/786, born in Oman, a leading grammarian, philologist and lexicographer of

Basra. He compiled the first Arabic dictionary: *Kitāb al-'Ayn*, and the first to codify the metres of Arabic poetry. His students included Sībawayh and al-Aṣma'ī.

kharaj: taxes imposed on agricultural land.

Khārijites: the earliest sect, who separated themselves from the body of the Muslims and declared war on all those who disagreed with them, stating that a wrong action turns a Muslim into an unbeliever.

Khaybar: Jewish colony to the north of Madina which was laid siege to and captured by the Muslims in the seventh year after the Hijra because of the Jews' continual treachery.

Khazraj: along with Aws, one of the two major tribes of Madīnah.

khums: the fifth taken from the booty which is given to the ruler for distribution.

Khusraw: the Persian emperor, also written as Khosrov, Khosrow, Chosroes or Osroes.

khuṭbah: a speech, and in particular a standing speech given by the imam before the *Jumu'ah* prayer and after the two *'Īd* prayers.

Khuzā'ah: an Azdī tribe who were concentrated around Makkah.

Kilāb: Banū Kilāb, a tribe that dominated central Arabia, originating from Najd.

Kinānah: a major Arab tribe in the Hijaz, located around Makkah and in Tihamah, Quraysh were a sub-branch.

kitābah: a contract for a slave to buy his freedom in instalments.

Kitābī: Someone who is one of the People of the Book, i.e. a Jew or Christian.

kufr: disbelief, to cover up the truth, to reject Allah and refuse to believe that Muhammad ﷺ is His Messenger.

kunyah: a respectful but intimate way of addressing people as "the father of so-and- so" or "the mother of so-and-so."

Kunāsah: a vast marketplace in Kufa, located outside the walls, which was a centre for caravans and a site for poetry recitation, storytelling, history and other activities.

Lā ilaha illā 'llāh: 'There is no god but Allah.'

lahd: a form of grave in which a niche is dug on the side of the grave facing qiblah into which the deceased is placed.

Lakhm: a large tribe that originated in Yemen and in pre-Islamic times created the Lakhmid kingdom in al-Ḥīrah, near Kufa, which acted as a buffer between the Arab tribes and Persian empire.

Al-Lāt: an idol worshipped by Thaqīf at Ṭā'if.

Lubad: the seventh vulture of Luqmān.
Luqmān: Luqmān ibn 'Ād, a figure known for his wisdom and longevity. He was granted the life span of the lives of seven vultures
Lūṭ: the Prophet Lot.
maddah: prolongation. There are three letters which are subject to prolongation in recitation of the Qur'an: *alif*, *wāw* and *yā'*.
Madyan: Midian, the people to whom the Prophet Shu'ayb was sent.
Maghrib: the sunset prayer; also the western part of Muslim lands. Today it means Morocco.
al-Mahdi: 'the Divinely Guided', the descendant of the Prophet ﷺ who will return at the end of time to establish justice.
Manāt: female idols worshipped by the Arabs in the Hijaz in the Jāhiliyyah.
mann: an Iraqi measure of weight.
Maqām of Ibrāhịm: the place of the stone on which the Prophet Ibrāhīm stood while he and Ismā'īl were building the Ka'bah, which marks the place of the two *rak'ah* prayer following *ṭawāf* of the Ka'bah.
marfū': 'elevated' , a narration from the Prophet ﷺ mentioned by a Companion, e.g. 'The Messenger of Allah ﷺ said...'
Marr az-Zahrān: site of one of the pre-Islamic marketplaces, located near a mountain, al-Aṣghar, about 24 Km from Makkah.
Maryam: Mary, the mother of 'Īsā.
Mash'ar al-Ḥarām: a venerated place in the valley of Muzdalifah where it is a sunnah to stop when doing *ḥajj*.
Masjid al-Ḥarām: the great mosque in Makkah.
Mathānī: lit. 'the often recited', said to be the first long *sūrah*s, or the *Fātiḥah* and also various other things.
mawālī: plural of *mawlā*.
mawla: a person with whom a tie of *walā'* has been established, usually by having been a slave and then set free.
mawqūf: 'stopped', a narration from a Companion without mentioning the Prophet ﷺ.
Mīkā'īl: the archangel Michael.
Minā: a valley five miles on the road to 'Arafah where the three *jamrah*s stand. It is part of the *ḥajj* to spend four or possibly three nights there over the course of the *ḥajj*.
mīqāt: plural *mawāqīt*, one of the designated places for entering *iḥrām* on *ḥajj* or *'umrah*.
mithqāl (plural *mathāqīl*): 'miskal', the weight of one dinar, the equivalent of 72 grains of barley (equals 4.4 grams).

mu'adhdhin: someone who calls the *adhan* (call to prayer).
muḍāf: in Arabic grammar in a possessive phrase, the *muḍāf* is the 'added' and *muḍāf ilayh* is what it is added to
mudabbar: a slave who has been given a *tadbīr*, a contract that he be freed after his master's death.
Muḍar: the ancestor of the Arabs.
mudd: a measure of volume. approximately a double-handed scoop.
Mudlij: an Arab tribe which was a branch of Kinānah.
muftī: someone qualified to give a legal opinion or fatwa.
Muhājirūn: Companions of the Messenger of Allah ﷺ who accepted Islam in Makkah and made hijrah to Madīnah.
muḥārib: a brigand, someone involved in *ḥirābah*.
Muḥarram: the first month of the Muslim lunar year.
muḥkam: perspicuous, a word or text conveying a firm and unequivocal meaning.
muḥrim: a person in *iḥrām*.
muḥṣan (or *muḥṣin*): a person who has been previously legally married.
mujtahid: a scholar who is qualified to carry out *ijtihād*.
mukātab: a slave who has been given a *kitābah*, a contract to buy his freedom.
munkar: "denounced", a narration reported by a weak reporter which goes against another authentic hadith.
Munkar and Nakīr: the two angels who come to question a person in his grave.
Murji'ites: the opponents of the Kharijites. The held that it is faith and not actions which are important. There is also a political position which suspends judgement on a person guilty of major sins.
mursal: a hadith where a man in the generation after the Companions quotes directly from the Prophet without mentioning the Companion from whom he got it.
Mūsā: the Prophet Moses.
Musaylimah: the false prophet of the Banū Ḥanīfah in Najd.
muṣḥaf: a physical copy of the Qur'an.
musinnah: a cow in its fourth year.
musnad: a collection of hadiths arranged according to the first authority in its *isnād*; also a hadith which can be traced back through an unbroken *isnād* to the Prophet.
Muṣṭaliq: a tribe that is a sub-clan of Khuzā'ah who were allied with Quraysh. The Muslims defeated them at al-Muraysi' in 5/626.

Mu'tah: an expedition in 8/629 under the command of Zayd ibn Ḥārithah against the Byzantines. After Zayd ibn Ḥārithah was killed, Ja'far ibn Abī Ṭālib took command and was killed, then 'Abdullāh ibn Rawāḥah who was also killed.
mutakallimūn: those who study the science of *kalām*, the science of investigating theological doctrine.
mutawātir: a hadith which is reported by a large number of reporters at all stages of the *isnād*.
Mu'tazilite: someone who adheres to the school of the Mu'tazilah which is rationalist in its approach to existence. Originally they held that anyone who commits a sin is neither a believer nor an unbeliever. They also held the Qur'an to be created.
Muzdalifah: a place between 'Arafah and Minā where, on *ḥajj*, the pilgrims returning from 'Arafah spend a night in the open between the ninth and tenth day of Dhū'l-Ḥijjah after performing *Maghrib* and *'Ishā'* there.
Muzaynah: a tribe that lived south of Madīnah on the caravan route to Makkah.
An-Naḍīr: a Jewish tribe in Madīnah.
nāfilah: (plural *nawāfil*): supererogatory act of worship.
Nafr: the 12th or 13th of Dhū al-Ḥijjah when the pilgrims on *ḥajj* leave Minā after having complete the rites at 'Arafah, Muzdalifah and Minā.
nafs: the lower self.
An-Naḥḥās: Abū Ja'far Aḥmad ibn Muḥammad an-Naḥḥās, d. 338/949, an Egyptian scholar of grammar and *tafsīr* in the Abbasid period.
Najd: the region around Riyadh in Arabia.
Najjār: the maternal tribe of the Prophet's grandfather who resided in Madīnah.
Najrān: a region in the southern Arabian peninsula which borders Yemen.
nawāfil: the plural of *nāfilah.*
Negus: a generic term for the ruler of Abyssinia.
niṣāb: the minimum amount of wealth of whatever kind that *zakat* can be deducted from.
Nūḥ: the Prophet Noah.
People of the Book: principally the Jews and Christians whose religions are based on the Divine Books revealed to Mūsā and 'Īsā; a term also used to refer to any other group who claim to be following a Book revealed prior to the Qur'an.

People of Hadith: 'the adherents of Hadith', the movement who considered only the Qur'an and hadith to be valid sources of fiqh.
People of Opinion (*ra'y*): a term used to describe those who use personal opinion to deduce judgement. It was a term used particularly to describe the early Ḥanafīs.
Preserved Tablet: *al-Lawḥ al-Maḥfūẓ*, also referred to as the *Umm al-Kitāb*, the source of the Qur'an, and the place where decrees are recorded.
qabā': a calf-length over-garment with sleeves.
Qābīl: Cain.
Qadariyyah: sect who said that people have power (*qadar*) over their actions and hence free will.
qāḍī: a judge, qualified to judge all matters in accordance with the Sharī'ah and to dispense and enforce legal punishments.
Qādisīyah: a decisive four day battle fought against the Persians in Iraq in 15/636.
qafīz: (plural *aqfizah*), 'cafiz', a measure of grain consisting of twelve *ṣā*'s' also a unit of area equal to 360 square cubits.
Qayrawān: a town in north-central Tunisia, founded in 50/670. It was chosen as the capital of the Maghrib by the Aghlabids in about 182/800. It was an important centre of learning.
qiblah: the direction faced in the prayer which is towards the Ka'bah in Makkah.
qirān: performing *ḥajj* and *'umrah* at the same time.
qirāṭ: plural *qarārīṭ*, a measure of weight with various meanings, either a twelfth of a dirham or a huge weight like that of Mount Uḥud.
Qinnasrin: a town in Syria originally known as Chalcis-on-Belus, 25 km southwest of Aleppo. It was the capital of one of the five provinces of Arab Syria.
Qubā': a village on the outskirts of Madīnah (originally about 5 km/3 miles outside the city) where the first mosque in Islam was built, also known as the Masjid at-Taqwā (Mosque of Fear of God).
Quraysh: one of the great tribes of Arabia. The Prophet Muḥammad ﷺ belonged to this tribe, which had great powers spiritually and financially both before and after Islam came. Someone from this tribe is called a Qurayshī.
Qurayẓah: one of the Jewish tribes of Madīnah.
ar-Rabadhah: a luxuriant oasis about 200 km northeast of Madīnah, located on a pilgrimage route.
Rabī'l-Awwal: the third month of the Muslim calendar.

Rabī'l-Ākhir: the fourth month of the Muslim calendar.
Rabī'ah: one of the two main branches of North Arabian tribes, the other being Muḍar.
Rāfiḍites: the Rawāfiḍ, a group of the Shī'ah known for rejecting Abū Bakr and 'Umar as well as 'Uthmān. It is a nickname, meaning "deserters".
Rajab: the seventh month of the Muslim calendar.
rak'ah: a unit of the prayer consisting of a series of standings, bowing, prostrations and sittings.
Ramadan: the month of fasting, the ninth month in the Muslim lunar calendar.
Rāshidūn: 'Rightly Guided', the title given to the first four caliphs in Islam: Abū Bakr, 'Umar, 'Uthmān and 'Alī.
ra'y: opinion, personal discretion. (see also People of Opinion.)
ribāṭ: the stronghold traditionally used by the Muslims to prepare for jihad against their enemy, situated on exposed points on the frontier.
Riddah: the defection of various Arab tribes after the death of the Prophet ﷺ which brought about the Riddah War.
ridā': an ample form of mantle.
Ridwān: the Pledge of Riḍwān was a pledge which the Muslims made with the Prophet ﷺ at Ḥudaybīyah to avenge 'Uthmān when they thought that Quraysh had murdered him in 6/628.
riṭl: or *raṭl*, a measurement of weight, approximately one pound.
rūḥ: (plural *arwāḥ*) the soul, vital spirit. 'The Purest Rūḥ' can also refer to 'Īsā or Jibrīl.
rukū': the bowing position in the prayer.
ṣā': a measure of volume equal to four *mudd*s.
ṣadaqah: charitable giving in the Cause of Allah.
sadd adh-dharā'i': a legal principle involving blocking the means which might lead to an illegal outcome.
Ṣafā and Marwah: two hills close to the Ka'bah; going back and forth between them constitutes one of the rites of *ḥajj* and 'umra.
Ṣafar: the second month of the Muslim lunar calendar.
ṣaḥīḥ: healthy and sound with no defects, used to describe an authentic hadith.
Ṣaḥīḥ: "the Sound", the title of the hadith collections of al-Bukhārī and Muslim.
sā'ibah: in the Jāhiliyyah, a she-camel let loose to graze, usually as a result of a vow to idols.
sajdah: prostration.

Sakīnah: calmness, tranquility, the Shekhinah which took the form of a cloud or wind.
Salaf: the early generations of the Muslims.
salām: the expression, *'as-salāmu 'alaykum,'* or 'Peace be upon you,' used as a greeting and to end the prayer.
Ṣāliḥ: the Prophet sent to the people of Thamūd.
Salimah: one of the tribes in Madīnah.
Sha'bān: the eighth month in the Muslim calendar.
shaddah: double letter.
shahādah: bearing witness, particularly bearing witness that there is no god but Allah and that Muhammad is the Messenger of Allah. It is one of the pillars of Islam. It is also used to describe legal testimony in a court of law.
Sham'ūn: Simon.
Sharī'ah: The legal modality of a people based on the revelation of their Prophet. The final Sharī'ah is that of Islam.
Shawwāl: the tenth month of the Muslim calendar.
Shayṭān: devil, particularly Iblīs, one of the jinn.
shirk: the unforgiveable wrong action of worshipping something or someone other than Allah or associating something or someone as a partner with Him.
Shu'ayb: the Prophet Jethro.
Sībawayh: Abū Bishr 'Amr ibn 'Uthmān ibn Qanbar al-Baṣrī, a famous Persian grammarian at Basra. He wrote the five volume *al-Kitāb* on the Arabic language. He died ca. 167/796.
Aṣ-Ṣiḥāḥ: the famous dictionary *Tāj al-'Arūs wa's-Ṣiḥāh al-'Arabīyah,* by Ismā'īl ibn Ḥammād al-Jawharī.
ṣiddīq: a man of truth, the ṣiddīq is the one who believes in Allah and His Messenger by the statement of the one who reports it, not from any proof except the light of belief which he experiences in his heart and which prevents him from hesitating and prevents any doubt entering him about the word of the Messenger who reported. It is the title given to Abū Bakr.
Ṣiffīn: a place in Syria near Raqqa where in 38/657 a battle took place between 'Alī ibn Abī Ṭālib and Mu'āwiyah. Part of it was the Night of Ḥarīr (Clamour) where the two armies fought into the night and all that could be heard was the sound of the clashing of swords.
Sīrah: biography, particularly biography of the Prophet ﷺ. The most famous is that of Ibn Isḥāq.

Ṣirāṭ: the narrow bridge which spans the Fire and must be crossed to enter the Garden. It is described as sharper than a sword and thinner than a hair. It will have hooks over it to catch people as they cross it.
siwāk: a small stick, usually from the arak tree, whose tip is softened and used for cleaning the teeth.
Ṣubḥ: dawn prayer.
Subḥāna'llāh: the Arabic expression, 'Glory be to Allah'.
Ṣuffah: a verandah attached to the Prophet's Mosque where the poor Muslims used to sleep.
sujūd: prostration.
sukūn: a diacritic mark that means that there is no sound after a consonant.
Sulaym: an Arab tribe that controlled part of the Hijaz in the pre-Islamic period. They were allies of Quraysh and initially hostile to the Prophet ﷺ, but became Muslim in the period in between the Battle of the Ditch and the conquest of Makkah.
Sulaymān: the Prophet Solomon.
sunan: plural of sunnah.
Sunnah: the customary practice of a person or group of people. It has come to refer almost exclusively to the practice of the Messenger of Allah ﷺ.
sūrah: a chapter of the Qur'an.
tā' marbūtah: a letter at the end of words which is not pronounced except when annexed to another word. It is written as a *hā'* with two overdots.
tabī': a male cow in its second year.
Tābi'ūn: the second generation of the early Muslims who did not meet the Prophet Muhammad ﷺ but learned the *dīn* of Islam from his Companions.
Tabūk: a town in northern Arabia close to Jordan.
tafsīr: commentary or explanation of the meanings of the Qur'an.
taḥrīm: a term used for entering a state of worship in which certain other actions are forbidden. The *taḥrīm* of the prayer is saying, *'Allahu akbar'* to start it.
Ṭā'if: a walled town south of Makkah known for its fertility. It was the home of the tribe of Thaqīf.
takbīr: saying *'Allāhu Akbar,'* 'Allah is greater'.
Ṭālūt: Saul.
Tamīm: one of the largest of the Arab tribes, located in Najd.
tanwīn: nunnation.
tanzīh: transcendence, disconnecting Allah from creation. The opposite of *tashbīh*.
taqdīs: proclaiming Allah's sanctity, often by certain formulae.

taqlīd: imitation; following the opinion of a *mujtahid* without considering the evidence.
taqwā: awe or fear of Allah, which inspires a person to be on guard against wrong action and eager for actions which please Him.
taṣawwuf: Sufism.
tasbīḥ: glorification of Allah by saying '*Subḥāna'llāh*'.
taslīm: giving the Islamic greeting of '*as-salāmu 'alaykum,*' 'Peace be upon you.' The prayer ends with a *taslīm.*
Tasnīm: the name of a spring in Paradise.
tathwīb: a repetition, the expression 'Prayer is better than sleep' pronounce twice in the adhan for *Fajr.*
ṭawāf: circumambulation of the Ka'bah, done in sets of seven circuits.
tawakkul: reliance, unshakeable trust in Allah.
tawḥīd: the doctrine of Divine Unity.
tawjīh: orientation, a supplication formula recited before starting the prayer.
Tayy': a large, ancient Arab tribe.
ta'zīr: discretionary punishment determined by the qāḍī.
Thamūd: a people to whom the Prophet Ṣāliḥ was sent, possibly a group of Nabateans. Madā'in Ṣāliḥ is located at al-Ḥijr in Najd about 180 miles north of Madina. The inscriptions on the tombs there date from 3 BC to 79 CE which are probably after the culture which once flourished there was destroyed.
Thaniyyat al-Wadā': a narrow pass in a mountain overlooking Madīnah to the north.
Thaqīf: a tribe based in the town of Ta'if, a branch of the tribe of Hawāzin.
Thawr: a mountain near Makkah where the cave Ḥirā' is located.
Tihāmah: the Red Sea coastal plain of Arabia.
Uḥud: a mountain just outside of Madīnah where five years after the Hijrah, the Muslims lost a battle against the Makkan idolaters. Many great Companions, and in particular Ḥamzah, the uncle of the Prophet, were killed in this battle.
Umayyah: the Banū Umayyah, the Umayyads.
Umm al-Kitāb: literally 'Mother of the Book'. It has a number of meanings, one of which is the celestial prototype of the Qur'an. It is also used for the Fātiḥah.
Umm al-Mu'minīn: literally 'Mother of the Believers', an honorary title given to the wives of the Prophet.

Umm al-Qur'ān: literally 'the Mother of the Qur'an', the opening *sūrah* of the Qur'an, *al-Fātiḥah.*
umm walad: a slavegirl who has had a child by her master and is freed on his death.
'umrah: the lesser pilgrimage to the Ka'bah in Makkah performed at any time of the year.
uqiyyah: unit of measurement equal to a 12th of a raṭl.
'ushr: land tax of one tenth of the produce if naturally watered and one twentieth if artificially irrigated.
uṣūl: plural of *aṣl*, the basic principles used in *fiqh* for arriving at a legal judgment.
uṣūlī: someone well-versed in the study of the fundamental principles (uṣūl) of Islamic law.
'Uzayr: Ezra.
Al-'Uzzā': a female idol worshipped by the pagan Arabs in the Hijaz in the Jāhiliyyah.
Verandah: as-Saqīfah, a roofed porch where the Muslims in Madīnah met after the death of the Prophet ﷺ to choose the first caliph.
Wādī al-Qurā: located near the Gulf of 'Aqabah north of the Red Sea where a Jewish settlement was located in the time of the Prophet ﷺ.
wakālah: agency, delegated authority..
walā': the tie of clientage established between a freed slave and the person who frees him, whereby the freed slave becomes integrated into the family of that person as a client (*mawlā*).
walī: (plural *awliyā'*) someone who is a 'friend' of Allah, thus possessing the quality of *wilāyah.* Also a relative who acts as a guardian.
waqf: also *habous*, an unalienable endowment for a charitable purpose which cannot be given away or sold to anyone.
waṣīlah: in the Jāhiliyyah, a she-camel that has given birth to two females with no male in between them. It was set loose to graze.
wasq: a measure of volume equal to sixty *ṣā*'s.
witr: literally 'odd', a single *raka'h* prayed after the *shaf'* which makes the number of sunnah prayers uneven.
wuḍū': ritual washing to be pure for the prayer.
Yahūdha: Judah.
Yaḥyā: the Prophet John the Baptist, the son of Zakariyyā.
Ya'jūj and Ma'jūj: the people of Gog and Magog who are to burst forth at the end of time to wreak destruction.
Yamāmah: a region to the east of the plateau of Najd.

Yamāmah, Battle of: also known as the Battle of ʻAqraba, the major battle of the Riddah War in which the Muslims defeated the forces of the false Prophet Musaylimah in 12/633.

Yaʻqūb: the Prophet Jacob, also called Isrāʼīl (Israel).

Yathrib: the ancient name for Madīnah.

Yūnus: the Prophet Jonah.

Yūsuf: the Prophet Joseph.

Zakariyyā: the Prophet Zachariah, the father of Yaḥyā, John the Baptist, and guardian of Maryam.

zakat: a wealth tax, one of the five pillars of Islam.

Zamzam: the well in the *Ḥaram* of Makkah.

zandaqah: heresy. This is an Arabicised Persian word. The term had been used for heterodox groups, especially Manichaeans, in pre-Islamic Persia, and hence it was originally applied to Magians.

zindīq: a term used to describe a heretic whose teaching is a danger to the community or state.

Ẓuhr: the midday prayer.

Zuṭṭ: a nomadic people from northern India who were in Iraq possibly before the Arab conquest.

www.ingramcontent.com/pod-product-compliance
Lightning Source LLC
Chambersburg PA
CBHW080933300426
44115CB00017B/2800
* 9 7 8 1 9 1 4 3 9 7 3 2 5 *